" . . . the first GMAT help book or course that I can recommend in terms of c[...]
and price . . . "

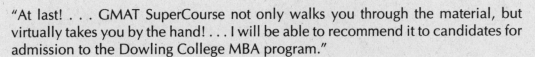

Kent Moore
MBA Director
Valdosta State College

"At last! . . . GMAT SuperCourse not only walks you through the material, but virtually takes you by the hand! . . . I will be able to recommend it to candidates for admission to the Dowling College MBA program."

Charles W. Rudiger, Dean
Graduate Business Administration
Dowling College

"My overall reaction was very positive. We at UND look forward to . . . recommending it to our MBA candidates."

Dennis J. Elbert
Associate Dean and MBA Director
University of North Dakota

"We find it to be a very good book for GMAT preparation . . . better than anything we have seen on the market."

Slimen J. Saliba, Dean
Andrews University

"I enjoyed reading the materials . . . the section on test anxiety was quite good."

Julie L. Granthen
Administrator of the MBA Program
Oakland University

" . . . well written and easy to follow . . . a useful book."

Debra M. Murphy
M.S.A. Program
Saint Michael's College

" . . . well written . . . the materials on general test-taking techniques . . . are very helpful."

Warren C. Weber, Professor
Management and Resources Department
California State Polytechnical University

ARCO

GMAT* CAT SuperCourse®

Thomas H. Martinson

Macmillan • USA

* GMAT is a registered trademark of the Graduate Management Admission Council, which does not endorse this book.

Photo Credits

page 1 © Conklin/Monkmeyer Press

page 39 © Rogers/Monkmeyer Press

page 471 © PhotoDisc, Inc.

Sixth edition

Macmillan Reference USA
A Simon & Schuster Macmillan Company
1633 Broadway
New York, NY 10019-6785

An ARCO Book

MACMILLAN and colophon is a registered trademark of Macmillan, Inc.
ARCO and colophon is a registered trademark of Prentice-Hall, Inc.

Manufactured in the United States of America

10 9 8 7 6 5 4 3 2 1

Library of Congress Number: 97-81046

ISBN: 0-02-861701-0

Contents

Part One   The Anatomy of a Test

Part Two   The Coaching Program

Part Three   Six Sample GMAT CATs

A Letter to the Reader

Dear Reader,

Here is a killer reason to buy this book:

It's worth somewhere between $500 and $800, depending on how conscientiously you use it.

How? This year, tens of thousands of students will spend big bucks—maybe even more than $1,000—for a test preparation course. Yet, this book can provide you with the same benefits. Are you skeptical?

I personally developed test preparation courses for two national companies. (Of course, I cannot mention the names.) The teachers for those companies lectured from lesson plans and notes that I created and wrote down. If you had a copy of the top-secret teacher's guide, then you wouldn't need to buy the test prep course.

This book is the teacher's guide. Now, you can prepare yourself for the GMAT CAT—on your own schedule, where it is convenient, and at substantial savings.

In my professional opinion, there is little offered by most commercial test preparation courses that you can't get for yourself by conscientious study of this book. Still skeptical? Look at the Contents page, where you will find an outline of a lesson plan that could have come directly from one of those expensive test prep companies. You also get 6 full-length practice exams with complete explanations.

Plus, even if you plan to take a test prep course, this book is your insurance policy. A teacher can forget to make an important point or run out of classtime before covering all the relevant material. A book does not have this weakness. And you can always use a little extra practice.

Good luck on the exam and on your career.

Thomas H. Martinson

Preface

There are three very important reasons for publishing this book at this time. One, it proves that it is possible to improve your GMAT CAT score. Two, it offers a reasonably priced alternative to expensive schools and tutoring services that now compete among themselves for your preparation dollars. Three, it stands as an antidote to the current mania for quick fixes rather than conscientious preparation and study.

First, this book shows that the GMAT CAT is not invincible—that it does have patterns or clues that are inherent in the structure of the test. If you understand these patterns or clues, you can pursue them to your advantage. Consider an example.

> At the beginning of a school year, a student receives a university loan of d dollars, which she deposits into a checking account. Each month, she receives p dollars from her parents and spends s dollars. If p is less than s, and the student makes up the difference by withdrawing from d, in how many months will d be exhausted?

Ⓐ $\dfrac{p-s}{d}$ Ⓑ $\dfrac{d}{s-p}$ Ⓒ $\dfrac{s-p}{d}$ Ⓓ $\dfrac{d-p}{s}$ Ⓔ $\dfrac{d}{p+s}$

This is a difficult math question. Perhaps no more than 15 to 20 percent of all test-takers would be able to answer it. But here is a strategy that lets you answer correctly even if you don't understand the algebra needed to set up a formula.

Just make the situation real by choosing some numbers for the letters in the problem. Assume, for example, that the loan was $1,000 ($d = 1,000$), that the student receives $200 per month from her parents ($p = 200$), and that she spends $300 per month ($s = 300$). The student is spending $100 per month more than her parents send her, which she withdraws from the checking account. At the rate of $100 per month, the checking account will be empty in $1,000 ÷ 100 = 10$ months.

So, on the assumption that $d = 1,000$, $p = 200$, and $s = 300$, the correct formula will yield the number 10. Just substitute the assumed values into the choices until you find the one that works:

Ⓐ $\dfrac{p-s}{d} = \dfrac{200-300}{1,000} = \dfrac{-100}{1,000} = -\dfrac{1}{10}$ (Wrong answer)

Ⓑ $\dfrac{d}{s-p} = \dfrac{1,000}{300-200} = \dfrac{1,000}{100} = 10$ (Correct)

Ⓒ $\dfrac{s-p}{d} = \dfrac{300-200}{1,000} = \dfrac{100}{1,000} = \dfrac{1}{10}$ (Wrong answer)

Ⓓ $\dfrac{d-p}{s} = \dfrac{1,000-200}{300} = \dfrac{800}{300} = \dfrac{8}{3}$ (Wrong answer)

Ⓔ $\dfrac{d}{p+s} = \dfrac{1,000}{200+300} = \dfrac{1,000}{500} = 2$ (Wrong answer)

Nor is success here a matter of luck. Since the GMAT math sections are multiple-choice tests, any problem like this one (which asks for an algebraic formula) can be attacked in this way. The correct answer is there for the testing.

Given that there are dozens of strategies like this, common sense dictates that test-takers who know the pattern of the GMAT CAT enjoy an important competitive edge over those who do not.

Second, this book is a viable alternative to expensive coaching schools. The 400-plus pages of instructional material are the equivalent of the thirty or forty hours of lecture included in those programs. Plus, you get hours of additional testing materials—all with complete analytical explanations.

Third, this book should help debunk a popular myth. There is currently in vogue an attitude that only a little preparation is needed. There is nothing really new in these approaches. They offer many of the strategies and methods that have been used effectively on multiple-choice tests for years. What is new, however, is the "hype" or indoctrination that accompanies the strategies. Students are encouraged to believe that by learning a few easy rules, they can attain a top score without really having to think. The idea is completely at odds with common sense.

Preparation is effective, but it requires a commitment of both time and effort. In point of fact, the only sure way to conquer the GMAT CAT is through conscientious preparation and hard work.

You can get a higher GMAT CAT score, but you'll have to earn it.

PART **ONE**

The Anatomy of a Test

Getting Started

Topics Covered

✓ **What is the GMAT CAT?**

What is the GMAC?

What is ETS?

How do you register for the GMAT CAT?

What Is the GMAT CAT?

The letters G-M-A-T stand for Graduate Management Admission Test. The letters C-A-T stand for Computer-Adaptive Test. So the GMAT CAT is the Graduate Management Admission Test Computer-Adaptive Test. GMAT CAT scores are required by or used by several hundred graduate management programs in the United States and in other countries. The GMAT CAT is entirely computer-based and is the only version of the test offered in the United States and most other areas of the world. The GMAT CAT is not yet available in some countries, so some international students may be required to take the older paper-based version of the test. (This book is effective preparation for either version of the test.)

The GMAT CAT is offered three weeks out of every month, six days a week, throughout the year. It is given at nearly 400 computer-based testing centers nationwide and at selected international sites.

The GMAT CAT includes both verbal and math questions. The questions are multiple-choice, and you indicate your answers by pointing and clicking with a mouse to darken a "bubble" on the monitor screen. The GMAT CAT also includes the Analytical Writing Assessment or AWA. The AWA is an essay test. You write essay responses to two "prompts" or topics by keyboarding (typing in) your answer.

On the multiple-choice parts of the GMAT CAT, the computer keeps track of your right and wrong answers and, at the end of the session, calculates your scores. At that point, you have the following options:

- Cancel your scores (before seeing them)
- Seeing your scores immediately (and receiving a written report in a few weeks)
- Waiting to receive a written score report in a few weeks

Your keyboarded responses to the AWA are not scored by the computer. Instead, copies of your responses are sent to a team of graders who read your essays and assign them a mark. Your AWA scores will be sent to you along with the written report containing your GMAT CAT scores.

If you are unhappy with your scores, you can retake the GMAT CAT once per calendar month.

What Is the GMAC?

The letters G-M-A-C stand for Graduate Management Admission Council. The GMAC is an association of representatives from over 120 graduate schools of management. The council describes itself as both a professional and service organization. As a professional organization, it seeks to provide a forum for the exchange of ideas among those concerned with education for management. As a service organization, it arranges for the development and administration of the GMAT CAT. You will not, however, need to be in contact with the GMAC. You will deal directly with the graduate schools to which you are applying and with ETS, the organization that is in charge of giving the GMAT CAT.

What Is ETS?

The letters E-T-S stand for Educational Testing Service. ETS is a private company with headquarters in Princeton, New Jersey, and offices in many other places. Educational Testing Service, as the name suggests, offers testing services. (ETS also writes and administers the SAT.)

How Do You Register for the GMAT CAT?

GMAT information and registration forms can be found in the *GMAT Bulletin*, which is available from your Career Placement Office or by contacting:

By Mail:	Graduate Management Admission Test
	Educational Testing Service
	P. O. Box 6103
	Princeton, NJ 08541-6103
By Phone:	(609) 771-7330
By e-mail:	gmat@ets.org
On-line:	http://www.gmat.org

You can register in either of the following two ways:
- On-line using the URL above if you have a Visa, MasterCard, or American Express card
- By phone by calling one of the hundreds of test centers listed in the *Bulletin*.

To schedule your test, you must call one of the designated test centers and make an appointment. While it is possible to make the appointment even just a few days before you would like to take the test, it is better to schedule a few weeks in advance to ensure that you get an appointment that is convenient for you.

A Quick Look at the GMAT CAT

✓ **Topics Covered**

Introducing the GMAT CAT

The GMAT CAT Verbal Question Types

The GMAT CAT Quantitative Question Types

The Analytical Writing Assessment

The Structure of the Test

Scoring the GMAT CAT

Introducing the GMAT CAT

The GMAT CAT has both a multiple-choice part and an essay part (called the Analytical Writing Assessment). The multiple-choice part is administered in two separately timed sections:

Multiple Choice
Verbal:	41 Questions—75 minutes
Quantitative:	37 Questions—75 minutes

The essay part is also administered in two separately timed sections:

Essay
Issue Topic:	1 topic—30 minutes
Argument Topic:	1 topic—30 minutes

You must write on the topics that are assigned. You may not write on a topic of your own choosing.

You will be given the opportunity to take two five-minute breaks—one after the Analytical Writing Assessment (which is administered first) and a second one between the two multiple-choice sections.

Verbal Section

The GMAT CAT uses three different kinds of verbal questions: reading comprehension, sentence correction, and critical reasoning.

Reading Comprehension

Reading comprehension questions are based upon a reading selection. The questions ask about the author's main point, the logic of the selection, some details mentioned in the selection, or the tone of the selection. To give you a better idea of what reading comprehension is like, here is an example of a brief reading selection with two questions. Later we will study longer selections.

Directions: Read the selection and answer the questions associated with it.

EXAMPLE:

Those who discover the people of Appalachia through quiet patience and open friendliness will rediscover something characteristically American. Part of it is awareness and appreciation of the individual, which have characterized every aspect of Appalachian history and culture. Since the romance of James

Fenimore Cooper's *The Leatherstocking Tales* on the "glimmerglass" of New York's Otsego Lake, Davy Crockett's tall tales of the Tennessee frontier, and the realistic character portrayals of North Carolina's mountain son Thomas Wolfe, there have been numerous efforts to "interpret" Appalachian life.

Even George Washington didn't fathom the ferocity of the Appalachian's claim to personal liberty—until the Whiskey Rebellion caused backwoodsmen to take up arms and march east in protest against excessive taxes on their mountain brew. Before and during the Civil War, mountain independence asserted itself once more; many of the Appalachian counties in Virginia, Tennessee, and North Carolina either seceded from their states or refused to support the Confederacy.

1. The author is primarily concerned with

    Ⓐ condemning the backwoodsmen for the Whiskey Rebellion

    Ⓑ describing the character of the people of Appalachia

    Ⓒ listing the main geographical divisions of Appalachia

    Ⓓ praising the people of Appalachia for ignoring the Civil War

    Ⓔ criticizing literary attempts to interpret Appalachian life

2. According to the author, which of the following are characteristics of the Appalachian people?

    I. Ferocity

    II. Independence

    III. Dishonesty

    Ⓐ I only   Ⓑ I and II only   Ⓒ I and III only   Ⓓ II and III only
    Ⓔ I, II, and III

The first question asks about the main point of the selection. The best answer is (B). (A), (D), and (E) are incorrect for pretty much the same reason. Though the author does mention those things, no condemnation, praise, or criticism is implied. As for (C), the author never gives such a list. (B) is the best description of the author's main point. The passage describes the important traits of the Appalachian people.

The second question asks about specific points mentioned in the selection. The best answer is (B). The first sentence of the second paragraph mentions ferocity, and the last sentence of the passage mentions independence. No mention, however, is made of dishonesty.

Sentence Correction

Sentence correction items require you to study a sentence, part or all of which is underlined, and to determine whether that underlined part is correctly written. Although the underlined parts of some items may be correct, most contain one or more errors of grammar or syntax.

EXAMPLES:

1. The rising tide of opposition to smoking in public places such as bus depots and restaurants <u>are prompting many state legislatures to consider</u> banning smoking in such location.

   Ⓐ are prompting many state legislatures to consider

   Ⓑ is prompting many state legislatures to consider

   Ⓒ are prompting many state legislatures considering

   Ⓓ is prompting many state legislatures considering

   Ⓔ is prompting many state legislatures' consideration of

2. <u>Thrown onto the stage by adoring fans, the prima ballerina knelt gracefully and gathered up the bouquets of red roses.</u>

   Ⓐ Thrown onto the stage by adoring fans, the prima ballerina knelt gracefully and gathered up the bouquets of red roses.

   Ⓑ Throwing onto the stage by adoring fans, the prima ballerina knelt gracefully and gathered up the bouquets of red roses.

   Ⓒ Thrown onto the stage by adoring fans, the prima ballerina had knelt gracefully before gathering up the bouquets of red roses.

   Ⓓ Thrown onto the stage by adoring fans, the bouquets of red roses were gathered up by the prima ballerina after she had knelt gracefully.

   Ⓔ The prima ballerina knelt gracefully and gathered up the bouquets of red roses that had been thrown onto the stage by adoring fans.

The best answer to the first item is (B). The subject of the sentence is *tide*, a singular noun. So the verb should also be singular, *is* rather than *are*. (C) fails to make the needed change. (D) and (E) make the needed change but introduce new errors. As for (D), the use of the gerund *considering* rather than the infinitive *to consider* is not idiomatic, and (E) is very awkward. (B) makes the needed change without introducing any new error.

The best answer to the second item is (E). This sentence is afflicted by the notorious dangling modifier. As written, the sentence implies that the prima ballerina was thrown onto the stage by the adoring fans. To avoid this ambiguity, the modifier should be placed closer to what it modifies, the bouquets. Only (D) and (E) make any attempt to correct the placement of the modifier. (D) attempts to correct the sentence by moving what is modified, but the resulting sentence is awkward. (E) is a better choice. (E) not only solves the problem of the dangling modifier, it is also a more direct way of rendering the thought.

Critical Thinking

Critical reasoning items ask you to evaluate an argument. The argument may be a single sentence or a short paragraph.

EXAMPLES:

1. I never wear a seat belt when I'm just going to the store, because I won't be driving more than 30 miles per hour.

    The speaker above apparently assumes that automobile accidents

    Ⓐ never occur when a car is traveling at exactly 30 miles per hour

    Ⓑ always occur when a car is traveling in excess of 30 miles per hour

    Ⓒ occur only when a car is traveling at 30 miles per hour or less

    Ⓓ occur only when a car is traveling at more than 30 miles per hour

    Ⓔ occur only when a driver is not in his own neighborhood

2. It is clear that television scenes depicting acts of violence can result in actual crimes. After a major network aired a movie in which a man is shown leaping to his death from a bridge, there were three such suicides.

    The author's primary concern is to

    Ⓐ refute a theory

    Ⓑ prove a causal connection

    Ⓒ appeal to an authority

    Ⓓ point out a contradiction

    Ⓔ make a statistical comparison

The best answer to the first question is (D). The question stem asks you to figure out what must have been on the speaker's mind when the statement was made. For the statement to make sense, it must be the case that the speaker feels that accidents just don't occur if you are driving at 30 miles per hour or less. If that's true, then the claim makes sense.

The best answer to the second question is (B). The author is attempting to demonstrate that the airing of the movie was responsible for three incidents similar to that depicted in the movie. So the best description of the paragraph is that the author is attempting to show a causal connection.

Quantitative Section

GMAT CAT quantitative questions test arithmetic, basic algebra, and elementary geometry. The specific topics that you should know are discussed later in the chapters on math. Math questions on the GMAT CAT have one of two different formats: problem-solving and data sufficiency.

Problem Solving

The problem-solving format is the one you're most likely to be familiar with. It includes manipulation questions, word problems, and geometry questions.

EXAMPLES:

If $x = 2$, then $2x(3x - 2) =$

Ⓐ –6   Ⓑ 0   Ⓒ 8   Ⓓ 12   Ⓔ 16

The answer to this algebraic manipulation is (E). You solve the problem by substituting 2 in place of *x* in the expression $2x(3x-2)$:

$$2(2)[3(2)-2] = 4[6-2] = 4(4) = 16$$

> Elizabeth reads at a constant rate of 45 pages per hour. If she reads without being interrupted, how long will it take her, in hours, to read a book 360 pages long?
>
> Ⓐ 4   Ⓑ 6   Ⓒ 8   Ⓓ 9   Ⓔ 10

The answer to this word problem is (C). To find the length of time, you divide the total number of pages by the rate at which Elizabeth reads:

$$\frac{360 \text{ pages}}{45 \text{ pages per hour}} = 8 \text{ hours}$$

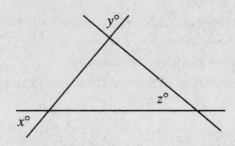

> In the figure above, if $x + y = 100$, then $z =$
>
> Ⓐ 40   Ⓑ 50   Ⓒ 60   Ⓓ 80   Ⓔ 90

The answer to this geometry problem is (D). Angles *x* and *y*, which are outside the triangle, are equal to their opposite angles inside the triangle.

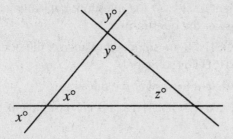

Since the sum of the angles inside a triangle is 180 degrees, we know that $x + y + z = 180$. Then, since $x + y = 100$, we know $100 + z = 180$. So $z = 80$.

Data Sufficiency

Data sufficiency math problems are in a format that is unique to the GMAT. These problems are governed by special directions:

Directions: Each data sufficiency problem consists of a question followed by two statements, labeled (1) and (2). You have to decide whether the data given in the numbered statements are *sufficient* to answer the question asked. Choose:

Ⓐ Statement (1) BY ITSELF is sufficient to answer the question, but statement (2) by itself is not sufficient to answer the question.

Ⓑ Statement (2) BY ITSELF is sufficient to answer the question, but statement (1) by itself is not sufficient to answer the question.

Ⓒ BOTH statements (1) and (2) TOGETHER are sufficient to answer the question, but NEITHER statement BY ITSELF is sufficient.

Ⓓ EACH statement BY ITSELF is sufficient to answer the question.

Ⓔ The two statements, even when taken TOGETHER are NOT sufficient to answer the question.

EXAMPLES:

1. Candy costs $1.50 a pound. How much did the candy in a certain box cost?

   (1) The box contains 2 pounds of candy.

   (2) The box contains 24 pieces of candy.

   Ⓐ Statement (1) BY ITSELF is sufficient to answer the question, but statement (2) by itself is not sufficient to answer the question.

   Ⓑ Statement (2) BY ITSELF is sufficient to answer the question, but statement (1) by itself is not sufficient to answer the question.

   Ⓒ BOTH statements (1) and (2) TOGETHER are sufficient to answer the question, but NEITHER statement BY ITSELF is sufficient.

   Ⓓ EACH statement BY ITSELF is sufficient to answer the question.

   Ⓔ The two statements, even when taken TOGETHER are NOT sufficient to answer the question.

2. Exactly how many puppies are there in a certain litter?

   (1) There are more than four puppies in the litter.

   (2) There are fewer than six puppies in the litter.

   Ⓐ Statement (1) BY ITSELF is sufficient to answer the question, but statement (2) by itself is not sufficient to answer the question.

   Ⓑ Statement (2) BY ITSELF is sufficient to answer the question, but statement (1) by itself is not sufficient to answer the question.

   Ⓒ BOTH statements (1) and (2) TOGETHER are sufficient to answer the question, but NEITHER statement BY ITSELF is sufficient.

   Ⓓ EACH statement BY ITSELF is sufficient to answer the question.

   Ⓔ The two statements, even when taken TOGETHER are NOT sufficient to answer the question.

3. One hundred twenty-five students were graduated from Eastern High School in 1984. How many students were graduated from Eastern High School in 1985?

   (1) Twenty-five more students were graduated from Eastern High School in 1985 than in 1984.

   (2) The number of students who were graduated from Eastern High School increased by 20 percent from 1984 to 1985.

   Ⓐ Statement (1) BY ITSELF is sufficient to answer the question, but statement (2) by itself is not sufficient to answer the question.

   Ⓑ Statement (2) BY ITSELF is sufficient to answer the question, but statement (1) by itself is not sufficient to answer the question.

   Ⓒ BOTH statements (1) and (2) TOGETHER are sufficient to answer the question, but NEITHER statement BY ITSELF is sufficient.

   Ⓓ EACH statement BY ITSELF is sufficient to answer the question.

   Ⓔ The two statements, even when taken TOGETHER are NOT sufficient to answer the question.

4. Bob took a multiple-choice test. What was the percent of all the questions on the test that he answered correctly?

   (1) Bob left 25 questions blank.

   (2) The test contained a total of 150 questions.

   Ⓐ Statement (1) BY ITSELF is sufficient to answer the question, but statement (2) by itself is not sufficient to answer the question.

   Ⓑ Statement (2) BY ITSELF is sufficient to answer the question, but statement (1) by itself is not sufficient to answer the question.

   Ⓒ BOTH statements (1) and (2) TOGETHER are sufficient to answer the question, but NEITHER statement BY ITSELF is sufficient.

   Ⓓ EACH statement BY ITSELF is sufficient to answer the question.

   Ⓔ The two statements, even when taken TOGETHER are NOT sufficient to answer the question.

The answer to Question 1 is (A). Statement (1) alone provides enough information to determine the cost of the candy: 2 pounds × $1.50/pound = $3.00. Statement (2) alone does not provide enough information to answer the question. Since statement (1) alone is sufficient but statement (2) alone is not, this item should be classified as (A).

The answer to Question 2 is (C). Neither statement alone provides enough information to answer the question, but the two statements taken together do. If there are more than four but fewer than six puppies in the litter, then there must be exactly five puppies in the litter. Since neither statement alone is sufficient to answer the question, but both taken together are, this item should be classified as (C).

The answer to Question 3 is (D). Statement (1) provides enough information to answer the question: 125 + 25 = 150 students who were graduated in 1985. Statement (2) also provides enough information to answer the question. The number of students who were graduated increased by 20 percent: 20% of 125 = 25, and 125 + 25 = 150 students who were graduated in 1985. Since each statement is in and of itself sufficient to answer the question, this item should be classified as (D).

The answer to Question 4 is (E). Neither statement alone provides enough information to answer the question. Further, even when both statements are taken together they do not provide enough information to answer the question: How many questions answered *correctly*? Since the statements, even when taken together, are not sufficient to answer the question, this item should be classified as (E).

Analytical Writing Assessment

The essay portion of the GMAT CAT consists of two separately timed parts. In each part, you are given a topic or prompt and must compose an essay on that topic at the computer keyboard within the time limit given. One of the topics will be an "issue" topic and the other will be an "argument" topic.

Issue Topic

People often complain that manufacturers consciously follow a policy of planned obsolescence and make products that are designed to wear out quickly. Planned obsolescence, they insist, wastes both natural and human resources. They fail to recognize, however, that the use of cheaper materials and manufacturing processes keeps costs down for the consumer and stimulates demand.

Which position do you find more persuasive, the complaint about planned obsolescence or the response to it? Explain your position, using relevant reasons and/or examples taken from experience, observations, or readings.

Argument Topic

All commercial airliners operating in the United States should be required to carry a computerized on-board warning system that can receive signals from the transponders of other aircraft. (A transponder is a radio device that signals a plane's course.) The system would be able to alert pilots to the danger of a collision and recommend evasive action. Installation of the system would virtually eliminate the danger of mid-air collisions.

Discuss the argument above. Analyze its logical structure and use of evidence. What, if anything, would make the argument more persuasive or would help you better to evaluate its conclusion?

The Structure of the Test

The following chart shows the structure of a typical GMAT CAT.

A TYPICAL GMAT CAT

Section	Number of Questions	Time
Warm-up Period		Untimed
Analytical Writing Assessment		
Issue Topic	1	30 min.
Argument Topic	1	30 min.
(optional break)		5 min.
Quantitative Section	37	75 min.
(optional break)		5 min.
Verbal Section	41	75 min.

The warm-up period is untimed and contains no questions that count toward a score. Instead, the warm-up period allows you to become familiar with the computer (the mouse and scroll bar functions in particular) and with the peculiarities of the program itself.

Scoring the GMAT CAT

The Scaled Scores

The multiple-choice sections of the GMAT CAT generate three scores: a verbal score, a quantitative score, and a composite score. The verbal and quantitative scores are reported on scales ranging from 0 to 60, and the composite score is reported on a scale ranging from 200 to 800.

The Algorithm

The most remarkable (and, admittedly, most mysterious) thing about the GMAT CAT is that at the moment you sit down at the testing carrel, there is no already-prepared test. In the computer's memory is a database containing test items, a few of which you will see, most of which you will not see. From this database of items, the computer literally builds your individualized test as you work through the GMAT CAT.

At the heart of this process is what is called an algorithm. An algorithm is a logically structured process. In essence, the algorithm tells the computer to move you up or down a ladder of difficulty according to whether you are answering questions correctly. If you answer correctly, then the computer gives you a more difficult item; if you answer incorrectly, then the computer gives you an easier item. The theory is that you will eventually reach a rung on the ladder of difficulty where further questions would simply move up one and back down or down one and back up, and so that rung on the ladder becomes your score.

Of course, the actual algorithm used for the GMAT CAT is immensely more complex than the simple model just described. According to its developers, it takes account not only of your answer on the last question but of your answers to all of the questions throughout the testing sequence. Further, it is designed make sure that your session covers all of the relevant concepts that are tested. Finally, the GMAT CAT algorithm is a carefully guarded corporate secret, so no one outside of ETS really knows very much about it.

None of this should worry you, however. It is out of your control, so you should just sit back and take the GMAT CAT, and let the computer worry about the details.

AWA Scores

The AWA or essay portion of the GMAT CAT is scored using a "holistic" grading system. Essays are assigned to two readers, each of whom assigns a grade independently on a scale of 0 (the minimum) to 6 (the maximum). If the scores assigned by the two readers are no more than one point apart, the score assigned to the essay is the average of those two scores. Thus, if one reader assigns an essay a "5" and the other assigns it a "4," the score for that essay is "4.5." If the scores assigned by the two readers are more than one point apart, say "3" and "5," the essay is given to a third reader. If the third score is "4," the average of the three scores, which is "4," is used. If the third score is "5," the "3" is discarded as unreliable, and a final score of "5" is assigned to the essay. A final Analytical Writing Assessment score is computed by averaging the scores on both essays and rounding off to the nearest one-half point.

The task is in some respects similar to that of the judges who evaluate Olympic athletics, such as gymnastics. It is the overall performance including writing skill and analysis that counts. Thus, just as two gymnastic routines that differ in level of difficulty and execution may receive similar scores, two Analytical Writing Assessment essays that are very different may receive the same score. According to the designers of the GMAT CAT, because readers are trained in advance to apply specified criteria, discrepant grades (grades more than one point apart) are very rare.

8 Ways to Tame the CAT

✓ **Topics Covered**

Get to Know the CAT

Practice the Tutorial

Dismiss the Directions

Take Your Optional Breaks

Keep up the Pace

Guess When You Have To

Answer All of the Questions

Don't Worry About How You Are Doing

CAT? Hey, No Problema

The GMAT is now a computer-based interactive exam. Is that a big deal? Only if you still use a rotary dial phone, pound a manual typewriter instead of using a word processor, or long for the "good old days" of black-and-white television. Otherwise, if you are like most adults under the age of 30, you have probably been dealing with computers on an almost daily basis for most your life. (And the research done by the GMAT division of ETS bears this out.) Therefore, the GMAT on computer is really no big deal.

Of course, a small minority of GMAT test-takers may fall into one of the disfavored categories mentioned above. If you do, then you may be disappointed that this chapter contains no "Gee Willy Whiz Bang Beat the Computer" strategies. But don't be disappointed because there simply aren't any. The GMAT on the computer is just the GMAT all over again. You need to concentrate on the substantive issues that are tested and not worry about the procedure used to deliver the test.

There are a few—but only a few—points to keep in mind about the new CAT delivery system.

Get to Know the CAT

You can increase your chances of scoring high on the CAT by practicing with the computer-based format in advance. One way is with ARCO's own simulated CATs, which offer you the chance to take as many CATs as you choose. This software is packaged with one version of this book. Another way to practice is to take the Official GMAT Practice Test. You can schedule an appointment for this test by calling your local GMAT testing center.

Practice the Tutorial

The testing session begins with an untimed tutorial that has no scored items. This is your chance to get the feel of the application and the hardware that is provided. This is free computer time. ETS does not refund you any money if you finish the tutorial session early. So take all the time you need.

Make sure that you feel completely comfortable with the hardware. The mouse may have a slightly different shape from the one that you are used to or be more or less sensitive. The commands such as "enter" and "confirm" may not have exactly the significance that you expect. So spend the time to make sure that you know how to use the tools effectively.

Dismiss the Directions

The directions for a question type may appear on the screen at various times during the testing session. You will probably have a tendency to think that they will time out—like a splash screen. But they don't. You have to point and click to make them go away.

Make that your first priority. By the time you actually sit down to take the GMAT CAT, the directions should be irrelevant. Instead, you should be able to recognize the question type presented just by its layout and know exactly what to do with an item.

Take Your Optional Breaks

You will be given the option of taking a five-minute break after the one-hour AWA part (the essay component) and another five-minute break after the first 75-minute section (whether it is verbal or math). Take these breaks! After you have finished a part, you may feel strong and think that you are on a roll, but you could crash and burn half-way through the next 75-minute section. At that point, you don't have the option of taking a break. So take advantage of the rest opportunities as they are presented.

Keep Up the Pace

You will be able to finish the Verbal Section of the GMAT CAT if you allow yourself approximately one and three-quarter minutes for each question. You can finish the Quantitative Section if you allow about two minutes per question. You will get a score even if you don't finish a section, but your chances of getting a good score are better if you manage to answer every one of the questions.

Guess When You Have To

Questions on the CAT are presented one at a time, and you can't move on from any one question until you have selected an answer and confirmed your choice. So this means you have to guess, right?

Not exactly. The issue of whether or not to guess on the GMAT has been pretty much made a non-issue by the CAT format. If you can't answer a question, you have to answer anyway. Is that a "guess," or is it just a "testing procedure"? That's a question of semantics that you don't have to worry about. When you sense that you are not making any progress on an item, eliminate as many choices as possible and then enter and confirm a response.

Is there a penalty for guessing incorrectly? Again, the question no longer makes sense so the answer is irrelevant. Since you have to answer (period), it doesn't make any sense to worry about a penalty. If you answer wrongly, the computer's algorithm will move you down a notch on the ladder of difficulty. But what's your alternative? You can sit there until you run out of time and get a really, really bad score. Or you can take your best shot (and get zinged if that happens) and move on, hoping to get back on track.

Answer All of the Questions

The scoring mechanism for the GMAT CAT has a curious feature. If you do not answer all of the questions in the allotted time, the computer assesses an automatic penalty: Your score is lowered proportionately for the number of questions you failed to answer.

Obviously, then, it is to your advantage to answer all questions, even if you are guessing at random as time begins to run out. (Statistical theory predicts that unless you are having the very worst day of your entire life, you will get some of them right and will show a net profit.)

What is the reason for this feature? The first CAT exams required a minimum number of responses and offered a maximum number of items, say between 24 and 30. The test-writers finally figured out that test-takers had figured out that they might as well work more slowly   answering just the minimum and ensuring that they answered the highest number correctly. Now, however, you must make sure that you finish the required number of questions.

Don't Worry About How You Are Doing

Of course, this is hard advice to follow. It is only natural to want to know "how are things going." You will try to feel whether you are moving up the ladder of difficulty or down. Unfortunately, this is a waste of psychic energy because knowing or not knowing cannot help you answer correctly. Just eat everything that is served— and as quickly as possible.

There is another reason for not worrying about where you are standing on the ladder of difficulty: Experimental questions are embedded in the sequence. Questions that are being tested for statistical features for possible use on future exams can appear at any point. And the test-writer might want to give an examinee who is doing very, very well an easy question just to see how it works. In other words, you could have the feeling that you are sailing along close to the ceiling of difficulty and then suddenly get a question that any first-grader could answer. It doesn't mean that you have suddenly fallen off the ladder of difficulty into the basement but rather that you have encountered an anomalous item.

In short, then, don't worry about how you are doing during the test. It cannot help you; it can only hurt you. Do your best, and let the computer do its job.

Demystifying the GMAT

✓ **Topics Covered**

ETS Is Just a Business

The Test-Makers Aren't Geniuses

The GMAT Isn't Perfect

The Testing Process Is No Cause for Alarm

Your Score Isn't Everything

ETS Is Just a Business

Many, even most, students experience a sense of dread or foreboding about the GMAT. For some, the feeling is no more than an uncomfortable and vague sense of uneasiness. For others, the dread can become unmanageable, leading to what is called test anxiety. In extreme cases, test anxiety can be crippling and can seriously interfere with a person's ability to take a test. This extreme anxiety, the fear of the GMAT as a final judgment, is created by a group of mistaken beliefs, or impressions. You do not have to experience all of the impressions to feel the strong sense of anxiety. What are these mistaken beliefs and impressions?

Most people regard the GMAT as having a kind of natural authority over them, something like the physical laws that govern the universe. Why is there a GMAT? Well, that's like asking why there is gravity. It's just there, a fact of the world. This impression is mistaken.

To see that this impression of natural authority is an error, you need only think about the nature of your relationship to the GMAT. When you register to take the GMAT, you are entering into a legal contract with ETS (the company that writes and administers the GMAT) and indirectly with the Graduate Management Admission Council. ETS is a company. You are paying that company a fee, and it agrees in turn to provide you with a service. That service is to administer to you a test and to report your scores to the schools you designate. Because you pay the fee, ETS has a legal obligation to you.

The registration form you sign and the information booklet you receive from ETS set forth in detail the specific provisions of your agreement with the company. Don't worry that all of this is not one single typed document, like a deed. It's still a legal contract. (In fact, most contracts are just verbal agreements, and they are still legally binding.) So you and ETS are parties to a business contract.

Two factors, however, tend to obscure the fact that the relationship between you and ETS is a business contract. First, ETS is a nonprofit corporation. People reason "since ETS is not in business to make a profit, they must administer the GMAT for altruistic reasons." This reasoning is mistaken. Though ETS does not show a profit, the people who operate the company are motivated by many of the same concerns that motivate the people who run General Motors or IBM. They are concerned about income, expenses, the quality of their product, their share of the market, customer relations, and so on. In fact, "GMAT" is a registered business trademark, like Coca-Cola.

This doesn't mean that the people who work at ETS don't believe in what they do. They believe that they produce a good product and they are proud of it. Just because they are a "nonprofit" corporation does not necessarily make them morally better than any other business.

The second factor that helps to create the impression of natural authority is size. ETS is very large and produces other tests such as the SAT. For this reason, ETS seems almost like a government agency. But the same can be said of many other large businesses, like power companies. You buy electricity from a particular business because it is the one that services your area. So, too, the GMAT "services" a large market. Interestingly, ETS does have competitors. Perhaps we will soon see an increase in competition in the area of standardized testing, just as we have seen an increase in competition in telephone communications.

In any event, the GMAT really has no natural authority over you. Your relationship is in the form of a contract—and it takes two parties to make a contract. You are an equal partner to the contract, and you have certain legal rights under the contract.

The Test-Makers Aren't Geniuses

The testing process also creates another mistaken impression. You sit down in a carrel at the testing center. You have to answer a lot of questions in a very short time. So, you begin to think that the person who wrote these questions must really be superhuman because you are expected to answer so many questions (and some of them are very difficult) in so short a time. This impression that genius is behind the test is an error. This test is not written by a single person, nor by two people, or even three. Rather, the test is the product of a large group of people, including teachers, reviewers, and statisticians. Each question is a group effort.

In fact, you will be involved in the process of creating GMAT questions. As a final check, experimental questions are embedded in your test. ETS then uses its computers to check for patterns. Do the experimental questions work in the way they want them to? Examinee responses on the experimental items of the GMAT are essential to the development of the exam.

The GMAT Isn't Perfect

A related impression conveyed by the testing process is that it is free from error. A misconception! In the first place, you are probably aware that every so often ETS slips up. You will find a newspaper report to the effect "Math Wiz Finds Test Error." But such errors do not occur very frequently.

The impression of infallibility is a mistake for a more important reason. Built into the scoring of the GMAT (for the composite score) is a 60-point range of error! The technical term for this is the "standard error of measurement." The standard error of measurement for the GMAT is 30 points. This means that two-thirds of all scores are within 30 points above or below the "true score."

So, for most students a GMAT score of 500 represents a true score of anywhere from 470 to 530. And for a full third of the test-takers, the score is even less accurate.

It is an error, therefore, to treat GMAT scores as though they are accurate to one or two points. The test is actually a very crude measuring device.

The Testing Process Is No Cause for Alarm

The testing process can also create a mistaken impression that ETS is all-powerful and that you are powerless. ETS sets the fees, the locations, and the conditions under which you will take the exam. It is true that you have very little say in these matters. Just remember, though, that this is the result of ETS's quasi-monopoly in the area of standardized testing.

ETS controls a large enough share of the market so that you have to do business with it. That is an economic fact of life, like public utilities. But ETS is no more omnipotent than your local electric, gas, or phone company.

This impression of omnipotence can also haunt you as you take the test. You are told where to sit, what you may and may not have with you, when you can use the rest room. And when you read the rules on the computer screen governing the testing procedure, it may sound as though you are hearing sentence passed. It may be difficult, but try to ignore this feeling. The supervisors maintain an air of authority to help them keep control of the situation.

Your Score Isn't Everything

One of the most important aspects of the fear of final judgment is the impression of finality created by the testing process. To a certain extent, the result of your test (barring a mistake in scoring) is final. Once a test is graded, that is the score you receive and it doesn't change. But many people have the mistaken impression that bad (or good) things are automatically going to happen as a result of the GMAT. In fact, the GMAT is a lot less important than you might think.

First, very few schools (if any) regard GMAT scores as either passing or failing. The score is just one more factor used in making a decision, like grades, activities, motivation, employment history, and so on. So a "poor" grade will not necessarily keep you out of a school, and a "good" grade will not guarantee you will get in.

Second, a year after you take the test no one else will care what your score was. Your professors will grade you on the basis of your course work. New acquaintances will accept you on the basis of your personality. Student associations will want you as a member for your motivation, energy, and ability.

In discussing the "myth" of final judgment, I do not mean to imply that anyone or any group set out to perpetrate a hoax. In particular, I am not suggesting that ETS or the GMAC consciously conspired to mislead people. In fact, if you read the information bulletin that comes with the registration materials for the GMAT, you will find that ETS and the GMAC say many of the same things I have just said.

I suppose that this mistaken impression of final judgment could be just an accident of history, but you do not have to live with it. (After all, at the time of Columbus, almost everyone believed the world was flat.) If you take care to avoid falling under the spell of any one of the individual misconceptions, you should be able to keep any fears you might have about the GMAT under control.

Unlocking the Mystery

✓ Topics Covered

GMAT Questions All Follow a Pattern

The Answers Are There in Front of You

Learning to Think Like Sherlock Holmes

Wouldn't it be great to take a test where you had all the questions in advance and the answers right there on the screen? Well, the GMAT comes close. First, it is almost possible to know in advance what questions will be asked. Second, the answers are actually given to you on the screen. These two features of the test form the basis for our system.

GMAT Questions All Follow a Pattern

Year after year the GMAT is given to hundreds of thousands of students; and, according to ETS, scores are comparable—not just from administration to administration within a given year, but even from year to year. But how is that possible, since the computer designs your test as you take it? The answer is found in the specifications for the test. Each question is written according to special formulas. A question is not acceptable for use on a GMAT unless it fits a particular pattern. These patterns are there for you to learn, and that is like having the questions before the test. Of course, you cannot literally have the exact questions that will appear on your particular GMAT, but certain patterns are so clearly identifiable that it almost amounts to the same thing.

The Answers Are There in Front of You

Additionally, you are actually given the answer to every question on your GMAT. Since every question on the exam is a multiple-choice question, the right answer is there on the screen. Of course, the correct answer is camouflaged in a group of wrong answers; but even though it is partially hidden, it's there for the taking. To demonstrate how important this is, we interrupt this discussion for a:

POP QUIZ

Who was the fourth Chief Justice of the United States Supreme Court?

Time's up! I am not going to give you the correct answer just yet. (If you do know the answer, that's good, and I would want you as my partner in a game of trivia. But for right now, let's assume that you do not know the answer.) It is not the answer to the question that is important to us, but the form of the question. With a question in this form, you have to come up with an answer from scratch. Either you know the name of the fourth Chief Justice of the Supreme Court or you do not. And if not, you must make a wild guess, so your chance of getting the right answer would be very small.

Things change, however, if the question is converted to a multiple-choice format.

POP QUIZ

Who was the fourth Chief Justice of the United States Supreme Court?
Ⓐ   xxxx xxxxx   Ⓑ   xxxx xxxxx   Ⓒ   xxxx xxxxx
Ⓓ   xxxx xxxxx   Ⓔ   xxxx xxxxx

Notice that the choices have been covered. Still, even though you cannot read the choices, you are in a much better position than you were before. Given the form of the earlier question, without the knowledge needed to answer the question you had literally no chance of getting credit for it. Now, even though you may not have knowledge that will allow you to answer with confidence, you at least have a fighting chance: pick any letter, and you have a one-out-of-five chance of getting credit for the question.

With real answer choices, you can tip the odds even more in your favor.

POP QUIZ

Who was the fourth Chief Justice of the United States Supreme Court?
Ⓐ   Julius Caesar   Ⓑ   Mickey Mouse   Ⓒ   Roger Taney
Ⓓ   David Letterman   Ⓔ   Madonna
Enter the letter of your choice here: _____

The answer is (C), and almost everyone can answer correctly even though they have never before seen the name Roger Taney.

How is it possible to answer correctly and even confidently when you don't have the historical fact needed to answer the question? "Easy," you say. "Just eliminate the four choices that could not possibly be correct, and select the one that remains."

This method of reasoning is called the Process of Elimination, and it takes advantage of an inherent weakness in the multiple-choice format. One—and only one—of the choices is correct. If you keep eliminating wrong choices, eventually only the correct choice will remain.

Granted, eliminating wrong choices on the GMAT will not usually be this easy, but the principle is the same. Even if you cannot eliminate four choices as incorrect, eliminating even one choice tips the odds in your favor and requires a guess.

Patterns and answers are inherent in the GMAT. Get rid of either one, and the GMAT is no longer the GMAT. Therefore, so long as there is a GMAT there will be patterns that can be learned and a multiple-choice format that can be taken advantage of.

Learning to Think Like Sherlock Holmes

5

You are probably familiar with Sherlock Holmes, the fictional detective created by the British writer Sir Arthur Conan Doyle. Using clues and logic, Holmes is able to solve case after case, even though to everyone else the situations seem to present insoluble mysteries. Most people are also familiar with the character of Dr. Watson, Holmes' good-natured friend. Watson, a medical doctor, is clearly a bright person; but his powers of investigation and logical reasoning do not quite equal those of his friend Holmes.

What would happen if these characters took the GMAT? I imagine that Watson would do fairly well. He would be able to answer a good many of the questions, but he would likely miss a lot of the more difficult ones. On the other hand, Holmes would surely do very well, getting answers to difficult questions by methods that seem almost magical.

In solving cases, Holmes relies heavily on two techniques: looking for established patterns and the process of elimination. First, in case after case, Holmes refers to his studies of patterns—footprints, cigar ashes, chemicals, and so on. Having foreknowledge of what to look for is often the key to Holmes' solution of a mystery.

Second, Holmes also uses logical reasoning, in particular the process of elimination. In "The Adventure of the Bruce-Partington Plans," Holmes explains to Watson, "When all other contingencies fail, whatever remains, however improbable, must be the truth." That is the process of elimination. Thus, Holmes succeeded where others failed because he was able to identify patterns and because he reasoned logically. You will notice that these two techniques are the same ones we talked about above.

If Holmes and Watson were to take the GMAT, here is what I think would happen.

ADVENTURES OF THE GMAT

The Case of the Missing Reading Passage

One day Watson came to his friend Holmes with a problem, "Holmes," said Watson, "I have a reading comprehension question that I must answer, but I seem to have lost the reading selection on which the question is based. Now I'll never be able to answer the question."

"Show me the question," insisted Holmes, taking the page offered by Watson. On the page was written:

> The author's attitude toward the new technique of literary criticism is
>
> Ⓐ apathetic   Ⓑ sentimental   Ⓒ scholarly
> Ⓓ careless   Ⓔ approving

"Why, Watson," exclaimed Homes, "this is a multiple-choice question. My methods are perfectly suited to it. If we can eliminate four of the five choices by any means whatsoever, then the one choice that remains must be the correct one."

Holmes studied the question for a moment before he spoke further. "We can infer," he began, "from the question itself that in the missing reading selection the author discussed some new technique of literary criticism. Now let us study the answer choices.

"In the first place, Watson, (A) does not seem to be a possible answer. The question stem informs us that the author has been writing about this new development. But if the author has gone to the trouble of writing an article about something, then it hardly seems likely that the author had no interest in the topic. We conclude, therefore, that the author is not apathetic.

"Now let us examine (B). Could the author's attitude be described as 'sentimental'? Before you answer yes, Watson, let's return to the question. The question asks about the author's attitude toward some new development. Is it possible that you would ever describe someone's attitude toward a new development as sentimental?"

"No," Watson agreed. "But the author might have regarded the old method with affection."

"Perhaps, Watson. But literary criticism does not seem the sort of thing about which one would feel sentimental. And in any case, the question asks for the author's attitude toward the new literary criticism—not the old criticism. So you see, (B) cannot be correct."

"So the correct choice must be (C)," offered Watson. "Literary criticism is a scholarly endeavor, so the missing reading passage must have been a scholarly work."

"Not too fast, my dear friend," Holmes interrupted. "Although I readily grant what you say, that does not prove that (C) is the answer we seek. The question does not ask about the author's style but about the author's opinion of the new development. I think you would agree that it makes little sense to say that the author's opinion is scholarly."

"So we must eliminate (C)," said Watson. "Holmes, even if we are not successful in eliminating one of the remaining choices, at least I shall have an even chance of selecting the correct one. It must be either (D) or (E)."

"Well, Watson, it seems to me that we can eliminate (D) on very much the same ground that we eliminated (C). Although 'careless' might describe the author's method in discussing a topic, it surely would not describe the author's attitude toward the new development."

"By Jove, you're right!" Watson exclaimed. "The correct solution is probably (E)."

"Not probably," insisted Holmes. "Certainly! We have eliminated all possibilities but (E) and that proves (E) is the correct solution. We now know in fact that the author approves of the new development discussed in the reading selection—even though we do not have a copy of the selection."

The Case of the Hidden Clue

One wintry afternoon, Holmes and Watson were riding in the compartment of a train on their way back to London. Watson, looking up from the book he was reading, blurted out, "Blast these critical reasoning questions, Holmes. I can't figure out why the correct answer to this one is correct." And he read to Holmes the following:

Advertising claim: Bernie's Electronics is the only department store where you can buy a 19-inch Commander color television for $195, and for that price get Bernie's special six-month warranty.

Which of the following, if true, proves that the advertising claim above is FALSE?

Ⓐ The Commander Television Company's factory outlet sells the same model television for $195 and backs the set with the same six-month warranty.

Ⓑ Al's Department Store sells the same model television for $195 and backs the set with a twelve-month warranty.

Ⓒ Trader John's department store sells the same model television for $185 and backs the set with a twelve-month warranty.

Ⓓ Honest Hal's Department Store sells a 25-inch Commander color television for $195 and backs it with a warranty containing the same terms as Bernie's warranty.

Ⓔ Jumpin' Jack's Department Store sells the same model television for $195 and backs it with the same warranty.

Holmes furrowed his brow and read the problem carefully. After a while he said, "Yes, Watson, I can understand your perplexity. But the verbal clues are there for you to read. The correct answer is (E)."

"As you know, Watson," continued Holmes, "when I visit the scene of a crime, I pay very careful attention to all details. And I am particularly careful not to allow preconceptions about what is ordinarily true to influence my judgment."

You, too, must learn this approach in order to solve successfully problems such as this.

"Notice how cleverly the advertising claim is worded. Bernie's is the only department store that offers this particular make and model for $195 and includes Bernie's six-month warranty. In essence, the claim states only that Bernie's is the only establishment that meets all of these criteria.

"Choice (A) does not contradict this claim, since Bernie's is careful to distinguish itself as a department store—not a factory outlet. That a different type of commercial establishment offers a similar arrangement does not, therefore, contradict Bernie's claim.

"As for choices (B), (C), and (D), the fact that other emporia offer arrangements that are even more favorable than those offered by Bernie does not contradict Bernie's claim that he does exactly what he claims to do: sells the set for $195 and backs it with a six-month warranty.

"Only (E) contradicts the wording of the claim, for (E) establishes that there is another, similar commercial entity that also does what Bernie's claims to do uniquely."

At this point Watson let out a sigh of frustration and said, "Well, if critical reasoning items require this much attention to detail, I don't see that I can ever hope to succeed in solving them."

"Don't despair, Watson. Rome wasn't built in a day. As you study more and more critical reasoning items, you will gain skill in the kind of observation that is needed to do well on them."

The Case of the Missing Numbers

Watson approached Holmes with the following math problem:

> During a sale, the price of a book is reduced by 20 percent. If the price of the book after the reduction is D dollars, what was the original price?
>
> Ⓐ 2D   Ⓑ 1.25D   Ⓒ 1.20D   Ⓓ 0.80D   Ⓔ 0.75D

"I was able to answer this question," announced Watson, "but the algebra took considerable time."

Holmes, smiling, said "Good, Watson! Though I think you might have saved yourself considerable trouble by employing my methods. In the first place, I immediately eliminated choices (D) and (E). They are both less than the final reduced price of D dollars, and I know that the original price must be greater than D dollars.

"Next I eliminated (A). If a price is reduced from 2D dollars to D dollars, it is cut in half. Cutting a price in half reduces it by 50 percent—not 20 percent."

At this point Watson interjected, "But now you are forced to guess. You do have a fifty-fifty chance, but with my approach I can answer with complete certainty."

"Not too quickly," Holmes said. "With one very simple calculation, I can easily arrive at the same position. Since no numbers are provided in the question, I will just supply my own. Let us assume that D, the new price is $1, a very convenient assumption.

"Now let's test (B). If D, as we assume, is $1, then 1.25D is $1.25. Is that consistent with what we are told in the question? Yes. We are told the original price was reduced by 20 percent, or $\frac{1}{5}$. One-fifth of $1.25 is $0.25, and if you reduce $1.25 by $0.25, the result is $1. This simple calculation proves that the original price was 1.25D. (B) is correct."

"But, Holmes," objected Watson, "you were merely lucky. Had you selected (C) instead of (B) for your experiment, you would then have had to do two calculations, not just one. And such calculations are time-consuming."

"Not so," countered Holmes. "Even had I selected (C) rather than (B) for my test, I still would have needed only one calculation. When a calculation showed (C) to be incorrect, that, in and of itself, would establish by the process of elimination that the one remaining choice, (B), was correct."

The more you are able to think like Holmes, the better you will do on the GMAT. In the chapters that follow, you will read about basic strategies that would be used by Dr. Watson. These strategies are sound, but they are not the final word on attacking the GMAT. So you will also learn Holmesian strategies like those discussed in the stories above that take advantage of the multiple-choice format of the GMAT.

PART TWO
The Coaching Program

Reading Comprehension

✓ Topics Covered

1. **Why Reading Comprehension Is Difficult**

   - **The choice of topics**

   - **The lack of a title**

   - **The way the selections are edited**

2. **The Six Types of Reading Comprehension Questions**

   - **Main idea questions**

   - **Specific detail questions**

   - **Logical structure questions**

   - **Implied idea questions**

   - **Further application questions**

   - **Tone questions**

3. **Reading Techniques**

4. **Question Patterns That Clue You In**

   - **Main idea questions**

   - **Specific detail questions**

   - **Logical structure questions**

   - **Implied idea questions**

   - **Further application questions**

   - **Tone questions**

5. **A Perfect Format for Holmes' Strategies**

Here are the instructions for reading comprehension:

> **Directions:** The passage below is followed by questions based on its content. After reading it, choose the best answer to each question and select the corresponding oval. Answer the questions on the basis of what is *stated* or *implied* in the passage.

This seems easy enough, but the impression of simplicity is misleading.

Why Reading Comprehension Is Difficult

Reading comprehension is not a test of speed reading. Some students attribute the difficulty of reading comprehension to their inability to read quickly enough. They imagine they would do better if they were able to do "speed reading." This conclusion is completely incorrect! The GMAT is not a test of "speed reading." First, the reading selections are only three or perhaps four paragraphs long—not so long as to need "speed reading" techniques and too short to be susceptible to them. Second, the selections are edited in such a way as to make them too dense for "speed reading." Third, the questions test depth of understanding; and, in general, "speed reading" emphasizes coverage at the expense of understanding.

1. GMAT reading selections can treat virtually any subject. The categories include:

Social Sciences, e. g., history, sociology, archaeology, government, economics

Physical Sciences, e. g., physics, chemistry, astronomy, geology

Biological Sciences, e. g., medicine, botany, zoology

Humanities, e. g., art, literary criticism, philosophy, music, folklore

And this list does not exhaust the possibilities. Since authors can write about any topic whatsoever, a reading comprehension selection can be about anything.

Obviously, a reading selection about an unfamiliar topic is more difficult to read than one about material you know something about, and the test-writers go out of their way to find unfamiliar material.

Let's put this into perspective. The test-writers don't select obscure reading selections simply to make the reading more difficult. Rather, they select obscure passages to make sure the questions test reading comprehension rather than knowledge of a subject. The theory is that if a reading selection is about, say, the obscure medieval composer Josquin des Pres, no one will be able to answer questions based on memory.

Additionally, since this is not a test of knowledge, the reading selection will contain everything needed to answer the question. For example, if a reading comprehension question asks "Why is Josquin des Pres so little known?", the basis for the correct answer will be provided in the reading selection itself.

Finally, don't let the reading selections intimidate you! Imagine the following as an opening sentence of a reading passage:

Until Josquin des Pres, Western music was liturgical, designed as an accompaniment to worship.

Your reaction to this could be "Who the dickens is this guy? I've never even heard the name before. Now, I'll never be able to answer any questions!" This reaction, while understandable, is the wrong one to have. Rather, you should be thinking "Here's one of those obscure topics that is typical of the GMAT. No one else has ever heard of this guy either; and anyway, everything I need is included in the selection."

2. A second factor that adds difficulty to the reading comprehension part of the GMAT is that you have to begin your reading without any idea of what is coming. Imagine the following opening sentence of a reading selection:

By far the most successful and visible aspect of the legal revolution in mental health has been the civil liberties and patient advocacy groups' concern for the patients' physical liberty and autonomy, as distinguished from their psychological well-being.

The sentence is really not that difficult to understand, and the topic it treats is probably one you have read about in the newspaper or in a news magazine. But the sentence seems more difficult than it really is because you don't have a point of reference from which to begin your reading.

Your reading would be much easier if a selection were accompanied by an explanatory headline:

NEW LEGAL RIGHTS FOR MENTAL PATIENTS
By far the most successful and visible aspect of the legal revolution in mental health has been the civil liberties and patient advocacy groups' concern for the patients' physical liberty and autonomy, as distinguished from their psychological well-being.

If you found this headline and article in a news magazine, you would begin your reading with an appropriate context.

Unfortunately, on the GMAT you will not be given this luxury. Instead, it's up to you to jump into the reading selection with both feet and learn as best you can what the selection is about. Just remember, however, everything you need is in the selection and everyone else is having the same problem.

3. The selections are edited so that they will "support" questions. Remember, the object of reading comprehension is not to test what you already know but how well you read. Each reading selection is taken from already published material and edited to fit the test design. The result is one or more highly compact paragraphs on which reading comprehension questions can be based.

Contrast the following two descriptions of the same events. The first is what you would expect to find in an American history textbook; the second, on the GMAT.

TYPICAL TEXTBOOK

Franklin D. Roosevelt became President in March of 1933. American agriculture had been nearly devastated. So, President Roosevelt promised a new farm relief program to help the farmers.

The result was the passage of the Agricultural Adjustment Act of 1933. This law created the Agricultural Adjustment Administration, or AAA for short. The legislation was based on the assumption that prosperity could be restored to the rural sector of the economy if farmers could be persuaded to control agricultural output. By controlling output, it would be possible to eliminate surplus agricultural production.

The method by which the AAA hoped to accomplish the control of surplus production was direct cash payments to farmers.

TYPICAL GMAT

When Franklin D. Roosevelt assumed the Presidency in 1933, he fulfilled his promise to bring immediate relief to the nearly devastated agricultural community by the establishment of the Agricultural Adjustment Administration (AAA). Operating on the assumption that agricultural prosperity could be restored by eliminating surpluses, the AAA offered cash inducements to farmers to control production.

6

Some information is lost, but not much. The second rendering uses fewer words to convey almost the same information, so it is more difficult to read.

The Six Types of Reading Comprehension Questions

Every GMAT reading comprehension question is an "open-book" test; the questions ask about a selection you can look at. And every GMAT reading comprehension question falls into one of six categories.

1. Main Idea Questions. These questions ask about the central theme that unifies the passage. They are often worded as follows:

Which of the following is the main point of the passage?

The primary purpose of the passage is to . . .

The author is primarily concerned with . . .

Which of the following titles best describes the content of the passage?

2. Specific Detail Questions. These questions ask about details that are explicitly mentioned in the passage. This type of question differs from a main idea question in that a specific detail is a point mentioned by the author as a part of the overall development of the main theme of the selection. These questions are often phrased:

The author mentions which of the following?

According to the author, . . .

The author provides information that would answer which of the following questions?

3. Logical Structure Questions. This type of question asks about the logical structure of the selection. Some such questions ask about the overall development of the passage and are sometimes phrased:

> The author develops the passage primarily by . . .

> The author proceeds primarily by . . .

Others ask about the role played by a specific detail. These are sometimes phrased:

> The author mentions . . . in order to . . .

> Which of the following best explains why the author introduces . . . ?

4. Implied Idea Questions. These questions ask not about what is specifically stated in the passage in so many words, but about what can be logically inferred from what is stated in the passage. For example, the passage might explain that a certain organism, X, is found only in the presence of another organism, Y. Then, an implied idea question might ask "If organism Y is not present, what can be inferred?" The answer would be "X is not present." The passage implies, and you can infer from the passage, that in the absence of Y, X cannot be present. Implied idea questions can be phrased:

> The passage implies that . . .

> The author uses the phrase " . . . " to mean . . .

> It can be inferred from the passage that . . .

> Which of the following can be inferred from the passage?

5. Further Application Questions. These questions are somewhat like implied idea questions, but they ask you to go one step further and apply what you have learned in the passage to a new situation. These are sometimes phrased:

> With which of the following statements would the author most likely agree?

> The author would probably consider which of the following a good example of her theory?

> The passage is most probably taken from which of the following sources?

6. Tone Questions. These questions ask you about the tone of the selection, that is, the attitude of the author. They can ask about the overall tone of the passage:

> The tone of the passage can best be described as . . .

Or they can ask about the author's attitude toward some specific detail:

> The author regards . . . as . . .

> Which of the following best describes the author's attitude toward . . . ?

There are many different ways of wording these six types of questions, but every GMAT reading comprehension question falls into one of the six categories.

The Six Types of Questions (Answers, page 65)

The passage below is followed by questions that illustrate the six different types of reading comprehension questions. Answer the questions on the basis of what is *stated* or *implied* in the passage.

To broaden their voting appeal in the Presidential election of 1796, the Federalists selected Thomas Pinckney, a leading South Carolinian, as running mate for the New Englander John Adams. But Pinckney's Southern friends chose to ignore their party's intentions and regarded Pinckney as a Presidential candidate, creating a political situation that Alexander Hamilton was determined to exploit. Hamilton had long been wary of Adams' stubbornly independent brand of politics and preferred to see his running mate, over whom he could exert more control, in the President's chair.

The election was held under the system originally established by the Constitution. At that time there was but a single tally, with the candidate receiving the largest number of electoral votes declared President and the candidate with the second largest number declared Vice-President. Hamilton anticipated that all the Federalists in the North would vote for Adams and Pinckney equally in an attempt to ensure that Jefferson would not be either first or second in the voting. Pinckney would be solidly supported in the South while Adams would not. Hamilton concluded if it were possible to divert a few electoral votes from Adams to Pinckney, Pinckney would receive more than Adams, yet both Federalists would outpoll Jefferson.

Various methods were used to persuade the electors to vote as Hamilton wished. In the press, anonymous articles were published attacking Adams for his monarchical tendencies and Jefferson for being overly democratic, while pushing Pinckney as the only suitable candidate. In private correspondence with state party leaders the Hamiltonians encouraged the idea that Adams' popularity was slipping, that he could not win the election, and that the Federalists could defeat Jefferson only by supporting Pinckney.

Had sectional pride and loyalty not run as high in New England as in the deep South, Pinckney might well have become Washington's successor. New Englanders, however, realized that equal votes for Adams and Pinckney in their states would defeat Adams; therefore, eighteen electors scratched Pinckney's name from their ballots and deliberately threw away their second votes to men who were not even running. It was fortunate for Adams that they did, for the electors from South Carolina completely abandoned him, giving eight votes to Pinckney and eight to Jefferson.

In the end, Hamilton's interference in Pinckney's candidacy lost even the Vice-Presidency for the man from South Carolina. Without New England's support, Pinckney received only 59 electoral votes, finishing third to Adams and Jefferson. He might have been President in 1797, or as Vice-President a serious contender for the Presidency in 1800; instead, stigmatized by a plot he had not devised, he served a brief term in the United States Senate and then dropped from sight as a national influence.

Main Idea Questions

1. The main purpose of the passage is to

    (A) propose reforms of the procedures for electing the President and Vice-President

    (B) condemn Alexander Hamilton for interfering in the election of 1796

    (C) describe the political events that lead to John Adams' victory in the 1796 Presidential election

    (D) contrast the political philosophy of the Federalists to that of Thomas Jefferson

    (E) praise Thomas Pinckney for his refusal to participate in Hamilton's scheme to have him elected President

2. Which of the following titles best describes the content of the passage?

    (A) The Failure of Alexander Hamilton's Plan for Thomas Pinckney to Win the 1796 Presidential Election

    (B) The Roots of Alexander Hamilton's Distrust of John Adams and New England Politics

    (C) Important Issues in the 1796 Presidential Campaign as Presented by the Federalist Candidates

    (D) The Political Careers of Alexander Hamilton, John Adams, and Thomas Pinckney

    (E) Political and Sectional Differences between New England and the South in the Late 1700s

Specific Detail Questions

3. According to the passage, which of the following was true of the Presidential election of 1796?

    (A) Thomas Jefferson received more electoral votes than did Thomas Pinckney.

    (B) John Adams received strong support from the electors of South Carolina.

    (C) Alexander Hamilton received most of the electoral votes of New England.

    (D) Thomas Pinckney was selected by Federalist party leaders to be the party's Presidential candidate.

    (E) Thomas Pinckney received all 16 of South Carolina's electoral votes.

4. According to the passage, Hamilton's plan included all BUT which of the following?

    (A) Articles published in newspapers to create opposition to John Adams

    (B) South Carolina's loyalty to Thomas Pinckney

    (C) Private contact with state officials urging them to support Thomas Pinckney

    (D) John Adams' reputation as a stubborn and independent New Englander

    (E) Support that the New England states would give to John Adams

5. The passage supplies information that answers which of the following questions?

Ⓐ How many votes were cast for John Adams in the 1796 Presidential election?

Ⓑ Under the voting system originally set up by the Constitution, how many votes did each elector cast?

Ⓒ Who was Jefferson's running mate in the 1796 Presidential election?

Ⓓ What became of Alexander Hamilton after his plan to have Thomas Pinckney elected President failed?

Ⓔ How many more electoral votes did Jefferson receive in the 1796 Presidential election than Pinckney?

Logical Structure Questions

6. Why does the author refer to the election procedure established by the original Constitution?

Ⓐ To prove to the reader that New England as a whole had more electoral votes than the state of South Carolina

Ⓑ To persuade the reader that Thomas Pinckney's defeat could have been avoided

Ⓒ To alert the reader that the procedure used in 1796 was unlike that presently used

Ⓓ To encourage the reader to study Constitutional history

Ⓔ To remind the reader that the President and Vice-President of the United States are chosen democratically

7. The overall development of the passage can best be described as

Ⓐ refuting possible explanations for certain phenomena

Ⓑ documenting a thesis with specific examples

Ⓒ offering an explanation of a series of events

Ⓓ making particular proposals to solve a problem

Ⓔ attacking the assumption of an argument

Implied Idea Questions

8. The passage implies that some electors voted for John Adams because they were

Ⓐ in favor of a monarchy

Ⓑ persuaded to do so by Hamilton

Ⓒ afraid South Carolina would not vote for Pinckney

Ⓓ concerned about New England's influence over the South

Ⓔ anxious to have a President from their geographical region

9. Which of the following can be inferred from the passage?

   Ⓐ   Thomas Pinckney had a personal dislike for Jefferson's politics.

   Ⓑ   The Federalists regarded themselves as more democratic than Jefferson.

   Ⓒ   The Hamiltonians contacted key Southern leaders to persuade them to vote for Adams.

   Ⓓ   Electors were likely to vote for candidates from their own geographical region.

   Ⓔ   New England states cast more electoral votes for Jefferson than did the South.

10. It can be inferred that had South Carolina not cast any electoral votes for Jefferson, the outcome of the 1796 election would have been a

   Ⓐ   larger margin of victory for John Adams

   Ⓑ   victory for Thomas Jefferson

   Ⓒ   Federalist defeat in the Senate

   Ⓓ   victory for Thomas Pinckney

   Ⓔ   defeat of the Federalist Presidential candidate

Further Application Questions

11. The electors who scratched Pinckney's name from their ballots behaved most like which of the following people?

   Ⓐ   A newspaper publisher who adds a special section to the Sunday edition to review the week's political events

   Ⓑ   A member of the clergy who encourages members of other faiths to meet to discuss solutions to the community's problems

   Ⓒ   An artist who saves preliminary sketches of an important work even after the work is finally completed

   Ⓓ   A general who orders his retreating troops to destroy supplies they must leave behind so they cannot be used by the enemy

   Ⓔ   A runner who sets too fast a pace during the early stages of a race and has no energy left for the finish

12. Hamilton's strategy can best be summarized as

   Ⓐ   divide and conquer

   Ⓑ   retreat and regroup

   Ⓒ   feint and counterattack

   Ⓓ   hit and run

   Ⓔ   camouflage and conceal

Tone Questions

13. The tone of the passage can best be described as

   Ⓐ   witty   Ⓑ   comical   Ⓒ   scholarly
   Ⓓ   frivolous   Ⓔ   morose

14. The author's attitude toward Hamilton's plan can be described as

    Ⓐ angry   Ⓑ approving   Ⓒ analytical
    Ⓓ regretful   Ⓔ disinterested

Reading Techniques

"You see, Watson," said Holmes. "The tail wags the dog."

Since Watson, like most people, believes the GMAT reading comprehension is just "reading," he would read the selections just as he might a chapter from a textbook or an article in a magazine. That is an error.

You have just learned that each reading selection is an "excuse" to ask one of the six questions. The test writers don't just find an interesting article and ask questions about it. Instead, they write a passage (by adapting and editing published material) just so they can ask several of the six questions. In other words, the tail is wagging the dog.

Knowing this, the Holmesian strategy for reading the selections is to "read for the six types of questions." Now, this does not mean that you try to anticipate the exact wording of every question that might be asked. (There are many possibilities.) Rather, this means that you adapt your reading techniques to fit the exercise.

GMAT reading comprehension questions are set up to test three levels of reading: appreciation of the general theme, understanding of specific points, and evaluation of the text. The first level, appreciation of the general theme, is the most basic. Main idea questions and questions about the overall development of the selection test whether you understand the passage at the most general level.

The second level of reading, understanding of specific points, takes you deeper into your reading of the selection. Specific detail questions and questions about the logical role of details test whether you read carefully. The third level of reading, evaluation of the text, takes you still deeper. Implied idea questions, further application questions, and tone questions ask not just for understanding—they ask for a judgment or an evaluation of what you have read. This is why implied idea questions and further application questions are usually the most difficult.

This does not mean, however, that the three different levels are reached at completely different times. A good reader will be constantly moving back and forth, but there is a logical priority to the levels. That is, without the first level of general understanding, you can't hope to have the precise understanding of the second level. And without the precise understanding of the second level, you can't hope to evaluate or criticize the selection.

The proper method for reading a GMAT selection could be represented as a pyramid. The base of the pyramid represents the basic level of reading on which the other two levels rest, and the second level is needed to support the third level. The easiest questions are usually those on the bottom level, and the most difficult questions are usually found at the top. (Note, however, that tone questions are often not very difficult.)

Your first task when you begin reading is to answer the question "What is the topic of the selection?" You may find it useful to scroll down and preview the first sentence of each paragraph.

The first sentence of a paragraph is often the topic sentence, and it may give you a summary of the content of the paragraph. Here are the first sentences from the paragraphs in a sample passage.

> In the art of the Middle Ages, the personality of the artist as an individual is never present; rather, it is diffused through the artistic genius of centuries embodied in the rules of religious art.
>
> Mathematics, too, was an important element of this iconography.
>
> Every painting is also an allegory, showing us one thing and inviting us to see another.
>
> Within such a system even the most mediocre talent was elevated by the genius of the centuries, and the first artists of the Renaissance broke with tradition at great risk.

A preview of the first sentences should give you a pretty good idea of the subject discussed in the selection. The passage treats art in the Middle Ages. Additionally, it states that art in the Middle Ages was governed by rules and had numerical and allegorical features. Renaissance painting, however, broke with this tradition.

Given this framework, here is the selection broken down by paragraphs. As you read, consciously ask yourself what point the author is trying to make. And as you come across each new particular point, ask yourself why the author has introduced the point:

> In the art of the Middle Ages, the personality of the artist as an individual is never present; rather, it is diffused through the artistic genius of centuries embodied in the rules of religious art. For art of the Middle Ages is first and foremost a sacred script, the symbols and meanings of which were well settled. The circular halo placed vertically behind the head signifies sainthood, while the halo impressed with a cross signifies divinity. A tower with a window indicates a village; and should an angel be watching from the battlements, that city is thereby identified as Jerusalem.

In the first sentence the author introduces the topic of art in the Middle Ages. In the second sentence, we learn that this art is like a script or writing governed by rules. What function does the rest of the paragraph serve in the overall development? The author provides some illustrations of the assertion about art. The second paragraph continues the discussion.

> Mathematics, too, was an important element of this iconography. "The Divine Wisdom," wrote Saint Augustine, "reveals itself everywhere in number," a doctrine derived from the neo-Platonists who revived the teachings of Pythagoras. And numbers require symmetry. At Chartres, a stained-glass window shows the four prophets Isaac, Ezekiel, Daniel, and Jeremiah carrying on their shoulders the four evangelists Matthew, Mark, Luke, and John.

Why does the author mention mathematics? Because it, too, was part of the rules for painting. And why does the author quote Saint Augustine? To show the importance of numbers in the Middle Ages.

Now, let us introduce another reading technique. This is an "open-book" test, and you can always go back to the selection. Therefore, if something is highly technical or difficult to understand, don't dwell on it. Bracket the information mentally. You can always come back to it. You should probably do this with the reference to the neo-Platonists. Who were they? It really doesn't matter. Just recognize that they had something to do with numbers, and if you need to learn more about them to answer a question, you can return to the paragraph.

What is the purpose of referring to the stained-glass window in Chartres? It illustrates the way in which numbers might influence art in the Middle Ages. Now we move to the third paragraph.

> Every painting is also an allegory, showing us one thing and inviting us to see another. In this respect, the artist was asked to imitate God, who had hidden a profound meaning behind the literal and who wished nature to be a moral lesson to man. In a painting of the final judgment, we see the foolish virgins at the left hand of Jesus and the wise at his right, and we understand that this symbolizes those who are lost and those who are saved.

In this paragraph, the author describes another characteristic of painting in the Middle Ages: it contains an allegory. What does the next sentence mean when it compares the artist to God? That's hard to say. If a question asks about the analogy between art and Creation, you can always return to the selection to study. And why is the painting of the final judgment mentioned at this point? It's an example of an allegorical painting.

Finally, we read the fourth paragraph.

> Within such a system even the most mediocre talent was elevated by the genius of the centuries, and the first artists of the Renaissance broke with tradition at great risk. Even when they are great, they are no more than the equals of the old master who passively followed the sacred rules; and then they are not outstanding, they scarcely avoid banality and insignificance in their religious works.

What is the meaning of the first sentence of the final paragraph? Roughly, that even mediocre artists could produce good work as long as the rules were followed. Then, the selection mentions the first artists of the Renaissance. Why? Because that was the next historical period, and also because it demonstrates how important the rules were to art in the Middle Ages.

Let's summarize the procedure for reading a GMAT reading comprehension selection.

Step 1: Scrolling, begin with a preview of the first sentence of each paragraph.

Step 2: Read the selection, consciously asking what the author is trying to do.

Step 3: When you encounter material in the selection that seems difficult to understand, bracket it mentally. Try to understand why the author introduced it even if you don't understand exactly what it means.

Previewing and Reading (Answers, page 66)

The passage below is followed by questions based on its content. Follow the suggestions indicated for reading GMAT passages. Then answer the questions on the basis of what is *stated* or *implied* in the passage.

The liberal view of democratic citizenship that developed in the 17th and 18th centuries was fundamentally different from that of the classical Greeks. The pursuit of private interests with as little interference as possible from government was seen as the road to human happiness and progress rather than the public obligations and involve-
(5) ment in the collective community that were emphasized by the Greeks. Freedom was to be realized by limiting the scope of governmental activity and political obligation and not through immersion in the collective life of the *polis*. The basic role of the citizen was to select governmental leaders and keep the powers and scope of public authority in check. On the liberal view, the rights of citizens against the state were the focus of
(10) special emphasis.

Over time, the liberal democratic notion of citizenship developed in two directions. First, there was a movement to increase the proportion of members of society who were eligible to participate as citizens—especially through extending the right of suffrage—and to ensure the basic political equality of all. Second, there was a broadening of the
(15) legitimate activities of government and a use of governmental power to redress imbalances in social and economic life. Political citizenship became an instrument through which groups and classes with sufficient numbers of votes could use the state power to enhance their social and economic well-being.

Within the general liberal view of democratic citizenship, tensions have developed
(20) over the degree to which government can and should be used as an instrument for promoting happiness and well-being. Political philosopher Martin Diamond has categorized two views of democracy as follows. On the one hand, there is the "libertarian" perspective that stresses the private pursuit of happiness and emphasizes the necessity for restraint on government and protection of individual liberties. On the other hand, there is
(25) the "majoritarian" view that emphasizes the "task of the government to uplift and aid the common man against the malefactors of great wealth." The tensions between these two views are very evident today. Taxpayer revolts and calls for smaller government and less government regulation clash with demands for greater government involvement in the economic marketplace and the social sphere.

1. The author's primary purpose is to
   Ⓐ   study ancient concepts of citizenship
   Ⓑ   contrast different notions of citizenship
   Ⓒ   criticize modern libertarian democracy
   Ⓓ   describe the importance of universal suffrage
   Ⓔ   introduce means of redressing an imbalance of power

2. It can be inferred from the passage that the Greek word *polis* means
   Ⓐ   family life   Ⓑ   military service   Ⓒ   marriage
   Ⓓ   private club   Ⓔ   political community

3. The author cites Martin Diamond (line 21) because the author

    Ⓐ   regards Martin Diamond as an authority on political philosophy

    Ⓑ   wishes to refute Martin Diamond's views on citizenship

    Ⓒ   needs a definition of the term "citizenship"

    Ⓓ   is unfamiliar with the distinction between libertarian and majoritarian concepts of democracy

    Ⓔ   wants voters to support Martin Diamond as a candidate for public office.

4. According to the passage, all of the following are characteristics of the liberal idea of government that would distinguish the liberal idea of government from the Greek idea of government EXCEPT

    Ⓐ   the emphasis on the rights of private citizens

    Ⓑ   the activities government may legitimately pursue

    Ⓒ   the obligation of citizens to participate in government

    Ⓓ   the size of the geographical area controlled by a government

    Ⓔ   the definition of human happiness

5. A majoritarian would be most likely to favor legislation that would

    Ⓐ   eliminate all restrictions on individual liberty

    Ⓑ   cut spending for social welfare programs

    Ⓒ   provide greater protection for consumers

    Ⓓ   lower taxes on the wealthy and raise taxes on the average worker

    Ⓔ   raise taxes on the average worker and cut taxes on business

Step 1:   Preview the first sentence of each paragraph:

The liberal view of democratic citizenship that developed in the 17th and 18th centuries was fundamentally different from that of the classical Greeks.

Over time, the liberal democratic notion of citizenship developed in two directions.

Within the general liberal view of democratic citizenship, tensions have developed over the degree to which the government can and should be used as an instrument for promoting happiness and well-being.

These three sentences, taken together, tell you that the topic of the passage is citizenship. The selection begins by defining the liberal view of citizenship. Then, the second paragraph states that the liberal view has evolved into two different ideas. Finally, the third paragraph apparently amplifies what was discussed in the second.

Step 2:   Preview the question stems.

Question 1 provides no useful information.

Question 2 tells you to flag the word *polis* when you find it. It will be the basis of that question.

Question 3 tells you that the author will quote Martin Diamond (whoever he may be) and that you will need to know why.

Questions 4 and 5, when taken in conjunction with your preview of the first sentences, might be very helpful. They contain key words. Question 4 tells you that one of the topics for discussion will be the difference between classical Greek notions of democracy and liberal notions of democracy. Similarly, question 5 alerts you to the fact that majoritarian democracy will be discussed.

Step 3: Read the passage.

The first paragraph defines the liberal idea of citizenship by contrasting it with the Greek idea. Several specifics are mentioned.

The second paragraph discusses the development of the liberal view in two directions and describes each.

The third paragraph discusses the significance of the division.

Now you are in a position to answer questions.

Question Patterns That Clue You In

Like most test-takers, Watson is completely preoccupied with finding a correct answer to particular questions; but Holmes is keenly aware that answers fall into patterns. Once you know what makes right answers right and wrong answers wrong, you will be able to eliminate incorrect choices and spot the correct answer more easily. Right now, just read through the following selection and familiarize yourself with it. There are no question stems yet.

The Aleuts, residing on several islands of the Aleutian Chain, the Pribilof Islands, and the Alaskan Peninsula, have possessed a written language since 1825, when the Russian missionary Ivan Veniaminov selected appropriate characters of the Cyrillic alphabet to represent Aleut speech sounds, recorded the main body of Aleut vocabulary and formulated grammatical rules. The Czarist Russian conquest of the proud, independent sea hunters was so devastatingly thorough that tribal traditions, even tribal memories, were almost obliterated. The slaughter of the majority of an adult generation was sufficient to destroy the continuity of tribal knowledge, which was dependent upon oral transmission. As a consequence, the Aleuts developed a fanatical devotion to their language as their only cultural heritage.

The Russian occupation placed a heavy linguistic burden on the Aleuts. Not only were they compelled to learn Russian to converse with their overseers and governors, but they had to learn Old Slavonic to take an active part in church services as well as to master the skill of reading and writing their own tongue. In 1867, when the United States purchased Alaska, the Aleuts were unable to break sharply with their immediate past and substitute English for any one of their three languages.

To communicants of the Russian Orthodox Church a knowledge of Slavonic remained vital, as did Russian, the language in which one conversed with the clergy. The Aleuts came to regard English education as a device to wean them from their religious faith. The introduction of compulsory English schooling caused a minor renascence of Russian culture as the Aleut parents sought to counteract the influence of the schoolroom. The harsh life of the Russian colonial rule began to appear more happy and beautiful in retrospect.

Regulations forbidding instruction in any language other than English increased its unpopularity. The superficial alphabetical resemblance of Russian and Aleut linked the two tongues so closely that every restriction against teaching Russian was interpreted as an attempt to eradicate the Aleut tongue. From the wording of many regulations, it appears that American administrators often had not the slightest idea that the Aleuts were clandestinely reading and writing their own tongue or even had a written language of their own. To too many officials, anything in Cyrillic letters was Russian and something to be stamped out. Bitterness bred by abuses and the exploitations the Aleuts suffered from predatory American traders and adventurers kept alive the Aleut resentment against the language spoken by Americans.

Gradually, despite the failure to emancipate the Aleuts from a sterile past by relating the Aleut and English languages more closely, the passage of years has assuaged the bitter misunderstandings and caused an orientation away from Russian toward English as their second language, but Aleut continues to be the language that molds their thought and expression.

Main Idea Questions

EXAMPLES:

The author is primarily concerned with describing

(A) the Aleuts' loyalty to their language and American failure to understand it

(B) Russian and United States treatment of Alaskan inhabitants both before and after 1867

(C) how the Czarist Russian occupation of Alaska created a written language for the Aleuts

(D) United States government attempts to persuade the Aleuts to use English as a second language

(E) the atrocities committed by Russia against the Aleuts during the Czarist Russian occupation

The best answer is (A). To answer a main idea question, look for a choice that covers the main elements of the passage without making reference to material not discussed in the passage. (B) can be eliminated because it goes beyond the scope of the passage. The passage is not concerned with the treatment of Alaskan inhabitants in general, but with the treatment of one particular group. (C), (D), and (E) can be eliminated because they are too narrow. Each of these three choices does mention one aspect of the passage, but none of them summarizes the overall point of the selection.

Here is a different kind of main idea question:

The author is primarily concerned with

(A) describing the Aleuts' loyalty to their language and American failure to understand it

(B) criticizing Russia and the United States for their mistreatment of the Aleuts

(C) praising the Russians for creating a written language for the Aleuts

(D) condemning Russia for its mistreatment of the Aleuts during the Czarist Russian occupation

(E) ridiculing American efforts to persuade the Aleuts to adopt English as a second language

Again, (A) is correct. You should be able to see that this second main idea question is really the first one presented in a different form. Here, the choices are possible completions of the question stem. Notice that each wrong choice begins with a word expressing a value judgment: criticize, praise, condemn, ridicule. None of those terms correctly describes the overall idea of the passage. In attacking a question in sentence completion form, eliminate as many choices as possible on the basis of the first word. Then treat the remaining choices as you would any other main idea question, looking for the one that is sufficiently broad without being overly broad.

Finally, a main idea question might also look like this:

> Which of the following titles best fits the passage?
> Ⓐ Aleut Loyalty to Their Language: An American Misunderstanding
> Ⓑ Failure of Russian and American Policies in Alaska
> Ⓒ Russia's Gift to the Aleuts: A Written Language
> Ⓓ Mistreatment of Aleuts During Russian Occupation
> Ⓔ The Folly of American Attempts to Teach Aleuts English

The correct choice is (A). This is essentially the same main idea question presented in yet another form. The trick is to find the title that best captures the content of the passage. The criterion is the same as that for other main idea questions; it must cover all the important points without going beyond the passage.

Once more, (C), (D), and (E) fail because they describe too little of the selection, and (B) fails because it is too broad. (A), though not a perfect title, is the best of the five.

Whatever the form of a main idea question, the answer will summarize the main theme of the selection without going beyond the scope of the passage.

Specific Detail Questions

EXAMPLE:

According to the passage, which of the following was the most important reason for the Aleuts' devotion to their language?
Ⓐ Invention of a written version of their language
Ⓑ Introduction of Old Slavonic for worship
Ⓒ Disruption of oral transmission of tribal knowledge
Ⓓ Institution of compulsory English education
Ⓔ Prohibition against writing or reading Russian

The correct choice is (C). Since this is a specific detail question, the information you need is somewhere explicitly given in the passage—though not in exactly the same words. The reference you need is the last two sentences of the first paragraph. The Russians killed the majority of Aleut adults, so there was no one left to teach the children the Aleut traditions. All that remained for the younger generation was the language they had already learned.

As for (A), though the passage states that a Russian missionary invented the written form of the Aleut language, this is not the cause of the Aleuts' devotion to their language. (B), too, is connected with the passage. We are told that the Aleuts learned Old Slavonic, the language of the Russian Orthodox Church, but that does not explain their loyalty to their own language. (D) and (E) fail for the same reason. Though these events are mentioned in the passage, they occurred after the events that triggered the special devotion the Aleuts feel toward their language.

An answer choice for a specific detail question can be attractive because it is mentioned somewhere in the selection, yet still be wrong because it is not responsive to the question. Take (D) as an example. The passage does specifically mention such a requirement (end of the third paragraph), and (D) would be a perfectly good answer to a question such as "Why did the Aleuts resent the Americans?" But that is not the question asked.

> The correct choice for a specific detail question must both be explicitly mentioned in the passage and answer the question asked.

6

Logical Structure Questions

Some logical structure questions ask about the overall development of the passage. These are like main idea questions, but the focus is on the form of the passage rather than the specific content.

EXAMPLE:

The passage is developed primarily by

Ⓐ   testing the evidence supporting a theory

Ⓑ   describing causes and effects of events

Ⓒ   weighing the pros and cons of a plan

Ⓓ   projecting the future consequences of a decision

Ⓔ   debating both sides of a moral issue

The answer is (B). We are looking for the best description of the overall development of the selection. The author discusses several events in terms of cause and effect. For example, the Russian brutality caused the Aleut devotion to their language, and American misunderstanding caused a renascence of Russian culture.

You can eliminate each of the other choices. As for (A), though the author uses historical evidence for his position, he is not testing evidence supporting a theory. As for (C), though the author points to some of the effects of Russian and American policies, the passage doesn't really "weigh" pros and cons. As for (D), though the author does state that the attitude of the Aleuts toward English is changing slowly, the passage is not primarily speculation about where this change might lead. Finally, as for (E), though the question of the morality of the Russian and American actions is implicit in the discussion, the passage is not developed by debating the morality of those actions.

> A logical structure question that asks about the overall development of the passage should be treated like a main idea question. Find the choice that best describes the structure of the selection.

Logical structure questions can also ask about the "why" of specific details.

EXAMPLE:

Why does the author mention that the Russians killed the majority of adult Aleuts?

Ⓐ To call attention to the immorality of foreign conquest

Ⓑ To urge Russia to make restitution to the children of those killed

Ⓒ To stir up outrage against the Russians for committing such atrocities

Ⓓ To explain the extreme loyalty Aleuts feel to their language

Ⓔ To prove that the Aleuts have a written language

The answer is (D). This question is somewhat like a specific detail question, except here the question is not *what* the author said but *why* he or she said it. (A), (B), and (C) are all incorrect because they do not explain why the author mentions the atrocities. The passage is not condemning Russian behavior. As for (E), though the author does state that the Aleuts have a written language, this is not why he mentions the Russian atrocities. Rather, he mentions the devastation of the Aleuts in order to show why Aleuts are so devoted to their language.

> The key to answering a logical detail question is to locate the needed reference and ask *why*: Why did the author do this?

Implied Idea Questions

EXAMPLES:

Which of the following statements about the religious beliefs of the Aleuts can be inferred from the passage?

Ⓐ Prior to the Russian occupation they had no religious beliefs.

Ⓑ American traders and adventurers forced them to abandon all religious beliefs.

Ⓒ At no time in their history have the Aleuts had an organized religion.

Ⓓ Aleut leaders adopted the religious beliefs of the American officials following the 1867 purchase.

Ⓔ The Russians forced Aleuts to become members of the Russian Orthodox Church.

The correct choice is (E), and you can justify (E) as a matter of logic. In paragraph two the passage states that the Aleuts "had to learn Old Slavonic to take an active part in church services." Which church was that? It must be the Russian Orthodox Church mentioned by name in the next paragraph. And how do we know the Aleuts were forced to convert? Since Old Slavonic was required of church members, and since at the time of the Russian conquest the Aleuts did not know Old Slavonic, they could not have been members of the sect at that time. Therefore, we logically infer that the Russian conquerors forced the Aleuts to become members of the Russian Orthodox Church.

The answer to an implied idea question will not be explicitly stated in the passage, but it will be strongly supported by the passage. You can create a logical argument for the answer.

The wrong choices cannot be justified by similar reasoning. As for (A), there is no basis in the passage for the conclusion that the Aleuts had no religion at all prior to the Russians. They might have had one; they might not. The point is that the passage is logically consistent with either position. The same is true for both (B) and (D). These statements could be either true or false given the information supplied in the passage. As for (C), this is clearly false. The passage does state that at one time the Aleuts were members of the Russian Orthodox Church.

> The passage implies that
> (A) the Cyrillic alphabet was invented for the Aleut language
> (B) all of the Cyrillic characters were used in writing the Aleut language
> (C) Russian and the Aleut language have some similar speech sounds
> (D) English is also written using the Cyrillic alphabet
> (E) the Cyrillic alphabet displaced the original Aleut alphabet

The answer is (C). This question asks about something not explicitly stated in the passage, but only implied. (C) is logically supported by the passage. The Russian missionary Ivan Veniaminov used Cyrillic letters (which already represented certain Russian speech sounds) to represent appropriate Aleut speech sounds. This is feasible only if the sounds are sufficiently similar (even if they don't mean the same thing in both languages).

None of the other choices can be logically deduced from the selection. (A) and (E) are contradicted by the passage. The Cyrillic alphabet already existed and was adapted to the Aleut language. And since this was the first written form of the language, no Aleut alphabet could have existed before then. As for (B), Veniaminov may not have needed the entire Cyrillic alphabet, only parts of it.

Finally, (D) is almost contradicted by the passage. The Cyrillic alphabet seems to be definitely not like English.

> To answer an implied idea question, look for a choice that is logically supported by the passage,

Further Application Questions

In many ways, these are the most difficult of all questions. They ask you to take what you have learned from the passage and apply it to a new situation.

> **EXAMPLE:**
>
> Distributing which of the following publications would be most likely to encourage Aleuts to make more use of English?
> (A) Russian translations of English novels
> (B) English translations of Russian novels
> (C) An English-Russian bilingual text devoted to Aleutian culture
> (D) An Aleut-English bilingual text devoted to Aleutian culture
> (E) A treatise about religions other than the Russian Orthodox Church written in English

The correct choice is (D). You must apply what you have learned in the passage to this new situation. What is the problem the author sees? The Aleuts have never really embraced English as a second language because of the events described. So what would most likely encourage them to embrace English? Something that would respect the integrity of their own culture while bringing it closer to English (and thereby minimizing the holdover effect of the Russian occupation). (A) and (B) will not do the trick since Russian-English books would not necessarily be relevant to the experience of an Aleut. (C) is closer, but still off the mark. The task is to get the Aleuts to embrace English—not Russian. As for (E), there is no reason given in the passage to believe the Aleuts have an interest in other religions. The task is to find English writings that would be of interest to the Aleuts.

> To answer a further application question, find the answer choice that is best supported by the information provided in the passage.

Tone Questions

The final category is tone questions.

EXAMPLE:

The author's attitude toward the Aleuts can best be described as one of

(A) understanding and sympathy

(B) callousness and indifference

(C) condemnation and reproof

(D) ridicule and disparagement

(E) awe and admiration

The correct choice is (A). With a tone question it is sometimes useful to arrange the choices in some kind of order. In this case, the order is from positive to negative feelings:

POSITIVE FEELINGS
awe and admiration
understanding and sympathy
callousness and indifference
ridicule and disparagement
condemnation and reproof
NEGATIVE FEELINGS

Now try to locate the author's attitude toward the Aleuts along this spectrum. First you can eliminate the extremes of "awe and admiration." Although the tone of the passage does seem mildly positive, it is not as strong as "awe and admiration." Then start from the other end. You can surely eliminate "condemnation and reproof" and "ridicule and disparagement," because there are no strong negative feelings toward the Aleuts. Finally, you should eliminate "callousness and indifference," since the author does seem to have mildly positive feelings about the Aleuts. The best choice, therefore, is "understanding and sympathy."

Some Final Words of Advice from Holmes

Earlier, reading comprehension was likened to a pyramid, with easier questions at the base and more difficult questions at the top. Remember, however, that reading comprehension questions are not necessarily arranged according to a ladder of difficulty. The first question on a selection might be the most difficult one and the last, the easiest. So don't get bogged down by the first or second question.

Additionally, certain questions (further application questions and some implied idea questions) can be extremely difficult. But on balance, there are enough of the easier kinds for you to do well on reading comprehension even if you can't answer a further application or a difficult implied idea question. Again, don't spend too much time trying to crack a difficult nut.

Remember also that you have your own particular strengths, and you will react differently to different topics. For example, if you are very interested in music but relatively less knowledgeable about chemistry, you will find a passage about music easier than one about chemistry. You don't have to do the passages in the order in which they are presented. If you start on one that seems so difficult that you're going nowhere, abandon it and try another.

A Perfect Format for Holmes' Strategies

EXAMPLE:

According to the passage, which of the following factors caused the Aleuts to resist adopting English as a second language?

I. Government regulations prohibiting teaching in any language other than English

II. Threats by members of the clergy of the Russian Orthodox Church to excommunicate Aleuts who learned English

III. Abuse suffered by the Aleuts at the hands of English speakers such as traders and adventurers

Ⓐ I only   Ⓑ II only   Ⓒ III only   Ⓓ I and II only   Ⓔ I and III only

The answer is (E). With a format such as this, the process of elimination becomes a very powerful logical tool. Start with I. If you look back at the passage on the Aleuts, you will find that this is mentioned as a factor that discouraged the Aleuts from adopting English. Once you know this, you can eliminate any choice that does not include I. So you eliminate (B) and (C). Next, you try II. Nowhere is such a factor mentioned, but let's assume that you have your doubts. You are worried you have overlooked something. Go on to the next statement, III. You will find that III is specifically mentioned, which means that III must be a part of the correct choice. Now you know the correct choice must include both I and III—even though you are still in doubt about it. But that is enough to answer the question. Only one choice includes both I and III, and that is (E). With this Roman-numeral format, you must always use the process of elimination to narrow down your choices and then make a guess.

Summary

1. Reading comprehension is made difficult by the variety of topics, lack of a reference point before starting, and compactness of the selections. Don't let the passages intimidate you.
2. Reading comprehension questions fall into one of six categories: main idea, specific detail, logical structure, implied idea, further application, and tone.
3. Your reading proceeds on three levels. Begin by previewing first sentences of the parangraphs in the selection. As you read, try to identify as quickly as possible the main theme of the selection. Then, as each new point is introduced, try to fit it into the overall development. If material is too difficult, bracket it mentally. Make sure you understand why it is in the passage (even if you don't understand what it says) and continue your reading.
4. Hints for answering questions:

    For a main idea question, find an answer that is not too broad and not too narrow. If the choices are supposed to complete the question stem, start by checking the first words. Eliminate any choice that does not correspond to the author's treatment of the topic.

    For a specific detail question, locate the reference you need in the passage. Don't be distracted by choices that make true or partially true statements but are not responsive to the question.

    Logical structure questions ask either about the overall development of the selection or a particular detail. Treat a question about the overall logical development of a passage as you would a main idea question. For a logical detail question, find the appropriate reference and determine why the author made the point.

    For an implied idea question, find a choice that is *logically* supported by the passage. The chain of reasoning will not be very long— only one or two steps. But the correct choice must be inferable from what is explicitly given.

    For a further application question, find the choice that is best supported by the passage. This means that you will have to apply what you have learned in the passage. Remember, this is perhaps the hardest question type, but you can get a good score even if you omit some difficult items.

Explanatory Answers

EXERCISE 1

Main Idea Questions

1. **(C)** The passage describes a series of political events that resulted in the election of John Adams as President.

2. **(A)** The central theme is Hamilton's plan to capture the Presidency for Pinckney and why that plan failed.

Specific Detail Questions

3. **(A)** In the last paragraph, the passage explicitly states that Pinckney finished third in the voting, behind Jefferson.

4. **(D)** (A), (B), (C), and (E) are all mentioned as elements of Hamilton's plan, but (D) is not. Although the selection does say that Hamilton did not like Adams' stubborn and independent politics, it nowhere says that this was to be a part of Hamilton's plan to help Pinckney win the Presidency.

5. **(B)** In the next to last paragraph, it is stated that electors had two votes to cast.

Logical Structure Questions

6. **(C)** This question asks why the author mentions the fact that the 1796 election took place under the rules established in the original Constitution. (C) provides the best explanation. Under current procedures, a vote is cast specifically for a Presidential candidate and another for a Vice-Presidential candidate. Under the original system, electoral votes were cast without distinction, and the candidate receiving the most was elected President and the runner-up was elected Vice-President. Without this crucial piece of information, the author's analysis makes no sense. So in the first sentence of the second paragraph he specifically reminds the reader of this fact.

7. **(C)** The passage explains the series of events that lead to the election of John Adams as President in 1796.

Implied Idea Questions

8. **(E)** At the beginning of the next to last paragraph, the author states that sectional pride was high in New England and that John Adams, the New England politician, received the New Englanders' votes. We may infer that many of them voted for Adams because of their desire to have a President from their own region.

9. **(D)** At various places in the passage you can find references to the idea of regional loyalty.

6

10. **(A)** South Carolina cast 16 votes, eight for Pinckney and eight for Jefferson. So each elector cast one vote for each. Had they not voted for Jefferson, for whom could they have voted? They could not have voted for Pinckney (they had already voted for him). They could have voted either for Adams or for some unknown candidate. Either way, Jefferson loses votes and Adams does not (he could actually have gained). So the net result is a larger margin of victory for Adams.

Further Application Questions

11. **(D)** Here you are asked to apply what you have learned from the passage to an entirely new situation. Exactly what did the electors in question do? They wasted their second vote so that neither Pinckney nor Jefferson could benefit from them.

12. **(A)** Hamilton's strategy was to divide the Federalist vote: weaken party support for Adams and let Pinckney pick up the pieces.

Tone Questions

13. **(C)** How would you describe the tone of the passage? It is very neutral and analytical, so a good description would be "scholarly."

14. **(C)** The author's treatment of the series of events is neutral and objective.

EXERCISE 2

1. **(B)** The author discusses three different concepts of government and citizenship (classical Greek, libertarian, and majoritarian), outlining the important differences among them.

2. **(E)** In the first paragraph the author contrasts the Greek idea of citizenship with the more modern, liberal idea. A series of parallels is set up. The liberal notion emphasizes pursuit of individual interests and limitation of government power, while the Greek notion emphasized participation in community affairs. The *polis,* we may infer, is the location of public life. So it must mean "political community."

3. **(A)** This is a logical detail question. The author has already mentioned that liberalism has moved in two directions. He introduces a political philosopher as an authority to support his position.

4. **(D)** This is a specific detail question. (A), (B), (C), and (E) are mentioned at various points in the selection, but (D) is not.

5. **(C)** This is an application question. From the last paragraph we learn that majoritarians are likely to favor greater government control of the marketplace (as opposed to libertarians, who favor less government involvement).

Reading Comprehension Drills

1. **Walk-Through Drills**
2. **Warm-Up Drills**

This chapter contains reading comprehension drills. The first three drills are "walk-throughs" and have answers and discussion facing the questions so that you can walk through the exercises as you read the explanations. The second three are "warm-up" drills, which should be done within the time limit given. Answers and explanations for the warm-up drills begin on page 89.

Walk-Through 1

Directions: The passage below is followed by questions based on its content. After reading the passage, choose the best answer to each question. Answer the questions on the basis of what is *stated* or *implied* in the passage.

The mental health movement in the United States began with a period of considerable enlightenment. Dorothea Dix was shocked to find the mentally ill in jails and alms houses and crusaded for the establishment of asylums in which people could receive humane care in hospital-like environments and treatment which might help restore them to sanity. By the mid-1800s, 20 states had established asylums, but during the late 1800s and early 1900s, in the face of economic depression, legislatures were unable to appropriate sufficient funds for decent care. Asylums became overcrowded and prisonlike. Additionally, patients were more resistant to treatment than the pioneers in the mental health field had anticipated, and security and restraint were needed to protect patients and others. Mental institutions became frightening and depressing places in which the rights of patients were all but forgotten.

These conditions continued until after World War II. At that time, new treatments were discovered for some major mental illnesses theretofore considered untreatable (penicillin for syphilis of the brain and insulin treatment for schizophrenia and depressions), and a succession of books, motion pictures, and newspaper exposés called attention to the plight of the mentally ill. Improvements were made, and Dr. David Vail's Humane Practices Program is a beacon for today. But changes were slow in coming until the early 1960s. At that time, the Civil Rights Movement led lawyers to investigate America's prisons, which were disproportionately populated by blacks, and they in turn followed prisoners into the only institutions that were worse than the prisons—the hospitals for the criminally insane. The prisons were filled with angry young men who, encouraged by legal support, were quick to demand their rights. The hospitals for the criminally insane, by contrast, were populated with people who were considered "crazy" and who were often kept obediently in their place through the use of severe bodily restraints and large doses of major tranquilizers. The young cadre of public interest lawyers liked their role in the mental hospitals. The lawyers found a population that was both passive and easy to champion. These were, after all, people who, unlike criminals, had done nothing wrong. And in many states they were being kept in horrendous

institutions, an injustice which, once exposed, was bound to shock the public, and, particularly, the judicial conscience. Patients' rights groups successfully encouraged reform by lobbying in state legislatures.

Judicial interventions have had some definite positive effects, but there is growing awareness that courts cannot provide the standards and the review mechanisms that assure good patient care. The details of providing day-to-day care simply cannot be mandated by a court, so it is time to take from the courts the responsibility for delivery of mental health care and assurance of patient rights and return it to the state mental health administrators to whom the mandate was originally given. Though it is a difficult task, administrators must undertake to write rules and standards and to provide the training and surveillance to assure that treatment is given and patients' rights are respected.

1. The main purpose of the passage is to

    Ⓐ   discuss the influence of Dorothea Dix on the mental health movement

    Ⓑ   provide a historical perspective on problems of mental health care

    Ⓒ   increase public awareness of the plight of the mentally ill

    Ⓓ   shock the reader with vivid descriptions of asylums

    Ⓔ   describe the invention of new treatments for mental illness

2. According to the passage, which of the following contributed to the deterioration of the asylum system?

    I.   Lack of funds to maintain the asylums ✓

    II.   Influx of more patients than the system was designed to handle

    III. Lack of effective treatments for many mental illnesses ✓

    Ⓐ   I only

    Ⓑ   III only

    Ⓒ   I and II only

    Ⓓ   I and III only

    Ⓔ   I, II, and III

1. **(B)** This is a main idea question. As discussed in the lesson, the idea is to find a statement that summarizes all of the main points of the selection without going beyond the scope of the selection. The passage does summarize the history of mental health care in the United States, so (B) is a good choice. You can eliminate (D) on the basis of the word "shock." There are no vivid images, and there is nothing in the passage that would shock a reader. You can eliminate (C) for a similar reason. Although a side effect of the selection may be to make some readers aware of a problem, the primary purpose of the passage is to describe, not to increase awareness.

    Finally, (A) and (E) violate that part of the main idea rule that states that the correct answer cannot be too narrow. Both (A) and (E) refer to interesting points made by the author, but neither is the main theme of the selection.

2. **(E)** This is a specific detail question. Seek out the particular references you need. All three statements are specifically supported by the first paragraph. There it is mentioned that funds dried up because of the depression, asylums were filled with too many patients, and many illnesses could not be effectively treated. So the correct choice must include I, II, and III.

3. It can be inferred from the passage that, of the
   following factors, which contributed to postwar
   reform of state mental institutions?

   I.   Heightened public awareness of the unaccept-
        able conditions in the institutions
   II. Discovery of effective treatments for illnesses
        previously considered untreatable
   III. Enactment of state legislation to improve
        conditions in mental institutions

   Ⓐ I only
   Ⓑ III only
   Ⓒ I and II only
   Ⓓ II and III only
   Ⓔ I, II, and III

4. The author's attitude toward people who are patients
   in state institutions can best be described as

   Ⓐ inflexible and insensitive
   Ⓑ detached and neutral
   Ⓒ understanding and sympathetic
   Ⓓ enthusiastic and supportive
   Ⓔ uncaring and unemotional

3. **(E)** This is an implied idea question. Which
   of the statements can be logically deduced
   from the selection?

   We need to focus on the second paragraph since the question asks about the
   causes of post-war reform. In that paragraph,
   the author mentions books, motion pictures,
   and newspaper exposés. Why would these
   be effective tools of reform? By creating a
   new public awareness of a problem. So statement I must be part of the correct choice.

   Statement II is also inferable, for the author mentions in passing that new treatments had been discovered. This, too, must
   have been one of the factors encouraging
   reform.

   Finally, the author states that patients'
   rights groups encouraged reform by lobbying. Since these efforts were successful, we
   can infer that the lobbying resulted in some
   reform legislation.

   So all three factors can be inferred to be
   part of the post-war reform.

4. **(C)** This is a tone question. Arrange all five
   choices to create a spectrum of attitudes
   ranging from positive to negative:

   POSITIVE ATTITUDE
   enthusiastic and supportive
   understanding and sympathetic
   detached and neutral
   uncaring and unemotional
   inflexible and insensitive
   NEGATIVE ATTITUDE

   Start by dividing the range in the middle.
   Does the passage tend toward the negative
   or positive direction? The author's attitude
   inclines more to the positive side. The passage speaks of the "plight" of the patient, a
   term that would not be used by someone
   who was detached, uncaring, or insensitive.
   Now the question is one of degree. How
   positive is the tone? Although the attitude
   toward patients might be described as
   either "sympathetic" or "supportive,"
   "understanding" is a better description than
   "enthusiastic." The author seems to understand the position of the patient, but he is
   not a cheerleader for the patient.

5. The passage provides information that would help answer all of the following questions EXCEPT

Ⓐ Who are some people who have had an important influence on the public health movement in the United States?

Ⓑ What were some of the mental illnesses that were considered untreatable until the 1950s?

Ⓒ What were some of the new treatments for mental illnesses that were adopted in the 1950s?

Ⓓ What were some of the most important legal cases that contributed to the new concern for patients' rights?

Ⓔ What effect did the Civil Rights Movement have on the rights of prisoners?

6. It can be inferred from the passage that had the Civil Rights Movement not prompted an investigation of prison conditions,

Ⓐ states would never have established asylums for the mentally ill

Ⓑ new treatments for major mental illnesses would likely have remained untested

Ⓒ the Civil Rights Movement in America would have been politically ineffective

Ⓓ conditions in mental hospitals might have escaped judicial scrutiny

Ⓔ many mentally ill prisoners would have been transferred from hospitals back to prisons

5. **(D)** This is a specific detail question. You will find information in the passage that would be useful in answering four of the five questions. As for (A), two names, Dorothea Dix and Dr. David Vail, are mentioned in the passage. As for (B) and (C), help for answering these questions can be found in the second sentence of the second paragraph. And as for (E), an answer to this question is contained later in the second paragraph. (D), however, cannot be answered on the basis of the passage, for no specific case names are included.

6. **(D)** This is an implied idea question. The author states that civil rights lawyers who represented black prisoners were drawn naturally into representing patients in mental hospitals. In other words, *x* caused *y*. The question stem asks us to assume that *x* did not occur, and on that basis we can infer that *y* might not have occurred. This is (D).

(A) is incorrect, for the cause of the establishment of the asylum system was Dorothea Dix's crusade. (B) is incorrect, for the passage does not state that judicial activism resulted in the discovery of any new treatments (even though it may have resulted in better treatment). (C) goes far beyond the scope of the passage. We cannot conclude that a failure in the area of prison reform would have meant complete failure of the Civil Rights Movement. Finally, as for (E), nothing in the passage suggests that judicial activism resulted in the transfer of prisoners to hospitals, so a lack of judicial activism would not necessarily have this effect.

7. The tone of the final paragraph can best be described as

- (A) stridently contentious
- (B) overly emotional
- (C) cleverly deceptive
- (D) cautiously optimistic
- (E) fiercely independent

7. **(D)** This is an author's attitude question that focuses on the final paragraph. There the author makes a specific proposal, which, he acknowledges, will require effort to implement. Since the author made the proposal, he must be optimistic about its chance for success. And since he acknowledges that it will not be easy, we can call the author cautious as well.

As for (A) and (B), though the author does make an argument in that paragraph, he does so in rather neutral terms. The paragraph is not contentious or strident or emotional. As for (C), there is nothing in the selection to suggest that the author is attempting to mislead the reader. You may or may not agree with the author's suggestion in that last paragraph, but there is no warrant for the conclusion that he is trying to fool you. Finally, as for (E), although the author evidently does his own thinking, the tone of the final paragraph cannot be described in these terms.

Walk-Through 2

Directions: The passage below is followed by questions based on its content. After reading the passage, choose the best answer to each question. Answer the questions on the basis of what is *stated* or *implied* in the passage.

President Roosevelt's administration suffered a devastating defeat when, on January 6, 1936, the Agricultural Adjustment Act was declared unconstitutional. New Deal planners quickly pushed through Congress the Soil Conservation and Domestic Allotment Act of 1935, one purpose of which was conservation, but which also aimed at controlling surpluses by retiring land from production. The law was intended as a stopgap measure until the administration could formulate a permanent farm program that would satisfy both the nation's farmers and the Supreme Court. Roosevelt's landslide victory over Landon in 1936 obscured the ambivalent nature of his support in the farm states. Despite extensive government propaganda, many farmers still refused to participate in the Agricultural Adjustment Administration's voluntary production control programs, and the burdensome surpluses of 1933 were gone—not the result of the AAA, but a consequence of great droughts.

In February of 1937, Secretary of Agriculture Wallace convened a meeting of farm leaders to promote the concept of the ever-normal granary, a policy that would encourage farmers to store crop surpluses (rather than dump them on the market) until grain was needed in years of small harvests. The Commodity Credit Corporation would grant loans to be repaid when the grain was later sold for a reasonable profit. The conference chose a Committee of Eighteen, which drafted a bill, but the major farm organizations were divided. Since ten of the eighteen members were also members of the American Farm Bureau Federation, the measure was quickly labeled a Farm Bureau bill, and there were protests from the small, but highly vocal, Farmer's Holiday Association. When debate on the bill began, Roosevelt himself was vague and elusive and didn't move the proposed legislation into the "desirable" category until midsummer. In addition, there were demands that the New Deal's deficit spending be curtailed, and opponents of the bill charged that the AAA was wasteful and primarily benefited corporations and large-scale farmers.

The Soil Conservation and Domestic Allotment Act had failed to limit agricultural production as the administration had hoped. Farm prices and consumer demand were high, and many farmers, convinced that the drought had ended the need for crop controls, refused to participate in the AAA's soil conservation program. Without direct crop controls, agricultural production skyrocketed in 1937, and by late summer there was panic in the farm belt that prices would again be driven down to disastrously low levels.

Congressmen began to pressure Roosevelt to place a floor under farm prices by making loans through the CCC, but Roosevelt made such loans contingent upon the willingness of Congress to support the administration's plan for a new system of crop controls. When the price of cotton began to drop, Roosevelt's adroit political maneuver finally forced congressional representatives from the South to agree to support a bill providing for crop controls and the ever-normal granary. The following year Congress passed the Agricultural Adjustment Act of 1938.

1. The primary purpose of the passage is to

   (A) analyze the connection between changes in weather conditions and the movement of agricultural prices

   (B) call attention to the economic hardship suffered by farmers during the 1930s

   (C) discuss the reasoning that led the Supreme Court to declare the Agricultural Adjustment Act of 1933 unconstitutional

   (D) describe the events that led to the passage of the Agricultural Adjustment Act of 1938

   (E) pinpoint the weaknesses of the agricultural policies of Roosevelt's New Deal

1. **(D)** This is a main idea question. The author begins by stating that the Agricultural Adjustment Act of 1933 was declared unconstitutional and then goes on to describe the administration's reaction to that decision. Specifically, the author details the difficulties of the administration in working out a second and permanent agricultural policy, the Agricultural Adjustment Act of 1938. This development is described by (D).

(A) is incorrect for two reasons. First, the author doesn't really analyze the connection between changes in the weather and fluctuations in farm prices. When he uses such information in the article, he simply takes it for granted. Second, the connection is only a part of the overall discussion. As for (B), though a reader might learn something about farmers during the depression, this is not the author's purpose in writing the selection. As for (C), though the author's starting point is the declaration of unconstitutionality, the author does not discuss the Supreme Court's reasoning. Finally, as for (E), though the passage might be used to argue that Roosevelt's policy had some weaknesses (e.g., failure to secure consensus in the farm sector), finding weaknesses is not the main point of the passage.

2. Which of the following is NOT a statement made by the author about the Soil Conservation and Domestic Allotment Act?

   (A) It was intended to be a temporary measure.

   (B) It aimed at reducing agricultural production.

   (C) It aimed at soil conservation.

   (D) It was largely ineffective.

   (E) It was drafted primarily by the Farm Bureau.

2. **(E)** This is a specific detail question—with a thought-reverser. The ideas suggested by (A), (B), and (C) are mentioned in the first paragraph. One aim of the law was conservation, but it was also intended to reduce output by taking land out of use. And it was considered a stop-gap or temporary measure. The idea suggested by (D) is mentioned in the final paragraph. In the first sentence of that paragraph, the author states that the law did not work. Finally, however, the idea mentioned by (E) represents a misreading of the selection. It was the Agricultural Adjustment Act of 1938, not the Soil Conservation and Domestic Allotment Act, that was drafted largely by members of the Farm Bureau.

3. According to the passage, the Roosevelt administration wanted agricultural legislation with all of the following characteristics EXCEPT

(A) It would not be declared unconstitutional by the Supreme Court.

(B) It would be acceptable to the nation's farmers.

(C) It would dismantle the Agricultural Adjustment Administration.

(D) It would provide loans to help farmers store surplus grain.

(E) It would provide for direct control of agricultural production.

4. The passage provides information that would help answer which of the following questions?

I. Who was Secretary of Agriculture during Roosevelt's second term?

II. Who was Roosevelt's major opponent in the 1936 Presidential election?

III. Who was president of the American Farm Bureau Federation in 1937?

(A) I only

(B) II only

(C) I and II only

(D) I and III only

(E) I, II, and III

5. According to the passage, all of the following were impediments to the passage of the Agricultural Adjustment Act of 1938 EXCEPT

(A) initial lack of clear Presidential support

(B) prosperity enjoyed by the nation's farmers

(C) opposition to the idea of a Farm Bureau bill

(D) doubts about the constitutionality of the bill

(E) lack of clear support for the bill in farm states

3. **(C)** This, too, is a specific detail question with a thought-reverser. The ideas suggested in (A) and (B) are mentioned in the middle of the first paragraph. The ideas suggested by (D) and (E) are mentioned in the final sentence of the selection. (And the idea of the ever-normal granary is explained in greater detail in the second paragraph.) The idea suggested by (C) is not mentioned anywhere in the passage. In fact, in the second sentence of the final paragraph, the author states that one of the criticisms leveled at the new act was the wastefulness of the existing AAA. We can almost infer from this that the new act continued the AAA.

4. **(C)** This is another specific detail question. In the opening sentence of the second paragraph, the name of the Secretary of Agriculture is given so statement I must be part of the answer. The name of Roosevelt's opponent in 1936 is given in the first paragraph, so II must be a part of the correct response. The passage does not mention by name anyone from the Farm Bureau, so III cannot be part of the correct answer.

5. **(D)** This is another specific detail question with a thought-reverser. The idea suggested by (A) is clearly mentioned in the second paragraph. The idea suggested by (B) is developed in the final paragraph. The idea suggested by (C) can be found in the second paragraph and that suggested by (E) in the first. The selection does not mention, however, the idea suggested by (D). Although the administration wanted a bill that would not be struck down, the passage does not indicate that constitutional concerns were an impediment to the bill's passage.

6. The author implies which of the following conclusions?

    (A) Roosevelt's ability to gain passage of the Agricultural Adjustment Act of 1938 depended on the large harvests of 1937.
    (B) Secretary of Agriculture Wallace alienated members of the American Farm Bureau Federation by proposing an ever-normal granary.
    (C) The Agricultural Adjustment Act of 1933 was declared unconstitutional because it was written by the Farm Bureau.
    (D) The Commodity Credit Corporation was created to offer farmers incentives for taking land out of production.
    (E) The compulsory production controls of the Agricultural Adjustment Act of 1933 were effective in eliminating surpluses.

6. **(A)** This is an implied idea question. In the final paragraph, the author describes the sequence of events that led to the passage of the 1938 legislation, and he shows how Roosevelt used the changing economic conditions to his advantage. In this discussion, the author implies that the changing economic conditions were a critical factor in the passage of the bill. As for (B), the author does state that some farm groups were displeased with the new bill because it was written primarily by members of the Farm Bureau, but we should not infer from this that the Secretary of Agriculture was blamed for this. (C) represents a confused reading of the passage. The author never states why the 1933 Act was voided but later does say that it was the new legislation (which would finally become the 1938 Act) that was written by members of the Farm Bureau. As for (D), there are two references to the CCC, but both mention that the CCC made loans. You cannot infer from this that the CCC encouraged taking land out of production. That confuses the Soil Conservation and Domestic Allotment Act with the CCC. Finally, (E) is incorrect because the passage says only that the voluntary production controls of that legislation were not the reason for the elimination of the surplus of 1933. Economic conditions finally eliminated the surplus.

7. Which of the following best describes the author's treatment of Roosevelt's farm policies?

    (A) Scholarly but appreciative
    (B) Objective but critical
    (C) Analytical but abrasive
    (D) Biased and condemnatory
    (E) Noncommittal and indifferent

7. **(A)** This is a tone question. The tone of the passage is neutral, like a scholarly journal, so you should eliminate (D) immediately. Next, (E) is not a good description of the tone of the passage, because the author makes very definite statements. The first words of the remaining choices seem correct. You might describe the selection variously as scholarly, objective, or analytical. (B) fails, however, because the author doesn't offer a negative assessment of the policies; and (C) fails because the tone of the passage is not abrasive. As for (A), appreciative is supported by the author's reference to Roosevelt's "adroit" political maneuver, which indicates that the author appreciates the significance of that move.

Walk-Through 3

Directions: The passage below is followed by questions based on its content. After reading the passage, choose the best answer to each question. Answer the questions on the basis of what is *stated* or *implied* in the passage.

In the summer of 999, Leif Ericsson voyaged to Norway and spent the following winter with King Olaf Tryggvason. Substantially the same account is given by both the Saga of Eric the Red and the Flat Island Book.
(5) Of Leif's return voyage to Greenland the latter says nothing, but according to the former it was during this return voyage that Leif discovered America. The Flat Island Book, however, tells of another and earlier landfall by Biarni, the son of a prominent man named
(10) Heriulf, and makes of this Leif's inspiration for the voyage to the new land. In short, like Leif, Biarni and his companions sight three countries in succession before reaching Greenland, and to come upon each new land takes 1 "doegr" more than the last until Biarni
(15) comes to land directly in front of his father's house in the last-mentioned country.

This narrative has been rejected by most later writers, and they may be justified. Possibly, Biarni was a companion of Leif when he voyaged from Norway to
(20) Greenland via America, or it may be that the entire tale is but a garbled account of that voyage and Biarni another name for Leif. It should be noted, however, that the stories of Leif's visit to King Olaf and Biarni's to that king's predecessor are in the same narrative in The
(25) Flat Island Book, so there is less likelihood of duplication than if they were from different sources. Also, Biarni landed on none of the lands he passed, but Leif apparently landed on one, for he brought back specimens of wheat, vines, and timber. Nor is there any good
(30) reason to believe that the first land visited by Biarni was Wineland. The first land was "level and covered with woods," and "there were small hillocks upon it." Of forests, later writers do not emphasize them particularly in connection with Wineland, though they are often
(35) noted incidentally; and of hills, the Saga says of Wineland only that "wherever there was hilly ground, there were vines."

Additionally, if the two narratives were taken from the same source we should expect a closer resemblance
(40) of Helluland. The Saga says of it: "They found there hellus" (large flat stones). According to the Biarni narrative, however, "this land was high and mountainous." The intervals of 1, 2, 3, and 4 "doegr" in both narratives are suggestive, but mythic formulas of this
(45) kind may be introduced into narratives without altogether destroying their historicity. It is also held against the Biarni narrative that its hero is made to come upon the coast of Greenland exactly in front of his father's home. But it should be recalled that Heriulfsness lay
(50) below two high mountains which served as landmarks for navigators.

I would give up Biarni more readily were it not that the story of Leif's voyage, contained in the supposedly more reliable Saga, is almost as amazing. But Leif's
(55) voyage across the entire width of the North Atlantic is said to be "probable" because it is documented in the narrative of a preferred authority, while Biarni's is "improbable" or even "impossible" because the document containing it has been condemned.

1. The author's primary concern is to demonstrate that

    Ⓐ Leif Ericsson did not visit America
    Ⓑ Biarni might have visited America before Leif
        Ericsson
    Ⓒ Biarni did not visit Wineland
    Ⓓ Leif Ericsson visited Wineland first
    Ⓔ Leif Ericsson was the same person as Biarni

2. The passage provides information that defines
    which of the following terms?

    I.   Doegr
    II. Hellus
    III. Heriulfsness

    Ⓐ I only
    Ⓑ II only
    Ⓒ III only
    Ⓓ I and II only
    Ⓔ II and III only

3. According to the passage, Wineland was character-
    ized by which of the following geographical features?

    I.   Woods
    II. Flat rocks
    III. Hills

    Ⓐ I only
    Ⓑ III only
    Ⓒ I and III only
    Ⓓ II and III only
    Ⓔ I, II, and III

1. **(B)** This is a main idea question. The author offers several reasons for the conclusion that the Biarni narrative does not describe the same series of events described by the Saga. And if he can pull this off, then he can claim that Biarni visited America before Leif Ericsson did. This is summarized by (B). (A) misinterprets the author's strategy. The author doesn't need to prove that Leif Ericsson did not visit America, only that Biarni did so before him. (C) is too narrow. It is true that the author wants to show that the two voyages are to some extent dissimilar, and that is why he tries to prove that Biarni did not visit Wineland. But this is a small part of the overall development. As for (D), as was just noted, the author only needs to argue that Biarni did not visit the same three lands later visited by Leif Ericsson. Finally, (E) would be fatal to the author's argument, so this is a point he wishes to disprove.

2. **(E)** The author explicitly defines hellus as meaning "stone," so it is part of the correct answer. You can now eliminate (A) and (C). III is defined implicitly in the passage. The author refers to Heriulfsness in the sentence following the reference to Biarni's father's home. And given the fact that Heriulf is identified as Biarni's father, we can conclude that Heriulfsness must be the father's home. Statement I, however, is not defined. For all that is stated in the selection, "doegr" could be a day, two days, a week, a fort-night, or a month.

3. **(C)** This is a specific detail question. The material you need is contained in the sec-ond paragraph. At the end of that paragraph, the author says that Wineland is described as having forests or woods and a hilly ter-rain. So both statements I and III must be part of the correct choice. II, however, is an idea mentioned in the following paragraph, and flat rocks are characteristic of Helluland—not Wineland.

4. It can be inferred from the passage that scholars who doubt the authenticity of the Biarni narrative make all of the following objections BUT

   (A) Biarni might have accompanied Leif Ericsson on the voyage to America, and that is why a separate, erroneous narrative was invented.

   (B) The similarity of the voyages described in the Saga and in the Flat Island Book indicates that there was but one voyage, not two voyages.

   (C) It seems very improbable that a ship, having sailed from America to Greenland, could have found its way to a precise point on the coast of Greenland.

   (D) The historicity of the Saga of Eric the Red is well-documented, while the historicity of the Flat Island Book is very doubtful. ✓

   (E) Both the Saga of Eric the Red and the Flat Island Book make use of mythical formulas, so it is probable that they were written by the same person.

4. (E) This is an implied idea question. The author doesn't give us a list of the objections to the historicity of the Biarni narrative, but we can infer what some of those objections must be from the refutations of them offered in the selection. As for (A), in the second paragraph, the author acknowledges that Biarni might have been a companion of Leif Ericsson's and that the narrative of Biarni might be a garbled tale of that adventure. We can infer, therefore, that the objectors try to explain away the "other voyage" in this way. As for (B), since the author spends so much effort in attempting to prove that the two voyages did not include exactly the same countries, we can infer that the objectors use the similarity between the two voyages as proof that there was but one voyage. As for (C), in the third paragraph, the author argues that it is not unreasonable to believe that Biarni could sail directly to his father's house since the house was situated by a known navigational landmark. So we infer that the objectors argue that the event was improbable and that this makes the Biarni narrative less believable. And as for (D), the author specifically attributes this objection to them in the closing sentences.

(E), however, is not an objection that would undermine the historicity of the narrative of Biarni. The similarity of the sequence of "doegr" might suggest the two accounts were based on the same events, and this could be an objective that might be raised against the historicity of the Biarni narrative. But this would not prove the two narratives were written by the same author. Further, someone who rejects the Biarni narrative would surely not want to suggest it has the same source as the saga, the supposedly authentic story.

5. The author mentions the two high mountains (line 50) in order to show that it is

    Ⓐ   reasonable for Biarni to land precisely at his father's home
    Ⓑ   possible to sail from Norway to Greenland without modern navigational equipment
    Ⓒ   likely that Biarni landed on America at least 100 years before Leif Ericsson
    Ⓓ   probable that Leif Ericsson followed the same course as Biarni
    Ⓔ   questionable whether Biarni required the same length of time as Leif Ericsson to complete his voyage

6. All of the following are mentioned as similarities between Leif Ericsson's voyage and Biarni's voyage EXCEPT

    Ⓐ   both visited Norway
    Ⓑ   on the return voyage, both visited three different lands
    Ⓒ   both returned to Greenland
    Ⓓ   both sighted Wineland
    Ⓔ   both sighted Helluland

5. **(A)** This is a logical detail question. As noted above, one of the objections to the Biarni narrative is that it would have been difficult for Biarni to navigate so accurately. But the author points out that the location of Heriulf's house was clearly indicated by mountains. So the author mentions the mountains to prove that Biarni could have found the location.

6. **(D)** This is a specific detail question with a thought-reverser. Four of the five ideas are specifically stated in the selection. (A), (B), and (C) are mentioned in the first paragraph and (E) is mentioned in the third. But the author is at pains to prove that Biarni did not visit Wineland as the first of his three lands.

Directions: The passage below is followed by questions based on its content. After reading the passage, choose the best answer to each question. Answer the questions on the basis of what is *stated* or *implied* in the passage.

The beginning of what was to become the United States was characterized by inconsistencies in the values and behavior of its population, inconsistencies that were reflected by its spokesmen, who took conflicting stances
(5) in many areas; but on the subject of race, the conflicts were particularly vivid. The idea that the Caucasian race and European civilization were superior was well entrenched in the culture of the colonists at the very time that the "egalitarian" republic was founded.
(10) Voluminous historical evidence indicates that, in the mind of the average colonist, the African was a heathen, he was black, and he was different in crucial philosophical ways. As time progressed, he was also increasingly captive, adding to the conception of deviance. The
(15) African, therefore, could be justifiably (and even philanthropically) treated as property according to the reasoning of slave traders and slaveholders.

Although slaves were treated as objects, bountiful evidence suggests that they did not view themselves
(20) similarly. There are many published autobiographies of slaves, and Afro-American scholars are beginning to know enough about West African culture to appreciate the existential climate in which the early captives were raised and which, therefore, could not be totally
(25) destroyed by the enslavement experience. This was a climate that defined individuality in collective terms. Individuals were members of a tribe, within which they had prescribed roles determined by the history of their family within the tribe. Individuals were inherently a
(30) part of the natural elements on which they depended, and they were actively related to those tribal members who once lived and to those not yet born.

The colonial plantation system that was established and into which Africans were thrust did virtually
(35) eliminate tribal affiliations. Individuals were separated from kin; interrelationships among kin kept together were often transient because of sales. A new identification with those slaves working and living together in a given place could satisfy what was undoubtedly a
(40) natural tendency to be a member of a group. New family units became the most important attachments of individual slaves. Thus, as the system of slavery was gradually institutionalized, West African affiliation tendencies adapted to it.

(45) This exceedingly complex dual influence is still reflected in black community life, and the double consciousness of black Americans is the major characteristic of Afro-American mentality. DuBois articulated this divided consciousness as follows:

(50) The history of the American Negro is the history of this strife—this longing to attain self-conscious manhood, to merge his double self into a better and truer self. In this merging, he wishes neither of the older selves to be best.

(55) Several black political movements have looked upon this duality as destructively conflictual and have variously urged its reconciliation. Thus, the integrationists and the black nationalists, to be crudely general, have both been concerned with resolving the conflict,
(60) but in opposite directions.

1. Which of the following would be the most appropriate title for the passage?

   Ⓐ The History of Black People in the United States
   Ⓑ West African Tribal Relations
   Ⓒ The Origin of Modern Afro-American Consciousness
   Ⓓ Slavery: A Democratic Anomaly
   Ⓔ The Legacy of Slavery: A Modern Nation Divided

2. The author states which of the following about the Africans who were brought to America?

   I. In Africa, they had acquired a sense of intertribal unity in which all were regarded as belonging to the same group.
   II. They did not regard themselves as objects of someone else's ownership.
   III. They formed new groups to replace the tribal associations that had been destroyed.

   Ⓐ I only
   Ⓑ II only
   Ⓒ III only
   Ⓓ I and II only
   Ⓔ II and III only

3. Which of the following can be inferred about the viewpoint expressed in the second paragraph of the passage?

    Ⓐ It is a reinterpretation of slave life based on new research done by Afro-American scholars.

    Ⓑ It is based entirely on recently published descriptions of slave life written by slaves themselves.

    Ⓒ It is biased and overly sympathetic to the views of white, colonial slaveholders.

    Ⓓ It is highly speculative and supported by little actual historical evidence.

    Ⓔ It is supported by descriptions of slave life written by early Americans who actually owned slaves.

4. The author puts the word *egalitarian* in line 9 in quotation marks to

    Ⓐ emphasize his admiration for the early Americans

    Ⓑ ridicule the idea of democracy

    Ⓒ remind the reader of the principles of the new nations

    Ⓓ underscore the fact that equality did not extend to everyone

    Ⓔ express his surprise that slavery could have existed in America

5. The tone of the passage could best be described as

    Ⓐ informed and anecdotal
    Ⓑ critical and argumentative
    Ⓒ impassioned and angry
    Ⓓ analytical and objective
    Ⓔ caustic and humorous

6. It can be inferred that which of the following pairs are the two elements of the "dual influence" mentioned in line 45?

    Ⓐ slavery and West African culture

    Ⓑ tribal affiliations in West Africa and family affiliations in West Africa

    Ⓒ a sense of individuality and a sense of tribal identification

    Ⓓ the history of West Africa and modern black political movements

    Ⓔ integrationism and black nationalism

7. The author's argument logically depends upon which of the following assumptions?

    Ⓐ The duality that characterized the consciousness of modern black Americans is so deeply rooted that it cannot be eliminated by political action.

    Ⓑ African captives who were brought to North America had learned a basic orientation toward the world that remained with them.

    Ⓒ The white Americans at the time of the beginning of the United States were not aware of the contradiction between the notion of equality and the institution of slavery.

    Ⓓ The influence of the slavery experience on the West Africans was more powerful than the remembrance of West African attitudes.

    Ⓔ Black Americans today are knowledgeable about the world view that was dominant in West Africa at the time of the beginning of slavery in America.

Directions: The passage below is followed by questions based on its content. After reading the passage, choose the best answer to each question. Answer the questions on the basis of what is *stated* or *implied* in the passage.

Two techniques have recently been developed to simplify research and reduce the number of nonhuman primates needed in studies of certain complex hormonal reactions. One technique involves the culturing of
(5) primate pituitary cells and the cells of certain human tumors. In the other, animal oviduct tissue is transplanted under the skin of laboratory primates. Both culturing techniques complement existing methods of studying intact animals.
(10) With an in vitro culturing technique, researchers are deciphering how biochemical agents regulate the secretion of prolactin, the pituitary hormone that promotes milk production. The cultured cells survive for as long as a month, and they do not require serum, a
(15) commonly used culture ingredient that can influence cellular function and confound study results. One primate pituitary gland may yield enough cells for as many as 72 culture dishes, which otherwise would require as many animals.
(20) The other technique allows scientists to monitor cellular differentiation in the reproductive tracts of female monkeys. While falling short of the long-sought goal of developing an in vitro model of the female reproductive system, the next best alternative was
(25) achieved. The method involves transplanting oviduct tissue to an easily accessible site under the skin, where the grafted cells behave exactly as if they were in the normal environment. In about 80 percent of the grafts, blood vessels in surrounding abdominal skin grow into
(30) and begin nourishing the oviduct tissue. Otherwise, the tissue is largely isolated, walled off by the surrounding skin. A cyst forms that shrinks and swells in tandem with stages of the menstrual cycle. With about 80 percent of the grafts reestablishing themselves in the new site, a
(35) single monkey may bear as many as 20 miniature oviducts that are easily accessible for study. Because samples are removed with a simple procedure requiring only local anesthesia, scientists can track changes in oviduct cells over short intervals. In contrast, repeated
(40) analysis of cellular changes within the oviduct itself would require abdominal surgery every time a sample was taken—a procedure that the animals could not tolerate.

Scientists are using the grafting technique to study
(45) chlamydia infections, a leading cause of infertility among women. By infecting oviduct tissues transplanted into the abdominal skin of rhesus monkeys, researchers hope to determine how the bacteria cause pelvic inflammatory disease and lesions that obstruct the oviduct. Such
(50) research could eventually lead to the development of antibodies to the infectious agent and a strategy for producing a chlamydia vaccine.

1. This passage deals primarily with
   Ⓐ reproductive organs of nonhuman primates
   Ⓑ diseases of the pituitary glands
   Ⓒ in vitro studies of pituitary hormones
   Ⓓ techniques for studying hormonal reactions
   Ⓔ new anesthesia techniques

2. According to the passage, the primary benefit of the new research is that
   Ⓐ scientists can study the pituitary gland for the first time
   Ⓑ the procedures are simpler and require fewer laboratory animals
   Ⓒ the study of intact laboratory animals has now been rendered obsolete
   Ⓓ researchers were able to discover prolactin
   Ⓔ an in vitro model of the reproductive system was developed

3. Which of the following conclusions about the culturing technique can be inferred from the passage?
   I. It produces more reliable results than research done with cells requiring serum.
   II. Cultured cells can be implanted in a living animal several times without harming the animal.
   III. A single pituitary gland may generate sufficient cells for a number of experiments.
   Ⓐ I only
   Ⓑ II only
   Ⓒ III only
   Ⓓ I and III only
   Ⓔ I, II, and III

4. All of the following are true of the transplantation technique EXCEPT

    Ⓐ It avoids the need for subjecting a laboratory subject to repeated major surgery.
    Ⓑ It permits scientists to monitor changes frequently. ✓
    Ⓒ The transplanted cells grow as they would in their normal site.
    Ⓓ The transplanted cells can be easily grown in vitro. ✓
    Ⓔ The transplant operation is usually successful. ✓

5. According to the passage, chlamydia causes infertility in women by

    Ⓐ causing tissue changes that block the oviduct ✓
    Ⓑ shrinking and swelling tissues in conjunction with the menstrual cycle
    Ⓒ allowing skin tissue to encyst reproductive tissue
    Ⓓ necessitating abdominal surgery to remove damaged tissue
    Ⓔ diverting the blood supply from the reproductive organs to the skin

6. It can be inferred from the passage that an in vitro model of the female reproductive system is

    Ⓐ currently available but prohibitively expensive
    Ⓑ currently available and widely used
    Ⓒ theoretically possible but of no real scientific value
    Ⓓ theoretically possible but as yet technically impossible
    Ⓔ theoretically impossible

7. The author's attitude toward the developments described in the passage is

    Ⓐ indifference
    Ⓑ concern
    Ⓒ enthusiasm
    Ⓓ disgust
    Ⓔ approval

Directions: The passage below is followed by questions based on its content. After reading the passage, choose the best answer to each question. Answer the questions on the basis of what is *stated* or *implied* in the passage.

Because some resources must be allocated at the national level, we have created policies which reflect the aggregated attributes of our society. The federal budget determines the proportion of federal resources to (5) be invested in social welfare programs and how these resources are distributed among competing programs. The budget is arrived at through a reiterative aggregative political process which mediates the claims of groups interested in health, education, welfare, and so on, thus (10) socializing the continuing conflict generated by their separate aspirations. The test of whether a policy is "good" under this system is whether it can marshal sufficient legitimacy and consent to provide a basis for cohesion and action. Technical criteria may play a role in (15) the process, but the ultimate criteria are political and social.

Whether a policy that is "good" in the aggregate sense is also "good" for a particular person, however, is a different matter. If everyone had identical attributes, (20) these criteria of goodness would produce identical outcomes. With any degree of complexity or change, however, these criteria will always produce different outcomes. Any policy negotiated to attain an aggregate correctness will be wrong for every individual to whom (25) the policy applies. The less a person conforms to the aggregate, the more wrong it will be.

When a policy is not working, we normally assume that the policy is right in form but wrong in content. It has failed because insufficient intelligence has informed (30) its construction or insufficient energy its implementation. We proceed to replace the old policy by a new one of the same form. This buys time, since some time must elapse before the new policy can fully display the same set of symptoms of failure as the old. We thus continue to (35) invest our time, energy, and other resources as if every new discovery of a nonworking policy is a surprise, and a surprise that can be corrected with some reorganized model. But if policies based on complex, aggregated information are always wrong with respect to the (40) preferences of every person to whom they apply, we should concentrate on limiting such policies to minima or "floors." Rather than trying for better policies, we should try for fewer policies or more limited aggregated ones. Such limitations could be designed to produce (45) policies as spare and minimal as possible, for the resources not consumed in their operation would then be usable in nonaggregative, person-specific ways—that is, in a disaggregated fashion. This will require more than just strengthened "local" capacity; it will require the (50) development of new procedures, institutions, roles, and expectations.

1. Which of the following best states the central theme of the passage?

    (A) Policies designed to meet the needs of a large group of people are inherently imperfect and should be scaled down.

    (B) Policies created by the democratic process are less effective than policies designed by a single, concentrated body of authority.

    (C) The effectiveness of a social policy depends more upon the manner in which the policy is administered than upon its initial design.

    (D) Since policies created on the federal level are inherently ineffective, all federal social welfare programs should be discontinued.

    (E) Because state, county, and city officials are more knowledgeable about local conditions, responsibility for all social welfare programs should be shifted to the local level.

2. According to the passage, the test of whether a policy is successful in the aggregate sense is whether or not it

    (A) applies to a large number of people

    (B) satisfies the needs of the people to whom it applies

    (C) appeals to a sufficiently large number of people

    (D) can be revised periodically in response to changing conditions

    (E) can be administered by existing federal agencies

3. Which of the following would the author probably
    regard as an example of a policy based on a process
    of aggregation?

    I. A school dietitian prepares menus based on a
        survey of the taste preferences of students.
    II. A state requires licensed drivers to take an eye
        examination only once every ten years
        because most people's eyes do not change
        radically in a shorter period of time.
    III. The trainer for a baseball team prescribes
         exercises for injured team members according
         to the nature of the injury and the physical
         makeup of the player.

    Ⓐ I only
    Ⓑ II only
    Ⓒ I and II only
    Ⓓ I and III only
    Ⓔ I, II, and III

4. The author places the word *good* in quotation marks
    (line 17) in order to

    Ⓐ emphasize that the word is ambiguous when
        applied to public policies
    Ⓑ stress that no two people will agree on what is
        "good" and what is not
    Ⓒ minimize the need to describe public policies
        in value terms
    Ⓓ point out that the word can be applied to
        individuals but not to groups
    Ⓔ remind the reader that the word is a technical
        term

5. Which of the following words, when substituted for
    the word *aggregate* in line 17, would LEAST
    change the meaning of the sentence?

    Ⓐ extreme
    Ⓑ group
    Ⓒ average
    Ⓓ quantity
    Ⓔ difference

6. The author regards the use of aggregative policies as

    Ⓐ enlightened but prohibitively expensive
    Ⓑ undesirable but sometimes necessary
    Ⓒ wasteful and open to corruption
    Ⓓ essential and praiseworthy
    Ⓔ ill-conceived and unnecessary

Explanatory Answers

Warm-Up 1

1. **(C)** Here we have a main idea question presented in the "name that passage" format. We'll go down the list of choices, eliminating those that are too narrow or too broad.

   (A) is too broad. Most of the discussion focuses on an early period of this country's history, even though there is one paragraph that points out the modern implications of this history. This hardly constitutes an entire history of black people in the United States. (B) is too narrow. Though the discussion of West African tribal relations is an important element of the passage, it is not the main theme. The correct answer must be a title that also includes reference to the implications of these cultural elements. (C) gives us what we are looking for. The passage contrasts white attitudes toward slaves with the attitudes the Africans held about themselves and then shows what implications this cultural history has for modern black Americans. You can eliminate (D), since the main theme of the passage is not really the relationship between slavery and democracy. The anomaly of slavery in a supposedly egalitarian society is only a small part of the discussion. Finally, (E) has the merit of using the phrase "legacy of slavery," which is an important element in the discussion. But the division mentioned in the final paragraph is a division of consciousness—not the division of a nation.

2. **(E)** This is a specific detail question. You will find II specifically stated in the first sentence of the second paragraph, and you will find III explicitly mentioned in the third paragraph. So II and III must be included in the correct choice. This conclusion lets us eliminate (A), (B), (C), and (D)—even without discussing statement I.

   In fact, statement I is contradicted by the passage. The author states that West Africans felt a *tribal* unity, not an *intertribal* unity.

3. **(A)** This is an implied idea question. It's difficult because you have to pick up on the key phrase "Afro-American scholars are beginning to know"; but the question stem doesn't tell you that this is the key to the question.

   That phrase implies that something new has been learned that has prompted scholars to change their ideas about the experience of slavery. In other words, the scholars have rejected the traditional view of what Africans thought of slavery. So we infer that the position outlined in the last two paragraphs is a new interpretation, and (A) correctly describes this.

   (B) is incorrect since the author mentions evidence other than the published autobiographies. And in any case, it is the information about West African culture that has been newly discovered, not the autobiographies. (C) is incorrect since the second paragraph doesn't even deal with the attitudes of the white slaveholders.

   Next, given that the author cites two sources in support of his interpretation (autobiographies and new research), we can eliminate (D). Finally, (E) is incorrect since the paragraph in question does not discuss the attitudes of those who owned slaves.

7

4. **(D)** This is a logical structure question. Why does the author place the term *egalitarian* in quotation marks? The term appears in the first paragraph, where the author is discussing the contradictions in early American attitudes, which are particularly evident in the area of race. These "egalitarian" thinkers believed that they were superior to the Africans.

The author places the term in quotation marks to indicate that he thinks the early white Americans were not really egalitarian. This surely eliminates (A) and (C). (B), however, overstates the case. The author is not implying that democracy, as a concept, is indefensible—only that the early American thinkers did not do a very good job of implementing the idea. Additionally, you can eliminate (E) because the passage does not express surprise. It treats slavery as a historical fact.

5. **(D)** This is a tone question using answer choices with two words. On the basis of first words, we can eliminate both (C) and (E). Although the topic is obviously of interest to the author, the treatment does not qualify as impassioned. Further, though the author's use of quotation marks to surround the word *egalitarian* might qualify as irony or even sarcasm, the overall tone of the passage is not caustic.

Next, using the second words, we eliminate (A) and (B). The author does not tell stories, so the tone cannot be anecdotal. Finally, the tone is not argumentative. Though the passage develops logically and has the form of a logical argument, it cannot be described as argumentative. Argumentative means "contentious and aggressive."

6. **(A)** This is an implied idea question. In the final paragraph, the author refers to the "dual influence" but does not name those influences. Given the context, however, we may conclude that the two influences are slavery and the elements of West African culture that survived. (B) is, therefore, only partially correct. West African culture is only one of the two influences. (C) is a dichotomy mentioned in the selection, but it is not the one to which the author is referring in the final paragraph. (D) is only partially correct. The elements of West African culture constitute one of the two influences, but modern black political movements could not be one of the *origins* mentioned by the author (though it is an outcome of the dual influences). Finally, as for (E), the author does mention these two contrasting movements, but they are a reflection of the duality, not the origin of the duality.

7. **(B)** Although this question uses the word *logically,* it is an implied idea question rather than a logical structure question. The question asks you to identify one of the choices as being a hidden premise of the argument. (B) is essential to the argument. For the argument regarding the West African influences to go through, it must be assumed that the West Africans had learned a world view that survived their being uprooted and transported to America. Without that critical assumption, the argument about the influence of West African culture fails.

(A) is not necessary to the author's argument. The author tries to prove the existence of such a duality, but he does not make any suggestion about how it might be eliminated. (C) is incorrect because the author merely states that there was such a contradiction. Whether white Americans were aware of the inconsistency in their behavior and beliefs is irrelevant. (D) is incorrect because the author merely states that there was the "dual" influence. He does not suggest that one or the other was more important in shaping the structure of modern black American consciousness. Finally, as for (E), though the author must assume that West African culture did survive in some form, he need not assume that black Americans today are still familiar with the elements of West African culture during the time of slavery. The legacy of that culture can survive even without conscious knowledge of its elements.

Warm-Up 2

1. **(D)** This is a main idea question. You are looking for the choice that best describes the content of the passage. (D) fits. The passage is primarily a discussion of two new research techniques.

    You can eliminate (A) as too narrow. Though the author does mention the reproductive organs of nonhuman primates such as monkeys, that is only one of the two techniques discussed. You can eliminate (C) for the same reason. The in vitro technique using cultured cells is but one half of the passage. Finally, you can eliminate (B) and (E) because the passage mentions no diseases of the pituitary gland nor any new anesthesia techniques.

2. **(B)** This is a specific detail question. The task is to find the right spot in the passage. Although the passage mentions the benefits of the new research techniques at several places, the first sentence neatly summarizes the point. (A) is incorrect since the passage does not state that this is the first time scientists have been able to study the pituitary gland. (C) is incorrect since the passage states only that the new techniques reduce the need for animals, not that they make laboratory animals unnecessary. (D) is incorrect for the same reason as (A). The passage does not state that the new techniques led to the discovery of prolactin. Finally, (E) is specifically denied in the second sentence of the third paragraph

3. **(D)** This is an implied idea question. It asks about the first technique, so you will need to study the second paragraph. Additionally, the Roman-numeral format gives you an advantage over the test structure.

    Statement I is inferable from the passage. The author states that cultured cells do not require serum, and that serum may confuse test results. We may infer, therefore, that research using cultured cells produces more reliable results than research using cells requiring serum. At this point, you can safely eliminate choices (B) and (C).

    Statement II is not inferable from the passage. Nothing suggests that these cells are implanted in animals. In fact, II represents a confusion. It is the second technique, transplantation, that implants cells. Having eliminated it, you would also eliminate (E).

    Our choice has been narrowed to (A) and (D). Our decision, therefore, depends on III. III is inferable. One of the advantages of the culturing technique (mentioned in the last sentence of the second paragraph) is the large yield of these cells. So III must also be part of the correct choice, and the right answer must be (D).

4. **(D)** This is a specific idea question. Given the thought-reverser (EXCEPT), we are looking for the one thing that is not mentioned in the selection. In the third paragraph, you will find (A), (B), (C), and (E) all explicitly stated. The procedure does avoid the problem of repeated major surgery; it does allow frequent monitoring; the cells do behave normally; and the transplants are usually successful. (D), however, represents a confused reading of the selection. The in vitro culturing of cells belongs to the first technique.

5. **(A)** This is a specific detail question. The technique for answering this kind of question is to find the particular reference you need. In this case, you'll find the discussion in the final paragraph. There the author states that the infection causes lesions that obstruct the oviduct. This is summarized by (A). (B) and (C) are incorrect because these ideas, though mentioned in the selection, are not responsive to the question. They provide information about how the research proceeds but not about the causes of infertility in women. (E) is closely related to (B) and (C). In the grafting technique, blood is apparently diverted to the grafts, but this is not responsive to the question. Finally, (D) is perhaps the second best answer. It at least has the merit of mentioning the tissue damage. But the passage never mentions the need for surgery to remove damaged tissue. Although you might infer that this could sometimes be a proper medical procedure, such a procedure is not specifically mentioned in the selection. Remember the answer to a specific detail question will be explicitly given in the selection.

6. **(D)** This is an inference question. In the second sentence of the third paragraph, the author states that the grafting technique falls "short of the long-sought goal of developing an in vitro model." From this remark we can infer, first, that an in vitro model does not yet exist, thus eliminating choices (A) and (B). Second, we can infer from the phrase "long-sought" that such a model is believed to be scientifically possible and of real value. On this basis we can eliminate both (C) and (E). Thus, (D) is the correct choice. And the remark just cited implies that such a procedure is possible but has not yet been achieved.

7. **(E)** This is an author's attitude question. If you can, arrange the choices on a spectrum. Here you can classify the various responses as suggesting either negative or affirmative reactions:

    (–)   disgust   concern   indifference   approval   enthusiasm   (+)

    Remember that in the passage, the author describes the advantages of these new techniques. So we can eliminate choices (B) and (D) with their negative overtones, and with them choice (A). Now we must choose between "approval" and "enthusiasm." Had the author said something like "These new techniques are long-sought-after breakthroughs," we might describe the treatment as enthusiastic. As it is, the author, in very neutral language, describes the techniques and some of the advantages of using them. The best description of this treatment is "approval."

Warm-Up 3

1. **(A)** This is a main idea question. In the first paragraph, the author introduces the idea of an aggregative policy, that is, a policy that is designed to meet the needs of a group of people. In the second paragraph, he explains that such policies are inherently imperfect because no single individual meets the group profile. In the final paragraph, he reaches the conclusion that we should rely less on policies that are necessarily imperfect. Choice (A) summarizes this development.

    (B) is incorrect and represents a confused reading of the first paragraph. It is not the fact that the policies are created by a democratic political process that makes them ineffective; rather, it is the fact that they are aimed at a group. An aggregative policy enacted by an absolute monarch would be open to the same indictment.

(C) is incorrect because the author indicts the design, not the implementation, of the programs. (D) is wrong for two reasons. First, the author is not describing just federal programs (though he uses the federal level as an example); he is attacking all aggregative policies. Second, (D) overstates the author's point. The author calls for minimizing such programs—not totally eliminating them. Finally, (E), too, goes beyond the scope of the passage. The author does call for minimizing aggregative policies, but it is not clear that this would mean just reducing their geographic scope. The author might very well favor eliminating a lot of programs altogether.

2. **(C)** This is a specific detail question. In the first paragraph, the author states that the measure of whether an aggregate policy is a success is essentially political and social. That is, a "good" policy is one that commands public support. Thus, (C) is the best response. (A) is incorrect, for this is part of the definition of an aggregate policy—not the measure of its worth. (B) is incorrect because this would be the measure of the value of a policy from the standpoint of the individual (see the second paragraph). As for (D), though the author does mention that aggregate policies are often changed, he says this is done in a futile attempt to make them work. To the extent that it is possible for a policy to be revised to meet individual circumstances, then it is not an aggregate policy. Finally, as for (E), though federal policies are aggregative policies, this is not the measure of the value of such a policy.

3. **(C)** This is a further application question. You must take what you have learned about aggregate policies from the passage and apply that information to these new situations. Remember that the defining characteristic of an aggregative policy is that it is based upon the characteristics of a group. The situations in both I and II fit this description, and the author would probably say of those programs that they are defective in this respect. A menu based on a survey will meet the needs of some summary of the group, but it will not satisfy exactly the desires of any one student. Similarly, requiring eye exams once every ten years won't catch people whose eyes deteriorate more quickly than the norm and is unnecessary for those whose eyes don't change at all. Statement III, however, is not an aggregative situation. The trainer creates policies that are tailored to each individual player.

4. **(A)** This is an implied idea question. The author discusses two different senses of "good" in this context: the aggregate level and the individual level. We can infer he places the word in quotations to emphasize this ambiguity. (B) overstates the case. As for (C), the author himself makes such a value judgment when he says that aggregate policies are imperfect. As for (D), it is not that the word cannot be applied to groups; it's just that when the word is applied to groups, it has a meaning different from the one it has when applied to individuals. Finally, (E) might be a good choice if the word in question were a technical word such as *aggregate* or *minima,* but it is not.

5. **(C)** This is an implied idea question. The author never explicitly defines aggregate, but you can learn from the passage what it means. Aggregate policies are aimed at a group of people and take into account what the "typical" person in the group would require. Thus, such policies are based on the needs of the "average" person even though, according to the author, no such person really exists.

6.   **(B)** This is an author's attitude question. The author presents a fairly powerful logical argument to show the weakness in all aggregative policies. So his attitude is one of disapproval. But that disapproval is not unqualified. The author calls for reducing the number and scale of aggregate policies but not for total elimination. Thus, implicit in the argument is the recognition that it may be necessary to have some such programs (the "minima" or "floors"). This attitude is best described by (B).

    (A) can be eliminated because the author regards aggregative policies as inherently weak, not enlightened. (C), however, overstates the case. Although the author believes that such programs do not make the best use of resources, this is not attributable to corruption but to the design of the programs. As for (D), though the author does consider that such programs are essential, he does not praise the programs. Finally, (E) overstates the point. The author does consider aggregative policies (in the main) to be ill-conceived, but he does not regard them as completely unnecessary.

English Grammar and Usage Diagnostic Test

✓ Topics Covered

How much English grammar do I need to know?

Do I need a general review of English grammar?

What specific areas of English usage am I weak in?

GMAT Sentence Correction items test English grammar, sentence structure, and usage. To help you decide what you must study, here is a diagnostic test.

ENGLISH DIAGNOSTIC TEST
30 Questions
No Time Limit

> **Directions:** Each of the following sentences contains an error of grammar, sentence structure, or usage. Circle the letter of the underlined part of the sentence containing the error. Although there is no time limit, you should work as quickly as possible. After you have finished, review your work using the explanations that follow.

1. Her and the other members of the team spoke to the press after their final victory.
   A   B   C   D

2. In early America, there has been very little to read except for the books sent from
                              A   B   C   D
   Europe.

3. Still remaining in the ancient castle are the Duke's collection of early Dutch
          A   B
   paintings which will be donated to a museum.
             C   D

4. After having took the entrance examination, she was absolutely sure that she
                   A   B   C
   would be admitted to the college.
          D

5. Most students preferred courses in the liberal arts to courses in science—unless
                  A   B   C
   they are science majors.
   D

6. The point of the coach's remarks were obviously to encourage the team and
                                   A   B
   to restore its competitive spirit.
   C   D

7. When Mozart wrote "The Marriage of Figaro," the Emperor was shocked at
                A   B
   him using mere servants as main characters.
   C   D

8. Since he was called back for a third reading, the actor expected being chosen for
   A   B   C   D
   the part.

9. For a young woman who is ready to join the work force, there now exists
                    A   B
   many more opportunities than existed for her mother.
   C   D

10. Movie fans claim there is no greater director than him, although most critics
                 A   B   C
    would mention the names of Bergman or Kurosawa.
    D

11. When the Senate meeting was televised, the first issue to be discussed were
    ___A___   ___B___ ___C___   _____D___
    federal grants and loans for higher education.

12. Although the average person watches a news program every day, they do not
    ___A___   ___B___   ___C___
    always understand the issues discussed.
                          ___D___

13. It was said of the noted author Marcel Proust that he goes out only at night.
                                                 ___A___ __B__ __C__   ___D___

14. Most people do not realize that white wines, including champagne, are actually
                 _____A_____ __B__   ___C___
    made of red grapes.
    ___D___

15. The earliest architecture in the New World resembled neither that of the Euro-
                                                ___A___   __B__
    pean Renaissance or that of the early Baroque period, but rather the medieval
                     __C__   ___D___
    architecture of European towns.

16. Like many composers of the period, Debussy was familiar and admired contem-
    ___A___   ___B___   __C__
    porary poetry and used it as the inspiration for his music.
                     _____D_____

17. Americans used to go to the movies as often as they watched television; but now
                                       ___A___
    that they can watch movies in their homes, they are doing more of it.
        __B__   ___C___   ___D___

18. After hearing Joan Sutherland perform live at the Metropolitan Opera on
    ___A___   __B__
    December 1, 1984, I am convinced that she is greater than any prima donna
                                                _____C_____
    of this century.
    ___D___

19. Like Andy Warhol, the "pop art" of Roy Lichtenstein is filled with familiar
                   ___A___   ___B___
    images such as cartoon characters.
    ___C__ __D__

20. Because the project had been a team effort, we had divided the bonus equally
    ___A___   ___B___
    among the five of us.
    __C__   __D__

21. Postponing marriage and having little or no children are not revolutionary
    _____A_____ ___B___   ___C___
    choices for women; they were choices made by the grandmothers of many
                       ___D___
    postwar women.

22. Being that black bears are large and powerful, most people fear them even
    ___A___   __B__   __C__
    though the bears are really quite shy.
                      ___D___

23. Because consumers believe there to be a correlation between price and quality,
    ___A___   __B__   __C__
    the cost of computer software is steadily raising.
                                  _____D_____

24. Travel to countries with less than ideal sanitary conditions increases the amount
    ___A___   _____B_____   ___C___   ___D___
    of victims of hepatitis.

25. The fuel truck overturned on the highway, stopped traffic for over four hours
                   ___A___   _____B_____
    during the busiest part of the day.
    __C__   __D__

26. Primarily found in the remote mountainous regions of the southeastern states,
    very few people die of the bite of the copperhead or highland moccasin because
    <u>A</u>   <u>B</u>
    very few people come into contact with them.
    <u>C</u>   <u>D</u>

27. When Peter started the business in 1982, it was hardly nothing more than a one-
    <u>A</u>   <u>B</u>
    room operation with a single telephone line, but today Peter has offices in six
                                            <u>C</u>   <u>D</u>
    different states.

28. Unlike the 1960s, when drugs were used primarily by "hippies," cocaine is used
    <u>A</u>   <u>B</u>
    today by people in all walks of life, including lawyers.
        <u>C</u>   <u>D</u>

29. While the Reagan–Gorbachev summit cannot be described as a complete waste
                                            <u>A</u>   <u>B</u>
    of time, nothing particular significant was accomplished during the ten-day
        <u>C</u>   <u>D</u>
    meeting.

30. There are some people who are unusually sensitive to bee stings and who may
    <u>A</u>   <u>B</u>
    experience allergic reactions including swelling, chills, nausea, fever, and
                            <u>C</u>
    they may even become delirious.
        <u>D</u>

8

Explanatory Answers

1. **(A)** *Her* is an object pronoun and cannot be used as a subject.

2. **(A)** The verb tense is incorrect. The past tense, *was*, is needed here.

3. **(B)** The subject here is the *collection* of paintings, which is singular; therefore the verb should be singular.

4. **(A)** The past participle for *to take* is *taken*, not *took*.

5. **(A)** The sentence suffers from an illogical combination of verb tenses, a problem that can be corrected by changing *preferred* to *prefer*.

6. **(A)** The subject here is *point*, which is singular; therefore the plural verb *were* is incorrect.

7. **(C)** The modifier is intended to modify the gerund; *him* should be *his*.

8. **(D)** The infinitive is required here; *he expected to be chosen*.

9. **(B)** The subject is *many opportunities*, which is plural. The verb should be *exist*.

10. **(C)** The subject pronoun is required for the predicate nominative; *him* should be *he*.

11. **(D)** The subject here is *issue*, which is singular, so the verb should also be singular—*was*.

12. **(C)** *They* represents a shift in subject from *the average person*. The correct pronoun would be *he* or *she*.

13. **(C)** Since the first verb is in the past tense, the second verb cannot be in the present tense.

14. **(D)** This is an error of idiomatic expression. The wines are made *from* red grapes, not *of* red grapes.

15. **(C)** The correct expression in English is *neither/nor*; here *or* is incorrect.

16. **(C)** This is an incomplete construction. The sentence should say that Debussy was familiar *with* and admired.

17. **(D)** Here the pronoun *it* has no specific referent.

18. **(C)** This is not a logical statement. The sentence says that Joan Sutherland is greater than herself. It should say that she is greater than any *other* prima donna.

19. **(A)** This is an illogical comparison; the sentence compares the art of Lichtenstein to Andy Warhol, not to his art.

20. **(B)** The use of the past perfect tense here is unnecessary. The simple past is required.

21. **(B)** This is a mistake of expression. The correct expression is *few*, not *little*.

22. **(A)** *Being that* is low-level usage for *since* or *because* and should not be used.

23. **(D)** This is an error in diction. The correct word here is *rising*.

24. **(D)** The sentence contains an error in diction. The correct word is *number*, not *amount*.

25. **(B)** *Stopping* should be used instead of *stopped* to indicate simultaneous action and to avoid a run-on sentence.

26. **(A)** The sentence contains a dangling modifier. The sentence does not mean to say that people are found in the remote mountainous regions, but that the snakes are found in those regions.

27. **(B)** The sentence contains a double negative: *hardly nothing*.

28. **(A)** The sentence contains a dangling modifier. The phrase *the 1960s* cannot modify *cocaine*.

29. **(D)** *Particular* is an adjective and cannot be used to modify another adjective. The correct word would be *particularly*.

30. **(D)** The sentence suffers from faulty parallelism.

8

Sentence Correction

✓ **Topics Covered**

1. **Principles of Grammar**
   - **Subject-Verb Agreement**
   - **Pronoun Usage**
   - **Adjective vs. Adverb**
   - **Double Negatives**
2. **Sentence Structure**
   - **Parallelism**
   - **Incomplete Split Constructions**
   - **Verb Tenses**
   - **Logical Errors**
   - **Sentence Fragments**
   - **Punctuation**
   - **Directness and Conciseness**
   - **Misplaced Modifiers**
3. **Idiomatic Expression**
   - **Wrong Prepositions**
   - **Right Idea, Wrong Word**
   - **Gerund vs. Infinitive**
   - **Unacceptable Expressions**

9

One kind of verbal question that will appear in your GMAT verbal section is sentence correction. Here are the directions for sentence correction items and an example.

Directions: In this type of question, part or all of a sentence is underlined. Following each sentence are five different ways of wording the underlined part. Answer choice (A) always repeats the original; the other four choices are different. If you think that the sentence as originally written is the best way of wording the underlined part, choose answer (A); otherwise, select the best alternative.

Questions of this type test your ability to identify correct and effective expression. Evaluate the answer choices by the requirements of standard written English. Pay attention to elements of grammar, diction (choice of words), and sentence construction. Select the answer choice that best renders the thought presented in the original sentence. The correct choice will be clear and precise and free of awkwardness, needless repetition, or ambiguity.

EXAMPLE:

Psychological tests indicate that Helen's son, Edward, has a natural ability for math and science, but he shows little interest <u>in subjects rather than</u> art and music.

Ⓐ in subjects rather than

Ⓑ for subjects other than

Ⓒ for subjects rather than

Ⓓ in subjects than

Ⓔ in subjects other than

The answer is (E). As a matter of idiomatic expression, the sentence must read *interest in* and not *interest for*. Additionally, to make a logical statement the sentence must read *in subjects other than* instead of *in subjects rather than*.

Sentence correction items are essentially a test of English grammar and usage, so the best preparation for them is a review of the most common errors tested by this question type.

Holmes' Attic

In the Sherlock Holmes stories, Dr. Watson occasionally remarks on the curious imbalance in the detective's learning. Holmes had remarkably detailed knowledge of some areas, such as the geography of London and the effects of exotic poisons, but no knowledge at all of other areas that most people would think important, like literature or politics. To explain this seeming shortcoming, Holmes draws an analogy between the mind and an attic. The mind, like an attic, is a storage facility—with limited space. To make effective use of the space, you have to be sure you don't clutter it up with things you don't need. You probably don't clutter up your mind with the formal principles of English grammar and usage. You have a working knowledge of them that allows you to write as clearly and effectively as you need to. But as you get ready to take the GMAT, you may find it necessary to take some of those principles down from the attic and dust them off—thus the title of this part of the lesson.

This part of the lesson contains a review of the principles of grammar, sentence structure, and usage most often tested by sentence corrections in the verbal section of the GMAT. (**Note:** Sentence correction items always include five answer choices; but in order to keep the presentation from becoming unmanageable, the illustrative examples will include only two choices, a wrong choice and a correct choice.)

Principles of Grammar

Most of the grammar errors tested by sentence correction fall into one of four categories.

1. Subject–Verb Agreement

As you know, a subject must agree with its verb.

> **EXAMPLE:**
>
> The professor were traveling in Europe when she received notice of her promotion.
>
> Ⓐ The professor were traveling in Europe
> Ⓑ The professor was traveling in Europe
> Ⓒ * * *
> Ⓓ * * *
> Ⓔ * * *

The construction *were traveling* is an error. The subject is *professor*, a singular noun. The verb *were traveling* should be *was traveling*. In this example choice (B) corrects the error.

The error in the sentence above is too easy for the GMAT. In order to make GMAT questions a bit more subtle, a question writer who wanted to test your ability to spot such errors might use one of three tricks: separate the subject and verb, use an inverted sentence structure, or use a subject that you might not recognize as singular (or plural).

First, in order to disguise the failure of subject verb agreement, a question writer can separate the subject matter from the verb by inserting a phrase or a clause.

EXAMPLES:

The professor voted Teacher of the Year by the students <u>were traveling in Europe</u> when she received notice of her promotion.

Ⓐ were traveling in Europe

Ⓑ * * *

Ⓒ was traveling in Europe

Ⓓ * * *

Ⓔ * * *

Most teachers, unless they have an appointment to a prestigious university, <u>earns relatively less as a teacher than they might in business.</u>

Ⓐ earns relatively less as a teacher than they might in business

Ⓑ * * *

Ⓒ earn relatively less as a teacher than they might in business

Ⓓ * * *

Ⓔ * * *

Many nutritionists now <u>believe that a balanced diet and not large doses of vitamins are</u> the best guarantee of health.

Ⓐ believe that a balanced diet and not large doses of vitamins are

Ⓑ * * *

Ⓒ * * *

Ⓓ * * *

Ⓔ believe that a balanced diet and not large doses of vitamins is

Television comedies in which there is at least one really detestable character <u>captures the interest of viewers.</u>

Ⓐ captures the interest of viewers

Ⓑ * * *

Ⓒ * * *

Ⓓ capture the interest of viewers

Ⓔ * * *

In the first example, the subject, *the professor*, is singular, yet the verb, *were traveling*, is plural. This is more difficult to spot in this version of the sentence because of the proximity of the noun *students*, which might be mistaken for the subject of the verb. The sentence sounds correct to the ear: . . . *students were* . . .

The answer to the second question is (C). The subject of *earns* is *teachers. Teachers earns* is incorrect. The correct construction is *teachers earn*. But it's easy to mistake *university* for the true subject of the sentence.

The third sentence is incorrect because the true subject of the verb *are* is *diet*. The phrase *not large doses* is not part of the subject. The correct construction is *diet . . . is*. (E) is the correct choice.

The answer to the fourth question is (D). The true subject of the verb *captures* is *comedies*. The correct construction is *comedies . . . capture*.

Second, the connection between the subject and verb may be obscured in an inverted sentence, which is one in which the verb comes before the subject.

EXAMPLES:

Though this is the wealthiest country in the world, within a few blocks of the White House <u>there is scores of homeless people who live</u> on the streets.

Ⓐ there is scores of homeless people who live

Ⓑ * * *

Ⓒ there are scores of homeless people who live

Ⓓ * * *

Ⓔ * * *

Just a few miles from the factories and skyscrapers <u>stand a medieval castle, which looks</u> exactly as it did in the twelfth century.

Ⓐ stand a medieval castle, which looks

Ⓑ stands a medieval castle, which looks

Ⓒ * * *

Ⓓ * * *

Ⓔ * * *

The answer to the first question is (C). The subject of the verb is not *there* but *scores*, which is plural. The correct construction is *there are scores*.

The answer to the second question is (B). The subject of the verb *stand* is *castle*. The correct construction is *stands a medieval castle*.

Third, there are some subjects that are a bit tricky.

EXAMPLES:

Either the governor or one of his close aides <u>prefer not to have</u> the senator at the head table, where he would be conspicuous.

Ⓐ prefer not to have

Ⓑ * * *

Ⓒ prefers not to have

Ⓓ * * *

Ⓔ * * *

Surrounded by layers of excelsior, none of the crystal goblets <u>were broken when the workers dropped the crate.</u>

Ⓐ were broken when the workers dropped the crate

Ⓑ * * *

Ⓒ * * *

Ⓓ * * *

Ⓔ was broken when the workers dropped the crate

John, his wife, and the rest of his family <u>plans to attend the awards dinner to be given</u> by the company for the employees with the most seniority.

Ⓐ plans to attend the awards dinner to be given

Ⓑ plan to attend the awards dinner to be given

Ⓒ * * *

Ⓓ * * *

Ⓔ * * *

The answer to the first question is (C). When a subject consists of two or more parts joined by *or*, the verb must agree with the element that follows the *or*. So, for the purpose of agreement, the subject of the sentence is *one*. The correct construction is *one . . . prefers.*

The answer to the second question is (E). The subject of the verb *were broken* is *none*. And *none* is singular. The correct construction is *none . . . was broken.*

The answer to the third question is (B). A subject consisting of two or more elements joined by *and* is plural. The correct construction is *John, his wife, and the rest of his family plan.*

2. Pronoun Usage

There are three areas of pronoun usage tested by sentence correction: whether a pronoun has a proper antecedent, agreement between pronoun and antecedent, and choice of pronoun case.

First, a pronoun is a word that takes the place of a noun, so a properly used pronoun will have an antecedent (also called a referent). This is the word the pronoun substitutes for. Setting aside certain idioms, such as *It's raining*, in which the *it* does not have an identifiable antecedent, a pronoun that lacks a clear antecedent is used incorrectly.

> **EXAMPLES:**
>
> During her rise to fame, she betrayed many of her friends, <u>and because of it,</u> very few people trust her.
>
> Ⓐ and because of it
>
> Ⓑ * * *
>
> Ⓒ and because of her behavior
>
> Ⓓ * * *
>
> Ⓔ * * *

> In New York City, <u>they are brusque and even rude</u> but quick to come to one another's assistance in a time of crisis.
>
> Ⓐ they are brusque and even rude
>
> Ⓑ * * *
>
> Ⓒ the people are brusque and even rude
>
> Ⓓ * * *
>
> Ⓔ * * *

> Ten years ago, the United States imported ten times as much French wine as Italian wine, <u>but today Americans are drinking more of it.</u>
>
> Ⓐ but today Americans are drinking more of it
>
> Ⓑ but today Americans are drinking more Italian wine
>
> Ⓒ * * *
>
> Ⓓ * * *
>
> Ⓔ * * *

The answer to the first question is (C). A pronoun must have an antecedent, but *it* doesn't refer to anything. *It* wants to refer to the woman's behavior, but that word doesn't appear in the original sentence. Corrected, the sentence reads *because of her behavior.*

The answer to the second question is (C). This construction might be called the ubiquitous *they*. *They* are everywhere: In New York, *they* are rude; in Chicago, *they* like the Cubs; in Atlanta, *they* speak with a southern accent; in California, *they* like parties. *They* do get around! The trouble with this use of *they* is that it has no antecedent.

In conversation, the ubiquitous *they* may be acceptable, but not in standard written English. The second sentence above is corrected by using the word *people* in place of *they*.

The answer to the third question is (B). The antecedent of *it* is unclear. Does the sentence mean to state that Americans are drinking more French wine or more Italian wine? It could be either. The sentence is corrected by specifying which.

Second, a pronoun must agree with its antecedent, both in number and person.

EXAMPLES:

Although a police officer used to be a symbol of authority, today they receive little respect from most people.

Ⓐ today they receive little respect from most people

Ⓑ * * *

Ⓒ * * *

Ⓓ * * *

Ⓔ today he or she receives little respect from most people

The Abbot was an effective administrator who attempted to assign each monk a task particularly suited to their talents and training.

Ⓐ particularly suited to their talents and training

Ⓑ particularly suited to his talents and training

Ⓒ * * *

Ⓓ * * *

Ⓔ * * *

After three years of college education, a person should be allowed to apply to graduate school, because by that time you are ready to choose a profession.

Ⓐ by that time you are ready to choose a profession

Ⓑ * * *

Ⓒ * * *

Ⓓ * * *

Ⓔ by that time one is ready to choose a profession

The answer to the first question is (E). The pronoun *they* refers to *police officer*, which is singular. The best way to correct it is to say *he or she is*. The answer to the second question is (B). *Their* refers to *each monk*. But *their* is plural and *each monk* is singular. The sentence is corrected by changing *their* to *his*.

The answer to the third question is (E). *You* refers to *person*. But *you* is a second-person pronoun and *person* requires a third-person pronoun. The sentence is corrected by changing *you are* to *one is*. This last error is called the error of shifting subject.

EXAMPLE:

If one wishes to apply for a scholarship, <u>you must submit a completed application</u> by March 1.

Ⓐ you must submit a completed application

Ⓑ * * *

Ⓒ * * *

Ⓓ a completed application must be submitted

Ⓔ * * *

(D) corrects the original by eliminating the incorrect pronoun altogether.

Third, pronouns have case, and a pronoun's function in a sentence determines which case should be used. Subjective case (also called nominative case) pronouns are used as subjects of sentences; objective case pronouns are used as objects (direct objects, indirect objects and objects of prepositions); and possessive case pronouns are used to show possession.

EXAMPLES:

The Judges were unable to make a final decision on a single winner, <u>so they divided first prize between John and he</u>.

Ⓐ so they divided first prize between John and he

Ⓑ * * *

Ⓒ so they divided first prize between John and him

Ⓓ * * *

Ⓔ * * *

Although Peter had been looking forward to the debate for weeks, a sore throat <u>prevented him taking part</u>.

Ⓐ prevented him taking part

Ⓑ prevented his taking part

Ⓒ * * *

Ⓓ * * *

Ⓔ * * *

The answer to the first question is (C). *He* cannot serve as the object of a preposition since it is a subject pronoun. The correct pronoun here is the object pronoun *him*.

The answer to the second question is (B). *Him* modifies *taking*, but the correct choice of pronouns is *his*. (When a pronoun modifies a gerund, the *-ing* form of a verb, you must use the possessive case.)

3. Adjective vs. Adverb

Adjectives are used to modify nouns. Adverbs are used to modify verbs or adjectives.

> **EXAMPLES:**
>
> Some psychologists maintain that a child who has seen violence on television is more likely to react violent in situations of stress.
>
> (A) is more likely to react violent
>
> (B) * * *
>
> (C) * * *
>
> (D) * * *
>
> (E) is more likely to react violently

> The recent created commission has done nothing to address the problem except to approve the color of its stationery.
>
> (A) The recent created commission has done nothing to address the problem
>
> (B) * * *
>
> (C) * * *
>
> (D) The recently created commission has done nothing to address the problem
>
> (E) * * *

The answer to the first question is (E). *Violent* is intended to modify *to react*, a verb form. So the adverb *violently* is required.

The answer to the second question is (D). *Recent* is intended to modify *created*, which is an adjective form modifying *commission*. So *recent* should be *recently*.

4. Double Negatives

Double negatives are not acceptable usage in standard written English.

> **EXAMPLES:**
>
> Not hardly a sound could be heard in the auditorium when the speaker approached the dais to announce the result of the contest.
>
> (A) Not hardly a sound could be heard in the auditorium
>
> (B) * * *
>
> (C) Hardly a sound could be heard in the auditorium
>
> (D) * * *
>
> (E) * * *

> Although she had been hired by the magazine to write book reviews, she knew scarcely nothing about current fiction.
>
> (A) she knew scarcely nothing about current fiction
>
> (B) she knew scarcely anything about current fiction
>
> (C) * * *
>
> (D) * * *
>
> (E) * * *

The answer to the first question is (C). *Not hardly* is a double negative. The sentence must begin *Hardly a sound.*

The answer to the second question is (B). *Scarcely nothing* is a double negative. The sentence must read *scarcely anything.*

(Answers, page 129)

Directions: The following exercise contains 25 sentences. Each sentence makes a grammatical error of the sort just reviewed. Circle the letter of the underlined part of the sentence containing the error.

1. The professor deals <u>harsh</u> with students <u>who are not prepared</u>, and <u>he is even</u>

                 A   **B**   **C**
    <u>more severe</u> with those who plagiarize.

   D

2. A recent study <u>indicates</u> that the average person <u>ignores</u> most commercial adver-

              A   **B**
    tising and <u>does not buy</u> products <u>because of them.</u>

         C   **D**

3. <u>Despite the fact</u> that New York City is <u>one of the most</u> densely populated areas in

   A   **B**
    the world, <u>there are</u> many parks where one can sit on a bench under the trees and

        C
    <u>you can read a</u> book.

  D

4. Charles Dickens <u>wrote</u> about the <u>horrifying</u> conditions in the English boarding

            A   **B**
    <u>schools, which</u> he learned about on one of <u>his</u> trips to Yorkshire.

   C   **D**

5. Andre Breton <u>initiated</u> the Surrealist movement <u>with the publication</u> of a mani-

          A   **B**
    festo, and <u>it</u> incorporated the theories of Freud <u>as well as his</u> own.

     C   **D**

6. The review of the concert <u>published</u> in the morning paper mentioned that the

                  A
    <u>soloist is</u> a very promising talent and <u>that</u> the orchestra <u>played capable.</u>

  B   **C**   **D**

7. <u>During the war</u> there were many people in the Polish countryside <u>that</u> sheltered

   A   **B**
    <u>those</u> who <u>had escaped</u> from concentration camps.

 C   **D**

8. The dean <u>lectured</u> to <u>we students</u> on the <u>privilege of and responsibility</u> of <u>attending</u>

         A   **B**   **C**   **D**
    the university.

9. <u>You taking the initiative</u> in the negotiations <u>will profit</u> the company <u>to a great</u>

          A   **B**   **C**   **D**
    degree.

10. The members of the club <u>insisted that</u> <u>I be</u> the representative of the organization

                    A   **B**
    at the <u>conference, which</u> was something <u>I had hoped</u> to avoid.

      C   **D**

11. <u>No one</u> knows for sure <u>whether there was</u> a real person <u>about which</u>

  A   **B**   **C**
    Michelangelo <u>wrote</u> his poems.

       D

12. <u>Although</u> the director of the zoo <u>takes</u> great pains <u>to recreate</u> the natural habitats

  A   **B**   **C**
    of the animals, none of the exhibits <u>are completely</u> accurate in every detail.

                        D

13. Climatic differences between the north and south of <u>some</u> countries <u>helps to</u>

                                 A   **B**
    <u>account for the differences</u> in temperament of the inhabitants <u>of the two</u> regions.

          C   **D**

9

14. The month of August was particularly cold; hardly no daily temperatures
    _____A_____B_____
    were recorded above 80 degrees and none was recorded above 90 degrees.
    _____C_____   _____D_____

15. The diaries of Stendhal, which make entertaining reading, also provides a great
                              _____A_____   ___B___
    wealth of information about musical taste and performance practice in the last
                          _____C_____   ___D___
    century.

16. Given the evidence of the existence of a complicated system of communication
    _____A_____
    used by whales, it is necessary to acknowledge its intelligence.
    ____B_____   ____C____   __D__

17. Him being at the rally does not necessarily mean that the congressman agrees
    _____A_____   _____B_____ __C__   ___D__
    with the President's entire platform.

18. Although there is no perfect form of government, representative democracy,
    as it is practiced in America, is a system that is working well and
    _____A_____   ___B___   ___C___
    more than satisfactory.
    _____D_____

19. Alfred Stieglitz launched the career of Georgia O'Keeffe, who he later married,
                     ___A___   __B_ _C_ ___D___
    by exhibiting her paintings in his gallery.

20. After driving past Trinity Church, the bus stopped at the recent constructed World
               ____A____   _____B_____
    Trade Towers, the tallest buildings in the city, to allow the passengers to take the
              _____C_____   _____D_____
    special elevators to the observation tower.

21. The student senate passed a resolution banning smoking in the cafeteria
                      __A__   _____B_____
    with scarcely any dissenting votes, which angered many members of the faculty.
    _____C_____   _____D_____

22. Most employers assume that one's professional personality and work habits
                  __A__
    are formed as a result of your early work experience.
    __B__   __C__   __D__

23. Only a small number of taxi drivers fail to insure their vehicles, but usually
                         __A__   ____B____
    these are the ones who need it most.
    ____C____   __D__

24. Angered by the double standard society imposed on women, Edna St. Vincent
                      __A__   ___B___
    Millay wrote candid about her opinions and her personal life.
              ___C___   __D__

25. Unless they hire players who are better hitters, the fans will gradually lose
          __A__   __B_ _C_   _____D_____
    interest in the team despite the fine efforts of the pitching staff.

Sentence Structure

The GMAT also tests your ability to distinguish correct and incorrect sentence structures. In analyzing the structure of a sentence, ask four things: Are the elements of the sentence parallel? Do the verb tenses correctly reflect the action? Are any split constructions correctly completed? Does the sentence say what it means to say?

1. Parallelism

In a correctly written sentence, similar elements must have a similar form.

> **EXAMPLES:**
>
> To abandon their homes, leave behind their families, <u>and traveling across the ocean required</u> great courage on the part of the immigrants who moved to America.
>
> (A) and traveling across the ocean required
>
> (B) and travel across the ocean required
>
> (C) ***
>
> (D) ***
>
> (E) ***

> The review praised the wit, charm, <u>and interpreting of the recitalist</u> but never once mentioned her voice.
>
> (A) and interpreting of the recitalist
>
> (B) ***
>
> (C) ***
>
> (D) ***
>
> (E) and interpretation of the recitalist

> <u>To acknowledge that one has something to learn is taking</u> the first step on the road to true wisdom.
>
> (A) To acknowledge that one has something to learn is taking
>
> (B) ***
>
> (C) ***
>
> (D) To acknowledge that one has something to learn is to take
>
> (E) ***

The answer to the first question is (B). The three verb forms *abandon, leave,* and *travel* should be parallel. The sentence is corrected by changing *traveling* to *travel*.

The answer to the second question is (E). *Wit* and *charm* are nouns, so *interpreting*, too, should be a noun. The sentence is corrected by changing *interpreting* to *interpretation*.

The answer to the third question is (D). The sentence has a structure similar to a mathematical equation: *This* is the same as *that*. Both parts of the "equation" must have the same form. The sentence is corrected by changing *taking* to *to take*.

2. Incomplete Split Constructions

A split construction is a sentence structure in which two otherwise separate ideas are joined together by a later element. For example, *The Mayor knew or should have known about the corruption.* This is a perfectly acceptable split construction in which the ideas *knew* and *should have known* are joined together by the single object *corruption.* In some split constructions, one half or the other never gets completed.

EXAMPLES:

The students are critical of the dean because he is either unfamiliar or doesn't care about the urgent need for new student housing on campus.

- (A) because he is either unfamiliar or doesn't care about
- (B) because he is either unfamiliar with or doesn't care about
- (C) * * *
- (D) * * *
- (E) * * *

Baseball has and probably always will be the sport that symbolizes for people in other countries the American way of life.

- (A) Baseball has and probably always will be
- (B) * * *
- (C) * * *
- (D) * * *
- (E) Baseball has been and probably always will be

The answer to the first question is (B). The split construction *is either unfamiliar or doesn't care* never gets completed. Leave out the idea following the or and the sentence reads *is unfamiliar the urgent need.* Nonsense! The sentence should read *is either unfamiliar with or doesn't care about.*

The answer to the second question is (E). The first half of the split verb construction is never completed. Leave out the second idea and the sentence reads *Baseball has be the sport.* The sentence should read *Baseball has been and probably always will be.*

3. Verb Tenses

The choice of verb tenses in a correctly written sentence reflects the sequence of events described. Some GMAT questions contain errors involving choice of verb tenses.

EXAMPLES:

The teacher began to discuss the homework assignment when he will be interrupted by the sound of the fire alarm.

- (A) when he will be interrupted by
- (B) * * *
- (C) when he was interrupted by
- (D) * * *
- (E) * * *

The conductor announced that the concert would resume <u>as soon as the soloist replaces</u> the broken string on her violin.

(A) as soon as the soloist replaces

(B) * * *

(C) * * *

(D) as soon as the soloist replaced

(E) * * *

Many patients begin to show symptoms again <u>after they stopped taking</u> the drug.

(A) after they stopped taking

(B) after they stop taking

(C) * * *

(D) * * *

(E) * * *

The answer to the first question is (C). The sentence reads *The teacher began . . . and will be interrupted.* One or the other verb tense is wrong. Since the second verb is underlined and not the first, it is the second that is incorrect. The sentence is corrected by changing *will be interrupted* to *was interrupted.*

The answer to the second question is (D). There is a mismatch between the verbs *would resume* and *replaces.* The sentence reads *the concert would resume as soon as the soloist replaces.* Since the second verb is underlined, it is the one that is incorrect. The sentence should read *the concert would resume as soon as the soloist replaced.*

The answer to the third question is (B). The sentence reads *patients . . . show symptoms again after they stopped.* The sentence can be corrected by changing *stopped* to *stop.*

4. Logical Errors

Sometimes a sentence will "want" to say one thing but end up saying something completely illogical.

EXAMPLES:

The great pianist Vladimir Horowitz plays the music of the romantic era <u>better than any pianist in history.</u>

(A) better than any pianist in history

(B) * * *

(C) * * *

(D) better than any other pianist in history

(E) * * *

Educators are now expressing their concern that American schoolchildren <u>prefer watching television to books.</u>

(A) prefer watching television to books

(B) prefer watching television to reading books

(C) * * *

(D) * * *

(E) * * *

The novels of Nathaniel Hawthorne contain characters who are every bit as sinister and frightening <u>as the master of cinematic suspense,</u> Alfred Hitchcock.

Ⓐ as the master of cinematic suspense

Ⓑ * * *

Ⓒ as those of the master of cinematic suspense

Ⓓ * * *

Ⓔ * * *

A Japanese firm has developed a computer so small <u>that users can carry it in their briefcase.</u>

Ⓐ that users can carry it in their briefcase

Ⓑ * * *

Ⓒ * * *

Ⓓ * * *

Ⓔ that users can carry it in their briefcases

The answer to the first question is (D). As written, the sentence asserts that Vladimir Horowitz is better than anyone—including himself. But that is a logical impossibility. The sentence should read *better than any other pianist in history.*

The answer to the second question is (B). The sentence makes an illogical comparison between *watching television* and *books. Watching television* is an activity; *books* are objects. The sentence should read *prefer watching television to reading books.*

The answer to the third question is (C), and it, too, commits the error just discussed. The sentence literally compares the characters in the novels of Nathaniel Hawthorne to Alfred Hitchcock, the person. The sentence should read *as sinister and frightening as those of the master.*

The answer to the fourth question is (E). As written, the sentence asserts that all of the users have but a single, jointly owned briefcase. What the sentence means to say is that users can carry the new computer in their *briefcases* (plural).

5. Sentence Fragments

A sentence must have a main verb.

EXAMPLE:

Postmodern art, with its vibrant colors and bold shapes, <u>and taking its inspiration from artists such as Cézanne but reacting against the pastel indistinctness of the Impressionist canvases.</u>

Ⓐ and taking its inspiration from artists such as Cézanne but reacting against the pastel indistinctness of the Impressionist canvases

Ⓑ * * *

Ⓒ * * *

Ⓓ took its inspiration from artists such as Cézanne but reacted against the pastel indistinctness of the Impressionist canvases

Ⓔ * * *

The answer to the question is (D). The original sentence lacks a main verb. This is corrected by changing *taking* and *reacting,* which function as adjectives modifying *art,* to *took* and *react.*

6. Punctuation

The GMAT also tests some simple points of punctuation.

> **EXAMPLES:**
>
> After months of separation, Gauguin finally joined Van Gogh <u>in Arles in October of 1888, Gauguin left a few weeks later.</u>
>
> Ⓐ in Arles in October of 1888, Gauguin left a few weeks later
>
> Ⓑ * * *
>
> Ⓒ * * *
>
> Ⓓ * * *
>
> Ⓔ in Arles in October of 1888, but left a few weeks later

> The nineteenth-century composers Wagner and Mahler did more than just write <u>music, they conducted their own works.</u>
>
> Ⓐ music, they conducted their own works
>
> Ⓑ * * *
>
> Ⓒ music; they conducted their own works
>
> Ⓓ * * *
>
> Ⓔ * * *

The answer to the first question is (E). Two main clauses cannot be spliced together using only a comma. If you want to join two main clauses, you can use a conjunction (such as *and*) plus a comma, or just a semicolon. The sentence above could have been written: *in Arles, in October of 1888; a few weeks later he left* or *in Arles in October of 1888, but a few weeks later he left.* (E) is correct and illustrates the point that when punctuation is tested at all, it is usually bound up with questions of expression. In this case, it is possible to reduce the entire second clause to a few words and incorporate that idea into the first clause.

The answer to the second question is (C). Here the second clause survives. To join it to the first clause without using a conjunction, you must use a semicolon.

7. Directness and Conciseness

Another thing that is tested by sentence correction is clarity of expression. A few sentence correction originals plus many wrong answers are characterized by awkwardness. We can use the two items above to illustrate the point:

> After months of separation, Gauguin finally joined Van Gogh <u>in Arles in October of 1888, Gauguin left a few weeks later.</u>
>
> Ⓐ in Arles in October of 1888, Gauguin left a few weeks later
>
> Ⓑ * * *
>
> Ⓒ in Arles in October of 1888, although Gauguin left a few weeks later
>
> Ⓓ * * *
>
> Ⓔ in Arles in October of 1888, but left a few weeks later

9

The nineteenth-century composers Wagner and Mahler did more than just write music, they conducted their own works.

(A) music, they conducted their own works

(B) * * *

(C) music; they conducted their own works

(D) * * *

(E) music; as conductors, they did their own works

In the first question, (C) is incorrect because the phrasing is awkward and needlessly wordy. Notice that the correct choice, (E), says the same thing more clearly and in fewer words.

In the second question, (E) is incorrect because it is awkward and needlessly wordy. The very same idea can be expressed more directly as shown by the correct choice, (C).

Unfortunately, there is no single rule by which you can judge whether a sentence is awkward or too wordy. But given a certain phrasing, if it is possible to express the same idea more clearly or more directly, then the original is almost surely wrong.

8. Misplaced Modifiers

Another error that frequently comes up on sentence correction questions is the problem of the misplaced modifier.

EXAMPLES:

Wrapped in several thicknesses of newspaper, packed carefully in a strong cardboard carton, and bound securely with tape, the worker made sure that the fragile figurines would not be broken.

(A) Wrapped in several thicknesses of newspaper, packed carefully in a strong cardboard carton, and bound securely with tape, the worker made sure that the fragile figurines would not be broken.

(B) * * *

(C) * * *

(D) * * *

(E) To make sure that the figurines would not be broken, the worker wrapped them in several thicknesses of newspaper, packed them carefully in a strong cardboard carton, and securely bound the carton with tape.

Riding in a coach and wearing the crown jewels, the crowd cheered the royal couple.

(A) the crowd cheered the royal couple

(B) * * *

(C) the royal couple was cheered by the crowd

(D) * * *

(E) * * *

The answer to the first question is (E). The sentence as originally written suggests that it was the worker who was wrapped, packed, and bound. In general, a modifier should be placed as closely as possible to the part of the sentence it is to modify.

The answer to the second question is (C). The sentence as originally written suggests that the crowd is wearing the crown jewels and riding in the carriage.

(Answers, page 130)

Directions: The following exercise contains 25 sentences. Each sentence makes an error in sentence structure of the sort just reviewed. Circle the letter of the underlined part of the sentence containing the error.

1. The owner of the collection <u>requested that</u> the museum <u>require</u> all
    A · B
    <u>people with a camera</u> to <u>leave them</u> at the door.
    C · D

2. The young comic <u>found</u> that capturing the audience's attention was easy,
    A
    but <u>to maintain</u> <u>their</u> interest <u>was</u> difficult.
    B · C · D

3. <u>Written in almost total isolation from the world</u>, Emily Dickinson <u>spoke</u> of love
    A · B
    <u>and</u> death in <u>her</u> poems.
    C · D

4. <u>Early in his career</u>, the pianist entertained thoughts <u>of becoming</u> a composer; but
    A · B
    after receiving bad reviews for his own work, <u>he</u> had <u>given it up</u>.
    C · D

5. The praying mantis <u>is welcomed</u> by homeowners for <u>its</u> ability <u>to control</u> destruc-
    A · B · C
    tive garden pests, <u>unlike the</u> cockroach, which serves no useful function.
    D

6. The fact that she is bright, articulate, and <u>has charisma</u> <u>will serve</u> her well in her
    A · B
    campaign for governor, <u>particularly</u> since her opponent <u>has none</u> of those
    C · D
    qualities.

7. Puritans such as William Bradford <u>displaying</u> the courage and piety
    A
    <u>needed to survive</u> in the New World, a world <u>both</u> promising and threatening,
    B · C
    <u>which</u> offered unique challenges to their faith.
    D

8. The baseball game was halted due to rain and <u>rescheduled</u> for the following day,
    A
    <u>even though</u> <u>the fans</u> would <u>not leave</u> the stadium.
    B · C · D

9. Unfortunately, <u>before</u> cures are found for diseases such as cancer, many lives
    A
    <u>would have been</u> lost and millions of dollars in medical services <u>spent</u> to treat
    B · C
    symptoms <u>rather than</u> provide a cure.
    D

10. <u>Being highly qualified for the position</u>, the bank president <u>will conduct</u> a final
    A · B
    interview of the new candidate tomorrow, <u>after which</u> he will <u>make</u> her a job offer.
    C · D

11. For many people it is difficult <u>to accept</u> compliments graciously and
    A
    even more difficult <u>taking</u> criticism <u>graciously</u>.
    B · C · D

12. The literature of Native Americans <u>has been overlooked</u> by <u>most</u> scholars, and
    A · B
    the reason is <u>because</u> most university courses in literature <u>are taught</u> in depart-
    C · D
    ments that also teach languages, such as French.

121

13. The French poet Artaud believes that, following the climax of a drama, the
    _____   ____   _____
         A   B   C
    audience experienced a violent catharsis and is thereby "reborn."
             _____
                  D

14. In broken English, the police officer patiently listened to the tourist ask for
    _____
         A
    directions to Radio City Music Hall, after which she motioned the tourist and his
                                         _____   _____
                                              B   C
    family into the squad car and drove them to their destination.
                                       ____
                                        D

15. Bullfighting remains a controversial sport and many are repulsed by it, since
                 _____   ____   _____
                    A   B   C
    Hemingway was an aficionado of the sport and glorified it in his writing.
                                                          __
                                                           D

16. Wagering on the Kentucky Derby favorite is a bad betting proposition, for in the
    _____   __   _____
        A   B   C
    last 15 years, the horse that was the crowd favorite at post time of the Kentucky
    Derby loses the race.
          _____
            D

17. Following the recent crash of the stock market, Peter bought a book on
    _____   _____
                      A   B
    portfolio management in order to learn methods to protect his investments
                        _____
                             C
    from a well-known investment banker.
         _____
                      D

18. During the years she spent searching for a cure for the disease, Dr. Thompson
    _____   _____
           A   B
    interviewed hundreds of patients, ran thousands of tests, and cross-checking
                                                                   _____
                                                                         C
    millions of bits of data.
             _____
                   D

19. Since we have a broader technological base, American scientists believe that our
    _____   _____
      A   B
    space program will ultimately prove superior to the Soviet Union.
                 _____   _____
                         C   D

20. Although a person may always represent himself in a judicial proceeding,
                                           _____
                                              A
    licensed lawyers only may represent others in such proceedings for a fee.
                     ____   _____ __
                       B   C   D

21. Unlike the pale and delicately built ballerinas of romantic ballet, Judith Jamison's
    _____
                                    A
    movement seems more African than European-American and her physical
             _____ _____
               B   C
    appearance reinforces the contrast.
               _____
                   D

22. Market experts predict that in ten years, when the harmful effects of caffeine
                  _____
                     A
    become more generally known, the number of tons of decaffeinated coffee
           _____
                   B
    consumed by Americans each year will exceed coffee containing caffeine.
    _____   _____
         C   D

23. Illiteracy, a widespread problem in the United States, undermines productivity
                _____ _____
                                  A   B
    because many mistakes are made by workers who do not know how to read
                          ___
                           C
    on the job.
    _____
        D

24. Because sailors are often assigned to ships that remain at sea for months at a
                    _____   _____
                           A   B
    time, men in the Navy spend more time away from home than any branch of the
                          _____   _____
                            C   D
    service.

25. Like A. J. Ayer, much of Gilbert Ryle's philosophical argumentation relies on an
         _____   _____
             A   B
    analysis of the way people ordinarily use language.
                        _____ _____
                          C   D

Idiomatic Expression

Some GMAT sentences contain usages that are incorrect because they are not idiomatic. An expression that is not idiomatic is one that is not acceptable English for any of several reasons.

1. Wrong Prepositions

In English, as in other languages, only certain prepositions can be used with certain verbs.

> **EXAMPLES:**
>
> <u>In contrast of the prevailing opinion</u>, the editorial places the blame for the strike on the workers and their representatives
>
> Ⓐ In contrast of the prevailing opinion
>
> Ⓑ In contrast to the prevailing opinion
>
> Ⓒ * * *
>
> Ⓓ * * *
>
> Ⓔ * * *

> Although ballet and modern dance <u>are both concerned in</u> the movement in space to musical accompaniment, the training for ballet is more rigorous than that for modern dance.
>
> Ⓐ are both concerned in
>
> Ⓑ * * *
>
> Ⓒ are both concerned with
>
> Ⓓ * * *
>
> Ⓔ * * *

The answer to the first question is (B). The expression *in contrast of* is not idiomatic. The expression should be *in contrast to*.

The answer to the second question is (C). The expression *concerned in* is not idiomatic. It should read *concerned with*.

2. Right Idea, Wrong Word

Some sentences are incorrect because they use a word that does not mean what is intended. The confusion is understandable because of the similarity between the correct and the chosen word.

> **EXAMPLES:**
>
> By midnight the guests still had not been served anything to eat <u>and they were ravishing</u>.
>
> Ⓐ and they were ravishing
>
> Ⓑ * * *
>
> Ⓒ * * *
>
> Ⓓ * * *
>
> Ⓔ and they were ravenous

9

The raise in the number of accidents attributable to drunk drivers has prompted a call for stiffer penalties for driving while intoxicated.

(A) The raise in the number of accidents attributable to drunk drivers

(B) The rise in the number of accidents attributable to drunk drivers

(C) * * *

(D) * * *

(E) * * *

The answer to the first question is (E). The sentence intends to state that the guests were very hungry, but that is not the meaning of the word *ravishing*. The sentence can be corrected by changing *ravishing* to *ravenous*.

The answer to the second question is (B). The sentence is corrected by changing *raise* to *rise*.

3. Gerund vs. Infinitive

The infinitive is the *to* form of a verb, and the gerund is one of the *-ing* forms of a verb. Both are used as nouns. In some circumstances you can use either; "Adding an extra room to the house is the next project," or "To add an extra room to the house is the next project." In some circumstances, however, gerund and infinitive are not interchangeable.

EXAMPLES:

The idea of trying completing the term paper by Friday caused Ken to cancel his plans for the weekend.

(A) The idea of trying completing

(B) * * *

(C) The idea of trying to complete

(D) * * *

(E) * * *

Psychologists think that many people eat satisfying a need for affection that is not otherwise fulfilled.

(A) many people eat satisfying a need

(B) * * *

(C) many people eat to satisfy a need

(D) * * *

(E) * * *

The answer to the first question is (C). Although *completing* can be a noun, here you need the infinitive. The sentence should read *trying to complete*.

The answer to the second question is (C). Again, you need the infinitive, not the gerund. The sentence should read *eat to satisfy*.

4. Unacceptable Expressions

There are a few expressions that are heard frequently in conversation that are regarded as low-level usages and unacceptable in standard written English.

EXAMPLES:

<u>Being that the hour was late</u>, we agreed to adjourn the meeting and reconvene at nine o'clock the following morning.

Ⓐ Being that the hour was late

Ⓑ Since the hour was late

Ⓒ * * *

Ⓓ * * *

Ⓔ * * *

<u>Why some whales beach themselves</u> in what seems to be a kind of suicide remains a mystery to marine biologists.

Ⓐ Why some whales beach themselves

Ⓑ * * *

Ⓒ * * *

Ⓓ That some whales beach themselves

Ⓔ * * *

<u>The reason Harriet fired her secretary is because</u> he was frequently late and spent too much time on personal phone calls.

Ⓐ The reason Harriet fired her secretary is because

Ⓑ * * *

Ⓒ * * *

Ⓓ * * *

Ⓔ The reason Harriet fired her secretary is that

I read in a magazine <u>where scientists believe that they have discovered</u> a new subatomic particle.

Ⓐ where scientists believe that they have discovered

Ⓑ that scientists believe that they have discovered

Ⓒ * * *

Ⓓ * * *

Ⓔ * * *

9

The answer to the first question is (B). *Being that* is not acceptable in standard written English. The sentence is corrected by changing the phrase to *Since.*

The answer to the second question is (D). *Why* cannot be the subject of a sentence. The sentence is corrected by changing *Why* to *That.*

The answer to the third question is (E). *Because* cannot introduce a noun clause. The sentence is corrected by changing *because* to *that.*

The answer to the fourth question is (B). *Where* cannot introduce a noun clause. The sentence is corrected by changing *where* to *that.*

(Answers, page 132)

Directions: The following exercise contains 15 sentences. Each sentence makes an error of the sort just reviewed. Circle the letter of the underlined part of the sentence containing the error.

1. Economists <u>have established</u> that there is a <u>relation</u>—albeit an indirect one—
   A   B
   between the <u>amount</u> of oil imported into this country and the <u>number</u> of traffic
   C   D
   accidents.

2. Ironically, Elizabeth I and <u>her</u> rival for the English throne, Mary Stuart, <u>whom</u>
   A   B
   she had executed, <u>lay</u> side <u>by</u> side in Westminster Abbey.
   C   D

3. Although the script is interesting and well-written, it is not clear <u>whether</u> it
   A
   can be <u>adopted</u> for television since the original story contains scenes that
   B
   <u>could not be broadcast</u> <u>over</u> the public airwaves.
   C   D

4. If he <u>had known</u> how difficult law school would be, he <u>would of chosen</u> a differ-
   A   B
   ent profession or perhaps even <u>have followed</u> the <u>tradition</u> of going into the
   C   D
   family business.

5. When shopping malls and business complexes <u>get built</u>, quite often the needs of
   A
   the handicapped <u>are</u> not considered; as a result, it later becomes necessary to
   B
   make <u>costly</u> modifications to structures to make them <u>accessible</u> to persons of
   C   D
   impaired mobility.

6. Researchers <u>have found</u> that children <u>experience</u> twice as much deep sleep <u>than</u>
   A   B   C
   adults, <u>a fact which</u> may teach us something about the connection between age
   D
   and learning ability.

7. <u>Despite</u> the ample evidence that smoking <u>is hazardous</u> to one's health, <u>many</u>
   A   B   C
   people seem to find the warnings neither frightening <u>or</u> convincing.
   D

8. No matter how <u>many</u> encores the audience demands, Helen Walker
   A
   is <u>always willing</u> to sing <u>yet</u> another song <u>pleasing</u> the audience.
   B   C   D

9. In light of <u>recent</u> translations of stone carvings <u>describing</u> scenes of carnage,
   A   B
   scholars are now questioning <u>as to whether</u> the Incas were <u>really</u> a peace-loving
   C   D
   civilization.

10. In galleries containing works of both Gauguin and Cézanne, you will find an
    equal <u>number</u> of admirers <u>in front</u> of the works of <u>each</u>, but most art critics agree
    A   B   C
    that Gauguin is not of the same artistic stature <u>with</u> Cézanne.
    D

11. The board of education will never be fully responsive to the needs of Hispanic
                             A   B   C
    children in the school system so long that the mayor refuses to appoint a Hispanic
                                      D
    educator to the board.

12. The judge sentenced the president of the corporation to ten years in prison for
             A
    embezzling corporate funds but gave his partner in crime less of a sentence.
       B   C   D

13. Scientists have recently discovered that mussels secrete a powerful adhesive that
             A   B
    allows them attaching themselves to rocks, concrete pilings, and other stone or
               C   D
    masonry structures.

14. Wall paintings found recently in the caves of Brazil are convincing evidence that
                                          A
    cave art developed in the Americas at an earlier time as it did on other continents.
          B   C D

15. The drop in oil prices and the slump in the computer industry account for the
        A   B
    recent raise in unemployment in Texas and the associated decline in the value of
         C   D
    real estate in the region.

Some Final Clues

9

Sometimes an error can be analyzed in isolation from the rest of the sentence.

EXAMPLE:

John, having took his seat at the head of the table, announced that the dinner would feature specialties from Thailand.

  Ⓐ John, having took his seat at the head of the table

  Ⓑ John, having taken his seat at the head of the table

  Ⓒ * * *

  Ⓓ * * *

  Ⓔ * * *

The answer is (B). There is no context in which *having took* could be correct. *Having took* must be changed to *having taken*.

Other times, however, an underlined part contains an error because of its connection with other parts of the sentence.

EXAMPLE:

The winter was so severe that several of Hilary's prize rosebushes had sustained serious damage.

  Ⓐ had sustained serious damage

  Ⓑ * * *

  Ⓒ sustained serious damage

  Ⓓ * * *

  Ⓔ * * *

The answer to the question is (C). Given the other verb in the sentence, *was*, *had sustained* must be simply *sustained*.

The error is not, strictly speaking, found only in the underlined part of the sentence but in the connection between the underlined part and another part of the sentence.

You can assume that the nonunderlined parts of the sentence are correct. That is, if you think you have found an error but cannot correct it by changing only one underlined part, then what you have found is not an error.

As you come to new items, begin your attack by reading through the sentence for meaning. Often this first reading will reveal to you an obvious error. If so, mark your answer sheet. To save time, don't read the first choice. It always repeats the original sentence.

If the first reading doesn't turn up an error, then read the sentence a second time more slowly. If you get the vague feeling that there is an error somewhere, then look carefully at the underlined part. If that doesn't pinpoint the error, then look at the connections between the underlined parts and the nonunderlined portion of the sentence.

If a sentence seems to be incorrect, but you don't find a single obvious error, run through the list of possible errors covered in this lesson. (A checklist of those errors is provided below in the Summary.)

If the checklist doesn't turn up an error, then use the answer choices for inspiration. Compare each choice with the original to see whether or not it improves the original. Then, if you find a mistake, compare answer choices to each other until you find the best formulation.

Finally, don't be afraid to select the first choice if you believe the sentence as originally written is correct. About one out of five sentence correction items does have the original as the correct answer.

Summary

The following is a checklist of common errors tested by sentence correction items.

1. Subject–verb agreement
2. Pronoun usage (antecedents, ambiguity, case)
3. Adjectives and adverbs (correct modification)
4. Double negatives (incorrect)
5. Parallelism (similar elements in similar form)
6. Split constructions properly completed
7. Logical choice of verb tenses
8. Logical expression
9. Sentence fragments
10. Punctuation
11. Directness and conciseness
12. Misplaced modifiers
13. Prepositions (idiomatic usage)
14. Correct choice of words
15. Gerund vs. infinitive
16. Low-level usage (*being that, why* as a subject, *because* in a noun phrase, *where* in a noun phrase)

Explanatory Answers

EXERCISE 1

1. **(A)** *Harsh* is intended to modify *deals*, a verb. The adverb *harshly* is needed here.

2. **(D)** *Them* is intended to be a pronoun substitute for *advertising*, but *advertising* is singular, not plural. *It* should replace *them*.

3. **(D)** *You* is intended to refer to *one*, but *one* is in the third person while *you* is in the second person. The sentence could be corrected simply by omitting the second pronoun altogether.

4. **(C)** *Which* has no clear referent. *Which* might refer either to *horrifying conditions* or to *English boarding schools.* The ambiguity could be avoided by rewording the sentence: ". . . about the horrifying conditions in the English boarding schools, conditions which he learned about. . . ."

5. **(C)** *It* has no clear referent. *It* might refer either to the movement or to the manifesto. The sentence can be corrected by including an appropriate noun to clarify the speaker's meaning, e.g., ". . . of a manifesto, a work that incorporated. . . ."

6. **(D)** *Capable* is intended to modify *played*, a verb. So the adverb form must be used: ". . . played capably."

7. **(B)** *Who* and *whom* are the correct pronouns to use for people. ". . . countryside who sheltered. . . ."

8. **(B)** *We* cannot be used as the object of *to*. The correct choice of pronoun is *us*.

9. **(A)** When a pronoun is used to modify a gerund, the pronoun must be in the possessive case: "Your taking the initiative. . . ."

10. **(C)** *Which* has no clear antecedent. Had the speaker hoped to avoid the conference or just being selected to be the representative of the group at the conference? To avoid the ambiguity the sentence will have to be substantially revised: ". . . at the conference, and I had hoped to avoid the conference altogether."

11. **(C)** *Whom* should be used here instead of *which*, since the pronoun refers to *person*.

12. **(D)** The subject of the main clause is *none*, a singular pronoun, so the verb should be *is* rather than *are*.

13. **(B)** The subject of the sentence is *differences*, a plural noun, so the verb should be *help* rather than *helps*.

14. **(B)** *Hardly no* is a double negative. The sentence should read *hardly any*.

15. **(B)** The subject of the sentence is *diaries*, a plural noun. So the verb should be *provide* rather than *provides*.

16. **(D)** *Its* intends to refer to *whales*, so the sentence should use the plural pronoun *their*.

17. **(A)** A pronoun used to modify a gerund must be in the possessive case: "His being at the rally. . . ."

18. **(D)** *Satisfactory* is intended to modify either *working* or *system*. If it modifies *working*, then the adverb should be used: ". . . and more than satisfactorily." If the word modifies *system*, then another verb is required: ". . . and is more than satisfactory."

19. **(B)** *Who* is intended to be the object of the verb *married*, so the objective case pronoun *whom* is required.

20. **(B)** *Recent* is intended to modify *constructed*, an adjective. But an adjective cannot be used to modify another adjective. Here the adverb *recently* should be used.

21. **(D)** *Which* has no clear referent. Were the faculty angry because the resolution passed or because it passed with few dissenting votes? The sentence must be rewritten to clarify the speaker's intention.

22. **(D)** *Your* is intended to refer to *one's*, so you need some kind of third-person pronoun, for example, *his* or *her*.

23. **(D)** *It* lacks a referent. *It* seems to refer to something like *insurance*, but there is no such noun in the sentence. The sentence could be corrected by using the noun *insurance* in place of the pronoun *it*.

24. **(C)** *Candid* is intended to modify *wrote*, so the sentence must use the adverb *candidly*.

25. **(A)** The sentence commits the "ubiquitous *they*" error. The sentence can be corrected by using a noun in place of the *they*.

EXERCISE 2

1. **(C)** The sentence commits an error of logical expression because it implies that all the people coming into the museum have but a single camera. The sentence could be corrected by changing *camera* to *cameras*.

2. **(B)** The sentence is flawed by faulty parallelism. It could be corrected by changing *to maintain* to *maintaining*.

3. **(A)** The sentence is afflicted with a dangling modifier. As written, the sentence implies that Emily Dickinson herself was written. To correct this error, the sentence would have to be rewritten to bring the introductory modifier closer to the noun it modifies, *poems*: "The poems by Emily Dickinson, written in almost total isolation from the world, spoke of love and death."

4. **(D)** The use of the perfect tense *had given up* is not consistent with the use of the past tense *entertained*, for the use of the perfect tense implies that the pianist gave up his attempt to become a composer before he even entertained the idea of becoming one. The sentence can be corrected by substituting *gave it up* for *had given it up*.

5. **(D)** The final phrase is out of place. As written, the sentence implies that the cockroach is unlike destructive garden pests, but the speaker means to say that the cockroach is not like the praying mantis. The sentence can be corrected by relocating the offending phrase closer to the noun it modifies: "The praying mantis, unlike the cockroach, which serves no useful function, is welcomed by homeowners. . . ."

6. **(A)** The sentence is flawed by a lack of parallelism, an error that can be corrected by substituting the adjective *charismatic* for the phrase *has charisma.*

7. **(A)** This item is a sentence fragment that lacks a conjugated verb. The fragment can be changed into a complete sentence by substituting *displayed* for *displaying.*

8. **(B)** The sentence commits an error of illogical expression, for, as written, it implies that the fans' leaving the stadium would ordinarily be sufficient to halt a game and reschedule it for later. The problem of illogical expression can be corrected by substituting the conjunction *but* for *even though.* (This particular error of logical expression is called illogical subordination.)

9. **(B)** The use of the subjunctive *would have been* is illogical. The use of the subjunctive incorrectly implies that the loss of lives and money is contingent upon some event, but no such event is mentioned in the sentence. The sentence can be corrected by substituting *will have been.*

10. **(A)** The sentence is afflicted with a dangling modifier. As written, it implies that the bank president is highly qualified for the position. The sentence needs substantial revision: "The bank president will conduct a final interview of the new candidate tomorrow. Since the candidate is highly qualified for the position, the president will make her a job offer after the interview."

11. **(C)** The sentence suffers from a lack of parallelism. This deficiency can be corrected by changing *taking* to *to take.* (In any event, the use of the gerund, *taking,* instead of the infinitive, *to take,* is not idiomatic, a point taken up in the next part of this lesson.)

12. **(C)** The sentence commits an error of logical expression by implying that the reason is an effect of some other cause, when the speaker really means to say that the reason and the cause are the same thing, the explanation for the phenomenon. The error can be corrected by substituting *that* for *because.* (Note: This use of *because* to introduce a noun clause can also be considered an example of an expression that is not acceptable in English usage, a point taken up in the next part of this lesson.)

13. **(D)** The tense of the first verb is not consistent with the tense of the second verb. The sentence can be corrected by substituting *experiences* for *experienced.*

14. **(A)** The sentence contains a dangling modifier. As written, the sentence implies that the police officer is listening in broken English (not listening to broken English). The sentence can be corrected by relocating the modifier: "The police officer patiently listened to the tourist ask in broken English for directions to Radio City Music Hall, . . ."

15. **(C)** The choice of *since* is illogical because *since* implies that there is a causal or explanatory connection between Hemingway's view of bullfighting and the fact that bullfighting is a controversial sport that repulses some people. The problem of illogical subordination can be corrected by substituting *but* for *since.*

16. **(D)** The use of the present tense *loses* is illogical and inconsistent with the use of the past tense *was* earlier in the sentence. The error can be corrected by substituting *lost* for *loses.*

9

17. **(D)** The sentence contains a misplaced modifier. As written, the sentence implies that Peter hopes to learn how to protect his investments from the threat posed by a well-known investment banker. The sentence must be re-written: ". . . in order to learn from a well-known investment banker methods to protect his investments."

18. **(C)** The elements of the sentence are not parallel. The sentence would be correct if *cross-checked* were substituted for *cross-checking*.

19. **(D)** The sentence makes an error of logical expression, for it seems to compare our space program to the Soviet Union. The error can be eliminated by inserting the phrase *to that of the Soviet Union* immediately after *superior*.

20. **(B)** The sentence contains a misplaced modifier. The placement of *only* seems to imply a restriction on the verb rather than on the subject. The sentence can be easily corrected by moving *only* and placing it just before *licensed lawyers.*

21. **(A)** The sentence contains a dangling modifier and seems to compare balleri-nas of the romantic ballet with the movement of Judith Jamison. To correct this error, the sentence would have to be substantially rewritten: "Judith Jamison's movement seems more African than European-American, and her physical appearance, which is unlike that of the pale and delicately built ballerinas of romantic ballet, reinforces the contrast."

22. **(D)** The sentence contains an error of logical expression. It attempts to com-pare an amount of decaffeinated coffee with coffee containing caffeine. The sentence can be corrected by inserting clarifying phrases: ". . . the number of tons of coffee containing caffeine consumed by Americans."

23. **(D)** The sentence contains a misplaced modifier. As written, it implies that the workers are illiterate because they don't know how to read on the job. The sentence can be corrected by relocating the offending phrase so that it is closer to the noun it modifies: ". . . many mistakes are made on the job by workers. . . ."

24. **(D)** The sentence makes an illogical statement. It attempts to compare *time* and *branch of the service.* The sentence can be corrected by inserting a clari-fying phrase: ". . . than do men in any other branch. . . ."

25. **(A)** The sentence contains a dangling modifier. As written, it implies a com-parison between A. J. Ayer, the person, and the philosophical writings of Gilbert Ryle. The error can be corrected in the following way: "Like the writing of A. J. Ayer, much of. . . ."

EXERCISE 3

1. **(B)** Substitute *relationship.*

2. **(D)** Substitute *lie.*

3. **(B)** Substitute *adapted.*

4. **(B)** Substitute *would have chosen.*

5. **(A)** Substitute *are built.*

6. **(C)** Substitute *as.*

7. **(D)** Substitute *nor.*

8. **(D)** Substitute *to please.*

9. **(C)** Substitute *whether.*

10. **(D)** Substitute *as.*

11. **(D)** Substitute *as.*

12. **(D)** Substitute *a shorter sentence.*

13. **(C)** Substitute *to attach.*

14. **(C)** Substitute *than.*

15. **(C)** Substitute *rise.*

9

Sentence Correction Drills

1. **Walk-Through Drills**
2. **Warm-Up Drills**

This lesson contains two walk-through and two warm-up sentence correction drills. The "walk-throughs" have answers and discussion on the page opposite the questions so that you can "walk-through" the problems. The "warm-ups" you should do under the specified time limit. The answers and explanations for the timed drills begin on page 153.

10

Walk-Through 1

Directions: In each of the following sentences, part or all of the sentence is underlined. Following each sentence are five different ways of wording the underlined part. Answer choice (A) always repeats the original; the other four choices are different. If you think that the sentence as originally written is the best way of wording the underlined part, choose answer (A); otherwise, select the best alternative.

1. The Bichon Frisé is a breed of nonsporting dog, descending from the water spaniel and originating in ancient times in the Mediterranean area.

   Ⓐ The Bichon Frisé is a breed of nonsporting dog, descending from the water spaniel and originating
   Ⓑ The Bichon Frisé, which is a breed of nonsporting dog descending from the water spaniel, originated
   Ⓒ The Bichon Frisé, a breed of nonsporting dog descended from the water spaniel, originated
   Ⓓ The Bichon Frisé, a breed of nonsporting dog, descended from the water spaniel which originated
   Ⓔ A Bichon Frisé is a breed of nonsporting dog, descended from the water spaniel, and has its origin

1. **(C)** The original sentence contains two similar errors. First, there is an error of diction. To show bloodlines, the sentence needs the word *descended*, not *descending*. *Descending*, used here suggests the dog is walking down a staircase. Second, the use of the present participle, *originating*, fails to show that the action of originating is completed and in the past. To reflect the correct sequence of events the sentence should use a verb to show past action. (B) makes the second correction but not the first. (D) makes both needed changes, but the way in which the second change is made changes the intended meaning of the original sentence. (D) implies that it is the water spaniel that originated in ancient times in the Mediterranean area, but in the original, this phrase modifies *Bichon Frisé*. (E) makes the first correction and attempts the second one, but the use of *has* (the present perfect tense) implies that the action is still continuing. Only (C) makes both needed changes without introducing another error.

2. The bicameral system is a legislative system in which the power of making laws is vested in two chambers, or houses, both of which must approve a bill before it can become a law.

   Ⓐ both of which must approve a bill before it can become
   Ⓑ both of which must approve a bill when it becomes
   Ⓒ which must approve a bill before it can become
   Ⓓ which must give their approval to a bill before it can become
   Ⓔ the approval of both of which is necessary before a bill

2. **(A)** The original sentence is correct. (B) introduces an error of logical subordination. The use of *when* implies that the approval of both chambers coincides with the bill's becoming law, a change from the meaning of the original sentence. (C) also changes the meaning of the original. Since the *which* refers to chambers, (C) implies that the two houses vote jointly rather than separately. (D) makes the same error and is needlessly wordy as well. Finally, (E) is awkward compared to the original.

3. The most important food-energy source <u>of three-fourths of the world's population are grains</u>.

   Ⓐ of three-fourths of the world's population are grains

   Ⓑ for three-fourths of the world's population are grains

   Ⓒ for three-fourths of the world's population is grains

   Ⓓ for three-fourths of the worlds' population is grains

   Ⓔ for three-fourths of the world's population is grain

4. The possibility of massive earthquakes <u>are regarded by most area residents with</u> a mixture of skepticism and caution.

   Ⓐ are regarded by most area residents with

   Ⓑ is regarded by most area residents with

   Ⓒ is regarded by most area residents as

   Ⓓ is mostly regarded by area residents with

   Ⓔ by most area residents is regarded with

5. All of the students except George and <u>she intends on ordering</u> the newest edition of the textbook.

   Ⓐ she intends on ordering

   Ⓑ her intends on ordering

   Ⓒ her intends to order

   Ⓓ her intend to order

   Ⓔ she intend to order

3. **(E)** The original sentence contains an error of grammar. The verb *are* fails to agree in number with its subject, *source*. The correct verb is *is*. Additionally, the *of* is not idiomatic, for *of* here creates the impression of ownership, e. g., that the population is in possession of the source. Finally, the use of *grains* is not idiomatic; *grain* would be preferable. (B) corrects the second error but not the first and third. (C) and (D) correct the first and second errors but not the third. Additionally, (D) changes the meaning of the original by implying that the sentence is describing several different worlds. Only (E) corrects all three errors.

4. **(B)** The original sentence contains an error of grammar. The verb *are* fails to agree with its subject, *possibility*. The correct verb is *is*. Each of the other choices makes the needed correction, but three of them introduce new problems. (C) changes the meaning of the original. The use of *as* implies that the residents think earthquakes are like a mixture of skepticism and caution. (D) changes the meaning of the original by qualifying *the belief* with *mostly* (a low-level usage in itself) and failing to quantify the number of residents who hold the belief. Finally, in (E), the use of *by* implies that the residents will themselves cause the earthquakes.

5. **(D)** The original sentence contains three errors. First, the verb *intends* does not agree with its subject, *all*. (Don't be distracted by *she*.) Second the use of *she* is grammatically incorrect. Since *she* is intended to be the object of the preposition *except*, the objective case *her* is needed. Finally the expression *intends on* is not idiomatic. (B) corrects only the error of pronoun usage. (C) corrects the pronoun error and the problem of idiom but fails to correct the verb error. (E) corrects two errors but fails to correct the pronoun error. Only (D) corrects all three errors.

6. Most of the dancers in the company, they supported the striking musicians and refused to cross picket lines for either rehearsals or performances.

   (A) Most of the dancers in the company, they supported
   (B) Most of the dancers in the company supported
   (C) Most of the dancers in the company provided support for
   (D) The dancers in the company, most of them supported
   (E) Of the dancers in the company, most supported

6. **(B)** The *they* in the original is not only superfluous; its placement following the comma is likely to give a reader the mistaken impression that everything before the comma is intended to modify what comes immediately after the comma. (B) is correct because it eliminates the superfluous *they*. The resulting sentence is more concise and avoids any ambiguity. (C) makes the needed change and one that is not needed. This second change is not only not needed, it introduces a new error. The phrase *provided support for* implies that the dancers gave something to the striking musicians, such as money. (D) eliminates the *they*, but the resulting structure contains a structural problem similar to that found in the original. Finally, (E) is needlessly indirect. By comparison, (B)'s straightforward wording is preferable.

7. According to current law, only licensed dental hygienists can practice their trade under the direct supervision of a licensed dentist; they are not allowed to open their own practices.

   (A) only licensed dental hygienists can practice their trade
   (B) only licensed dental hygienists can practice their trades
   (C) licensed dental hygienists only can practice their trade
   (D) licensed dental hygienists can practice only their trade
   (E) licensed dental hygienists can practice their trade only

7. **(E)** In the original sentence, the placement of the modifier *only* creates an illogical statement. As originally written, the sentence implies that licensed dental hygienists are the only people who can work for a dentist. The original sentence intends to say that it is only under the supervision of a licensed dentist that a hygienist can practice his or her trade. The placement of *only* in (E) makes this clear. (B) fails to correct the error and introduces a new error. The use of *trades* is not logical because a hygienist can have only one trade as a hygienist. (Although a hygienist might be a tinker or tailor as well, she would not be practicing those trades under the supervision of a dentist.) (C) fails to eliminate the ambiguity of the original. (D) eliminates the original ambiguity but introduces a new one. The placement of *only* implies that a hygienist can only perform certain duties for a dentist.

8. Fluoride helps protect a child's teeth while the teeth grow, but it is unharmful to their bodies.

   (A) but it is unharmful to their bodies.
   (B) and it is unharmful to their bodies.
   (C) and it is not harmful to their bodies.
   (D) and it is not harmful to the bodies.
   (E) and it is not harmful to the body.

8. **(E)** The original sentence contains three errors. First, the use of *but* creates an illogical contrast between the two thoughts in the sentence. Second, *unharmful* is not idiomatic. Third, *their bodies* refers to *child*, which is singular, not plural. (B) corrects the first error but not the other two. (C) corrects the first two errors but not the third. But (D) implies that a child has several bodies. Only (E) corrects all three errors.

9. Certain infections are <u>made up by both viral and bacterial elements that makes</u> treatment of those infections difficult.

    (A) made up by both viral and bacterial elements that makes

    (B) composed of both viral and bacterial elements; this combination makes

    (C) composed of both viral and bacterial elements which make

    (D) composed by both viral as well as bacterial elements, and they make

    (E) including both viral as well as bacterial elements that make

9. **(B)** The original sentence contains two errors. First, *made up by* illogically implies that the infections are created by, not composed of, viral and bacterial elements. Second, the *which* lacks a referent. *Which* cannot refer to *elements*, because it is not the elements that make treatment difficult—it is the mix of those elements. The *which* wants to refer to something like *combination* or *mix*, but no such noun appears in the sentence. (B) eliminates both errors. (C) corrects the first error but not the second. (D) attempts to correct the first error, but the resulting phrase still implies that the elements create the infection. Additionally, the use of *they* is no better than *which*. Although *they* clearly refers to *elements*, the resulting sentence does not render correctly the intended meaning of the original. Finally, (E) attempts to correct only the first error, but the resulting phrase (*are including*) is not idiomatic. Additionally, the use of *as well as* implies that one element is more important than the other, a change in meaning from the original.

10. <u>According to tradition,</u> Vishnu appeared as Krishna to rid the world of a tyrannical king named Kamsa, the son of a demon.

    (A) According to tradition

    (B) Due to tradition

    (C) Because of tradition

    (D) Tradition has it that

    (E) Traditionally

10. **(A)** The original sentence is correct. (B) and (C) both imply that it was tradition that caused Vishnu to appear as Krishna. (In any event, *due to* is not acceptable in standard written English as a substitute for *because*.) (D) is low-level usage. In any case, you should not make a change from the original unless you know that the change is an improvement over the original. Finally, (E) implies that Vishnu often appeared as Krishna. *Traditionally* is an adverb, so *traditionally* cannot modify *Vishnu*, a noun. The next closest word to *traditionally* is *appeared*. So *traditionally* would seem to modify *appeared*, but that is not the sense of the original.

11. Biofeedback is <u>a technique by which patients monitor their own bodily functions</u> in an attempt to alter those functions.

    Ⓐ   a technique by which patients monitor their own bodily functions

    Ⓑ   the technique by which patients monitor their own body functioning

    Ⓒ   the technique by which patients monitor their own body's functioning

    Ⓓ   a technique so that patients monitor their own bodily functions

    Ⓔ   a technique which patients use for the monitoring of bodily functions of their own

11. **(A)** The original sentence is correct. (B) substitutes a nonidiomatic phrase, *own bodily functioning*, for an idiomatic one. Additionally, the use of the definite article *the* rather than the indefinite *a* implies that there is but one technique by which a person can monitor bodily functions, a sense not present in the original. (C) also makes this latter mistake. Additionally, (C) results in the illogical assertion that all of the patients possess but a single body. In (D), the use of *so* creates an illogical connection between the technique and the result of the technique. (D) implies that the reason biofeedback is even considered a technique is to allow patients to monitor their bodily functions, a fairly strange idea. Finally, (E) is needlessly wordy and awkward.

Walk-Through 2

Directions: In each of the following sentences, part or all of the sentence is underlined. Following each sentence are five different ways of wording the underlined part. Answer choice (A) always repeats the original; the other four choices are different. If you think that the sentence as originally written is the best way of wording the underlined part, choose answer (A); otherwise, select the best alternative.

1. Recent increases in the price of steel have made it profitable to reopen iron mines once closed because the quality of ore taken from them <u>was less than</u> other, more profitable mines.

    (A) was less than
    (B) is less than
    (C) is lower than that of
    (D) was lower than
    (E) was lower than that of

1. **(E)** Although the underlined part of the sentence is only three words long, it contains two errors. First, the use of *less* to compare quality is not idiomatic. The correct word would be *lower*. Second, the original sets up an illogical comparison between *quality* and *mines.* (B) fails to correct either error and manages, with its change, to introduce another problem of logical expression. The mines were closed (in the past) because the ore that was being taken out (in the past) was of low quality (again in the past, because that ore is now gone). (C) corrects the errors of the original but introduces the new error just discussed. As for (D), even though it avoids the new error created by both (B) and (C), it fails to correct one of the two mistakes in the original. Finally, (D) corrects both of the errors in the original and avoids making a new mistake.

2. Several hundred residents were evacuated as the fire neared Andersonville, but <u>three days later, they were allowed to return to their homes that were nearly destroyed</u>.

   Ⓐ three days later, they were allowed to return to their homes that were nearly destroyed

   Ⓑ three days later, they were allowed to return to their homes, which were nearly destroyed

   Ⓒ they were allowed, three days later, to return to their homes that were nearly destroyed

   Ⓓ they were allowed to return to their homes that were nearly destroyed three days later

   Ⓔ they were allowed to return to their homes, nearly destroyed, three days later

3. <u>Greek fire, a gelatinous, incendiary mixture, was used in warfare before gunpowder was invented.</u>

   Ⓐ Greek fire, a gelatinous, incendiary mixture, was used in warfare before gunpowder was invented.

   Ⓑ Greek fire, a gelatinous, incendiary mixture, was used during warfare before the invention of gunpowder.

   Ⓒ Greek fire, a gelatinous, incendiary mixture before the invention of gunpowder, was used in warfare.

   Ⓓ A gelatinous, incendiary mixture, warfare involved the use of Greek fire, before the invention of gunpowder.

   Ⓔ Gelatinous and incendiary, Greek fire was a mixture that was used in warfare before the invention of gunpowder.

2. **(B)** The original sentence contains one error. The use of the restrictive clause (*that were nearly destroyed*) illogically implies that the residents had other homes that were not almost destroyed. (Compare *Mine is the blue house, which has a chimney* with *Mine is the blue house that has a chimney*. In the first, the *chimney* is not needed to identify the house indicated. The second implies that there are several blue houses and the one spoken of can be identified by its chimney.) (B) corrects the problem of the original and makes it clear that the final phrase is intended to modify *homes* almost as an aside rather than identify the homes spoken of. (C) fails to correct the mistake contained in the original, and the placement of the phrase *three days later* disrupts the flow of the sentence. (D) not only fails to correct the error of the original, but implies that it is a defining characteristic of the homes that they were nearly destroyed three days later—clearly not the intended meaning of the original. Finally, (E), too, changes the intended meaning of the original.

3. **(A)** The sentence is correct as originally written. The use of *during* in (B) is not idiomatic. (C) changes the meaning of the original by illogically implying that Greek fire was only a gelatinous, incendiary mixture before the invention of gunpowder and that it then became something else. (D) is not only awkward when compared with the original; the proximity of *warfare* to the introductory modifier implies that warfare is a gelatinous, incendiary mixture. Finally, (E), too, is needlessly awkward. Additionally, reducing *gelatinous and incendiary* to an introductory modifier suggests that these aspects were merely incidental to Greek fire and not its defining characteristics.

4. After weighing out, the jockey who rode the horse that finished second picked up the telephone, called the stewards' box, <u>and claimed that the winning horse allegedly had committed interference with his mount in the stretch</u>.

    Ⓐ and claimed that the winning horse allegedly had committed interference with his mount in the stretch

    Ⓑ and claimed that the winning horse had interfered with his mount in the stretch

    Ⓒ and claimed that the winning horse in the stretch had interfered with his mount

    Ⓓ claiming that the winning horse had allegedly interfered with his mount in the stretch

    Ⓔ to claim that in the stretch his mount had been allegedly interfered with by the winning horse

5. A recently published report warns parents to monitor the time their children spend watching television, <u>because television viewing only ranks second</u> to sleeping in terms of the number of hours per day the average child devotes to any activity.

    Ⓐ because television viewing only ranks second

    Ⓑ because only television viewing ranks second

    Ⓒ noting only television viewing ranks second

    Ⓓ noting television viewing ranks second only

    Ⓔ only because television viewing ranks second

4. **(B)** The original sentence contains two errors one of which is fairly subtle. First, the expression *committed interference with* is not idiomatic. Second, and this is perhaps more difficult to find, the original sentence asserts that the losing jockey claimed *alleged interference.* The sentence should say either that the jockey claimed there was interference or that he alleged there was interference. (B) corrects both of the errors. (C) corrects both of the original errors, but the placement of the phrase *in the stretch* introduces a new problem by implying that the horse that caused the interference was winning only in the stretch—not that the horse was the winner of the race. (D) fails to eliminate the redundancy of the original and destroys the parallelism of the verb elements as well. Finally, (E) fails to eliminate the redundant element of the original and also disrupts the parallel structure of the original.

5. **(D)** The original sentence contains two errors. First, the relationship between the second clause and the first is ambiguous. Is the fact that children watch too much television the cause of the report or the reason parents should monitor their children's time more carefully? Second, the placement of *only* illogically implies that the report expresses concern that television is not ranked first. (B) fails to correct the first error and eliminates the second error only by introducing yet another problem. It implies the report states that television does not share the second-place ranking with any other activity. (C) is also afflicted with this latter problem, although it does eliminate the first error contained in the original. (E) fails to eliminate the error created by *because* and compounds that error with its placement of *only.*

6. When it rains outside, most parents prefer small children to play indoors.

Ⓐ When it rains outside, most parents prefer small children to play indoors.

Ⓑ Most parents prefer the indoors for their children's play when it rains.

Ⓒ Most parents prefer that small children play indoors when it rains.

Ⓓ When raining outside, most parents prefer small children to play indoors.

Ⓔ When raining, most parents prefer small children to play indoors.

7. Scholars recognized immediately after publication that the language experiments in *Finnegan's Wake* are different than any other novel.

Ⓐ publication that the language experiments in *Finnegan's Wake* are different than

Ⓑ publication that the language experiments in *Finnegan's Wake* are different from

Ⓒ publication that the language experiments in *Finnegan's Wake* are different from those of

Ⓓ publication that the language experiments in *Finnegan's Wake* differ from

Ⓔ its publication that the language experiments in *Finnegan's Wake* are different from those of

8. Otto Wagner, the father of modern Viennese architecture, designed buildings that earned him an international reputation and influenced an entire generation of artists and architects.

Ⓐ designed buildings that earned him an

Ⓑ who designed buildings that earned him an

Ⓒ whose design of buildings earned him the

Ⓓ designed buildings which earned him an

Ⓔ designed buildings earning him an

6. **(C)** The original sentence is potentially ambiguous, because it could be read to assert a comparison between small children and indoor play. Additionally, the *outside* is redundant. (C) eliminates the danger of ambiguity and the redundant element. (B) eliminates the problems of the original, but not as concisely as (C). (D) and (E) both introduce a new problem by implying that it is the parents who are raining.

7. **(E)** The original sentence contains three errors. First, the original sentence does not clearly connect the prepositional phrase *after publication* with another element in the sentence. Consequently, the sentence seems to imply that the scholars were published. Second, the expression *different than* is not idiomatic. (**Note:** While some authorities would allow *different than* for comparing verbs, here it is nouns that are compared.) Third, the original sets up an illogical comparison between *experiments* and *novel*. (B) corrects the second error but not the first or third. (C) corrects the second and third errors but not the first. (D) corrects the first and second errors but not the third. Only (E) corrects all three errors.

8. **(A)** The sentence as originally written is correct. (B) and (C) both reduce the main clause of the sentence to a relative clause, with the result that the entire sentence becomes a sentence fragment with no main verb. (D) changes the meaning of the original by implying that it was the simple fact that Wagner designed some buildings that earned him a reputation. Finally, the use of *earning* in (E) creates a problem because it is not clear what function *earning* has in the sentence. Is it a poor choice of verb form (*designed buildings and earned*)? Or is *earning* intended as an adjective to modify *building*? (An illogical idea.)

9. Although completely ineffective as a fire-retardant, the researchers concluded that the compound might nonetheless have some other applications.

    (A) Although completely ineffective as a fire-retardant, the researchers concluded that the compound

    (B) Although the compound was completely ineffective for fire-retarding, the researchers concluded that it

    (C) The researchers, although completely ineffective as a fire-retardant, concluded that the compound

    (D) The researchers concluded, though completely ineffective as a fire-retardant, that the compound

    (E) The researchers concluded that, though completely ineffective as a fire-retardant, the compound

10. After having had Ann Boleyn beheaded, the next day King Henry VIII was betrothed to Jane Seymour.

    (E) After having had Ann Boleyn beheaded, the next day King Henry VIII was betrothed to Jane Seymour.

    (B) After having had Ann Boleyn beheaded, King Henry VIII was betrothed to Jane Seymour the next day.

    (C) Having had Ann Boleyn beheaded, King Henry VIII was betrothed to Jane Seymour the next day.

    (D) On the day after he had Ann Boleyn beheaded, King Henry VIII was betrothed to Jane Seymour.

    (E) On the day after having had Ann Boleyn beheaded, King Henry VIII was betrothed to Jane Seymour.

9. **(B)** The original sentence is afflicted with a dangling modifier. The sentence implies that the researchers themselves were not an effective fire-retardant. (B) corrects this ambiguity by making it clear that it is the compound that was considered a possible fire-retardant. (C) suffers from the same problem as the original. (C) also implies that it is the researchers who have failed as a fire-retardant. As for (D) and (E), the placement of the offending modifier is such that it is not clear what it is supposed to modify.

10. **(D)** The errors in this sentence are fairly subtle. First, the *after* is superfluous. The phrase *having had* adequately indicates a past action completed before another past action. Second, the placement of the phrase *the next day* directly after the element modified by the introductory modifier is annoying, because on first reading the sentence seems to say the next day was responsible for Ann Boleyn's execution. Finally, the use of the introductory participial phrase does clearly express the logical relationship between the elements of the sentence. The participial phrase is an adjective. Even setting aside the problem of ambiguity mentioned above, as an adjective, the participial phrase can only modify a noun, *King Henry VIII*. By modifying a noun, however, the phrase loses its ability to describe the temporal or verb sequence, which is the real intent of the sentence. Only (D) and (E) make an attempt to correct this last problem. (E), however, fails to correct the first problem.

11. Curare has little effect when ingested, <u>but few</u> <u>people are known to recover from its effects</u> when the poison is introduced directly into the bloodstream.

    Ⓐ   but few people are known to recover from its effects

    Ⓑ   but few people are known to have recovered from its effects

    Ⓒ   but its effects are known to allow few people to recover

    Ⓓ   and few people are known to recover from its effects

    Ⓔ   since few people are known to recover from its effects

11. (B) The original sentence contains one error. The use of *to recover* rather than *to have recovered* illogically implies that recovery is an ongoing or permanent characteristic of certain people. (B) makes it clear that the recovery is a past action. (C) is very awkward. (D) suffers from the same problem as the original. Additionally, the substitution of *and* for *but* destroys the contrast between the two ideas that is present in the original. Finally, (E) is afflicted with the same problem as the original. Moreover, the use of *since* subordinates the second idea to the first, destroying the sense of the original.

Directions: In each of the following sentences, part or all of the sentence is underlined. Following each sentence are five different ways of wording the underlined part. Answer choice (A) always repeats the original; the other four choices are different. If you think that the sentence as originally written is the best way of wording the underlined part, choose answer (A); otherwise, select the best alternative.

---

1. Quintus Marcius, the Roman legate in the war against Persius, wanted to gain time for the reason that he needed to wait for reinforcements to arrive.

   (A) time for the reason that he needed to wait for reinforcements to arrive
   (B) time because he was waiting for reinforcements to arrive
   (C) time since he needed was waiting for the arriving of reinforcement
   (D) time, the reason why he was waiting for reinforcements to arrive
   (E) time, and he was waiting for reinforcements to arrive

2. It was us Americans who first became obsessed with the idea of physical fitness, but the madness has now spread to Europe.

   (A) It was us Americans who first became obsessed with
   (B) It was us Americans who first became obsessed by
   (C) It was we Americans whose first obsession was
   (D) It was we Americans who first became obsessed with
   (E) We Americans were first obsessed by

3. The new tax reform bill may be as important, if not more important than, any other piece of legislation introduced in the Congress in the past decade.

   (A) important, if not more important than, any other
   (B) important, if not more important than, any
   (C) important as, if not more important than, any
   (D) important as, if not more important than, any other
   (E) important as, if not more important,

4. Much of the Wall Street jargon one reads in the financial pages are taken from the game of poker such as the phrase "blue chip" stocks.

   (A) pages are taken from the game of poker such as the phrase "blue chip" stocks
   (B) pages such as "blue chip" stocks, is actually taken from the game of poker
   (C) pages, such as "blue chip" stocks, is taken from the game of poker
   (D) pages, such as "blue chip" stocks, are actually derived from the game of poker
   (E) pages is derived from the game of poker such as "blue chip" stocks

5. The primary aims of the Greenback Party, formed in 1875, was the adoption of a new monetary policy and the federal issuance of paper currency not backed by gold.

   (A) The primary aims of the Greenback Party, formed in 1875, was
   (B) The primary aims, formed in 1875, of the Greenback Party, were
   (C) The primary aims of the Greenback Party, formed in 1875, were
   (D) The Greenback Party's primary aims, formed in 1875, were
   (E) Formed in 1875, the primary aims of the Greenback Party were

6. There is new evidence to suggest that a child's personality is developed more by everyday interactions rather than by traumatic events.

   (A) developed more by everyday interactions rather than by
   (B) developed more by everyday interactions than by
   (C) developed more by everyday interactions and not by
   (D) developed more by everyday interactions instead of
   (E) being developed more by everyday interactions than by

7. <u>Required by law to register by the end of the year, the post office was crowded with legal aliens attempting to comply with the law before the deadline.</u>

    Ⓐ Required by law to register by the end of the year, the post office was crowded with legal aliens attempting to comply with the law before the deadline.

    Ⓑ Required by law to register, the post office, by the end of the year, was crowded with legal aliens who were attempting to comply with the law before the deadline.

    Ⓒ Required by law to register before the deadline at the end of the year, legal aliens crowded into the post office in order that they might attempt compliance with the law.

    Ⓓ Required by law to register, legal aliens, who were attempting to comply with the law before the deadline, crowded into the post office by the end of the year.

    Ⓔ Legal aliens, who are required by law to register by the end of the year, crowded into the post office in an attempt to comply with the law before the deadline.

8. <u>One of the greatest enterprises of modern times was the laying of the first Trans-Atlantic cable.</u>

    Ⓐ One of the greatest enterprises of modern times was the laying of the first Trans-Atlantic cable.

    Ⓑ Of all the modern enterprises, the laying of the first Trans-Atlantic cable, was one of the greatest.

    Ⓒ The first Trans-Atlantic cable's laying was among man's greatest enterprises.

    Ⓓ In modern times, the laying of the first Trans-Atlantic cable, was among man's greatest enterprises.

    Ⓔ One of the greatest enterprises of modern times was the lying of the first Trans-Atlantic cable.

9. Throughout the New Deal era, the economic troubles of the nation's people <u>spurred our political leaders on constantly</u> to new, creative heights in social legislation.

    Ⓐ spurred our political leaders on constantly

    Ⓑ spurred on our political leaders constantly

    Ⓒ spurred constantly on our political leaders on

    Ⓓ was the reason why our political leaders were spurred on

    Ⓔ constantly spurred on our political leaders

10. Many experts agree that the <u>rise in the number of street crimes reported due to increased unemployment and homelessness</u> is a problem that can be solved only by providing jobs and homes to those who need them.

    Ⓐ rise in the number of street crimes reported due to increased unemployment and homelessness

    Ⓑ rising number of reported street crimes due to increasing unemployment and homelessness

    Ⓒ rise in the number of street crimes reported because of increased unemployment and homelessness

    Ⓓ rise in the number of reported street crimes, which is attributable to increased unemployment and homelessness,

    Ⓔ rise in the number of street crimes reported is because of increased unemployment and homelessness which

11. <u>Although many tantalizing clues were found and the manhunt intensive,</u> the infamous killer Jack the Ripper eluded the police.

    Ⓐ Although many tantalizing clues were found and the manhunt intensive

    Ⓑ Although many tantalizing clues were found and the manhunt was intensive,

    Ⓒ Although many tantalizing clues were found and an intensive manhunt

    Ⓓ Many tantalizing clues were found, and the manhunt was intensive, although

    Ⓔ Although many clues which were tantalizing were found and the manhunt was intensive

Directions: In each of the following sentences, part or all of the sentence is underlined. Following each sentence are five different ways of wording the underlined part. Answer choice (A) always repeats the original; the other four choices are different. If you think that the sentence as originally written is the best way of wording the underlined part, choose answer (A); otherwise, select the best alternative.

1. <u>Being that she was Asian and a woman,</u> she was denied several promotions that were later given to men.

    Ⓐ Being that she was Asian and a woman,
    Ⓑ Because she was Asian and a woman,
    Ⓒ Because of the fact that she was a woman and Asian,
    Ⓓ Due to her being a woman and Asian,
    Ⓔ Her being a woman and Asian was the reason why

2. Pets such as turtles and iguanas, which require very little personal attention, <u>and are rapidly becoming popular in families having everyone working or in school</u>.

    Ⓐ and are rapidly becoming popular in families having everyone working or in school
    Ⓑ are rapidly becoming popular in families in which everyone is either working or in school
    Ⓒ and becoming popular rapidly in families that have everyone working or in school
    Ⓓ and in families where everyone is either working or in school are becoming popular
    Ⓔ have been becoming popular in families having everyone working or in school

3. It is only through the cooperation of all the forces of production and distribution that we can obtain a higher standard of living <u>and ensuring a better future for</u> our children.

    Ⓐ and ensuring a better future for
    Ⓑ and ensure a better future for
    Ⓒ and so to ensure
    Ⓓ thereby ensure
    Ⓔ and ensure a better future on behalf of

4. <u>Fought on April 19, 1775, Concord, Massachusetts, was the first serious engagement of the American Revolution.</u>

    Ⓐ Fought on April 19, 1775, Concord, Massachusetts, was the first serious engagement of the American Revolution.
    Ⓑ The first serious engagement of the American Revolution was Concord, Massachusetts, fought on April 19, 1775.
    Ⓒ The Battle of Concord, Massachusetts, was the first serious engagement of the American Revolution fought on April 19, 1775.
    Ⓓ The first serious engagement of the American Revolution was the Battle of Concord, Massachusetts, fought on April 19, 1775.
    Ⓔ The American Revolution's first serious engagement was the Battle of Concord, Massachusetts, fought on April 19, 1775.

5. Other desirable qualities of concrete, the only major building material that can be delivered to the job site in a pliable state, include its strength, economy, and <u>the fact that it lasts a long while.</u>

    Ⓐ the fact that it lasts a long while
    Ⓑ because it lasts a long while
    Ⓒ heavy-duty wear and tear
    Ⓓ durability
    Ⓔ great ability to last

6. Though the sun has been the subject of scientific study for decades, there is no agreement among scientists <u>for what caused the sun's beginning.</u>

    Ⓐ for what caused the sun's beginning
    Ⓑ for what was the cause of the sun's beginning
    Ⓒ as to what caused the sun's beginning
    Ⓓ as to the origin of the sun
    Ⓔ on the sun's origin

7. If enacted into law, the Compassion Pain Relief Act
    would allow American physicians prescribing
    heroin to the terminally ill in a hospital or hospice, a
    course of treatment which has long been available to
    British physicians.

    (A) prescribing heroin to
    (B) to prescribe heroin to
    (C) the option of prescribing heroin to
    (D) the option to prescribing heroin in
    (E) the options of prescriptions of heroin for

8. As the first order of business, we were advised
    of the importance of regular and timely class
    attendance, told we could not smoke in the class-
    room, and were admonished to stay current with the
    reading at all times.

    (A) of the importance of regular and timely class
         attendance, told we could not smoke in the
         classroom, and were
    (B) of the importance of regular and timely class
         attendance, told we could not smoke in the
         classroom, and
    (C) of the importance of regular and timely class
         attendance and that we could not smoke in the
         classroom and
    (D) that regular and timely class attendance would
         be important, that we could not smoke in the
         classroom, and were
    (E) that regular and timely class attendance would
         be important, we could not smoke in the
         classroom, and were

9. Advances in metallurgy have often been inspired by
    war, since Bessemer steel was the direct outcome of
    the attempts to correct the deficiencies of the
    artillery used in the Crimean War.

    (A) often been inspired by war, since Bessemer
         steel
    (B) often been inspired by war, for example;
         Bessemer steel
    (C) often been inspired by war; Bessemer steel,
         for example,
    (D) been inspired often by war; Bessemer steel,
         for example,
    (E) been inspired often by war; Bessemer steel, as
         an example,

10. A plant turns toward a light because the light
    reduces the concentration of auxin, a growth
    hormone, on the more brightly lighted side of the
    stem.

    (A) because the light reduces the concentration of
         auxin, a growth hormone, on
    (B) because the light reduces the concentration of
         auxin, a growth hormone on
    (C) because the concentration of auxin, a growth
         hormone, is reduced on
    (D) to reduce the concentration of auxin, a growth
         hormone, on
    (E) to reduce the concentration of auxin, a growth
         hormone on

Explanatory Answers

Warm-Up 1

1. **(B)** The original sentence contains two errors. First, *for the reason that* is a clumsy way of saying *because*. Second, the phrase *he needed to* is illogical. Quintus Marcius was not stalling for time because he needed to stall for time; rather, he was stalling for time because he was waiting for reinforcements. (B) corrects both errors. As for (C), the phrase *waiting for the arriving of* is not idiomatic. As for (D), the *reason* seems to be an appositive, but there is no noun in the first part of the sentence that *reason* could be in apposition to. Finally, (E) joins the two ideas with a coordinate conjunction, destroying the subordination of the original and creating an illogical statement.

2. **(D)** The original sentence contains an error of pronoun usage. Subject pronouns, not object pronouns, must follow copulative verbs (state of being verbs), so *we* is the correct pronoun here. (B) fails to correct the error of the original and makes a gratuitous change. Both *obsessed with* and *obsessed by* are idiomatic. (C) and (E) both correct the pronoun error but change the intended meaning of the original.

3. **(D)** The original sentence contains an incomplete split construction that is not idiomatic. The correct idiom is *as important as*, but that idiom never gets completed. (B) fails to make the needed correction. (C), (D), and (E) make the needed correction, but (C) and (E) introduce new errors. As for (C), without the other, the comparison seems to include the new tax reform bill itself, which implies that the new bill is as important as, if not more important than, itself. As for (E), without *than*, the resulting sentence would not be idiomatic.

4. **(C)** The original sentence contains two errors. First, the verb *are* does not agree in number with its subject, *much*. Second, the phrase *such as the phrase "blue chip" stocks* is too far from the noun it is intended to modify, *jargon*. As written, the sentence seems to imply that the phrase *"blue chip" stocks* is a type of poker game. (B) eliminates the subject verb error and relocates the misplaced phrase to its logical position, but without setting the phrase off in commas. As a consequence, the resulting sentence may be read to imply that *"blue chip" stocks* are a type of financial page. (D) fails to correct the error of agreement, and (E) fails to correct the ambiguous placement of the final phrase.

5. **(C)** The original sentence contains an error of subject-verb agreement. The subject of the sentence is *aims*, so the correct verb form is *were*. (B) makes the needed correction but changes the intended meaning of the original. (B) implies that it was the aims of the party, rather than the party itself, that were formed in 1875. (D) not only suffers from the same problem as (B), but it is also worded in a very awkward way. The phrase *the Greenback Party's primary aims* does not read smoothly. Finally, (E), too, implies that it was the aims, rather than the party, that were formed in 1875.

10

6. **(B)** The original sentence contains one error. The correct English idiom is "more by x than by y." (B) uses the correct idiom. (C) suffers from two problems. First, it is not idiomatic to say *more by . . . and not by . . .* Second, (C) changes the intended meaning of the original by saying that traumatic events do not influence a child's personality at all. (D) also makes this second error and so must be incorrect. As for (E), either it means to say the same thing as the original, in which case the *is being* is not idiomatic, or it means to say a particular child's personality is in the process of development, in which case (E) is incorrect because it departs from the meaning of the original sentence. Only (B) corrects the error of the original without introducing a new error and without changing the intended meaning of the original sentence.

7. **(E)** The original sentence is afflicted with the notorious dangling modifier. As written, the sentence seems to imply that the post office is required to register by the end of the year. (E) eliminates this problem by relocating the introductory phrase nearer to the noun it is intended to modify, *aliens.* Despite some changes, (B) still gives the impression that it is the post office that is required to register. (C) eliminates the problem of the original, but it is very awkward. As for (D), the placement of *by the end of the year* creates the impression that the aliens were trying to crowd into the post office by a certain time.

8. **(A)** The sentence is correct as written. (B) is incorrect for two reasons. First, it is awkward. Second, (B) changes the emphasis if not the meaning of the original sentence by creating a category called modern enterprises. (C) is very awkward. The phrase *first Trans-Atlantic cable's laying* just does not read as well as *laying of the first Trans-Atlantic cable.* As for (D), the proximity of the phrase *in modern times* to *laying* suggests that it was the fact that the cable was laid in modern times that made the achievement great. Finally, (E) contains an error of diction. *Laying* is the wording needed here, not *lying.*

9. **(E)** The original sentence contains two errors. First, the material that intervenes between the two elements of the idiom *spurred on* make it difficult to see the connection between those two words. Second—and this error is related to the first error—the placement of the adverb, *constantly,* is such that it is not immediately clear what is being modified. (B) corrects the first problem but not the second. (C) attempts to correct both errors but falls just short because *spurred* and *on* are still separated. By comparison, (E) is more idiomatic than (C), for in (E) there is no doubt about what *constantly* modifies. Finally, (D) is needlessly wordy and awkward.

10. **(D)** The original sentence is ambiguous. It seems to say that the rise in the reports of street crime, and not the rise in crimes themselves, is due to unemployment and homelessness. (B) attempts to correct the error of the original but introduces two new problems. First, the phrase *reported street crimes* is awkward and potentially ambiguous, because it seems to create a new category of crime. Second, the problem addressed in the sentence is not a rising number but the increase in the number of crimes. (C) fails to eliminate the ambiguity of the original. Finally, (E) simply reinforces the error of the original. (D) eliminates the ambiguity without introducing a new error.

11. **(B)** The original sentence contains an incomplete split construction. The adjective *intensive* is intended as a predicate adjective modifying *manhunt.* The sentence also gives the impression that those two ideas are joined by the *were* earlier in the sentence, but the verb *were* is plural and *manhunt* is singular.

The sentence can be corrected by adding another verb: *the manhunt was intensive.* (B) makes this correction. (C) fails to make the needed correction and commits the additional sin of implying that the manhunt was found along with the clues. (D) suffers from a variety of problems. It is awkward, it changes the meaning of the original (by de-emphasizing the importance of finding the clues), and it introduces an additional problem of illogical subordination (*Although*). Finally, (E) is needlessly wordy.

Warm-Up 2

1. **(B)** The original sentence is wrong because the phrase *being that* is nonstandard English. (B) is incorrect because it is awkward. (C) uses the awkward construction *because of the fact.* (D) is wrong because *due to* should not be used in place of *since* or *because.* (E) is wrong because it is hopelessly wordy and awkward.

2. **(B)** The original sentence is not a sentence at all but a sentence fragment. Additionally, the phrase *having everyone working or in school* is not idiomatic. (C) is incorrect because it, too, is a fragment and contains the unidiomatic phrase *that have everyone working.* (D) is awkward because *are becoming popular* is too far from its subject. Finally, (E) is wrong because the verb tense is incorrect, and, again, the phrase having *everyone working or in school* is not idiomatic.

3. **(B)** The original sentence is afflicted with faulty parallelism. (B) makes the needed correction by replacing *ensuring* with *ensure.* (C) fails to make the needed correction. As for (D), though *ensure* is the correct verb form, the *thereby* with no *and* disrupts the compound verb (*obtain and ensure*), and, as a result, the final phrase no longer has any logical connection to the rest of the sentence. Finally, as for (E), the change from *for* to *on behalf of* is not only unneeded; *on behalf of* implies that the action does not benefit the children directly but only indirectly.

4. **(D)** The original sentence asserts, illogically, that Concord, Massachusetts, a location, is the same thing as a battle. (B) fails to correct this error. (C) corrects the error of the original but introduces a new mistake. (C) implies that the Battle of Concord was the first serious engagement of the day on April 19, 1775. Finally, (E) is wordy and the phrase *the American Revolution's first serious engagement* is awkward. Only (D) corrects the error of the original without creating any new problems.

5. **(D)** The original sentence suffers from a lack of parallelism. The first two objects of the verb *include* are nouns, but the third object is a clause. (B) fails to correct the problem of parallelism. (C), (D), and (E) all address the problem of the original. (C) and (E), however, are not idiomatic.

6. **(D)** The original sentence contains two errors. First, there is the problem of the nonidiomatic phrase *agreement for.* The correct idiom is *agreement on.* Second, the phrase *sun's beginning* is not idiomatic. The sentence could be corrected by using the infinitive *sun to begin* or, better, by using a phrase such as *sun's origin* or *origin of the sun.* (B) fails to correct either error and just complicates things further. (C) corrects the first error but not the second. (E) fails to correct the second error. Moreover, although (E) does, technically speaking, eliminate the first error, it does so at the cost of introducing another, similar error. The phrase *agreement on* is an acceptable English idiom, but the

kinds of things people agree on are things such as theories, suggestions, proposals, etc. One could agree on an explanation for the origin of the sun—but not on the origin of the sun itself.

7. **(C)** The sentence suffers from two defects. First, the use of the gerund *prescribing* is not idiomatic. Second, and this error is a bit more subtle, the phrase *course of treatment* seems to be an appositive, but there is no noun earlier in the sentence to support that function. The correct choice, therefore, will eliminate the problem of the nonidiomatic construction and supply a noun for the appositive treatment. (B) fails to correct the second error. (C), (D), and (E) all correct the second error, but (D) and (E) create new problems of idiom.

8. **(B)** The sentence suffers from faulty parallelism. The first *were* is intended to govern all three of the verb elements, so the second *were* is superfluous. Additionally, the second *were* takes *admonished . . . times* outside of the scope of the first *were*. As a result, that part of the sentence has no logical connection to any other part of the sentence. By eliminating the second *were*, (B) provides a logical connection for that part of the sentence with the rest of the sentence; it is one part of a three-part, compound verb. In each of the other three choices, a *that* disrupts the parallelism of the verb elements.

9. **(C)** The sentence suffers from illogical subordination. The *since* implies that the event described in the second clause was the cause of the event described in the first clause, but that is not the intended meaning of the original. (C) corrects this problem. (B) eliminates the problem of subordination but implies that war is an example of some category. As for (D), the placement of *often* suggests that it is possible to inspire particular advances several times. (E), too, makes this error. Additionally, the expression *as an example* is not idiomatic.

10. **(A)** The original sentence is correct. (B) introduces an ambiguity by eliminating the second comma. (B) implies auxin is a growth hormone that is found only on the more brightly lighted side of the plant. (C) fails to reproduce the meaning of the original, since (C) does not specify the agency by which the concentration of auxin is reduced. (D) changes the meaning of the original by implying that the plant makes a conscious decision to turn toward the light to accomplish some result. (E) shares this error as well as the error of ambiguity found in (B).

Critical Reasoning

✓ **Topics Covered**

Anatomy of a Critical Reasoning Question

Important Facts about Critical Reasoning

- **Topics**
- **The Rule of 2 Out of 5**

Holmes and the Magnifying Glass

The Structure of Critical Reasoning

Locating and Understanding the Conclusion of an Argument

Hidden Premises

Evaluating Inferences

- **Causal Sequences**
- **Generalizations**

11

Anatomy of a Critical Reasoning Question

All critical reasoning items consist of three parts: an initial statement or statements, a question stem, and answer choices. The initial statement or statements contain an argument, that is, a line of analysis or reasoning. The question stem then asks you to evaluate that argument, e.g., to describe it, to identify any missing parts, to defend it, or to attack it. Finally, one of the five answer choices will best respond to the question stem; the other choices will be distractors.

> **EXAMPLE:**
>
> In her address to the City-Wide Association of Dairy Products Distributors, the mayor cited the success of Redwood Farms, which has increased its sales in the city by 23 percent. She encouraged all distributors to make similar efforts, concluding that the overall increase in business would benefit the city.
>
> Which of the following, if true, points out a serious weakness in the mayor's reasoning?
>
> (A) Milk and other dairy products contain important nutrients that are vital to the health and well-being of citizens, particularly children.
>
> (B) Redwood Farms achieved the increase in sales by offering discounts to businesses that purchased a complete line of Redwood Farms products.
>
> (C) The mayor made a speech on a previous occasion to the city's chamber of commerce in which she proposed city tax abatements to attract new industry.
>
> (D) During the year cited, Redwood Farms showed only a 15-percent increase in before-tax profits over the previous year.
>
> (E) The size of the market in the city is relatively fixed, so any increase in sales by one firm must come at the expense of sales by other firms.

The initial statements present an argument (or logical analysis). The question stem asks you to find a logical weakness in the argument. The correct answer to this critical reasoning item is (E). The mayor applauds the success of one company in increasing its business and encourages other companies to do the same. If, however, the gains of Redwood Farms came at the expense of other firms in the same business, then it is logically impossible for every other firm to achieve the same success.

Important Facts About Critical Reasoning

1. Topics

Like reading comprehension passages, the initial statement of a critical reasoning item can treat any topic—art, science, history, philosophy, government, sports, and so on. The advice you were given in the lesson on reading comprehension is applicable here as well: Don't let the subject matter of the item intimidate you. Even if the topic is something you have never before heard of, everything you need to answer the question will be given to you.

2. The Rule of 2 Out of 5

A fundamental principle of the construction of critical reasoning items is that one out of the five choices must be identifiably better than the others. However, it should not be so obviously better than the others that the question becomes too easy.

This principle presents a dilemma to the writer of critical reasoning items. If a question stem asks you to attack an argument, one of the choices must represent a legitimate objection to the logic of the initial statement. This will be the "credited response." The other choices—the distractors—must be deficient in some respects, but they cannot be so deficient as to make the item ridiculously easy.

Preparing workable distractors is actually more difficult than writing the credited response. As a consequence, usually only two of the answer choices have any real merit (one being the correct choice). The other three choices, while related to the general topic of the initial statement, ignore the logical structure of the argument.

EXAMPLE:

Over the past fifteen years, the largely urbanized Northeastern United States has shown more and more the influence of the Southwestern portion of the country. Once, very few people in New York City could be found sporting cowboy boots and Stetson hats, and no major radio station boasted twenty-four-hour-a-day programming of country and western music. The latest development is the rapid proliferation of restaurants serving chili, nachos, burritos, and other Tex-Mex dishes.

The passage above makes which of the following assumptions?

Ⓐ The lifestyle of people in the Northeast has been enriched by the influence of the Southwestern states.

Ⓑ Most residents of the Southwestern states regularly eat at Tex-Mex restaurants.

Ⓒ Over the last fifteen years, residents of the Southwestern United States have increasingly adopted lifestyles similar to those of the Northeast.

Ⓓ Tex-Mex dishes are an element of the regional cuisine of the Southwestern states.

Ⓔ People in the Northeastern United States eat out more frequently than they did fifteen years ago.

The best answer to this item is (D). The author claims that the Northeast has absorbed elements of the culture of the Southwest and provides three examples. A tacit assumption (one which is not proved) of the argument is that a certain mode of dress, a kind of music, and a type of cuisine are found in the Southwest. (D) articulates this assumption.

Three of the remaining choices are really just "flak." They lack any real plausibility after a reasonably careful reading. These are (A), (C), and (E).

(A) goes beyond the scope of the initial statement. The author simply states that certain cultural elements of the Southwest have been transplanted to the Northeast, but no value judgment is contained in the paragraph about that process.

(C) reverses the causal linkage described by the initial statement. According to the author, the Southwest has influenced the Northeast—not vice versa.

(E) goes beyond the scope of the initial statement. Nothing in the argument suggests that people in the Northeast are eating out more frequently than they did fifteen years ago—only that there are more Tex-Mex restaurants in the region than there were fifteen years ago.

To most people, (B) will probably seem to be the second-best answer. It at least has the merit of being fairly closely connected to the argument in the initial statement. It *might* be true that people in the Southwest regularly patronize the Tex-Mex restaurants. That, however, is not necessarily an assumption of the argument. All that is required for the argument is that there exist in the Southwest such restaurants—not that residents of that area patronize those restaurants with any frequency.

Holmes and the Magnifying Glass

In several of the Sherlock Holmes stories, Watson describes how Holmes takes out a magnifying glass from his pocket and proceeds to study the scene of a crime in excruciating detail, a means by which Holmes finds clues that Watson, using only his ordinary vision, overlooked. On the exam, you must use a "mental magnifying glass" to study critical reasoning problems, for this part of the exam tests careful reading as well as critical reasoning.

Most of the time we are reading or listening, we are just passively absorbing information. For example, when you are reading a newspaper or watching the television, you probably simply accept whatever is said as correct without studying the information too carefully. This applies to your reading of college textbooks as well. You read to learn the content of the textbook—but you take it for granted that what is written in the book is correct.

You can prove this to yourself by thinking about the advertising you encounter in the media. You are barraged by advertising, and even if you don't pay very much attention to it, you can probably recite a dozen or so key phrases from advertisements and sing parts of several jingles. Most people are surprised when they examine the actual content of the advertisements.

The claims of many advertisements are very carefully and sometimes very cleverly worded. Here are some of my old favorites, but you can probably find illustrations of your own. No brand names will be mentioned, but some of the advertisements may be familiar.

One television commercial for chewing gum runs roughly as follows:

> Chew Brand X Sugarless Gum. Four out of five dentists surveyed recommend sugarless gum for their patients who chew gum.

This is a claim you may have heard. On a first and casual hearing, the advertisement may give the impression that 80 percent of all dentists recommend that people chew Brand X Sugarless Gum. A closer examination reveals, however, that the claim is much less ambitious.

First, the advertisement does not claim that the dentists surveyed recommend Brand X Sugarless Gum over any other brand of sugarless gum. The advertisement states only that the dentists stated they would recommend a sugarless gum for patients who chew gum.

Second, the advertisement does not state that the dentists recommend that patients chew gum at all. The claim is that the dentists recommend that patients who intend to chew gum should chew a sugarless gum. Actually, the dentists surveyed might be universally opposed to all gum-chewing but regard the chewing of a sugarless gum as the lesser of two evils.

Finally, the advertisement does not really make a claim about dentists in general. Notice that the claim contains the qualifier "of dentists surveyed." The ad does not state how many dentists were in the survey. (Given the wording, the survey might have included only five dentists. Indeed, it seems strange that a survey should yield a number so precise—instead of something like 82.1 percent or 77.3 percent.) Moreover, the ad does not state whether more than one survey was conducted. It is possible, given the wording of the claim, that several such surveys were taken, yielding unsatisfactory results, until one survey yielding the desired result was finally obtained. At that point, the company could proudly make its claim.

Once you understand the clever way in which the claim is qualified, you can see the claim really doesn't provide any really good reason for chewing Brand X Sugarless Gum.

Another tactic used by advertising copywriters is the literally true but vacuous claim. One antiperspirant is advertised on television in the following way:

> Only Brand X gives you twenty-four full hours of protection and the special Brand X scent.

The obvious intent of the advertisement is to persuade the viewer that Brand X antiperspirant has some unique advantage over all of the other antiperspirants that are available; and on a first and casual hearing, you might think that Brand X is the only antiperspirant that provides the user with twenty-four-hour protection. This is, not, however, what the advertisement claims. What it really says is that Brand X is the only product to provide both the twenty-four-hour protection and the special Brand X scent. This is hardly surprising. The Brand X scent probably is unique to Brand X products.

In fact, advertisers are so confident that readers and viewers are not really attending very carefully that they sometimes even include in the advertising a disclaimer about the claim they are making. Another gum manufacturer, we will say Brand Y, used a television advertisement that claimed, "Brand Y has twice as much flavor as Brand Z." The camera focused on the pieces of gum:

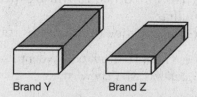

Brand Y   Brand Z

While this image appeared on screen an actress chanted, "I can see it! I can see it!" In other words, the comparison was based on the relative size of the sticks of gum, and that is why the character in the commercial was literally able to see the difference in taste. (Of course, if you wanted to have the same intensity of taste from Brand Z gum, you need only put two pieces in your mouth.)

None of this is particularly new; it's been going on for years. The following anecdote appeared recently in a New York City newspaper, though the source declined to state that he knew for certain that it is true.

> At the turn of the century, the producers of canned tuna and the producers of canned salmon were pitched in a merchandising battle against each other, and the salmon people were winning. So the tuna producers came up with a new marketing slogan that promised, "Our product is guaranteed not to turn red in the can!"

The claim was, of course, true, but not very interesting.

You might be thinking that such lack of substance might be found only in advertising. But if you carefully study news reports, you will find quite a few reports that are seemingly unbelievable. Here is the substance of a recent television news report:

> Today, the Federal Aviation Administration released the results of a study of airport safety in which agents attempted to smuggle weapons past security checkpoints at passenger boarding areas. Of a nationwide total of slightly over 2,000 attempts, 20 percent of the attempts were successful. The worst security performance was recorded at the Las Vegas airport, where nearly 60 percent of the weapons were not detected. The best security performance was found in Alaska, where the failure rate was only 1 percent.

There are many questions you might want to ask about the report before you conclude that airport security is or is not lax, for example, what kinds of weapons were used, exactly how the attempts were made, and so on. Aside from such questions, there is something very odd about the statistics—in particular, the 1 percent. According to the report, just over 2,000 agent-initiated smuggling attempts were made nationwide. If the number of attempts was divided equally among the 50 states, the result would be roughly 40 attempts in each state. If 40 tests were run at airports in Alaska (and given that Alaska is one of the less populated areas, you would expect even fewer), then the 1-percent rate translates into 1 percent of 40, or 0.4 successes. But how could part of one attempt have succeeded?

Here is another example:

> A local prosecutor had promised to reduce the incidence of crime related to drug use and to that end had established a special court to handle certain cases. After a while, the media grew critical of the plan, suggesting that virtually nothing or at best very little had really been accomplished. Few cases had been tried and fewer convictions won. To these objections, the prosecutor responded, "In 90% of the drug cases that we have pursued we have obtained convictions."

You might wonder whether the media and the prosecutor were discussing the same problem until you examine the prosecutor's claim carefully.

In the first place, the prosecutor qualifies the claim with the phrase "we have pursued." But what proportion of the cases were "pursued," and how is that term being used? It's possible that most of the arrests made were simply dismissed for any number of reasons, but even granting that a significant number of cases were pursued, the claim is weak. For what crimes were the accused convicted? It's possible that the prosecutor accepted a plea bargain, thereby obtaining a conviction—but for a crime considerably less serious than the one actually committed.

If you examine carefully the substance of what you read and hear, you can find similar examples almost every day. This is the type of careful and considered analysis that is rewarded by the GMAT.

11

The Structure of Critical Reasoning

Sherlock Holmes was a scientific detective who combined acute powers of observation with chains of reasoning to reach his conclusions. In the preceding part of this lesson, I stressed the importance of reading carefully for clues; in this part, I describe how to evaluate the logic of an argument. An argument is a group of statements, one of which is the conclusion and one or more of which are the premises. The premises and the conclusion are tied together by inference.

When we think of logical arguments, the first thing that may come to mind is something like this:

> All men are mortal.
> Socrates is a man.
> Therefore, Socrates is mortal.

In this argument, the conclusion is supported by two premises. Of course, the inference does not appear on the page. The inference is the movement of thought from the premises to the conclusion.

An argument need not have exactly two premises. An argument might have just one premise:

> No fish are mammals.
> Therefore, no mammals are fish.

An argument might have several premises:

> If John attends the party, then Ken attends the party.
> If Ken attends the party, then Lisa attends the party.
> If Lisa attends the party, then Mary attends the party.
> If Mary attends the party, then Ned attends the party.
> John attends the party.
> Therefore, Ned attends the party.

The arguments just presented are obviously valid, which is to say, they are correct. The conclusions clearly follow from the premises. The type of argument in which the conclusion necessarily follows from the premises is called a deductive argument.

In our day-to-day lives, however, we rarely have occasion to make such nice, neat, and precise deductive arguments. The kinds of arguments we ordinarily make are more apt to sound like this:

> Upon returning to the apartment I see that the mail is
> still in the mail box.
> It is my roommate's habit to pick up the mail from the
> box upon returning home.
> Therefore, my roommate has not returned home.

Though this argument does have its conclusions and its premises, the inference that joins them is not quite the same as the inference of the deductive arguments given above. In a deductive argument, the conclusion follows from the premises as a matter of necessity. That is, if the premises are true, then the conclusion must also be true. Here, however, it is possible for the premises to be true and yet the conclusion false.

Under what circumstances might the premises be true and yet the conclusion false? It's not difficult to imagine several possibilities: the roommate returned home before the mail was delivered or the roommate returned home but for any number of different reasons was either unable or unwilling to pick up the mail. The premises would still be true (the mail is there and it is the roommate's habit to pick it up) yet the conclusion is false.

Arguments of this sort are *inductive* arguments (as opposed to deductive arguments). They are also called probabilistic arguments, because the conclusion does not follow from the premises with certainty but only with probability.

The GMAT utilizes some deductive arguments as initial statements, but most of the arguments used fall into the second category. The question stem may ask you to do one of several different things. You may be asked to find the conclusion of an argument, or to draw a conclusion from a set of premises. You may be asked to identify a premise, particularly an unstated premise of an argument. Often you are asked to examine the linkage between the premises and the conclusion and to assess the strength or weakness of the inference of the argument.

All critical reasoning items focus on one or more of these three elements, so we will examine each in greater detail.

Locating and Understanding the Conclusion of an Argument

When speaking of an argument, it is customary to say that the conclusion follows from the premises; and often, the conclusion is the last sentence in an argument.

EXAMPLE:

A diet high in fiber is believed to reduce the risk of heart disease, colon cancer, and diabetes. Yet, consumers seeking to follow a high-fiber diet are hampered by the failure of food packages to list fiber content. Congress should mandate the inclusion of fiber content on all nutrition labels.

Here the conclusion of the argument is the final sentence, "Congress should mandate the inclusion of fiber content on all nutrition labels."

There is no requirement, however, that the conclusion appear last. The same argument could be rewritten:

Congress should mandate the inclusion of fiber content on all nutrition labels. A diet high in fiber is believed to reduce the risk of heart disease, colon cancer, and diabetes. Yet, consumers seeking to follow a high-fiber diet are hampered by the failure of food packages to list fiber content.

Now the conclusion appears first, but the logic of the argument remains unchanged. The conclusion could even appear in the middle of the argument:

A diet high in fiber is believed to reduce the risk of heart disease, colon cancer, and diabetes. Congress should mandate the inclusion of fiber content on all nutrition labels. But, consumers seeking to follow a high-fiber diet are hampered by the failure of food packages to list fiber content.

Now the conclusion is situated in the middle of the argument. Again, the logic of the argument remains the same, but this last revision introduces certain problems of style. The argument no longer reads smoothly.

The problem of style, however, can be easily corrected by simply adding one or two transitional words to inform the reader about the logical structure of the argument:

11

A diet high in fiber is believed to reduce the risk of heart disease, colon cancer, and diabetes. Therefore, <u>Congress should mandate the inclusion of fiber content on all nutrition labels</u>, because consumers seeking to follow a high-fiber diet are hampered by the failure of food packages to list fiber content.

With the addition of the transitional words *therefore* and *because,* the logic of the argument is once again clear.

Because the conclusion of the argument can appear anywhere, writers usually include signals for the reader. Here is a list of words and phrases that are often used to signal a conclusion:

> therefore
> thus
> so
> hence
> consequently
> as a result
> it follows that
> it can be inferred that
> which shows that
> which suggests that
> which proves that
> which means that

At other times, the author may use transitional words to signal which are the premises:

> since
> because
> for
> as
> inasmuch as
> insofar as

Sometimes, you may need to dissect the argument to find the conclusion. To do this, you must consciously ask yourself, "What is the author trying to prove here?"

EXAMPLE:

For many poor families, the desire to move from dependency to self-sufficiency founders on the problem of health insurance. A person leaving welfare for a job may earn too much to qualify for Medicaid, the federal health insurance for the poor; and low-paying entry-level jobs rarely provide for employee health coverage.

The argument consists of three propositions:

1. The desire to move from dependency to self-sufficiency founders on the problem of health insurance.
2. A person leaving welfare for a job may earn too much to qualify for Medicaid.
3. Entry-level jobs do not provide health coverage.

You can find the conclusion by asking, "Is this the point the author is trying to prove?" For statements 2 and 3, the answer is "no." The author is not trying to prove that a person leaving welfare may earn too much to qualify for Medicaid. That is one of the starting points of the reasoning. Similarly, the author is not trying to prove that entry-level jobs do not provide health coverage. Again this is a starting point of the argument.

The author is, however, trying to prove statement 1. He wants to prove that lack of health insurance is a disincentive for workers to move off welfare rolls. Statements 2 and 3 provide support for the argument. The two statements cite two different factors contributing to the health insurance problem. Were we to diagram the argument, it would have the following structure:

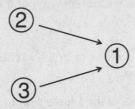

Often, a premise of an argument will support the ultimate conclusion of the argument only indirectly.

EXAMPLE:

It is immoral to take something that one has not earned. Gambling winnings are unearned, so gambling is immoral. Therefore, a state government that operates a lottery is acting immorally.

This argument consists of four propositions:

1. It is immoral to take something that one has not earned.
2. Gambling winnings are unearned.
3. Gambling is immoral.
4. State governments that operate lotteries are acting immorally.

The ultimate conclusion to be proved here is contained in statement 4. Statement 3 is a premise of that conclusion, but statement 3 also functions as the conclusion of a subargument, of which statements 1 and 2 are the premises. So the diagram of this argument would look like this:

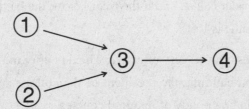

Since arguments are organized around their conclusions, finding the conclusion is the important first step in analyzing arguments. The following exercise allows you to practice identifying the conclusions of arguments. The exercise gets progressively more difficult as the arguments get more complex.

(Answers, page 183)

Directions: Underline the conclusion of each of the following arguments:

> **EXAMPLE:**
>
> The hammer is either in the toolbox or in the kitchen. <u>It must be in the kitchen,</u> because it is not in the toolbox.

1. Every winter for the past ten years, I have caught at least one cold. So this winter, I'll probably catch one or more colds.

2. Ann has not yet taken a foreign language course. Since only students who have passed at least one foreign language course are eligible for graduation, Ann is not a graduate.

3. All members of the Board of Trustees are graduates of the college, so Irving, who is a Trustee, is a graduate of the college.

4. Every time Allen comes to a dinner party, he brings his friend Bob, who tells that same joke about the whale and the pirate. Frank invited Allen to his dinner party tonight, so tonight I will hear the joke about the whale and the pirate.

5. The company rules require a supervisor to discipline a habitually tardy employee by either docking his pay or firing him. Since Smith has been late every day this week, he will either be docked or fired.

6. If a nail is lost, the shoe is lost; and if the shoe is lost, the horse is lost; and if the horse is lost, the rider is lost; and if the rider is lost, the battle is lost; therefore, if a nail is lost, the battle is lost.

7. The student protest proved very effective. The day after the students first occupied the administration building, the president of the college announced he would reverse the longstanding policy of required courses.

8. Officer, I could not have been exceeding the speed limit. I was moving at the same speed as the train on the tracks that run parallel to the highway here. The speed limit for trains along that stretch of track is less than the speed limit on this highway.

9. It is possible to reduce our reliance on foreign energy sources, because the United States relies heavily on imported oil as an energy source, despite the fact that we have considerable nuclear energy capacity that remains idle.

10. This country doesn't need a five-cent cigar. What it needs is no cigar at all. There is convincing scientific evidence that smoke not only harms the smoker himself but those in proximity to him who must breathe the smoke he creates. The federal government should enact a total ban on the sale of all tobacco products in this country.

11. The tuition and other costs of getting a college education continue to soar, and recent cutbacks in government aid for students have made it even more difficult for families of even moderate means to finance their children's education. We may soon see the day when a college education is once again the prerogative of only the very rich.

12. A band saw is more efficient than a reciprocating saw. The blade of a band saw travels at the rate of from 8,000 to 10,000 feet per minute, whereas a reciprocating saw making 200 strokes of 18 inches each minute would have a cutting speed of only 300 feet per minute.

13. The Federal Reserve Board must have moved last month to slow the growth of the money supply. Following a month in which prices rose more than the month before, interest rates rose noticeably, and in similar situations in the past the Board has moved to counteract inflation.

14. Contrary to the misrepresentations of my opponent, this administration has been one of the most free from corruption in the history of our city. Of the previous five administrations, a total of 23 persons were accused of criminal offenses relating to their performance of their public duties. Fifteen resigned under pressure, and four were convicted of wrongdoing. In this administration, only two people have been accused of any wrongdoing, and they quickly took leaves of absence from their positions until they were able to exonerate themselves.

15. Protectionists argue that an excess of exports over imports is essential to maintaining a favorable balance of trade. The excess can then be "cashed in" as precious metals. This means, however, that the most favorable of all trade balances will occur when a country exports its entire national product and, in turn, imports only gold and silver. Since one cannot eat gold and silver, the protectionists must surely be wrong.

16. The use of balls originated in the Middle East as part of religious ceremonies, and the earliest written references to balls of the sort we associate with games are found in the writings of Christian theologians who condemned the use of a ball as a form of Saturnalia. Apparently, the use of balls was transmitted to Europe by the Moors during the time of their invasion of Spain, for the first and condemnatory references to balls follow the time of the Moorish occupation of Europe.

11

17. *Nicholas Nickleby,* the second novel of Charles Dickens, has been referred to by some commentators as romantic, but the novel is actually highly realistic. Dickens collected material for his novel on a journey to Yorkshire during which he investigated for himself the deplorable conditions of the cheap boarding schools which produced broken bones and deformed minds in the name of education.

18. Given the ages and health of the justices currently on the Supreme Court, the present administration will likely get to appoint only one more nominee. Then, assuming that the Democrats will win the presidency in the upcoming election, they should be able to appoint two or perhaps three new justices during the next administrations, bringing the balance between conservative and liberal forces roughly into line. Now the Democrats should expedite the appointment of Judge Bork, so as not to antagonize the Republicans, who will surely repay in kind when considering nominees in the future.

19. A blanket ballot is one on which all the nominees of a single group or party are linked together and a voter can choose the entire "slate" simply by making one mark. With such a ballot, the support for a single popular candidate is transmitted to others on the "slate" without the voter's conscious decision to cast his vote for or against them. The Australian ballot is more democratic. All candidates are listed by office, and this requires the voter to think about each selection individually.

20. Administration officials say to scrap oil taxes, import fees, and subsidies for alternative fuels. The free market, they say, will produce the right amount of oil at the right price. That has always been a glib analysis. Now, in light of the administration's willingness to risk lives and dollars in the defense of oil from the Persian Gulf, it seems totally absurd. The real cost of oil should include the cost of military forces protecting supplies.

Hidden Premises

Perhaps the most striking feature of the literary genre called detective fiction is that the detective usually has certain privileged information, which the reader is denied by the author. This is, after all, what makes a "whodunit" fun to read. Only at the end of the book do you learn that "the uncle's wife's lover and the parson are really the same person, and he killed the high school principal because the principal was blackmailing him." In logical terms, the detective has relied on a hidden or supposed premise to reach his conclusion.

Above we discussed procedures for isolating the conclusions of arguments. Since every relevant proposition in an argument is either the conclusion or one of the premises, the procedures also enable you to find the explicit premises of an argument.

Most arguments, however, rely on premises that are not explicitly stated.

EXAMPLE:

Premise: Theft is an action that hurts another person.
Conclusion: Therefore, theft is immoral.

The conclusion here does not follow logically from the single, explicit premise. The argument requires yet another premise:

Premise (Explicit): Theft is an action that hurts another person.
Premise (Implicit): Actions that hurt others are immoral.
Conclusion: Therefore, theft is immoral.

Now the conclusion does follow from the two premises taken together.

Most arguments rely on such hidden premises. This is not because the speaker intends to deceive listeners by concealing information (although that may sometimes be the case). Rather, the reason most arguments rely on hidden premises is for economy of communication. If you think that you and your listener enjoy a common view, for instance, that actions that hurt others are immoral, then there is no need for you to articulate that premise. Your argument will have its persuasive appeal even though it rests upon a suppressed premise.

The role of suppressed premises is highlighted when two parties in discussion agree on all of the explicit premises of an argument but disagree about the conclusion.

EXAMPLE:

Mary: Rembrandt is the greatest painter of all times. His dramatic yet highly realistic representations give us an accurate picture of the people of his time.
Alan: No, Van Gogh is the greatest painter of all times. His impassioned use of color and authoritative brushstrokes let us feel the anguish through which he interpreted the world.

This exchange illustrates a discussion in which the two parties are probably not going to resolve their differences easily because each is committed to a host of implicit premises that the other does not share. In Mary's view, the measure of a painter is his ability to depict people or events in a highly accurate and realistic manner, while in Alan's view, the measure of a painter is his ability to communicate emotion. So, while there may not be disagreement about the explicit premises, that is, the important elements of the style of each painter, there is considerable disagreement about the import of those elements.

Many GMAT items ask you to uncover implicit or hidden premises. Sometimes, a careful reading of the stimulus material will allow you to anticipate one or more implicit premises, particularly if the argument is relatively simple.

> **EXAMPLE:**
>
> The legislature's decision to require doctors to prescribe generic alternatives to brand name drugs, when an alternative is available, is an excellent one. Now, patients will be able to save a lot of money and yet get the same medical treatment.

You can probably detect a very important premise in the argument: generic alternatives have the same effect as brand name drugs. Otherwise, patients won't pay less for the same treatment. This is the most obvious hidden assumption, but there are some others. For example, the speaker implicitly assumes that the difference in cost between brand name and generic drugs is sufficient to make an important difference, and further that there are enough generic alternatives to make a difference.

Sometimes it may not be so easy to isolate the hidden premises. In that case, you will use the available answer choices as "prompts." Look at each and ask yourself, "Is the author committed to this idea?"

> **EXAMPLE:**
>
> During the miserably hot weather of the first week of June, residents of our city were unable to cool off in the municipal pools. Why not? Because the pools were not scheduled to open until the first week after the end of the school year, but the school year did not end until the second week of June. To avoid this problem in the future, the Parks Department should schedule the opening of the pools for the first day of June.
>
> The argument above makes which of the following assumptions?
>
>   I. The warm weather of the first week of June is typical weather for the first week of June.
>
> II. The staff needed to operate the pools would be available during the first week of June.
>
> III. The fee charged for admission to the city's pools is not sufficient to meet the operating expenses of the pools.
>
>   (A) I only   (B) II only   (C) III only   (D) I and II only   (E) I, II, and III

The answer to this item is (D), for I and II are hidden premises of the argument. You should test each of the statements by asking whether or not the author is (implicitly) committed to that idea. As for statement I, the basis for the demand for an earlier scheduled opening is the hot weather experienced during the first week of June. Since the author uses this as the basis for a recommendation about the future, he is implicitly committed to the idea that this year's weather is typical of June weather. As for II, the author is also implicitly committed to the general idea that opening the pools earlier is feasible and therefore to the more specific idea that staff can be found to open them. Finally, as for III, the author is not committed to this idea. If anything, he probably leans in the other direction, that is, that the increased cost of opening earlier would not be very significant.

When we talk about premises, we often say that a conclusion "rests" on its premises or that the premises "support" the conclusion. The logical function of a premise is analogous to that of the foundation of a building. For this reason, premises play an extremely important role in the attack and defense of an argument. If a key premise can be shown to be false, then the argument, like a building with a weakened foundation, will collapse.

Some GMAT questions ask you to find an idea that weakens an argument. Others ask you to find one that strengthens an argument. The correct answer to both types of questions is often a hidden premise. In the case of a question that asks for an attack on the argument, the correct choice will be a statement that an implicit assumption is false, while in the case of a question that asks for a defense of an argument, the correct choice will be a statement that an implicit assumption is true.

EXAMPLES:

Now that the Federal Government has passed legislation allowing states to raise their speed limits from 55 miles per hour to 65 miles per hour, our legislature should move quickly to raise our speed limit. Most people currently drive at 65 miles per hour anyway, and this widespread disobedience tends to encourage disrespect for the law. The new speed limit would allow people to drive at a reasonable speed without encouraging people to break the law.

Which of the following, if true, would most weaken the argument above?

(A) When the speed limit is raised to 65 miles per hour, people will drive 75 miles per hour.

(B) Newer, relatively more efficient cars do not use significantly more fuel driving at 65 miles per hour than at 55 miles per hour.

(C) Many people who drive in excess of the posted speed limit use electronic devices to detect police radar and avoid being caught.

(D) The legal speed at which drivers are allowed to operate their vehicles has no effect on the incidence of drunken driving.

(E) During periods in which police give extra attention to the speed limit, more speeders are apprehended and eventually required to pay fines.

The answer is (A). A hidden premise of this argument is that once the speed limit is raised, people will obey the higher limit—rather than go 10 miles per hour faster than that limit. (A) most weakens the argument because it attacks this premise.

Notice also that the question asks you to accept each of the choices as true. Of course, (A) may or may not be true in reality, but for the purpose of argument you are to accept it as true. In fact, we could transform the example above into a "strengthening" question. In that case, the correct answer would probably be something like:

(A) Most people will obey a 65-miles-per-hour limit because that is the speed at which most cars are designed to cruise. Again, I am not saying this is true—just that if we assume it is true, then it strengthens the argument above by proving one of its implicit premises.

Here is an example of a "strengthening" question:

> More and more couples are entering into prenuptial agreements in which they specify before the marriage ceremony a distribution of property to be implemented should the marriage end in divorce. In this way, the parties can avoid lengthy and costly divorce proceedings.
>
> Which of the following, if true, would most strengthen the analysis above?
>
> (A) Not every dissolution of a marriage ends in a bitter divorce.
>
> (B) A party to a divorce is precluded from contesting the fairness of a prenuptial agreement.
>
> (C) More than two-thirds of marriages end in divorce.
>
> (D) Couples who have lived together prior to marriage may have accumulated considerable joint property.
>
> (E) The emotional impact of a prenuptial agreement may actually deter some people from marriage.

The answer to the item above is (B). The argument asserts that prenuptial agreements have the beneficial effect of allowing couples to avoid lengthy and costly divorce disputes over the distribution of property. The author implicitly assumes, though it is not explicitly stated, that such agreements cannot themselves become the center of a dispute. If that implicit assumption is true, as (B) states, then the argument is much strengthened.

Thus, we see that GMAT questions often test your ability to find suppressed premises in an argument by asking you to identify them or by asking you to weaken or strengthen the argument. The following exercise will give you some practice in both types of questions. Remember, to determine whether an idea is a hidden premise of an argument, ask yourself whether the author, by the logic of the argument, is committed to that idea.

(Answers, page 185)

Directions: Each of the following items asks you to isolate the hidden premises (assumptions) of an argument. Mark the best answer.

1. Edward was just elected president of the Student Senate, so he must be a senior.

   The statement above makes which of the following assumptions?

   I.   Only seniors can be members of the Student Senate.
   II. Only seniors can be president of the Student Senate.
   III. Only members of the Student Senate can be seniors.

   Ⓐ I only   Ⓑ II only   Ⓒ III only   Ⓓ I and III only   Ⓔ I, II, and III

2. If these cabinets were built after 1975, then they were not made out of oak plywood.

   The statement above depends upon which of the following assumptions?

   Ⓐ All cabinets made after 1975 were made out of oak plywood.
   Ⓑ All cabinets made in 1975 or earlier were made out of oak plywood.
   Ⓒ Only cabinets made of oak plywood were built in 1975 or earlier.
   Ⓓ No cabinets made in 1975 or earlier were made of oak plywood.
   Ⓔ No cabinets made after 1975 were made of oak plywood.

3. *Max:* Every painting done by Picasso is a masterpiece.
   Ernst: That's not true. Several masterpieces by David and Delacroix hang in the Louvre in Paris.

   Ernst apparently assumes that Max said
   Ⓐ only masterpieces were painted by Picasso.
   Ⓑ all masterpieces were painted by either David or Delacroix.
   Ⓒ only masterpieces by Picasso hang in the Louvre.
   Ⓓ only masterpieces by David and Delacroix hang in the Louvre.
   Ⓔ some of Picasso's masterpieces do not hang in the Louvre.

4. Students at Duns Scotus High must get a better education than students at Erasmus High because the grade point average of students at Duns Scotus High is higher than that of students at Erasmus High.

   The claim above depends upon which of the following assumptions?

   I.   The average grade earned by students is a good measure of the quality of education that a student receives.
   II. Extracurricular activities at Duns Scotus High are given more emphasis than at Erasmus High.
   III. The grading standards at the two high schools are roughly the same.

   Ⓐ I only   Ⓑ III only   Ⓒ I and III only   Ⓓ II and III only   Ⓔ I, II, and III

11

5. A government survey released today shows that 80 percent of the people who fly are satisfied with the service they receive from the airlines in this country. Three interviewers stood outside a major airline and asked people leaving the terminal, "Do you have any complaints about the flight you just got off?" Only 20 percent responded "yes!"

Which of the following, if true, would most undermine the conclusion of the argument above?

Ⓐ Sixty percent of the people coming out of the airline terminal were not people who had just gotten off a flight.

Ⓑ One percent of the people approached by the interviewers refused to respond to their inquiries.

Ⓒ The interviewers began their inquiry just after passengers were discharged from a flight that was 40 minutes late.

Ⓓ The interviewers were able to speak to only 70 percent of the people leaving the terminal, but those people were selected at random.

Ⓔ For six months following the day of the interviews, no official complaints were filed by any passenger with the Federal agency that regulated the airlines.

6. Colonel Mustard did not commit the murder in the dining room with the candlestick; therefore Mrs. Peacock committed the murder in the conservatory with the knife.

The argument above depends upon which of the following assumptions?

I. The murder was committed either with the candlestick or with the knife.
II. The murder was committed either in the dining room or in the conservatory.
III. The murder was committed either by Colonel Mustard or by Mrs. Peacock.
IV. The murder was committed either by Colonel Mustard in the dining room with the candlestick or by Mrs. Peacock in the conservatory with the knife.

Ⓐ I only Ⓑ IV only Ⓒ I and III only Ⓓ I, II, and III only Ⓔ I, II, III, and IV

7. An efficiency expert made the following suggestion to the manager of a shirt factory: Purchase larger spools of sewing thread. With more thread to a spool, your operators will not need to stop production as often to change spools. This will reduce your labor costs.

The efficiency expert apparently assumes that

Ⓐ thread wound on larger spools is not as strong as thread wound on smaller spools
Ⓑ sewing machines do not break down and do not require routine maintenance
Ⓒ workers in the factory are paid by the hour rather than on a piecework basis
Ⓓ machine operators are not allowed to leave their machines during the work period
Ⓔ speeding up production will improve the quality of the shirts made at the factory

8. A major insurance company reported that approximately 80 percent of all traffic accidents never result in an insurance claim. So we can conclude that about 80 percent of all losses due to theft also go unreported.

The argument above assumes that

I. Statistics about automobile insurance claims are applicable to claims for theft losses.
II. Traffic accidents represent a more serious danger to the individual than do thefts.
III. The average dollar value of a traffic accident claim is equal to the average dollar value of a theft loss claim.

Ⓐ I only   Ⓑ II only   Ⓒ III only   Ⓓ I and II only   Ⓔ I and III only

9. The continuing and increased reliance on computers represents a serious threat to the privacy of the individual. Recently, we have seen numerous examples of teenage and other "hackers" breaking the security codes of stores and banks and obtaining sensitive financial information about customers.

The argument above depends upon which of the following assumptions?

   I. People who obtain sensitive financial information about others will not share it.
  II. It is not possible to develop a security system for a computer that cannot be broken.
  III. Computers are not more efficient than other systems of record keeping.

  Ⓐ I only   Ⓑ II only   Ⓒ III only   Ⓓ I and III only   Ⓔ II and III only

10. The need for drug and sex counseling for teenagers has been overemphasized. Instead, we should channel the money spent on those programs into marriage counseling and other programs designed to hold the family together. Lower the rate of family dissolution, and you will reduce the incidence of teen drug use and pregnancies.

The author makes which of the following assumptions?

   I. Marriage counseling and other programs are effective in maintaining the unity of the family.
  II. Family dissolution contributes to problems of teen drugs and sex.
  III. People presently working in teen counseling programs can be reemployed as marriage counselors.

  Ⓐ I only   Ⓑ II only   Ⓒ I and II only   Ⓓ II and III only   Ⓔ I, II, and III

Evaluating Inferences

On the GMAT you will be asked to recognize that an argument contains an error; you may also be asked to describe that error in nontechnical terms or to correct it. Two types of inferences are found in GMAT critical reasoning items with sufficient frequency to make it worthwhile to single them out.

Causal Sequences

One common type of GMAT question tests your ability to analyze a causal relation.

Some questions ask you to recognize that the initial statement contains a causal analysis.

EXAMPLE:

In May, new-home sales dropped 14.9 percent, the largest decline in over five years. At the same time, mortgage interest rates increased from 9 percent to 10.5 percent. Evidently, many first-time buyers, who normally purchase less expensive homes, were driven out of the market by higher mortgage rates.

The argument above is primarily concerned with

Ⓐ offering an explanation of a phenomenon
Ⓑ refuting a traditional theory
Ⓒ questioning the reliability of statistics
Ⓓ criticizing government policies
Ⓔ casting doubt on the credibility of a source

11

The answer is (A). The initial statement seeks to provide a causal explanation for the decline of new-home sales during the month cited.

A question stem may also ask that you find an answer choice that weakens (or strengthens) a causal explanation. Usually, the correct answer to such a question points to the existence (or nonexistence) of what is called an alternative causal linkage.

EXAMPLE:

In May, new-home sales dropped 14.9 percent, the largest decline in over five years. At the same time, mortgage interest rates increased from 9 percent to 10.5 percent. Evidently, many first-time buyers, who normally purchase less expensive homes, were driven out of the market by higher mortgage rates.

Which of the following, if true, would most weaken the conclusion of the argument above?

(A) During the first six months of the year, the economy experienced an annualized growth rate of 4.5 percent.

(B) During the first six months of the year, a nationwide strike in the building trade brought new construction to a virtual standstill.

(C) People are today able to afford their first new home at a younger age than were people ten years ago.

(D) Nationwide, per capita disposable income rose by 0.5 percent during the month of June.

(E) Many people live in urban areas where single family homes are scarce and very expensive.

The answer to this item is (B). (B) points to a causal explanation other than the one suggested by the initial paragraph.

Sometimes the answer to a question about causal sequences will be one that mentions some unforeseen consequences of an action.

EXAMPLE:

Good health and grooming habits should be taught in school, and one such habit is the use of a cotton swab to remove wax from the ear canal. This prevents a buildup of excess wax.

Which of the following, if true, would constitute a valid criticism of the suggestion above?

I. Some good health and grooming habits can be learned by even very young children and should be taught before a child enters school.

II. When a cotton swab is inserted into the ear canal, it pushes wax ahead of itself, and this can result in wax buildup and infection in the inner ear.

III. Removal of ear wax exposes the delicate tissues of the ear canal to dirt and other elements that may cause infection.

(A) II only   (B) III only   (C) I and III only   (D) II and III only   (E) I, II, and III

The correct answer to this item is (D). Both II and III point to unanticipated consequences which undermine the value of the suggestion.

Generalizations

Another form of reasoning used by many disciplines is induction or generalization, in which a broad conclusion is based upon a limited number of examples.

EXAMPLE:

Every household interviewed on this block responded that crime is a serious problem in this area. Therefore, most residents in this town probably believe that crime is a serious problem here.

This is a simple illustration of a very common form of reasoning. There is nothing inherently correct or incorrect about such arguments. Rather, generalizations are stronger or weaker depending upon the evidence used to support the conclusion. The argument above could be strong or weak depending on the number of households surveyed and their representativeness of the area described.

Questions about generalizations are likely to focus on the issue of "representativeness."

EXAMPLES:

Every household interviewed on this block responded that crime is a serious problem in this area. Therefore, most residents in this town probably believe that crime is a serious problem here.

The argument above depends upon which of the following assumptions?

(A) The incidence of crime in the town surveyed is typical of the incidence of crime nationwide.

(B) The incidence of crime in the town surveyed is growing.

(C) The households surveyed included at least one person who had been a victim of a crime.

(D) In the town cited, violent crime is a greater problem than nonviolent crime.

(E) The households surveyed are representative of the households in the town.

The answer is (E), for (E) articulates the hidden assumption of the generalization—that the data upon which the generalization is based are representative.

Using the same initial statement, a question stem might ask you to defend the argument:

Every household interviewed on this block responded that crime is a serious problem in this area. Therefore, most residents in this town probably believe that crime is a serious problem here.

Which of the following, if true, would most strengthen the argument above?

(A) The incidence of crime in the town surveyed is typical of the incidence of crime nationwide.

(B) The incidence of crime in the town surveyed is growing.

(C) The households surveyed included at least one person who had been a victim of a crime.

(D) In the town cited, violent crime is a greater problem than nonviolent crime.

(E) The households surveyed are representative of the households in the town.

Again the answer is (E). If the assumption of representativeness is true, then the argument is much stronger.

Conversely, a question stem might ask that you attack the argument:

> Every household interviewed on this block responded that crime is a serious problem in this area. Therefore, most residents in this town probably believe that crime is a serious problem here.
>
> Which of the following, if true, would most weaken the argument above?
>
> Ⓐ The incidence of crime in the town surveyed is typical of the incidence of crime nationwide.
>
> Ⓑ The incidence of crime in the town surveyed is growing.
>
> Ⓒ The households surveyed included at least one person who had been a victim of a crime.
>
> Ⓓ In the town cited, violent crime is a greater problem than nonviolent crime.
>
> Ⓔ The households surveyed are located in the most commercial area of the town, where the crime rate is the highest.

Again the answer is (E), for (E) essentially says that the sample upon which the generalization is based is not representative of the entire town.

Another type of generalization projects conditions into the future:

> Per capita income in Country X rose from $2,000 to $2,500 from 1978 to 1988. Therefore, by the year 1998, per capita income in Country X will be $3,000.

Like a generalization, a projection is strong or weak depending on whether or not the time period on which the projection is based is "representative" of the future, that is, whether factors existing at present will continue into the future. Question stems will likely focus on these issues.

EXAMPLE:

> *Archaeologist:* In the past eight months, we have recovered fifteen ancient weapons from this dig. At this rate, by the time we have finished excavating the site next year, we will have recovered almost forty such items.
>
> The logic of the reasoning above is most similar to which of the following?
>
> Ⓐ *Economist:* When the money supply is tightened, the interest rates of savings and loans institutions rise more slowly than those of other state institutions because of state regulations. As a result, money flows out of savings and loans into other sectors.
>
> Ⓑ *Attorney:* The new appointment to the Supreme Court gives the conservative bloc more voting power, so we can expect to see earlier decisions on civil and individual rights read in a fairly restrictive manner.
>
> Ⓒ *Doctor:* The condition of this patient is caused by a lack of vitamin C. A vitamin supplement high in vitamin C should restore the patient to good health.
>
> Ⓓ *Astronomer:* Since no one has yet been able to prove that black holes do not exist, we can conclude that the theory that certain stars eventually become pointal masses is correct.
>
> Ⓔ *Political Scientist:* So far, six of the 15 Presidents elected in this century have been Democrats. This means the remaining three elections in this century are critical. If the Democrats are not successful again this century, we can expect to see only six Democratic Presidents in the 21st century.

The answer to this item is (E). The initial statement makes a projection based on past experience, as does (E).

You might also be asked to weaken (or strengthen) a projection, in which case the correct response would likely point out that conditions are not likely to continue (or are likely to continue) into the future.

> **EXAMPLE:**
>
> *Political Scientist:* So far, six of the 15 Presidents elected in this century have been Democrats. This means the remaining three elections in this century are critical. If the Democrats are not successful again this century, we can expect to see only six Democratic Presidents in the 21st century.
>
> Which of the following point out a logical weakness in the argument above?
>
> (A) The author presupposes that Democrats make better Presidents than do members of any other political party.
>
> (B) The author assumes that political conditions of one century will be repeated in the next century.
>
> (C) The author believes that most people in the 21st century will vote in presidential elections.
>
> (D) The author fails to consider the possibility that a new form of government will be enacted that doesn't include elected officials.
>
> (E) The author doesn't prove that most people prefer the policies of the Republican party to those of the Democratic party.

The answer to this item is (B). The initial paragraph is a straightforward projection into the future. The weakness in the argument is that it presupposes the same events will be repeated one hundred years later—without regard to possible changes in political conditions. (D) is perhaps the second-best answer. It at least has the merit of saying that political conditions may not repeat exactly. The problem with (D) is that it fails to point out the general logical flaw in the argument. Yes, it is true that the author does fail to consider this possibility, and this is one of the possibilities that might invalidate the author's prediction, but there are many others as well. (B), because it is a more general attack on the structure of the argument, is a stronger attack.

11

Summary

1. In general, only two of the answer choices in a critical reasoning item will have any real merit. You'll have to think carefully about those two choices. In general, you must read and reason carefully—more carefully than you do in your day-to-day activities.

2. An argument consists of a conclusion, a premise or premises, and an inference, and a critical reasoning item could ask about any of these elements.

   A. The conclusion may or may not be the last sentence of the argument and may or may not be signaled by a transitional word such as *therefore*. Be prepared to dissect the argument by asking yourself, "Is this what the author is trying to prove?"

   B. Once you have found the conclusion, every other sentence in the argument (if it is relevant) must be a premise of the argument, but not all premises are explicitly stated. If an item asks you to identify an assumption made by the argument, test each choice by asking, "Is this essential to the argument?" Often the correct answer to a weakening or strengthening question identifies a hidden premise of the argument.

   C. The GMAT frequently uses arguments that make a causal statement or that are generalizations.

      i. When you analyze an argument that asserts a causal connection, be alert for the possibility of alternative causal sequences.

      ii. When you analyze an argument that makes a generalization, try to determine whether the sample on which the generalization is based is adequate to support the conclusion. Similarly, if the author makes a projection, try to determine whether conditions are likely to repeat themselves.

Explanatory Answers

EXERCISE 1

1. Every winter for the past ten years, I have caught at least one cold. <u>So this winter, I'll probably catch one or more colds.</u>

2. Ann has not yet taken a foreign language course. Since only students who have passed at least one foreign language course are eligible for graduation, <u>Ann is not a graduate.</u>

3. All members of the Board of Trustees are graduates of the college, so <u>Irving,</u> who is a Trustee, <u>is a graduate of the college.</u>

4. Every time Allen comes to a dinner party, he brings his friend Bob, who tells that same joke about the whale and the pirate. Frank invited Allen to his dinner party tonight, so <u>tonight I will hear the joke about the whale and the pirate.</u>

5. The company rules require a supervisor to discipline a habitually tardy employee by either docking his pay or firing him. Since Smith has been late every day this week, <u>he will either be docked or fired.</u>

6. If a nail is lost, the shoe is lost; and if the shoe is lost, the horse is lost; and if the horse is lost, the rider is lost; and if the rider is lost, the battle is lost; therefore, <u>if a nail is lost, the battle is lost.</u>

7. <u>The student protest proved very effective.</u> The day after the students first occupied the administration building, the president of the college announced he would reverse the longstanding policy of required courses.

8. Officer, <u>I could not have been exceeding the speed limit.</u> I was moving at the same speed as the train on the tracks that run parallel to the highway here. The speed limit for trains along that stretch of track is less than the speed limit on this highway.

9. <u>It is possible to reduce our reliance on foreign energy sources,</u> because the United States relies heavily on imported oil as an energy source, despite the fact that we have considerable nuclear energy capacity that remains idle.

10. This country doesn't need a five-cent cigar. What it needs is no cigar at all. There is convincing scientific evidence that smoke not only harms the smoker himself but those in proximity to him who must breathe the smoke he creates. <u>The federal government should enact a total ban on the sale of all tobacco products in this country.</u>

11. The tuition and other costs of getting a college education continue to soar, and recent cutbacks in government aid for students have made it even more difficult for families of even moderate means to finance their children's education. <u>We may soon see the day when a college education is once again the prerogative of only the very rich.</u>

11

12. The band saw is more efficient than a reciprocating saw. The blade of a band saw travels at the rate of from 8,000 to 10,000 feet per minute, whereas a reciprocating saw making 200 strokes of 18 inches each minute would have a cutting speed of only 300 feet per minute.

13. The Federal Reserve Board must have moved last month to slow the growth of the money supply. Following a month in which prices rose more than the month before, interest rates rose noticeably, and in similar situations in the past the Board has moved to counteract inflation.

14. Contrary to the misrepresentations of my opponent, this administration has been one of the most free from corruption in the history of our city. Of the previous five administrations, a total of 23 persons were accused of criminal offenses relating to their performance of their public duties. Fifteen resigned under pressure, and four were convicted of wrongdoing. In this administration, only two people have been accused of any wrongdoing, and they quickly took leaves of absence from their positions until they were able to exonerate themselves.

15. Protectionists argue that an excess of exports over imports is essential to maintaining a favorable balance of trade. The excess can then be "cashed in" as precious metals. This means, however, that the most favorable of all trade balances will occur when a country exports its entire national product and, in turn, imports only gold and silver. Since one cannot eat or wear gold and silver, the protectionists must surely be wrong.

16. The use of balls originated in the Middle East as part of religious ceremonies, and the earliest written references to balls of the sort we associate with games are found in the writings of Christian theologians who condemned the use of a ball as a form of Saturnalia. Apparently, the use of balls was transmitted to Europe by the Moors during the time of their invasion of Spain, for the first and condemnatory references to balls follow the time of the Moorish occupation of Europe.

17. *Nicholas Nickleby,* the second novel of Charles Dickens, has been referred to by some commentators as romantic, but the novel is actually highly realistic. Dickens collected material for his novel on a journey to Yorkshire during which he investigated for himself the deplorable conditions of the cheap boarding schools which produced broken bones and deformed minds in the name of education.

18. Given the ages and health of the justices currently on the Supreme Court, the present administration will likely get to appoint only one more nominee. Then, assuming that the Democrats win the presidency in the upcoming election, they should be able to appoint two or perhaps three new justices during the next and following administration, bringing the balance between conservative and liberal forces roughly into line. Now, the Democrats should expedite the appointment of Judge Bork, so as not to antagonize the Republicans, who will surely repay in kind when considering nominees in the future.

19. A blanket ballot is one on which all the nominees of a single group or party are listed together and a voter can choose the entire "slate" simply by making one mark. With such a ballot, the support for a single popular candidate is transmitted to others on the "slate" without the voter's conscious decision to cast his vote for or against them. <u>The Australian ballot is more democratic</u>. All candidates are listed by office, and this requires the voter to think about each selection individually.

20. Administration officials say to scrap oil taxes, import fees, and subsidies for alternative fuels. The free market, they say, will produce the right amount of oil at the right price. That has always been a glib analysis. Now, in light of the administration's willingness to risk lives and dollars in the defense of oil from the Persian Gulf, <u>it seems totally absurd</u>. The real cost of oil should include the cost of military forces protecting supplies.

EXERCISE 2

1. B
2. E
3. C
4. C
5. A
6. B
7. C
8. A
9. B
10. C

11

Critical Reasoning Drills

1. **Walk-Throughs**
2. **Warm-Up Drills**

This lesson includes two walk-through and two warm-up critical reasoning drills. The "walk-throughs" have answers and discussion on the page opposite the questions so that you can "walk through" the problems. The "warm-ups" you should do under the specified time limit. The answers and explanations for the timed drills begin on page 205.

Walk-Through 1

Directions: Each question or group of question is based on a passage or set of conditions. For each question, select the best answer choice given.

Archaeologists have uncovered evidence that even as early as paleolithic times, human beings had a belief in an afterlife. Burial sites located close to ancient settlements have been found in which the dead were buried along with clothing, tools, and weapons. This is the earliest known evidence of a belief in life after death.

1. Which of the following is an assumption underlying the argument above?

   Ⓐ The placement of burial sites near settlements indicates a feeling of piety toward the dead.
   Ⓑ Belief in life after death is a central tenet of most religious faiths.
   Ⓒ The clothing, tools, and weapons found in the burial sites belonged to those buried nearby.
   Ⓓ Religious belief is a characteristic of most civilized societies.
   Ⓔ Only people who believe in life after death would bury artifacts with the dead.

1. **(E)** This is a question that asks you to identify a hidden assumption of the argument. (E) does this. The conclusion of the argument is that early humans believed in a life after death. The evidence for this conclusion is the discovery of certain articles buried with the dead. For this evidence to support the conclusion, the argument must implicitly presuppose that such articles would be buried with the dead only by people who had such beliefs.

   (A) is incorrect, for what is needed for this argument is a connection between the articles buried and a belief in an afterlife—not a feeling of piety toward the dead. After all, one might venerate one's ancestors even though one did not hold a belief in an afterlife. As for (B), this goes beyond the scope of the argument. The author's conclusion, as delimited by the wording of the passage, is that certain early humans held a belief in the afterlife—not that such beliefs are widespread. (C) is incorrect because the ownership of the articles is not important—only that the articles were placed there for use by the deceased. Finally, (D) makes essentially the same error that (B) does; it goes beyond the scope of the argument.

Some of the most popular television advertisements are those employing humor. But as an advertising technique, humor has its drawbacks. Studies have shown that, while many viewers of humorous advertisements vividly recall the commercials, far fewer recall the name of the product being promoted. This casts doubt on the ability of humorous commercials, no matter how funny or expensive, to increase product sales.

2. Which of the following is assumed by the passage above?

   Ⓐ Humorous commercials tend to reduce the credibility of products in the eyes of viewers.
   Ⓑ Though enjoyable, humorous commercials are often less memorable than serious commercials.
   Ⓒ A commercial that fails to create product name recognition does not increase sales of the product.
   Ⓓ Humorous commercials may alienate almost as many viewers as they entertain.
   Ⓔ The ultimate goal of advertising is to increase the name recognition of the product being promoted.

Religious leaders in our country were once expected to express and articulate lasting moral values. This is no longer the case. Today, we see spokespersons for major religious denominations entering into debate over merely political matters formerly reserved for members of the secular community.

3. The logical structure of the passage above depends upon the author's assumption that the expressing of lasting moral values is

   Ⓐ a strictly religious function
   Ⓑ no longer deeply valued
   Ⓒ essentially nonpolitical
   Ⓓ reserved for secular society
   Ⓔ the most important role of religion

2. **(C)** This question, too, asks about a hidden assumption of the argument. The conclusion of the argument is that humorous ads are not effective. Supporting this conclusion is an explicit premise. Consumers remember the humor but not the product name. This conclusion also depends on a suppressed premise; name recognition is essential to sales. Answer (C) correctly identifies this hidden premise.

As for (A), this goes beyond the scope of the argument. The speaker merely says that such ads are not effective, not that they are damaging as well. As for (B), the author never states that viewers don't remember the ad, only that they don't remember the product. (D) makes the same error made by (A). The author does not say that the ads are damaging, only that they are ineffective in promoting the product.

(E) is perhaps the most attractive of the distractors here. But a careful reading of the argument will show that (E) is incorrect. The conclusion of the argument is that humorous ads do not increase sales. We should infer, therefore, that the ultimate objective of advertising is to increase sales and that name recognition is merely a means to that end.

3. **(C)** This item asks you to identify a hidden assumption of the argument. The speaker argues that religion is creeping into the political sphere. Critical to this argument is the assumption that there are two distinct and separate spheres, religion and politics. (C) correctly points out that this is an assumption of the argument.

Those in the business community who decry government regulation claim that it increases the costs of doing business and reduces beneficial competition, ultimately harming both business and the community as a whole. They point to industries such as trucking, airlines, and telecommunications, in which deregulation has apparently brought greater economic efficiency. These commentators ignore the industries, such as financial services, in which government regulation is essential; indeed, without government intervention in the 1930s, some whole segments of that industry might have permanently collapsed.

4. The author's point is made primarily by

   Ⓐ offering a counterexample to rebut his opponents' argument
   Ⓑ calling into question the motives of his opponents
   Ⓒ pointing out an inconsistency in his opponents' use of terms
   Ⓓ drawing a distinction between valid and invalid methods of argument
   Ⓔ underscoring the subjectivity of his opponents' basic assumptions

Landmark preservation laws unfairly impinge on the freedom of owners to develop their own property as they see fit. In some cases, owners of hotels and office buildings designated as landmarks have been forbidden to make changes in the original facades or interiors, even though they reasonably believed that the changes would enhance the structures and make them more valuable.

5. Which of the following statements, if true, seriously weakens the author's argument?

   Ⓐ Altering the appearance of a historic structure sometimes does not enhance its beauty or value.
   Ⓑ In traditional legal doctrine, ownership of a property implies the right to alter it at will.
   Ⓒ Only buildings over 75 years old are normally affected by landmark preservation laws.
   Ⓓ Landmark designations must be approved by a local regulatory body before taking effect.
   Ⓔ Historic buildings represent a cultural heritage which the community has a legitimate stake in preserving.

4. **(A)** This item asks you to describe the logical structure of the argument. The author cites the position of those who oppose government regulations and mentions some of the reasons they give for their position. Then the author introduces an example in which regulation was essential and successful. (A) best describes that attack.

As for (B), when you attack the motives of an opponent, as opposed to the argument of the opponent, you make what is called an *ad hominem* attack, but the speaker here doesn't make such an attack. As for (C), though the author does attack the position he cites, he does so by counterexample, not by pointing to any contradiction. As for (D), the author never raises the issue of what constitutes a proper mode of argumentation. Without any such theoretical justification, he simply launches his attack by counterexample. Finally, as for (E), the author never suggests that any of the terms or judgments involved are based on anything but objective, economic facts.

5. **(E)** This question asks that you weaken an argument. Often, the correct answer to such a question states that a key hidden assumption of the argument is false. In this case, the conclusion of the argument is that landmark preservation laws deprive landlords of their right to use their own property. This argument presupposes a clear distinction between public and private property and further that the building owned by a landlord is purely private property in which the community has no legitimate interest. (E) comes to grips with this assumption by noting that a landmark building may not be purely private property and that some part of the building (the heritage) may belong to the community at large.

(A) is perhaps the second-best response. It does seem to attack the landlord's judgment that his actions in altering a historical structure will be valuable. The difficulty with (A) is that it represents only a partial attack on the argument. It questions whether this or that alteration would be useful or valuable but seems to grant the main philosophical point that the community, in some cases, should be able to substitute its judgment for that of the landlord.

As for (B), this seems to strengthen the speaker's claim that landmark preservation laws represent an unwarranted interference with the rights of the landlord. (C) fails to come to grips with the issue here—even if the building is over 75 years old, doesn't it still belong to the owner and not to the community? Finally, (D) makes the same kind of error. Even if we grant that landmark status must be approved by a public body, that doesn't explain why a public body should be allowed to substitute its judgment for that of the building's owner in the first place.

The cleaning and restoration of Michelangelo's frescoes on the ceiling of the Sistine Chapel were undertaken by some of the world's finest art restorers under the close supervision of an international team of art experts and historians. Nonetheless, the results have produced a storm of controversy. Most modern viewers, it seems, had become accustomed to seeing the frescoes with their colors dulled by layers of yellowing glue and varnish and with the contours of the figures obscured by centuries' accumulation of grime.

6. The passage implies that Michelangelo's frescoes

Ⓐ have been the subject of intense controversy over their artistic merit

Ⓑ suffered until recently from centuries of obscurity and neglect

Ⓒ should not have been cleaned and restored without more careful planning

Ⓓ have been obscured by dirt during the recent process of restoration

Ⓔ were originally much brighter and more vivid than most modern viewers realize

6. **(E)** This item asks you to determine what is implied by the argument, that is, what is implicit in the argument. (E) is the correct choice. The speaker states that modern viewers, accustomed to the dull colors, were startled and even offended by the result of the restoration. We may infer from this that the cleaning restored the original, brighter colors.

As for (A), the passage deals with the restoration, not with the artistic merit of the work itself. (B) and (D) both represent misreadings of the paragraph. The author implies that the damage was the result of the natural process of the passing of centuries. Finally, as for (C), the author is not critical of the restoration. He even notes that it was conducted under the supervision of a team of experts. If anything, the author implies criticism of those who did not like the result of the restoration.

Questions 7–8

"In general," stated Professor Charney, "the athletes now attending the university are more interested in studies than athletes of ten years ago. The proof is that more and more of my students who are athletes attend class on a regular basis."

7. The conclusion of Professor Charney depends upon which of the following assumptions?

   Ⓐ Professor Charney's student athletes show greater interest in studies because Professor Charney is a better teacher now than she was ten years ago.

   Ⓑ Student athletes are more concerned about getting good grades because it is more difficult to become a professional athlete now than it was ten years ago.

   Ⓒ Whether or not a student attends class on a regular basis is a good measure of whether a student is interested in his or her studies.

   Ⓓ Professors should not expect the same commitment to studies from student athletes that they require of students in general.

   Ⓔ An interest in studies is something that a student must learn very early in his or her academic career.

8. Which of the following is a possible weakness in Professor Charney's reasoning?

   Ⓐ The athletes who enroll in her classes are not typical of student athletes in general.

   Ⓑ Many other students who are not athletes are very interested in their studies.

   Ⓒ Professor Charney does not take into account the special demands placed on students who are also athletes.

   Ⓓ Professor Charney does not explain why student athletes are more motivated today than they were ten years ago.

   Ⓔ Some student athletes may be provided with special tutoring to ensure that their grades will make them eligible for participation in athletics.

7. **(C)** This question asks about a hidden assumption. Start by isolating the conclusion of the line of reasoning:

Athletes are now more interested in studies than before.

The explicit premise that supports that conclusion is:

My student athletes are attending class more regularly.

Now you should look to each choice and ask yourself, "Is the speaker committed to this idea?"

As for (A) and (B), the speaker is not necessarily committed to either of these ideas. The conclusion is a statement of fact: things have changed. The speaker is not necessarily committed to any particular explanation of that change. (D) makes the mistake of going beyond the scope of the statement. Although this is a judgment that someone might make, there is no warrant for attributing it to this particular speaker. For all we know, the speaker may feel that student athletes should be held to the same standard as other students. Finally, (E) is a fairly weak response to the question, for nothing in the structure of the argument commits the author to analyze the development of study habits.

8. **(A)** The answer to this question is also a hidden assumption of the argument. The explicit premise of the argument is:

My student athletes are attending class more regularly.

However, the conclusion is much broader, referring as it does to student athletes in general. Thus, the structure of the argument is a generalization; and, as you learned in the lesson on critical reasoning, often the best attack on such an argument is to point out that the sample is not representative of the population as a whole. This is the burden of choice (A).

(D) and (E) will probably both attract some support as the correct choice, though neither is really a very good choice. (D), however, makes the error of trying to force the speaker to take on a greater burden than she has been willing to assume. The speaker says only, "Student athletes are more interested in studies, and here is my proof." It is not a logical weakness in that she has not also assumed the burden of explaining the "why" of this change. As for (E), this would be more relevant to an argument that claims "Athletes are now better students." (E) just isn't relevant to the claim actually made by the speaker.

(B) and (C) make the same kind of mistake made by (E)—they aren't really relevant to the statement made. As for (B), the speaker's comparison is of student athletes of today and those of another time—not of student athletes and other types of students. As for (C), the speaker does not analyze the reason for the change or for the original phenomenon.

Walk-Through 2

Directions: Each question or group of question is based on a passage or set of conditions. For each question, select the best answer choice given.

In an effort to increase the number of taxicabs available during the hours from 8:00 p.m. to 6:00 a.m., the Taxi Commission, which sets fares, has proposed a $1.00-per-ride surcharge during those hours. This is unlikely to have any effect on the availability of taxis. The fleet owners who lease cabs to drivers on a shift basis will simply raise the per-shift charge for those hours, thus eliminating any incentive for the individual driver to work the nighttime hours.

1. Which of the following, if true, most weakens the argument above?

 Ⓐ   Fleet owners usually have unleased cars during the nighttime hours covered by the Commission's proposal.

 Ⓑ   Most people who need a taxi during the nighttime hours would not mind paying the $1.00 surcharge.

 Ⓒ   The majority of licensed cabs are owned by individual drivers who do not lease them from fleet owners.

 Ⓓ   The previous year the Commission approved a 10-percent increase in taxi fares.

 Ⓔ   Passengers would not treat the surcharge as part of the driver's tip.

1. **(C)** The correct answer to this question aims at a hidden assumption of the argument. The argument offers a causal analysis: The fleet owners will raise the rent on cabs, so drivers will pay more; thus there will be no additional economic incentive to drive at night. (C) attacks this analysis by suggesting that a substantial number of cabs are owned by individual drivers and not fleets. This would mean the increase would go directly into the pocket of the driver, thus providing an economic incentive to drive at night.

  As for (A), this seems to strengthen the proposal rather than weaken it (and thereby it weakens the speaker's analysis). If cabs are idle during the night hours, then raising the price that can be charged for those hours should increase the supply of cabs during those hours. As for (B), this too seems to strengthen the Commission's proposal by eliminating a possible objection to the surcharge. (D) is not clearly relevant to the argument, and to attempt to justify (D) as the correct choice, you would have to engage in considerable speculation, thus taking you far beyond the scope of the argument as given. Finally, (E) seems to strengthen rather than weaken the argument by precluding a possible unforeseen consequence of the proposal that would render it ineffective.

Sentence had little effect why? strengthen.

A landlord was recently found guilty of hiring thugs to harass legal tenants to force them from a decaying building so that the apartments could be renovated and sold as high-priced cooperatives. The judge sentenced the landlord to convey ownership of the property to a nonprofit organization that would convert the building into housing for the homeless. Yet, the sentence will not deter other landlords in the future from trying similar strongarm tactics.

2. The argument above is most strengthened if which of the following is true?

    Ⓐ The current tenants will be allowed to continue to live in their apartments even after the transfer of ownership.

    Ⓑ The value of the unrenovated building to the landlord was virtually nothing.

    Ⓒ The landlord could have continued to make a profit on the rental units in the building even without improving the property.

    Ⓓ Tenants have clearly defined rights under the landlord tenant law including the right to quiet enjoyment of the premises.

    Ⓔ A building begins to decay only when the rental income from the property is insufficient to justify further investment in the property.

If Robert attends the party, then Sally, Tess, and Victor will also attend the party.

3. If the statement above is true, which of the following statements must also be true?

    Ⓐ If Robert does not attend the party, then Sally does not attend the party.

    Ⓑ If Sally, Tess, and Victor attend the party, then Robert will also attend the party.

    Ⓒ If Robert and Sally attend the party, then Tess, and Victor will not attend the party.

    Ⓓ If Victor does not attend the party, then Robert does not attend the party.

    Ⓔ If Tess does not attend the party, then Sally does not attend the party.

2. **(B)** This question asks you to strengthen the argument. The conclusion of the argument is: Landlords will not be deterred by this sentence, but the speaker does not explain why not. There must be a hidden assumption, as (B) correctly points out. If the forfeiture of a building is not painful to a landlord, it must be the case that the building isn't worth anything in the first place.

    (A) and (D), although generally related to the subject matter of the statement, are irrelevant to the structure of the argument. They don't aim at the connection between the sentence and deterrence. (C) and (E) at least have the merit of bearing on that connection, but (C) seems to weaken the speaker's argument. If the building is valuable, then the landlord did lose something of value, and the sentence might have some deterrent value. As for (E), to the extent that it hints at what (B) states specifically, (E) is an interesting answer. But the very fact that (B) makes the point explicitly makes (B) a better choice.

3. **(D)** This is a logical deduction question, focusing on the structure of an "if, then" statement. The correct choice is (D). If Robert attends the party, then the other three also do. From this we can infer "If it is not the case that Sally, Tess, and Victor attend, then Robert does not attend." The conditional element of this statement is equivalent to "If Sally does not attend, or Tess does not attend, or Victor does not attend." Thus, if Victor does not attend, Robert does not attend.

Based on the results of a pilot program providing health care for elderly patients in their homes, the state concludes that such a system is considerably cheaper than providing the same care in a nursing home. The study does not mention, however, that the dramatic cost savings are achieved by severely undervaluing the work of home attendants. A system which perpetuates low wages is not the best way of providing health care services to the elderly.

4. The criticism above would be most strengthened if which of the following were true?

  Ⓐ Approximately 90 percent of the cost of providing health care to elderly patients in their homes is compensation for home attendants.

  Ⓑ Many elderly patients would prefer to live in communities with others of similar age and receive health care there.

  Ⓒ Most elderly patients lack the financial resources to purchase at-home health care without some government assistance.

  Ⓓ The state is planning to implement a testing and licensing procedure for home attendants who provide health care services to the elderly.

  Ⓔ In the past decade, unions representing hospital and nursing home workers have been able to secure substantial increases in wages and fringe benefits for their members.

Researchers have found that cushioned running shoes absorb energy, thus working against the runner. A highly elastic, rather than soft, sole would return energy to the runner's leg, allowing the runner to run faster. It is clear that the best running shoes in the future will be those that have highly elastic soles.

5. Which of the following, if true, would most weaken the argument above?

  Ⓐ Running shoes with highly elastic soles will be cheaper to manufacture than those with soft soles.

  Ⓑ With better training techniques, runners today are already breaking more and more track records.

  Ⓒ A highly elastic sole places great stress on joints and increases significantly the chance of serious injury.

  Ⓓ Many people who purchase running shoes use them as everyday shoes and not for training purposes.

  Ⓔ Present-day soft-soled running shoes represent a considerable advance over the leather-soled running shoes of thirty years ago.

4. (A) The conclusion of the argument is that the cost savings claimed are obtainable only by undervaluing the services of some workers. The conclusion depends on the hidden assumptions that the cost of those services is an important component of the total cost of care and therefore of the total savings that are obtained by alternative care programs. (A) strengthens this argument because it documents this hidden assumption.

(B), (C), and (D) fail to come to grips with the logical structure of the argument. (E) is perhaps the second-best answer, for it at least has the merit of focusing upon the economics of the argument. As for (E), that workers received wage increases in the past does not necessarily mean that current levels are not still too low.

5. (C) This question asks for you to identify an unforeseen causal consequence. As (C) correctly points out, a stiffer sole may have advantages in efficiency but disadvantages in other ways. Thus, (C) weakens the argument.

(A), if anything, seems to strengthen the argument by pointing to another advantage of stiffer soles. (B), (D), and (E) are all irrelevant to the question of the value of elastic versus inelastic soles.

A recent study conducted by a national market research firm reported that only 11 percent of college-bound women would consider an all-women's college. It is clear that women's colleges must become coeducational if they are to survive.

6. Which of the following, if true, most weakens the reasoning above?

   (A) Graduates of women's colleges have better records for getting into medical and other professional schools than do women graduates of coeducational colleges.

   (B) Fewer than 10 percent of all college-bound men would consider attending an all-men's college.

   (C) The total capacity of all-women's colleges can accommodate only 2 percent of the nation's college-bound female students.

   (D) Many women's colleges report a decline in the number of large alumnae contributions over the past few years.

   (E) The total pool of college-bound high school graduates is projected to shrink during the next ten years.

When a large manufacturing business decides to relocate, the community suffers an economic loss beyond that of the immediate unemployment of those who had been employed at the factory. For example, the automotive service industry in the area is depressed as well. Unemployed workers no longer use their cars for the daily commute to and from work, thus reducing the need for fuel and tires and for services to maintain the cars.

7. The author's point is made primarily by

   (A) posing a question and answering it

   (B) appealing to an authority

   (C) attacking the credibility of a speaker

   (D) presenting an analogy

   (E) analyzing a causal relationship

6. **(C)** This argument rests upon a hidden assumption: fewer women want to attend an all-women's college than there are seats available. The support for this conclusion, however, is a percentage figure—not an absolute number. The argument works only if the number of interested applicants (11 percent of the total pool) is less than the number of available seats. But the total pool may be so large that even a relatively small percentage, such as 11 percent, means more applicants than seats. (C) correctly points out this weakness.

As for (A), the quality of education is irrelevant to the speaker's claim that there aren't enough applicants. As for (B), conditions for all-men colleges are not relevant to the argument. As for (D), although this is not related to the logical structure of the argument, as an independent point it would, if anything, actually strengthen the argument: Not only are there fewer applicants, there are budgetary pressures as well. The same reasoning applies to (E). This, if anything, strengthens the argument, and the number of interested women will decline.

7. **(E)** This question just asks that you describe the argument. The author traces out the causal implications of a certain phenomenon, so (E) is the best description.

College tuition has risen sharply over the past decade and will continue to rise in the future. Yet colleges and universities have the means to reverse this trend. Every such institution has a considerable endowment. They should use these funds to reduce tuition costs.

8. Which of the following, if true, would most weaken the argument above?

  Ⓐ Most college students are able to meet tuition and other educational expenses even if they have to take out student loans.

  Ⓑ The costs incurred by colleges in providing educational services have risen more rapidly than have tuition costs to students.

  Ⓒ Donors who make gifts to the endowment funds usually restrict the uses to which their gifts can be put by the institution.

  Ⓓ More college students are able to find part-time work during the academic year, which helps them to meet the rising costs of an education.

  Ⓔ Non-tuition costs of a college education have increased more rapidly than the cost of tuition.

8. (C) The conclusion of the argument is that colleges could slow the increase in tuition by dipping into their endowments. This conclusion rests upon the hidden assumption that colleges have the authority to use their endowments in this way. (C) weakens the argument by attacking this assumption. As for (A) and (D), the author doesn't claim that students cannot find ways of meeting increasing tuitions—only that colleges should not force them to do so. As for (B), the fact that institutional costs are increasing doesn't deny the author's point. In fact, the author might accept (B) and simply add, "Yes, I know that, but still tuition doesn't have to increase at all." Finally, as for (E), again the author might accept this and add "Yes, and this makes it all the more urgent to hold the line on tuition."

Directions: Each of the following questions asks you to analyze and evaluate the reasoning presented in a statement or short paragraph. For some questions, all of the choices may arguably be answers to the question asked, but you are to select the *best* answer to the question. In evaluating the choices to a question, do not make assumptions that violate common standards by being implausible, redundant, irrelevant, or inconsistent.

The existence of flying saucers, unidentified flying objects supposedly piloted by extraterrestrial beings, has been shown to be illusory. Skeptical researchers have demonstrated that a number of photographs purportedly showing flying saucers are either crude forgeries or misinterpreted images of such earthly objects as clouds, birds, weather balloons, or small private planes.

1. If the photographs mentioned above are accurately explained in the passage, which of the following is the best argument AGAINST the conclusion drawn?

   Ⓐ Not all unidentified flying objects can be conclusively shown to be manmade objects.

   Ⓑ The fact that a number of photographs of flying saucers are fake does not generally disprove the phenomenon.

   Ⓒ Some of those who claim to have witnessed flying saucers have no apparent motive for lying.

   Ⓓ Given the size and complexity of the universe, it seems unreasonable to assume that life exists only on Earth.

   Ⓔ Researchers who are skeptical about flying saucers inevitably bring their own biases and preconceptions to their work.

All the members of the Student Rights Coalition signed the petition calling for a meeting with the university trustees. Philip must be a member of the Student Rights Coalition, since his signature appears on the petition.

2. Which of the following best states the central flaw in the reasoning above?

   Ⓐ Some members of the Student Rights Coalition may not support all of the organization's positions.

   Ⓑ Philip's signature on the petition was not forged by a member of the Student Rights Coalition.

   Ⓒ Any member of the student body is eligible to sign a petition dealing with university affairs.

   Ⓓ Philip may also be a member of the school's debating society.

   Ⓔ Some of those who signed the petition may not be members of the Student Rights Coalition.

For the purposes of this study, ten qualities of a livable city were chosen, including a low crime rate, cleanliness, cultural attractions, and other amenities. For each city in the study, scores from 1 (lowest) to 10 (highest) were assigned for each of the ten qualities. The ten scores for each city were then averaged, yielding a total livability score for each city. We hope the resulting ratings will help you in choosing your next place of residence.

3. The passage above makes which of the following assumptions?

   I. It is possible to assign an accurate numerical score to each of a city's amenities.

   II. Each of the ten qualities of a livable city is equally important.

   III. Most people enjoy some degree of personal choice in where they reside.

   Ⓐ I only   Ⓑ II only   Ⓒ III only
   Ⓓ I and II only   Ⓔ II and III only

Foreign-made electronics products gained popularity in the United States during the 1970s primarily because of their low cost. In recent years, changes to the exchange rates of United States and other currencies have increased the prices of imported electronics products relative to those produced in the United States. However, sales of imported electronics products have not declined in recent years.

4. Which of the following, if true, would help to explain why sales of imported electronics products remain high?

   Ⓐ Trade ministries in foreign nations have pursued policies that prevented prices of electronics products from rising even faster.

   Ⓑ The cost of manufacturing electronics products abroad is rising faster than it is in the United States.

   Ⓒ A coming shortage in consumer credit in the United States is expected to depress sales of imported products during the next two years.

   Ⓓ American consumers now perceive the quality of imports as being high enough to justify the increased prices.

   Ⓔ Efforts to convince Americans to buy U.S.-made products for patriotic reasons have yet to bear fruit.

Young people who imagine that the life of a writer is one of glamour, riches, or fame soon discover not only the difficulties of the craft but the long odds against achieving any measure of recognition or financial security. Upon being asked, "Aren't most editors failed writers?" T. S. Eliot is said to have remarked, "Yes, but so are most writers."

5. The statement by T. S. Eliot conveys which of the following ideas?

    (A) Editing can be just as creative and challenging as writing.

    (B) Few writers are fortunate enough to attain real success in their profession.

    (C) For a writer, success is measured more by influence exerted than by material gain achieved.

    (D) Many writers find that a stint at editorial work is a beneficial apprenticeship for their craft.

    (E) There are no clear-cut standards of success and failure for writers, but there are such standards for editors.

In an extensive study of the reading habits of magazine subscribers, it was found than an average of between four and five people actually read each copy of the most popular weekly news magazine. On this basis, we estimate that the 12,000 copies of *Poets and Poetry* that are sold each month are actually read by 48,000 to 60,000 people.

6. The estimate above assumes that

    (A) individual magazine readers generally enjoy more than one type of magazine

    (B) most of the readers of *Poets and Poetry* subscribe to the magazine

    (C) the ratio of readers to copies is the same for *Poets and Poetry* as for the weekly news magazine

    (D) the number of readers of the weekly news magazine is similar to the number of readers of *Poets and Poetry*

    (E) most readers enjoy sharing copies of their favorite magazines with friends and family members

In reaction against the heavy, ornate designs favored by the neoclassical architects of the Victorian era, architectural critics and historians in the first half of this century went to the opposite extreme, declaring that only what was stripped-down, light, and free of decoration could be beautiful. Today, an overdue reevaluation of this esthetic is under way, as exemplified by the current exhibition of designs from the Beaux Arts school of the nineteenth century.

7. It can be inferred from the passage above that the present movement among architectural critics is toward

    (A) a renewed appreciation of the use of decorative motifs in building designs

    (B) a rejection of neoclassical standards of beauty in architectural design

    (C) a greater admiration of the light, simple designs characteristic of the early twentieth century

    (D) the adaptation of Victorian styles in the work of today's younger architects

    (E) a deeper understanding of the esthetic values of underlying post-neoclassical theory

In national surveys taken between 1970 and 1985, the percentage of respondents who reported that they regularly attended weekly religious services rose from 28 percent to 34 percent. However, statistics compiled during the same period by the nation's major religious denominations showed a gradual decline in attendance at weekly services.

8. Each of the following, if true, could help explain the apparent contradiction in the statements above EXCEPT

    (A) There was a sharp drop in the number of persons who attended religious services on an occasional basis.

    (B) Attendance statistics compiled by the religious denominations are often highly inaccurate.

    (C) As older churchgoers died, they were replaced by an equal number of younger churchgoers.

    (D) There was a significant increase in attendance among religious groups outside the major denominations.

    (E) Those responding to the surveys were not representative of the population as a whole.

Directions: Each of the following questions asks you to analyze and evaluate the reasoning presented in a statement or short paragraph. For some questions, all of the choices may arguably be answers to the question asked, but you are to select the *best* answer to the question. In evaluating the choices to a question, do not make assumptions that violate common standards by being implausible, redundant, irrelevant, or inconsistent.

If Whirlaway wins the Georgia Derby, then the Georgia Derby must be a fixed race.

1. The statement above depends upon which of the following assumptions?

    (A) Whirlaway can win a race only if the race is fixed.

    (B) Whirlaway can win the Georgia Derby only if the Georgia Derby is fixed.

    (C) No horse can win the Georgia Derby unless the race is fixed.

    (D) No horse can win any race unless the race is fixed.

    (E) Whirlaway will not win the Georgia Derby.

Philosophy should be taught to students at a very early age. It will instill in them a healthy skepticism toward values that they might otherwise accept without question.

2. The argument above makes which of the following assumptions?

    I. Unless students are exposed to philosophy at an early age, they will accept every idea.

    II. Even at an early age, students are able to understand some philosophical concepts.

    III. It is a good idea for students to question traditional values.

    (A) II only   (B) III only   (C) I and II only

    (D) II and III only   (E) I, II, and III

A: The plays and poems attributed to William Shakespeare, a poorly educated country bumpkin, were in fact written by Queen Elizabeth I, who had the intelligence and learning demanded by such works of genius.

B: Your claim is highly unlikely. If Elizabeth I had written plays such as *Hamlet* and *Macbeth,* she would quickly have become known as the greatest woman author in history. Yet, she has no such reputation.

3. B's argument assumes that it is improbable that

    (A) Elizabeth I's authorship of the plays would have been kept a secret

    (B) an uneducated person could have written plays like *Hamlet* and *Macbeth*

    (C) Elizabeth I had the artistic gifts necessary for great literary achievement

    (D) education and talent as a creative writer necessarily go hand in hand

    (E) a woman in Elizabethan times could not have attained greatness as an author

Between 1960 and 1970, ivory poachers in the African nation of Zinbaku killed over 6,500 elephants. During that period, the total elephant population in Zinbaku fell from about 35,000 to just under 30,000. In 1970, new antipoaching measures were implemented in Zinbaku, and between 1970 and 1980 over 800 poachers were arrested and expelled from the country. Nevertheless, by 1980, the elephant population in Zinbaku had fallen to about 21,000.

4. Which of the following, if true, would best help to explain the apparent paradox present above?

    (A) The poachers arrested in Zinbaku between 1970 and 1980 were rarely sentenced to long prison terms.

    (B) Because of highly publicized campaigns against the slaughter of elephants, demand for ivory fell between 1970 and 1980.

    (C) The elephant population in neighboring Mombasa rose slightly between 1970 and 1980.

    (D) Prior to 1970, the antipoaching laws passed by parliament in Zinbaku were rarely enforced.

    (E) In Zinbaku, between 1970 and 1980, thousands of acres of forest, the elephant's natural habitat, were cleared for farming.

Secondary school graduates in Japan score significantly higher on tests of science and mathematics than do students at the same level in the United States. Some educational reformers in the United States attribute this difference to the more rigid and rigorous Japanese secondary school program, which emphasizes required courses, long hours of study and homework, and memorization to a far greater degree than do schools in the United States.

5. Which of the following, if true, would most seriously weaken the conclusion drawn by the educational reformers cited?

Ⓐ The Japanese elementary school program is far less rigid and structured than the elementary school programs in most U.S. schools.

Ⓑ Many Japanese parents and educators decry the Japanese educational system, saying that it stifles independent thinking on the part of the students.

Ⓒ Secondary schools in the U.S. that emphasize creativity and flexible student schedules usually produce students with science and math scores higher than those earned by their Japanese counterparts.

Ⓓ On average, Japanese students score lower than U.S. students on tests of logical thinking, language arts, and communications skills.

Ⓔ A higher percentage of U.S. students go on to higher education than in Japan.

If the wind is strong, kites are flown. ✓
If the sky is not clear, kites are not flown.
If the temperature is high, kites are flown. ⌄

6. Assuming the statements above are true, if kites are flown, which of the following statements must be true?

I. The wind is strong. ⌄
II. The sky is clear.
III. The temperature is high.

Ⓐ I only   Ⓑ II only   Ⓒ III only
Ⓓ I and III only   Ⓔ II and III only

Last year, the number of cases of rape reported by women in this city increased by 20 percent. Ironically, these statistics have been cited with approval by advocates of women's rights.

7. Which of the following, if true, would logically explain the seemingly paradoxical approval of the women's rights advocates?

Ⓐ A new city policy of encouraging women to report cases of rape has sharply diminished the number of unreported cases.

Ⓑ The rate of convictions in rape cases in the city has increased steadily over the past three years.

Ⓒ Rape prevention has long been a high priority for leaders of women's rights organizations.

Ⓓ Most of the increase in reported cases of rape occurred in three particularly dangerous neighborhoods of the city.

Ⓔ Local judges have begun to deal more harshly with those found guilty of committing rape.

Superficially, today's problems with the abuse of illegal drugs such as heroin and cocaine resemble the problems of alcohol abuse during the 1920s, when many people kept drinking in spite of Prohibition. There is, however, a significant difference. The use of drugs such as heroin and cocaine has never been a widespread, socially accepted practice among most middle-class, otherwise law-abiding Americans.

8. An underlying assumption of the passage is that

Ⓐ during Prohibition, drinking of alcohol was commonly accepted among most Americans

Ⓑ as long as drugs are available, they will be used despite laws to the contrary

Ⓒ most Americans consider heroin and cocaine to be in the same category as alcohol

Ⓓ in a democracy, laws must be based on the fundamental beliefs and values of the majority of citizens

Ⓔ American popular opinion has always been molded primarily by the values of the middle class

Explanatory Answers

Warm-Up 1

1. **(B)** The logical structure of this argument is an attempt to conclude from the failure to prove "A," that "not A" is true. It says, in essence, "No one has proved that flying saucers exist; therefore, they do not exist." (B) correctly notes this logical structure.

2. **(E)** This argument has the following logical structure:

   All S are P.
   F is a P.

   Therefore, F is an S.
   The argument is fatally flawed. It's like arguing:

   All soft drinks are liquids.
   Water is a liquid.
   Therefore, water is a soft drink.

   (E) correctly notes this logical flaw.

3. **(D)** This item asks you to identify hidden assumptions in the argument. Test each statement. Statement I is an assumption of the argument, for the author states that he has assigned numerical values for the various aspects, which assumes that some sort of quantitative measure is possible. II, also, is an assumption, for the author treats each variable as a separate, independent measure, and the scores were averaged. Finally, however, III is not necessarily an assumption of the argument. The author does address those who do have flexibility in their living plans (otherwise he would not have prepared the study), but this does not commit him to the assumption that people in general enjoy such flexibility.

4. **(D)** This question asks you to examine a causal linkage. Ordinarily, we would expect higher prices to result in less demand for a product. Yet, according to the speaker, in the face of higher prices for imported electronics, demand has not weakened. (D) gives a good alternative causal explanation that could account for this.

5. **(B)** The main point of the passage is that most writers don't fare well. And this is why the author quotes T. S. Eliot, who, somewhat ironically, points out that even most people who claim to be writers really aren't successful writers.

6. **(C)** This argument is really kind of a generalization. It assumes that what is true of one magazine is true of other magazines as well. (C) points out that the argument is implicitly committed to this idea.

7. **(A)** This item asks that you draw a further inference from the material given. The speaker claims that for years architects were not interested in ornamentation, but instead wanted simple, light lines. Then the author states that we are seeing a reevaluation of this attitude—as exemplified by a current exhibit. We may infer from this that the reexamination is prompting a renewed appreciation of the function of ornamentation.

12

8. **(C)** This is one of those items that asks you to find alternative causal explanations. Here you are asked to find the one choice that does not provide an alternative explanation that would help eliminate the paradox. Every choice but (C) suggests a way of eliminating the paradox. (C), however, if anything, strengthens the paradox by eliminating a possible way of explaining away the paradox.

Warm-Up 2

1. **(B)** This item asks you to identify a hidden assumption of the claim. The claim states that Whirlaway's winning entails that the race be fixed. So the claim depends on the hidden assumption that Whirlaway can win the Georgia Derby only if the race is fixed. (A) is incorrect, for the speaker claims only that Whirlaway's winning (and not some other horse's winning) means that the race is fixed. (D) is wrong for the reasons that both (A) and (C) are wrong. Finally, as for (E), the author specifically allows that Whirlaway might win.

2. **(D)** This item asks you to identify hidden assumptions in the argument. Test each statement. Statement I is not an assumption of the argument, for the author need not commit himself to the view that children accept every idea— just that, given philosophical training, they would be more critical of ideas. The author is, however, committed to II. If children were not able to grasp philosophical concepts, then it would make no sense to try to teach them the concepts. The author is also committed to III. Implicit in the argument is the premise that it is a good idea to have students question ideas—otherwise, the author would be content to let them absorb the ideas without question.

3. **(A)** This item asks you to identify the assumptions made by B. B merely denies A's claim that Elizabeth I wrote the works ordinarily attributed to Shakespeare. In other words, B says "Elizabeth I did not write Shakespeare. Had she, she would have been famous." B doesn't have to take on any other burden. He doesn't have to prove who actually wrote the works—only that Elizabeth I did not write them.

4. **(E)** This question asks you to look for an alternative causal linkage. The passage implies that, given the legal actions to stop poaching, the elephant population should not have declined, but it did. What would explain that? (E) gives a very good explanation—another cause was working at the same time.

5. **(C)** Focus on the claim that you are asked to assess. The reformers claim that the critical difference between the math and science scores of Japanese and American children is the discipline of the Japanese educational system. (C) directly contradicts this claim. It says, in essence, that this cannot be the proper causal explanation because American students, in their highly flexible environments, actually outscore the Japanese students in their rigid environments.

6. **(B)** This is a problem involving deductive arguments. Assume that the initial statements are true, then test each choice. Statement I is not necessarily true. For example, even though it is true that when it is raining, there are clouds in the sky, you cannot conclude from the fact that there are clouds in the sky that it is raining. And III makes the same error. II, however, is inferable. It follows this reasoning: When there are no clouds in the sky, it is not raining. It is raining; therefore, there are clouds in the sky.

7. **(A)** Again, you are looking for an alternative causal explanation. The explanation for the paradoxical result is that there was no increase in the incidence of rape, but there was an increase in the number of cases reported.

8. **(A)** This item asks for an underlying assumption. The author claims that the situation with the abuse of heroin and cocaine is unlike that which existed with respect to alcohol during Prohibition. What is the difference? According to the author, heroin and cocaine are not middle-class drugs of preference. Thus, we can infer (though the author never specifically says so) that alcohol, even during Prohibition, was a middle-class drug of preference.

12

Diagnostic Math Test

Topics Covered

1. Arithmetic
2. Basic Algebra
3. Geometry

13

The GMAT tests arithmetic, basic algebra, and elementary geometry. To do well, you obviously will need to be familiar with certain principles. To help you decide whether you need to do any review of mathematics, here is a diagnostic test.

If you can answer all of the items in the diagnostic test, you almost surely do not need to do any outside review. If you are generally successful on the test but have trouble with a few items, the three lessons that follow the diagnostic test probably contain sufficient review material to refresh your memory on these points. However, if you have difficulty with several items, or if you are not confident of your ability to do the basic mathematical operations, you should review basic math concepts in any standard textbook.

MATH DIAGNOSTIC TEST

40 Questions

No Time Limit

Directions: Enter your answers to the following questions in the blanks provided. Use the available space for scratch work. Although there is no time limit for the exercise, you should work as quickly as possible. After you have finished, review your work using the explanations that follow.

---

1. To increase the number 12,345,678 by exactly 10,000, it is necessary to increase which digit by one? _____

2. $\dfrac{(7+2)\,(16 \div 4)}{(2 \times 3)\,(6 \div 2)} =$ _____

3. List all of the factors of 36: _____

4. List all of the prime numbers greater than 10 but less than 30:

   _____

Questions 5–7

Indicate whether or not the following must always be an even number. Enter *yes* or *no.*

5. Even Number × Odd Number _____

6. Odd Number + Odd Number _____

7. Even Number ÷ Even Number _____

8. In a string of consecutive odd numbers, what is the fifth number following the number 13? _____

9. $\dfrac{\left(\dfrac{5}{6}+\dfrac{1}{2}\right) \times \left(\dfrac{4}{3} \times \dfrac{1}{4}\right)}{\left(\dfrac{3}{2}-\dfrac{1}{3}\right)-\left(\dfrac{2}{3} \div \dfrac{8}{2}\right)} =$ _____

10. Convert $2\dfrac{2}{5}$ to a decimal: _____

11. Convert 1.125 to a fraction: _____

12. $0.001 + 0.01 + 0.227 - 0.027 =$ _____

13. $0.1 \times 0.01 =$ _____

14. $1.5 \div 0.75 =$ _____

15. Convert $2\frac{3}{4}$ to a percent: _____

16. 2 is what percent of 10? _____

17. The price of a certain item increased from \$2.00 to \$2.50. What was the percent increase in the price? _____

18. $\dfrac{(3-6)\,(12 \div -2)}{(6-8)} =$ _____

19. Bob's average score on five tests was 85. If he received scores of 90, 80, 78, and 82 on four of the five tests, what was his score on the remaining test? _____

20. In a certain class, a student's final grade is a function of the grades she receives on a midterm exam, a final exam, and a term paper. The term paper counts twice as much as the final exam, and the final exam counts twice as much as the midterm exam. If a student receives a midterm score of 75, a final exam score of 80, and a grade of 90 on the term paper, what is the student's final grade for the course? _____

21. A jar contains black and white marbles in the ratio 2:3. If the jar contains a total of 30 marbles, how many of the marbles are black? _____

22. In a certain game, if 2 wixsomes are worth 3 chags, and 4 chags are worth 1 plut, then 6 pluts are worth how many wixsomes? _____

23. In the proportion $\dfrac{x}{6} = \dfrac{12}{24}$, $x =$ _____

24. What is the value of 3 raised to the third power? _____

25. $\sqrt{4} + \sqrt{9} =$ _____

26. $y - x + 3x - 4y + 3y =$ _____

27. $\dfrac{\left(x^3 y^4\right)^2}{\left(x^2 y^2\right)\left(x^4 y^6\right)} =$ _____

28. $(a + b)(a + b) =$ _____

29. Factor the expression $12x^3 + 3x^2 + 18x$: _____

30. Factor the expression $x^2 + 2xy + y^2$: _____

31. If $2x + y = 12$ and $y - x = 3$, then $x =$ _____

32. If $x^2 + x = 2$, and $x > 0$, then $x =$ _____

33. If $x + y \leq 5$ and $y \geq 2$, then what is the maximum possible value of x?

_____

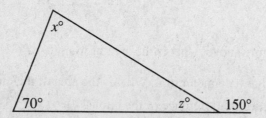

34. In the figure above, what is the value of x? _____

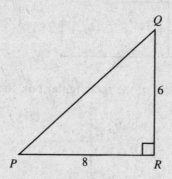

35. In the figure above, what is the length of side PQ? _____

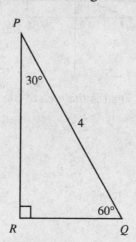

36. In the figure above, what is the length of sides PR and RQ?

PR: _____ RQ: _____

13

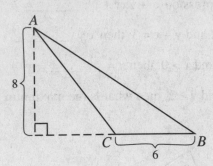

37. In the figure above, what is the area of triangle *ABC*? _____

38. A circle has a diameter of 4. What is the area of the circle? _____
What is the circumference of the circle? _____

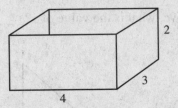

39. What is the volume of the rectangular box shown above? _____

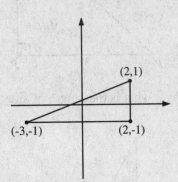

40. In the figure above, what is the area of the triangle? _____

Explanatory Answers

1. Changing the digit 4 to 5 will increase the number by 10,000, to 12,355,678.

2. 2

$$\frac{(7+2)\,(16 \div 4)}{(2 \times 3)\,(6 \div 2)} = \frac{(9)\,(4)}{(6)\,(3)} = \frac{36}{18} = 2$$

3. 1 and 36; 2 and 18; 3 and 12; 4 and 9; and 6 and 6

4. 11, 13, 17, 19, 23, and 29

5. Yes. For example, 2×3 is 6, which is even.

6. Yes. For example, $3 + 5$ is 8, which is even.

7. No. For example, $2 \div 4$ is a fraction and therefore not an even number.

8. 23

	First	Second	Third	Fourth	Fifth
13	15	17	19	21	23

9. $\frac{4}{9}$

$$\frac{\left(\frac{5}{6}+\frac{1}{2}\right) \times \left(\frac{4}{3} \times \frac{1}{4}\right)}{\left(\frac{3}{2}-\frac{1}{3}\right)-\left(\frac{2}{3} \div \frac{8}{2}\right)} = \frac{\left(\frac{8}{6}\right)\left(\frac{4}{12}\right)}{\left(\frac{7}{6}\right)-\left(\frac{1}{6}\right)} = \frac{\frac{4}{9}}{1} = \frac{4}{9}$$

10. 2.4

$$2\frac{2}{5} = \frac{12}{5} = 2.4$$

11. $1\frac{1}{8}$

$$1.125 = 1 + 0.125 = 1 + \frac{125}{1,000} = 1 + \frac{1}{8} = 1\frac{1}{8}$$

12. 0.211

$$
\begin{array}{r}
0.001 \\
0.010 \\
+\ 0.227 \\
\hline
0.238 \\
-\ 0.027 \\
\hline
0.211
\end{array}
$$

13

13. 0.001

$$
\begin{array}{r}
0.01 \\
\times \quad .1 \\
\hline
0.001
\end{array}
$$

14. 2

$$0.75\overline{)1.50}$$ with quotient 2

15. 275%

$$2\frac{3}{4} = \frac{11}{4} = 2.75 = 275\%$$

16. 20%

$$\frac{2}{10} = 0.20\% = 20\%$$

17. 25%

$$\frac{\text{Increase}}{\text{Original Price}} = \frac{\$0.50}{\$2.00} = \frac{1}{4} = 25\%$$

18. –9

$$\frac{(3-6) \times (12 \div -2)}{(6-8)} = \frac{-3 \times -6}{-2} = \frac{18}{-2} = -9$$

19. 95

$$\frac{90+80+78+82+x}{5} = 85$$

$$\frac{330+x}{5} = 85$$

$$330 + x = 85(5)$$

$$x = 425 - 330$$

$$x = 95$$

20. 85

$$\frac{75+2(80)+4(90)}{7} = \frac{595}{7} = 85$$

21. 12

There are 2 + 3 = 5 ratio parts. So each part has the value 30 ÷ 5 = 6. Two of the parts are black marbles, and 2 × 6 = 12.

22. 16

Since 2 wixsomes equal 3 chags, 8 wixsomes equal 12 chags. Since 4 chags equal 1 plut, 12 chags equal 3 pluts. Therefore, 8 wixsomes equal 3 pluts, and 16 wixsomes equal 6 pluts.

23. $x = 3$
Cross-multiply: $24x = 72$.
Divide by 24: $x = 3$.

24. 27

$3 \times 3 \times 3 = 27$

25. 5

$\sqrt{4} = 2$ and $\sqrt{9} = 3$, and 2 + 3 = 5

26. $2x$

$y - x + 3x - 4y + 3y = 3x - x + y - 4y + 3y = 2x$

27. 1

$$\frac{\left(x^3 y^4\right)^2}{\left(x^2 y^2\right)\left(x^4 y^6\right)} = \frac{x^6 y^8}{x^6 y^8} = 1$$

28. $a^2 + 2ab + b^2$

29. $3x(4x^2 + x + 6)$

30. $(x + y)(x + y)$

31. $x = 3$

Since $y - x = 3$, $y = 3 + x$. Therefore,

$2x + (3 + x) = 12$

$3x + 3 = 12$

$3x = 9$

$x = 3$

13

32. $x = 1$
Rewrite the original equation: $x^2 + x - 2 = 0$.
Factor: $(x + 2)(x - 1) = 0$.
So the two solutions are $x = -2$ or $x = +1$.

33. 3
x will be the greatest when y is the least. So let's use the minimum possible value for y: $x + 2 \leq 5$, so $x \leq 3$. The maximum value for x is 3.

34. 80°
z with the 150° angle forms a straight line, for a total of 180°. Therefore z is 180° less 150°, or 30°. Then, the interior angles of the triangle total 180°. So:
$70° + 30° + x° = 180°$
$x + 100 = 180$
$x = 80$

35. 10
This is a right triangle, so you can use the Pythagorean Theorem to find the length of the hypotenuse:
$PR^2 + QR^2 = PQ^2$
$(8)^2 + (6)^2 = PQ^2$
$64 + 36 = PQ^2$
$PQ^2 = 100$
$PQ = 10$

36. $PR = 2\sqrt{3}$ and $RQ = 2$
In a triangle with angles of 30°, 60°, and 90°, the side opposite the 30° angle is one-half the length of the hypotenuse, while the side opposite the 60° angle is one-half the length of the hypotenuse times the square root of 3.

37. 24
The area of a triangle is equal to $\frac{1}{2} \times$ altitude $\times$ base. So $\frac{1}{2} \times 8 \times 6 = 24$.

38. The radius of a circle is one-half the diameter, so the radius of this circle is 2.
Area $= \pi r^2 = \pi(2)^2 = 4\pi$
Circumference $= 2\pi r = 2\pi(2) = 4\pi$

39. 24
To find the volume of a rectangular solid, multiply the length by the width by the depth: $2 \times 3 \times 4 = 24$.

40. 5
The length of the altitude is 2; the length of the base is 5; so the area is $\frac{1}{2}(2)(5) = 5$.

Problem Solving: Introduction

✓ **Topics Covered**

14

14

Problem Solving: Introduction

Topics Covered

- The Directions for Problem Solving
- What Tested in Problem Solving?
- Arithmetic Manipulation
- Arithmetic Application
- Algebra Manipulation
- Algebra Application
- Geometry Manipulation
- Geometry Application
- Important Test-Prep Problem-Solving Hints

The GMAT uses two different kinds of math questions: problem solving and data sufficiency. Problem-solving items are standard, five-answer multiple-choice questions. Data sufficiency items involve special instructions that are analyzed in Lesson 19.

The Directions for Problem Solving

Here are the directions for Problem Solving:

Directions: Solve the problem and indicate the best answer choice.

Numbers: All values are real numbers.

Figures: A figure accompanying a problem-solving item is intended to supply information that would be useful in solving the problem. The figures are drawn as accurately as possible unless a figure is accompanied by a note specifically stating that the figure is not drawn to scale. Unless otherwise indicated, all figures lie in a plane.

One point does need clarification. Unless otherwise specifically noted, the figures included as illustrations are drawn to scale.

14

EXAMPLE:

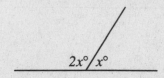

In the figure above, $x =$

ⓐ 15   ⓑ 30   ⓒ 45   ⓓ 60   ⓔ 120

Since the sum of the measures in degrees of the angles of a straight line is 180, $2x + x = 180°$. So $3x = 180°$, and $x = 60°$. If you measure angle x with a protractor, you will find it is indeed 60°.

Sometimes, however, a figure will include a warning note.

EXAMPLE:

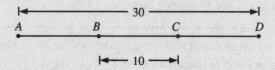

Note: Figure not drawn to scale.

In the figure above, $AB =$

ⓐ 5   ⓑ 10   ⓒ 15   ⓓ 20
ⓔ Cannot be determined from the information given.

In the figure above, $AB + CD =$

ⓐ 5   ⓑ 10   ⓒ 15   ⓓ 20
ⓔ Cannot be determined from the information given.

The answer to the first question is (E) The length of AB cannot be determined from the information given. Although AB, BC, and CD appear to be equal in the drawing, we cannot conclude that they are equal since (as we are warned) the figure is not drawn to scale. It is possible that $AB > 10$:

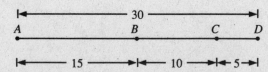

And it is also possible that $AB < 10$:

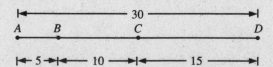

The answer to the second question, however, is (D)—not (E). Although the note indicates that the figure is not drawn to scale, you may assume that points $ABCD$ are on line AD in the order shown. Therefore, regardless of the accuracy of the drawing, you can deduce mathematically that $AB + CD$ must be 20. The entire line segment AD is 30 units long. BC is 10 units long, so the other two segments together, AB plus CD, must be $30 - 10 = 20$.

Here are other examples to illustrate the difference between valid and invalid conclusions based on figures that are not drawn to scale:

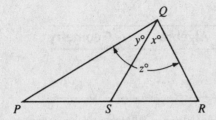

Note: Figure not drawn to scale.

Which of the following must be true?

I. $PS < SR$

II. $z = 90$

III. $x > y$

Ⓐ I only   Ⓑ I and II only   Ⓒ I and III only

Ⓓ I, II, and III   Ⓔ Neither I, II, nor III

Which of the following must be true?

I. $PR > PS$

II. $z > x$

III. $x + y = z$

Ⓐ I only   Ⓑ I and II only   Ⓒ I and III only

Ⓓ I, II, and III   Ⓔ Neither I, II, nor III

The answer to the first question is (E). Although all three statements look like they are true the way the figure is drawn, the figure might also be drawn as follows:

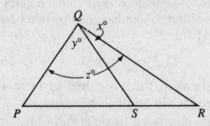

Notice that the lines and points in this redrawn figure are in the same position relative to each other as they are above. But in this figure, it appears that all three statements are false. Therefore, none of the three statements is necessarily true.

The answer to the second question, however, is (D). No matter how the figure is drawn, all three of these statements must be true. Statement I must be true, since PS is only a part of PR. For the same reason, II must be true; angle x is only a part of angle z. And III must be true since x and y are the only two parts of z.

What Is Tested in Problem Solving?

Problem-solving items test arithmetic, basic algebra, and elementary geometry. Some of the questions will look as though they might have been taken from one of your math textbooks; others will require you to apply your knowledge of math to new situations.

14

Therefore, we can classify problem-solving questions according to whether they just test your ability to do mathematical manipulation or require you to do some original thinking:

	Arithmetic	Algebra	Geometry
Manipulation	1	3	5
Application	2	4	6

Your methods for attacking a particular problem will depend on what type of problem you have. The following problems illustrate the six categories.

1. Arithmetic Manipulation

> **EXAMPLE:**
>
> What is the average of 8.5, 7.8, and 7.7?
>
> (A) 8.3   (B) 8.2   (C) 8.1   (D) 8.0   (E) 7.9

No original thinking is needed to solve this question. To find the average of the three numbers, you simply total them and divide the sum by 3:

$$\frac{8.5 + 7.8 + 7.7}{3} = \frac{24}{3} = 8.0$$

So the answer is (D).

2. Arithmetic Application

> **EXAMPLE:**
>
> If the price of fertilizer has been decreased from 3 pounds for $2 to 5 pounds for $2, how many more pounds of fertilizer can be purchased for $10 than could have been purchased before?
>
> (A) 2   (B) 8   (C) 10   (D) 12   (E) 15

The operations required here are the basic ones of arithmetic, but applying them to this new situation requires some original thinking.

To solve the question, you have to determine how many pounds of fertilizer could have been purchased at the old price and how many can be purchased at the new price. With $10, it's possible to buy five $2 measures of fertilizer (10 ÷ 2 = 5). At the old price, this would mean 5 × 3 = 15 pounds. At the new price, this would be 5 × 5 = 25 pounds. Therefore, it's possible to buy 25 – 15 = 10 more pounds at the new price than at the old price. So the correct choice is (C).

3. Algebra Manipulation

> **EXAMPLE:**
>
> If $x - 5 = 3 - x$, then $x =$
>
> (A) –8   (B) –2   (C) 2   (D) 4   (E) 8

To answer this question, you need only to solve for *x*—one of the basic manipulations of algebra:

$x - 5 = 3 - x$

Add *x* to both sides: $x - 5 + x = 3 - x + x$

$2x - 5 = 3$

Add 5 to both sides: $2x - 5 + 5 = 3 + 5$

$2x = 3 + 5$

$2x = 8$

Divide both sides by 2: $2x \div 2 = 8 \div 2$

$x = 4$

So the correct choice is (D).

4. Algebra Application

EXAMPLE:

A vending machine dispenses *k* cups of coffee, each at a cost of *c* cents, every day. During a period *d* days long, what is the amount of money in dollars taken in by the vending machine from the sale of coffee?

Ⓐ $\dfrac{100kc}{d}$ Ⓑ kcd Ⓒ $\dfrac{dk}{c}$ Ⓓ $\dfrac{kcd}{100}$ Ⓔ $\dfrac{kc}{100d}$

This question requires more than just basic manipulation. You must apply your knowledge of algebra to a new situation. Let's first find the total amount of money received by the vending machine in cents. It sells *k* cups each day at *c* cents per cup, so it takes in *k* times *c* or *kc* cents every day. And it does this for *d* days, so the total taken in (in cents) is *kc* times *d*, or *kcd*. But the question asks for the amount expressed in dollars. Since there are 100 cents in every dollar, we need to divide *kcd* by 100. So the final answer is $\frac{kcd}{100}$, or (D).

5. Geometry Manipulation

EXAMPLE:

If a circle has a radius of 1, what is its area?

Ⓐ $\dfrac{\pi}{2}$ Ⓑ π Ⓒ 2π Ⓓ 4π Ⓔ π^2

This very easy question just requires that you substitute 1 into the formula πr^2:
$\pi(1)^2 = \pi(1 \times 1) = \pi(1) = \pi$

Very few GMAT geometry questions are as easy as this. Virtually all require that you apply your knowledge of formulas to a new situation.

14

6. Geometry Application

EXAMPLE:

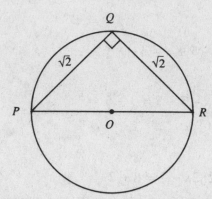

In the figure above, a triangle is inscribed in a circle with center O. What is the area of the circle?

Ⓐ $\dfrac{\pi}{2}$ Ⓑ $\dfrac{\pi}{\sqrt{2}}$ Ⓒ π Ⓓ $\pi\sqrt{2}$ Ⓔ 2π

To answer this question, we will have to find the radius of the circle. Since the hypotenuse of the triangle is also the diameter of the circle, we can find the radius of the circle by calculating the length of the hypotenuse of the triangle. First we use the Pythagorean Theorem:

$$PR^2 = PQ^2 + QR^2$$

$$PR^2 = (\sqrt{2})^2 + (\sqrt{2})^2$$

$$PR^2 = 2 + 2 = 4$$

$$PR = \sqrt{4} = 2$$

So the diameter of the circle is 2, which means the radius of the circle = 1. Now we use the formula for calculating the area of a circle, just as we did above: $\pi r^2 = \pi(1)^2 = \pi$. So the correct choice is (C).

Some Words to the Wise

The wrong answer choices for problem-solving items are very carefully selected. In fact, from a question writer's perspective, each wrong choice is as important as the correct answer. Why? Since the correct answer is one of the five, it has to be carefully camouflaged by the wrong choices. To accomplish this, a question writer keeps in mind four points.

First, the correct choice must blend into the background of the wrong answers. Study the following "dummy" question.

Xx x xxxxxx xxxx, xxx xxxxxx xx xxxxx xxx xxxxxxxxx xxxx Xxxx Xxxx Xxxxxx xxx xxxxx xxx xxxxxx xx xxxx. Xx xxx xx xxx xxxxx xxx xxx xx xxx xxxx xxxx xx xxxxxx xxxxxxxxxxx xxxxx xxxxxxxxxx, xxxx xxxxxxxx xx xxx xxxxxxxxx xxxx xxxx xxxx xx xxxxxx xxxxxxxxxxx xxxxx xxxxxxxxxx?

Ⓐ $\dfrac{5}{36}$ Ⓑ $\dfrac{16}{27}$ Ⓒ $\dfrac{7}{9}$ Ⓓ $\dfrac{29}{36}$ Ⓔ $\dfrac{31}{36}$

Even without a real question stem, you can see that each choice seems at least a plausible answer. The answer is hidden by the camouflage of wrong responses.

You would never have an array of choices like this:

Ⓐ π^3 Ⓑ $\sqrt{143.111}$ Ⓒ $\dfrac{7}{9}$ Ⓓ k^{33} Ⓔ $120°$

In this array, the wrong choices could not conceal the right one. Given an actual question stem, one of these choices would stick out as obviously correct.

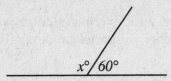

$x°$ $60°$

In the figure above, $x =$

Ⓐ π^3 Ⓑ $\sqrt{143.111}$ Ⓒ $\dfrac{7}{9}$ Ⓓ k^{33} Ⓔ $120°$

The answer is obviously (E)—the only choice that makes any sense. So the choices will be similar enough to one another that you can't spot the correct one at a glance.

On the other hand, the choices are not so similar that the question becomes a test of "donkey" math. You would never find a question on the GMAT such as the following:

$142,130.7016 + 222,143.1901 + 579,101.7913 + 143,241.1087 =$

Ⓐ 1,086,614.7   Ⓑ 1,086,615.7   Ⓒ 1,086,616.7
Ⓓ 1,086,617.7   Ⓔ 1,086,618.7

Such a question really wouldn't have any validity. If exam writers wished to test your ability to add decimals, they might use the following item:

$10 + 1 + 0.1 + 0.01 =$

Ⓐ 10.001   Ⓑ 10.011   Ⓒ 10.111   Ⓓ 11.11   Ⓔ 111.11

The correct choice is (D). The arithmetic really isn't that much work, but the problem does test whether you know how to add decimals (without the silly burden of adding large numbers).

This explains why you are not permitted to bring a calculator to the exam. On the one hand, the test-writers want to determine whether you truly understand the mathematical principles they are testing (as opposed to some procedure for pushing buttons on a calculator). And on the other hand, you really don't need a calculator. All of the arithmetic operations can be done either in your head or on the scratch paper provided.

Third, you can see that the answer choices are arranged in an order. Sometimes they are arranged from smallest to largest, sometimes from largest to smallest; but they are always in some order. Even algebraic expressions are arranged in some order:

Ⓐ x Ⓑ x^2 Ⓒ x^3 Ⓓ x^4 Ⓔ x^5

Or:

Ⓐ x Ⓑ $x + y$ Ⓒ $x^2 + y$ Ⓓ $x^2 + y^2$ Ⓔ $(x + y)^2$

14

The only exception to this rule would be a question like the following.

> Which of the following fractions is the largest?
>
> (A) $\dfrac{12}{29}$ (B) $\dfrac{108}{129}$ (C) $\dfrac{76}{130}$ (D) $\dfrac{11}{12}$ (E) $\dfrac{101}{200}$

In a question like this, choices will not be arranged in order for the obvious reason that the order would give away the solution. Here, the largest answer (and correct choice) is (D).

Fourth, and finally, many answer choices correspond to possible mistakes (incorrect reading or some other misunderstanding). The following example illustrates this point:

> In a certain year, the number of girls who graduated from City High School was twice the number of boys. If $\frac{3}{4}$ of the girls and $\frac{5}{6}$ of the boys went to college immediately after graduation, what fraction of the graduates that year went to college immediately after graduation?
>
> (A) $\dfrac{5}{36}$ (B) $\dfrac{16}{27}$ (C) $\dfrac{7}{9}$ (D) $\dfrac{29}{36}$ (E) $\dfrac{31}{36}$

The correct choice is (C), and the problem requires that you apply your knowledge of fractions. Since the ratio of girls to boys was 2:1, girls were $\frac{2}{3}$ of the graduating class and boys $\frac{1}{3}$. Let us write this as $\frac{2}{3}T$ and $\frac{1}{3}T$, where T stands for Total (all graduates). Of the $\frac{2}{3}T$, $\frac{3}{4}$ went directly to college: $\frac{3}{4}$ of $\frac{2}{3}T = \frac{3}{4} \times \frac{2}{3}T = \frac{6}{12}T = \frac{1}{2}T$. Of the $\frac{1}{3}T$, $\frac{5}{6}$ went directly to college: $\frac{5}{6}$ of $\frac{1}{3}T = \frac{5}{6} \times \frac{1}{3}T = \frac{5}{18}T$. The fraction of boys and girls combined was $\frac{1}{2}T + \frac{5}{18}T = \frac{28}{36}T = \frac{7}{9}T$, so $\frac{7}{9}$ of all the graduating students went directly to college.

The wrong choices, however, represent possible misreadings or misunderstandings. Take (D) as an example. Suppose that you carelessly misread the question thinking that $\frac{5}{6}$ of the girls and $\frac{3}{4}$ of the boys went directly to college (rather than vice versa). Given that misreading, you would multiply: $\frac{5}{6}$ of $\frac{2}{3}T = \frac{5}{9}T$ and $\frac{3}{4}$ of $\frac{1}{3}T = \frac{1}{4}$; and adding $\frac{5}{9}T + \frac{1}{4}T = \frac{29}{36}T$, which is choice (D).

Or imagine that you read the problem correctly and got as far as $\frac{1}{2}$ and $\frac{5}{18}$, but then multiplied instead of adding: $\frac{1}{2} \times \frac{5}{18} = \frac{5}{36}$, which is choice (A).

Such wrong answers are "distractors" (they distract attention from the correct choice). Distractors are an important part of the design of a question. After all, imagine what would happen if you made one of the mistakes described above but couldn't find a choice to fit your solution. Obviously, you would try another tack. So distractors are like misleading clues that lead you to a wrong conclusion.

Don't be misled by sloppy detective work!

Although this part of the GMAT is a "math" test, you must also read carefully. While this is always important, there are two special cases where it becomes even more important: capitalized and underlined words.

First, pay very careful attention to any words in the question stem that are capitalized. When a question stem contains a thought-reverser, it is usually capitalized. Why? To catch your attention. A thought-reverser is a negative word that turns a question around.

EXAMPLE:

A jar contains black and white marbles. If there are ten marbles in the jar, which of the following could NOT be the ratio of black to white marbles?

Ⓐ 9:1   Ⓑ 7:3   Ⓒ 1:1   Ⓓ 1:4   Ⓔ 1:10

Ordinarily, questions are phrased in the affirmative, such as "Which of the following is . . . ?" or "Which of the following could be . . . ?" This question, however, contains the thought-reverser NOT. So a wrong answer here would ordinarily be a right answer, and vice versa.

The answer is (E). Since there are ten marbles, the number of ratio parts in the ratio must be a factor of 10. (E) is not possible since $1 + 10 = 11$, and 10 is not evenly divisible by 11.

The question above might also have been phrased as:

A jar contains black and white marbles. If there are ten marbles in the jar, all of the following could be the ratio of black to white marbles EXCEPT

Ⓐ 9:1   Ⓑ 7:3   Ⓒ 1:1   Ⓓ 1:4   Ⓔ 1:10

Or as:

A jar contains black and white marbles. If there are ten marbles in the jar, which of the following CANNOT be the ratio of black to white marbles?

Ⓐ 9:1   Ⓑ 7:3   Ⓒ 1:1   Ⓓ 1:4   Ⓔ 1:10

Another word that functions like a thought-reverser is "LEAST."

EXAMPLE:

If n is a negative number, which of the following is the LEAST?

Ⓐ $-n$ Ⓑ $n - n$ Ⓒ $n + n$ Ⓓ n^2 Ⓔ n^4

The word *least* is capitalized here to make sure that you don't do what most of us would ordinarily do, which is to look for the largest value. The correct choice is (C). Since n is a negative number, (A), (D), and (E) are all positive. Then (B) is just zero, since it is one number subtracted from itself. (C) is the smallest since a negative added to a negative yields a negative number.

The second group of words requiring special attention contains those that are underlined. If the question is one that requires an answer choice in special units, the test-writer may underline the special units to avoid a possible misunderstanding.

14

EXAMPLE:

If a machine produces 240 thingamabobs per hour, how many minutes are needed for the machine to produce 30 thingamabobs?

Ⓐ 6   Ⓑ 7.5   Ⓒ 8   Ⓓ 12   Ⓔ 12.5

The answer is (B). A machine that produces 240 units per hour produces 240 units/ 60 minutes = 4 units/minute. To produce 30 units will take $30 \div 4 = 7.5$ minutes.

Additionally, anytime there is the possibility of a misunderstanding, the test-writer may underline a word or phrase.

EXAMPLE:

Of the 120 people in a room, $\frac{3}{5}$ are women. If $\frac{2}{3}$ of the people are married, what is the maximum number of women in the room who could be <u>unmarried</u>?

Ⓐ 80   Ⓑ 72   Ⓒ 48   Ⓓ 40   Ⓔ 32

In this question, there is a potential for confusion since the stem specifies the number of people who are married but asks for the maximum number of women who could be unmarried. To minimize this danger and ensure that the question doesn't become unnecessarily tricky, the question-writer underlines the key word. The answer is (D). In the room there are $\frac{3}{5} \times 120 = 72$ women and $\frac{2}{5} \times 120 = 48$ men, with a total of $\frac{2}{3} \times 120 = 80$ people being married and 40 unmarried. Even assuming all of the men are married, this still leaves $80 - 48 = 32$ others who are married, and those others are women. So at least 32 women must be married, which means the maximum possible number of women who are unmarried is $72 - 32 = 40$.

Since capitalized and underlined words are emphasized in order to catch your attention, you should make sure you understand their significance. After you have found your solution, stop and ask yourself, "Did I solve for the right thing?" In this case, you would ask, "Did I find the maximum number of women who could be *unmarried?*"

Summary

1. Unless otherwise indicated, a figure is drawn to scale. If a figure is not accompanied by any disclaimer, then you can rely upon the apparent magnitudes (angles, lines, etc.). If a figure is accompanied by the disclaimer "**Note**: Figure not drawn to scale," then you cannot rely upon the apparent magnitudes, but you can trust that lines drawn s straight are straight and that points are in the order shown.
2. Problem solving tests both basic manipulations and further applications of arithmetic, algebra, and geometry.
3. The distractors are carefully selected and represent possible misreadings or misunderstandings.
4. Circle any word in the question stem that is emphasized (capitalized or underlined). Once you've finished a problem, consciously ask yourself whether you have answered what the question asked.

(Answers, page 234)

Directions: The following questions are difficult problem-solving items. As you work them, be alert for possible Watson–type errors. Eliminate any choice that is a number found in the problem itself. If you try an approach that generates an easy answer, eliminate that answer and try again.

---

1. Peter walked from point P to point Q and back again, a total distance of 2 miles. If he averaged 4 miles per hour on the trip from P to Q and 5 miles per hour on the return trip, what was his average walking speed for the entire trip?

   Ⓐ $2\frac{2}{9}$ Ⓑ 4 Ⓒ $4\frac{4}{9}$ Ⓓ $4\frac{1}{2}$ Ⓔ 5

2. A square floor with sides of 8 feet is to be completely covered with non-overlapping square tiles, each with sides of 1 foot. If every tile along the outer edge of the floor is black and all other tiles are white, how many black tiles are needed?

   Ⓐ 28 Ⓑ 29 Ⓒ 30 Ⓓ 32 Ⓔ 64

3. After a 20% decrease in price the cost of an item is D dollars. What was the price of the item before the decrease?

   Ⓐ $0.75D$ Ⓑ $0.80D$ Ⓒ $1.20D$ Ⓓ $1.25D$ Ⓔ $1.524324D$

4. On a certain trip, a motorist drove 10 miles at 30 miles per hour, 10 miles at 40 miles per hour, and 10 miles at 50 miles per hour. What portion of her total driving time was spent driving 50 miles per hour?

   Ⓐ $\frac{5}{7}$ Ⓑ $\frac{5}{12}$ Ⓒ $\frac{1}{3}$ Ⓓ $1\frac{13}{51}$ Ⓔ $\frac{12}{47}$

   Pile A   Pile B

   | 1 | 2 | 3 | | 4 | 5 | 6 |

5. In a certain game, to determine how many spaces to move, a player selects a card from pile A and another card from pile B. If the player then moves a number of spaces equal to the sum of the two cards selected, how many different possible moves are there?

   Ⓐ 5 Ⓑ 6 Ⓒ 7 Ⓓ 8 Ⓔ 9

6. What is the largest number of non-overlapping sectors that can be created when a circle is crossed by three straight lines?

   Ⓐ 3 Ⓑ 4 Ⓒ 5 Ⓓ 6 Ⓔ 7

14

7. At Glenridge High School, 20 percent of the students are seniors. If all of the seniors attended the school play, and 60 percent of all the students attended the play, what percent of the non-seniors attended the play?

   Ⓐ 20%   Ⓑ 40%   Ⓒ 50%   Ⓓ 60%   Ⓔ 100%

8. Sally has an amount of money equal to the amount Charles has, plus $6. If the amount Charles has is equal to 0.6 the amount Sally has, then how much money does Charles have?

   Ⓐ $9   Ⓑ $12   Ⓒ $36   Ⓓ $100   Ⓔ $120

9. On a certain street, the houses on the west side have consecutive odd numbers and those on the east side have consecutive even numbers. If only the houses on the east side with numbers 122 through 182 are painted blue, how many houses on the street are painted blue?

   Ⓐ 120   Ⓑ 60   Ⓒ 59   Ⓓ 31   Ⓔ 30

10. The ratio of Victor's weight to Mike's weight is 2:7, and the ratio of Victor's weight to Hank's weight is 3:5. What is the ratio of Hank's weight to Mike's weight?

    Ⓐ 6:35   Ⓑ 5:12   Ⓒ 10:21   Ⓓ 12:5   Ⓔ 35:6

Water Usage in Cubic Feet

| 7 | 1 | . | 1 | 1 | 1 |

11. The water meter at a factory displays the reading above. What is the MINIMUM number of cubic feet of water the factory must use before four of the five digits on the meter are the same?

    Ⓐ 10,000   Ⓑ 1,000   Ⓒ 999   Ⓓ 666   Ⓔ 9

12. During a certain chess tournament, each of six players will play every other player exactly once. How many matches will be played during the tournament?

    Ⓐ 12   Ⓑ 15   Ⓒ 18   Ⓓ 30   Ⓔ 36

13. A telephone call from City X to City Y costs $1.00 for the first three minutes and $0.25 for every minute thereafter. What is the maximum length of time (in minutes) that a caller could talk for $3.00?

    Ⓐ 8   Ⓑ 10   Ⓒ 11   Ⓓ 12   Ⓔ 13

14. For a certain student, the average of ten test scores is 80. If the highest and the lowest test scores are dropped, the average of the remaining scores is 82. What is the average of the highest and lowest scores?

    Ⓐ 68   Ⓑ 72   Ⓒ 78   Ⓓ 81
    Ⓔ Cannot be determined from the information given.

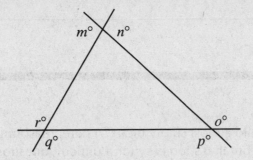

15. In the figure above, $m + n + o + p + q + r =$

ⓐ 360   ⓑ 540   ⓒ 720   ⓓ 900

ⓔ Cannot be determined from the information given.

14

Explanatory Answers

1. **(C)** Watson would almost surely pick (D) here, reasoning that $4\frac{1}{2}$ is the average of 4 and 5, but that's too easy for a difficult question. And, in fact, (D) is incorrect.

    The average speed for the entire trip is the total distance traveled divided by the total time of the trip. Since the entire trip was 2 miles, each leg was 1 mile. Therefore, the time it took Peter to walk from P to Q was $\frac{1}{4}$ hour, and the time it took to walk back from Q to P was $\frac{1}{5}$ hour. So the total walking time was $\frac{1}{4} + \frac{1}{5} = \frac{9}{20}$ hours. The total distance walked was 2 miles, so the average rate of travel was $2 \div \frac{9}{20} = 2 \times \frac{20}{9} = 4\frac{4}{9}$.

2. **(A)** Most likely, Watson will pick (D), reasoning that there are four sides to a square and that $4 \times 8 = 32$. But this is much too easy. This reasoning overlooks the fact that a corner tile belongs to both of its sides:

8	9	10	11	12	13	14	15
7							16
6							17
5							18
4							19
3							20
2							21
1	28	27	26	25	24	23	22

3. **(D)** Here Watson is likely to pick (C) (or perhaps (B)), reasoning that $1.2D - .2D = 1D = D$. But the fact that this is so easy should make him suspicious. The correct answer is $1.25D$: 20% of $1.25D = .25D$ and $1.25 D - .25D = D$.

4. **(E)** In this item, there are several misleading clues for Watson to use. He could add 30, 40, and 50 to get 120, and put 50 over that: $\frac{50}{120} = \frac{5}{12}$. Too easy, and wrong. Or he might place 50 over 30 plus 40: $\frac{50}{70} = \frac{5}{7}$. Again, easy but wrong. He might even be so foolish as to think "the leg driven at 50 miles per hour was one of three legs of the journey and 1 out of 3 is $\frac{1}{3}$" and pick (C). (Ouch!)

    $$10 \div 30 = \frac{1}{3}$$

    $$10 \div 40 = \frac{1}{4}$$

    $$10 \div 50 = \frac{1}{5}$$

    Total: $\frac{47}{60}$

    So the fraction of the time spent driving at 50 miles per hour was $\frac{1}{5} \div \frac{47}{60} = \frac{12}{47}$.

5. (A) Again there are two easy mistakes for Watson to make. Since there are three cards in each pile, he can reason that $3 + 3 = 6$ or $3 \times 3 = 9$. Both are too easy, and both are wrong!

The easiest way to get the correct answer is just to test all of the possibilities. The addition is easy and there aren't that many.

$A + B =$	$A + B =$	$A + B =$
$1 + 4 = 5$	$2 + 4 = 6$	$3 + 4 = 7$
$1 + 5 = 6$	$2 + 5 = 7$	$3 + 5 = 8$
$1 + 6 = 7$	$2 + 6 = 8$	$3 + 6 = 9$

How many *different* moves are possible? Only five: five, six, seven, eight, and nine spaces.

6. (E) Here we have a difficult geometry question with several appealing distractors. First, on a bad day, Watson might think "three lines, three sectors." But that's clearly wrong. On second reading, he might draw a figure:

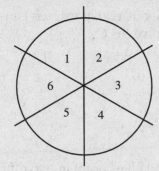

But that's too obvious, so it must be wrong. Trying again:

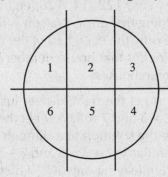

No improvement. At this point, a Holmesian test-taker would reason, "It's got to be more than 6, so the correct choice must be (E)." And (E) it is.

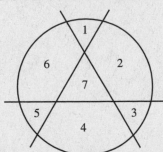

14

7. **(C)** Now we're learning how to avoid the typical errors. In this problem it is very unlikely that (A) or (D) will be correct. And it's a foregone conclusion that (B) is wrong. Since $60 - 20 = 40$, (B) is too easy and must be wrong.

 The solution requires more thought. From the number of those who attended the play, take away the number of seniors:

 60% of student body − 20% of student body = 40% of student body

 This 40 percent of the student body comes from the 80 percent who are not seniors. So half, or 50 percent , of non-seniors must have attended.

8. **(A)** Here, Watson would be very content to select either (B) $(6 + 6 = 12)$ or, more likely, (C) $(6 \times 6 = 36)$. The answer, however is (A).

 Using $2S$ to stand for the amount Sally has and C for the amount Charles has, we can express the information as follows:

 $S = C + 6$

 $C = 0.65$

 Treating these simultaneous equations, we can substitute $C + 6$ for S in the second equation and solve for C:

 $C = 0.6(C = 6)$

 $C = 0.6C + 0.36$

 $0.4C = 0.36$

 $C = 9$

9. **(D)** Here, the misleading clues point in two different directions. One, a careless reader might overlook the fact that the east side of the street uses consecutive even numbers, e.g., 122, 14, 126, etc. That mistake leads to (B) or (C). Two, even disregarding that error, Watson is likely to reason: $182 - 122 = 60$, and (since we have only the even half of the numbers, not the odds) $60 \div 2 = 30$. Too easy! The trick is that house number 122 is also painted blue, so there are $30 + 1 = 31$ blue houses.

10. **(C)** Here you can almost get the right answer just by eliminating misleading clues. If you multiply 2×3 and 7×5, you get the numbers 6 and 35. Such a simple process can't be the solution to a difficult problem, so you can eliminate both (A) and (E). Similarly, $2 + 3 = 5$ and $7 + 5 = 12$; also too easy, so you can eliminate (B) and (D), leaving only (C), which is correct.

 The solution requires that you find a common multiple for 2 and 3 and change the rations so that the Victor term is the same in both:

 $$\frac{2}{7} = \frac{2 \times 3}{7 \times 3} = \frac{6}{21}$$
 $$\frac{3}{5} = \frac{3 \times 2}{5 \times 2} = \frac{6}{10}$$

 Now you have the ratios:

 Victor:Mike::6:21

 Victor:Hank::6:10

 So Hank:Mike::10:21

11. **(D)** The most common error here would b (A). Watson recognizes that 71,111 plus 10,000 is equal to 81,111— a number in which four of the digits are the same. The difficulty with this reasoning is that 10,000 is not the smallest number that will do the trick. 71,111 plus 666 is equal to 71,777—a number in which four of the digits are the same.

12. **(B)** Here, Watson is likely to be tempted to do something as easy as multiplying 6 × 6 to get 36. But it's too easy. So in an attempt to think like Holmes, Watson reasons, "That's too easy. I bet I need to divide or multiply by 2. So it's either (C) or (E)." Good try, Watson, but that's still too easy.

    The solution is to see that each player plays the other five players 6 × 5 = 30. But each match involves two players: 30 ÷ 2 = 15.

13. **(C)** By this point we may assume that Watson has learned not to take the bait, so there is no chance that he will think 3.00 ÷ 0.25 = 12. So the correct choice cannot be (D). Once over this hurdle, if he reasons carefully, he can answer correctly. Out of the $3.00, the first dollar is for the first three minutes. this leaves $2.00 for the additional minutes: $2.00 ÷ $0.25 = 8. So the total time is the original three minutes plus the additional eight, or 11 minutes.

14. **(B)** The one thing Watson should not guess here is (E). Remember, it is unlikely that the answer to a difficult question will be "cannot be determined." The correct choice is (B). Since the average of the ten scores is 80, the total of the ten scores is $80 \times 10 = 800$. The total of the eight scores remaining after the high and low scores are cropped is $8 \times 82 = 656$. This means that the two dropped scores totaled $800 - 656 = 144$, so their average is $144 \div 2 = 72$.

15. **(C)** Here we have a similar situation. Watson will be tempted to pick (E), since the drawing doesn't provide much information. But the solution is supposed to be difficult, since this is a difficult question.

    One way of understanding the problem is to see that each of the lettered angles, when combined with an angle of the triangle, forms a straight line:

$m + x = 180$

$n + x = 180$

$o + y = 180$

$p + y = 180$

$q + z = 180$

$r + z = 180$

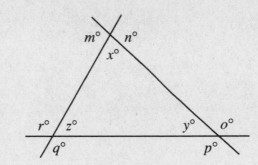

This means that:

$m + x + n + x + o + y + p + y + q + z + r + z = 6(180)$

$m + n + o + p + q + r + x + y + z + x + y + z = 6(180)$

And since $x + y + z = 180$:

$m + n + o + p + q + r + 180 + 180 = 6(180)$

$m + n + o + p + q + r = 4(180) = 720$

Problem Solving: Arithmetic

✓ **Topics Covered**

1. **Arithmetic Manipulations**

   - **Simplifying**

   - **Factoring**

   - **Calculation Shortcuts**

2. **Arithmetic Applications**

3. **Common Types of Problem Solving**

   - **Properties of Numbers**

   - **Percents**

   - **Ratios**

   - **Averages**

   - **Proportions**

4. **Testing the Test**

15

In this lesson, we discuss three topics: techniques for handling pure arithmetic manipulations, strategies for dealing with problems that require some original thinking, and hints for dealing with some often-used question types.

Arithmetic Manipulations

Some easy problem-solving questions ask for nothing more than simple addition, subtraction, multiplication, or division. These are Watson's favorites, since the obvious and correct strategy is to perform the indicated operation.

FOR SIMPLE ARITHMETIC MANIPULATIONS, JUST DO THE OPERATIONS.

EXAMPLES:

$$\frac{8}{7} \quad \frac{7}{8} =$$

Ⓐ $\frac{1}{72}$ Ⓑ $\frac{15}{72}$ Ⓒ $\frac{1}{7}$ Ⓓ $\frac{1}{8}$ Ⓔ $\frac{15}{17}$

The answer is (A), and the arithmetic is so simple that you should not hesitate to perform the subtraction indicated:

$$\frac{8}{9} - \frac{7}{8} = \frac{64 - 63}{72} = \frac{1}{72}$$

$$\sqrt{1 - \left(\frac{2}{9} + \frac{1}{36} + \frac{1}{18}\right)} =$$

Ⓐ $\frac{1}{5}$ Ⓑ $\sqrt{\frac{2}{3}}$ Ⓒ $\frac{5}{6}$ Ⓓ 1 Ⓔ $\sqrt{3}$

Again, the arithmetic is not that complicated, so you should perform the indicated operations:

$$\sqrt{1 - \left(\frac{2}{9} + \frac{1}{36} + \frac{1}{18}\right)} =$$

$$\sqrt{1 - \left(\frac{8}{36} + \frac{1}{36} + \frac{2}{36}\right)} =$$

$$\sqrt{1 - \frac{11}{36}} = \sqrt{\frac{36}{36} - \frac{11}{36}} = \sqrt{\frac{25}{36}} = \frac{5}{6}$$

Holmes Helps

Other manipulation questions are so complicated that it would take too long to perform them as written. In such cases, the questions were not written to test whether you know the basic manipulation but whether you can find an alternative solution. The test-writer has provided you with an escape route from the maze—if you can find it.

IF THE ARITHMETIC IS TOO COMPLICATED, LOOK FOR ONE OF THE FOLLOWING ESCAPE ROUTES: SIMPLIFYING, FACTORING, OR APPROXI-MATING.

1. Simplifying

EXAMPLE:

$$\frac{1}{2} \times \frac{2}{3} \times \frac{3}{4} \times \frac{4}{5} \times \frac{5}{6} \times \frac{6}{7} \times \frac{7}{8} =$$

(A) $\frac{1}{56}$ (B) $\frac{1}{8}$ (C) $\frac{28}{37}$ (D) $\frac{41}{43}$ (E) $\frac{55}{56}$

The fact that performing this operation as it is written would be tedious is a clue that an alternate route has been provided. The alternative is to simplify by canceling:

$$\frac{1}{\cancel{2}} \times \frac{\cancel{2}}{\cancel{3}} \times \frac{\cancel{3}}{\cancel{4}} \times \frac{\cancel{4}}{\cancel{5}} \times \frac{\cancel{5}}{\cancel{6}} \times \frac{\cancel{6}}{\cancel{7}} \times \frac{\cancel{7}}{8} = \frac{1}{8}$$

2. Factoring

EXAMPLES:

$$48(1) + 48(2) + 48(3) + 48(4) =$$

(A) 48   (B) 96   (C) 480   (D) 960   (E) 7,200

You could do the operations as indicated, but the fact that the process would be very time-consuming indicates that there is an alternate solution. You can factor:

$$48(1) + 48(2) + 48(3) + 48(4) =$$
$$48(1 + 2 + 3 + 4) = 48 \times 10 = 480$$

So the correct choice is (C).

$$86(37) - 37(85) =$$

(A) 0   (B) 1   (C) 37   (D) 85   (E) 86

Again, factoring is the shorter route:

$$86(37) - 37(85) = 37(86 - 85) = 37(1) = 37$$

So the correct choice is (C).

There are three factoring patterns you should memorize and always be alert for.

LEARN THE FOLLOWING PATTERNS AND BE ON THE LOOKOUT FOR OPPORTUNITIES TO USE THEM.

$$m^2 - n^2 = (m + n)(m - n)$$

$$m^2 + 2mn + n^2 = (m + n)(m + n)$$

$$m^2 - 2mn + n^2 = (m - n)(m - n)$$

The first is the most important. The second is less important, but it is still used occasionally. The third is the least important, but it is something you should know, and it is a pattern that is easily spotted.

The first pattern is called the "difference of two squares." (It is the square of one number minus the square of another.)

EXAMPLES:

$74^2 - 26^2 =$

Ⓐ 26   Ⓑ 48   Ⓒ 74   Ⓓ 4,800   Ⓔ 5,678

The answer is (D):

$$74^2 - 26^2 = (74 + 26)(74 - 26) = 100 \times 48 = 4,800$$

$125^2 - 25^2 =$

Ⓐ 25   Ⓑ 100   Ⓒ 125   Ⓓ 175   Ⓔ 15,000

The answer is (E):

$$125^2 - 25^2 = (125 + 25)(125 - 25) = 150 \times 100 = 15,000$$

Here are some questions in the second pattern.

EXAMPLES:

$36^2 + 2(36)(64) + 64^2 =$

Ⓐ 3,600   Ⓑ 6,400   Ⓒ 10,000   Ⓓ 10,300   Ⓔ 14,400

The answer is (C):

$$36^2 + 2(36)(64) + 64^2 = (36 + 64)(36 + 64) = 100 \times 100 = 10,000$$

$14^2 + 2(14)(16) + 16^2 =$

Ⓐ 28   Ⓑ 48   Ⓒ 360   Ⓓ 900   Ⓔ 2,700

The answer is (D):

$$14^2 + 2(14)(16) + 16^2 = (14 + 16)(14 + 16) = 30 \times 30 = 900$$

Finally, here is a question using the last pattern.

EXAMPLE:

$25^2 - 2(25)(15) + 15^2 =$

Ⓐ 100   Ⓑ 400   Ⓒ 900   Ⓓ 1,600   Ⓔ 2,500

The answer is (A):

$$25^2 - 2(25)(15) + 15^2 = (25 - 15)(25 - 15) = 10 \times 10 = 100$$

15

3. Approximation

> **EXAMPLES:**
>
> $2\dfrac{0.2521 \times 8.012}{1.014}$ is approximately equal to
>
> (A) 0.25   (B) 0.5   (C) 1.0   (D) 1.5   (E) 2.0

The operations indicated here are very tedious, so you are not expected to do all the arithmetic. Instead, you are specifically invited to approximate. Round 0.2521 to 0.25, 8.012 to 8, and 1.014 to 1:

$$\frac{0.25 \times 8}{1} = 2$$

And (E) must be the correct answer.

> Which of the following fractions is the largest?
>
> (A) $\dfrac{111}{221}$ (B) $\dfrac{75}{151}$ (C) $\dfrac{333}{998}$ (D) $\dfrac{113}{225}$ (E) $\dfrac{101}{301}$

One way of comparing fractions is to convert them to decimals by dividing the numerator by the denominator. That process, however, would obviously be time-consuming, so there must be an alternative.

The alternative is to approximate. A quick glance reveals that (A), (B), and (D) are all very close to $\frac{1}{2}$. (Their denominators are just about twice their numerators.) (C) and (E) are closer to $\frac{1}{3}$. Since $\frac{1}{3} < \frac{1}{2}$, you can eliminate (C) and (E).

Now take a closer look at the remaining three choices. (A) and (D) are both slightly more than $\frac{1}{2}$ (the numerator is a little more than double the denominator), but (B) is slightly less than $\frac{1}{2}$ (the numerator is slightly less than double the denominator). So we eliminate (B).

Now the choice is between (A) $\frac{111}{221}$ and (D) $\frac{113}{225}$. Since $\frac{1}{221}$ is larger than $\frac{1}{225}$, (A) is slightly larger than (D). And that's all that's needed to prove that (A) is the answer.

$$\boxed{\textbf{Calculation Shortcuts}}$$

Here are some hints to help you do calculations more quickly.

1. Divisibility

If a number is even, then it is divisible by 2; for example, 9,999,992 is divisible by 2. If a number ends in 0 or 5, it is divisible by 5; for example, 1,005 and 1,230 are divisible by 5.

If the sum of the digits of a number is divisible by 3, then the number is divisible by 3; for example, 12,327. Since $1 + 2 + 3 + 2 + 7 = 15$ and 15 is divisible by 3, 12,327 is divisible by 3

2. The Flying-X

Ordinarily when we add or subtract fractions, we look for a lowest common denominator. But that's only because we want the result in lowest terms for reasons of convenience. As long as you are prepared to reduce your final result, you don't really need to use a lowest common denominator. Instead, you can add or subtract any two fractions in the following way:

THE FLYING-X METHOD OF ADDING AND SUBTRACTING FRACTIONS

$$\frac{a}{b} + \frac{c}{d} = \frac{a}{b} + \frac{c}{d} = \frac{ad + bc}{bd}$$

$$\frac{a}{b} - \frac{c}{d} = \frac{a}{b} - \frac{c}{d} = \frac{ad - bc}{bd}$$

The method is called the "flying-x" because of the picture it creates—an x flying above the ground. (Also, it helps you fly through the calculation.) The steps are:

1. Find the new denominator by multiplying the old denominators.
2. Multiply the numerator of the first fraction by the denominator of the second fraction.
3. Multiply the denominator of the first fraction by the numerator of the second fraction.
4. Add (or subtract) the results of steps (2) and (3).

EXAMPLES:

$$\frac{4}{5} + \frac{3}{4} = \frac{4}{5} + \frac{3}{4} = \frac{16 + 15}{20} = \frac{31}{20}$$

$$\frac{4}{5} - \frac{3}{4} = \frac{4}{5} - \frac{3}{4} = \frac{16 - 15}{20} = \frac{1}{20}$$

Of course, this method does not guarantee your results will be in lowest terms, but you can correct that by reducing.

3. Decimal/Fraction Equivalents

You should memorize the following decimal/fraction equivalents:

$$\frac{1}{2} = 0.50$$

$$\frac{1}{3} = 0.33\frac{1}{3} = 0.333\ldots$$

$$\frac{1}{4} = 0.25$$

$$\frac{1}{5} = 0.20$$

$$\frac{1}{6} = 0.16\frac{2}{3} = 0.1666\ldots$$

$$\frac{1}{7} = 0.14\frac{2}{7} = 0.1428\ldots$$

$$\frac{1}{8} = 0.125$$

$$\frac{1}{9} = 0.11\frac{1}{9} = 0.1111\ldots$$

15

What about fractions like $\frac{4}{9}$ or $\frac{5}{8}$? There is no need to memorize more equivalents; just multiply. Since $\frac{1}{9}$ is approximately 0.111, $\frac{4}{9}$ is approximately 4×0.111, or 0.444; and since $\frac{1}{8}$ is 0.125, $\frac{5}{8}$ is 5×0.125, or 0.625.

Sometimes it is easier to use fractions than decimals in a calculation.

EXAMPLES:

$0.125 \times 0.125 \times 64 =$

Ⓐ 0.625   Ⓑ 0.125   Ⓒ 0.5   Ⓓ 1   Ⓔ 8

The answer is (D). The problem can be solved quickly if you convert 0.125 to its fraction equivalent, $\frac{1}{8}$.

$\frac{1}{8} \times \frac{1}{8} \times 64 = \frac{1}{64} \times 64 = 1$

$\dfrac{0.111 \times 0.666}{0.166 \times 0.125}$ is approximately

Ⓐ 6.8   Ⓑ 4.3   Ⓒ 3.6   Ⓓ 1.6   Ⓔ 0.9

Convert the decimals to their fractional approximations.

$$\dfrac{\dfrac{1}{9} \times \dfrac{2}{3}}{\dfrac{1}{6} \times \dfrac{1}{8}} = \dfrac{2}{27} \div \dfrac{1}{48} = \dfrac{2}{27} \times 48 =$$

$$\dfrac{96}{27} = 3\dfrac{5}{9} \cong 3.555$$

The final conversion can even be done in your head. Since $\frac{1}{9} \cong .111$, $\frac{5}{9} \cong 5 \times .111 = .555$.

Arithmetic Manipulations (Answers, page 271)

1. $\dfrac{1}{9} + \dfrac{1}{10} =$

   Ⓐ $\dfrac{1}{90}$ Ⓑ $\dfrac{1}{45}$ Ⓒ $\dfrac{2}{19}$ Ⓓ $\dfrac{19}{90}$ Ⓔ $\dfrac{1}{3}$

2. $\dfrac{1}{3} + \dfrac{1}{4} + \dfrac{1}{5} =$

   Ⓐ $\dfrac{1}{60}$ Ⓑ $\dfrac{1}{20}$ Ⓒ $\dfrac{1}{10}$ Ⓓ $\dfrac{47}{60}$ Ⓔ $\dfrac{65}{64}$

3. $\dfrac{12}{11} - \dfrac{11}{12} =$

   Ⓐ $\dfrac{1}{121}$ Ⓑ $\dfrac{1}{12}$ Ⓒ $\dfrac{1}{11}$ Ⓓ $\dfrac{23}{132}$ Ⓔ $\dfrac{1}{2}$

4. $\dfrac{8}{7} - \dfrac{8}{9} =$

   Ⓐ $-\dfrac{16}{63}$ Ⓑ 0 Ⓒ $\dfrac{16}{63}$ Ⓓ $\dfrac{1}{4}$ Ⓔ 4

5. $\dfrac{\dfrac{3}{5} \times \dfrac{5}{9} \times \dfrac{9}{13}}{\dfrac{13}{12} \times \dfrac{12}{11} \times \dfrac{11}{3}} =$

   Ⓐ $\dfrac{9}{169}$ Ⓑ $\dfrac{12}{123}$ Ⓒ $\dfrac{7}{47}$ Ⓓ $\dfrac{3}{5}$ Ⓔ 1

6. $\dfrac{3}{11} \times \dfrac{11}{13} \times \dfrac{13}{15} \times \dfrac{15}{17} =$

   Ⓐ $\dfrac{1}{17}$ Ⓑ $\dfrac{1}{11}$ Ⓒ $\dfrac{3}{17}$ Ⓓ $\dfrac{1}{5}$ Ⓔ $\dfrac{1}{3}$

7. Which of the following numbers is divisible by both 3 and 88?
   Ⓐ 88,888,888   Ⓑ 8,888,888   Ⓒ 888,888   Ⓓ 88,888   Ⓔ 8,888

8. Which of the following numbers is divisible by both 11 and 3?
   Ⓐ 111,111,111   Ⓑ 11,111,111   Ⓒ 1,111,111   Ⓓ 111,111   Ⓔ 11,111

9. $(0.506 \times 4.072) \div 4.08$ is approximately

   Ⓐ $\dfrac{1}{4}$ Ⓑ $\dfrac{1}{2}$ Ⓒ 1 Ⓓ 2 Ⓔ 4

15

10. $\left(\dfrac{0.889}{0.666}\right) \div \left(\dfrac{0.333}{0.625}\right)$ is approximately

    Ⓐ $\dfrac{1}{27}$ Ⓑ $\dfrac{1}{16}$ Ⓒ $\dfrac{1}{2}$ Ⓓ $\dfrac{5}{7}$ Ⓔ $\dfrac{5}{2}$

11. Which of the following fractions is the LEAST?

    Ⓐ $\dfrac{12}{119}$ Ⓑ $\dfrac{1}{10}$ Ⓒ $\dfrac{2}{21}$ Ⓓ $\dfrac{4}{39}$ Ⓔ $\dfrac{7}{69}$

12. $12{,}345(1) + 12{,}345(2) + 12{,}345(3) + 12{,}345(4) =$

    Ⓐ 66,667   Ⓑ 81,818   Ⓒ 99,999   Ⓓ 123,450   Ⓔ 127,978

13. $510^2 - 490^2 =$

    Ⓐ 16,000   Ⓑ 18,917   Ⓒ 19,470   Ⓓ 20,000   Ⓔ 24,000

14. $16^2 + 2(9)(16) + 81 =$

    Ⓐ 444   Ⓑ 500   Ⓒ 625   Ⓓ 875   Ⓔ 900

15. $\dfrac{1}{10^{22}} - \dfrac{1}{10^{23}} =$

    Ⓐ $\dfrac{1}{10}$ Ⓑ $\dfrac{9}{10^{23}}$ Ⓒ $\dfrac{1}{10^{23}}$ Ⓓ $\dfrac{-1}{10}$ Ⓔ $\dfrac{-1}{10^{22}}$

Arithmetic Applications

Some arithmetic questions require original thinking, and Watson often has difficulty with these items. Why should Watson have trouble with arithmetic questions? Because he fails to attack them in a systematic fashion. When Watson can't envision the needed sequence of operations all at once, he goes off in just any direction, adding and subtracting, multiplying and dividing, until he finally gets a wrong answer or gets so discouraged he abandons the problem as too difficult.

Holmes, on the other hand, thrives on such items because he analyzes them step by step. He knows that the question stem gives him all the clues needed to solve the mystery, if he can only put them together in the right order.

Holmes' Method for Solving Complicated Problems

---

1. What is the question to be answered?
2. What information have I been given?
3. How can I bridge the gap between (1) and (2)?
4. Execute the needed operations.

Notice that Holmes doesn't start doing arithmetic (4) until he has formulated his solution to the problem.

Here is how the method works:

EXAMPLE:

If the senior class has 360 students, of whom $\frac{5}{12}$ are women, and the junior class has 350 students, of whom $\frac{4}{7}$ are women, how many more women are there in the junior class than in the senior class?

Ⓐ $(350 - 360)\left(\frac{4}{7} - \frac{5}{12}\right)$

Ⓑ $\dfrac{(350 - 360)\left(\frac{4}{7} - \frac{5}{12}\right)}{2}$

Ⓒ $\left(\frac{4}{7} \times \frac{5}{12}\right)(360 - 350)$

Ⓓ $\left(\frac{4}{7} \times 350\right) - \left(\frac{5}{12} \times 360\right)$

Ⓔ $\left(\frac{5}{12} \times 360\right) - \left(\frac{4}{7} \times 350\right)$

15

This is a good question to illustrate logical thinking, because you don't even have to do the arithmetic. All you need to do is set up the problem.

Step 1:   **What is the question to be answered?** If the senior class has 360 students, of whom $\frac{5}{12}$ are women, and the junior class has 350 students, of whom $\frac{4}{7}$ are women, how many more women are there in the junior class than in the senior class?

Depending on how complex the problem is, Holmes might make a note of what is required on scratch paper:

Women Juniors—Women Seniors

Step 2:   **What information am I given?** The question states the total number of students in each class and the fraction who are women.

Step 3:   How can I bridge the gap? Multiplying the total number by the fraction who are women will fill in the blanks in the statement in Step 1.

Step 4:   Execute. The solution is ($\frac{4}{7} \times 350$) minus ($\frac{5}{12} \times 360$), which is choice (D).

Here is another question to illustrate how Holmes breaks a solution down into several steps:

EXAMPLE:

If the price of candy increases from 5 pounds for $7 to 3 pounds for $7, how much less candy (in pounds) can be purchased for $3.50 at the new price than at the old price?

Ⓐ $\frac{2}{7}$ Ⓑ $1\frac{17}{35}$ Ⓒ $3\frac{34}{35}$ Ⓓ 1   Ⓔ 2

Step 1:   **What is the question to be answered?** If the price of candy increases from 5 pounds for $7 to 3 pounds for $7, how much less candy (in pounds) can be purchased for $3.50 at the new price than at the old price?

In other words, you are looking for the amount $3.50 used to buy minus the amount it now buys. And because the question is fairly complex, Holmes might write this down:

amt. $3.50 old – amt. $3.50 new

Step 2:   **What information am I given?** The question gives pounds and dollars for two different prices.

Step 3:   **How can I bridge the gap?** Find the cost per pound and divide the amount you have to spend by the cost per pound. The result is the quantity you can buy.

Step 4:   **Execute.** If $7 buys 5 pounds, the cost is $7 \div 5 = \frac{7}{5}$ dollars per pound. $3.50 = \frac{7}{2}$ dollars, and $\frac{7}{2} \div \frac{7}{5} = \frac{7}{2} \times \frac{5}{7} = \frac{5}{2}$. If $7 buys 3 pounds, the cost is $7 \div 3 = \frac{7}{3}$ dollars per pound, and $\frac{7}{2} \div \frac{7}{3} = \frac{7}{2} \times \frac{3}{7} = \frac{3}{2}$. Finally, $\frac{5}{2} - \frac{3}{2} = 1$. So the correct answer is (D). (As was suggested above, we used fractions rather than decimals. This made the arithmetic in Step 4 easier.)

Learning to think in a systematic way is not easy, nor is it a skill that can be acquired just by reading about it. In this respect, systematic thinking is like playing a sport or a musical instrument. You can't just read a book about basketball or the violin and expect to become a star player or virtuoso overnight. Still, the more you practice logical thinking, the better you'll become at it. So as you do practice problems later in this book, try to break down your solutions to difficult questions into steps.

Some Common Types of Problem Solving

There are some common types of math problems that appear so frequently that you must be familiar with them and know how to solve them almost automatically.

Properties of Numbers

You should be familiar with the following principles of odd and even numbers:

EVEN + EVEN = EVEN (and EVEN − EVEN = EVEN)
EVEN + ODD = ODD (and EVEN − ODD = ODD)
ODD + ODD = EVEN (and ODD − ODD = EVEN)
EVEN × EVEN = EVEN
EVEN × ODD = EVEN
ODD × EVEN = EVEN
ODD × ODD = ODD

Note: The multiplication properties do not hold for division. This is because division may not result in a whole number; for example, $2 \div 4 = \frac{1}{2}$, a fraction. Odd and even are properties of integers, not fractions.

Questions based on these principles usually ask that you make a judgment about the "structure" of a number.

EXAMPLE:

If n is an odd integer, which of the following must also be odd?

I. $n + n$
II. $n + n + n$
III. $n \times n \times n$

Ⓐ I only   Ⓑ II only   Ⓒ III only   Ⓓ II and III only   Ⓔ I, II, and III

The answer is (D). As for I, since n is odd, $n + n$ must be even. As for II, since $n + n$ is even, $n + (n + n)$ must be odd. And as for III, since n is odd, $n \times n$ is odd, and so $n \times (n \times n)$ also is odd.

In the example just studied, the question specifies that n is an odd number. You get a different answer if the question is changed to specify that n is an even number.

15

EXAMPLE:

If n is an even integer, which of the following must also be even?

I. $n + n$

II. $n + n + n$

III. $n \times n \times n$

Ⓐ I only   Ⓑ II only   Ⓒ III only   Ⓓ II and III only   Ⓔ I, II, and III

Now the answer is (E).
Some structures are odd or even no matter what the value of n.

EXAMPLE:

If n is an integer, which of the following must be even?

I. $2n$

II. $2n + n$

III. $2n \times n$

Ⓐ I only   Ⓑ II only   Ⓒ III only   Ⓓ I and II only   Ⓔ I and III only

The answer is (E). As for item I, $2n$ has the structure $2 \times n$, so no matter what the value of n, $2n$ must be even. As for III, since $2n$ is even, $2n \times n$ must be even (an even number times any other number always yields an even number.) II, however, may or may not be even. Although we know that $2n$ is even, $2n + n$ will be even only if n is even (even plus even); if n is odd, $2n + n$ will be odd (even plus odd).

A variation on this type of question uses the phrase *consecutive integers*.
CONSECUTIVE INTEGERS ARE INTEGERS IN A ROW: 3, 4, 5, AND 6 ARE CONSECUTIVE INTEGERS, AS ARE –2, –1, 0, 1, AND 2.

Since a number in a series of consecutive integers is just one more than its predecessor and one less than its successor, consecutive integers can be represented as: n, $n + 1$, $n + 2$, $n + 3$, and so on.

EXAMPLE:

Which of the following represents the product of two consecutive integers?

Ⓐ $2n + 1$ Ⓑ $2n + n$ Ⓒ $2n^2$ Ⓓ $n^2 + 1$ Ⓔ $n^2 + n$

The answer is (E). If n is an integer, the next larger consecutive integer is just one more: $n + 1$. And the product of n and $n + 1$ is $n(n + 1) = n^2 + n$. Sometimes a question will ask about consecutive even numbers or consecutive odd numbers.

EXAMPLES:

If n is an odd number, which of the following represents the third odd number following n?

Ⓐ $n + 3$ Ⓑ $n + 4$ Ⓒ $n + 6$ Ⓓ $3n + 3$ Ⓔ $4n + 4$

The answer is (C). If n is an odd number, the next odd number is $n + 2$, then $n + 4$, then $n + 6$.

If n is the first number in a series of three consecutive even numbers, which of the following represents the sum of the three numbers?

Ⓐ $n + 2$ Ⓑ $n + 4$ Ⓒ $n + 6$ Ⓓ $3n + 6$ Ⓔ $6(3n)$

The answer is (D). Since n is even, the next even number is $n + 2$ and the one following that is $n + 4$. The sum of n, $n + 2$, and $n + 4$ is $n + n + 2 + n + 4 = 3n + 6$.

Notice that in the two previous examples, it was stipulated that n was either odd or even. This is important, because $n + 2$ can be either odd or even, depending on whether n is odd or even.

> **EXAMPLES:**
>
> If n is any integer, which of the following is always an odd integer?
>
> Ⓐ $n - 1$ Ⓑ $n + 1$ Ⓒ $n + 2$ Ⓓ $2n + 1$ Ⓔ $2n + 2$

The answer is (D). Since n can be either even or odd, $n - 1$, $n + 1$ and $n + 2$ can be either even or odd. $2n + 1$, however, must always be odd. No matter what n is, $2n$ is even, and $2n + 1$ must be odd. By the same reasoning, (E) must always be even.

The behavior of positive and negative numbers is also a basis for questions. You should know the following principles:

POSITIVE × POSITIVE = POSITIVE (and POSITIVE ÷ POSITIVE = POSITIVE)
POSITIVE × NEGATIVE = NEGATIVE (and POSITIVE ÷ NEGATIVE = NEGATIVE)
NEGATIVE × POSITIVE = NEGATIVE (and NEGATIVE ÷ POSITIVE = NEGATIVE)
NEGATIVE × NEGATIVE = POSITIVE (and NEGATIVE ÷ NEGATIVE = POSITIVE)

> If n is a negative number, which of the following must be positive?
>
> I. $2n$
> II. n^2
> III. n^5
>
> Ⓐ I only   Ⓑ II only   Ⓒ III only   Ⓓ I and II only   Ⓔ II and III only

The answer is (B). Since n is negative, $2n$ must also be negative. As for III, since n is negative, $(n \times n) \times (n \times n) \times n$ is a positive times a positive, which is a positive, multiplied by a negative. So the final result is negative. II, however, must be positive, since n^2 is just $n \times n$, and a negative times a negative yields a positive.

Finally, fractions have a peculiar characteristic that might be the basis for a question.

> THE RESULT OBTAINED FROM MULTIPLYING A FRACTION BY ITSELF IS SMALLER THAN THE ORIGINAL FRACTION; FOR EXAMPLE, $\frac{1}{2} \times \frac{1}{2} \times \frac{1}{2} = \frac{1}{8}$ AND $\frac{1}{8} < \frac{1}{2}$.

> **EXAMPLE:**
>
> If $0 < x < 1$, which of the following is the largest?
>
> Ⓐ x Ⓑ $2x$ Ⓒ x^2 Ⓓ x^3 Ⓔ $x + 1$

The answer is (E). When a fraction is raised to a power, the result is smaller than the original fraction, so (C) and (D) are smaller than (A). (B), however, is double (A), so (B) is larger. But finally, (E) is larger than (B). $2x$ is equal to $x + x$, and since $1 > x$, (E) must be larger than (B).

If you know the general principles just discussed and apply them correctly, you should be able to handle any question about properties of numbers. If, however, you find that you are having trouble, fall back on the simplistic, yet very effective, technique of substitution.

15

AS A LAST RESORT, TRY SUBSTITUTING NUMBERS.

Just pick some values and test them in the choices.

> **EXAMPLE:**
>
> If $-1 < x < 0$, which of the following is the largest?
>
>   Ⓐ -1 Ⓑ x Ⓒ $2x$ Ⓓ x^3 Ⓔ $x-1$

The correct choice is (D), but the problem is a little tricky. You might want to test a value, for example, $-\frac{1}{2}$. On the assumption that $x = -\frac{1}{2}$, the choices have these values:

  Ⓐ -1 Ⓑ $-\frac{1}{2}$ Ⓒ -1 Ⓓ $-\frac{1}{8}$ Ⓔ $-1\frac{1}{2}$

The largest of these is $-\frac{1}{8}$.

Properties of Numbers (Answers, page 272)

1. If n is an even number, all of the following must also be even EXCEPT
    Ⓐ n^3 Ⓑ n^2 Ⓒ $2n$ Ⓓ $2n + n$ Ⓔ $2n + 5$

2. If $3n$ is an even number, which of the following must be an odd number?
    Ⓐ n Ⓑ $2n$ Ⓒ $n + 1$ Ⓓ $n + 2$ Ⓔ n^2

3. If n is an integer, which of the following must be an odd number?
    Ⓐ $n + 1$ Ⓑ $2n$ Ⓒ $2n + 1$ Ⓓ $2(n + 1)$ Ⓔ $3(n + 1)$

4. If $m, n, o, p,$ and q are integers, then $m(n + o)(p - q)$ must be even when which of the following is even?
    Ⓐ $m + n$ Ⓑ $n + p$ Ⓒ m Ⓓ o Ⓔ p

5. If n is an integer, which of the following *must* be even?
    Ⓐ $n - 1$ Ⓑ $n + 1$ Ⓒ $3n + 1$ Ⓓ $2n + 2$ Ⓔ $2n + n$

6. If p is the smallest of three consecutive integers, $p, q,$ and r, what is the sum of q and r expressed in terms of p?
    Ⓐ $3p + 3$ Ⓑ $3p + 1$ Ⓒ $2p + 3$ Ⓓ $2p + 1$ Ⓔ $2p$

7. If the fifth number in a series of five consecutive integers has the value $n + 3$, what is the first number in the series expressed in terms of n?
    Ⓐ 0 Ⓑ 1 Ⓒ $n - 1$ Ⓓ $n - 3$ Ⓔ $-4n$

8. If n is negative, all BUT which of the following must also be negative?
    Ⓐ n^5 Ⓑ n^3 Ⓒ $\dfrac{1}{n}$ Ⓓ $\dfrac{1}{n^2}$ Ⓔ $\dfrac{1}{n^3}$

9. If $x = -1$, which of the following is the largest?
    Ⓐ $2x$ Ⓑ x Ⓒ $\dfrac{x}{2}$ Ⓓ x^2 Ⓔ x^3

10. If x is greater than zero but less than 1, which of the following is the largest?
    Ⓐ $\dfrac{1}{x^2}$ Ⓑ $\dfrac{1}{x}$ Ⓒ x Ⓓ x^2 Ⓔ x^3

15

Percents

Aside from the very basic operation of taking a percent of some number (for example, 25 percent of 60 = 15), there are really only two different kinds of percent questions. One question asks for the ratio of two numbers expressed as a percent (for example, 4 is what percent of 20?); the other asks about percent change in a quantity.

All percent questions in the first category can be solved by a simple Holmesian device called the "this-of-that" strategy. Compare the following questions:

> What percent is 4 of 20?
>
> 4 is what percent of 20?
>
> Of 20, what percent is 4?

The questions are equivalent, for they all ask for the same thing: express $\frac{4}{20}$ as a percent. Notice also that in each there is the phrase "of 20" and the other number, 4.

Generally, then, these questions all have the form:

> What percent is this of that?
>
> This is what percent of that?
>
> Of that, what percent is this?

You can solve any question of this type using the "this-of-that" strategy.

> THIS-OF-THAT: CREATE A FRACTION IN WHICH THE NUMBER IN THE PHRASE "OF THAT" IS THE DENOMINATOR AND THE OTHER NUMBER IN THE QUESTION (THE "THIS") IS THE NUMERATOR. CONVERT THE FRACTION TO A PERCENT.

EXAMPLES:

If a jar contains 24 white marbles and 48 black marbles, then what percent of all the marbles in the jar are black?

   Ⓐ 20%   Ⓑ 25%   Ⓒ $33\frac{1}{3}$% Ⓓ 60%   Ⓔ $66\frac{2}{3}$%

Using the "this-of-that" strategy, we create a fraction:

$$\frac{\text{black marbles}}{\text{of all marbles}} = \frac{48}{24 + 48} = \frac{48}{72} = \frac{2}{3} = 66\frac{2}{3}\%$$

Three friends shared the cost of a tape recorder. If Andy, Barbara, and Donna each paid $12, $30, and $18, respectively, then Donna paid what percent of the cost of the tape recorder?

   Ⓐ 10%   Ⓑ 30%   Ⓒ $33\frac{1}{3}$% Ⓓ 50%   Ⓔ $66\frac{2}{3}$%

In this question, the phrase "of the cost" establishes the denominator. The cost is 12 + 30 + 18 = 60. The numerator is the other item in the question. Donna's contribution:

$$\frac{\text{Donna's}}{\text{Total}} = \frac{18}{60} = \frac{3}{10} = 30\%$$

The other type of percent question asks about the percent change in a quantity. The Holmesian strategy for such questions is the "change-over" formula.

EXAMPLE:

If the price of an item increased from $5.00 to $5.25, what was the percent increase in the price?

Ⓐ 50%   Ⓑ 25%   Ⓒ 20%   Ⓓ 5%   Ⓔ 4%

The answer is (D).

CHANGE-OVER STRATEGY: TO FIND PERCENT CHANGE, CREATE A FRACTION. PUT THE CHANGE IN THE QUANTITY OVER THE ORIGINAL AMOUNT. CONVERT THE FRACTION TO A PERCENT.

$$\frac{\text{Change}}{\text{Original Amount}} = \frac{5.25 - 5.00}{5.00} = \frac{0.25}{5.00} = 0.05 = 5\%$$

The "change-over strategy" works for decreases as well.

EXAMPLE:

If the population of a town was 20,000 in 1970 and 16,000 in 1980, what was the percent decline in the town's population?

Ⓐ 50%   Ⓑ 25%   Ⓒ 20%   Ⓓ 10%   Ⓔ 5%

$$\frac{\text{Change}}{\text{Original Amount}} = \frac{20,000 - 16,000}{20,000} = \frac{4,000}{20,000} = \frac{1}{5} = 20\%$$

So there was a 20-percent decline in the town's population.

Be careful that you don't confuse the two strategies. Compare the following three questions.

EXAMPLES:

If 20 people attended Professor Rodriguez's class on Monday and 25 attended on Tuesday, the number of people who attended on Monday was what percent of the number who attended on Tuesday?

Ⓐ 5%   Ⓑ 20%   Ⓒ 25%   Ⓓ 80%   Ⓔ 125%

If 20 people attended Professor Rodriguez's class on Monday and 25 attended on Tuesday, the number of people who attended on Tuesday was what percent of the number who attended on Monday?

Ⓐ 5%   Ⓑ 20%   Ⓒ 25%   Ⓓ 80%   Ⓔ 125%

If 20 people attended Professor Rodriguez's class on Monday and 25 attended on Tuesday, what was the percent increase in attendance from Monday to Tuesday?

Ⓐ 5%   Ⓑ 20%   Ⓒ 25%   Ⓓ 80%   Ⓔ 125%

Only the third question asks about percent change; the first two questions are of the form "this-of-that." So the answer to the first question is $\frac{20}{25} = \frac{4}{5} = 80\%$, or (D). The answer to the second question is $\frac{25}{20} = \frac{5}{4} = 125\%$, or (E). And the answer to the third question, using the "change-over" strategy, is $\frac{25-20}{20} = \frac{5}{20} = \frac{1}{4} = 25\%$, or (C).

15

Percents (Answers, page 273)

1. A certain company has 120 employees. If 24 of the employees are in the union, what percent of the employees are not in the union?

   Ⓐ 12%　Ⓑ 24%　Ⓒ 48%　Ⓓ 80%　Ⓔ 96%

2. In 1960, a certain tree was 12 meters tall. If the tree measured 15 meters in 1985, by what percent did its height increase?

   Ⓐ 3%　Ⓑ 25%　Ⓒ 40%　Ⓓ 80%　Ⓔ 125%

3. At 9:00 a.m. on Monday the price of gold was $450 an ounce. If the price of gold at 3:00 that same day was $441 per ounce, what was the percent decrease in the price of gold during the day?

   Ⓐ 98%　Ⓑ 9.8%　Ⓒ 9%　Ⓓ 2%　Ⓔ 0.2%

4. In 1940, the price of a certain item was $0.20. If the same item cost $1.00 in 1987, what was the percent increase in the price of the item?

   Ⓐ 20%　Ⓑ 80%　Ⓒ 120%　Ⓓ 400%　Ⓔ 500%

5. In a certain school, 40 percent of the students are boys. If there are 80 boys in the school, what is the total number of students in the school?

   Ⓐ 32　Ⓑ 50　Ⓒ 120　Ⓓ 200　Ⓔ 320

6. The price of an item increased by 25 percent. If the price of the item after the increase is $2.00, what was the original price?

   Ⓐ $1.50　Ⓑ $1.60　Ⓒ $1.75　Ⓓ $2.50　Ⓔ $3.20

Average Price of Metal X (per ounce)	
1991	$10
1992	$11
1993	$12
1994	$15
1995	$18
1996	$21

7. The greatest percent increase in the average price per ounce of metal X occurred during which period?

    Ⓐ 1991–1992 Ⓑ 1992–1993 Ⓒ 1993–1994
    Ⓓ 1994–1995 Ⓔ 1995–1996

Use the following table for questions 8–10.

Number of Fires in City Y	
1992	100
1993	125
1994	140
1995	150
1996	135

8. The number of fires in 1992 was what percent of the number of fires in 1993?

    Ⓐ 25% Ⓑ $66\frac{2}{3}$% Ⓒ 80% Ⓓ 100% Ⓔ 125%

9. The number of fires in 1996 was what percent of the number of fires in 1995?

    Ⓐ 90% Ⓑ 82% Ⓒ 50% Ⓓ 25% Ⓔ 10%

10. What was the percent decrease in the number of fires from 1995 to 1996?

    Ⓐ 10% Ⓑ 25% Ⓒ 50% Ⓓ 82% Ⓔ 90%

15

Ratios

In addition to understanding the basic idea of a ratio, you may be asked to divide a quantity according to ratio parts or to work with a three-part ratio. First, you may be asked to divide a quantity according to a ratio.

TO DISTRIBUTE A QUANTITY ACCORDING TO A RATIO, DIVIDE THE QUANTITY BY THE TOTAL NUMBER OF RATIO PARTS. THEN MULTIPLY THAT RESULT BY THE NUMBER OF PARTS TO BE DISTRIBUTED.

EXAMPLE:

A groom must divide 12 quarts of oats between two horses. If Dobbin is to receive twice as much as Pegasus, how many quarts of oats should the groom give to Dobbin?

Ⓐ 4   Ⓑ 6   Ⓒ 8   Ⓓ 9   Ⓔ 10

The answer is (C). The oats must be divided according to the ratio 2:1. There are 2 + 1 = 3 ratio parts, so each part is 12 ÷ 3 = 4 quarts. Dobbin gets two parts, or 2 × 4 = 8 quarts.

The other type of ratio question involves three parts.

EXAMPLE:

If the ratio of John's allowance to Lucy's allowance is 3:2, and the ratio of Lucy's allowance to Bob's allowance is 3:4, what is the ratio of John's allowance to Bob's allowance?

Ⓐ 1:6   Ⓑ 2:5   Ⓒ 1:2   Ⓓ 3:4   Ⓔ 9:8

The answer is (E). In a problem like this, the middle term (the one that appears in both ratios) joins the other two terms like a common denominator. Here, the common term is Lucy's allowance. Adjust the ratios so that the "Lucy" term has the same value in both ratios. The ratio of John's allowance to Lucy's is 3:2, and that is equivalent to 9:6. The ratio of Lucy's allowance to Bob's is 3:4, and that is equivalent to 6:8. So the ratio John:Lucy:Bob is 9:6:8, and the ratio John:Bob is 9:8.

Ratios (Answers, page 274)

1. In a certain box of candy, the ratio of light chocolates to dark chocolates is 4:5. If the box contains 36 candies, how many of the candies are dark chocolates?

   Ⓐ 9   Ⓑ 18   Ⓒ 20   Ⓓ 24   Ⓔ 27

2. In a certain school, the ratio of Seniors to Juniors is 5:4, and the ratio of Seniors to Sophomores is 6:5. What is the ratio of Sophomores to Juniors?

   Ⓐ 2:3   Ⓑ 25:24   Ⓒ 1   Ⓓ 24:25   Ⓔ 3:2

3. In a certain library, the ratio of fiction to nonfiction books is 3:5. If the library contains a total of 8,000 books, how many of the books are nonfiction?

   Ⓐ 2,400   Ⓑ 3,000   Ⓒ 3,600   Ⓓ 4,800   Ⓔ 5,000

4. In a certain game, 3 nurbs are equal to 2 zimps, and 6 clabs are equal to 1 zimp. 4 clabs are equal to how many nurbs?

   Ⓐ 1   Ⓑ 2   Ⓒ 3   Ⓓ 4   Ⓔ 5

5. A $1,000 bonus is to be divided among three people so that Jane receives twice as much as Robert, who receives $\frac{1}{5}$ as much as Wendy. How much money should Wendy receive?

   Ⓐ $100   Ⓑ $125   Ⓒ $250   Ⓓ $375   Ⓔ $625

15

Averages

Aside from the very simple question that asks you to calculate the average of several numbers, there are two questions about averages that you should know about.
The first kind asks about a missing element.

> **EXAMPLE:**
>
> If the average of 35, 38, 41, 43, and x is 37, what is x?
>
> Ⓐ 28   Ⓑ 30   Ⓒ 31   Ⓓ 34   Ⓔ 36

The answer is (A). Using the general idea of average:

$$\frac{35+38+41+43+x}{5} = 37$$

So: $35 + 38 + 41 + 43 + x = (5)37$

$157 + x = 185$

$x = 28$

THE DIFFERENCE OF THE SUMS METHOD FOR FINDING THE MISSING QUANTITY (OR QUANTITIES) OF AN AVERAGE:

(1) FIND THE SUM OF ALL THE QUANTITIES BY MULTIPLYING THE AVERAGE BY THE TOTAL NUMBER OF QUANTITIES.

(2) ADD UP THE KNOWN QUANTITIES.

(3) SUBTRACT THE RESULT OF (2) FROM THE RESULT OF (1). THE DIFFERENCE IS THE MISSING QUANTITY (OR THE SUM OF THE MISSING QUANTITIES.)

In the question above, the total of all five elements in the average had to be 185. But the total of the four we were given was only 157. So the missing element had to be 185 – 157 = 28.
There is a Holmesian shortcut you can use with this type of problem.

THE AVERAGE IS THE "MIDPOINT" OF THE NUMBERS AVERAGED.

So if the average of 35, 38, 41, 43, and x is 37, the values in excess of 37 must equal the values below 37. Instead of doing an "official" calculation, you can reason that 35 is 2 below the average, or –2; 38 is one over, or +1; 41 is 4 over, or +4; and 43 is 6 over, or +6. Now you add up those numbers: –2 + 1 + 4 + 6 = + 9. To offset this overage and bring the average down to 37, the missing number must be 9 less than 37, or 28. You can check this result by calculating the average using 28.
As you might have already guessed, there are some variations on this theme, but all can be solved in essentially the same way.

> **EXAMPLES:**
>
> For a certain student, the average of ten test scores is 80. If the high and low scores are dropped, the average is 81. What is the average of the high and low scores?
>
> Ⓐ 76   Ⓑ 78   Ⓒ 80   Ⓓ 81   Ⓔ 82

The answer is (A). The sum of the ten test scores is $80 \times 10 = 800$. The sum of the eight scores after the two scores have been dropped is $8 \times 81 = 648$. So the two scores that were dropped total $800 - 648 = 152$. And since there are two of them, their average is $152 \div 2 = 76$.

> In a certain shipment, the average weight of six packages is 50 pounds. If another package is added to the shipment, the average weight of the seven packages is 52 pounds. What is the weight (in pounds) of the additional package?
>
> Ⓐ 2　　Ⓑ 7　　Ⓒ 52　　Ⓓ 62　　Ⓔ 64

The answer is (E). The total weight of the original six packages is $6 \times 50 = 300$ pounds. The total weight of the seven packages is $7 \times 52 = 364$ pounds. So the weight of the final package is $364 - 300 = 64$ pounds.

The other unusual average question that you might encounter is a weighted average.

> **EXAMPLES:**
>
> In a certain course, a student's final exam grade is weighted twice as heavily as his midterm grade. If a student receives a score of 84 on his final exam and 90 on his midterm, what is his average for the course?
>
> Ⓐ 88　　Ⓑ 87.5　　Ⓒ 86　　Ⓓ 86.5　　Ⓔ 85

The answer is (C). You have to be sure you weight the final exam grade twice as much as the midterm grade:

$$\frac{90 + 2(84)}{3} = \frac{258}{3} = 86$$

In calculating a weighted average, there are two things to watch out for. One, make sure you have the average weighted properly. Two, make sure you divide by the correct number of quantities.

> In a certain group of children, three of the children are ten years old and two of the children are five years old. What is the average age in years of the children in the group?
>
> Ⓐ 6　　Ⓑ 6.5　　Ⓒ 7　　Ⓓ 7.5　　Ⓔ 8

The answer is (E).

$$\frac{3(10) + 2(5)}{5} = \frac{40}{5} = 8$$

Notice that we weight the ages according to the number of children in the group, and then we divide by 5 (the number of children in the group).

15

Averages (Answers, page 275)

1. If the average of six numbers—12, 15, 18, 14, 13, and x—is 14, what is x?

    Ⓐ 10   Ⓑ 11   Ⓒ 12   Ⓓ 13   Ⓔ 14

2. The average weight of four packages on a scale is 16 pounds. When one of those packages is removed, the average of the remaining three packages is 14 pounds. What is the weight in pounds of the package that was removed?

    Ⓐ 16   Ⓑ 18   Ⓒ 21   Ⓓ 22   Ⓔ 24

3. Herman purchased three books that cost $2, five books that cost $3, and one book that costs $6. What was the average cost of the books?

    Ⓐ $3   Ⓑ $4   Ⓒ $5   Ⓓ $6   Ⓔ $7

4. On a certain toll road, the toll charge is 10 cents per mile for the first 50 miles, 20 cents per mile for the next 20 miles, and 30 cents per mile for the last 10 miles. What is the average cost per mile (in cents) for the entire trip?

    Ⓐ 10.5   Ⓑ 12   Ⓒ 12.5   Ⓓ 15   Ⓔ 18

5. The average weight of ten people sitting in a boat is 145 pounds. If one person gets out of the boat, the average weight of the remaining people is 150 pounds. What is the weight in pounds of the person who got out of the boat?

    Ⓐ 90   Ⓑ 100   Ⓒ 120   Ⓓ 150   Ⓔ 175

Proportions

The simplest of all problems with a proportion asks that you solve for an unknown quantity.

EXAMPLE:

If $\frac{2}{3} = \frac{x}{12}$, $x =$

Ⓐ 3   Ⓑ 4   Ⓒ 6   Ⓓ 8   Ⓔ 9

To solve, you cross-multiply:

$\frac{2}{3} = \frac{x}{12}$

$2(12) = 3x$

$3x = 24$

Then you divide both sides by 3:

$3x \div 3 = 24 \div 3$

$x = 8$

Proportions also provide you with a powerful Holmesian strategy for solving word problems that ask about things like cost, output, distance, and so on.

IF A QUESTION INVOLVES QUANTITIES THAT CHANGE IN THE SAME DIRECTION WITH ONE ANOTHER, USE A PROPORTION TO SOLVE FOR UNKNOWN QUANTITIES.

EXAMPLES:

If 4.5 pounds of chocolate cost $10, how many pounds of chocolate can be purchased for $12?

Ⓐ $4\frac{3}{4}$ Ⓑ $5\frac{2}{5}$ Ⓒ $5\frac{1}{2}$ Ⓓ $5\frac{3}{4}$ Ⓔ 6

This is not a difficult question, and Watson will probably get it right. He reasons that $10 buys $4\frac{1}{2}$ pounds of chocolate, so the cost per pound is $10 \div 4\frac{1}{2} = \$2\frac{2}{9}$. (We use a fraction to avoid the repeating decimal 2.222 . . . .) Next, Watson divides: $12 \div 2\frac{2}{9} = 5\frac{2}{5}$. So (B) is the answer.

There is nothing conceptually wrong with what Watson has done, but the same result can be achieved more easily by using a proportion:

$\frac{\text{Amount } x}{\text{Amount } y} = \frac{\text{Cost } x}{\text{Cost } y}$

Cross-multiply: $\frac{4.5}{x} = \frac{10}{12}$

$54 = 10x$

Solve for x: $x = 5\frac{2}{5}$

15

At a certain school, 45 percent of the students purchased a yearbook. If 540 students purchased yearbooks, how many students did not buy a yearbook?

  Ⓐ 243   Ⓑ 540   © 575   Ⓓ 660   Ⓔ 957

Set up a proportion. Since 45 percent bought a yearbook, 55 percent did not.

$$\frac{45\%}{55\%} = \frac{540}{x}$$

First, you can cancel the percent signs:

$$\frac{45}{55} = \frac{540}{x}$$

Cross-multiply: $45x = 55(540)$

Solve for x: $x = \dfrac{55(540)}{45} = \dfrac{11(540)}{9} = 660$

This method will work in all of the following situations and more:

The greater (or less) the quantity, the greater (or less) the cost (and vice versa).

The greater (or less) the quantity, the greater (or less) the weight (and vice versa).

The greater (or less) the number, the greater (or less) the percent of the whole (and vice versa).

The longer (or shorter) the working time, the greater (or less) the output, assuming constant rate of operation (and vice versa).

The longer (or shorter) the travel time, the greater (or less) the distance traveled, assuming constant speed (and vice versa).

The only things to watch for are those situations in which the quantities vary indirectly.

EXAMPLE:

Walking at a constant rate of 4 miles per hour, it takes Jill exactly one hour to walk home from school. If she walks at a constant rate of 5 miles per hour, how many minutes will the trip take?

  Ⓐ 48   Ⓑ 54   © 56   Ⓓ 72   Ⓔ 112

In this case, the faster the speed, the shorter the time. So we use an indirect proportion. Set up the proportion as usual (being sure to group like terms):

$$\frac{60}{x} = \frac{4}{5}$$

Then invert the right side of the proportion:

$$\frac{60}{x} = \frac{5}{4}$$

And solve for x:

$$5x = 4\,(60)$$

$$x = \frac{4(60)}{5} = 48 \text{ minutes}$$

Proportions (Answers, page 275)

1. A roll of metal ribbon that weighs 12 pounds is cut into two pieces. One piece is 75 feet long and weighs 9 pounds. What was the length, in feet, of the original roll?

   Ⓐ 60   Ⓑ 90   Ⓒ 100   Ⓓ 120   Ⓔ 150

2. A car traveling at a constant 50 miles per hour covers the same distance in one hour as a car traveling at a constant 25 miles per hour for how many hours?

   Ⓐ $\frac{1}{3}$ Ⓑ $\frac{1}{2}$ Ⓒ 1   Ⓓ 2   Ⓔ 3

3. A recipe calls for three eggs and two cups of milk. If a quantity of the recipe is prepared using eight eggs, how many cups of milk should be used?

   Ⓐ 4   Ⓑ $4\frac{2}{3}$ Ⓒ $5\frac{1}{3}$ Ⓓ $5\frac{1}{2}$ Ⓔ $5\frac{2}{3}$

4. If 8 pounds of coffee cost $50, how much do 12 pounds of coffee cost?

   Ⓐ $25.00   Ⓑ $62.50   Ⓒ $75.00   Ⓓ $80.00   Ⓔ $84.00

5. Three printing presses can finish a certain job in 60 minutes. How many minutes will it take five such printing presses to do the same job?

   Ⓐ 15   Ⓑ 20   Ⓒ 30   Ⓓ 36   Ⓔ 100

6. If 4 gallons of water occupy 30 cubic feet of space, how many gallons are needed to fill a tank with a capacity of 360 cubic feet?

   Ⓐ 12   Ⓑ 24   Ⓒ 30   Ⓓ 36   Ⓔ 48

7. A repair shop can paint three cars every four hours. At that rate, how many hours will it take the shop to paint five cars?

   Ⓐ $6\frac{1}{3}$ Ⓑ $6\frac{2}{3}$ Ⓒ $7\frac{1}{3}$ Ⓓ $7\frac{1}{2}$ Ⓔ $7\frac{3}{4}$

8. If a machine seals cans at the rate of $4\frac{1}{2}$ cans every three seconds, how many minutes will it take the machine to seal 720 cans?

   Ⓐ 6   Ⓑ 8   Ⓒ 18   Ⓓ 36   Ⓔ 48

9. At a certain factory, it takes five metal fasteners to attach a muffler to a car. If a box containing 500 fasteners costs $42, how much will it cost to buy the exact number of fasteners needed to attach 300 mufflers?

   Ⓐ $14   Ⓑ $36   Ⓒ $56   Ⓓ $126   Ⓔ $4,200

10. In a certain population, only 0.03 percent of the people have physical trait X. On the average, it will be necessary to screen how many people to find six with trait X?

    Ⓐ 180   Ⓑ 200   Ⓒ 1,800   Ⓓ 2,000   Ⓔ 20,000

15

> **Testing the Test**

It cannot be said often enough that the correct answer to every single math problem is right there on the page. This sets up a Holmesian strategy that can be applied to many different kinds of problems:

TEST THE TEST

Instead of trying to devise a mathematical solution to a problem, just test the available choices until you find one that works.

> **EXAMPLE:**
>
> Which of the following is the larger of two numbers the product of which is 600 and the sum of which is five times the difference between the two?
>
> Ⓐ 10   Ⓑ 15   Ⓒ 20   Ⓓ 30   Ⓔ 50

It would be foolish to try to devise some mathematical approach to this question. All you need to do is test answers until you find one that works. First, we can eliminate (A), (B), and (C). Though those are factors of 600, they are not the *larger* of their respective pairs, as required by the question.

Next we test (D). $30 \times 20 = 600$, and $30 + 20 = 50$, which is $5 \times 30 - 20 = 10$. Since 30 meets the requirements, it must be the correct choice.

Testing the Test (Answers, page 278)

Directions: Solve each of the following questions by testing answer choices.

1. If $\frac{1}{3}$ of a number is 3 more than $\frac{1}{4}$ of the number, then what is the number?

Ⓐ 18   Ⓑ 24   Ⓒ 30   Ⓓ 36   Ⓔ 48

2. If $\frac{3}{5}$ of a number is 4 more than $\frac{1}{2}$ of the number, then what is the number?

Ⓐ 20   Ⓑ 28   Ⓒ 35   Ⓓ 40   Ⓔ 56

3. When both 16 and 9 are divided by n, the remainder is 2. What is n?

Ⓐ 3   Ⓑ 4   Ⓒ 5   Ⓓ 6   Ⓔ 7

4. The sum of the digits of a three-digit number is 16. If the tens digit of the number is 3 times the units digit, and the units digit is $\frac{1}{4}$ of the hundreds digit, then what is the number?

Ⓐ 446   Ⓑ 561   Ⓒ 682   Ⓓ 862   Ⓔ 914

5. If the sum of five consecutive integers is 40, what is the smallest of the five integers?

Ⓐ 4   Ⓑ 5   Ⓒ 6   Ⓓ 7   Ⓔ 8

15

Summary

1. If a problem presents an easy arithmetic manipulation, just do the indicated operations. If the indicated operations are too complex, look for an alternative approach such as simplifying, factoring, or approximating.

2. If a problem is very complicated, break your solution of the problem down into steps:
    (1) What is the question to be answered?
    (2) What information have I been given?
    (3) How can I bridge the gap between (1) and (2)?
    (4) Execute the needed operations.

3. The following principles are often tested:
    (a) properties of numbers (odd and even, positive and negative, and fractions)
    (b) percents (the "this of that" and the "change over" strategies)
    (c) ratios (basic ratios and ratio parts)
    (d) averages (simple averages and weighted averages)
    (e) proportions (direct and indirect)

4. Sometimes the best attack strategy is just to test answer choices until you find the correct one.

Explanatory Answers

EXERCISE 1

1. **(D)** This is a case for the "flying x":

$$\frac{1}{9}+\frac{1}{10} = \frac{9+10}{90} = \frac{19}{90}$$

2. **(D)** Don't worry about common denominators. Just perform the "flying x" twice.

$$\frac{1}{3}+\frac{1}{4} = \frac{4+3}{12} = \frac{7}{12}$$

$$\frac{7}{12}+\frac{1}{5} = \frac{35+12}{60} = \frac{47}{60}$$

3. **(D)** Again, the "flying x."

$$\frac{12}{11}-\frac{11}{12} = \frac{144-121}{132} = \frac{23}{132}$$

4. **(C)** The mighty "flying x."

$$\frac{8}{7}-\frac{8}{9} = \frac{72-56}{63} = \frac{16}{63}$$

5. **(A)** The escape route out of this maze of calculations is canceling to simplify:

$$\frac{\frac{3}{5}\times\frac{5}{9}\times\frac{9}{13}}{\frac{13}{12}\times\frac{12}{11}\times\frac{11}{3}} = \frac{3}{13}\div\frac{13}{3} = \frac{3}{13}\times\frac{3}{13} = \frac{9}{169}$$

6. **(C)** Again, you can cancel:

$$\frac{3}{11}\times\frac{11}{13}\times\frac{13}{15}\times\frac{15}{17} = \frac{3}{17}$$

7. **(C)** A quick check shows that (B) and (D) are not divisible by 88. After that, if a number is divisible by 3, then the sum of its digits is divisible by 3. As for (A), the sum of the digits, $8\times 8 = 64$, is not divisible by 3. As for (E), the sum of the digits is $4\times 8 = 32$, not divisible by 3. But the sum of the digits of (C) is $6\times 8 = 48$, which is divisible by 3.

8. **(D)** Only (B) and (D) are divisible by 11. (B) is not divisible by 3, since the sum of the digits is 8. But the sum of the digits of (D) is divisible by 3.

9. **(B)** The question specifically invites approximation:

$(0.5\times 4.0)\div 4 = 0.5$, which is $\frac{1}{2}$.

15

10. **(E)** You are specifically invited to approximate, and approximation makes the operations manageable. 0.889 is approximately $\frac{8}{9}$; 0.666 is approximately $\frac{2}{3}$; 0.333 is approximately $\frac{1}{3}$; and 0.625 is $\frac{5}{8}$.

$$\frac{8}{9} \div \frac{2}{3} = \frac{8}{9} \times \frac{3}{2} = \frac{4}{3}$$

$$\frac{1}{3} \div \frac{5}{8} = \frac{1}{3} \times \frac{8}{5} = \frac{8}{15}$$

$$\frac{4}{3} \div \frac{8}{15} = \frac{4}{3} \times \frac{15}{8} = \frac{5}{2}$$

11. **(C)** Look for a benchmark. In this case, $\frac{1}{10}$ will do very well. Since $\frac{12}{120} = \frac{1}{10}$, $\frac{12}{119}$ is larger than $\frac{1}{10}$; (A) can be eliminated. Similarly, $\frac{4}{39}$ and $\frac{7}{69}$ are larger than $\frac{1}{10}$ and can be eliminated. Finally, since $\frac{2}{20}$ would be exactly $\frac{1}{10}$, (C) is slightly smaller than $\frac{1}{10}$. So (C) is the smallest fraction.

12. **(D)** Look for an escape. In this case, you can factor:

    12,345(1) + 12,345(2) + 12,345(3) + 12,345(4) =

    12,345(1 + 2 + 3 + 4) = 12,345 × 10 = 123,450

13. **(D)** Notice that this expression is the difference of two squares. Factor:

    $510^2 - 490^2 = (510 + 490)(510 - 490) = 1{,}000 \times 20 = 20{,}000$

14. **(C)** Finding the escape route here is a little more difficult. $81 = 9^2$, and $16^2 + 2(9)(16) + 9^2$ is the second pattern you were asked to learn:

    $16^2 + 2(9)(16) + 9^2 = (16 + 9)(16 + 9) = (25)(25) = 625$

15. **(B)** Here, your escape is accomplished by factoring.

    $$\frac{1}{10^{22}} - \frac{1}{10^{23}} = \frac{1}{10^{22}}\left(1 - \frac{1}{10}\right) = \frac{1}{10^{22}}\left(\frac{9}{10}\right) = \frac{9}{10^{23}}$$

EXERCISE 2

1. **(E)** $2n$ must be even, so $2n + 5$, which is an even number plus an odd number, must be odd. Or, you could substitute a number such as 2 into each choice. (E) turns out to be $2(2) + 5 = 9$, an odd number.

2. **(C)** The only way 3 times n can be even is if n is even. Since n is even, $n + 1$ is odd.

3. **(C)** Since $2n$ will be even no matter what the value of n, $2n + 1$ must be odd. Again, you can substitute numbers to prove to yourself that the other choices do not guarantee an odd number.

4. **(C)** Regardless of whether $n + o$ or $p - q$ is even, as long as m is even the entire number is even.

5. **(D)** Regardless of whether n is itself odd or even, $2n$ must be even, and $2n + 2$ must be even as well.

6. **(C)** Since p is the smallest of the three, the next number is $p + 1$ and the one after that is $p + 2$. So the sum of the next two consecutive integers is $p + 1 + p + 2 = 2p + 3$.

7. **(C)** Since these are consecutive integers, each number in the series is one less than the number that follows it. So the number before $n + 3$ is $n + 2$; the number before that is $n + 1$; the one before that is just n; and the one before that is $n - 1$. So the first of the five numbers is $n - 1$.

8. **(D)** A negative times a negative is a positive, so n^2 must be positive. So $\dfrac{1}{n^2}$ is positive.

9. **(D)** Just substitute -1 for x in each choice:

   (A) $2x = 2(-1) = -2$

   (B) $x = -1$

   (C) $\dfrac{x}{2} = \dfrac{-1}{2} = -\dfrac{1}{2}$

   (D) $x^2 = (-1)(-1) = 1$

   (E) $x^3 = (-1)(-1)(-1) = -1$

10. **(A)** When a positive, proper fraction is raised to a power, the result is smaller than the original fraction. Therefore, (D) and (E) are both smaller than (C). On the other hand, when you divide by a positive, proper fraction, the result is larger than the number divided, so both (A) and (B) are larger than 1 and so larger than (C). Between (A) and (B), since x^2 is smaller than x, $\dfrac{1}{x^2}$ will be larger than $\dfrac{1}{x}$. You can arrive at the same conclusion by testing a number such as $\dfrac{1}{2}$.

EXERCISE 3

1. **(D)** $120 - 24 = 96$ are not in the union. Next, use the "this-of-that" strategy.

   $$\frac{\text{Nonmembers}}{\text{Of Employees}} = \frac{96}{120} = 0.8 = 80\%$$

2. **(B)** This is a percent increase question. Use the "change-over" strategy. Change $= 15 - 12 = 3$. Original amount $= 12$. $\dfrac{3}{12} = \dfrac{1}{4} = 25\%$.

3. **(D)** Though this question involves a percent decrease, you still use the "change-over" strategy. Change $= 450 - 441 = 9$. Original amount $= 450$. $\dfrac{9}{450} = 0.02 = 2\%$.

4. **(D)** This question asks about percent change, so you use the "change-over" strategy. Change $= 1.00 - 0.20 = 0.80$. Original amount $= 0.20$. $\dfrac{0.80}{0.20} = 4 = 400\%$.

5. **(D)** This question can be answered using the "this-of-that" strategy. $\dfrac{80}{\text{Total}} = 40\%$. $80 = 40\%$ of Total, so Total $= \dfrac{80}{0.4} = 200$.

15

6. **(B)** This question can be answered with the "change-over" strategy even though you don't know the change or the original price. The key is to see that the original price is equal to $2.00 minus the change.

$$\frac{\text{Change}}{\$2.00 - \text{Change}} = 25\%$$

Let C stand for Change:

$$\frac{C}{2-C} = 0.25$$

$$C = 0.25\,(2 - C)$$

$$C = 0.5 - 0.25C$$

$$C + 0.25C = 0.5 - 0.25C + 0.25C$$

$$1.25C = 0.5$$

$$C = 0.5 \div 1.25$$

$$C = 0.4$$

So the change was $0.40, which means the original price was $2.00 – $0.40 = $1.60. You can check this result by using the "change-over" formula to calculate the percent increase from 1.60 to 2.00.

7. **(C)** This question calls for the "change-over" strategy. Since you are only interested in finding the largest percent growth, you can compare your fractions and skip the step of converting them to percents:

(A) $\dfrac{1}{10}$ (B) $\dfrac{1}{11}$ (C) $\dfrac{3}{12}$ or $\dfrac{1}{4}$ (D) $\dfrac{3}{15}$ or $\dfrac{1}{5}$ (E) $\dfrac{3}{18}$ or $\dfrac{1}{6}$

8. **(C)** Use the "this-of-that" strategy. $\dfrac{100}{125} = \dfrac{4}{5} = 80\%$.

9. **(A)** Use the "this-of-that" strategy. $\dfrac{135}{150} = \dfrac{9}{10} = 90\%$.

10. **(A)** Use the "change-over" strategy. Change = 150 – 135 = 15.

    $\dfrac{15}{150} = \dfrac{1}{10} = 10\%$.

EXERCISE 4

1. **(C)** Add the ratio parts: 4 + 5 = 9. Divide the total quantity by that result: 36 ÷ 9 = 4. So each ratio part is worth 4. Since five of the ratio parts are dark chocolates, the number of dark chocolates is 5 × 4 = 20.

2. **(B)** "Seniors" must function as a common term. Change 5:4 to 30:24, and 6:5 to 30:25. The ratio of Seniors to Juniors is 30:24, and the ratio of Seniors to Sophomores is 30:25. So the ratio of Sophomores to Juniors is 25:24.

3. **(E)** Find the total number of ratio parts: 3 + 5 = 8. Divide: 8,000 ÷ 8 = 1,000. Then multiply by the number of parts that are nonfiction: 5 × 1,000 = 5,000.

4. **(A)** Since 6 clabs = 1 zimp, 12 clabs = 2 zimps. Therefore, 3 nurbs = 12 clabs, and 4 clabs = 1 nurb.

5. **(E)** The tricky thing here is setting up the ratio. The ratio of Robert's share to Wendy's share is 1:5, and the ratio of Robert's share to Jane's share is 1:2. So the ratio of the shares of Wendy:Jane:Robert is 5:2:1. Now you add ratio parts: $5 + 2 + 1 = 8$. Divide: $\$1,000 \div 8 = \$125$. And finally, multiply by the number of parts Wendy is to receive: $5 \times \$125 = \$625$.

EXERCISE 5

1. **(C)** The total of all the numbers must be $14 \times 6 = 84$. The total of the known quantities is only 72. So the missing number is $84 - 72 = 12$.

    Or, you might have used the "midpoint" method. 12 is 2 below 14, for -2. 15 is 1 above 14, and (keeping a running total) $-2 + 1 = -1$. Then, 18 is 4 above 14, and $4 - 1 = +3$. 14 is equal to 14, so our running total is still $+3$. Finally, 13 is 1 less than 14, which brings our running total to $+3 - 1 = +2$. This means that the missing number must offset this $+2$ by being 2 less than 14, or 12.

2. **(D)** The total weight of the four packages is $16 \times 4 = 64$. The weight of the remaining three is $3 \times 14 = 42$. The difference is $64 - 42 = 22$. So the package that was removed weighed 22 pounds.

3. **(A)** Here you must use a weighted average:

    $$\frac{3\,(\$2) + 5\,(\$3) + 1\,(\$6)}{9} = \frac{6 + 15 + 6}{9} = \frac{27}{9} = 3$$

4. **(D)** Here again you can use a weighted average:

    $$\frac{50\,(10) + 20\,(20) + 10\,(30)}{80} = \frac{500 + 400 + 300}{80} = \frac{1200}{800} = 15 = 15 \text{ cents}$$

5. **(B)** The weight of the ten people is $145 \times 10 = 1,450$. The weight of the remaining nine is $9 \times 150 = 1,350$. So the person who got out of the boat weighed $1,450 - 1,350 = 100$ pounds.

EXERCISE 6

1. **(C)** The longer the piece, the greater the weight. So you can use a direct proportion:

    $$\frac{\text{Length } x}{\text{Length } y} = \frac{\text{Weight } x}{\text{Weight } y}$$

    $$\frac{75}{x} = \frac{9}{12}$$

    Simplify: $\dfrac{75}{x} = \dfrac{3}{4}$

    Cross-multiply: $4(75) = 3x$

    Solve for x: $x = \dfrac{4(75)}{3} = 100$

15

2. **(D)** The faster the speed, the shorter the time (and vice versa). So here you must use an indirect proportion. Set up a normal proportion, being sure to group like terms:

$$\frac{\text{Speed } x}{\text{Speed } y} = \frac{\text{Time } x}{\text{Time } y}$$

$$\frac{50}{25} = \frac{1}{x}$$

Invert the right side: $\dfrac{50}{25} = \dfrac{x}{1}$

Cross-multiply: $50(1) = 25x$

Solve for x: $x = \dfrac{50}{25} = 2$

3. **(C)** The more eggs, the more milk, so you should use a direct proportion:

$$\frac{\text{Eggs } x}{\text{Eggs } y} = \frac{\text{Milk } x}{\text{Milk } y}$$

$$\frac{3}{8} = \frac{2}{x}$$

Cross-multiply: $3x = 16$

Solve for x: $x = \dfrac{16}{3} = 5\dfrac{1}{3}$

4. **(C)** The more of a thing purchased, the greater the cost. Use a direct proportion:

$$\frac{\text{Quantity } x}{\text{Quantity } y} = \frac{\text{Cost } x}{\text{Cost } y}$$

$$\frac{18}{12} = \frac{50}{x}$$

Cross-multiply: $8x = 50(12)$

Solve for x: $x = \dfrac{50\,(12)}{8} = 75$

5. **(D)** The more machines working, the shorter the time needed to do a job. Here you need an indirect proportion. Set up a proportion, being sure to group like terms:

$$\frac{\text{Number of Machines } x}{\text{Number of Machines } y} = \frac{\text{Time } x}{\text{Time } y}$$

$$\frac{3}{5} = \frac{60}{x}$$

Invert the right side: $\dfrac{3}{5} \times \dfrac{x}{60}$

Cross-multiply: $5x = 3(60)$

Solve for x: $x = \dfrac{3\,(60)}{5} = 36$

6. **(E)** The more water, the greater the space occupied. So you can use a direct proportion:

$$\frac{\text{Water } x}{\text{Water } y} = \frac{\text{Space } x}{\text{Space } y}$$

$$\frac{4}{x} = \frac{30}{360}$$

Cross-multiply: $30x = 4(360)$

Solve for x: $x = \frac{4(360)}{30} = 48$

7. **(B)** The greater the number of cars, the longer the time needed for the job. So use a direct proportion:

$$\frac{\text{Cars } x}{\text{Cars } y} = \frac{\text{Time } x}{\text{Time } y}$$

$$\frac{3}{5} = \frac{4}{x}$$

Cross-multiply: $3x = 4(5)$

Solve for x: $x = \frac{4(5)}{3} = 6\frac{2}{3}$

8. **(B)** The more cans, the longer the time. So you can use a direct proportion, but you must take care that the final result is expressed in minutes and not seconds. First, set up a proportion to find how many seconds will be needed.

$$\frac{\text{Cans } x}{\text{Cans } y} = \frac{\text{Time in Seconds } x}{\text{Time in Seconds } y}$$

$$\frac{4\frac{1}{2}}{720} = \frac{3}{x}$$

Cross-multiply: $4\frac{1}{2}x = 3(720)$

Solve for x: $x = 3(720) \div 4\frac{1}{2} = 480$ seconds.

To convert that number of seconds to minutes, divide by 60:

$$480 \div 60 = 8 \text{ minutes}$$

9. **(D)** This problem is a bit complex, but we will take it step by step. To find the total cost of the fasteners, we must first find how many we need. Since more mufflers means more fasteners, use a direct proportion:

$$\frac{\text{Mufflers } x}{\text{Mufflers } y} = \frac{\text{Fasteners } x}{\text{Fasteners } y}$$

$$\frac{1}{300} = \frac{5}{x}$$

Cross-multiply: $x = 1,500$

15

Now to figure cost, you set up another direct proportion:

$$\frac{\text{Cost } x}{\text{Cost } y} = \frac{\text{Number } x}{\text{Number } y}$$

$$\frac{500}{1,500} = \frac{42}{x}$$

Cross-multiply: $500x = 42(1,500)$

Solve for x: $x = \dfrac{42\,(1,500)}{500} = 126$

10. (E) Here, too, you can use a direct proportion:

$$\frac{\text{Percent } x}{\text{Percent } y} = \frac{\text{Number } x}{\text{Number } y}$$

$$\frac{0.03\%}{100\%} = \frac{6}{x}$$

Clear the percents: $\dfrac{0.03}{100} = \dfrac{6}{x}$

Cross-multiply: $0.03x = 6(100)$

Solve for x: $x = \dfrac{600}{0.03} = 20,000$

EXERCISE 7

1. (D) 36

$\frac{1}{3}$ of 36 = 12. $\frac{1}{4}$ of 36 = 9. And 12 is 3 more than 9. So (D) fits the requirements.

2. (D) 40

$\frac{3}{5}$ of 40 = 24. $\frac{1}{2}$ of 40 = 20. And 24 is 4 more than 20. So (D) fits the requirements.

3. (E) 7

16 ÷ 7 = 2 plus remainder 2. 9 ÷ 7 = 1 plus remainder 2. So (E) fits the requirements.

4. (D) 862

The sum of the three digits of 862 is 8 + 6 + 2 = 16. The tens digit is 6, which is three times the units digit, which is 2. Finally, 2, the units digit, is $\frac{1}{4}$ of 8, the hundreds digit.

5. (C) 6

If the smallest integer is 6, then the sum is 6 + 7 + 8 + 9 + 10 = 40.

Problem Solving: Algebra

✓ Topics Covered

1. Testing the Test
2. Algebraic Manipulations
   - Evaluating Expressions
   - Exponents
   - Factoring
   - Defined Functions
   - One Equation with One Variable
   - One Equation with Two Variables
   - Two Equations with Two Variables
   - Quadratic Equations
3. Algebraic Applications

16

We now move to algebra, and some of the same observations made with regard to arithmetic are relevant here—as are some strategies. First, if you encounter a simple, straight-forward algebra questions, then just do the indicated operations:

EXAMPLE:

If $a^3 + b = 3 + a^3$, then $b =$

   Ⓐ 33   Ⓑ $3\sqrt{3}$ Ⓒ 3   Ⓓ $^3\sqrt{3}$ Ⓔ $-\sqrt{3}$

The problem is solved by a simple manipulation. Subtract a^3 from both sides of the equation:

$$a^3 + b - (a^3) = 3 + a^3 - (a^3)$$

$$a^3 - a^3 + b = 3 + a^3 - a^3$$

$$b = 3$$

So the answer is (C). Of course, not all algebra problems are so simple. Here is one of moderate difficulty:

EXAMPLE:

Diana spent $\frac{1}{2}$ of her allowance on a book and another \$3 on lunch. If she still had $\frac{1}{6}$ of her original allowance, how much is Diana's allowance?

   Ⓐ \$24   Ⓑ \$18   Ⓒ \$15   Ⓓ \$12   Ⓔ \$9

You can solve the problem by setting up an equation. In words, the problem states:

Diana's allowance minus $\frac{1}{2}$ her allowance minus another \$3 is equal to $\frac{1}{6}$ of Diana's allowance.

If you use x for Diana's allowance, your equation is:

$$x - \frac{1}{2}x - 3 = \frac{1}{6}x$$

16

And now you solve for x. First, combine like terms:

$$\left(x - \frac{1}{2}x\right) - 3 = \frac{1}{6}x$$

$$\frac{1}{2}x - 3 = \frac{1}{6}x$$

Next, get all of the x terms on one side (by subtracting $\frac{1}{6}x$ from both sides of the equation):

$$\left(\frac{1}{2}x - \frac{1}{6}x\right) - 3 = \frac{1}{6}x - \frac{1}{6}x$$

$$\left(\frac{3}{6}x - \frac{1}{6}x\right) - 3 = 0$$

$$\frac{2}{6}x - 3 = 0$$

$$\frac{1}{3}x - 3 = 0$$

Then, isolate the x term by adding 3 to both sides of the equation:

$$\frac{1}{3}x - 3 + 3 = 0 + 3$$

$$\frac{1}{3}x = 3$$

Finally, solve for x by multiplying both sides by 3:

$$(3)\frac{1}{3}x = 3(3)$$

$$x = 9$$

The solution was described in excruciating detail. The problem can actually be solved in fewer steps. Even so, wouldn't it be nice if there were a way to avoid the algebra altogether? Well, there is an alternative.

If Holmes were studying the above problem, he would begin by thinking, "The guilty party is one of the five suspects. I only need to prove which one." This sets up two Holmesian strategies which we will discuss before we talk any further about algebra.

One of the Five Suspects: Testing the Test

We concluded our discussion of arithmetic problems with the topic "Testing the Test." You learned that it is sometimes possible to get a right answer just by testing choices. That principle can be extended to cover algebra questions.

Let's apply the principle to the problem of Diana's allowance. Start by testing (A). If Diana's allowance is $24, then after she spends $\frac{1}{2}$ on a book, she has $12. Subtract the $3 for lunch, and she has $9. But $\frac{9}{24}$ is not equal to $\frac{1}{6}$, so (A) cannot be correct.

Next, try (B). If her allowance is $18, then she has $9 after she buys the book and $6 after she pays for lunch. But $\frac{6}{18}$ is not $\frac{1}{6}$, so (B), too, is incorrect.

Next, try (C), $15. Half of that is $7.50, which, less the $3 for lunch, leaves Diana with $4.50. But $\frac{4.5}{15}$, which is $\frac{9}{2} \div 15 = \frac{9}{30}$, is not $\frac{1}{6}$. So you would try (D), $12. Half of $12 is $6, which less $3 more for lunch is $3; but $\frac{3}{12}$ is not $\frac{1}{6}$.

By this point you know that the correct answer must be (E). But we will check it anyway. Half of $9 is $4.50, which less $3 is $1.50. And $\frac{1.5}{9} = \frac{3/2}{9} = \frac{3}{18} = \frac{1}{6}$.

But, you object, that is too many calculations! Yes and no. Yes, but the algebra itself required several steps. And with the "five suspects" strategy, at least you may be able to do something if the algebra proves impossible. And no, because the process really doesn't require all of those calculations.

Answer choices to questions like this one are arranged in order, from largest to smallest or vice versa. This cuts the calculations to a maximum of two. Start by testing choice (C). Your result is $\frac{3}{12}$, which is $\frac{1}{4}$ (which proves (C) is wrong). So ask yourself, is (C) incorrect because $15 is too much money or too little? Since $\frac{1}{4}$ is more than $\frac{1}{6}$, $15 must be too much money. So you should test the next smaller number.

You test (D). It doesn't work. By the process of elimination, (E) must be correct—and you don't need to do that calculation (unless you are ahead of schedule and can afford the time for a fail-safe check).

We will apply this "five suspects" strategy to some other problems.

EXAMPLES:

In a certain game, a player had five successful turns in a row, and after each one the number of points added to his total score was double what was added the preceding turn. If the player scored a total of 465 points, how many points did he score on the first play?

    Ⓐ 15   Ⓑ 31   Ⓒ 93   Ⓓ 155   Ⓔ 270

Start with (C). If the player scored 93 points on the first turn, he scored $2 \times 93 = 186$ on the second, for a total of $93 + 186 = 279$. Then, on the third turn, he scored $2 \times 279 = 558$. But wait! This cannot possibly be the correct answer. We have already exceeded the total number of points scored.

Which suspect should we grill next? If 93 generated a result that was too large, logically, we should try the next smaller number. Assuming the player won 31 points on the first turn, he won $2 \times 31 = 62$ on the second, for a total of $31 + 62 = 93$. On the third, he won $2 \times 62 = 124$, for a total of $93 + 124 = 217$. On the fourth, he won $2 \times 124 = 248$, for a total of $217 + 248 = 465$, with still another round to go. (B) must be wrong.

16

By the process of elimination, therefore, (A) is correct. And if you care, you can prove it by doing the calculation.

Notice that in both of our examples, the answer was located at the extreme—either (E) or (A). This was to demonstrate that even with the worst luck, only two calculations are required. Sometimes you will be lucky and hit upon the correct choice on the first try.

The principle of the five suspects gives rise to another strategy called "If you don't see what you want, ask for it." This "ask for it" strategy is useful when the problem asks you to invent a formula.

> At a certain firm, d gallons of fuel are needed per day for each truck. At this rate g gallons of fuel will supply t trucks for how many days?
>
> (A) $\dfrac{dt}{g}$ (B) $\dfrac{gt}{d}$ (C) dgt (D) $\dfrac{t}{dg}$ (E) $\dfrac{g}{dt}$

This is a fairly difficult question. And what makes it difficult is the use of unknowns. The question wouldn't be difficult if it read:

> At a certain firm, 20 gallons of fuel are needed per day for each truck. At this rate 1,000 gallons of fuel will supply five trucks for how many days?

You would reason that five trucks using 20 gallons of fuel per day would consume $5 \times 20 = 100$ gallons per day. So 1,000 gallons would be used up in $1,000 \div 100 = 10$ days.

Numbers are what you want. You don't see them, so ask for them. Or rather, make them up as we just did. On the assumption that there are five trucks ($t = 5$), and that each truck consumes 20 gallons per day ($d = 20$), and that we have 1,000 gallons of fuel ($g = 1,000$), the correct formula should generate the number 10.

(A) $\dfrac{dt}{g} = \dfrac{20\,(5)}{1,000} = \dfrac{100}{1,000} = \dfrac{1}{10}$ (Wrong answer.)

(B) $\dfrac{gt}{d} = \dfrac{1,000\,(5)}{20} = \dfrac{5,000}{20} = 250$ (Wrong answer.)

(C) $dgt = (20)(1,000)(5) = 100(1,000)$ (Wrong answer.)

(D) $\dfrac{t}{dg} = \dfrac{5}{(20)\,(1,000)} = \dfrac{5}{20,000}$ (Wrong answer.)

(E) $\dfrac{g}{dt} = \dfrac{1,000}{20\,(5)} = \dfrac{1,000}{100} = 10$ (BINGO!)

> Y years ago Paul was twice as old as Bob. If Bob is now 18 years old, how old is Paul in terms of Y?
>
> (A) $36 + Y$ (B) $18 + Y$ (C) $18 - Y$ (D) $36 - Y$ (E) $36 - 2Y$

In our first example, we used realistic numbers. A truck might use 20 gallons of fuel per day, and a firm might have five trucks and a 1,000-gallon tank. But an unknown can stand for any number at all (as long as you don't divide by zero). So pick numbers that are easy to work with.

For starters, why not assume that Y = zero, which is to say that right now Paul is twice as old as Bob. Since Bob is now 18, Paul is 36. So with Y = zero, the correct formula should generate the value 36.

    Ⓐ $36 + Y = 36 + 0 = 36$

    Ⓑ $18 + Y = 18 + 0 = 18$

    Ⓒ $18 - Y = 18 - 0 = 18$

    Ⓓ $36 - Y = 36 - 0 = 36$

    Ⓔ $36 - 2Y = 36 - 0 = 36$

What happened? Our strategy yielded three choices, not one. There's nothing wrong with the strategy. The problem is with the value we used. (A), (D), and (E) all yielded 36 because –0, +0, and –2(0) are all zero. To eliminate the two incorrect choices, just pick another easy number.

    Assume that $Y = 1$. On that assumption, a year ago Bob was 17 years old and Paul was 34 years old. And today, one year later, he is $34 + 1 = 35$. So if $Y = 1$, the correct choice should yield 35:

    Ⓐ $36 + Y = 36 + 1 = 37$ (Definitely incorrect.)

    Ⓓ $36 - Y = 36 - 1 = 35$ (Bingo!)

    Ⓔ $36 - 2Y = 36 - 2 = 34$ (Wrong.)

You may also encounter a problem if you use the value 1, because $1 \times 1 = 1 \div 1$. For example, if you assume that $X = 1$, the formula XY will give you the same result as the formula $\frac{Y}{X}$. This doesn't mean you should never use 1. You can and should use 1 as an assumption; but if you get more than one seemingly correct formula, try another set of numbers.

16

It Must Be One of the Five (Answers, page 304)

Directions: Solve the following problems using one of the two strategies just discussed. Don't even be tempted to use algebra.

1. On a shopping trip, Peter spent $\frac{1}{3}$ of his money for a jacket and another $5 for a hat. If Peter still had $\frac{1}{2}$ of his money left, how much money did he have originally?

   Ⓐ $18   Ⓑ $24   Ⓒ $30   Ⓓ $48   Ⓔ $60

2. After filling the car's fuel tank, a driver drove from P to Q and then to R. She used $\frac{2}{5}$ of the fuel driving from P to Q. If she used another 7 gallons to drive from Q to R and still had $\frac{1}{4}$ of a tank left, how many gallons does the tank hold?

   Ⓐ 12   Ⓑ 18   Ⓒ 20   Ⓓ 21   Ⓔ 35

3. A school meeting was attended only by sophomores, juniors, and seniors. $\frac{5}{12}$ of those who attended were juniors, and $\frac{1}{3}$ were seniors. If 36 sophomores attended, what was the total number of students who attended the meeting?

   Ⓐ 108   Ⓑ 144   Ⓒ 252   Ⓓ 288   Ⓔ 300

4. If p pounds of coffee costs d dollars, how many pounds of coffee can be purchased for x dollars?

   Ⓐ $\dfrac{pd}{x}$ Ⓑ $\dfrac{x}{pd}$ Ⓒ $\dfrac{xp}{d}$ Ⓓ $\dfrac{d}{xp}$ Ⓔ xpd

5. If p pounds of coffee costs d dollars, how many pounds of coffee can be purchased for $x + 10$ dollars?

   Ⓐ $\dfrac{pd}{x+10}$ Ⓑ $\dfrac{x+10}{pd}$ Ⓒ $\dfrac{10px}{d}$ Ⓓ $\dfrac{p(x+10)}{d}$ Ⓔ $pd(x + 10)$

6. If pencils cost x cents each, how many pencils can be purchased for y dollars?

   Ⓐ $\dfrac{100}{xy}$ Ⓑ $\dfrac{xy}{100}$ Ⓒ $\dfrac{100y}{x}$ Ⓓ $\dfrac{y}{100x}$ Ⓔ $100xy$

7. If the profit on an item is $2 and the sum of the cost and the profit is $10, what is the cost of the item?

   Ⓐ $6   Ⓑ $8   Ⓒ $10   Ⓓ $12   Ⓔ $14

8. A candy bar weighing 4 ounces costs c cents. If the size of the candy bar is reduced to 3.6 ounces while the price remains the same, then the old price per ounce is what fraction of the new price per ounce?

   Ⓐ $\dfrac{10c}{9}$ Ⓑ $\dfrac{9c}{10}$ Ⓒ $\dfrac{10}{9c}$ Ⓓ $\dfrac{9}{10c}$ Ⓔ $\dfrac{9}{10}$

9. A merchant increased the original price of an item by 10 percent. If she then reduces the new price by 10 percent, the final result in terms of the original price is

Ⓐ a decrease of 11 percent

Ⓑ a decrease of 1 percent

Ⓒ no net change

Ⓓ an increase of 1 percent

Ⓔ an increase of 11 percent

10. Harold is twice as old as Jack, who is three years older than Dan. If Harold's age is five times Dan's age, how old in years is Jack?

Ⓐ 2   Ⓑ 4   Ⓒ 5   Ⓓ 8   Ⓔ 10

11. A tank with capacity T gallons is empty. If water flows into the tank from Pipe X at the rate of X gallons per minute, and water is pumped out by Pipe Y at the rate of Y gallons per minute, and X is greater than Y, in how many minutes will the tank be filled?

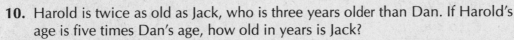

Ⓐ $\dfrac{T}{Y-X}$ Ⓑ $\dfrac{T}{X-Y}$ Ⓒ $\dfrac{T-X}{Y}$ Ⓓ $\dfrac{X-Y}{60T}$ Ⓔ $\dfrac{60T}{XY}$

12. If 144 pencils cost d dollars, how many pencils can be purchased for $0.50?

Ⓐ $72d$ Ⓑ $288d$ Ⓒ $\dfrac{72}{d}$ Ⓓ $\dfrac{d}{72}$ Ⓔ $\dfrac{720}{d}$

13. Machine X produces w widgets in five minutes. Machine X and Machine Y, working at the same time, produce w widgets in two minutes. How long will it take Machine Y working alone to produce w widgets?

Ⓐ 2 min. 30 sec.

Ⓑ 2 min. 40 sec.

Ⓒ 3 min. 20 sec.

Ⓓ 3 min. 30 sec.

Ⓔ 3 min. 40 sec.

14. If a train travels m miles in h hours and 45 minutes, what is its average speed in miles per hour?

Ⓐ $\dfrac{m}{h+\frac{3}{4}}$ Ⓑ $\dfrac{m}{1\frac{3}{4}h}$ Ⓒ $m\left(h+\dfrac{3}{4}\right)$ Ⓓ $\dfrac{m+45}{h}$ Ⓔ $\dfrac{h}{m+45}$

15. In a playground, there are x seesaws. If 50 children are all riding on seesaws, two to a seesaw, and five seesaws are not in use, what is x?

Ⓐ 15   Ⓑ 20   Ⓒ 25   Ⓓ 30   Ⓔ 35

16. Of a group of 27 students, 18 belong to the French Club and 15 belong to the Spanish Club. If each student belongs to at least one club, how many students belong to both clubs?

Ⓐ 3   Ⓑ 6   Ⓒ 8   Ⓓ 10   Ⓔ 24

16

17. In a certain population group, 57 percent of the people have characteristic X and 63 percent have characteristic Y. If every person in the group has at least one of the two characteristics, what percent of the people have both X and Y?

Ⓐ 6%   Ⓑ 12%   Ⓒ 18%   Ⓓ 20%   Ⓔ 23%

18. Mike is older than Ned but younger than Oscar. If m, n, and o are the ages of Mike, Ned, and Oscar, respectively, then which of the following is true?

Ⓐ $m < n < o$

Ⓑ $n < m < o$

Ⓒ $o < n < m$

Ⓓ $o < m < n$

Ⓔ $n < o < m$

19. If $2 < x < 5$ and $3 < y < 6$, which of the following describes all of the possible values of $x + y$?

Ⓐ $1 < x + y < 6$

Ⓑ $1 < x + y < 11$

Ⓒ $2 < x + y < 6$

Ⓓ $3 < x + y < 5$

Ⓔ $5 < x + y < 11$

20. If $2 < x < 5$ and $3 < y < 6$, which of the following describes all of the possible values of $x - y$?

Ⓐ $-4 < x - y < 1$

Ⓑ $-4 < x - y < 2$

Ⓒ $-1 < x - y < 1$

Ⓓ $-1 < x - y < 11$

Ⓔ $5 < x - y < 11$

Algebraic Manipulations

A few math problems may require algebraic manipulation. And sometimes there is no better way to attack the problem than to do the operations indicated. We will divide our discussion of algebraic manipulations into two parts: rewriting expressions and solving equations.

Rewriting Expressions

1. Evaluating Expressions

A problem may ask you to change an algebraic expression into a number by having you substitute values. This is called "evaluating an expression."

EXAMPLE:

If $x = 2$, what is the value of $x^2 + 2x - 2$?

Ⓐ -2 Ⓑ 0 Ⓒ 2 Ⓓ 4 Ⓔ 6

We use the same strategy here that we would employ for an analogous arithmetic problem: if the operations are manageable, just do them. Here, you substitute 2 for x and do the easy arithmetic:

$$x^2 + 2x - 2 = 2^2 + 2(2) - 2 = 4 + 4 - 2 = 8 - 2 = 6$$

A test-writer might try to make a problem like this more difficult by using fractions.

EXAMPLE:

If $x = 2$, then $\dfrac{1}{x^2} + \dfrac{1}{x} - \dfrac{x}{2} =$

Ⓐ $-\dfrac{3}{4}$ Ⓑ $-\dfrac{1}{4}$ Ⓒ 0 Ⓓ $\dfrac{1}{4}$ Ⓔ $\dfrac{1}{2}$

The answer is (B). Just substitute 2 for each occurrence of x:

$$\frac{1}{x^2} + \frac{1}{x} - \frac{x}{2} = \frac{1}{2^2} + \frac{1}{2} - \frac{2}{2}$$

$$\frac{1}{4} + \frac{1}{2} - 1 = \frac{3}{4} - 1 = -\frac{1}{4}$$

And just as was the case with arithmetic manipulations, there is a limit to the complexity of manipulations. You might find something like this.

EXAMPLE:

If $p = 1$, $q = 2$, and $r = 3$, then $\dfrac{(q \times r)(r - q)}{(q - p)(p \times q)} =$

Ⓐ -3 Ⓑ -1 Ⓒ 0 Ⓓ 3 Ⓔ 6

16

You just substitute for the different letters and execute:

$$\frac{(q \times r)(r - q)}{(q - p)(p \times q)} = \frac{(2 \times 3)(3 - 2)}{(2 - 1)(1 \times 2)} = \frac{(6)(1)}{(1)(2)} = \frac{6}{2} = 3$$

Such manipulations shouldn't get any more complicated than this; but if they do, you know to look for an escape route.

2. Exponents

A knowledge of the rules for manipulating exponents is essential for many algebraic manipulations:

1. $(x^m)(x^n) = x^{m+n}$

2. $\left(\dfrac{x^m}{x^n}\right) = x^{m-n}$

3. $\left(x^m\right)^n = x^{m \cdot n}$

4. $\left(x^m \cdot y^m\right)^n = x^{mn} \cdot y^{mn}$

5. $\left(\dfrac{x^m}{y^m}\right)^n = \dfrac{x^{mn}}{y^{mn}}$

Occasionally, you may be asked to demonstrate your knowledge of these rules.

EXAMPLE:

$$\frac{9\left(x^2 y^3\right)^6}{\left(3x^6 y^9\right)^2} =$$

  Ⓐ 1   Ⓑ 3   Ⓒ $x^2 y^3$ Ⓓ $3x^2 y^3$ Ⓔ $x^{12} y^{12}$

The answer is (A).

$$\frac{9\left(x^2 y^3\right)^6}{\left(3x^6 y^9\right)^2} = \frac{9\left(x^{2 \cdot 6} y^{3 \cdot 6}\right)}{3^2 x^{6 \cdot 2} y^{9 \cdot 2}} = \frac{9x^{12} y^{18}}{9x^{12} y^{18}} = 1$$

3. Factoring

Although factoring of algebraic expressions is an important part of most high school algebra classes, it's really not that important for the GMAT. Of course, you might be asked to do simple factoring.

EXAMPLE:

$2x^3 + 4x^2 + 6x =$

Ⓐ $2x(2x^2 + 2x + 6)$

Ⓑ $2x(x^2 + 2x + 3)$

Ⓒ $2x(x + 5)$

Ⓓ $3x(x + 2x + 2)$

Ⓔ $6x(x + 2x + 1)$

The answer is (B), as you can prove to yourself by multiplying:

$$2x(x^2 + 2x + 3) = 2x^3 + 4x^2 + 6x$$

Generally, the factoring procedures you learned in the chapter on arithmetic are all you need to know. If you need to factor a quadratic expression, you follow the formats you learned in the preceding chapter:

$$x^2 - y^2 = (x + y)(x - y) \text{ (Called the difference of two squares)}$$

$$x^2 + 2xy + y^2 = (x + y)(x + y) \text{ (Also written } [x + y]^2)$$

$$x^2 - 2xy + y^2 = (x - y)(x - y) \text{ (Not used that often, but easy to recognize)}$$

Whenever you see one of these three expressions, you should have an irresistible urge to factor.

EXAMPLE:

$$\frac{x^2 - y^2}{x + y}$$

Ⓐ $x^2 - y^2$ Ⓑ $x^2 + y^2$ Ⓒ $x^2 + y$ Ⓓ $x + y^2$ Ⓔ $x - y$

The answer is (E). Just factor the numerator, using the method for the difference of two squares:

$$\frac{x^2 - y^2}{x + y} = \frac{(x + y)(x - y)}{x + y} = x - y$$

It is theoretically possible, though unlikely, that you could be asked to factor a quadratic expression that is not one of the three shown above. But then you would look for an escape route:

EXAMPLE:

$$\frac{x^2 - x - 6}{x + 2} =$$

Ⓐ $x^2 - \frac{1}{2}x - 3$ Ⓑ $x^2 - 2$ Ⓒ $x - 2$ Ⓓ $x - 3$ Ⓔ x

The answer is (D). And the trick is to see that $x + 2$ must be a factor of $x^2 - x - 6$. (Otherwise, what is the question doing on the GMAT?) Now you can figure out what the other factor is:

$$(x + 2) \,(?\ \ ?) = x^2 - x - 6.$$

The first question mark must be filled in by an x. That's the only way to get x2 in the final result:

$$(x + 2) \,(x\ \ ?) = x^2 - x - 6.$$

The second question mark must be 3:

$$(x + 2) \,(x\ \ 3) = x^2 - x - 6.$$

16

Finally, to get –6 in the final result, the sign must be:

$$(x + 2)(x - 3) = x^2 - 3x + 2x - 6 = x^2 - x - 6.$$

Once you know this, you rewrite the original expression:

$$\frac{x^2 - x - 6}{x + 2} = \frac{(x + 2)(x - 3)}{x + 2} = x - 3$$

And what happens if you fail to see the trick? You can use one of the other techniques we have already used to good advantage. Try numbers. Assume that $x = 1$:

$$\frac{x^2 - x - 6}{x + 2} = \frac{1^2 - 1 - 6}{1 + 2} = \frac{1 - 1 - 6}{3} = -\frac{6}{3} = -2$$

So substituting 1 for x into the correct choice will yield –2:

(A) $x^2 - \dfrac{1}{2}x - 3 = 1^2 - \dfrac{1}{2}(1) - 3 = -3\dfrac{1}{2}$ (Wrong.)

(B) $x^2 - 2 = 1^2 - 2 = 1 - 2 = -1$ (Wrong.)

(C) $x - 2 = 1 - 2 = -1$ (Wrong.)

(D) $x - 3 = 1 - 3 = -2$ (Correct.)

(E) $x = 1$ (Wrong.)

4. Defined Functions

In algebra, you learned about the expression $f(\ )$, which signals a function. $f(x)$ tells you to do something to the term inside the parentheses. Algebraic functions are tested by the GMAT using strange drawings.

EXAMPLE:

If $\boxed{x} = x^2 - x$ for all whole numbers, then $\boxed{-2} =$

(A) –6   (B) –2   (C) 0   (D) 4   (E) 6

The answer is (E). The weird drawing does the job of $f(\ )$. $\bigtriangledown$ tells you to take whatever is inside the $\bigtriangledown$ and do "$x^2 - x$" to it. If $x = -2$, then $\boxed{x} = (-2^2) - (-2) = 4 + 2 = 6$.

Some function questions are easy (the one above), while others are fairly difficult. But even the easy ones can seem difficult because of the unusual format. To make them seem more familiar, you might want to give them a name, say, your own name. If your name is Ted, you could analyze a function in the following way:

EXAMPLE:

If $\boxed{x} = x^2 - x$ for all whole numbers, then $\boxed{\boxed{3}} =$

(A) 27   (B) 30   (C) 58   (D) 72   (E) 121

The answer is (B). You must ted the result of tedding 3. To ted 3, you square 3 and subtract 3 from that result: $3^2 - 3 = 9 - 3 = 6$. Now you do ted to that. To ted 6, you square 6 and subtract 6 from that result: $6^2 - 6 = 36 - 6 = 30$. The main thing is to take the problem one step at a time.

Sometimes functions come in pairs. Then, the first question will just ask that you perform the defined operation on a number. The second will ask for something more complicated.

EXAMPLES:

For all numbers, $x * y = xy + y$

What is $4 * 5$?

Ⓐ 12   Ⓑ 18   Ⓒ 24   Ⓓ 25   Ⓔ 30

For all numbers, $x * y = xy + y$.

If $3 * 2 = 7 * k$, then $k =$

Ⓐ 1   Ⓑ 2   Ⓒ 3   Ⓓ 4   Ⓔ 5

The first question just asks you to apply the definition of "*." Using Ted's name (or your own), 4 ted 5 means 4 times 5 plus 5: $(4 \times 5) + 5 = 20 + 5 = 25$. So the correct choice is (D).

The second question is more difficult. First, let's find the value of 3 ted 2. 3 ted 2 means 3 times 2 plus 2: $(3 \times 2) + 2 = 6 + 2 = 8$. So $7 * k = 8$, but what is k? Fall back on one of our strategies. Test the choices starting with (C).

$7 * 3$ means 7 times 3 plus 3: $(7 \times 3) + 3 = 21 + 3 = 24$. But that is not equal to 8, so (C) is wrong. Since (C) is too large, try (B).

$7 * 2$ means 7 times 2 plus 2: $(7 \times 2) + 2 = 14 + 2 = 16$. Again too large, so the correct choice must be (A): $7 * 1$ means 7 times 1 plus 1: $(7 \times 1) + 1 = 7 + 1 = 8$. So (A) is correct.

Solving Equations

---

1. One Equation with One Simple Variable

These questions are generally require nothing more than that you solve for x.

EXAMPLE:

If $(2 + 3)(1 + x) = 25$, then $x =$

Ⓐ $\dfrac{1}{5}$ Ⓑ $\dfrac{1}{4}$ Ⓒ 1   Ⓓ 4   Ⓔ 5

The answer is (D).
Solve for x:

$(2 + 3)(1 + x) = 25$

$5(1 + x) = 25$

Divide both sides by 5:

$$\frac{5(1 + x)}{5} = \frac{25}{5}$$

$1 + x = 5$

16

Subtract 1:
$$1 + x(-1) = 5 - 1$$
$$x = 4$$

It is possible to employ our "test the test" technique by substituting the choices back into the equation. But given that the equation is so simple, it's probably easier to solve for x directly. You may, however, use the testing technique to check your solution. Substitute 4 back into the original equation: $(2 + 3)(1 + 4) = 5(5) = 25$. This proves our solution is correct.

Sometimes the test-writers will attempt to jazz up their simple equations a bit by using decimals or fractions, but this really doesn't change things much.

EXAMPLE:

If $T \times \dfrac{3}{7} = \dfrac{3}{7} \times 9$, then $T =$

(A) $\dfrac{1}{9}$ (B) $\dfrac{1}{7}$ (C) 1   (D) 7   (E) 9

Once you divide both sides by $\dfrac{3}{7}$ to eliminate the fractions, the equation becomes $T = 9$. So there's no need for a strategy other than just doing the simple algebra.

There is one variation on this theme for which you might look for something different.

EXAMPLE:

If $2x + 3 = 7$, then $2x =$

(A) 4   (B) 6   (C) 8   (D) 14   (E) 21

The correct choice is (A), and it would not be wrong to solve for x. $2x = 4$, so $x = 2$. Therefore, $2x = 2(2) = 4$. You don't really need to do the last two steps. Once you have $2x = 4$, you have your solution.

EXAMPLE:

If $\dfrac{1}{3}x = 10$, then $\dfrac{1}{6}x =$

(A) $\dfrac{1}{15}$ (B) $\dfrac{2}{3}$ (C) 2   (D) 5   (E) 30

The answer is (D). And again it would not be wrong to solve for x and then substitute your solution for x in $\dfrac{1}{6}x$. But you can save a few seconds if you can see that $\dfrac{1}{6}$ is one-half of $\dfrac{1}{3}$, so $\dfrac{1}{6}x$ is half of $\dfrac{1}{3}x$. Therefore, half of 10 is 5.

In general, then, if the problem is an equation with one simple variable, you are safe solving for the variable. But if the question asks for a multiple or a fraction of the variable, you can save a little time if you can compare things directly without solving for the variable itself.

2. One Equation with Two Variables

With one equation and one variable, you can solve for the variable. But with two variables and only one equation, you won't be able to get a solution for either variable alone.

EXAMPLE:

If $x + y = 3$, then $2x + 2y =$

   Ⓐ $\dfrac{2}{3}$ Ⓑ $\dfrac{1}{2}$ Ⓒ $\dfrac{3}{2}$ Ⓓ 6

Ⓔ Cannot be determined from the information given.

The answer is (D). Although it is not possible to find values for x and y individually, $2x + 2y = 2(x + y)$, so $2x + 2y$ is double 3, which is 6.

For questions with two variables and only one equation, look for a way of transforming the first expression into the second. The transformation will give you a solution.

3. Two Equations with Two Variables

With two equations and two variables, you solve using the technique of simultaneous equations:

Given two equations with two variables, x and y, to solve for x:

Step 1: **In one of the equations, define y in terms of x ($y =$ some form of x).**

Step 2: **Substitute the value of y (from step 1) for every occurrence of y in the other equation.** (This will eliminate the ys, leaving only xs.)

Step 3: **Solve for x.** (And, if necessary, substitute the value of x for x into either equation to get the value of y.)

In simplest form, such problems look like this:

EXAMPLE:

If $2x + y = 8$ and $x - y = 1$, then $x =$

   Ⓐ –2   Ⓑ –1   Ⓒ 0   Ⓓ 1   Ⓔ 3

The answer is (E).

First, use one of the equations to define y in terms of x. Since the second is simpler, use it:

$$x - y = 1$$
$$x = 1 + y$$
$$x - 1 = y, \text{ so } y = x - 1$$

Second, substitute $x - 1$ into the other equation for every occurrence of y. (There is only one occurrence of y in the other equation.)

$$2x + y = 8$$
$$2x + (x - 1) = 8$$

Third, solve for x:

$$2x + (x - 1) = 8$$
$$3x - 1 = 8$$
$$3x = 9$$
$$x = 3$$

16

Sometimes it may be necessary to continue the process to solve for the second variable.

EXAMPLE:

If $2x + y = 8$ and $x - y = 1$, then $x + y =$

Ⓐ −1   Ⓑ 1   Ⓒ 2   Ⓓ 3   Ⓔ 5

The answer is (E), and this is the question we just answered, except that we are looking for $x + y$, not just x. You follow the same procedure, and once you know $x = 3$, substitute 3 for x into either equation. Since the second is simpler, we will use it:

$x - y = 1$

$3 - y = 1$

$y = 2$

So $x + y = 5$.

If you keep your eyes open, you might find a chance to make a direct substitution, thereby avoiding some algebra.

EXAMPLE:

If $7x = 2$ and $3y - 7x = 10$, then $y =$

Ⓐ 2   Ⓑ 3   Ⓒ 4   Ⓓ 5   Ⓔ 6

The answer is (C). The problem can be solved using the procedure outlined above, but in solving for x, you get a fraction. And fractions are a pain in the neck. You can avoid the problem, however, if you see not only that $7x = 2$ but that $7x$ is one of the terms of the second equation. Just substitute 2 for $7x$ in the second equation.

$3y - 2 = 10$

$3y = 12$

$y = 4$

And such shortcuts become absolutely necessary with more difficult problems.

EXAMPLE:

If $4x + 5y = 12$ and $3x + 4y = 5$, then $7(x + y) =$

Ⓐ 7   Ⓑ 14   Ⓒ 49   Ⓓ 77   Ⓔ 91

The answer is (C). You could, if you had to, solve for both x and y, but it would be a tedious process. The best attack on this question is to see that the final answer requires the sum of x and y $(x + y)$, not the individual values of x and y.
We can simply rewrite our equations so that we get a value for $x + y$:

$$
\begin{array}{rr}
4x + 5y = & 12 \\
- [3x + 4y = & 5] \\
\hline
x + y = & 7
\end{array}
$$

Since $x + y = 7$, then $7(x + y) = 7(7) = 49$.

In general, then, "two equation/two variable" questions should be attacked as simultaneous equations, unless that process would be too complicated. Then look for an alternative.

4. Quadratic Equations (Equations with a Squared Variable)

Perhaps one of the most important topics in high school algebra is solving quadratic equations. These are equations with squared variables.

> **EXAMPLE:**
>
> If $x^2 - 3x = 4$, then which of the following shows all possible values of x?
>
> Ⓐ 4, 1   Ⓑ 4, –1   Ⓒ –4, 1   Ⓓ –4, –1   Ⓔ –4, 1, 4

To solve a quadratic equation:

Step 1: Set all the terms equal to zero.

Step 2: Factor.

Step 3: Set each of the factors equal to zero.

Step 4: Solve each equation.

First, set all the terms equal to zero:

$$x^2 - 3x = 4$$

$$x^2 - 3x - 4 = 0$$

Next, factor:

$$(x - 4)(x + 1) = 0$$

Now, create equations with each of the factors equal to zero:

$$x - 4 = 0 \text{ or } x + 1 = 0$$

Finally, solve each equation

$$x - 4 = 0 \text{ or } x + 1 = 0$$

$$x = 4 \qquad x = -1$$

And if you need to, you can check these solutions by reinserting 4 and –1 in the original equation.

Although this procedure is a big deal in math class, you probably will not need to do it on the GMAT. And in the extremely unlikely event that you do need to do it, the factoring will probably fit one of three patterns:

$$x^2 - y^2 = (x - y)(x + y)$$

$$x^2 + 2xy + y^2 = (x + y)(x + y)$$

$$x^2 - 2xy + y^2 = (x - y)(x - y)$$

You should recognize these three patterns. They are the same three you were asked to memorize in Lesson 15 as a way of avoiding lengthy calculations. Once again, the first and second are more important than the third. In the context of algebra, it is possible you could get a problem like the following.

16

EXAMPLE:

If $x^2 - y^2 = 0$ and $x + y = 1$, then $x - y =$

Ⓐ −1   Ⓑ 0   Ⓒ 1   Ⓓ 2

Ⓔ Cannot be determined from the information given.

The answer is (B). Factor:

$x^2 - y^2 = 0$

$(x + y)(x - y) = 0$

Either $x + y = 0$ or $x - y = 0$.

The question stipulates that $x + y = 1$ and not zero, so $x - y$ must be zero.

In general, then, you probably will not need to solve a quadratic equation. If you should, it will probably fit one of the two patterns: $x^2 - y^2$ or $x^2 + 2xy + y^2$. And remember, most quadratic equations have two solutions. (Some, like $x^2 - 2x + 1 = 0$, have only one solution.)

Algebraic Manipulations (Answers, page 308)

1. Which of the following is equal to $3x^3 + 3x^2 + 3x$?

   (A) $9x^6$ (B) $3x^6$ (C) $3x(x^3 + x^2 + x)$ (D) $3x(3x^2 + 3x + 3)$ (E) $3x(x^2 + x + 1)$

2. $\dfrac{x^2 + 2xy + y^2}{x + y} =$

   (A) $x + y$ (B) $x - y$ (C) $x^2 + y$ (D) $x + y^2$ (E) $x^2 + y^2$

3. If $x - y = 3$, then $\dfrac{x^2 - y^2}{x + y} =$

   (A) 0   (B) 1   (C) 3   (D) 9

   (E) Cannot be determined from the information given.

4. $(x + y)^2 - (x - y)^2 =$

   (A) $4xy$ (B) x^2 (C) $x + y$ (D) $x - y$ (E) $x^2 + y^2$

5. $\dfrac{x^2 + 2x + 1}{x + 1} =$

   (A) x (B) $x + 1$ (C) $x - 1$ (D) x^2 (E) x^3

6. If $\lfloor x \rfloor$ denotes the greatest integer that is less than or equal to x, then $\lfloor -0.1 \rfloor + \lfloor 0.1 \rfloor =$

   (A) -2 (B) -1 (C) 0   (D) 1   (E) 2

Questions 7 and 8

For all numbers x and y, $x \lozenge y = xy + x$.

7. $4 \lozenge 5 =$

   (A) 9   (B) 24   (C) 25   (D) 36   (E) 41

8. If $2 \lozenge 3 = x \lozenge 7$, then $x =$

   (A) 0   (B) 1   (C) 4   (D) 5   (E) 7

Questions 9 and 10

For all real numbers except 0, $x \lozenge y \lozenge z = \dfrac{x + y}{z}$

9. $9 \lozenge 3 \lozenge 1 =$

   (A) 1   (B) 3   (C) 9   (D) 10   (E) 12

10. $x \lozenge y \lozenge (x \lozenge y \lozenge z) =$

   (A) $\dfrac{z}{x + y}$ (B) $\dfrac{x + y}{z}$ (C) x (D) y (E) z

11. If $n + n + 1 + n + 2 = 12$, then $n =$

   (A) 0   (B) 1   (C) 2   (D) 3   (E) 4

12. If $\dfrac{1}{x} + \dfrac{1}{x} = 4$, then $x =$

   (A) $\dfrac{1}{4}$ (B) $\dfrac{1}{2}$ (C) 1   (D) 2   (E) 4

13. If $x + y = 9$, then $\frac{1}{3}x + \frac{1}{3}y =$

   Ⓐ 1   Ⓑ 3   Ⓒ 18   Ⓓ 27   Ⓔ 54

14. If $2x + y = 5$ and $x + y = 3$, then $x =$

   Ⓐ 0   Ⓑ 1   Ⓒ 2   Ⓓ 4   Ⓔ 5

15. If $3m = 5$ and $4n - 3m = 3$, then $n =$

   Ⓐ 0   Ⓑ 1   Ⓒ 2   Ⓓ 4   Ⓔ 8

16. If $7m - 2 = 3k$, then $\dfrac{7m - 2}{3} =$

   Ⓐ $\dfrac{k}{3}$ Ⓑ k Ⓒ $3k$ Ⓓ $9k$ Ⓔ $27k$

17. If $x = 4y$, then $12y - 3x =$

   Ⓐ 0   Ⓑ 1   Ⓒ 7   Ⓓ 15

   Ⓔ Cannot be determined from the information given.

18. If $x + \dfrac{1}{3} = \dfrac{x + 2}{3}$, then $x =$

   Ⓐ $\dfrac{1}{2}$ Ⓑ 1   Ⓒ $\dfrac{3}{2}$ Ⓓ 2   Ⓔ 3

19. If $(x + y)^2 = x^2 + y^2$, then $xy =$

   Ⓐ 0   Ⓑ 1   Ⓒ 2   Ⓓ 5

   Ⓔ Cannot be determined from the information given.

20. If $(x + y)^2 - (x - y)^2 = 20$, then $xy =$

   Ⓐ 0   Ⓑ 1   Ⓒ 2   Ⓓ 5

   Ⓔ Cannot be determined from the information given.

Algebraic Applications

Some questions ask for you to apply your algebra skills to practical situations. The problems in Exercise 1 are examples. And this raises an interesting question. If it is possible to solve algebra questions by testing choices or by assuming numbers, why bother with algebra at all?

There are two answers to this question. One, sometimes you may not be able to find an alternative solution, in which case, you can use the "official" algebra approach. Two, a direct solution using algebra may be faster than working backwards or assuming numbers.

You can brush up on your algebra by doing the following problems.

16

Algebraic Applications (Answers, page 311)

Directions: These problems appeared in Exercise 1. Solve them using algebra. To make sure you don't try to use your Holmesian strategies, there are no answer choices. You will have to arrive at your own solutions.

1. On a shopping trip, Peter spent $\frac{1}{3}$ of his money for a jacket and another $5 for a hat. If Peter still had $\frac{1}{2}$ of his money left, how much money did he have originally? _____

2. After filling the car's fuel tank, a driver drove from *P* to *Q* and then to *R*. She used $\frac{2}{5}$ of the fuel driving from *P* to *Q*. If she used another 7 gallons to drive from *Q* to *R* and still had $\frac{1}{4}$ of a tank left, how many gallons does the tank hold? _____

3. A school meeting was attended only by sophomores, juniors, and seniors. $\frac{5}{12}$ of those who attended were juniors, and $\frac{1}{3}$ were seniors. If 36 sophomores attended, what was the total number of students who attended the meeting? _____

4. If *p* pounds of coffee costs *d* dollars, how many pounds of coffee can be purchased for *x* dollars? _____

5. If *p* pounds of coffee costs *d* dollars, how many pounds of coffee can be purchased for *x* + 10 dollars? _____

6. If pencils cost *x* cents each, how many pencils can be purchased for *y* dollars? _____

7. If the profit on an item is $2 and the sum of the cost and the profit is $10, what is the cost of the item? _____

8. A candy bar weighing 4 ounces costs *c* cents. If the size of the candy bar is reduced to 3.6 ounces while the price remains the same, then the old price per ounce is what fraction of the new price per ounce? _____

9. A merchant increased the original price of an item by 10 percent. If she then reduces the new price by 10 percent, what is the final result in terms of the original price? _____

10. Harold is twice as old as Jack, who is three years older than Dan. If Harold's age is five times Dan's age, how old in years is Jack? _____

11. A tank with capacity *T* gallons is empty. If water flows into the tank from Pipe *X* at the rate of *X* gallons per minute, and water is pumped out by Pipe *Y* at the rate of *Y* gallons per minute, and *X* is greater than *Y*, in how many minutes will the tank be filled? _____

12. If 144 pencils cost *d* dollars, how many pencils can be purchased for $0.50? _____

13. Machine *X* produces *w* widgets in five minutes. Machine *X* and Machine *Y*, working at the same time, produce *w* widgets in two minutes. How long will it take Machine *Y* working alone to produce *w* widgets? _____

14. If a train travels *m* miles in *h* hours and 45 minutes, expressed in terms of *m* and *h*, what is its average speed in miles per hour? _____

Summary

1. Some problems require simple algebraic manipulations such as evaluating an expression, working with exponents, or factoring. Do the operations.

2. Defined functions use a nonstandardized symbol to define a short series of algebraic operations. Do the indicated operations step by step. For a difficult function problem, try working backwards from the answer choices.

3. If the question stem is an equation (or equations), solve for an unknown or find a way of directly transforming one expression into another.

4. The Holmesian principle "one of the five suspects" is the basis for two powerful strategies: (a) test answer choices, and (b) assume actual numbers for unknowns.

16

Explanatory Answers

EXERCISE 1

1. **(C)** Test choices starting with (C). If Peter spent $\frac{1}{3}$ of his money for a jacket, he spent $\frac{1}{3}$ of $30 = $10. This would leave him with $30 − $10 = $20. Take away another $5 for the hat, and he is left with $20 − $5 = $15. And $\frac{15}{30}$ is equal to $\frac{1}{2}$, so (C) is correct.

2. **(C)** Test choices starting with (C). On the assumption that the tank originally contained 20 gallons, the driver used $\frac{2}{5}$ of 20, or 8, gallons going from P to Q, which left her with $20 − 8 = 12$ gallons. Take away another 7 gallons, and she is left with $12 − 7 = 5$. $\frac{5}{20}$ is $\frac{1}{4}$, so (C) is correct.

3. **(B)** We will test choices, but first we must determine what fraction of the students are not sophomores. $\frac{5}{12} + \frac{1}{3} = \frac{5}{12} + \frac{4}{12} = \frac{9}{12} = \frac{3}{4}$. If $\frac{3}{4}$ are not sophomores, $\frac{1}{4}$ are sophomores. So 36 over the total number must be $\frac{1}{4}$. Start with (C). $\frac{36}{252}$ is not $\frac{1}{4}$, so (C) is wrong. And since $\frac{36}{252}$ is less than $\frac{1}{4}$, the number of students is less than 252, so we should try a smaller number. (The smaller the denominator, the larger the fraction.) So we try (B). $\frac{36}{144} = \frac{1}{4}$. So (B) is correct.

4. **(C)** Assume some numbers. Suppose coffee costs $5 for 2 pounds and that you have $10. You could buy 4 pounds. So if $p = 2$, $d = 5$, and $x = 10$, the correct formula generates the value 4:

   (A) $\dfrac{pd}{x} = \dfrac{2(5)}{10} = \dfrac{10}{10} = 1$ (Wrong.)

   (B) $\dfrac{x}{pd} = \dfrac{10}{2(5)} = \dfrac{10}{10} = 1$ (Wrong.)

   (C) $\dfrac{xp}{d} = \dfrac{10(2)}{5} = \dfrac{20}{5} = 4$ (Correct.)

   (D) $\dfrac{d}{xp} = \dfrac{5}{10(2)} = \dfrac{5}{20} = \dfrac{1}{4}$ (Wrong.)

   (E) $xpd = (10)(2)(5) = 100$ (Wrong.)

5. **(D)** Again, assume that $p = 2$ and $d = 5$. And let's assume that $x = 0$. If $x = 0$, then $x + 10 = 10$, and so again the correct answer should be 4.

   (A) $\dfrac{pd}{x+10} = \dfrac{(2)(5)}{0+10} = \dfrac{10}{10} = 1$ (Wrong.)

   (B) $\dfrac{x+10}{pd} = \dfrac{0+10}{(2)(5)} = \dfrac{10}{10} = 1$ (Wrong.)

   (C) $\dfrac{10px}{d} = \dfrac{10(2)(0)}{5} = \dfrac{0}{5} = 0$ (Wrong.)

   (D) $\dfrac{p(x+10)}{d} = \dfrac{2(0+10)}{5} = \dfrac{20}{5} = 4$ (Correct.)

   (E) $pd(x + 10) = 2(5)(0 + 10) = 100$ (Wrong.)

6. **(C)** Assume some numbers. Assume pencils cost 2 cents apiece and that you have $2 to spend. You can buy 100 pencils. So if $x = 2$ and $y = 2$, the correct formula generates 100.

(A) $\dfrac{100}{xy} = \dfrac{100}{(2)(2)} = \dfrac{100}{4} = 25$ (Wrong.)

(B) $\dfrac{xy}{100} = \dfrac{(2)(2)}{100} = \dfrac{4}{100} = \dfrac{1}{25}$ (Wrong.)

(C) $\dfrac{100y}{x} = \dfrac{100(2)}{2} = \dfrac{200}{2} = 100$ (Correct.)

(D) $\dfrac{y}{100x} = \dfrac{2}{100(2)} = \dfrac{2}{200} = \dfrac{1}{100}$ (Wrong.)

(E) $100xy = 100(2)(1) = 200$ (Wrong.)

7. **(B)** Test numbers, starting with (C). If the cost of the item is $10, then the sum of the cost and profit is $10 + $2 = $12, which is more than $10. So try a smaller number, (B). If the cost of the item is $8, then the sum of the cost and profit is $8 + $2 = $10. So (B) is correct.

8. **(E)** Assume some numbers. Since the numbers you assume will have to be divided by both 4 and 3.6, choose 36. So the cost per ounce at the old price was 36 cents per 4 ounces = 9 cents per ounce. At the new price, it is 36 cents per 3.6 ounces = 10 cents per ounce. So if $c = 36$, the correct choice will yield the value $\dfrac{9}{10}$.

You don't even need to calculate for (A) through (D). You can see immediately that once you put in 36 for c, they will not equal $\dfrac{9}{10}$. Only (E) is $\dfrac{9}{10}$ — but (E) doesn't have c as part of it. That is true. And the correct formula should not have c as part of it.

9. **(B)** Assume some numbers. Assume the original price of the item is $100. Increase that by 10 percent: 10% of $100 = $10, and $100 + $10 = $110. Now decrease $110 by 10 percent: 10% of $110 = $11, and $110 − $11 = $99. The original price was $100 and the new price is $99, so there is a net decrease of 1 percent. (Change/Original Total = $\dfrac{\$1}{\$100} = 1\%$.)

10. **(C)** Test choices starting with (C). If Jack is five, then Harold (who is twice as old) is ten. And Dan must be two (Jack is three years older than Dan). If Harold is ten and Dan is two, then Harold is five times older than Dan. So (C) is correct.

16

11. **(B)** Assume some numbers. Assume the tank has a capacity of 10 gallons, and that water is flowing in at the rate of 2 gallons per minute and being pumped out at the rate of 1 gallon per minute. That's a net gain of 1 gallon per minute, and at that rate it will take $10 \div 1 = 10$ minutes to fill the tank. So on the assumption that $T = 10$, $X = 2$, and $Y = 1$, the correct formula generates 10.

(A) $\dfrac{10}{1-2} = \dfrac{10}{-1} = -10$ (Wrong.)

(B) $\dfrac{10}{2-1} = \dfrac{10}{1} = 10$ (Correct.)

(C) $\dfrac{10-2}{1} = \dfrac{8}{1} = 8$ (Wrong.)

(D) $\dfrac{2-1}{60(10)} = \dfrac{1}{600}$ (Wrong.)

(E) $\dfrac{60(10)}{(2)(1)} = \dfrac{600}{2} = 300$ (Wrong.)

12. **(C)** Assume numbers. Assume that 144 pencils cost \$1, so for 50 cents you can get $\frac{1}{2}$ of 144, or 72. So assuming $d = 1$, the correct choice will generate 72.

(A) $72d = 72(1) = 72$

(B) $288d = 288(1) = 288$ (Wrong.)

(C) $\dfrac{72}{d} = \dfrac{72}{1} = 72$

(D) $\dfrac{d}{72} = \dfrac{1}{72}$ (Wrong.)

(E) $\dfrac{720}{d} = \dfrac{720}{1} = 720$ (Wrong.)

And we seem to have two right answers. But that sometimes happens when you use 1. So let's try again with $d = 2$. If 144 pencils cost \$2, for 50 cents you can buy $\frac{1}{4}$ of 144, or 36.

(A) $72(2) = 144$ (Wrong.)

(C) $\dfrac{72}{2} = 36$ (Correct.)

13. **(C)** Assume some numbers. Assume that w is 100 widgets—a nice round number that is easily divided by a lot of other numbers. On that assumption, Machine X operates at $100 \div 5 = 20$ widgets per minute. At that rate, when the two machines are working together, Machine X contributes at the rate of 20 widgets per minute, which means Machine X produces only 40 of the 100 widgets. So Machine Y produces the other 60 in two minutes, which is 30 widgets per minute. To produce 100 widgets would take Machine Y $100 \div 30$ $= 3\frac{1}{3}$ minutes, which is three minutes and 20 seconds.

14. **(A)** Assume some numbers, and let's make them easy. Say that the train traveled for $2\frac{3}{4}$ hours and covered 275 miles. That would be 100 miles per hour. So assuming that $m = 275$ and $h = 2$, the correct formula generates 100.

   (A) $\dfrac{275}{2\frac{3}{4}} = \dfrac{275}{2.75} = 100$ (Correct.)

   (B) $\dfrac{275}{1\frac{3}{4}(2)} = \dfrac{275}{1.75(2)} = \dfrac{275}{3.5} = 78\frac{4}{7}$ (Wrong.)

   (C) $275\left(2+\dfrac{3}{4}\right) = 275 \times 2.75$ (Wrong.)

   (D) $\dfrac{275+45}{2} = \dfrac{320}{2} = 160$ (Wrong.)

   (E) $\dfrac{2}{275+45} = \dfrac{2}{320} = \dfrac{1}{160}$ (Wrong.)

15. **(D)** Test numbers, starting with (C). Since 50 children need 25 seesaws, if x (the total number of seesaws in the park) is 25, all the seesaws are in use. So 25 is too small; try (D). If there are 30 seesaws in the park and five are not in use, that makes 25 seesaws in use. So (D) is correct.

16. **(B)** Test numbers. Start with(C). If 8 students belong to both clubs, that means that there are $(18 + 15) – 8 = 25$ total students. But that is incorrect. Since 25 is less than 27, fewer than eight must belong to both clubs. So try (B). $(18 + 15) – 6 = 27$. So (B) is correct.

    Incidentally, this sets up a very easy method of solving problems like this. The total membership of the two clubs is $18 + 15 = 33$, but there are only 27 different students. So $33 – 27 = 6$ must belong to both clubs.

17. **(D)** Test choices, starting with (C). If 18 percent have both characteristics, then $(57 + 63) – 18 = 102$ percent. But the total population cannot exceed 100 percent. So try the next larger number: $(57 + 63) – 20 = 100$ percent.

    And now you can use the method devised in our explanation to the previous question. $(57 + 63) – 100 = 20$.

18. **(B)** You can make up numbers for the ages. Assume that Mike is two, and Ned (who is younger) is one, and Oscar (who is older) is three. So $m = 2$, $n = 1$, and $o = 3$. The proper order is n, m, o.

19. **(E)** You don't need any fancy algebraic technique to answer this question. Just try to figure out under what circumstance $x + y$ will be the largest, and under what conditions it will be the smallest. Since x must be larger than 2 and y larger than 3, $x + y$ must be larger than 5. And since x is smaller than 5 and y is smaller than 6, $x + y$ must be smaller than 11, which is choice (E).

20. **(B)** Though this item is a little trickier than the last, you can use the same technique of picking numbers. The least value for $x – y$ will come with the smallest possible value for x and the largest possible value for y: $2 – 6 = –4$. So the smallest possible value for $x – y$ is greater than –4. And the largest value will come with the largest possible value for x and the smallest possible value for y: $5 – 3 = 2$. So $x – y$ must be less than 2.

16

EXERCISE 2

1. **(E)** Factor by removing the common factor of $3x$ from each of the terms: $3x^3 + 3x^2 + 3x = 3x(x^2 + x + 1)$.

2. **(A)** The numerator fits the second of the three factoring patterns you learned: $(x + y)(x + y)$. Simplify by canceling the $(x + y)$. The final result is $x + y$.

3. **(C)** Again, you should have an irresistible urge to factor. The numerator of the expression is the difference of two squares, the first of the three factoring patterns you learned. So the numerator is equal to $(x + y)(x - y)$. Next, cancel the $(x + y)$ terms. The result is $x - y$, which is said to be equal to 3.

4. **(A)** Do the indicated operations, and subtract.

    $$(x + y)^2 = (x + y)(x + y) = x^2 + 2xy + y^2$$

    $$(x - y)^2 = (x - y)(x - y) = \frac{x^2 - 2xy + y^2}{0 + 4xy + 0}$$

5. **(B)** $x^2 + 2x + 1$ fits the pattern $x^2 + 2xy + y^2$, where $y = 1$. But even if you didn't recognize that, you should think that $(x + 1)$ is one of the factors of the numerator and work backwards to find the other factor, which is also $(x + 1)$. Then cancel, and the final result is $x + 1$.

6. **(B)** This is a function problem. To "ted" a number (perform the defined operation on it), you do one of two things. If the number is already an integer, the number stays the same. If the number is not an integer, it is rounded down to the next lowest integer. So tedding -0.1 yields -1. (-1 is the next integer smaller than -0.1.) And tedding 0.1 yields 0. And $-1 + 0 = -1$.

7. **(B)** Here is the first of a pair of function questions. Use the name Ted (or your own name, if you prefer). To ted means to multiply the first number by the second and add to that product the first number. So 4 ted 5 is (4 times 5) plus $4 = 20 + 4 = 24$.

8. **(B)** This question is more difficult than the previous one. But you can solve it by working backwards. 2 ted 3 is equal to $(2 \times 3) + 2 = 8$. Which of the answer choices, when substituted for x, will yield 8? Try (C). 4 ted 7 is equal to $(4 \times 7) + 4 = 32$. (C) is too large, so try the next smaller choice. 1 ted 7 is equal to $(1 \times 7) + 1 = 8$. Which proves that (B) is correct.

9. **(E)** The first question of this pair just requires that you plug in numbers. 9 ted 3 ted 1 means 9 plus 3 divided by 1, which is equal to 12.

10. **(E)** This second question is more difficult, because you must work with unknowns. First, x ted y ted z means $\frac{x+y}{z}$. Now we use that result as the third element of another ted. x ted y ted $\frac{x+y}{z}$ is equal to $x + y$ divided by $\frac{x+y}{z}$. $x + y \div \frac{x+y}{z} = (x + y)(\frac{z}{x+y}) = z$.

11. **(D)** Solve for n:

    $n + n + 1 + n + 2 = 12$

    $3n + 3 = 12$

    $3n = 9$

    $n = 3$

12. **(B)** Solve for x:

$$\frac{1}{x} + \frac{1}{x} = 4$$

$$\frac{2}{x} = 4$$

$$2 = 4x$$

$$x = \frac{2}{4} = \frac{1}{2}$$

13. **(B)** Before you start solving for x, look for a way of converting $x + y$ to $\frac{1}{3}x + \frac{1}{3}y$. You can do that by multiplying $x + y$ by $\frac{1}{3}$: $\frac{1}{3}(x + y) = \frac{1}{3}x + \frac{1}{3}y$. So $\frac{1}{3}x + \frac{1}{3}y$ must be equal to $\frac{1}{3}(9)$, or 3.

14. **(C)** Two variables and two equations calls for the simultaneous equations technique. To solve for x, first isolate y in one of the equations. We will use the second, since it is simpler:

$$x + y = 3$$

$$y = 3 - x$$

Now substitute $3 - x$ for y in the first equation:

$$2x + (3 - x) = 5$$

And solve for x:

$$2x + 3 - x = 5$$

$$2x - x + 3 = 5$$

$$x + 3 = 5$$

$$x = 2$$

15. **(C)** Simultaneous equations again, so to solve for n, you isolate m: $3m = 5$, so $m = \frac{5}{3}$. Now substitute $\frac{5}{3}$ for m in the second equation:

$$4n - 3\left(\frac{5}{3}\right) = 3$$

$$4n - 5 = 3$$

$$4n = 8$$

$$n = 2$$

Or you might have recognized that since $3m = 5$, you can substitute 5 for $3m$ in the second equation without solving for m.

16

16. **(B)** You could solve for m in the first equation, getting m in terms of k:

$$7m = 3k + 2$$

$$m = \frac{3k + 2}{7}$$

Then substitute this into $\frac{7m - 2}{3}$:

$$\frac{7\left(\frac{3k + 2}{7}\right) - 2}{3} = \frac{3k + 2 - 2}{3} = \frac{3k}{3} = k$$

That's conceptually correct, but it's too much work. Instead, you should see that you can turn $7m - 2$ into $\frac{7m - 2}{3}$ by dividing by 3. So $\frac{7m - 2}{3} = \frac{3k}{3} = k$.

17. **(A)** Notice that $12y$ is 3 times $4y$ and that $3x$ is 3 times x. Start by multiplying $x = 4y$ by 3.

$$3(x) = 4y(3)$$

$$3x = 12y$$

Now, to turn $3x = 12y$ into $12y - 3x$, subtract $3x$ from both sides of the equation:

$$3x = 12y$$

$$3x - 3x = 12y - 3x$$

$$0 = 12y - 3x$$

So $12y - 3x$ is equal to 0.

18. **(A)** You can solve for x.

First, multiply both sides of the equation by 3:

$$3(x + \frac{1}{3}) = x + 2$$

$$3x + 1 = x + 2$$

$$2x = 1$$

$$x = \frac{1}{2}$$

Or, if you need to, you can use the technique of substituting numbers.

19. **(A)** The natural starting point is to do the indicated multiplication. It's one of the patterns you memorized.

$(x + y)^2 = (x + y)(x + y) = x^2 + 2xy + y^2$

So, $x^2 + 2xy + y^2 = x^2 + y^2$.

Subtract x^2 and y^2 from both sides. The result is:

$2xy = 0$

So $xy = 0$.

20. **(D)** First do the multiplication. You should be able to do this by memory.

$(x + y)^2 = x^2 + 2xy + y^2$

$(x - y)^2 = x^2 - 2xy + y^2$

So:

$x^2 + 2xy + y^2 - (x^2 - 2xy + y^2) = 20$

$x^2 + 2xy + y^2 - x^2 + 2xy - y^2 = 20$

$x^2 - x^2 + 2xy + 2xy + y^2 - y^2 = 20$

$4xy = 20$

$xy = 5$

EXERCISE 3

1. 30

The original amount minus $\frac{1}{3}$ of the original amount minus another \$5 is equal to $\frac{1}{2}$ of the original amount. With x designating the original amount, in algebra:

$x - \dfrac{1}{3}x - 5 = \dfrac{1}{2}x$

$\dfrac{2}{3}x - 5 = \dfrac{1}{2}x$

$\dfrac{2}{3}x - \dfrac{1}{2}x = 5$

$\dfrac{1}{6}x = 5$

$x = 30$

16

2. 20

A tank full minus $\frac{2}{5}$ of a tank minus another 7 gallons is equal to $\frac{1}{4}$ of a tank. Let x be the number of gallons the tank holds:

$$x - \frac{2}{5}x - 7 = \frac{1}{4}x$$

$$\frac{3}{5}x - 7 = \frac{1}{4}x$$

$$\frac{3}{5}x - \frac{1}{4}x = 7$$

$$\frac{7}{20}x = 7$$

$$x = 7(\frac{20}{7}) = 20$$

3. 144

$\frac{5}{12}$ of the total number who attended plus $\frac{1}{3}$ of the total number who attended plus 36 students is equal to the total number who attended. Let T represent the total number who attended:

$$\frac{5}{12}T + \frac{1}{3}T + 36 = T$$

$$\frac{9}{12}T + 36 = T$$

$$36 = T - \frac{3}{4}T$$

$$36 = \frac{1}{4}T$$

$$T = 36 \times 4 = 144$$

4. $\frac{xp}{d}$

To find how much of something can be purchased for a certain amount, you divide the amount of money by the cost. The cost of coffee is d dollars per p pounds, or $\frac{d}{p}$. Then divide x dollars by $\frac{d}{p}$: $x \div \frac{d}{p} = x(\frac{p}{d}) = \frac{xp}{d}$.

5. $\frac{p(x+10)}{d}$

Follow the same procedure. The cost of coffee is $\frac{d}{p}$. Next, divide $x + 10$ by $\frac{d}{p}$: $(x + 10) \div \frac{d}{p} = (x + 10)(\frac{p}{d}) = \frac{p(x+10)}{d}$.

6. $\frac{100y}{x}$

Again, divide the amount available by the cost. The cost of a pencil is $\frac{x}{1}$. The available amount is y dollars, which is $100y$ cents. $100y \div x = \frac{100y}{x}$.

7. 8

Cost plus $2 = $10. Let C be cost:

$C + 2 = 10$

$C = 8$

8. $\dfrac{9}{10}$

The old price was $\dfrac{c}{4}$ ounces, and the new price is $\dfrac{c}{3.6}$ ounce. Using the "this-of-that" strategy:

old price per ounce/new price per ounce =

$$\dfrac{\dfrac{c}{4}}{\dfrac{c}{3.6}} = \dfrac{c}{4} \times \dfrac{3.6}{c} = \dfrac{3.6}{4} = \dfrac{9}{10}$$

9. 1%

Let P be the original price. The price increases by 10 percent, or $\dfrac{1}{10}$: $P + 0.1P = 1.1P$. Then that price decreases by 10 percent: $1.1P - 0.11P = 0.99P$. So the net decrease was $0.01P$, and the percent decrease was $\dfrac{0.01P}{P} = 0.01 = 1\%$.

10. 5

Harold's age is twice Jack's age; Jack's age is 3 more than Dan's; and Harold's age is 5 times Dan's age. Let H, J, and D stand for the ages of Harold, Jack, and Dan.

$H = 2J$ and $J = D + 3$ and $H = 5D$

Since $H = 2J$, substitute $2J$ for H in the third equation:

$H = 5D$, so $2J = 5D$

Solve for D:

$2J = 5D$

$D = \dfrac{2}{5}J$

Now substitute $\dfrac{2}{5}J$ for D in the equation $J = D + 3$:

$J = \dfrac{2}{5}J + 3$

$J - \dfrac{2}{5}J = 3$

$\dfrac{3}{5}J = 3$

$J = 3\left(\dfrac{5}{3}\right) = 5$

16

11. $\left(\dfrac{T}{X-Y}\right)$

Since water comes in at X gallons per minute and goes out at Y gallons per minute, the net gain is $X - Y$. To find how long it will take to fill the tank, divide the capacity of the tank by the net rate at which the tank is being filled: $T \div (X - Y)$, which is $\dfrac{T}{X-Y}$.

12. $\dfrac{72}{d}$

Divide the available amount by the cost of each pencil. The available amount is 50 cents. Pencils cost d dollars, or $100d$ cents per 144. $50 \div \left(\dfrac{100d}{144}\right) = 50\left(\dfrac{144}{100d}\right)$ $= \dfrac{144}{2d} = \dfrac{72}{d}$.

13. 3 minutes, 20 seconds.

Machine X operates at the rate of w widgets per five minutes. Machines X and Y together operate at the rate of w widgets per two minutes. Take away Machine X's contribution, and you will have the rate at which Machine Y operates.

Rate of X and Y together – Rate of X = Rate of Y

$$\dfrac{w \text{ widgets}}{2 \text{ minutes}} - \dfrac{w \text{ widgets}}{5 \text{ minutes}} = \dfrac{w \text{ widgets}}{x \text{ minutes}}$$

$$\dfrac{w}{2} - \dfrac{w}{5} = \dfrac{w}{x}$$

$$\dfrac{5w - 2w}{10} = \dfrac{w}{x}$$

$$\dfrac{3w}{10} = \dfrac{w}{x}$$

$$x = w\left(\dfrac{10}{3w}\right) = \dfrac{10}{3}, \text{ which is 3 minutes and 20 seconds.}$$

14. $\dfrac{m}{h+\dfrac{3}{4}}$

The speed is to be expressed in miles per hour. Miles traveled is m, and time traveled is h hours plus another $\frac{3}{4}$ of an hour, or $h + \frac{3}{4}$. So the speed was $\dfrac{m}{h+\frac{3}{4}}$.

Problem Solving: Geometry

✓ **Topics Covered**

1. Angles
2. Triangles
3. Rectangles and Squares
4. Circles
5. Solids
6. Coordinate Geometry
7. Complex Figures
8. Nonformulaic Techniques
   - "Guestimating"
   - Measuring
   - "Meastimating"

Some problems will test your knowledge of *geometry.* You won't be asked to give formal proofs of theorems, but you will need to use logic and your knowledge of basic formulas to do things like finding the size of an angle, the length of a line, or the area of a figure.

Holmes' Attic

Although the term *geometry* covers a lot of knowledge, relatively few principles are tested by the GMAT. These are the ones to keep in your "attic."

Angles

THE NUMBER OF DEGREES OF ARC IN A CIRCLE IS 360.

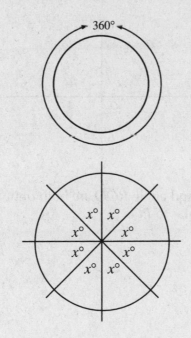

EXAMPLE:

In the figure above, $x =$

(A) 15   (B) 30   (C) 45   (D) 60   (E) 75

The answer is (C).

$$x + x + x + x + x + x + x + x = 360$$

$$8x = 360$$

$$x = 45$$

17

THE MEASURE IN DEGREES OF A STRAIGHT ANGLE IS 180.

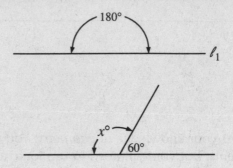

EXAMPLE:

In the figure above, $x =$

Ⓐ 45   Ⓑ 60   Ⓒ 75   Ⓓ 90   Ⓔ 120

The answer is (E).

$x + 60 = 180$

$x = 120$

THE NUMBER OF DEGREES IN A RIGHT ANGLE IS 90.

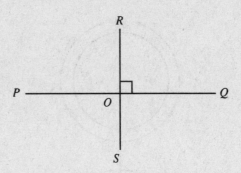

In the figure above, POR and angle ROQ are both right angles, so each measures 90°. And RS is perpendicular to PQ.

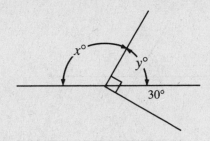

| **EXAMPLE:**

In the figure above, $x =$

Ⓐ 45   Ⓑ 60   Ⓒ 90   Ⓓ 105   Ⓔ 120

The answer is (E).

$$y + 30 = 90$$

$$y = 60$$

$$x + y = 180$$

$$x + 60 = 180$$

$$x = 120$$

WHEN PARALLEL LINES ARE CUT BY A THIRD LINE, THE RESULTING ANGLES ARE RELATED AS FOLLOWS:

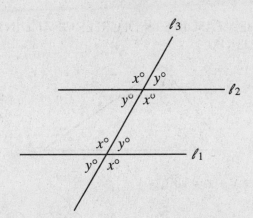

$x = x = x = x$; $y = y = y = y$; and $x + y = 180$. This is the "big angle, little angle" theorem. All the big angles are equal; all the little angles are equal; and any big angle plus any little angle equals 180. (In the event the third line intersects the parallel lines on the perpendicular, then all angles equal 90°.)

17

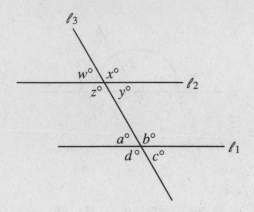

EXAMPLE:

In the figure above, which of the following must be true?

I. $w = a$

II. $y + b = 180°$

III. $x + d = 180°$

Ⓐ I only   Ⓑ II only   Ⓒ I and II only
Ⓓ II and III only   Ⓔ I, II, and III

The answer is (C). w and a are "small" angles, so they are equal, and statement I is true. y is a "small" angle and b is a "large" angle, so their sum is 180°, and II is true. III, however, is not true. x and d are both "large" angles. They would total 180° only in the special case where both are 90°.

THE SUM OF THE MEASURES IN DEGREES OF THE INTERIOR ANGLES OF A TRIANGLE IS 180°.

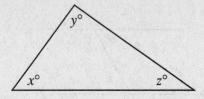

In the figure above, $x + y + z = 180$.

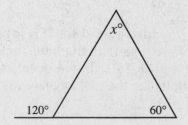

EXAMPLE:

In the figure above, $x =$

Ⓐ 30   Ⓑ 45   Ⓒ 60   Ⓓ 75   Ⓔ 90

The answer is (C). Let y be the measure of the third and unlabeled angle inside the triangle:

$120 + y = 180$

$y = 60$

$x + y + 60 = 180$

$x + 60 + 60 = 180$

$x + 120 = 180$

$x = 60$

THE SUM IN DEGREES OF THE INTERIOR ANGLES OF A POLYGON OF N SIDES IS $180(N - 2)$.

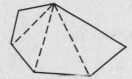

The figure above has six sides, so the sum of the six angles is $180(6 - 2) = 180(4) = 720°$. Instead of memorizing the formula just given, you can reason that the figure is composed of four triangles, each with angles totaling $180°$.

EXAMPLE:

In the figure above, what is the sum of the indicated angles?

Ⓐ 540   Ⓑ 720   Ⓒ 900   Ⓓ 1,080   Ⓔ 1,260

The answer is (C). Divide the figure into triangular regions:

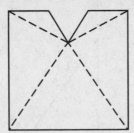

There are five triangles, so the sum of the angles is $5(180) = 900°$.

Note: This principle gives you the sum of the interior angles of the polygon. You might be asked about the average size of the angles. In that case, divide the sum of the angles by the total number of angles inside the figure.

17

Triangles

WITHIN A TRIANGLE, IF TWO ANGLES ARE EQUAL, THE LENGTHS OF THEIR OPPOSITE SIDES ARE EQUAL, AND VICE VERSA.

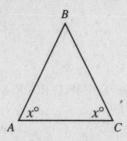

In the figure above, $AB = BC$.

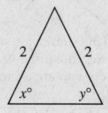

In the figure above, $x = y$.

THE PYTHAGOREAN THEOREM: IN A RIGHT TRIANGLE, THE SQUARE OF THE LONGEST SIDE (THE HYPOTENUSE) IS EQUAL TO THE SUM OF THE SQUARES OF THE OTHER TWO SIDES.

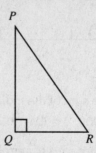

In the figure above, $PR^2 = PQ^2 + QR^2$.

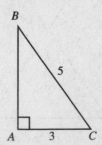

EXAMPLE:

In the figure above, $AB =$

  Ⓐ 2   Ⓑ $2\sqrt{3}$ Ⓒ 4 Ⓓ $4\sqrt{2}$ Ⓔ 8

The answer is (C).

$$BC^2 = AB^2 + AC^2$$

$$5^2 = AB^2 + 3^2$$

$$25 = AB^2 + 9$$

$$AB^2 = 16$$

$$AB = \sqrt{16} = 4$$

ANY TRIANGLE WITH SIDES OF 3, 4, AND 5 (OR MULTIPLES THEREOF) IS A RIGHT TRIANGLE.

This a two-edged sword. First, any triangle having sides that fit the Pythagorean Theorem is a right triangle. Since $3^2 + 4^2 = 5^2$, a triangle with those sides must be a right triangle. Additionally, any triangle with sides that are multiples of 3, 4, and 5 is a right triangle. For example, since $6^2 + 8^2 = 10^2$, a triangle with sides of 6, 8, and 10 is a right triangle (as are triangles with sides of 18, 24, and 30; 30, 40, and 50; and so on).

The other edge of the sword gives you an easy method for finding the length of a side in such triangles.

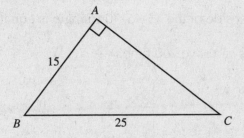

EXAMPLE:

In the figure above, what is the length of *AC*?

Ⓐ 5   Ⓑ 10   Ⓒ 12   Ⓓ 16   Ⓔ 20

The answer is (E). Since ABC is a right triangle, you can use the Pythagorean Theorem. Or, you can save time by reasoning that one side is 3×5 and the hypotenuse is 5×5, so the missing length must be $4 \times 5 = 20$.

IN A TRIANGLE WITH ANGLES OF 45°, 45°, AND 90°, THE LENGTH OF THE HYPOTENUSE IS EQUAL TO THE LENGTH OF EITHER SIDE MULTIPLIED BY $\sqrt{2}$, AND EACH OF THE SHORTER SIDES IS EQUAL TO $\frac{1}{2}$ TIMES THE LENGTH OF THE HYPOTENUSE TIMES $\sqrt{2}$.

17

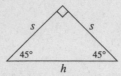

Both of these conclusions follow from the Pythagorean Theorem (coupled with the rule that sides opposite equal angles are equal in length).

$h^2 = s^2 + s^2$

$h^2 = 2s^2$

$h = s\sqrt{2}$

Which is to say, the hypotenuse of the 45-45-90 triangle is equal to either side times $\sqrt{2}$. Conversely,

$s^2 + s^2 = h^2$

$2s^2 = h^2$

$s^2 = \dfrac{h^2}{2}$

$s = \dfrac{h}{\sqrt{2}} = \left(\dfrac{1}{2}\right)\left(h\sqrt{2}\right)$

Which is to say, either side of the 45-45-90 triangle is equal to $\frac{1}{2}$ times the hypotenuse times $\sqrt{2}$.

These conversions can save you time.

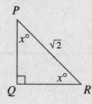

EXAMPLE:

In the figure above, $PQ =$

Ⓐ 1   Ⓑ $\sqrt{2}$ Ⓒ $2\sqrt{2}$ Ⓓ 4   Ⓔ 5

The answer is (A). Since the triangle contains a right angle and two equal angles, it must be a 45-45-90 triangle. Rather than use the general form of the Pythagorean Theorem, just reason that PQ, one of the sides, is equal to $\frac{1}{2}$ times the length of the hypotenuse times $\sqrt{2}$: $\frac{1}{2}(\sqrt{2} \times \sqrt{2}) = \frac{1}{2}(2) = 1$.

IN A TRIANGLE WITH ANGLES OF 30°, 60°, AND 90°, THE LENGTH OF THE SIDE OPPOSITE THE 30° ANGLE IS $\frac{1}{2}$ TIMES THE LENGTH OF THE HYPOTENUSE, AND THE LENGTH OF THE SIDE OPPOSITE THE 60° ANGLE IS $\frac{1}{2}$ TIMES THE LENGTH OF THE HYPOTENUSE TIMES $\sqrt{3}$.

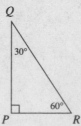

In the figure above, $PR = \frac{1}{2}QR$, and $PQ = \frac{1}{2}QR\sqrt{3}$.

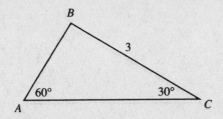

EXAMPLE:

In the triangle above, what is the length of *AC*?

  Ⓐ 2   Ⓑ $\sqrt{3}$ Ⓒ $2\sqrt{3}$ Ⓓ $3\sqrt{3}$ Ⓔ 6

The answer is (C). Since two of the angles of the triangle are 30° and 60°, the remaining angle must be 90°. So we have a 30-60-90 triangle, in which the side opposite the 60° angle is equal to $\frac{1}{2}$ times the length of the hypotenuse times $\sqrt{3}$.

$$BC = \frac{1}{2}AC\sqrt{3}$$

$$3 = \frac{1}{2}AC\sqrt{3}$$

$$6 = AC\sqrt{3}$$

$$AC = \frac{6}{\sqrt{3}} = \frac{6\sqrt{3}}{3} = 2\sqrt{3}$$

AN EQUILATERAL TRIANGLE (3 EQUAL SIDES) HAS THREE 60° ANGLES. CONVERSELY, A TRIANGLE WITH THREE EQUAL ANGLES IS EQUILATERAL.

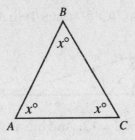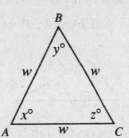

In the figure on the left, $x = 60$, and $AB = BC = AC$. In the figure on the right, because all three sides are equal, $x = y = z = 60$.

THE PERIMETER OF A TRIANGLE IS THE SUM OF THE LENGTHS OF ITS SIDES.

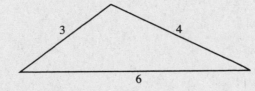

In the figure above, the perimeter is $3 + 4 + 6 = 13$.

17

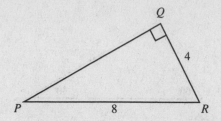

EXAMPLE:

In the figure above, the perimeter of triangle PQR =
Ⓐ $12 + \sqrt{3}$ Ⓑ $12 + 2\sqrt{3}$ Ⓒ $12 + 4\sqrt{3}$ Ⓓ   28
Ⓔ   Cannot be determined from the information given.

The answer is (C). To find the perimeter of the triangle, you must first find the length of PQ.

$PR^2 = PQ^2 + QR^2$

$8^2 = PQ^2 + 4^2$

$64 = PQ^2 + 16$

$PQ^2 = 64 - 16 = 48$

$PQ = \sqrt{48} = \sqrt{16 \times 3} = 4\sqrt{3}$

So the perimeter is $4 + 8 + 4\sqrt{3} = 12 + 4\sqrt{3}$

You can skip over a large number of the steps we just did if you remember the facts about a 30-60-90 triangle. PQR is a right triangle in which one of the sides is half the hypotenuse. So PQR must be a 30-60-90 triangle and QR is opposite the 30° angle. This means that $PQ = 4\sqrt{3}$.

THE AREA OF A TRIANGLE IS EQUAL TO $\frac{1}{2}$ TIMES THE ALTITUDE TIMES THE BASE.

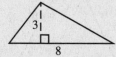 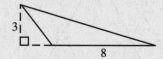

The area of the triangle on the left is $\frac{1}{2} \times 3 \times 8 = 12$. And the area of the triangle on the right is also $\frac{1}{2} \times 3 \times 8 = 12$.

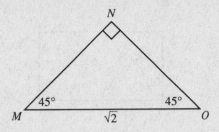

EXAMPLE:

What is the area of triangle *MNO*?

  Ⓐ $\frac{1}{2}$ Ⓑ $\frac{\sqrt{2}}{2}$ Ⓒ 1   Ⓓ $\sqrt{2}$ Ⓔ 2

The answer is (A). This is a 45-45-90 triangle, so each of the two shorter sides is $\frac{1}{2}$ $\times \sqrt{2} \times MO = \frac{1}{2} \times \sqrt{2} \times \sqrt{2} = \frac{1}{2} \times 2 = 1$. Since *MN* and *NO* form a right angle, we can use them as altitude and base:

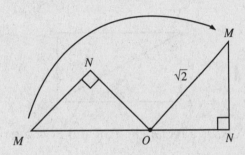

$$\frac{1}{2} \times 1 \times 1 = \frac{1}{2} \times 1 = \frac{1}{2}$$

Rectangles and Squares

THE PERIMETER OF A RECTANGLE IS EQUAL TO THE SUM OF THE LENGTHS OF THE FOUR SIDES. THE AREA OF A RECTANGLE IS EQUAL TO THE WIDTH MULTIPLIED BY THE LENGTH.

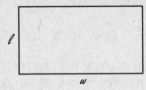

The perimeter of the rectangle above is $w + \ell + w + \ell = 2w + 2\ell$. The area is equal to w times $\ell = w\ell$.

17

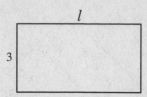

EXAMPLE:

If the area of the rectangle above is 18, what is the perimeter?

   Ⓐ 9   Ⓑ 12   Ⓒ 18   Ⓓ 24   Ⓔ 30

The answer is (C). The area of a rectangle is $w \times \ell$.

   $3 \times \ell = 18$

   $\ell = 18 \div 3 = 6.$

So the perimeter is $3 + 6 + 3 + 6 = 18$.

THE DIAGONAL OF A RECTANGLE IS THE HYPOTENUSE OF A RIGHT TRIANGLE WITH SIDES THAT ARE THE LENGTH AND WIDTH OF THE RECTANGLE.

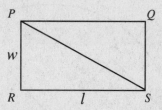

In the figure above, *PQRS* is a rectangle. *PSR* and *PQR* are right triangles, so $PR^2 = w^2 + \ell^2$.

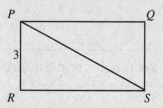

EXAMPLE:

In the figure above, *PQRS* is a rectangle. If *PS* = 5, then what is the area of the rectangle?

   Ⓐ 2   Ⓑ 3   Ⓒ 4   Ⓓ 8   Ⓔ 12

The answer is (E). *PSR* is a right triangle with hypotenuse of 5 and one side of 3, so the missing side must be 4. The area of the rectangle is $3 \times 4 = 12$.

A SQUARE IS A RECTANGLE WITH FOUR EQUAL SIDES. SO THE PERIM-
ETER OF A SQUARE IS 4 TIMES THE LENGTH OF A SIDE, AND THE AREA
IS SIDE TIMES SIDE.

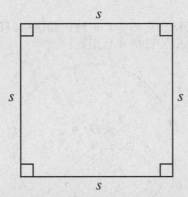

The perimeter of the square is $s + s + s + s = 4s$, and the area of the square is $s \times s$ $= s^2$.

THE DIAGONAL OF A SQUARE IS EQUAL TO ITS SIDE TIMES $\sqrt{2}$, AND
THE SIDE OF A SQUARE IS EQUAL TO $\frac{1}{2}$ TIMES ITS DIAGONAL TIMES $\sqrt{2}$.

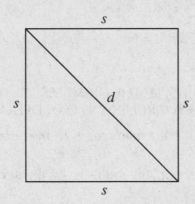

In the square above, $d = s\sqrt{2}$, and $s = \frac{1}{2} \times d\sqrt{2}$. This is just a variation on the Pythagorean Theorem. The two sides of the square and the diagonal create a 45-45-90 triangle.

GIVEN (1) THE SIDE, (2) THE DIAGONAL, OR (3) THE AREA OF A
SQUARE, YOU CAN DEDUCE THE OTHER TWO QUANTITIES.

(1) Given that the side has a length of s, the area is $s \times s = s^2$, and the diagonal $= s\sqrt{2}$

(2) Given that the diagonal has a length of d, the side is $\frac{1}{2} \times d\sqrt{2}$, and the area is

$$(\tfrac{1}{2} \times d\sqrt{2}) \times (\tfrac{1}{2} \times d\sqrt{2}) = \frac{2d^2}{4}$$

(3) Given that the area is s^2, the side is s, and the diagonal is $s\sqrt{2}$.

17

Circles

THE RADIUS OF A CIRCLE IS $\frac{1}{2}$ OF THE DIAMETER, AND THE DIAMETER OF A CIRCLE IS 2 TIMES THE RADIUS.

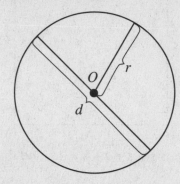

CIRCUMFERENCE = $2\pi r$

AREA = πr^2

If a circle has a radius of 3:

CIRCUMFERENCE = $2\pi(3) = 6\pi$

AREA = $\pi(3^2) = 9\pi$

GIVEN (1) THE RADIUS, (2) THE DIAMETER, (3) THE CIRCUMFERENCE, OR (4) THE AREA OF A CIRCLE, YOU CAN DEDUCE THE OTHER THREE.

(1) Given a radius of r, the diameter is $2r$, the circumference is $2\pi r$, and the area is πr^2.

(2) Given a diameter of d, the radius is $\frac{1}{2}d$, the circumference is $2\pi\left(\frac{d}{2}\right) = \pi d$, and the area is $\pi\left(\frac{d}{2}\right)^2 = \left(\frac{\pi d^2}{4}\right)$.

(3) Given a circumference of $2\pi r$, the radius is r, the diameter is $2r$, and the area is πr^2.

(4) Given an area of πr^2, the radius is r, the diameter is $2r$, and the circumference is $2\pi r$.

EXAMPLE:

If the area of a circle is 9π, which of the following is (are) true?

  I. The radius is 3.

 II. The diameter is 6.

III. The circumference is 6π.

Ⓐ I only   Ⓑ II only   Ⓒ III only   Ⓓ I and II only   Ⓔ I, II, and III

The answer is (E). If the area of the circle is 9π, then

$\pi r^2 = 9\pi$

$r^2 = 9$

$r = \sqrt{9} = 3$

So statement I is true. Then if $r = 3$, the diameter is 2×3, so II is also true. Finally, if $r = 3$, then the circumference is $2\pi(3) = 6\pi$.

Solids

THE VOLUME OF A RECTANGULAR SOLID (A BOX) IS THE WIDTH OF THE BASE MULTIPLIED BY THE LENGTH OF THE BASE MULTIPLIED BY THE HEIGHT OF THE SOLID.

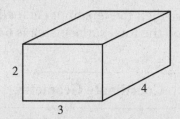

The volume of the rectangular solid above is $2 \times 3 \times 4 = 24$.

THE AREA OF THE FACE OF A RECTANGULAR SOLID (SIDE OF A BOX) IS THE PRODUCT OF THE LENGTH OF ONE EDGE OF THE FACE AND THE LENGTH OF AN ADJACENT EDGE.

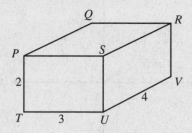

The area of $PTUS = 2 \times 3 = 6$.
The area of $SRVU = 2 \times 4 = 8$.
The area of $PQRS = 3 \times 4 = 12$.

THE TOTAL SURFACE AREA OF A RECTANGULAR SOLID (THE OUTSIDE OF A BOX) IS THE SUM OF THE AREAS OF THE SIX FACES.

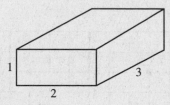

The front has an area of $1 \times 2 = 2$.
The side has an area of $1 \times 3 = 3$.
The bottom has an area of $2 \times 3 = 6$.
Since there are two of each (front = back, side = side, bottom = top), the total surface area is $(2 + 2) + (3 + 3) + (6 + 6) = 22$.

A CUBE IS A RECTANGULAR SOLID WITH THREE EQUAL DIMENSIONS. GIVEN (1) THE LENGTH OF AN EDGE, (2) THE AREA OF A FACE, (3) THE TOTAL SURFACE AREA OF THE CUBE, OR (4) THE VOLUME OF THE CUBE, YOU CAN DEDUCE THE OTHER THREE QUANTITIES.

17

(1) If the edge is s, then the area of each face is s^2, the total surface area is $6s^2$, and the volume is s^3.

(2) If the area of a face is s^2, then the length of each edge is s, the total surface area is $6s^2$, and the volume is s^3.

(3) If the total surface area is $6s^2$, then the area of a face is s^2, the length of each edge is s, and the volume is s^3.

(4) If the volume is s^3, then the length of each edge is s, the surface area of each face is s^2, and the total surface area is $6s^2$.

Coordinate Geometry

A COORDINATE PLANE IS DESCRIBED WITH REFERENCE TO AN X-AXIS (HORIZONTAL AXIS) AND A Y-AXIS (VERTICAL AXIS) WHICH ARE PERPENDICULAR TO EACH OTHER. THEIR INTERSECTION IS CALLED THE ORIGIN.

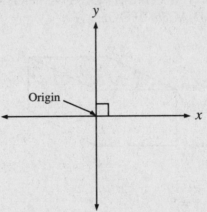

COORDINATE PAIRS ARE USED TO LOCATE POINTS ON THE PLANE. THE GENERAL FORM IS (x, y). THE FIRST ELEMENT GIVES LOCATION WITH REFERENCE TO THE X-AXIS, THE SECOND WITH REFERENCE TO THE Y-AXIS.

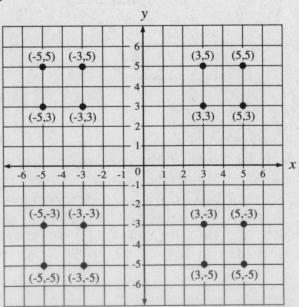

THE LENGTH OF A LINE PARALLEL TO AN AXIS IS THE DIFFERENCE
BETWEEN THE END-POINT COORDINATES FOR THAT AXIS.

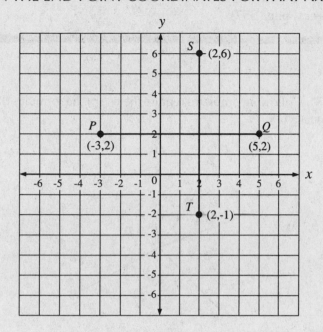

Line *PQ* runs from (–3,2) to (5,2) parallel to the *x*-axis. So the distance is just the
difference between the *x* coordinates, 5 and –3; 5 – (–3) = 5 + 3 = 8. Line *ST* runs
from (2,6) to (2,–2), so the length is the difference between the *y* coordinates:
6 – (–2) = 6 + 2 = 8.

THE LENGTH OF LINES NOT PARALLEL TO EITHER AXIS CAN BE
DETERMINED BY THE PYTHAGOREAN THEOREM.

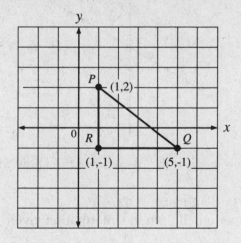

PQR is a right triangle. *PR* = 3, and *RQ* = 4. So *PQ* = 5.

17

Holmes' Attic (Answers, page 357)

Directions: The following problems require the use of the formulas discussed in the preceding section.

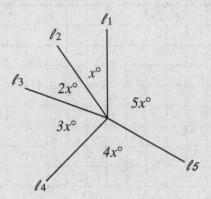

1. In the figure above, $x =$

Ⓐ 10   Ⓑ 15   Ⓒ 18   Ⓓ 24   Ⓔ 25

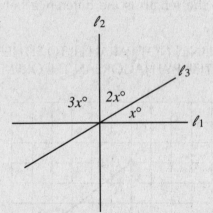

2. In the figure above, what is the measure of the angle formed by the intersection of ℓ_1 and ℓ_3?

Ⓐ 30°   Ⓑ 45°   Ⓒ 60°   Ⓓ 90°
Ⓔ Cannot be determined from the information given.

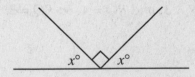

3. In the figure above, $x =$

Ⓐ 30   Ⓑ 45   Ⓒ 55   Ⓓ 60   Ⓔ 75

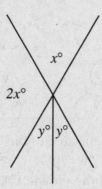

4. In the figure above, $y =$

   Ⓐ 15   Ⓑ 30   Ⓒ 45   Ⓓ 60

   Ⓔ Cannot be determined from the information given.

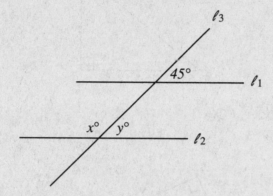

5. In the figure above, $x - y =$

   Ⓐ 0   Ⓑ 45   Ⓒ 60   Ⓓ 90   Ⓔ 135

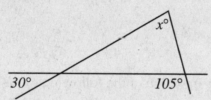

6. In the figure above, $x =$

   Ⓐ 25   Ⓑ 35   Ⓒ 45   Ⓓ 55   Ⓔ 75

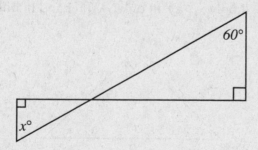

17

7. In the figure above, $x =$

   Ⓐ 15   Ⓑ 30   Ⓒ 45   Ⓓ 60

   Ⓔ Cannot be determined from the information given.

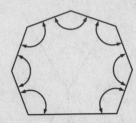

8. In the figure above, what is the sum of the indicated angles?

Ⓐ 360 Ⓑ 540 Ⓒ 720 Ⓓ 900

Ⓔ Cannot be determined from the information given.

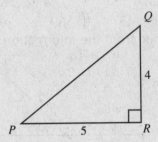

9. In the figure above, $PQ =$

Ⓐ 1 Ⓑ 3 Ⓒ $3\sqrt{2}$ Ⓓ $\sqrt{41}$ Ⓔ $\sqrt{47}$

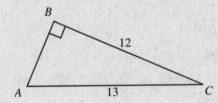

10. In the figure above, $AB =$

Ⓐ 1 Ⓑ 5 Ⓒ $5\sqrt{2}$ Ⓓ $5\sqrt{3}$ Ⓔ 11

11. Triangles with sides in which of the following ratios must be right triangles?

   I. $2 : 1 : \sqrt{3}$

   II. $1 : 1 : \sqrt{2}$

   III. $\sqrt{2} : \sqrt{2} : 2$

Ⓐ I only Ⓑ II only Ⓒ III only Ⓓ I and III only Ⓔ I, II, and III

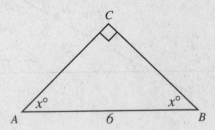

12. In the figure above, $AB =$

Ⓐ 3 Ⓑ $3\sqrt{2}$ Ⓒ $3\sqrt{3}$ Ⓓ 9 Ⓔ $\dfrac{9\sqrt{3}}{2}$

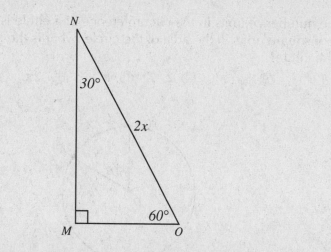

13. In the figure above, $NM =$

 Ⓐ x Ⓑ $x\sqrt{3}$ Ⓒ $3x$ Ⓓ $2x\sqrt{3}$ Ⓔ $3x\sqrt{3}$

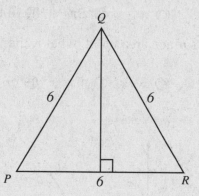

14. What is the area of triangle PQR?

 Ⓐ $2\sqrt{3}$ Ⓑ 9 Ⓒ $9\sqrt{3}$ Ⓓ 18 Ⓔ $18\sqrt{3}$

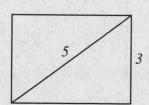

15. What is the area of the rectangle shown above?

 Ⓐ 8 Ⓑ 12 Ⓒ 15 Ⓓ 18 Ⓔ 30

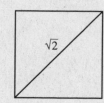

16. What is the area of the square shown above?

 Ⓐ 1 Ⓑ $\sqrt{2}$ Ⓒ 2 Ⓓ $2\sqrt{2}$ Ⓔ $4\sqrt{2}$

17

17. If the number of units in the circumference of a circle is equal to the number of square units in the area of the circle, what is the length of the radius of the circle?

　Ⓐ 1　　Ⓑ $\sqrt{2}$　　Ⓒ 2　　Ⓓ π　　Ⓔ 2π

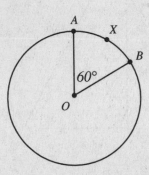

18. If the radius of Circle O, shown above, is 3, what is the length of arc AXB?

　Ⓐ $\frac{1}{6}\pi$　　Ⓑ $\frac{1}{3}\pi$　　Ⓒ π　　Ⓓ 3π　　Ⓔ 6π

19. If a cube has a total surface area of 54, what is the length of the edge of the cube?

　Ⓐ 3　　Ⓑ $2\sqrt{2}$　　Ⓒ $3\sqrt{2}$　　Ⓓ 6　　Ⓔ 9

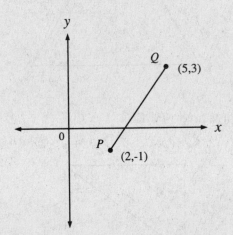

20. In the figure above, what is the length of PQ?

　Ⓐ 1　　Ⓑ $3\sqrt{2}$　　Ⓒ 4　　Ⓓ 5　　Ⓔ 7

Complex Figures

Thus far we have discussed the most commonly used principles of geometry as they apply to simple figures such as intersecting lines, triangles, squares, and circles. Some of the drawings used on the GMAT, however, may be made up of more than one figure.

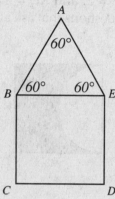

EXAMPLE:

If *BCDE* is a square with an area of 4, what is the perimeter of triangle *ABE*?

Ⓐ 3 Ⓑ 4 Ⓒ 6 Ⓓ 8 Ⓔ 12

The answer is (C). *ABE* has three 60° angles, so it is equilateral. To find the perimeter, you need to find the length of one of the sides. The only information given in the question is the area of the square. To bridge the gap, you must see that one side of the square is also a side of the triangle. If you can find the side of the square, you have everything you need to know.

Since the area of the square is 4, the side of the square is 2:

side × side = area

$s^2 = 4$

$s = \sqrt{4} = 2$

So the perimeter of the triangle is 2 + 2 + 2.

The key to such questions is to see that some line or angle serves two functions. Here is an example of greater difficulty:

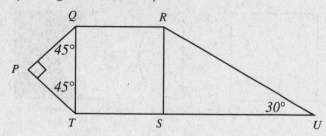

EXAMPLE:

In the figure above, if *QRST* is a square and $PQ = \sqrt{2}$, what is the length of *RU*?

Ⓐ $\sqrt{2}$ Ⓑ $\sqrt{6}$ Ⓒ $2\sqrt{2}$ Ⓓ 4 Ⓔ $4\sqrt{3}$

17

The question doesn't supply a lot of information—at least not explicitly. So it must be possible to deduce some further conclusions from what is given.

The hypotenuse of *PQT* is also a side of square *QRST*. And *RS* is not only a side of the square, it is a side of triangle *RSU*. If we can find the length of *QT*, we can deduce the length of *RU*. Since *PQT* is a 45-45-90 triangle and $PQ = \sqrt{2}$, $QT = \sqrt{2} \times \sqrt{2} = 2$. All four sides of a square are equal, so $RS = QT = 2$. *RS* is also a side in a 30-60-90 triangle (*RS* is perpendicular to *TU*). Since *RS* is opposite the 30° angle, it is $\frac{1}{2}$ the length of *RU*. So $\frac{1}{2} RU = 2$, and $RU = 4$.

A variation on this theme is questions that ask about shaded portions of a figure.

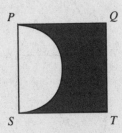

EXAMPLE:

In the figure above, *PQTS* is a square, and *PS* is the diameter of a semicircle. If $PQ = 2$, what is the area of the shaded portion of the diagram?

   Ⓐ $4 - 2\pi$ Ⓑ $4 - \pi$ Ⓒ $4 - \dfrac{\pi}{2}$ Ⓓ $8 - \pi$ Ⓔ $8 - \dfrac{\pi}{2}$

The answer is (C). What makes the problem a little tricky is that you are asked to find the area of a figure that looks like this:

And that is not a figure for which you have a ready-at-hand formula. The key to the solution is to see that the irregular shaded part of the figure is what's left over after you take away the semicircle from the square:

Square *PQTS* minus Semicircle = Shaded Area

So if you can find the area of the square and the area of the semicircle, you can answer the question.

Now we proceed as we did above. *PS* is not only a side of the square, it is the diameter of the semicircle. Since the side of the square is 2, the square has an area of 4. And since $PS = 2$, the semicircle has a radius of 1. The area of an entire circle with radius 1 is $\pi r^2 = \pi(1^2) = \pi$. And since this is half a circle, the semicircle has an area of $\frac{\pi}{2}$. So the area of the shaded portion of the figure is $4 - \frac{\pi}{2}$.

Monster Figures (Answers, page 360)

Take a quick glance at the three figures that follow. They are more complex than anything you should expect to see on your GMAT, but they make excellent practice.

The interesting thing about the drawings is that if you know the length of any line or the area of any part of the figure (no matter how weird its shape) you can find the length of every other line in the drawing and the area of every other shape.

Directions: Below each drawing is a table you are to fill in. You are asked to assume values for various aspects of the drawings and to deduce values for other parts of the drawings. In the explanations at the end of the lesson you will find a correctly completed table and an outline of the procedures to follow.

MONSTER DRAWING 1

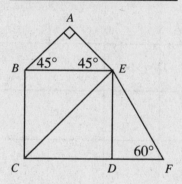

	AB	BC	CE	DF	EF	Area △ABE	Area △CDE	Area △EDF
AB = 1	1							
BC = 1		1						
CE = 1			1					
DF = 1				1				
EF = 1					1			

MONSTER DRAWING 2

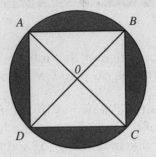

	AB	Radius	Area ABCD	Circum- ference of Circle	Area of Circle	Shaded Area
AB = 1	1					
Radius = 1		1				
Area of ABCD = 4			4			
Circumference of Circle = 2π				2π		
Area of Circle = 4π					4π	

MONSTER DRAWING 3

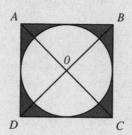

	AB	AO	Radius	Area ABCD	Circum-ference of Circle	Area of Circle	Shaded Area
AB = 1	1						
AO = 1		1					
Radius = 1			1				
Area ABCD = 16				16			
Circumference = 8 π					8 π		
Area Circle = 9 π						9 π	

17

IF YOU DON'T SEE WHAT YOU WANT, ASK FOR IT.

This is a strategy we developed for algebra problems, but it applies to some geometry questions as well.

EXAMPLE:

If the width of a rectangle is increased by 10 percent and the length of the rectangle is increased by 20 percent, the area of the rectangle increases by what percent?

Ⓐ 2%   Ⓑ 10%   Ⓒ 15%   Ⓓ 32%   Ⓔ 36%

The answer is (D) Assume that the original width of the rectangle is 10 and the original length is 10. (Yes, the width is equal to the length, but a square is a rectangle too, and 10 is a convenient number.)

On the assumption that $w = 10$ and $\ell = 10$, the original area is 100. Now increase the width by 10 percent from 10 to 11 and the length by 20 percent from 10 to 12. The new area is $11 \times 12 = 132$. Using the "change-over" formula, the change is $132 - 100 = 32$ and the original amount is 100, so the percent change is $\frac{32}{100} = 32\%$

ONE PICTURE IS WORTH A THOUSAND WORDS.

Some GMAT geometry questions do not come equipped with a figure, and this makes them more difficult. When no sketch is provided, make one yourself.

EXAMPLE:

If a circle of radius 1 is inscribed in a square, what is the area of the square?

Ⓐ 1   Ⓑ $\frac{\sqrt{2}}{2}$ Ⓒ $\sqrt{2}$ Ⓓ 2   Ⓔ 4

The answer is (E). This can be seen more easily if you draw the figure:

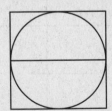

Now you can see that the diameter of the circle is equal to the side of the square. Since the radius of the circle is 1, the diameter is 2. So the side of the square is 2, and the area of the square is $2 \times 2 = 4$.

Sometimes you may be given a figure that is in some respect incomplete. To see the solution, you may need to add one or more lines to the drawing.

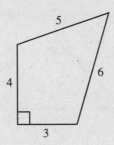

EXAMPLE:

What is the area of the quadrilateral above?

Ⓐ 6   Ⓑ $6 + \sqrt{3}$ Ⓒ 12   Ⓓ 18

Ⓔ Cannot be determined from the information given.

The correct choice is (D), and the numbers 3, 4, and 5 are highly suggestive of one of those famous triangles. Divide the quadrilateral into two triangles:

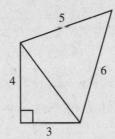

Now the problem turns into a composite figure problem. You have one triangle with an altitude and a base of 3 and 4. So it has an area of $\frac{1}{2} \times 3 \times 4 = 6$. As for the other triangle, it has a base of 6, but you need an altitude. So sketch it in:

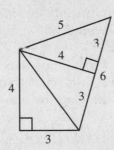

Since the altitude bisects the base (divides it in half), you have created two 3-4-5 triangles. So the area of the second triangle is $\frac{1}{2} \times 4 \times 6 = 12$. And the area of the entire quadrilateral is 6 + 12 = 18.

EXAMPLE:

An isosceles right triangle is inscribed in a semicircle with radius 1. What is the area of the triangle?

Ⓐ $\frac{1}{2}$ Ⓑ $\frac{\sqrt{2}}{2}$ Ⓒ 1   Ⓓ $\sqrt{2}$ Ⓔ $2\sqrt{2}$

17

The correct choice is (C), which is more easily seen if you draw the figure:

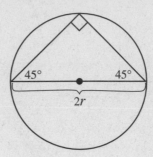

Now you can see that the diameter of the circle is the base of the triangle. But what about an altitude? Sketch that also:

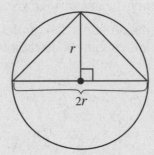

So the altitude is equal to the radius of the circle. And the area of the triangle is $\frac{1}{2} \times 2 \times 1 = 1$.

Out of the Attic

In the story of "The Musgrave Ritual," Holmes steps off the distances provided by a cryptic treasure map to find a family's hidden legacy. This is a simple, direct, and effective solution. And Holmes would find ample opportunity to use the same tactic on the GMAT.

You will recall from Lesson 14 that Problem-Solving drawings are rendered to scale (unless accompanied by the disclaimer "**Note:** Figure not drawn to scale"). Take advantage of the accurate drawings by estimating and measuring quantities instead of solving by formulas.

Three techniques will help you get the most out of the drawings: "guestimating," "measuring," and "meastimating."

1. "Guestimating"

Sometimes it is possible to arrive at a correct answer just by a rough approximation with the eye.

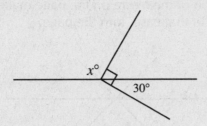

EXAMPLE:

In the figure above, what is the value of *x*?

   Ⓐ 30   Ⓑ 65   Ⓒ 120   Ⓓ 150   Ⓔ 170

A glance should show you that angle *x* is greater than a right angle. This allows you to eliminate both (A) and (B). But *x* is only 20 or 30 degrees bigger than a right angle, so (D) and (E) can also be eliminated. This leaves only choice (C). And if you do the geometry, you will confirm what we have already deduced.

    To develop your skill at "guestimating," study the following angles.

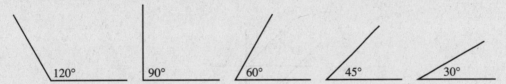

    If you can visualize them, you can arrive at a fairly accurate conclusion about the size of almost any angle.

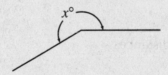

EXAMPLE:

In the figure above, *x* =

   Ⓐ 120   Ⓑ 150   Ⓒ 180   Ⓓ 210   Ⓔ 240

The answer is (D). The angle is larger than 180°, so you can eliminate (A), (B), and (C). But what about (D) and (E)? A quick sketch will help you:

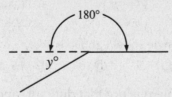

    What's your best estimate of the value of *y*? 30° or 60°? It must be 30°, and 180° + 30° = 210°.

17

Sometimes the position of the figure on the page makes it difficult to get a feel for the size of the angle. In that case, turn the page.

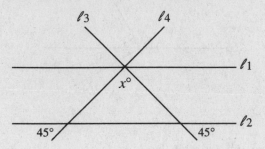

EXAMPLE:

If $\ell_1 \parallel \ell_2$, then $x =$

Ⓐ 45   Ⓑ 60   Ⓒ 90   Ⓓ 110   Ⓔ 125

The answer is (C). If you have trouble seeing that x is a right angle, turn your book until x looks like this:

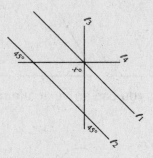

You can also "guestimate" distances.

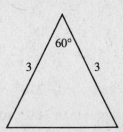

EXAMPLE:

The perimeter of the triangle shown above is

Ⓐ $3\sqrt{2}$ Ⓑ 6   Ⓒ 7.5   Ⓓ 9   Ⓔ 15

The answer is (D). The problem is not that difficult, and you can probably quickly deduce that the third side has a length of 3. But you can also tell that at a glance. It *looks* like it's 3 units long. So the perimeter is $3 + 3 + 3 = 9$.

Estimating Angles (Answers, page 361)

Directions: Visualize the following angles.

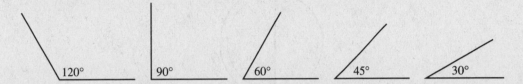

120°   90°   60°   45°   30°

Answer the following questions based solely on your ability to "guestimate." Use the answer choices to guide you. So you won't be tempted to use geometry, all information except the picture has been deleted.

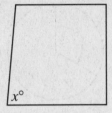

1. In the figure above, *x* =

    Ⓐ 15   Ⓑ 30   Ⓒ 60   Ⓓ 75   Ⓔ 85

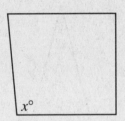

2. In the figure above, *x* =

    Ⓐ 120   Ⓑ 95   Ⓒ 85   Ⓓ 75   Ⓔ 60

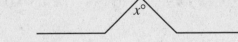

3. In the figure above, *x* =

    Ⓐ 15   Ⓑ 30   Ⓒ 45   Ⓓ 60   Ⓔ 90

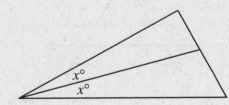

4. In the figure above, *x* =

    Ⓐ 15   Ⓑ 30   Ⓒ 45   Ⓓ 55   Ⓔ 70

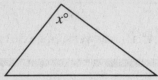

5. In the figure above, $x =$
 Ⓐ 20 Ⓑ 30 Ⓒ 45 Ⓓ 75 Ⓔ 90

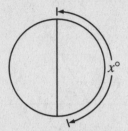

6. In the figure above, $x =$
 Ⓐ 210 Ⓑ 183 Ⓒ 175 Ⓓ 140 Ⓔ 120

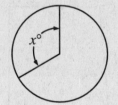

7. In the figure above, $x =$
 Ⓐ 60 Ⓑ 75 Ⓒ 90 Ⓓ 120 Ⓔ 150

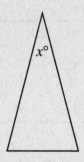

8. In the figure above, $x =$
 Ⓐ 15 Ⓑ 30 Ⓒ 45 Ⓓ 55 Ⓔ 60

9. In the figure above, the sum of the indicated angles is
 Ⓐ 180° Ⓑ 360° Ⓒ 540° Ⓓ 680° Ⓔ 720°

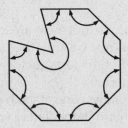

10. What is the average measure of the degrees of the angles indicated above?

Ⓐ 45   Ⓑ 60   Ⓒ 90   Ⓓ 120   Ⓔ 140

2. *Measuring*

"Guestimating" is a useful technique, but there are times when it won't be accurate enough. Then you should measure. It's true that you're not allowed to bring a protractor or a ruler to the test. But the test proctor is going to give you something that does both jobs: scratch paper!

Scratch paper has four right angles, one at each corner. You can use the corner for measuring angles. It will tell you immediately whether an angle is larger than, smaller than, or exactly 90°. Additionally, if you have trouble visualizing angles, the scatch paper will help you.

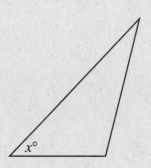

EXAMPLE:

In the figure above, $x =$

Ⓐ 30 Ⓑ 45 Ⓒ 60 Ⓓ 75 Ⓔ 90

If you have trouble seeing that the answer is (B), take a sheet of paper and line up a corner next to the angle in question:

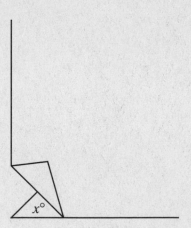

Pull up the edge. The angle seems to be half of the right angle formed by the corner of the page.

There are more ways of using the corner of scratch paper than can be described in a reasonable space. Just keep your mind open.

The scratch paper can also be used as a ruler. To be sure, it doesn't have inches or centimeters marked on it; but then, you don't need them.

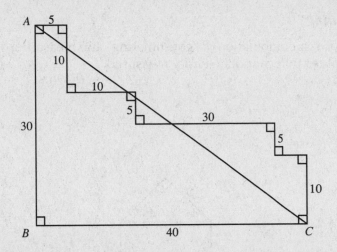

EXAMPLE:

In the figure above, *AC* =

Ⓐ $30\sqrt{2}$ Ⓑ 50   Ⓒ 75   Ⓓ $60\sqrt{2}$ Ⓔ 100

The answer is (B). You can work it out using the Pythagorean Theorem. But you can also use the edge of a sheet of paper to measure it.

Get a piece of notebook paper. Mark off the distance from A to C like this:

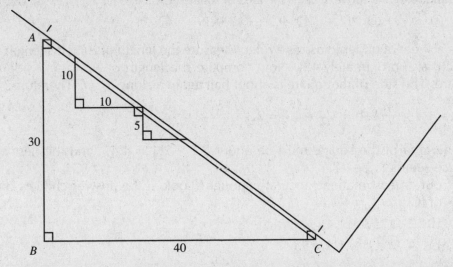

Now measure the distance on the edge of the paper against one of the distances in the problem:

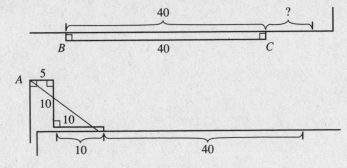

Repeat until you have the full measure of *AC*. It is 50.

3. "Meastimating"

"Meastimating" is a combination of "guestimating" and measuring. It uses approximations for values that cannot be easily measured.

$$\sqrt{2} = 1.4$$

$$\sqrt{3} = 1.7$$

$$\pi = 3.1$$

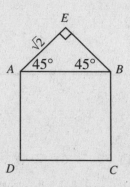

EXAMPLE:

In the figure above, what is the area of square *ABCD*?

Ⓐ 2   Ⓑ $\sqrt{2}$ Ⓒ 4   Ⓓ $4\sqrt{2}$ Ⓔ 8

Take a sheet of paper to use as a ruler. Measure the length of *AE*. This length is $\sqrt{2}$, which is approximately 1.4. Now compare the length of *AE* to any side of the square. The side of the square is about half again as long as *AE*. Therefore:

$$\text{side} \cong 1.4 + \frac{1}{2}(1.4) = 1.4 + 0.7 = 2.1$$

So the area of the square must be about 2.1 × 2.1 = 4.41, and the best answer choice seems to be (C).

Is our "meastimation" accurate enough? Look at the answer choices on both sides of (C):

(B) $2\sqrt{2} \cong 2 \times 1.4 = 2.8$

(D) $4\sqrt{2} \cong 4 \times 1.4 = 5.6$

So the best answer must be (C).

The Monster Revisited (Answers, page 362)

Directions: This exercise is based on one of the monster drawings from Exercise 2. Again, you are asked to assume values for various aspects of the drawing and complete a table. This time, however, complete the table by "meastimating." For example, if *AB* = 1, then *BE* must be about 1.7.

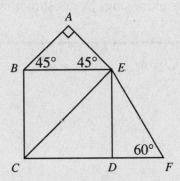

	AB	BC	CE	DF	EF	Area △ABE	Area BCDE	Area △EDF
AB = 1	1							
BC = 1		1						
CE = 1			1					
DF = 1				1				
EF = 1					1			

17

Summary

1. "Holmes' attic" contains all of the geometry principles you need for the GMAT.
2. Complex figures can be analyzed as two figures with a common feature.
3. Shaded areas can be analyzed as the difference between two common figures.
4. Instead of working with unknowns, assume values.
5. Unless otherwise noted, all figures are drawn to scale. Take advantage of the accuracy of the drawings by guestimating, measuring, or meastimating.

Explanatory Answers

EXERCISE 1

1. **(D)**

   $x + 2x + 3x + 4x + 5x = 360$

   $15x = 360$

   $x = 24$

2. **(A)**

   $x + 2x + 3x = 180$

   $6x = 180$

   $x = 30$

3. **(B)**

   $x + x + 90 = 180$

   $2x + 90 = 180$

   $2x = 90$

   $x = 45$

4. **(B)**

   $2x + x = 180$

   $3x = 180$

   $x = 60$

   $y + y = x$

   $y + y = 60$

   $2y = 60$

   $y = 30$

5. **(D)** Since $\ell 1 \parallel \ell 2$, you can use the "big angle/little angle" theorem.

   $y = 45$

   $x + y = 180$

   $x + 45 = 180$

   $x = 135$

   $x - y = 135 - 45 = 90$

17

6. **(E)** The angle inside the triangle and opposite the 30° angle is also 30°. The angle inside the triangle and next to the 105° angle is $180 - 105 = 75°$.

$30 + 75 + x = 180$

$105 + x = 180$

$x = 75$

7. **(D)** The third angle of the larger triangle is 30°. The angle directly opposite it (in the smaller triangle) is also 30°. So:

$90 + 30 + x = 180$

$120 + x = 180$

$x = 60$

8. **(D)** The figure has seven sides, so the sum of the degree measures of its interior angles is $180(7 - 2) = 900$. (Or, you can divide the polygon into five triangular regions.)

9. **(D)**

$PQ^2 = PR^2 + RQ^2$

$PQ^2 = 5^2 + 4^2$

$PQ^2 = 25 + 16$

$PQ^2 = 41$

$PQ = \sqrt{41}$

10. **(B)**

$AB^2 + BC^2 = AC^2$

$AB^2 = AC^2 - BC^2$

$AB^2 = 13^2 - 12^2$

$AB^2 = 169 - 144$

$AB^2 = 25$

$AB = \sqrt{25} = 5$

11. **(E)** A 30-60-90 triangle has sides in the ratio $2:1:\sqrt{3}$. A 45-45-90 triangle has sides in the ratio $1:1:\sqrt{2}$. And a triangle with sides of $\sqrt{2}:\sqrt{2}:2$ fits the Pythagorean Theorem:

$(\sqrt{2})^2 + (\sqrt{2})^2 = 2^2$

(Also, a triangle with sides in the ratio of $\sqrt{2}:\sqrt{2}:2$ is a 45-45-90 triangle.)

12. **(B)** AC is the hypotenuse of a 45-45-90 triangle, so AB is equal to $\frac{1}{2}$ times 6 times $\sqrt{2}$:

$AB = \frac{1}{2}(6)(\sqrt{2}) = 3\sqrt{2}$

13. **(B)** MNO is a 30-60-90 triangle. NM is equal to $\frac{1}{2}$ times NO times $\sqrt{3}$:

$$NM = \frac{1}{2}(2x)(\sqrt{3})$$

$$NM = x\sqrt{3}$$

14. **(C)** Since PQR is equilateral, the altitude creates two 30-60-90 triangles. The altitude is the side opposite the 60° angle, so it is equal to $\frac{1}{2}$ times 6 times $\sqrt{3}$:

$$\text{Altitude} = \frac{1}{2}(6)(\sqrt{3}) = 3\sqrt{3}$$

$$\text{Area } PQR = \frac{1}{2}(\text{alt.})(\text{base}) = \frac{1}{2}(3\sqrt{3})(6) = 9\sqrt{3}$$

15. **(B)** The diagonal creates a right triangle with a hypotenuse of 5 and side of 3. The remaining side, which is the length of the rectangle, is 4.

$$\text{Area} = \text{length} \times \text{width}$$

$$\text{Area} = 4 \times 3 = 12$$

16. **(A)** The diagonal of the square creates two 45-45-90 triangles. So the side of the square is equal to $\frac{1}{2}$ times the diagonal times $\sqrt{2}$:

$$\text{side} = \frac{1}{2}(\sqrt{2})(\sqrt{2}) = \frac{1}{2}(2) = 1$$

$$\text{Area of square} = \text{side} \times \text{side} = 1 \times 1 = 1$$

17. **(C)**

$$\text{Area} = \text{Circumference}$$

$$\pi r^2 = 2\pi r$$

$$r^2 = 2r$$

$$r = 2$$

Note: In algebra, $r = +2$ or -2. But r here indicates a distance that can only be positive.)

18. **(C)** The circumference of Circle O is $2\pi r = 2\pi(3) = 6\pi$. Since the entire circle measures 360°, $AXB = \frac{60}{360} = \frac{1}{6}$ of the circle. And $\frac{1}{6}$ of $6\pi = \pi$.

19. **(A)** Since a cube has six faces, each face has an area of $54 \div 6 = 9$. The area of a face is a function of the length of the edge or side: side $\times$ side $= 9$, $s^2 = 9$, $s = 3$.

20. **(D)** Drop a line from Q parallel to the Y-axis. Draw a line through P parallel to the X-axis. The point where the two intersect (call it R) is $(5, -1)$. PQ is the hypotenuse of the right triangle you have created. The triangle has sides with lengths of 3 and 4, so the length of PQ is 5.

17

EXERCISE 2

	AB	BC $BC = AB \times \sqrt{2}$	CE $CE = BE \times \sqrt{2}$	DF $DF = BE \div \sqrt{3}$	EF $EF = 2\,DF$	Area ABE $\frac{1}{2}(AB)(AE)$	Area $BCDE$ BE^2	Area EDF $\frac{1}{2}(ED \times DF)$
$AB = 1$	1	$\sqrt{2}$	2	$\frac{\sqrt{2}}{\sqrt{3}} = \frac{\sqrt{6}}{3}$	$\frac{2}{3}\sqrt{6}$	$\frac{1}{2}$	2	$\frac{\sqrt{3}}{3}$
$BC = 1$	$\frac{\sqrt{2}}{2}$	1	$\sqrt{2}$	$\frac{1}{\sqrt{3}} = \frac{\sqrt{3}}{3}$	$\frac{2}{3}\sqrt{3}$	$\frac{1}{4}$	1	$\frac{\sqrt{3}}{6}$
$CE = 1$	$\frac{1}{2}$	$\frac{\sqrt{2}}{2}$	1	$\frac{\sqrt{2}}{2\sqrt{3}} = \frac{\sqrt{6}}{6}$	$\frac{\sqrt{6}}{3}$	$\frac{1}{8}$	$\frac{1}{2}$	$\frac{\sqrt{3}}{12}$
$DF = 1$	$\frac{\sqrt{6}}{2}$	$\sqrt{3}$	$\sqrt{6}$	1	2	$\frac{3}{4}$	3	$\frac{\sqrt{3}}{2}$
$EF = 1$	$\frac{\sqrt{6}}{4}$	$\frac{\sqrt{3}}{2}$	$\frac{\sqrt{6}}{2}$	$\frac{1}{2}$	1	$\frac{3}{16}$	$\frac{3}{4}$	$\frac{\sqrt{3}}{8}$

	AB	Radius $r = \frac{1}{2} \times AB \times \sqrt{2}$	Area $ABCD$ AB^2	Circum- ference of Circle $2\pi r$	Area of Circle πr^2	Shaded Area $\pi r^2 - AB^2$
$AB = 1$	1	$\frac{\sqrt{2}}{2}$	1	$\sqrt{2}\,\pi$	$\frac{\pi}{2}$	$\frac{\pi}{2} - 1$
Radius $= 1$	$\sqrt{2}$	1	2	2π	π	$\pi - 2$
Area of $ABCD = 4$	2	$\sqrt{2}$	4	$2\sqrt{2}\,\pi$	2π	$2\pi - 4$
Circumference of Circle $= 2\pi$	$\sqrt{2}$	1	2	2π	π	$\pi - 2$
Area of Circle $= 4\pi$	$2\sqrt{2}$	2	8	4π	4π	$4\pi - 8$

	AB	AO	Radius	Area $ABCD$	Circum-ference of Circle	Area of Circle	Shaded Area
$AB = 1$	1	$\frac{\sqrt{2}}{2}$	$\frac{1}{2}$	1	π	$\frac{\pi}{4}$	$1 - \frac{\pi}{4}$
$AO = 1$	$\sqrt{2}$	1	$\frac{\sqrt{2}}{2}$	2	$\sqrt{2}\,\pi$	$\frac{\pi}{2}$	$2 - \frac{\pi}{2}$
Radius = 1	2	$\sqrt{2}$	1	4	2π	π	$4 - \pi$
Area $ABCD$ = 16	4	$2\sqrt{2}$	2	16	4π	4π	$16 - 4\pi$
Circumference $= 8\pi$	8	$4\sqrt{2}$	4	64	8π	16π	$64 - 16\pi$
Area Circle $= 9\pi$	6	$3\sqrt{2}$	3	36	6π	9π	$36 - 9\pi$

EXERCISE 3

1. **(E)** x is slightly less than a right angle, so the answer must be (E).

2. **(B)** x is slightly more than a right angle, so the answer must be (B).

3. **(E)** x appears to be a right angle. And no answer is close to 90° except (E). If you have trouble visualizing the angle, rotate the page.

4. **(A)** The entire angle consisting of x and x appears to be about 30°, so x must be 15°.

5. **(E)** x seems to be a right angle, which is choice (E). No other answer choice is close.

6. **(C)** The line through the circle seems to be a diameter, so it creates two 180° arcs. x is slightly less than 180°, so (C) must be the correct answer. (Notice how this reasoning allows us to distinguish between two numbers that are otherwise very close, 175 and 183.)

7. **(D)** x appears to take up about $\frac{1}{3}$ of the circle, so x should be $\frac{1}{3}$ of 360 = 120.

8. **(B)** This question is a bit more difficult than some of the earlier ones, but x seems to be about 30°.

9. **(E)** Our task here seems difficult, but let's give it a try. Those marked angles could be anywhere from 120° to about 140°. Let's assume they are about 130°. $6 \times 130 = 780$. Only (E) is in the ballpark.

17

10. **(E)** At first, it might seem impossible to do this question by visually estimating angles. After all, it's difficult to say whether some of them are 130° or 140° or 150°. Give the problem a try. Assume that the six angles that appear to be equal are each about 140°. Then the two acute angles seem to be about 60° each. So far we have (140 × 6) + (2 × 60) = 960. And you still have that large angle, which must be about 300°. (The unmarked angle is about 60°). So the sum of the angles is about 1,260. Since there are nine angles, the average is 1,260 ÷ 9 = 140, more or less. So (E) is the best bet. (In fact, (E) is correct, as you can prove using the formula for calculating the interior angles of a polygon.)

EXERCISE 4

	AB	$BE \cong AB \times 1.4$ BE	$CE \cong BE \times 1.4$ CE	$DF \cong BE \div 1.7$ DF	$EF = 2\,DF$ EF	$\frac{1}{2}(AB)(AE)$ Area △ABE	BE^2 Area BCDE	$\frac{1}{2}(ED \times DF)$ Area △EDF
AB = 1	1	1.4	2	.8	1.6	$\frac{1}{2}$	about 2	0.5 - 0.6
BC = 1	.7	1	1.4	0.5 - 0.6	1.0 - 1.2	about $\frac{1}{4}$	1	0.3
CE = 1	about $\frac{1}{2}$	.7	1	0.4	0.8	about $\frac{1}{8}$	about $\frac{1}{2}$	0.14
DF = 1	1.2	1.7	2.4	1	2	.7+	2.9+	0.8 - 0.9
EF = 1	0.6	0.8 - 0.9	1.2	$\frac{1}{2}$	1	0.18	0.64 - 0.81	0.2

Problem Solving Drills

1. Walk-Through Drills
2. Warm-Up Drills

This lesson contains two walk-through and two warm-up problem-solving drills. The "walk-throughs" have the answers and explanations for the questions printed on the same page so that you can "walk through" the drill. There is no time limit for the walk-throughs. The "warm-ups" should be done within the specified time limit. Answers and explanations for the warm-up drill start on page 380.

18

Walk-Through 1

Directions: Solve each of the following problems. You may use any available space in the section for scratchwork.

Numbers: All values are real numbers.

Figures: A figure accompanying a problem in this section is intended to supply information that would be useful in solving the problem. The figures are drawn as accurately as possible unless a figure is accompanied by a note specifically stating that the particular figure is not drawn to scale. Unless otherwise indicated, all figures lie in a plane.

1. A television rating survey found that out of a potential viewing audience of 161.3 million persons, 40.2 million watched a certain television program. Approximately what percent of the potential viewers watched the program?

    Ⓐ 0.2%   Ⓑ 2.5%   Ⓒ 16%
    Ⓓ 25%   Ⓔ 40%

2. To raise funds, a charitable organization conducted a raffle. If each ticket costs $0.50, and a total of $3,000 was raised from the sale of tickets, how many tickets were sold?

    Ⓐ 600   Ⓑ 1,500   Ⓒ 3,000
    Ⓓ 6,000   Ⓔ 15,000

1. **(D)** Notice that the question stem specifically invites you to approximate, so you don't need to work out a calculation to decimal-point precision. The question asks for:

    $$\frac{\text{Actual Viewers}}{\text{Potential Audience}}$$

    And matching the data to this solution statement is fairly easy:

    $$\frac{40 \text{ million}}{161 \text{ million}} = \frac{1}{4} = 25\%$$

2. **(D)** Start by making a note, either mentally or in writing, of what is required to answer the question:

    $$\frac{\text{Total Receipts}}{\text{Ticket Price}}$$

    And plug in the appropriate numbers:

    $$\frac{3,000}{\$0.50} = 6,000$$

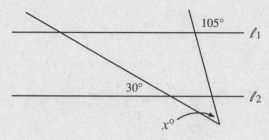

3. In the figure above if $\ell_1 \parallel \ell_2$, then $x =$

Ⓐ 20   Ⓑ 30   Ⓒ 45   Ⓓ 65   Ⓔ 130

4. During a special sale, eight shirts can be purchased for the price of five shirts. The savings per shirt is what percent of the usual price of a shirt?

Ⓐ 25%   Ⓑ $37\frac{1}{2}$%   Ⓒ 40%

Ⓓ 60%   Ⓔ $67\frac{1}{2}$%

3. **(C)** Here is one of those geometry questions that requires that you use given information to deduce some further conclusion: Since we have parallel lines, ℓ_1 and ℓ_2, and since opposite angles are equal, we deduce:

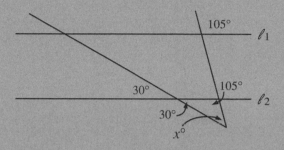

Now we have a triangle with angles 30, 105, and x:

$30 + 105 + x = 180$
$x = 45$

You might also note that this drawing is rendered to scale. Using the techniques of "guestimation," you could surely eliminate choices (A) and (E). Further, many people will also be able to see that x is not larger than 60° nor as small as 30°, and realize that (C) is the correct answer just by relying on a visual estimate of the size of x.

4. **(B)** Here we have one of those questions in which the information is presented neither in absolute numbers such as dollars nor as letters. One way of attacking the question is to use a letter such as d to represent a value such as the usual cost of five shirts. The question asks for:

$$\frac{\text{Savings}}{\text{Usual Cost}}$$

On the assumption that the usual cost for five shirts is d, one shirt usually costs $\frac{d}{5}$. During the sale you can buy eight shirts for d (the usual price of five shirts). So the sale price is $\frac{d}{8}$. Now we can express savings in terms of d:

$$\text{Savings} = \frac{d}{5} - \frac{d}{8} = \frac{8d - 5d}{40} = \frac{3d}{40}$$

Plugging this term into our solution statement:

$$\frac{\dfrac{3d}{40}}{\dfrac{d}{5}} = \frac{3d}{40} \times \frac{5}{d} = \frac{15}{40} = \frac{3}{8} = 37\frac{1}{2}\%$$

Another way of solving the problems is to assume concrete values for the unstated quantities. We might have used 40, since 40 is a multiple of 5 and 8. We assume that ordinarily five shirts cost $40, or $8 per shirt. During the sale, we can buy shirts at a special price of eight shirts for $40, or $5 per shirt. $5 per shirt is a $3-per-shirt savings over the usual price, and $\frac{3}{8}$ is $37\frac{1}{2}\%$.

5. Working independently, Machine X can fill an order in 15 hours. Working independently, Machine Y can fill the same order in ten hours. If Machine X works independently for 12 hours to fill an order and then Machine Y works independently to complete the order, how many hours does it take Machine Y to complete the order?

Ⓐ $\dfrac{1}{5}$ Ⓑ $\dfrac{3}{4}$ Ⓒ $\dfrac{4}{5}$ Ⓓ 1 Ⓔ 2

5. **(E)** This is a good question with which to illustrate the importance of defining a solution and working through the data to complete that solution. Our final answer will be:

Time for Y to complete

What data are we given? We know the rates at which X and Y operate, and we know the length of time X operates. So to find out what part of the job X has completed, we set up a direct proportion:

$$\frac{1 \text{ job}}{15 \text{ hours}} = \frac{X \text{ jobs}}{12 \text{ hours}}$$

and solve for X:

$$X = \frac{12}{15} = \frac{4}{5}$$

So X has completed $\frac{4}{5}$ of the job, leaving $\frac{1}{5}$ of the job for Y to do:

$$\frac{1 \text{ job}}{10 \text{ hrs.}} = \frac{\dfrac{1}{5} \text{ job}}{X \text{ hours}}$$

Solving for X:

$$X = \frac{1}{5}(10) = 2 \text{ hrs.}$$

6. Which of the following is equal to $\frac{4}{7}$ of 1.12 percent?

   (A) $\frac{49}{25}$ (B) $\frac{16}{25}$ (C) $\frac{8}{26}$

   (D) $\frac{3}{23}$ (E) $\frac{25}{49}$

6. (B) Here we have one of those questions in which the task is to match the answer choice to the data given in the question stem. We must rewrite "$\frac{4}{7}$ of 1.12" as a fraction. The manipulation is fairly easy:

$$\frac{4}{7} \times 1.12 = \frac{4.48}{7} = 0.64$$

Then we rewrite 0.64 to create a fraction that will bring the form of our calculation into conformity with the form of the answer choices:

$$\frac{64}{100} = \frac{16}{25}$$

It is also possible to solve the question by using an approximation and the distribution of answer choices. $\frac{4}{7}$ is slightly more than $\frac{1}{2}$, and $\frac{1}{2}$ of 1.12 would be .61 or about $\frac{3}{5}$. Looking at the choices, we see that (A) is greater than 1, which is too large, and that (C) is less than a third, which is too small. By the process of elimination, (B) must be the correct choice.

7. (D) This question presents information in graphic form, and your preview should include some study of the graphs. We find the percent of employees earning more than $15,000 but not more than $25,000 by the following method:

x = Total – (Over $25,000) – ($15,000 or less)

x = 100% – (30%) – (40%)

x = 100% – 70% = 30%

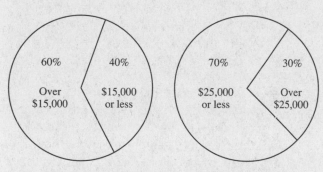

7. The graphs above show the percent of all employees of a company who earn the amounts shown. What percent of all employees earn more than $15,000 but not more than $25,000?

   (A) 10%   (B) 12%   (C) 28%
   (D) 30%   (E) 42%

8. A collector bought a stamp for $12, and later sold it for $48. What was the percent increase in the selling price of the stamp?

   (A) 400%   (B) 300%   (C) 75%

   (D) $33\frac{1}{3}$%   (E) 25%

8. (B) This question asks for percent change, so you can use the "change over" strategy discussed in the lesson:

$$\frac{\text{Change in Price}}{\text{Original Price}} \times 100 = \text{Percent Change}$$

And it is not difficult to match the data to the solution statement:

$$\frac{(48-12)}{12} = \frac{36}{12} = 3 = 300\%$$

Walk-Through 2

> *Directions:* Solve each of the following problems. You may use any available space in the section for scratchwork.
>
> *Numbers:* All values are real numbers.
>
> *Figures:* A figure accompanying a problem in this section is intended to supply information that would be useful in solving the problem. The figures are drawn as accurately as possible unless a figure is accompanied by a note specifically stating that the particular figure is not drawn to scale. Unless otherwise indicated, all figures lie in a plane.

1. A merchant bought a crate of water-damaged goods, estimating that only $\frac{1}{5}$ of the items would be salable, in which case her cost per salable item would have been \$1.20. If it turned out that $\frac{1}{4}$ of the items were salable, what was her actual cost per salable item?

    Ⓐ \$0.96 Ⓑ \$1.00 Ⓒ \$1.16
    Ⓓ \$1.24 Ⓔ \$1.50

1. **(A)** Look at the answer choices to this problem. You should be able to eliminate two of the five without doing a calculation. Since it turned out that the merchant actually got more salable items than she had expected, her cost per salable item will be less than, not more than, \$1.20, thus eliminating both (D) and (E). One way of solving the problem is to use an inverse proportion. An inverse proportion is to be used whenever two quantities vary indirectly (e.g., the faster the speed, the shorter the time or the better the mileage, the less the fuel consumed) as opposed to a direct proportion, which is used whenever two quantities vary directly (e.g., the more items, the greater the cost). Here the cost per salable item varies indirectly with the number of salable items in the lot; that is, the more salable items, the less the cost per item.

    To set up an indirect proportion, you first set up your ratios *grouping like terms*:

    $$\frac{\text{Cost(a)}}{\text{Cost(b)}} = \frac{\text{No. of Items(a)}}{\text{No. of Items(b)}}$$

    Then invert one side or the other:

    $$\frac{\text{Cost(b)}}{\text{Cost(a)}} = \frac{\text{No. of Items(a)}}{\text{No. of Items(b)}}$$

    Therefore:

    $$\frac{1.20}{x} = \frac{\frac{1}{5}}{\frac{1}{4}}$$

And invert one side:

$$\frac{x}{1.20} = \frac{\frac{1}{5}}{\frac{1}{4}}$$

And solve for x:

$$x = \frac{1}{5}(4)\,(1.20) = \$0.96$$

Or, you might have used the technique of assuming numbers. Since 20 is a multiple of both 4 and 5, let us assume that the lot contained 20 items. On the assumption of the original expectation, $\frac{1}{5}$ of those items, or 4 items, would have been salable. Since the merchant had expected a cost of \$1.20 per item, that meant she paid \$4.80 for the entire lot. Now if it turns out that she actually gets $\frac{1}{4}$ of 20, or 5, salable items, then the cost is $\frac{\$4.80}{5} = \$0.96$.

2. **(B)** This is a fairly typical "shaded area" question. The shaded area will be the whole square minus the four circles:

Shaded Area $= \square - (4 \times \bigcirc)$

Our entire solution statement is:

$$\frac{\text{Shaded Area}}{\text{Square}}$$

On the assumption that each circle has a radius of r, the side of the square must be $4r$, and the area of the square is $4r \times 4r = 16r^2$. This is the denominator of our solution statement and is also an element in our calculation of the shaded area. To complete our calculation of the shaded area, we reason that each square with radius r has an area of πr^2. So:

Shaded Area $= 16r^2 - 4\pi r^2$

Filling in the solution statement:

$$\frac{16r^2 - 4\pi r^2}{16r^2} = \frac{4r^2(4 - \pi)}{16r^2} = \frac{4 - \pi}{4}$$

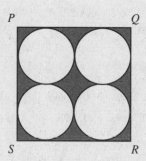

P   Q

S   R

2. In the figure above, *PQRS* is a square and each of the four circles has a radius of r. What fractional part of the area of the square is shaded?

Ⓐ $\dfrac{\pi - 4}{2}$ Ⓑ $\dfrac{4 - \pi}{4}$ Ⓒ $\dfrac{\pi}{4}$

Ⓓ $\dfrac{4}{\pi}$ Ⓔ π

You should also note that a little common sense goes a long way when applied to the answer choices. We can see from the figure that the shaded area is only about a fifth of the entire square. Yet, (C) asserts that the shaded area is about three quarters of the area of the square—and (D) and (E) are even larger. In fact, both (D) and (E) are greater than 1, asserting that the shaded area is larger than the square, an absurd conclusion. As for (A), since π is less than 4, (A) is a negative number, and that, too, is impossible. So common sense goes all the way to solve this problem, without your having to use the algebraic approach shown above.

3. Three automatic looms produced quantities of material in the ratios of 5:4:3 during operating times in the ratios of 1:2:3, respectively. What are the ratios of their respective operating speeds?

    Ⓐ 5:2:1   Ⓑ 4:2:1   Ⓒ 3:2:1
    Ⓓ 1:1:1   Ⓔ 1:2:3

3. **(A)** Use one of the alternative attack strategies: assume numbers. Simply assume that the quantities are 5 units, 4 units, and 3 units, respectively, and that the operating times are one hour, two hours, and three hours, respectively. The fastest machine produces 5 units per hour; the next fastest machine produces 4 units per two hours, or 2 units per hour; and the slowest machine produces 3 units per three hours, or 1 unit per hour. So their operating speeds are in the ratio of 5:2:1.

4. Attendance for a three-game series at a baseball park averaged 25,000 persons for the three games. If the second and third games drew crowds $1\frac{1}{2}$ and $2\frac{1}{2}$ times as large as the first game, respectively, what was the attendance for the second game?

    Ⓐ 15,000   Ⓑ 18,000   Ⓒ 22,500
    Ⓓ 25,000   Ⓔ 37,500

4. **(C)** This question is a fairly classic case for translating into "equationese." The solution statement is not that difficult; attendance of second game. To match the data to this statement, we use x to represent the number of people who attended the *first game*. Then it is easy to express the attendance of the second game as $1.5x$ and that of the third game as $2.5x$. If we average these three numbers together, we get 25,000:

$$\frac{x + 1.5x + 2.5x}{3} = 25,000$$

And solve for x:

$5x = 75,000$

$x = 15,000$

This, however, is not the answer to our question. This is the number of people who attended the first game, and we want the number who attended the second game. To find that, we multiply 15,000 by 1.5, and our answer is 22,500.

This problem also illustrates one of the limitations of our alternative attack strategies. It might be possible to test each answer choice, beginning with (C), but to do that you would have to take 22,500 and calculate the first game as being only $\frac{2}{3}$ of that, or 15,000. Then you would have to calculate the attendance of the third game as $2\frac{1}{2}$ of that, or 37,500. Finally, you would have to average those three together. To be sure, (C) is the correct answer, but the alternative attack strategy is almost unmanageably cumbersome.

5. **(E)** This question should seem almost familiar to you from our review of geometry problems. The task is to take the data given, starting with the area of square *PQRS*, and deduce conclusions sufficient to provide the area of triangle *RTU*. Our ultimate solution statement will require the altitude and base of *RTU*, that is, the lengths of *RT* and *TU*:

$$\text{Area} = \frac{1}{2}ab = \frac{1}{2}(RT)(TU)$$

We start with the only number we have: 4. If *PQRS* is a square with an area of 4, then it must have sides of 2:

Area of Square = Side × Side

$4 = s^2$

$s = 2$

QR, therefore, equals 2, and *QR* is also a leg of a special right triangle. *QRT* is a 30:60:90 triangle, and the sides of such a triangle are in the ratio $\frac{h}{2}:h\frac{\sqrt{3}}{2}:h$, which is to say that the side opposite the 60° angle is equal to the side opposite the 30° angle multiplied by $\sqrt{3}$:

$RT = QR\sqrt{3}$
$RT = 2\sqrt{3}$

Now we can fill in our solution statement:

$$\text{Area} = \frac{1}{2}(2\sqrt{3})(2\sqrt{3}) = 6$$

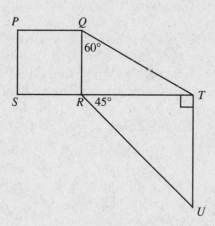

5. In the figure above, if *SRT* is a straight line and *PQRS* is a square with the area of 4, what is the area of triangle *RTU*?

ⓐ 2   ⓑ $2\sqrt{3}$ ⓒ 4   ⓓ $3\sqrt{3}$ ⓔ 6

An alternative way of attacking the question is to measure. You must reason that any side of the square *PQRS* is 2. Using your answer sheet as a straightedge, measure that distance. Then compare that distance against *RT* and *TU*. You should be able to see that each is about 3.5 units long. Using that for the altitude and base, the area would be:

$$\frac{1}{2}(3.5)(3.5) = 6.125$$

And (E) would be the best choice.

   Even if the idea of measuring did not occur to you, common sense eliminates three of the five choices. Is *RTU* larger than, smaller than, or equal to the square *PQRS*? You should be able to see that it is larger, but choice (C) is 4, and that could be true only if the square and the triangle were equal. So we eliminate (A), (B), and (C) on that ground alone.

6. A book dealer received an order in which $\frac{1}{5}$ of the books were hardcover books. The dealer sold $\frac{2}{3}$ of the books, including $\frac{3}{4}$ of the hardcover books. What fraction of the unsold books were hardcover books?

Ⓐ $\frac{1}{10}$ Ⓑ $\frac{3}{20}$ Ⓒ $\frac{1}{5}$ Ⓓ $\frac{11}{20}$ Ⓔ $\frac{4}{5}$

6. **(B)** This is a question without absolute numbers. The mathematical approach would assign a letter to represent the total number of books in the shipment, say *n*. We ultimately must find:

$$\frac{\text{Unsold Hardcover}}{\text{Total Unsold}}$$

Two-thirds of the books were sold, so $\frac{1n}{3}$ of the books were unsold:

$$\frac{\text{Unsold Hardcover}}{\frac{n}{3}}$$

Then $\frac{3}{4}$ of the hardcover books were sold, which means that $\frac{1}{4}$ of them went unsold. Since hardcover books account for $\frac{1}{5}$ of *n*, $\frac{1}{4}$ of $\frac{1}{5}$ of *n* were hardcover books that went unsold:

$$\frac{1}{4} \times \frac{1}{5} \times n = \frac{1}{20}(n)$$

Putting this in the numerator of our solution statement, we have:

$$\frac{\frac{n}{20}}{\frac{n}{3}} = \frac{3}{20}$$

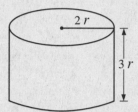

7. A container in the shape of a right circular cylinder with an inside radius $2r$ and height $3r$ is completely filled with water. If 30 glass marbles of radius $\frac{r}{2}$ are put into the container, displacing some of the water, in terms of r, what is the volume of water that remains in the container?

    (*Note:* Volume of sphere = $\frac{4}{3}\pi r^3$.)

    (A) πr^3 (B) $5\pi r^3$ (C) $7\pi r^3$
    (D) $12\pi r^3$ (E) $17\pi r^3$

For some people, it may be easier to assume a certain number of books. Sixty is a common multiple of the denominators of our fractions, 5, 3, and 4, and is not too unwieldy. Let us assume that the shipment contained 60 books. Then we reason that 40 of the books were sold, so 20 remained unsold. Only 12 of the books were hardcovers, of which nine were sold and three remain. So, 20 books remain unsold, of which three are hardcovers. Thus, hardcover books constitute $\frac{3}{20}$ of the unsold books.

7. **(C)** This is a three-dimensional variation on the shaded area concept. The irregular volume of the liquid is represented in our solution statement as:

Container – 30 Marbles = Water in Container

The volume of the container is calculated using the formula for the volume of a right circular cylinder: $\pi \times radius^2 \times$ height.

Volume of Container = $\pi(2r)^2(3r) = 12\pi r^3$

The volume of a sphere is given by the question stem. So, a marble with a radius of $\frac{r}{2}$ will have a volume of:

Volume of Marble = $\frac{4}{3}(\pi)\left(\frac{r}{2}\right)^3 = \left(\frac{\pi}{6}\right)r^3 = \frac{\pi r^3}{6}$

Substituting into the solution statement:

$$12\pi r^3 - 30\left(\frac{\pi r^3}{6}\right) = 12\pi r^3 - 5\pi r^3 = 7\pi r^3$$

8.   A music director has a group of five female vocal-
     ists and another group of five male vocalists. From
     the group of female vocalists she will select three
     persons to form a trio, and from the group of male
     vocalists she will select two persons to form a duo.
     What is the difference between the number of
     different trios she could choose and the number of
     different duos she could choose?

     Ⓐ 0   Ⓑ 1   Ⓒ 6   Ⓓ 10   Ⓔ 20

8. (A) This question is interesting in two respects. First, although the question seems
to require some fancy mathematical formula, in actuality it can be solved with common sense. Second, the italicized words are
of surpassing importance. Taking the second point first, we remind you again of the
importance of careful reading—even in the
math section. The question asks about the
different possible combinations. Some students will misread the stem and think the
question is asking "How many trios can be
made from five persons?" and "How many
duos can be made from five persons?" The
answer to these questions is one and two,
respectively, since three goes into five only
once and two goes into five twice—but this
is not the question asked. Our question asks
about the number of different possibilities.

How do we find the number of possibilities? To be sure, there is a special mathematical procedure for calculating what are
called "combinations," but we do not need
that. Instead, we ask ourselves, given five
people, how many different pairings are
possible? Assume that the people are *A*, *B*,
C, *D*, and *E*.

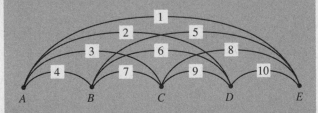

As the diagram shows, there are ten possible duos:

AB, AC, AD, AE, BC, BD, BE, CD, CE, DE

Apply similar reasoning to the question of
trios. A diagram for trios would be too clut-
tered to be useful, so count on your fingers,
e.g., thumb, index, middle; thumb, index,
ring; thumb, index, pinky, etc. Again, there
are ten different possibilities:

*ABC, ABD, ABE, ACD, ACE, ADE, BCD, BCE,
BDE, CDE*

Note that the order of presentation is not relevant, e. g., *ABC* = *BCA* = *CAB*, etc. So there are ten of each, and

10 – 10 = 0

and the answer is (A).

There is one final note I'd like to make. Though common sense is sufficient to answer the question, there is a more elegant solution. Take any group of five persons, and if you select two persons from the group, you have left behind three persons, and vice versa. In other words, since 2 + 3 = 5, the number of different duos that can be selected from a group of five is equal to the number of different trios that can be selected from a group of five. Of course, this insight is obscured by the fact that the question stem refers to two different groups of vocalists, but that distinction is not relevant to the mathematics underlying the question.

WARM-UP DRILL 1

Time: 12 Minutes

8 Questions

Directions: Solve each of the following problems. You may use any available space in the section for scratchwork.

Numbers: All values are real numbers.

Figures: A figure accompanying a problem in this section is intended to supply information that would be useful in solving the problem. The figures are drawn as accurately as possible unless a figure is accompanied by a note specifically stating that the particular figure is not drawn to scale. Unless otherwise indicated, all figures lie in a plane.

1. If $2x = 5y$, then $10y - 4x =$

    Ⓐ 0   Ⓑ 1   Ⓒ 2   Ⓓ 5

    Ⓔ Cannot be determined from the information given.

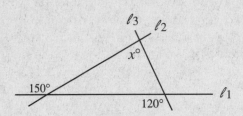

2. In the figure above, $x =$

    Ⓐ 30   Ⓑ 60   Ⓒ 75   Ⓓ 90   Ⓔ 105

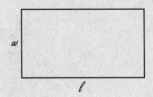

3. The figure above is a rectangle. If the width is increased by 20 percent and the length is decreased by 10 percent, expressed in terms of w and l, what is the new area of the rectangle?

    Ⓐ $.09\ wl$ Ⓑ $0.92\ wl$ Ⓒ $1.1\ wl$

    Ⓓ $1.08\ wl$ Ⓔ $1.3\ wl$

4. If n is an odd integer, all of the following are odd EXCEPT

    Ⓐ $n - 2$

    Ⓑ $2n + n$

    Ⓒ n^2

    Ⓓ $(n + 2)^2$

    Ⓔ $n^2 + n$

5. If n is an integer that is evenly divisible by 18, then all of the following must be an integer EXCEPT

    Ⓐ $\dfrac{n}{2}$ Ⓑ $\dfrac{n}{3}$ Ⓒ $\dfrac{n}{6}$ Ⓓ $\dfrac{n}{9}$ Ⓔ $\dfrac{n}{12}$

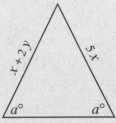

6. In the figure above, what is the ratio $x:y$?

    Ⓐ 4:1   Ⓑ 2:1   Ⓒ 1:1   Ⓓ 1:2   Ⓔ 1:4

7. In a game, special cards are printed with one of three symbols—a star, a circle, or a rectangle. A star is worth three points more than a circle and a circle is worth three points more than a rectangle. If three rectangles are worth x points, a player holding five circles and four stars has how many points?

    Ⓐ $3x + 12$

    Ⓑ $3x + 39$

    Ⓒ $3x + 42$

    Ⓓ $7x + 39$

    Ⓔ $7x + 42$

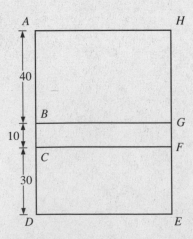

8. The figure above shows three rectangular garden plots that lie side by side. If *AE*, not shown, is equal to 100 feet, what is the area, in square feet, of plot *BCFG*?

    Ⓐ 240   Ⓑ 300   Ⓒ 360   Ⓓ 480   Ⓔ 600

Warm-Up 2

Time: 12 Minutes

8 Questions

Directions: Solve each of the following problems. You may use any available space in the section for scratchwork.

Numbers: All values are real numbers.

Figures: A figure accompanying a problem in this section is intended to supply information that would be useful in solving the problem. The figures are drawn as accurately as possible unless a figure is accompanied by a note specifically stating that the particular figure is not drawn to scale. Unless otherwise indicated, all figures lie in a plane.

1. At City High School, the marching band has 48 members and the orchestra has 36 members. If a total of 12 students belong to only one of the two groups and all students belong to at least one group, how many students belong to both groups?

    Ⓐ 12 Ⓑ 18 Ⓒ 36 Ⓓ 48 Ⓔ 72

2. If $x = 2k - 2$ and $y = 4k^2$, what is y in terms of x?

    Ⓐ $x + 2$ Ⓑ $(x + 2)^2$ Ⓒ $\dfrac{(x+2)^2}{2}$

    Ⓓ $\dfrac{(x+2)^2}{4}$ Ⓔ $x^2 + 4$

3. For all numbers x, y, and z, the operation $x * y = x - xy$. What is $x * (y * z)$?

    Ⓐ $x - xy + xyz$
    Ⓑ $x - xy - xz - xyz$
    Ⓒ $x + xy - xz + xyz$
    Ⓓ $x^2 - xy^2 - xyz$
    Ⓔ $x^2 - xy^2 - x^2yz$

4. If the cost of x meters of wire is d dollars, what is the cost, in dollars, of y meters of wire at the same rate?

    Ⓐ yd Ⓑ $\dfrac{yd}{x}$ Ⓒ $\dfrac{xd}{y}$ Ⓓ xd Ⓔ $\dfrac{xy}{d}$

5. The average (arithmetic mean) weight of five chemical samples is 0.5 grams. If the weight of the lightest of the five samples is 0.35 grams, which of the following could NOT be the weight, in grams, of the heaviest of the five samples?

    Ⓐ 0.55 Ⓑ 0.78 Ⓒ 0.99
    Ⓓ 1.06 Ⓔ 1.12

6. A group of three friends ate dinner at a restaurant. When they settled the check, Peter paid as much as John paid, and John paid as much as Ralph paid. What fraction of the check did John pay?

    Ⓐ $\dfrac{15}{24}$ Ⓑ $\dfrac{12}{31}$ Ⓒ $\dfrac{5}{24}$ Ⓓ $\dfrac{1}{6}$ Ⓔ $\dfrac{1}{24}$

7. In a race around an oval track, a race car made the second lap at a speed 25 percent greater than it made the first lap. The time required to make the second lap was what percent of the time required to make the first lap?

    Ⓐ 75% Ⓑ 80% Ⓒ 87.5%
    Ⓓ 120% Ⓔ 125%

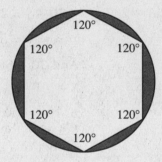

8. If the radius of the circle above is 2, then what is the area of the shaded portion of the diagram?

    Ⓐ $8\pi - \sqrt{3}$ Ⓑ $4\pi - 6\sqrt{3}$ Ⓒ $4\pi - \sqrt{3}$
    Ⓓ $2\pi - 6\sqrt{3}$ Ⓔ $2\pi - \sqrt{3}$

Explanatory Answers

Warm-Up 1

1. **(A)** Here you have one equation with two variables. It isn't possible to solve for either variable individually, and that's not what is required. The question asks for the value of $10y - 4x$. Either $2x = 5y$ can be rewritten as $10y - 4x$ or the answer is (E).

   Multiply both sides of $2x = 5y$ by 2:

   $(2)2x = (2)5y$

   $4x = 10y$

   And you need $10y - 4x$:

   $0 = 10y - 4x$

   The answer is (A).

2. **(D)** The task here is to deduce the value of x from the information already given, and there is really only one route to take. Assign the letter y to the angle inside the lower left vertex of the triangle and z to the angle inside the lower right vertex:

   $150 + y = 180$ and $120 + z = 180$

   $y = 30 \qquad\qquad z = 60$

   And $30 + 60 + x = 180$

   $x = 90$

   This line of reasoning is not that complex, but there is an alternative. Because the figure is drawn to scale, you can either "guestimate" or use the corner of a piece of paper to measure the size of the angle in question, which is 90°.

3. **(D)** This problem is more difficult than the last one. You might solve it using unknowns. The width of the rectangle increases by 20 percent from w to $1.2w$, and the length decreases by 10 percent from ℓ to 0.9ℓ. The area of a rectangle is width times length. So the old area was $(w)(\ell)$, and the new area is $1.2w \times 0.9\ell = 1.08w\ell$.

   If working with unknowns is not your cup of tea, then assume some numbers, for example, $w = 1$ and $\ell = 2$. The new dimensions are 1.2 and 1.8, and the new area is $2.16w\ell$. Now substitute 1 for w and 2 for ℓ into each answer choice. The correct one will generate the number 2.16:

   (A) $0.09(1)(2) = 1.8$ (Incorrect.)
   (B) $0.92(1)(2) = 1.84$ (Incorrect.)
   (C) $1.1(1)(2) = 2.2$ (Incorrect.)
   (D) $1.08(1)(2) = 2.16$ (Correct.)
   (E) $1.3(1)(2) = 2.6$ (Incorrect.)

4. (E) This question tests properties of numbers. One way of attacking the problem is to reason about each choice in the following way. Since n is odd:

(A) This is an odd minus 2, so the result is still odd.

(B) $2n$ is even, plus n, which is odd; so $2n + n$ is odd.

(C) An odd number times itself is odd.

(D) n plus 2 is still odd; so this is an odd times an odd and therefore odd.

(E) n^2 is odd; n itself is odd; so this is an odd plus an odd and that's an even number.

Or you could have substituted a number, say, 1. If $n = 1$, then:

(A) $n - 1 = 1 - 2 = -1$. (An odd number.)

(B) $2n + n = 2(1) + 1 = 2 + 1 = 3$. (An odd number.)

(C) $n^2 = (1)^2 = 1 \times 1 = 1$. (An odd number.)

(D) $(n + 2)^2 = (1 + 2)^2 = 3^2 = 9$. (An odd number.)

(E) $n^2 + n = (1)^2 + 1 = 1 + 1 = 2$. (An even number.)

5. (E) If n is divisible by 18, then it must also be divisible by all of the factors of 18 (in addition to 1 and 18): 2, 3, 6, and 9. But n is not necessarily divisible by 12. You can reach this same conclusion by testing some values for n, say, 18, the first number divisible by 18. You will find that n is divisible by 2, 3, 6, and 9, but not by 12.

6. (D) Since the two labeled sides are both opposite angles of $a°$, they must have equal lengths:

$$x + 2y = 5x$$

$$2y = 4x$$

$$y = 2x$$

$$\frac{x}{y} = \frac{1}{2}$$

7. (B) This question asks you to devise a formula. Use the letter s for star, c for circle, and r for rectangle. The answer choices are expressed in terms of x, so your formula will have to express s and c in terms of r and then in terms of x.

The question stem states that a circle is worth three points more than a rectangle, so $c = r + 3$. And a star is worth three points more than a circle, which means $s = c + 3$, and so $s = r + 6$. Since $3r = x$, $r = \frac{x}{3}$. Substituting $\frac{x}{3}$ for r: $s = \frac{x}{3} + 6$ and $c = \frac{x}{3} + 3$. So $5c$ and $4s$ is:

$$5\left(\frac{x}{3} + 3\right) + 4\left(\frac{x}{3} + 6\right) = \frac{5x}{3} + 15 + \frac{4x}{3} + 24 =$$

$$\frac{9x}{3} + 39 = 3x + 39$$

You can also use the principle "it's one of the five suspects." You might assume that $x = 1$, so that a rectangle is equal to $\frac{1}{3}$; but that already involves a fraction. A more convenient assumption is $x = 3$. Then a rectangle is worth one point. On that assumption, circles are worth $1 + 3 = 4$ and stars are worth $4 + 3 = 7$. And five circles plus four stars is worth $5(4) + 4(7) = 48$. So, on the assumption that $x = 3$, the correct formula yields 48:

18

(A) 3(3) + 12 = 21   (Incorrect.)

(B) 3(3) + 39 = 48   (Correct.)

(C) 3(3) + 42 = 51   (Incorrect.)

(D) 7(3) + 39 = 60   (Incorrect.)

(E) 7(3) + 42 = 63   (Incorrect.)

8. **(E)** The area of a rectangle is equal to its width times its length. The diagram already provides the width, so you'll have to find the length.

An important piece of information $AE = 100$, is not entered on the diagram. The first thing you should do is draw AE. This creates a right triangle with sides AD and DE and hypotenuse AE. And DE is not only a side of triangle ADE, it is the length of the rectangle. You know the length of AD and AE, so you can find DE with the Pythagorean Theorem:

$$AD^2 + DE^2 = AE^2$$

$$DE^2 = AE^2 - AD^2$$

$$DE^2 = 100^2 - 80^2$$

$$DE^2 = 10{,}000 - 6{,}400$$

$$DE^2 = 3{,}600$$

$$DE = \sqrt{3{,}600} = 60$$

The area of rectangle $BCFG$ is $10 \times 60 = 600$.

You can save yourself the calculation if you notice that 80 and 100 are multiples of 8 and 10, which are in turn multiples of 4 and 5. This triangle must have sides of 60, 80, and 100.

Or you can avoid all but the last step of the calculation by measuring to find the length of the rectangle. Using the edge of a sheet of paper (on the test, use your scratch paper), mark off the length of BC. Since $BC = 10$, the length shown on the edge of the paper is 10 units. Now measure the length of CF. Starting at C, mark 10 units on CF, then another 10, and so on. The final result: CF is 60 units long. Finish off the problem by multiplying 10×60.

Warm-Up 2

1. **(C)** A diagram can help you understand what's required:

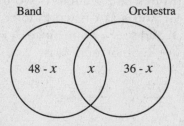

x is the number of students who are members of both groups. Since only 12 students are members of only one group:

$$48 - x + 36 - x = 12$$

$$84 - 12 = 2x$$

$$72 = 2x$$

$$x = 36$$

2. **(B)** Here you are asked to express one variable in terms of another. You have x in terms of k, and y in terms of k; so there must be a way of rewriting one equation to correspond to the other. Since it's usually easier to square something than to take the square root of something, work from k toward k^2.

To rewrite the first equation so that x is expressed in terms of k^2, you'll first need to get rid of the -2 on the right side:

$$x = 2k - 2$$

$$x + 2 = 2k$$

$$k = \frac{x+2}{2}$$

Before you square both sides, look at the answer choices to see what form your final result should take. You don't have to multiply $(x + 2)^2$:

$$\frac{(x+2)^2}{4} = k^2$$

Since y is also equal to $4k^2$, then:

$$y = (x + 2)^2$$

You can also attack the question by assuming numbers. Assume a value for k, say, 1. If $k = 1$, then $x = 2(1) - 2 = 0$, and $y = 4(1^2) = 4$. When you substitute 0 for x into the formulas in the choices, the correct choice will yield the value 4, which is y.

(A) $0 + 2 = 2$ (Incorrect.)

(B) $(0 + 2)^2 = 4$ (Correct?)

(C) $\dfrac{(0+2)^2}{2} = \dfrac{4}{2} = 2$ (Incorrect.)

(D) $\dfrac{(0+2)^2}{4} = \dfrac{4}{4} = 1$ (Incorrect.)

(E) $0^2 + 4 = 4$ (Correct?)

This first substitution eliminated all but (B) and (E).

Try another number for k, say, 2. If $k = 2$, then $y = 4(2^2) = 16$, and $x = 2(2) - 2 = 2$. So, when $x = 2$, the correct formula should generate 16:

(B) $(2 + 2)^2 = 16$ (Correct.)

(E) $2^2 + 4 = 8$ (Incorrect.)

3. **(A)** Here we have a defined function problem. Just take it one step at a time. First, $y * z = y - yz$. Second, $x * (y - yz) = x - x(y - yz) = x - xy + xyz$, which is (A). You can assume values for the three letters, but the arithmetic you would do would exactly parallel what we just did with letters. So there is no real advantage to using numbers.

18

4. (B) This question asks you to devise a formula. The easiest approach is to set up a direct proportion, using k as our unknown:

$$\frac{\text{Length } X}{\text{Length } Y} = \frac{\text{Cost } X}{\text{Cost } Y}$$

$$\frac{x}{y} = \frac{d}{k}$$

$$xk = yd$$

$$k = \frac{yd}{x}$$

You can also assume some values for the three unknowns. Assume that 2 meters of wire cost $4, so 5 meters will cost $10. On the assumption that $x = 2$, $d = 4$, and $y = 5$, the correct formula will yield 10:

(A) $5(4) = 20$ (Incorrect.)

(B) $\dfrac{5(4)}{2} = 10$ (Correct.)

(C) $\dfrac{2(4)}{5} = \dfrac{8}{5}$ (Incorrect.)

(D) $2(4) = 8$ (Incorrect.)

(E) $\dfrac{2(5)}{4} = \dfrac{10}{4}$ (Incorrect.)

5. (E) If Holmes were to attack this item, he would be able to eliminate choices (B), (C), and (D) without doing a calculation. The question stem gives you the average of the five samples and the weight of the lightest. It then asks which of the five choices could NOT be the weight of the heaviest. The correct answer must be either too large or too small, so it must be either (A) or (E).

The correct choice is (E). Assume that the weights of the three samples between the lightest and the heaviest are 0.35. I know that this is not possible, since the lightest sample weighs 0.35 grams, but this assumption will allow us to define the lower limit for the weights of those samples and, at the same time, the upper limit for the weight of the heaviest sample. The total weight of four samples each weighing 0.35 grams would be 1.40. This is the lower limit for the total weight of the four lightest samples. The total weight of the five samples is $5 \times 0.5 = 2.5$, so the upper limit on the weight of the heaviest is $2.5 - 1.4 = 1.1$.

6. **(C)** One way to attack this problem is to use algebraic variables. Let J, P, and R represent the fractions of the check paid by John, Peter, and Ralph, respectively. Since Peter paid only $\frac{4}{5}$ as much as John:

$$P = \frac{4}{5}J$$

And since John paid only $\frac{1}{3}$ as much as Ralph:

$$J = \frac{1}{3}R$$

$$R = 3J$$

Since the three friends together paid the entire check:

Total $= P + J + R$

And we can substitute $\frac{4}{5}J$ for P and $3J$ for R:

$$\text{Total} = \frac{4}{5}J + J + 3J$$

$$\text{Total} = 4\frac{4}{5}J$$

$$\text{Total} = \frac{24}{5}J$$

$$\frac{J}{\text{Total}} = \frac{5}{24}$$

Thus, John paid $\frac{5}{24}$ of the total check.

As an alternative, you might just assume some numbers. Since John paid only $\frac{1}{3}$ as much as Ralph, assume that Ralph paid $30. (Why $30? Because it's divisible by 3.) On the assumption that Ralph paid $30, John paid $10. And if John paid $10, then Peter paid $8, and the total check was $48. John paid $10 of the $48, so John paid $\frac{10}{48} = \frac{5}{24}$ of the check.

18

7. **(B)** One way to attack this item is to use an inverse proportion. Why an inverse proportion? Because the faster the speed, the shorter the time to cover a distance. First, set up an ordinary proportion, being sure to group like terms:

$$\frac{\text{Time (1)}}{\text{Time (2)}} = \frac{\text{Speed (1)}}{\text{Speed (2)}}$$

Then invert one side or the other:

$$\frac{\text{Time (2)}}{\text{Time (1)}} = \frac{\text{Speed (1)}}{\text{Speed (2)}}$$

Now let S be the speed at which the car covered the first lap. $1.25S$ is the speed at which it covered the second lap.

$$\frac{\text{Time (2)}}{\text{Time (1)}} = \frac{S}{1.25S}$$

$$\frac{\text{Time (2)}}{\text{Time (1)}} = 0.80 = 80\%$$

So the time needed to complete the second lap was only 80 percent of the time needed to complete the first lap.

As an alternative, you could assume some actual numbers. Assume that the track is exactly 1 mile around, and assume also that on the first lap the car traveled at a rate of 1 mile per hour. On that assumption, it took the car 1 hour to make the lap. If the car then traveled the second lap at 1.25 miles per hour, it took the car $1 \div 1.25 = 0.80$ hours to make the second lap, and 0.80 hours is 80 percent of 1 hour.

8. **(B)** This is a shaded area problem. The area of the shaded portion of the figure is the difference between the area of the circle and the area of the hexagon. Since the radius of the circle is 2, the area of the circle is 4π. Now we will find the area of the hexagon:

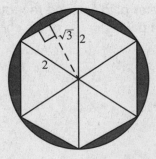

So each of the six triangles has an area of $\frac{1}{2}(2)(\sqrt{3}) = \sqrt{3}$. Therefore, the area of the shaded portion of the figure is $4\pi - 6(\sqrt{3})$.

Data Sufficiency

✓ Topics Covered

1. **Anatomy of a Data Sufficiency Item**
   - **The Directions**
   - **The Choices Illustrated**
   - **A Note About Figures**

2. **The "Good Enough" Principle**

3. **Data Sufficiency Items Using Arithmetic**
   - **Odd and Even Numbers**
   - **Consecutive Integers**
   - **Signs of Numbers**
   - **Multiples and Divisibility**
   - **Unique Integer Solutions**
   - **Fractions, Ratios, and Percents**
   - **Average**
   - **Rate**
   - **Algebra Operations**
   - **Geometry**

4. **Be Sure You Understand the Significance of Each Clue**

5. **Accentuate the Positive and Eliminate the Negative**

Data sufficiency is the "other" type of math question that appears on the GMAT, the one with the peculiar instructions.

Anatomy of a Data Sufficiency Item

The Directions

Here are the instructions for data sufficiency questions:

Directions: Each item of this type consists of a question followed by two statements, labeled (1) and (2). You must determine whether the information provided by the numbered statements is sufficient to answer the questions asked. In addition to the information provided in the numbered statements, you should rely on your knowledge of mathematics and ordinary facts (such as the number of minutes in an hour). Choose:

    A if statement (1) BY ITSELF is sufficient to answer the question but statement (2) by itself is not sufficient to answer the question

    B if statement (2) BY ITSELF is sufficient to answer the question but statement (1) by itself is not sufficient to answer the question

    C if BOTH statements (1) and (2) together are sufficient to answer the question but NEITHER statement BY ITSELF is sufficient to answer the question

    D if EACH statement BY ITSELF is sufficient to answer the question

    E if the two statements, even when taken TOGETHER, are NOT sufficient to answer the question

Numbers: All values are real numbers.

Figures: The figures with this question type will not necessarily reflect the information given in the numbered statements, but they will reflect the information provided in the question. Unless otherwise indicated, all figures lie in a plane; all lines shown as straight are straight; and the positions of all points, angles, regions, etc., are correctly depicted.

Example:

In $\triangle ABC$, what is the value of x?

(1) $y = 60$

(2) $AB = BC$

Explanation: Statement (1) is not sufficient to answer the question, for statement (1) provides no information about x or z. Statement (2) is not sufficient to answer the question. Statement (2) does establish that $y = z$, but that is not enough information to determine the value of x. Both statements together are sufficient to answer the question. Since $AB = BC$ and $y = z$, $z = 60$. Since $x + y + z = 180$, $x = 60$.

The Choices Illustrated

As the name "data sufficiency" implies, the task here is to determine whether or not information is sufficient to answer the question asked. The following problems illustrate the meanings of the five answer categories.

1. Choice (A)

The instructions state that an item is to be classified as (A) if statement (1) ALONE is sufficient to answer the question asked, but statement (2) alone is not sufficient to answer the question asked.

> **EXAMPLE:**
>
> Is Phil older than Raoul?
> (1) Laura is four years younger than Phil and two years younger than Raoul.
> (2) The average of Phil's age in years and Raoul's age in years is 17.

Statement (1) is by itself sufficient to answer the question asked. If Laura is four years younger than Phil and two years younger than Raoul, then Phil must be two years older than Raoul. Statement (2), however, is not by itself sufficient to answer the question. From the statement about the average of their ages in years, you can't draw any conclusion about their respective ages. Since statement (1) is by itself sufficient, but statement (2) is not, you should classify this question as (A).

2. Choice (B)

The instructions state that an item is to be classified as (B) if statement (2) ALONE is sufficient to answer the question asked, but statement (1) alone is not sufficient to answer the question asked.

> **EXAMPLE:**
>
> If a, b, and c are consecutive integers, is b even?
> (1) $a < b < c$
> (2) ac is an odd integer

Statement (1) is not sufficient to answer the question asked. Although statement (1) describes the order of the integers, it provides no information about which elements of the sequence are even and which are odd. Statement (2), however, is by itself sufficient to determine whether or not b is even. If ac is odd, then both a and c must be odd integers. In the series of three consecutive integers, at least one of the integers must be even. Therefore, b must be even. Since statement (2) alone is sufficient to answer the question asked, but statement (1) alone is not, you should classify this item as (B).

3. *Choice (C)*

EXAMPLE:

How many students are enrolled in Professor Torres' history class?
(1) If three more students sign up for the class and none drop out, more than 35 students will be enrolled in the class.
(2) If four students drop out of the class and no more sign up, fewer than 30 students will be enrolled in the class.

Statement (1) alone is not sufficient to answer the question asked, but (1) does imply that at least 33 students are enrolled in the class. Statement (2) alone is not sufficient to answer the question asked, but (2) does imply that no more than 33 students are enrolled in the class. Although neither statement alone is sufficient to answer the question, the two statements taken together are sufficient to answer the question. The number of students enrolled in the class is 33. Since neither statement alone is sufficient to answer the question but both together are sufficient, you should classify this item as (C).

4. *Choice (D)*

EXAMPLE:

What is the area of circular region *C*?
(1) *C* has a circumference of 4π.
(2) *C* has a diameter of 4.

Statement (1) alone is sufficient to answer the question asked. Since the circumference of a circle is equal to 2 times π times its radius, a circle with a circumference of 4π has a radius of 2. And a circle with a radius of 2 has an area of 4π. Statement (2) is also, in and of itself, sufficient to answer the question. A circle with a diameter of 4 has a radius of 2 and an area of 4π. Since each statement is by itself sufficient to answer the question, classify this item as (D).

5. *Choice (E)*

EXAMPLE:

Is $x < y$?
(1) $-0.25 < x < 0.25$
(2) $0.15 < y < 0.35$

Statement (1) alone is not sufficient to answer the question asked. Although statement (1) defines a range for x, the statement provides no information about y. Similarly, statement (2) alone is not sufficient to answer the question asked. Statement (2) defines a range for y but provides no information about x. Are both statements taken together sufficient to answer the question asked? No. Although x might be less than y, x also may be more than or even equal to y. Since the two statements, even when taken together, do not provide enough information to answer the question asked, you should classify this item as (E).

19

A Note About Figures

Previously, you learned Holmesian strategies for attacking problems based on a figure. These strategies had names such as "meastimation." Unfortunately, "meastimation" and the other strategies that utilize geometry figures cannot be used to attack data sufficiency items, because the figures that accompany data sufficiency items are not necessarily drawn to scale.

The fact that figures are not necessarily drawn to scale does not mean that the figures are superfluous. You can rely on the general configuration of the aspects of the figures; for example, lines drawn as straight are straight, and points, angles, regions, and so on are in the general order depicted. But you cannot rely on the apparent magnitude of these features to answer the question. In short, the figure itself is never sufficient to answer the question asked.

The distinction between legitimate and illegitimate uses of the figures is not that difficult to understand; and, after a little practice, you will make it without even thinking. To get used to the idea that the figure itself is not sufficient to answer the question asked, here are some data sufficiency problems that use figures.

EXAMPLES:

Is *R* the midpoint of line segment *PT*?
(1) *PS = QT*
(2) *QR = RS*

The figure is drawn such that *PR* is equal to *RT*, but this does not mean that the additional data provided in the numbered statements are sufficient to answer the question asked. The accompanying figure might have been drawn differently:

Is R the midpoint of line segment *PT*?
(1) *PS = QT*
(2) *QR = RS*

In this case, the figure is drawn so that *PR* does not appear equal in length to *RT*. Still, the answer will be the same.

Test each of the statements for sufficiency. Statement (1) is not sufficient to answer the question:

Nor is statement (2) sufficient to answer the question:

Both statements taken together, however, are sufficient to answer the question. Since *PR = PS – RS* and *RT = QT – QR*, given that *PS = QT* and *QR = RS*, *PR = RT*. Since neither statement alone is sufficient to answer the question, but both statements together are, you should classify this item as (C).

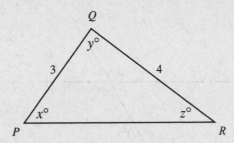

What is the length of *PR* in the figure above?
(1) $y = 90$
(2) $x + z = 90$

If the triangle is a right triangle, then it will be possible to determine the length of *PR* using the Pythagorean Theorem. The figure is drawn so that the triangle appears to be a right triangle, but you cannot use the appearance of the triangle as proof of the conclusion that the triangle is a right triangle. The problem could also have been presented in this way:

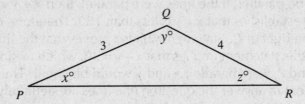

What is the length of *PR* in the figure above?
(1) $y = 90$
(2) $x + z = 90$

In this figure, *y* appears to be larger than 90, but, again, appearance is not dispositive of the issue. You must test each of the numbered statements for sufficiency. Statement (1) is, by itself, sufficient to establish that *PQR* is a right triangle, and from that conclusion you can deduce that the length of *PR* is 5. Statement (2) also is, by itself, sufficient to answer the question. Since the sum of the degree measures of the interior angles of a triangle is 180, if $x + z = 90$, then the remaining angle, *y*, must also be equal to 90. This proves that the triangle is a right triangle, and you can use the Pythagorean Theorem to deduce that the length of *PR* is 5. Since each statement is sufficient by itself, you should classify this item as (D).

19

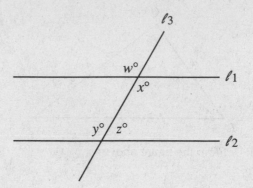

In the figure above, do ℓ_1 and ℓ_2 intersect somewhere to the right of ℓ_3?
(1) $x + z < 180$
(2) $y - w = 20$

Here, the lines in the figure appear to be parallel, but that is not a sufficient basis for concluding that they are. In fact, each of the numbered statements proves that the lines cannot be parallel. If the lines were parallel, then $x + y$ would equal 180; but statement (1) establishes that $x + y$ is less than 180. Therefore, ℓ_1 and ℓ_2 intersect somewhere to the right of ℓ_3. Statement (2) also proves that the lines are not parallel. Since $w = x$, this statement implies that $x - y = 20$, which means that x and y are not equal. If ℓ_1 and ℓ_2 were parallel, x and y would be equal. Thus each statement is by itself sufficient to answer the question (the lines are definitely not parallel), so you should classify this item as (D).

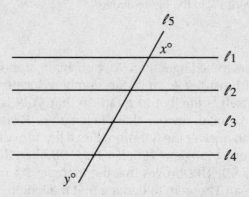

In the figure above, does $x = y$?
(1) $\ell_1 \parallel \ell_3$
(2) $\ell_2 \parallel \ell_4$

In the figure, the four lines seem to be parallel, and if ℓ_1 is parallel to ℓ_4, then x must be equal to y. But you cannot conclude from the appearance of the figure that the lines are parallel. In fact, the correct classification of this item is (E). Neither statement alone is sufficient to answer the question, because neither statement connects ℓ_1 to ℓ_4. Even taken together the statements are insufficient, for there is no way to determine whether ℓ_1 is parallel to ℓ_4.

The "Good Enough" Principle

Once you have determined that the statement, either alone or in conjunction with the other statement, is sufficient, that's "good enough." You don't necessarily have to do a calculation.

EXAMPLE:

What is the value of $\dfrac{(x^{12}y^{16}) - \left(\dfrac{x}{y}\right)}{11,234.221}$?

(1) $x = 4,321$

(2) $y = -0.0043$

Obviously, neither statement alone is sufficient to answer the question asked, for each provides information about the value of only one of the two variables in the problem. Both statements taken together are sufficient, for when the values are substituted for x and y in the expression in the stem, it will be possible to find the value of that expression. Of course, it would take a lot of time and work to do that calculation. Fortunately, it isn't necessary. Once you recognize that neither statement alone is sufficient to answer the question asked, but that both together are, that's "good enough." Mark (C) on the answer sheet and go to the next item.

In this part of the lesson we will review data sufficiency items that test your knowledge of the principles studied in lessons 15 through 17. You will notice that the presentation here follows the same general outline as the presentation in those chapters. If you have difficulty with an item in this lesson, you may want to refer to the appropriate material in the earlier lessons.

Data Sufficiency Items Using Arithmetic

Odd and Even Numbers

EXAMPLES:

If x is an integer, is x an even number?
(1) $3x$ is an even number.
(2) $x + 2$ is an even number.

Statement (1) alone is sufficient to answer the question. Since 3 is an odd number, if $3x$ is even, then x must be an even number. Statement (2) is also sufficient. If $x + 2$ is an even number, then x must be an even number. Since each statement is by itself sufficient, this item should be classified as (D).

If x is an integer, is x an odd number?
(1) When $x + 1$ is divided by 3, the remainder is 1.
(2) $3x$ is an odd number.

19

Statement (1) alone is not sufficient to answer the question. If $x + 1$, when divided by 3, generates a remainder of 1, then x is divisible by 3. Some multiples of 3 are odd (e.g., 3, 9, 15), but others are even (e.g., 6, 12, 18). Statement (2) alone is sufficient to answer the question. Since the question stem specifies that x is an integer, if $3x$ is an odd integer, then x must be odd. Thus, the correct classification for this item is (B).

Consecutive Integers

EXAMPLES:

If p, q, and r are consecutive integers, in that order, what is the value of q?
(1) $q = p + r$
(2) $pr = -1$

You will recall from earlier lessons that consecutive integers can be represented in the following way: If p is the least of the consecutive integers, then $p + 1$ is the next integer in the sequence, $p + 2$ is the third integer in the sequence, and so on. Thus statement (1) can be rewritten:

$$p + 1 = p + (p + 2)$$
$$p + 1 = 2p + 2$$
$$p = -1$$

And q is zero. Therefore, statement (1) is sufficient to answer the question. Statement (2) is also sufficient to answer the question.

$$p(p + 2) = -1$$
$$p^2 + 2p = -1$$
$$p^2 + 2p + 1 = 0$$
$$(p + 1)(p + 1) = 0$$

So $p = -1$ and $q = 0$. Since each statement is by itself sufficient to answer the question, the correct classification for this item is (D).

What is the average of three consecutive odd integers?
(1) One of the integers is –1.
(2) The sum of two of the integers is 4.

Statement (1) alone is not sufficient to answer the question asked, since –1 could be the first, second, or third odd integer in the series. Nor is statement (2) alone sufficient to answer the question. Let n represent the smaller of the two integers, whose sum is 4. They may be consecutive integers, in which case $n + (n + 2) = 4$, or they may be the first and third integers in the series, in which case $n + (n + 4) = 4$.

$$n + (n + 2) = 4$$
$$2n = 2$$
$$n = 1$$

or

$$n + (n + 4) = 4$$
$$2n = 0$$
$$n = 0$$

But since *n* is odd, *n* is 1 and the other integer is 3. This alone, however, is not sufficient to answer the question, for the series might contain –1, 1, and 3, or 1, 3, and 5. The two statements taken together, however, do answer the question, for statement (1) selects one of the two possible series implied by statement (2). The integers are –1, 1, and 3. Since neither statement alone is sufficient to answer the question, but both statements together are sufficient, this item should be classified as (C).

Signs of Numbers

EXAMPLES:

Is *xy* a positive number?
(1) x^2y is a positive number.
(2) $x \div y$ is a positive number.

Statement (1) alone is not sufficient to answer the question asked. The square of any number (except 0) is positive. So (1) implies that *y* is positive, but implies nothing about the sign of *x*. Statement (2) alone, however, is sufficient to answer the question. Since *x* divided by *y* is positive, *x* and *y* must have the same sign. Therefore, *x* times *y* must also be positive. Since statement (2) alone is sufficient to answer the question asked, but statement (1) alone is not, this item should be classified as (B).

Is $a - b > 0$?
(1) $a > b$
(2) $a^2 > b^2$

Statement (1) alone is sufficient to answer the question asked, for (1) can be rewritten as $a - b > 0$. Statement (2), however, is not sufficient. Although a^2 is greater than b^2, *a* might or might not be greater than *b*. (For example, *a* might be –5 and *b* 4.) Since statement (1) alone is sufficient to answer the question asked, but statement (2) is not, this item should be classified as (A).

Multiples and Divisibility

EXAMPLES:

What is the remainder when *x* is divided by 15?
(1) *x* is a multiple of 3.
(2) *x* is a multiple of 5.

Statement (1) alone is not sufficient to answer the question asked. Some multiples of 3, such as 30, are divisible by 15, but others, such as 27, are not. Similarly, statement (2) alone is not sufficient to answer the question asked. Some multiples of 5, such as 45, are divisible by 15, but others, such as 35, are not. The two statements taken together are sufficient to answer the question, for together they imply that *x* is a multiple of $3 \times 5 = 15$. Since neither statement alone is sufficient to answer the question asked, but both taken together are, this item should be classified as (C).

19

Is $\dfrac{x}{9}$ an integer?

(1) $\dfrac{x}{909,909}$ is an integer.

(2) $\dfrac{x}{567}$ is an integer.

Statement (1) alone is sufficient to answer the question asked. Since 909,909 is divisible by 9 (909,909 = 9 × 101,101), x is divisible by 9. Statement (2) alone is also sufficient to answer the question asked. Since 567 is divisible by 9 (567 = 9 × 63), x is also divisible by 9. Since each statement is by itself sufficient to answer the question asked, this item should be classified as (D).

Unique Integer Solutions

How many marbles are contained in a certain jar?
(1) The marbles can be evenly divided into groups, each group having a dozen marbles.
(2) There are more than 140 but fewer than 150 marbles in the jar.

Statement (1) alone is not sufficient to answer the question asked; the total could be any multiple of 12. Nor is statement (2) alone sufficient to answer the question asked, for (2) just defines a range for the total. But both statements taken together are sufficient to answer the question, for there is only one multiple of 12 between 140 and 150, and that is 144. Since neither statement alone is sufficient to answer the question, but both statements taken together are sufficient, this item should be classified as (C).

John paid $130 for tickets to a series of concerts. How many of the tickets cost $20?
(1) Each ticket cost either $15 or $20.
(2) More than two of the tickets cost $20.

Statement (1) alone is not sufficient to answer the question asked, for there are two combinations of tickets that would cost $130: two $20 tickets plus six $15 tickets, or five $20 tickets plus two $15 tickets. Nor is statement (2) by itself sufficient. Both statements taken together are sufficient because statement (2) eliminates one of the two possibilities implied by statement (1). Since neither statement alone is sufficient to answer the question, but both taken together are sufficient, this item should be classified as (C).

Fractions, Ratios, and Percents

A certain forest consists only of pines, oaks, and sycamores. Which type of tree is the most numerous?

(1) There are $\frac{4}{5}$ as many sycamores as there are oaks.

(2) There are $\frac{2}{3}$ as many oaks as there are pines.

Neither statement alone is sufficient to answer the question asked, for each statement provides information about only two of the three types. But both statements taken together are sufficient to answer the question asked. Statement (1) implies that there are fewer sycamores than oaks, and statement (2) implies that there are fewer oaks than pines. Therefore, the most numerous tree must be the pine. Since neither statement alone is sufficient to answer the question asked, but both taken together are, this item should be classified as (C).

In a certain English class, students choose between reading *Moby Dick* or *David Copperfield*, and some students who want extra credit read both books. What fraction of the students read both books?

(1) $\frac{3}{4}$ of the students read *Moby Dick*.

(2) $\frac{2}{3}$ of the students read *David Copperfield*.

Neither statement alone is sufficient to answer the question asked, for each provides information about the readers of one title but not about readers of the other title. Both statements taken together are sufficient to answer the question asked. $\frac{3}{4}+\frac{2}{3}=\frac{17}{12}$, and that means that $\frac{5}{12}$ of the students must have read both books. Since neither statement alone is sufficient to answer the question asked, but both taken together are, this item should be classified as (C).

Average

EXAMPLES:

If 20 students took the same test, what was the average score of the students?
(1) The highest score was 80 and the lowest score was 20.

(2) $\frac{1}{2}$ of the students scored 40 or higher and $\frac{1}{2}$ of the students scored lower than 40.

Statement (1) is obviously not sufficient to answer the question, for it provides no information about the scores of the other 18 students. Nor is statement (2) sufficient. Finally, even the two statements together are not sufficient. Although they define ranges for the scores, they supply no information about the distribution of scores within the ranges defined. Since the statements, even when taken together, don't answer the question asked, this item should be classified as (E)

19

Ten children are sitting at a table. What is the average age, in years, of the ten children?
(1) The average age of the six youngest children is 12 years.
(2) The average age of the four oldest children is 16 years.

Neither statement alone is sufficient to answer the question asked, but both taken together are. It is possible to set up a weighted average:

$$\frac{6(12) + 4(16)}{10} = \frac{136}{10} = 13.6$$

Thus, this item should be classified as (C).

John made five deposits to his savings account. What was the total of the deposits?
(1) The average of the deposits was $65.
(2) The largest deposit was $90 and the smallest deposit was $45.

Statement (1) alone is sufficient to answer the question asked. Since John made five deposits, the total deposited was 5 × $65 = $325. Statement (2), however, is not sufficient to answer the question asked. Since (1) alone is sufficient but (2) is not, you should classify this item as (A).

$$\boxed{\textbf{Rate}}$$

EXAMPLES:

Steve walked from his home to the store and back again. How long did it take him to make the entire trip?
(1) He walked from his home to the store at an average rate of 2 miles per hour.
(2) He walked from the store to his home at an average rate of 3 miles per hour.

Neither statement (1) nor (2) is sufficient to answer the question asked, for each provides information about only one of the two legs of the trip. Are the two statements taken together sufficient? No, because you have no information about the length of the trip. This item should be classified as an (E).

Al drove from City P to City Q and back again. What was his average speed for the entire trip?
(1) He drove from City P to City Q in two hours, and the return trip took three hours.
(2) The distance between P and Q is 100 miles.

Statement (1) alone is not sufficient to answer the question asked, because you have no information about the distance of the trip. Statement (2) is not sufficient because you have no information about the time needed to complete the journey. But both statements taken together are sufficient to answer the question asked. The total distance was 200 miles, and the total time for the trip was five hours. Therefore, the average speed was 40 miles per hour. Since neither statement alone is sufficient to answer the question asked, but both taken together are, this item should be classified as (C).

Dick drove from City P to City Q, a total of 600 miles. What was his average speed for the trip?

(1) Dick drove the first 300 miles at an average rate of 40 miles per hour.
(2) Dick drove the last 500 miles at an average rate of 50 miles per hour.

Neither statement alone is sufficient to answer the question asked, for each provides information about only a portion of the trip. And even when the two statements are taken together they are insufficient, for there is an overlap of 200 miles between the two statements. This item should be classified as an (E).

Algebra Operations

When a question stem indicates an operation, the solution to the problem usually requires the performance of that operation.

EXAMPLE:

What is the value of $\dfrac{p}{q} + \dfrac{r}{s}$?

(1) $ps + qr = 2$
(2) $qs = 2$

The correct classification for this item is (C), though you might not realize that unless you perform the operation indicated in the stem. Use the "flying x" method:

$$\frac{p}{q} + \frac{r}{s} = \frac{(ps + qr)}{qs}$$

Now you should be able to see that neither statement alone is sufficient, but both together are.

You may also need to "undo" operations like the one just shown.

EXAMPLE:

What is the value of $\dfrac{(x - y)}{x}$?

(1) $\dfrac{x}{y} = 2$

(2) $\dfrac{y}{x} = \dfrac{1}{2}$

The correct classification for this item is (D).

$$\frac{(x - y)}{x} = \frac{x}{x} - \frac{y}{x} = 1 - \frac{y}{x}$$

Thus, each statement establishes that the expression in the question stem is equal to $\frac{1}{2}$.

19

If a question stem contains a complex expression, try to simplify the expression.

EXAMPLE:

What is the value of $\dfrac{x^3y^2z^4}{z^3x^4y^2}$?

(1) $x = 2$

(2) $\dfrac{z}{x} = 2$

The correct classification for this item is (B), a conclusion more easily seen once the expression in the stem is simplified:

$$\frac{x^3y^2z^4}{z^3x^4y^2} = \frac{z}{x}$$

You should also be alert to the possibility of factoring an expression.

EXAMPLES:

What is the value of $\dfrac{\left(2pq + pq^2\right)}{pq}$?

(1) $p = 2$
(2) $q = 1$

The correct classification for this item is (B), a conclusion more easily seen once the expression in the stem is factored and simplified:

$$\frac{\left(2pq + pq^2\right)}{pq} = \frac{pq(2+q)}{pq} = 2 + q$$

What is the value of $x^2 + 2xy + y^2$?
(1) $x + y = 0$
(2) $x = -y$

The correct classification for this item is (D), a conclusion more easily seen once the expression has been factored:

$$x^2 + 2xy + y^2 = (x + y)(x + y)$$

Statement (1) is sufficient because it implies that the value of the entire expression is zero. Statement (2) is also sufficient, for it implies that $x + y = 0$.

To classify a data sufficiency item containing an equation, you will probably need to solve the equation.

EXAMPLE:

What is the value of x?
(1) $x + 2 = 8$

(2) $\dfrac{x}{3} = 2$

Each statement is sufficient to answer the question:

$$x + 2 = 8$$

$$x = 6$$

and

$$\frac{x}{3} = 2$$

$$x = 6$$

So the correct classification for this item is (D).

Be alert for the possibility of using two equations together as simultaneous equations.

> **EXAMPLE:**
>
> What is the value of x?
> (1) $x + 2y = 3$
> (2) $x - y = 0$

Neither statement alone is sufficient, since each is a single equation containing two unknowns, but both statements taken together create a system of simultaneous equations from which can be deduced the value of x:

$$x + 2y = 3$$

$$x - y = 0$$

Subtract the equations:

$$3y = 3$$

$$y = 1$$

So $x = 1$ also. Since neither statement alone is sufficient to answer the question asked, but both taken together are, the correct classification for this item is (C).

19

Geometry

Any of the principles included in "Holmes' Attic" in Lesson 17 could be the basis for a data sufficiency item, but some principles are more likely to be used than others. Especially popular with the test-writers are right triangles and equilateral figures.

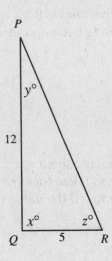

EXAMPLES:

What is the length of *PR*?
(1) $x = 90$
(2) $y + z = 90$

The correct classification for this item is (D), for each statement is sufficient to answer the question asked. Each statement establishes that *PQR* is a right triangle, so it is possible to use the Pythagorean Theorem to find the length of *PR*.

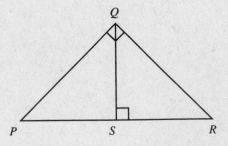

In the figure above, if $PQ = QR$, then what is the area of the triangle *PQR*?
(1) $QS = 1$
(2) $PQ = \sqrt{2}$

The correct classification for this item is (D), for each statement alone is sufficient to answer the question asked. Statement (1) alone is sufficient, since S must be the midpoint of *PR*, so $PR = 2$, and the area of the triangle is 1. Statement (2) alone is also sufficient. *PQ* and *QR* can be used as altitude and base of the triangle, so the triangle has an area of 1.

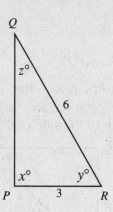

What is the area of Δ *PQR* above?
(1) The degree measures of *x*, *y*, and *z* are in the ratio of 3:2:1, respectively.
(2) $QP = 3\sqrt{3}$

Each statement alone is sufficient to answer the question. As for (1), let *a* represent the degree measure of the smallest angle:

$a + 2a + 3a = 180$

$6a = 180$

$a = 30$

The degree measures of the three angles are 30, 60, and 90, which means the triangle is a right triangle. Therefore, $QP = 3\sqrt{3}$, and *QP* and *PR* can be used as altitude and base to determine the area of the triangle: $\frac{1}{2}(3\sqrt{3})(3) = \frac{9\sqrt{3}}{2}$. Statement (2) is also sufficient. Since the sides of the triangle are in the ratio $1:\frac{1}{2}:\frac{\sqrt{3}}{2}$, the triangle must be a right triangle, so it is possible to find the area of the figure.

What is the area of triangle *ABC*?
(1) *ABC* is an equilateral triangle.
(2) The length of *AB* is 2.

The correct classification for this item is (C). Neither statement alone is sufficient to answer the question asked, but both taken together are. Given information about the length of the sides, the length of the altitude, or the area of an equilateral triangle, you can deduce the magnitude of the other quantities. Therefore, given that *ABC* is an equilateral triangle with a side of 2, you can deduce that the area is $\sqrt{3}$:

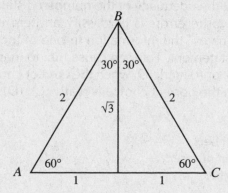

19

What is the area of square *PQRS*?
(1) The length of *PQ* is 4.
(2) The length of diagonal *PR* is $4\sqrt{2}$.

Each statement alone is sufficient to answer the question asked. Obviously, statement (1) is sufficient to determine that the area is 16. But statement (2) can also be used to determine that the length of the side of the square is 4:

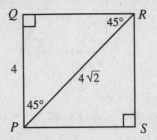

What is the area of a circle with center *O*?
(1) The circumference of the circle is 2π.
(2) The diameter of the circle is 2.

Each statement alone is sufficient to answer the question asked. Obviously, statement (2) is sufficient to determine that the radius of the circle is 1 and the area π. But statement (1) is also sufficient:

Circumference = $2\pi r$

$2\pi = 2\pi(r)$

$r = 1$

Be Sure You Understand the Significance

of Each Clue

Data sufficiency questions place special demands on your analytical faculties. The task here is to determine the sufficiency of the numbered statements to answer the question—not simply to answer the question. Thus, the sufficiency question is of a different order than the ordinary math question. Consequently, it is possible to know how to do the math needed to answer a question and yet miss the question by incorrectly assessing the adequacy of the numbered statements.

One of Watson's favorite errors is to classify an item incorrectly because he inadvertently "contaminates" the information in one of the statements with information from the other statement. This can cause him to mark (C) when the correct choice is (A), (B), or (D), or to mark (D) when the correct choice is (A), (B), or (C), or to mark (A) or (B) when the correct choice is really (C), (D), or (E).

EXAMPLE:

Is $x + 3$ an even number?
(1) $2x + 6$ is an even number.
(2) x is an odd number.

Watson is likely to classify this item as (C). He reads the stem and recognizes that $x + 3$ will be an even number just in case x is an odd number. Then he reads statement (1) and reasons correctly that it is not sufficient to answer the question: "Although $2x + 6$ is an even number, $x + 3$, which is half of $2x + 6$, might or might not be a whole number. So statement (1) is not sufficient." Then Watson reads statement (2) and thinks: "So x is an odd number. This statement supplies what is missing from statement (1). Together, the two statements answer the question, so I'll answer (C)."

This reasoning is erroneous. The correct answer is (B). If x is an odd number, then $x + 3$ must be odd. Statement (2), therefore, is sufficient to answer the question asked. So, statement (1) alone is not sufficient to answer the question, but statement (2) alone is sufficient to answer the question, so the correct classification is (B)—not (C).

A technique to help you avoid this problem is to read each of the clues separately, assessing its adequacy independently of the other clue. For example:

If $xy \neq 0$, what is the value of $x \div y$?

(1) $y \div x = -1$

(2) $-x = y$

Begin by reading the question as though the second statement did not exist:

If $xy \neq 0$, what is the value of $x \div y$?

(1) $y \div x = -1$

Is this statement sufficient to answer the question asked? Yes.

$$\frac{y}{x} = -1$$

$$y = -x$$

$$1 = -\frac{x}{y}$$

$$-1 = \frac{x}{y}$$

So, $x \div y = -1$. Now read the question a second time to test the sufficiency of the second statement:

If $xy \neq 0$, what is the value of $x \div y$?

(2) $-x = y$

Is this statement sufficient to answer the question? Yes.

$$-x = y$$

$$x = -y$$

$$\frac{x}{y} = -1$$

19

So, $x \div y = -1$. Since each statement is sufficient in itself to answer the question, the correct classification of the item is (D).

This technique of reading each statement and assessing its sufficiency in isolation of the other is important to "clear thinking" about data sufficiency items. Additionally, it has an important advantage in terms of economy of thought. One of the most difficult choices in this section occurs when you have determined that neither (1) alone nor (2) alone is sufficient to answer the question. It is then necessary to decide whether or not the two together answer the question or not (whether the answer is (C) or (E)). Unless you first read and assess each statement in isolation of the other, you will find that you begin to worry about this difficult "(C) versus (E)" question before it is necessary to do so.

So read each statement in isolation of the other statement. You may even want to cover up the other statement with your hand so that your judgment about the statement you are studying is not influenced by your reading of the other. To gain discipline in this approach, here is an exercise.

(Answers, page 415)

Directions: The following exercise consists of 25 questions. Go through the questions the first time trying to determine the sufficiency of statement (1). If you determine that statement (1) is sufficient to answer the question asked, mark "✔" on the answer sheet provided. Mark "x" if it is not sufficient. Then go through the questions again, following the same procedure for statement (2). Finally, go through the questions a third time and classify the items as (A), (B), (C), (D), or (E).

1. Which copy machine, *X* or *Y*, makes copies at the faster rate?

    (1) Machine *X* makes 90 copies per minute.

    (2) In three minutes, *X* makes 1.5 more copies than *Y*.

2. Lines ℓ_1, ℓ_2, and ℓ_3 lie in a plane. Is ℓ_1 parallel to ℓ_3?

    (1) ℓ_1 is perpendicular to ℓ_2.

    (2) ℓ_2 is perpendicular to ℓ_3.

3. How many cookies are in a 2-pound tin of Ronald's Cookies?

    (1) Each cookie weighs between 3.25 and 3.75 ounces.

    (2) Ronald's Cookies cost $6.25 per pound.

4. What is the value of *x*?

    (1) $x + 2y = 8$

    (2) $2 + x + y = 2y + 2x - y$

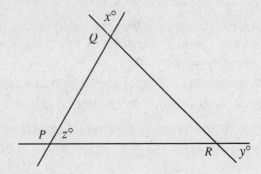

5. In *PQR* above, if *PQ* = *QR*, what is *z*?

    (1) $x = 65$

    (2) $y = 57\dfrac{1}{2}$

6. The membership of a certain school club is made up of only sophomores, juniors, and seniors. If the total membership of the club is 120, how many of the club's members are seniors?

   (1) $\frac{1}{5}$ of the club's members are sophomores and $\frac{1}{3}$ are juniors.

   (2) The ratio of juniors to sophomores is 5:3.

7. If x is a positive integer such that x is evenly divisible only by 1 and itself, what is the value of x?

   (1) $9 < x < 14$

   (2) $10 < x < 15$

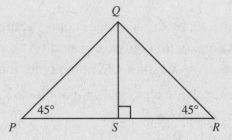

8. What is the perimeter of triangle PQR?
   (1) $PS = \sqrt{2}$
   (2) $PR = 2\sqrt{2}$

9. Is triangle ABC an isosceles triangle?

   (1) The number of degrees in angle A is not equal to the number of degrees in angle B.

   (2) Exactly two of the angles of ABC have the same number of degrees.

10. A horse ran and finished a race that consisted of two laps around an oval track. If the distance around the track is $1\frac{1}{4}$ miles, what was the horse's average running speed for the race?

    (1) The horse completed the first lap in 2 minutes and 36 seconds.

    (2) The horse's average speed for the second lap was 25 miles per hour.

11. How many people are seated in a certain theater?

    (1) If $\frac{1}{4}$ of the people in the theater left, the theater would be filled to $\frac{3}{5}$ of capacity.

    (2) If 20 more people entered the theater, it would be filled to capacity.

12. If w, x, y, and z are integers such that $w < x < y < z$, what is the value of x?
    (1) $w + z = 10$
    (2) $y = 3$

13. Is x an even integer?

    (1) $\frac{(x+x)}{2}$ is even.

    (2) $\frac{(x+x+x)}{6}$ is even.

14. Line ℓ is a straight line lying in the coordinate plane. Does line ℓ include the origin?

    (1) Line ℓ has a slope of -1.

    (2) Line ℓ includes those points with coordinates $(-1, 1)$ and $(1, -1)$

15. Is x an integer?

    (1) x^2 is an integer.

    (2) $2x$ is an integer.

16. If $p \neq 0$ and $q \neq 0$, is $\dfrac{(p+q)}{q}$ an integer?

    (1) $\dfrac{p}{q} = 2$

    (2) $p + q = 6$

17. What is the value of $\dfrac{2^x}{2^y}$?

    (1) $x = y$

    (2) $y - x = 0$

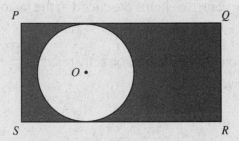

18. What is the area of the shaded part of the figure above?

    (1) The radius of the circle is 4.

    (2) $PQ = 16$ and $PS = 8$.

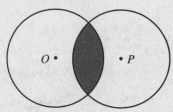

19. What is the area of the shaded part of the figure above?

    (1) The radius of circle O is 1.

    (2) The radius of circle P is 1.

20. What percent is x of y?

    (1) $2x = 3y$

    (2) $\dfrac{x}{y} = 1.5$

19

21. What is the value of integer x?

(1) $-3(x + 2) > 6$

(2) $-x + 5 > 1$

22. What is the value of $x^2 - y^2$?

(1) $x - y = 0$

(2) $x + y = 3$

23. Tickets to a play are for either the orchestra or the balcony. If tickets for balcony seats cost 25 percent less than tickets for orchestra seats, what is the ratio of revenues earned from sales of balcony tickets to revenues earned from sales of orchestra tickets?

(1) 20 percent more orchestra tickets were sold than balcony tickets.

(2) Balcony tickets cost $20.

24. Is $x^2 + 2xy + y^2 > 0$?

(1) $x + y > 0$

(2) $x > y$

25. What fraction of the items produced at a certain factory are defective?

(1) $\dfrac{1}{20}$ of the defective items produced at the factory are not detected by quality control inspectors.

(2) Quality control inspectors correctly reject $\dfrac{1}{1,000}$ of the items produced as defective.

	Statement (1)	Statement (2)	Answer Choice
1.			
2.			
3.			
4.			
5.			
6.			
7.			
8.			
9.			
10.			
11.			
12.			
13.			
14.			
15.			
16.			
17.			
18.			
19.			
20.			
21.			
22.			
23.			
24.			
25.			

Accentuate the Positive and

Eliminate the Negative

The data sufficiency format is fertile ground for cultivating Holmesian strategies. Partial information about either statement can be sufficient to eliminate two or even three answer choices:

Once you determine that statement (1) alone is sufficient to answer the question, eliminate (B), (C), and (E). (If [1] alone is sufficient, then the correct response must be either [A] or [D].)

Once you determine that statement (2) alone is sufficient to answer the question, eliminate (A), (C), and (E). (If [2] alone is sufficient, then the correct response must be either [B] or [D].)

Once you determine that statement (1) alone is NOT sufficient to answer the question, eliminate (A) and (D). (If [1] alone is not sufficient, then the correct response must be [B], [C], or [E].)

Once you determine that statement (2) alone is NOT sufficient, eliminate (B) and (D). (If [2] alone is not sufficient, then the correct response must be [A], [C], or [E].)

Make it a policy to put a mental "✔" or an "x" by each statement. If you are able to make a judgment about the sufficiency of one of the statements but not the other, then make a guess:

✔ (1) ⎫
? (2) ⎬ = (A) or (D)   ? (1) ⎫
                              ✔ (2) ⎬ = (B) or (D)

x (1) ⎫
? (2) ⎬ = (B), (C) or (E)   ? (1) ⎫
                              x (2) ⎬ = (A), (C), or (E)

Summary

1. Memorize the meanings of the lettered classifications. Remember that a figure in this section may not be drawn to scale.
2. With difficult data sufficiency items, expect the unexpected, and remember that the "good enough" principle applies to items in this section.
3. The same math principles tested in problem solving are tested in data sufficiency, but there are some peculiarities. Be familiar with them.
4. Study each statement in isolation from the other, so that you don't contaminate one statement with information learned from the other.
5. Be sure to eliminate answer choices and make a guess.

Answers

	Statement (1)	Statement (2)	Answer Choice
1.	X	✓	B
2.	X	X	C
3.	X	X	E
4.	X	✓	B
5.	X	X	C
6.	✓	X	A
7.	X	X	E
8.	✓	✓	D
9.	X	✓	B
10.	X	X	C
11.	X	X	C
12.	X	X	E
13.	✓	✓	D
14.	X	✓	B
15.	✓	X	A
16.	✓	X	A
17.	✓	✓	D
18.	X	✓	B
19.	X	X	E
20.	✓	✓	D
21.	X	X	E
22.	✓	X	A
23.	✓	X	A
24.	✓	X	A
25.	X	X	C

Data Sufficiency Drills

1. **Walk-Through Drills**
2. **Warm-Up Drills**

This lesson contains four data sufficiency drills. The first two drills are "walk-throughs." In these exercises, the answers and explanations for the questions are printed in the facing column so that you can "walk through" the drill. There is no time limit for the walk-through drills. The third and fourth drills are "warm-ups." Answers and explanations for the warm-up drills start on page 434.

Walk-Through 1

Directions: Each item of this type consists of a question followed by two statements, labeled (1) and (2). You must determine whether the information provided by the numbered statements is sufficient to answer the questions asked. In addition to the information provided in the numbered statements, you should rely on your knowledge of mathematics and ordinary facts (such as the number of minutes in an hour). Choose:

    A if statement (1) BY ITSELF is sufficient to answer the question but statement (2) by itself is not sufficient to answer the question

    B if statement (2) BY ITSELF is sufficient to answer the question but statement (1) by itself is not sufficient to answer the question

    C if BOTH statements (1) and (2) together are sufficient to answer the question but NEITHER statement BY ITSELF is sufficient to answer the question

    D if EACH statement BY ITSELF is sufficient to answer the question

    E if the two statements, even when taken TOGETHER, are NOT sufficient to answer the question

Numbers: All values are real numbers.

Figures: The figures with this question type will not necessarily reflect the information given in the numbered statements, but they will reflect the information provided in the question. Unless otherwise indicated, all figures lie in a plane; all lines shown as straight are straight; and the positions of all points, angles, regions, etc., are correctly depicted.

Example:

In $\triangle ABC$, what is the value of x?

(1) $y = 60$

(2) $AB = BC$

Explanation: Statement (1) is not sufficient to answer the question, for statement (1) provides no information about x or z. Statement (2) is not sufficient to answer the question. Statement (2) does establish that $y = z$, but that is not enough information to determine the value of x. Both statements together are sufficient to answer the question. Since $AB = BC$ and $y = z$, $z = 60$. Since $x + y + z = 180$, $x = 60$.

---

1. If a subway token cost $1.00 on January 1, 1997, by what percent did the price of a token increase between January 1, 1987 and January 1, 1997?
   (1) On January 1, 1987, a token cost $.60.
   (2) On July 1, 1989, the cost of a token was raised to $.75; on February 1, 1993, the cost of a token was raised to $.90; and on October 1, 1994, the cost of a token was raised to $1.00.

1. **(A)** Since the question stem states that the cost of a token on January 1, 1997, was $1.00, the only other piece of information needed to answer the question is the cost of a token on January 1, 1987. Examine each statement independently of the other to determine whether it provides that additional information.

   Statement (1) does provide the missing information, so statement (1) alone is sufficient to answer the question. (And we can eliminate choices [B], [C], and [E].) Statement (2) however, does not provide the needed information because statement (2) says nothing about the cost of a token on January 1, 1987. (Eliminate choice [D].) Since statement (1) alone is sufficient, but statement (2) alone is not sufficient, classify this item as (A).

2. What is the length of a rectangular swimming pool?
    (1) The perimeter of the pool is 80 meters.
    (2) The ratio of the width of the pool to its length
         is 1:3.

3. Is Al taller than Ken?
    (1) Al is taller than Sergio.
    (2) Ken is taller than Sergio.

2. **(C)** Statement (1) alone is not sufficient to answer the question because it provides no information about the relative sizes of the length of the pool and its width. Nor is statement (2) alone sufficient because it provides no information about actual lengths. (And you eliminate [A], [B], and [D].)

Now the issue is whether the two statements together answer the question, and they do. Expressed algebraically, statement (1) says:

$$2w + 2\ell = 80$$

(Where w and ℓ represent the width and the length of the pool, respectively.) And statement (2) says:

$$\frac{w}{\ell} = \frac{1}{3}$$

We have two equations with only two variables. It is possible to treat these as simultaneous equations and solve for w and ℓ. Since neither statement alone is sufficient to answer the question, but the two statements taken together are, classify this item as (C). (**Note:** There is no need to find the actual values of the variables. Since this is a data sufficiency item, once you determine that the two statements together are sufficient, that's "good enough.")

3. **(E)** Statement (1) alone is not sufficient because (1) provides no information about Ken's height. (Eliminate [A] and [D].) Statement (2) is not sufficient because (2) provides no information about Al's height. (Eliminate [B] as well.) Are the two statements together sufficient to answer the question? No; the two statements taken together establish:

(1) $A > S$
(2) $K > S$

But this is not sufficient to determine whether $A > K$. Since the statements, even when taken together, don't provide enough information to answer the question, classify this item as (E).

4. What is the value of 60 percent of x?

    (1) $\frac{1}{2}$ of 20 percent of $x = 5$

    (2) $4x = k$, $5y = k$, and $y = 40$

5. Three packages have a combined weight of 48 pounds. What is the weight of the heaviest package?
    (1) One package weighs 12 pounds.
    (2) One package weighs 24 pounds.

6. What is the value $(x + y)^2$?
    (1) $x^2 + xy = 3$
    (2) $y^2 + yx = 5$

4. **(D)** To answer this question, you need to find the value of x. Statement (1) alone is sufficient to determine the value of x:

$$\left(\frac{1}{2}\right)(20\%)x = 5$$

Since this is an equation with only one variable, it is possible to find the value of x. (Eliminate [B], [C], and [E].) Statement (2) alone is also sufficient to determine the value of x, since $y = 40$, $k = 200$, and $x = 50$. (Eliminate [A].) Since each statement is in and of itself sufficient to answer the question, classify this item as (D).

5. **(B)** Statement (1) is not sufficient to determine the weight of the heaviest package. It implies only that the combined weight of the other two packages is 36 pounds. (Eliminate [A] and [D].) Statement (2) alone is sufficient, for it implies that the combined weight of two of the packages is only 24 pounds. Since the weight of the 24-pound package is equal to the combined weight of the other two packages, the heaviest package must weigh 24 pounds. (Eliminate [C], and [E].) Since statement (2) alone is sufficient to answer the question, but statement (1) alone is not, classify this item as (B).

6. **(C)** First, do the multiplication indicated in the stem:

$$(x + y)^2 = x^2 + 2xy + y^2$$

Neither statement alone is sufficient to determine the value of this expression. (Eliminate [A], [B], and [D].) But the two statements taken together are sufficient. Add together the two equations:

$x^2 + xy = 3$

$y^2 + xy = 5$

$x^2 + 2xy + y^2 = 8$

Since neither statement alone is sufficient to answer the question, but the two statements taken together are, classify this item as (C).

7. How many books are there on a certain shelf?
   (1) If four books are removed, the number of books remaining on the shelf will be less than 12.
   (2) If three more books are placed on the shelf, the total number of books on the shelf will be more than 17.

8. What is the value of the positive integer x?
   (1) When 23 and 25 are divided by x, the remainders are 3 and 1, respectively.
   (2) When 24 is divided by x, the remainder is zero.

9. What is the value of $\dfrac{x-y}{y} + \dfrac{y-x}{x}$?
   (1) $(x-y)^2 = 12$
   (2) $xy = 6$

7. **(C)** Neither statement alone is sufficient to answer the question asked. Statement (1) alone implies only that the number of books on the shelf is 15 or fewer, and statement (2) alone implies only that the number of books on the shelf is 15 or more. (Eliminate [A], [B], and [D].) But the two statements taken together are sufficient to answer the question, for they imply that the number of books on the shelf is 15. (15 is the only integer that satisfies both [1] and [2].) Since neither statement alone is sufficient, but the two together are, classify this item as (C).

8. **(A)** Statement (1) alone is sufficient to answer the question asked. Since x, when divided into 23, generates a remainder of 3, x must be 4, 5, 10, or 20. Further, since x, when divided into 25, generates a remainder of 1, x must be 2, 3, 4, 6, 8, or 12. There is only one number common to both lists, 4, so x is 4. (Eliminate [B], [C], and [E].) Statement (2) alone, however, is not sufficient, for it implies only that x is a factor of 24, but that means that x could be 1, 2, 3, 4, 6, 8, 12, or 24. Since (1) alone is sufficient but (2) alone is not, classify this item as (A).

9. (C) Begin by performing the indicated operation:

$$\frac{x-y}{y} + \frac{y-x}{x} = \frac{x^2 - xy - xy + y^2}{xy} = \frac{x^2 - 2xy + y^2}{xy}$$

Neither statement alone is sufficient to answer the question. Although statement (1) implies that $x^2 - 2xy + y^2 = 12$, that information is not sufficient to determine the value of the expression above. Nor is statement (2) alone sufficient. (Eliminate [A], [B], and [D].) The two statements taken together are sufficient. They imply that the value of the expression above is $\frac{12}{6} = 2$. Since neither statement alone is sufficient to answer the question, but both statements taken together are, classify this item as (C).

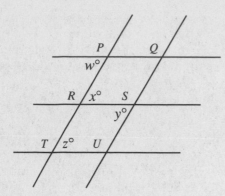

10. In the figure above, is *PQ* parallel to *TU*?
    (1) $w = z$
    (2) $x = y$

10. (A) Statement (1) alone is sufficient to answer the question. If $w = z$, then *PQ* must be parallel to *TU* (by the "big angle/little angle" theorem of parallel lines). (Eliminate [B], [C], and [E].) Statement (2) alone, however, is not sufficient to answer the question. Although (2) implies that *PT* is parallel to *QU*, it does not determine whether *PQ* is parallel to *TU*. (Eliminate [D].) Since (1) alone is sufficient, but (2) is not, classify this item as (A).

Walk-Through 2

Directions: Each item of this type consists of a question followed by two statements, labeled (1) and (2). You must determine whether the information provided by the numbered statements is sufficient to answer the questions asked. In addition to the information provided in the numbered statements, you should rely on your knowledge of mathematics and ordinary facts (such as the number of minutes in an hour). Choose:

  A if statement (1) BY ITSELF is sufficient to answer the question but statement (2) by itself is not sufficient to answer the question

  B if statement (2) BY ITSELF is sufficient to answer the question but statement (1) by itself is not sufficient to answer the question

  C if BOTH statements (1) and (2) together are sufficient to answer the question but NEITHER statement BY ITSELF is sufficient to answer the question

  D if EACH statement BY ITSELF is sufficient to answer the question

  E if the two statements, even when taken TOGETHER, are NOT sufficient to answer the question

Numbers: All values are real numbers.

Figures: The figures with this question type will not necessarily reflect the information given in the numbered statements, but they will reflect the information provided in the question. Unless otherwise indicated, all figures lie in a plane; all lines shown as straight are straight; and the positions of all points, angles, regions, etc., are correctly depicted.

Example:

In △ ABC, what is the value of *x*?

(1) $y = 60$

(2) $AB = BC$

Explanation: Statement (1) is not sufficient to answer the question, for statement (1) provides no information about *x* or *z*. Statement (2) is not sufficient to answer the question. Statement (2) does establish that $y = z$, but that is not enough information to determine the value of *x*. Both statements together are sufficient to answer the question. Since $AB = BC$ and $y = z$, $z = 60$. Since $x + y + z = 180$, $x = 60$.

---

1. Is point *P* located on the circumference of the circle with center *O* and radius of length 1?

    (1) Points *P*, *O*, and *R* are the vertices of an equilateral triangle.

    (2) Point *R* is located on the circumference of the circle with center *O* and radius of length 1.

1. (C) Statement (1) is not by itself sufficient to answer the question, for *P* might or might not be on the circle:

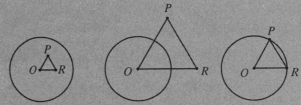

(Eliminate [A] and [D].) Nor is statement (2) alone sufficient to answer the question. (Eliminate [B].) The two statements together are sufficient to answer the question. Since *POR* is an equilateral triangle with one vertex at the center of the circle and the other on the circle, the third vertex must also be on the circle. Since neither statement alone is sufficient to answer the question, but both statements taken together are, classify this item as (C).

2. Is it cheaper to have employee *A* or employee *B* do a
    certain task?
    (1) *A* is paid 20 percent more per hour than *B*, but *B*
        takes two hours longer to complete the task
        than *A*.
    (2) *A* is paid $18.00 per hour.

2. **(E)** Statement (1) alone is not sufficient to answer the question, for whether it is cheaper to use employee *A* or *B* will depend on the length of time required to complete the task. This idea can be expressed algebraically. Let *b* represent the hourly wage of *B*, and *x* the number of hours needed for *A* to complete the task. The cost of having *B* do the task is:

Cost of $B = b(x + 2)$

And the cost of having *A* do the task is:

Cost of $A = 18(x)$

But without further information, it is impossible to determine whether the cost of *B* is greater than, less than, or equal to the cost of *A*. (Eliminate [A] and [D].) Obviously, (2) alone is not sufficient. (Eliminate [B].) And even taken together, the two statements do not answer the question. Since *A* makes 20 percent more per hour than *B*, $18 = 1.2b$ and $b = 15$. Therefore,

Cost of $B = 15(x + 2)$
Cost of $A = 18(x)$

The two costs will be equal when:

$$15(x + 2) = 18x$$
$$15x + 30 = 18x$$
$$3x = 30$$
$$x = 10$$

When $x < 10$, the cost of *B* is greater; but when $x > 10$, the cost of *A* is greater. If *x* is a number such as $\frac{1}{4}$, then the cost of *B* is greater; but if *x* is a number such as 5, then the cost of *A* is greater. Since the two statements, even when taken together, don't answer the question, classify this item as (E).

3. Is xy an odd integer?
   (1) $x + y$ is an even integer.
   (2) x and y are distinct prime numbers greater than 10.

4. A clock loses m minutes every h hours. How many minutes will the clock lose in 48 hours?
   (1) The clock loses 0.25 minutes every h hours.
   (2) Every two hours, the clock loses one minute.

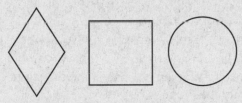

5. Each of the figures above is a different color—blue, green, or red. Which of the figures is red?
   (1) The red figure is next to the green figure.
   (2) The green figure is not next to the blue figure.

6. J and K are two different walls in a building. Is wall J parallel to wall K?
   (1) J and K are both perpendicular to ceiling C.
   (2) J and K are both perpendicular to wall W.

3. **(B)** Statement (1) alone is not sufficient to answer the question, for it implies only that either x and y are both even, or that x and y are both odd. (Eliminate [A] and [D].) Statement (2) alone is sufficient. Since x and y are both prime numbers and neither is 2, x and y must both be odd numbers. Therefore, xy is also an odd number. (Eliminate [C] and [E].) Since (2) alone is sufficient to answer the question, but (1) alone is not, classify this item as (B).

4. **(B)** Statement (1) alone is not sufficient to answer the question, for it provides no value for h. (Eliminate [A] and [D].) Statement (2), however, is sufficient by itself to answer the question. If the clock loses one minute every two hours, then it will lose 24 minutes in 48 hours. (Eliminate [C] and [E].) Since (2) alone is sufficient to answer the question, but (1) alone is not, classify this item as (B).

5. **(B)** This item does not, technically speaking, test "math," but it does test logical thinking. Statement (1) alone is not sufficient to answer the question. (Eliminate [A] and [D].) Statement (2), however, is sufficient by itself to answer the question, for (2) implies that the green and blue figures are the outside figures, which means that the red figure is the middle figure. (Eliminate [C] and [E].) Since statement (2) alone is sufficient to answer the question, but (1) is not, classify this item as (B).

6. **(B)** Statement (1) is not sufficient. Although the walls, which are vertical, are perpendicular to the ceiling, which is horizontal, the walls may or may not be parallel to each other. (Eliminate [A] and [D].) Statement (2), however, is sufficient. If J and K are both perpendicular to W, then J and K must be parallel to each other. (Eliminate [C] and [E].) Since (2) alone is sufficient to answer the question, but (1) is not, classify this item as (B).

7. What is the value of $5^x \div 5^y$?
   (1) $x - y = 2$
   (2) $x = 2y$

8. If the book value of a car is presently $3,600, what was its book value last year?
   (1) From last year to this year, the book value of the car declined by 24 percent.
   (2) From last year to this year, the book value of the car declined by $864.

9. What is the sum of three consecutive *odd* integers?
   (1) The smallest of the three integers is equal to $\frac{1}{5}$ of the sum of the three integers.
   (2) The sum of the three integers is greater than the average of the three integers.

7. **(A)** Statement (1) is, by itself, sufficient to answer the question. The expression in the question stem is equivalent to $5^{(x-y)}$, so (1) implies that the expression has the value 5^2, or 25. (Eliminate [B], [C], and [E].) Statement (2), however, is not by itself sufficient to answer the question, for (2) implies only that the expression is equivalent to $5^{(2y-y)} = 5y$. (Eliminate [D].) Since (1) alone is sufficient to answer the question, but (2) alone is not, classify this item as (A).

8. **(D)** Statement (1) alone is sufficient to answer the question, for it implies that $3,600 is 76 percent of the book value of the previous year. (Value − 24% Value = 76% value.) (Eliminate [B], [C], and [E].) Statement (2) alone is also sufficient to answer the question: $3,600 + $864 = $4,464. (Eliminate [A].) Since each statement is, by itself, sufficient to answer the question, classify this item as (D).

9. **(A)** Statement (1) is sufficient to answer the question. Let n represent the smallest of the three consecutive odd integers. The other two integers are $n + 2$ and $n + 4$:

$$n = \frac{1}{5}[n + (n + 2) + (n + 4)]$$

$$n = \frac{1}{5}(3n + 6)$$

$$n = \frac{3}{5}n + \frac{6}{5}$$

$$\frac{2}{5}n = \frac{6}{5}$$

$$n = 3$$

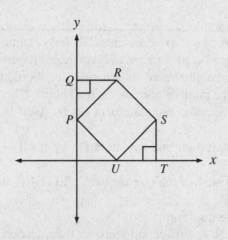

10. In the figure above, is *PRSU* a square?
    (1) *PQ* = *QR* and *UT* = *TS*
    (2) *PU* = *RS*

(Eliminate [B], [C], and [E].) Statement (2), however, is not sufficient to answer the question:

$$[n + (n + 2) + (n + 4)] > \frac{[n + (n + 2) + (n + 4)]}{2}$$

$$2(3n + 6) > 3n + 6$$

$$6n + 12 > 3n + 6$$

$$3n > -6$$

$$n > -2$$

(Eliminate [D].) Since statement (1) alone is sufficient to answer the question, but (2) alone is not, classify this item as (A).

10. **(E)** By using the technique of distorting the figure, we learn that even both statements taken together are not sufficient to answer the question:

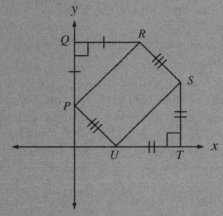

Since both statements taken together are insufficient, classify this item as (E).

Time: 12 minutes

10 Questions

Directions: Each item of this type consists of a question followed by two statements, labeled (1) and (2). You must determine whether the information provided by the numbered statements is sufficient to answer the questions asked. In addition to the information provided in the numbered statements, you should rely on your knowledge of mathematics and ordinary facts (such as the number of minutes in an hour). Choose:

    A if statement (1) BY ITSELF is sufficient to answer the question but statement (2) by itself is not sufficient to answer the question

    B if statement (2) BY ITSELF is sufficient to answer the question but statement (1) by itself is not sufficient to answer the question

    C if BOTH statements (1) and (2) together are sufficient to answer the question but NEITHER statement BY ITSELF is sufficient to answer the question

    D if EACH statement BY ITSELF is sufficient to answer the question

    E if the two statements, even when taken TOGETHER, are NOT sufficient to answer the question

Numbers: All values are real numbers.

Figures: The figures with this question type will not necessarily reflect the information given in the numbered statements, but they will reflect the information provided in the question. Unless otherwise indicated, all figures lie in a plane; all lines shown as straight are straight; and the positions of all points, angles, regions, etc., are correctly depicted.

Example:

In $\triangle ABC$, what is the value of x?

(1) $y = 60$

(2) $AB = B$

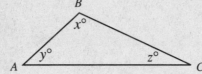

Explanation: Statement (1) is not sufficient to answer the question, for statement (1) provides no information about x or z. Statement (2) is not sufficient to answer the question. Statement (2) does establish that $y = z$, but that is not enough information to determine the value of x. Both statements together are sufficient to answer the question. Since $AB = BC$ and $y = z$, $z = 60$. Since $x + y + z = 180$, $x = 60$.

---

1. If m and n are positive numbers, what percent of n is m?

    (1) $m = \dfrac{4}{5}n$

    (2) $n = \dfrac{5}{4}m$

2. On December 31, 1985, only 20 people were members of a certain club. During which year did the club's membership first exceed 1,000?

    (1) In each year following 1985, membership in the club doubled.

    (2) On December 31, 1993, total membership in the club was 5,120.

3. If $3^n = xy$, what is the value of x?

    (1) $n = 2$

    (2) $x = y$

4. Is Paul older than John?

    (1) The average of Paul's age and John's age is 15.

    (2) Paul is two years older than the average of his age and John's age.

5. Three gymnasts, Debbie, Janet, and Molly, competed in a gymnastic meet. If each gymnast scored at least one point, which gymnast scored the most points?

    (1) Janet scored fewer points than Debbie but more points than Molly.

    (2) The total number of points scored by Janet and Molly is less than the number of points scored by Debbie.

6. What is the remainder when the positive integer x is divided by 2?

    (1) When $x + 1$ is divided by 2, the remainder is 1.

    (2) x is a multiple of 3.

7. If the ratio of teachers to students at Public School No. 10 in 1995 was 1 to 20, what was the ratio of teachers to students at Public School No. 10 in 1996?

    (1) Public School No. 10 had five more teachers in 1996 than in 1995.

    (2) Public School No. 10 had 100 more students in 1996 than in 1995.

8. Exactly how many stamps are in Mike's stamp
    collection?
    (1) Of all the stamps in Mike's collection, 375
        were issued on or before December 31, 1960.
    (2) Of all the stamps in Mike's collection, exactly
        $\frac{1}{4}$ were issued on or after January 1, 1961.

9. What is the value of the two-digit number n?
    (1) The sum of the two digits is 5.
    (2) The difference between the two digits is 3.

10. Is $xy > 0$?
    (1) $x^2y > 0$
    (2) $x^3y^2 > 0$

Time: 12 minutes

10 Questions

Directions: Each item of this type consists of a question followed by two statements, labeled (1) and (2). You must determine whether the information provided by the numbered statements is sufficient to answer the questions asked. In addition to the information provided in the numbered statements, you should rely on your knowledge of mathematics and ordinary facts (such as the number of minutes in an hour). Choose:

    A if statement (1) BY ITSELF is sufficient to answer the question but statement (2) by itself is not sufficient to answer the question

    B if statement (2) BY ITSELF is sufficient to answer the question but statement (1) by itself is not sufficient to answer the question

    C if BOTH statements (1) and (2) together are sufficient to answer the question but NEITHER statement BY ITSELF is sufficient to answer the question

    D if EACH statement BY ITSELF is sufficient to answer the question

    E if the two statements, even when taken TOGETHER, are NOT sufficient to answer the question

Numbers: All values are real numbers.

Figures: The figures with this question type will not necessarily reflect the information given in the numbered statements, but they will reflect the information provided in the question. Unless otherwise indicated, all figures lie in a plane; all lines shown as straight are straight; and the positions of all points, angles, regions, etc., are correctly depicted.

Example:

In $\triangle ABC$, what is the value of x?

(1) $y = 60$

(2) $AB = BC$

Explanation: Statement (1) is not sufficient to answer the question, for statement (1) provides no information about x or z. Statement (2) is not sufficient to answer the question. Statement (2) does establish that $y = z$, but that is not enough information to determine the value of x. Both statements together are sufficient to answer the question. Since $AB = BC$ and $y = z$, $z = 60$. Since $x + y + z = 180$, $x = 60$.

---

1. Is $a + b > p + q$?

    (1) $a > p$ and $q < b$.

    (2) $a = 5$, $b = 3$, $p = 0$, and $q = 2$.

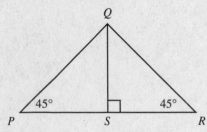

2. In the figure above, what is the length of QS?

    (1) $PQ = 2$

    (2) $PR = 2\sqrt{2}$

3. If $abc \neq 0$, what is the value of $\dfrac{a^5 b^5 c^3}{c^3 a^4 b^5}$?

    (1) $a = 2$ and $b = 6$.

    (2) $b = 6$ and $c = -1$.

4. What fractional part of the people watching a hockey match are wearing both a hat and a scarf?

    (1) Exactly $\dfrac{3}{4}$ of the people are wearing hats.

    (2) Exactly $\dfrac{2}{3}$ of the people are wearing scarves.

5. If x is an integer, what is the value of x?

    (1) $x^2 - 5x + 6 = 0$

    (2) $\dfrac{3}{4} > \dfrac{3}{(x + 2)}$

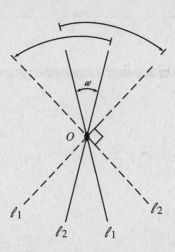

6. The figure above shows two lines intersecting at point O. If the lines are rotated about O in the directions indicated until they are first perpendicular to each other, what is the value of w?
   (1) Each line is rotated at the same rate.
   (2) Each line is rotated through 60°.

7. What is the value of $\dfrac{1}{x} + \dfrac{1}{y} + \dfrac{1}{z}$?

   (1) $xyz = 24$
   (2) $xy + xz + yz = 26$

8. Is the average of three positive numbers, p, q, and r, greater than q?
   (1) $p < q < r$
   (2) $q - r < q - p$

9. Is $a^2 - b^2$ a positive number?
   (1) $a + b$ is a positive number.
   (2) $a > b$

10. A homeowner offered her house for sale at an asking price that was 60 percent more than she paid for the house. How much did she originally pay for the house?
    (1) She finally accepted a bid that was 25 percent less than her asking price and sold the house for $36,000 more than she paid for it.
    (2) She sold the house for $216,000.

Explanatory Answers

Warm-Up Drill 1

1. **(D)** Statement (1) alone is sufficient to answer the question:

    $$m = \frac{4}{5}n$$

    $$m = 0.80n$$

    $$m = 80\% \text{ of } n$$

    And statement (2) is also sufficient:

    $$n = \frac{5}{4}m$$

    $$m = \frac{4}{5}n$$

    $$m = 0.80n = 80\% \text{ of } n$$

2. **(A)** Statement (1) alone is sufficient to answer the question. Since the club membership doubled every year after 1985, the total membership was 40 at the end of 1986, 80 at the end of 1987, 160 at the end of 1988, 320 at the end of 1989, 640 at the end of 1990, and 1,280 at the end of 1991. Thus, statement (1) implies that membership first exceeded 1,000 in 1991. Statement (2), however, is not sufficient. Therefore, you should classify this item as (A).

3. **(E)** Statement (1) alone is not sufficient to answer the question, for (1) implies only that $9 = xy$. Nor is statement (2) alone sufficient to answer the question (though it does imply that $n = 2$ or 4, or any even number). Both statements, even when taken together, also fail to answer the question, for x and y might both be +3 or they might both be –3.

4. **(B)** Statement (1) alone is not sufficient to answer the question because (1) says nothing about which person is older. Statement (2), however, is sufficient to answer the question. If Paul is older than the average of his age and John's age, then Paul must be the older of the two. Statement (2) can be expressed algebraically:

    $$P = \left(\frac{P+J}{2}\right) + 2$$

    $$P - 2 = \left(\frac{P+J}{2}\right)$$

    $$2P - 4 = P + J$$

    $$P = J + 4$$

    So Paul is four years older than John.

5. **(D)** Statement (1) is sufficient to answer the question, for it establishes that Debbie scored the most points, Janet the next largest number of points, and Molly the fewest points. Statement (2) is also sufficient. If Debbie scored more points than Janet and Molly combined, then Debbie scored the greatest number of points:

$$D > J + M$$

So Debbie must have scored more than Janet and more than Molly.

6. **(A)** Statement (1) alone is sufficient to answer the question. If, when $x + 1$ is divided by 2, the remainder is 1, then $x + 1$ is an odd number. Therefore, x is an even number. (And when an even number is divided by 2, the remainder is zero.) Statement (2), however, is not sufficient to answer the question. Positive multiples of 3 can be represented as $3n$, where n is a positive integer. When n is odd, $3n$ is also odd; when n is even, $3n$ is also even. Therefore, half the multiples of 3 leave a remainder of 1 when divided by 2, and the other multiples of 3 leave no remainder when divided by 2.

7. **(C)** Neither statement alone is sufficient to answer the question, for each provides information about only one of the two parts of the ratio, teachers or students, but not both parts. Are both statements together sufficient? Yes. Since students and teachers are added in the ratio of 1:20, the original ratio remains unchanged. (**Note:** Had the additional students and teachers been added in numbers other than the ratio 1:20, then the answer would have been [E].)

8. **(C)** Statement (1) alone is not sufficient to answer the question because it says nothing about stamps issued after December 31, 1960. Statement (2) alone is insufficient because it provides no information about stamps issued before January 1, 1961. Both statements together are sufficient, for together they imply that 375 stamps represent $\frac{3}{4}$ of all the stamps in the collection. ($375 = \frac{3}{4}$ of Total; therefore Total = 500.)

9. **(E)** Statement (1) alone is not sufficient to answer the question, for there are five two-digit numbers such that the sum of the digits is 5: 14, 41, 23, 32, and 50. Statement (2) is also insufficient since there is more than one number that satisfies that condition. Are both statements together sufficient? No. There are two numbers that satisfy both conditions, 14 and 41.

10. **(C)** Statement (1) alone is not sufficient to answer the question. Since $x^2y > 0$, x^2 cannot be zero. Therefore, x^2 is positive, and so y, too, must be positive. Although x^2 is positive, x itself might by positive or negative. Thus, (1) alone doesn't provide enough information to determine the sign of xy. For similar reasons, statement (2) is also insufficient. Statement (2) establishes that x is positive but implies nothing about the sign of y. The two statements taken together do imply that xy is positive. Statement (1) implies that y is positive and statement (2) implies that x is positive, so together they imply that xy is positive and therefore greater than zero.

Warm-Up Drill 2

1. **(D)** Statement (1) is sufficient to answer the question, for it establishes that $a > p$ and $b > q$. And statement (2) is also sufficient since it provides actual values for the variables.

2. **(D)** Statement (1) alone is sufficient to answer the question. *PQS* is a 45-45-90 degree right triangle, and information about any feature of that triangle is sufficient to deduce conclusions about every other feature of the triangle. If $PQ = 2$, then $QS = \sqrt{2}$. Statement (2) is also sufficient. Since *PR* is the hypotenuse of the 45-45-90 degree triangle *PQR*, if $PR = 2\sqrt{2}$, then $PQ = 2$ and $QS = \sqrt{2}$ (by the reasoning above). (Or you might reason that the altitude *QS* bisects *PR* and that $PS = QS$, so $QS = \sqrt{2}$.)

3. **(A)** Begin by simplifying the expression in the stem:

$$\frac{a^5 b^5 c^3}{c^3 a^4 b^5} = a^{(5-4)} b^{(5-5)} c^{(3-3)} = a$$

Since the expression is really equivalent to *a*, statement (1) alone is sufficient to answer the question, but statement (2) is not.

4. **(E)** Neither statement alone is sufficient to answer the question asked, for each gives information about one of the two relevant characteristics of the group but not about the other. Are both together sufficient? No. It could be that everyone who is wearing a scarf is also wearing a hat, but it could also be the case that some people wearing scarves are not wearing hats.

5. **(C)** Statement (1) alone is not sufficient to answer the question, for there are two solutions to that equation:

$$x^2 - 5x + 6 = 0$$

$$(x - 3)(x - 2) = 0$$

$$x - 3 = 0 \text{ or } x - 2 = 0$$

$$x = 3 \text{ or } x = 2$$

Nor is statement (2) alone sufficient, for that inequality does not determine a unique value of *x*. Are both statements taken together sufficient? Yes. Statement (1) implies that *x* is either 3 or 2, but only the first of those values satisfies the second statement ($\frac{3}{4} > \frac{3}{5}$, but $\frac{3}{4} = \frac{3}{4}$). Therefore, the two statements together imply that $x = 3$.

6. **(B)** Statement (1) is not sufficient to answer the question, for the rate at which the lines are rotated does not determine the "distance" they cover while rotating. Statement (2), however, is sufficient to answer the question:

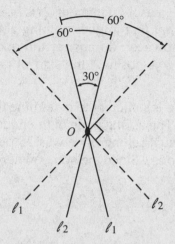

Since a complete circle describes a 360° arc, $w = 30$.

7. **(C)** Begin by performing the indicated addition:

$$\frac{1}{x} + \frac{1}{y} + \frac{1}{z} = \frac{y+x}{xy} + \frac{1}{z} = \frac{xy+yz+xz}{xyz} = \frac{xy+xz+yz}{xyz}$$

Statement (1) provides the value of the denominator of the expression, and statement (2) provides the value of the numerator. Thus, although neither statement alone is sufficient to determine the value of the entire expression, together they establish that the value of the expression is $\frac{26}{24} = \frac{13}{12}$.

8. **(E)** Expressed algebraically, the question is asking:

$$\frac{(p+q+r)}{3} > q?$$

$$p + q + r > 3q?$$

$$p + r > 2q$$

Statement (1) alone is not sufficient to answer the question. Although q is greater than p and less than r, whether $2q$ is less than the sum of p and r depends on how much less q is than r and how much greater q is than p. Nor is statement (2) sufficient:

$$q - r < q - p$$

$$-r < -p$$

$$r > p$$

Statement (2) adds nothing to what is already contained in the question stem, so the two together will not be sufficient.

20

9. **(C)** The expression $a^2 - b^2$ can be factored into $(a + b)(a - b)$. Statement (1) provides information about the sign of only one of the two factors. (And it isn't possible to deduce from $a + b > 0$ the sign of $a - b$.) So statement (1) is not sufficient. For the same reason, statement (2) is insufficient. Statement (2) does imply that $a - b > 0$, but that implies nothing about the sign of $a + b$. Both statements together, however, do answer the question. Given that $a + b$ is positive and that $a - b$ is positive, the sign of $(a + b)(a - b)$ must also be positive.

10. **(A)** Statement (1) alone is sufficient to determine that the original price of the house was $180,000. The asking price of the house was 1.6 times the cost of the house, and the actual selling price was 25 percent less than that, or 1.2 times the cost of the house. Since the homeowner sold the house for $36,000 more than it cost:

1.2 Cost – Cost = $36,000

0.2 Cost = $36,000

Cost = $180,000

Statement (2), however, is not sufficient to answer the question.

Analytical Writing Assessment

✓ Topics Covered

1. **Anatomy of an Analytical Writing Task**
2. **Two Sample Essay Topics**
3. **How Essays Are Graded**
4. **The "Issue" Essay**
   - **Content**
   - **Organization**
5. **The "Argument" Essay**
   - **Content**
   - **Organization**
6. **Mechanics of Essay Writing**
7. **Essay-Writing Style**

Lesson 21

Professional managers and educators increasingly have come to realize that good managers must possess effective communication skills. The Analytical Writing Assessment or essay component of the GMAT is designed to help admissions officers identify those applicants who have effective writing skills.

Anatomy of an Analytical Writing Task

As of this writing, the Analytical Writing Assessment consists of two separately timed 30-minute writing tasks, one requiring an analysis of an issue and the other requiring an analysis of an argument. The GMAT has said that it will announce as many as 180 possible AWA topics (90 of each type) in the official registration materials. Check those materials for the announced topics.

Can you prepare essay answers to all 180 in advance? You could try, but do you really think that you could memorize 180 essay responses? And why would you want to?

Instead, you can use the sample prompts in this chapter and the official topics as practice materials. Do several essays until you become comfortable with writing a response within the 30-minute limit. A good practice technique would be, after you become comfortable with the approach, to choose some topics at random—including some with which you are not familiar.

You will have to keyboard or type your essay using the provided GMAT word processing program. It uses fairly standard functionalities such as cut and paste and delete. If you are familiar with the functionalities of any widely used program, then you should have no trouble with this unusual aspect of the exam. If, however, you are not accustomed to using a word processing program, then it would probably be a good idea to visit your college's computer lab or your local public library where such facilities are almost surely available at no cost. Spend a few hours "at the wheel" so that you will feel comfortable on the day of your test.

Two Sample Essay Topics

The following topics are offered as examples of typical GMAT writing assignments.

Analysis of an Issue

People often complain that manufacturers consciously follow a policy of planned obsolescence and make products that are designed to wear out quickly. Planned obsolescence, they insist, wastes both natural and human resources. They fail to recognize, however, that the use of cheaper materials and manufacturing processes keeps costs down for the consumer and stimulates demand.

Which position do you find more persuasive, the complaint about planned obsolescence or the response to it? Explain your position, using relevant reasons and/or examples taken from experience, observations, or readings.

Analysis of an Argument

All commercial airliners operating in the United States should be required to carry a computerized on-board warning system that can receive signals from the transponders of other aircraft. (A transponder is a radio device that signals a plane's course.) The system would be able to alert pilots to the danger of a collision and recommend evasive action. Installation of the system would virtually eliminate the danger of mid-air collisions.

Discuss the argument above. Analyze its logical structure and use of evidence. What, if anything, would make the argument more persuasive or would help you to better evaluate its conclusion?

How Essays Are Graded

Each essay is graded on a scale of 0 (the minimum) to 6 (the maximum):

    0 Any essay that is totally illegible or obviously not written on the assigned topic.

    1 An essay that is fundamentally deficient.

    2 An essay that is seriously flawed.

    3 An essay that is seriously limited.

    4 An essay that is merely adequate.

    5 An essay that is strong.

    6 An essay that is outstanding.

We can learn something about what the readers will be looking for by examining a portion of the GMAT scoring guide for an "issue" essay:

OUTSTANDING (6)	SERIOUSLY FLAWED (2)
—explores ideas and develops a position on the issue with insightful reasons and/or persuasive examples	—is unclear or seriously limited in presenting or developing a position on the issue and provides few, if any, relevant examples
—is clearly well organized	—is disorganized
—demonstrates superior facility with the conventions of standard written English but may have minor flaws	—contains numerous errors in grammar, usage, or mechanics which interfere with meaning
—demonstrates superior control of language, including diction and syntactic variety	—has serious and frequent problems in the use of language

(**Note:** This language is used to describe the "issue" essay. That used for the "argument" essay is slightly different, but the underlying considerations are substantially the same.)

The four areas mentioned are content, organization, mechanics, and style; and we need to develop strategies that will help you to create a good impression in each. The areas of mechanics and style, which make up effective writing, are the same for both types of essays. Content and organization, however, must be treated separately. We will begin by discussing the content and organization of an "issue" essay. Then we will treat the content and organization of an "argument" essay. Finally, we will turn to the areas of mechanics and style.

"ISSUE" ESSAY

Content

A strong essay is obviously distinguished from a weak one in terms of content. The scoring guidelines given above note that the strong essay "develops a position on the issue," while the weak essay is "unclear or seriously limited in presenting or developing a position on the issue." So the first thing that an "issue" essay must do is take a *clear* stand on the issue:

I agree with the complaint.

or

I disagree with the complaint.

An essay that does not take a clear stand one way or the other will be graded down. You need not worry that by taking a clear stand you risk choosing the "wrong side" of the issue. An "issue" topic is worded carefully so that there can be no right or wrong answer—only different positions. In any event, there is no way around the requirement. The grading criteria are quite specific that the strong essay makes a clear statement of the writer's position.

The strong essay is further distinguished from the weak one by its use of "insightful reasons." Thus, the next task is to adduce some reasons in support of your position; and it is at this point that you may worry, "But what if I have nothing to say?" While that is a natural reaction (the topic, after all, is a surprise), your concerns should not be exaggerated. In the first place, taking a clear position will help you generate the ideas that will constitute the body of the essay. You may even want to flip a coin to determine which side of the issue you will support. Once you have taken a clear stand, you will then be forced to think of ideas to support your position.

Second, the topic itself will be worded in such a way as to suggest ideas to you and will contain prompts to encourage you to develop a position. The topic we are considering strongly suggests the following:

> Products are (are not) designed to wear out quickly. Planned obsolescence does (does not) waste resources. The use of cheaper materials and processes does (does not) result in lower consumer costs.
> Lower cost products do (do not) stimulate demand.

These ideas lie right on the "surface" of the topic and can be obtained without much analysis. Once you have taken your stand on the topic, then you will find that the list has suggestions for reasons that can be used to support your position. For example, let's say that we want to defend the response to the complaint about planned obsolescence. Our essay might develop along the following lines:

> I disagree with the complaint regarding planned obsolescence.
> In the first place, it is not clear that many manufacturers do intentionally design products to wear out quickly.
> Second, the fact that a product wears out does not necessarily mean that its design and manufacture represent a waste of resources.
> Third, often a more cheaply made product is just what consumers want because they cannot afford a more expensive version.

Of course, this sketch is not, in and of itself, a strong essay. To form a strong essay, the ideas outlined need to be developed in greater detail.

The third way of distinguishing a strong essay from a weak one in terms of content is the use of examples. The above grading criteria state that the strong essay uses "persuasive examples," while the weak essay provides "few, if any, relevant examples." And, according to the directions for the "issue" topic essay, these examples can be drawn from "experience, observations, or readings." Thus, the third point of our sketch might be developed in the following way:

> Third, often a more cheaply made product is just what consumers want because they cannot afford a more expensive version. A classic example of this phenomenon is the automobile industry. Indeed, the term "Cadillac" is often used to refer to any product that includes many expensive features and is priced accordingly.

Organization

The second distinction drawn by the grading criteria between the strong essay and the weak one focuses on organization. The strong essay is "clearly well organized," while the weak essay is "disorganized." It is interesting to note that the analysis describes the strong essay as "clearly well organized" and not simply "well organized." That distinction suggests that the strong essay is not just well organized, but that it has an organization that is apparent to the reader.

In fact, the distinction between "well organized" and "clearly well organized" is reflected in the age-old advice for public speakers: Tell your audience what you plan to tell them, then tell them, and then tell them what you told them. It is the first ("tell your audience what you plan to tell them") and last ("tell them what you told them") elements that make an implicit organization explicit or clear to the listener (or reader).

The heart of your "issue" essay will be three or perhaps four main ideas like those sketched above, and each of the three or four main ideas should be developed in separate paragraphs. This format will give you a "well organized" essay. Then, to make sure that your essay is "clearly well organized," you should begin with an opening paragraph that advises the reader about the organization that will follow:

> I disagree with the complaint for three reasons. First, it is not at all clear that many manufacturers engage in planned obsolescence. Second, the fact that a product eventually wears out does not necessarily mean that its manufacture was a waste of resources. Third, many so-called "cheap" products are made inexpensively because consumers want inexpensive products.

The three or four main reasons then become the body of the essay.

Each of the subsequent paragraphs should begin with a restatement (in somewhat different words) of a main reason:

> In the first place, the practice of planned obsolescence may or may not be widespread.
>
> * * *
>
> Second, the fact that a product wears out does not mean that the company that made the product or the consumer who bought it has wasted resources.
>
> * * *
>
> Finally, a product should not be called "cheap" just because it is less expensive.

And if time permits, a final concluding paragraph "telling the reader what you told the reader" can be added:

> Because the practice is not widespread, because so-called "cheap" products are not necessarily wasteful, and because there is a demand for inexpensive products, the complaint about planned obsolescence is unjustified.

Given that your essay is not likely to be overly complex, a conclusionary paragraph is optional.

Now it remains only to develop the three paragraphs that form the heart of the essay. All that is needed is two more sentences in each paragraph that amplify or provide examples of the idea set forth in the first or topic sentence of that paragraph:

> I disagree with the complaint for three reasons. First, it is not at all clear that many manufacturers engage in planned obsolescence. Second, the fact that a product eventually wears out does not necessarily mean that its manufacture was a waste of resources. Third, many so-called "cheap" products are made inexpensively because consumers want inexpensive products.
>
> In the first place, the practice of planned obsolescence may or may not be widespread. While it is sometimes politically fashionable to label the manufacturing industry as greedy, the actual evidence for planned obsolescence is slim. Automobile manufacturers, for example, are now offering more inclusive and longer warranties on new cars.
>
> Second, the fact that a product wears out does not mean that the company that made the product or the consumer who bought it has wasted resources. To prove that a product is a "waste," it would be necessary to show that the material and human resources could have been used more efficiently. In the case of a car, for example, it may be a good idea to replace it sooner rather than later because a newer model may include new safety features.
>
> Finally, a product should not be called "cheap" just because it is less expensive. Not every car should be a "Cadillac." Consumers have differing needs and differing financial resources.
>
> Because the practice is not widespread, because so-called "cheap" products are not necessarily wasteful, and because there is a demand for inexpensive products, the complaint about planned obsolescence is unjustified.

(**Note:** A conclusionary paragraph has been added to this essay, but you might choose to leave it out. The length and complexity of the analysis that precedes it is just barely sufficient to justify putting it in. Were the essay any shorter, the conclusionary paragraph might appear to be make-weight.)

If we now abstract from the content of the essay we have just written, you will see that we have created a "template" that can be used for any "issue" topic essay:

Introductory Paragraph	I agree (disagree) . . . for three reasons. First, . . . Second, . . . Third, . . .
Second Paragraph	In the first place, (topic sentence restating the first reason). Plus two sentences developing the idea of that topic sentence.
Third Paragraph	Second, (topic sentence restating the second reason). Plus two sentences developing the idea of that topic sentence.
Fourth Paragraph	Third, (topic sentence restating the third reason). Plus two sentences developing the idea of that topic sentence.
Optional Final Paragraph	Thus, . . .

If you consciously use this "template," you will be guaranteed that your "issue" essay will be "clearly well organized."

"ARGUMENT" ESSAY

Content

A good way to begin our discussion of the "argument" essay is to return to the directions for it. After setting forth the prompt regarding the installation of computerized on-board warning systems for commercial airlines, the instructions continue:

> Discuss the argument above. Analyze its logical structure and use of evidence. What, if anything, would make the argument more persuasive or would help you better to evaluate its conclusion?

The outline of what you are to do with the "argument" prompt is noticeably different from that for the "issue" prompt. So, too, our approach to the content aspect of this essay must be different. Fortunately, the nature of the prompt once again helps to provide the content of the essay.

The most striking aspect of the "argument" prompt we are studying is that it calls for the adoption of a proposal: Put these devices in all commercial airliners. And any argument for the adoption of some proposal can be analyzed in cost-benefit terms. It does not matter whether the proposal under consideration is a plan for a military invasion of a foreign country, a plan to build a new wing on the local school, a plan to enroll a child in day care, or a plan to change the family's regular dinner time from 6:00 to 6:30. All such proposals can be analyzed by asking four questions:

1. What is the extent of the problem to be solved?
2. Are there less drastic, alternative solutions?
3. Will the proposed solution really work?
4. Would the proposal have any adverse consequences?

Whether or not a proposal ought to be adopted depends on the answers to these questions. Let's apply them to the "argument" prompt:

> All commercial airliners operating in the United States should be required to carry a computerized on-board warning system that can receive signals from the transponders of other aircraft. (A transponder is a radio set that signals a plane's course.) The system would be able to alert pilots to the danger of a collision and recommend evasive action. Installation of the system would virtually eliminate the danger of mid-air collisions.

The first question to ask of this argument is whether it identifies a problem sufficiently serious to warrant the plan that it proposes. You should immediately observe that this argument fails to provide any information about the extent of the problem it is supposed to solve. What presently is the danger of a mid-air collision between commercial airliners? How many such collisions have occurred in the past? What was the cost of these collisions in terms of life and property lost? To ask these questions is not to prove that the installation of the devices in question would be a waste; rather, it is to challenge the proponent of the plan to show that any change from or addition to the present system is needed. This type of question is asking for quantification.

The second question assumes for the purpose of analysis that it can be established that a sufficiently serious problem exists to warrant some sort of action but asks whether or not there might be some less drastic alternatives to the proposal set forth. For example, even assuming that there is a quantifiable and significant risk of mid-air collisions, might not that risk be eliminated by requiring pilots to file more detailed flight plans, or by having air-traffic controllers monitor commercial flights more carefully, or by changing flight schedules to eliminate overcrowding of the airways? Again, to ask these questions is not to prove that any one of these suggestions is a clearly better alternative than the installation of a new computer system, but it is to recognize that the desirability of the proposal must be measured against the benefits that could be achieved by less onerous means. This type of question is asking for entrenchment, that is, whether the problem is sufficiently entrenched in the system that we need a radical change.

The third question assumes for the purpose of analysis that a sufficiently serious problem exists that cannot be solved by any other readily available means and goes on to ask whether or not the proposal under consideration would really work. Will the transponders provide information far enough in advance to enable the new system to process the data and make recommendations in time for pilots to take evasive action? Is this type of radio communication sufficiently reliable in all types of weather so that the desired results will actually be achieved? Is a situation in which there is a danger of a mid-air collision so complex that no computer program can effectively be substituted for human judgment? Obviously, if the answer to one or more of these questions strongly suggests that the device will not work, then there is no reason to adopt the proposal. This type of question asks about the feasibility of the plan.

The fourth question assumes for the purpose of analysis that a problem exists, that it cannot otherwise be solved, that the proposal would in fact solve the problem, and goes on to ask whether or not the cost and other consequences of adopting the proposal might not outweigh the desirable effects that it could achieve. How much will it cost to install the new devices? Would that cost be more than the projected cost of the mid-air collisions that would otherwise occur? Might not the new devices actually increase the risk of mid-air collisions by recommending that pilots take dangerous evasive action when it is not really warranted? If it should turn out that the cost (however measured) of using the proposal to eliminate the problem would be greater than that of the problem it hopes to eliminate, then common sense would recommend against installing the new devices. These questions, then, ask about the disadvantages (cost and other) of the proposed change.

When we consider these four challenges in a purely formal way, we can easily see that they are generally applicable to any proposal or plan of action. Of course, one or more of the issues may have been addressed by the proponent of the change, say quantification of the problem in terms of the number of lives and dollar value of property lost. Even so, it would still be open to an opponent to challenge the proposal on the other grounds; and it would of course be a legitimate argumentative strategy to challenge the reliability of the evidence used to quantify the problem.

Organization

Just as the organization of the "issue" essay emerged naturally from the content, so too the content of the "argument" essay generates a template that guarantees that your essay will score points for organization. Again, we have an opening paragraph to alert the reader to what will follow:

> The argument . . . is inconclusive for four reasons. First, it fails to quantify the problem. Second, less drastic alternatives may be available. Third, the plan may not work. Fourth, the costs of the plan might outweigh any benefits.

The second, third, fourth, and fifth paragraphs of the essay then set forth in turn each of our four challenges:

> In the first place, the argument fails to demonstrate that a serious problem exists. (Followed by two sentences asking for quantification.)
> Second, simpler means may solve any problem that does exist. (Followed by two sentences suggesting alternatives to the plan.)
> Third, the plan may simply not work. (Followed by two sentences suggesting why the plan may not work as hoped.)
> Fourth, the proposal is likely to entail some fairly substantial costs. (Followed by two sentences suggesting why the plan may have unwanted side effects.)

And, of course, you may want to include a concluding paragraph to summarize the development of your analysis.

Applying the template to the topic we have been considering, we might get the following essay:

> The argument for the installation of computerized on-board warning systems is inconclusive for four reasons. First, it fails to establish that there is a serious danger at present. Second, less drastic alternatives may be available to ensure public safety. Third, the radio equipment and computers may simply not work. Fourth, the costs of the plan might outweigh any benefits.
>
> In the first place, the argument fails to demonstrate that a serious problem exists. Before implementing such extensive measures, it would be necessary to know the likelihood of a mid-air collision. Additionally, it would be important to know what would be the cost in terms of dollars and loss of life.
>
> Second, simpler means may solve any problem that does exist. A change in the way that air-traffic controllers monitor flights might achieve the same result. Or altering flight schedules to spread traffic out over time might effectively eliminate any danger of mid-air collisions.
>
> Third, the computerized system may simply not work. It would have to be shown that the information transmitted by navigational transponders would give a warning sufficiently far in advance. Further, it would be necessary to know that a pilot could act on that warning effectively.
>
> Finally, the proposal is likely to entail some fairly substantial costs. In dollars and cents terms alone, the cost of developing, installing, and maintaining the system could be greater than that of all the mid-air collisions that have ever occurred combined. The plan might even result in more collisions if the equipment malfunctions or the computer program contains bugs.

Mechanics of Essay Writing

The area of "mechanics" covers all of those elements that normally determine whether writing measures up as standard written English, including grammar, sentence structure, idiom, and punctuation. Fortunately, you have already had a substantial review of mechanics: the Sentence Correction lessons earlier in this book. As you proofread your essays, you should ask:

1. Does each sentence have a conjugated (main) verb?
2. Does each verb agree with its subject?
3. Does each pronoun have a referent (antecedent)?
4. Does each pronoun agree with its referent (antecedent)?
5. Do similar elements in each sentence have parallel form?
6. Do the modifiers make sense?
7. Does each sentence say what it means to say?
8. Is each sentence direct and concise?

If you are not clear on the significance of any of these questions, you should review once again the relevant material in the lessons on Sentence Correction.

There is one aspect of mechanics that could use some further attention: punctuation. The punctuation that is tested by Sentence Correction is very basic and usually only incidental to some other question of clarity or logical expression. Since Sentence Correction is not, *per se,* a test of punctuation, we did not cover some rules of punctuation there and so will do so here.

Punctuation

1. Commas

Use a comma before *and, but, so, yet, or,* and *nor* when those words are used to join two main clauses.

EXAMPLES:

I think that Doré's illustrations of Dante's *Divine Comedy* are excellent, but my favorite drawing is "Don Quixote in His Library."

Practically all nitrates are crystalline and readily soluble, and they are characterized by marked decrepitation when heated on charcoals by a blowpipe.

The general rule stated above should be qualified in two respects. First, when the two clauses joined by the conjunction are very short, the comma is optional. For this reason, each of the following sentences is correct.

EXAMPLE:

The door was ajar and the house had been ransacked.

The door was ajar, and the house had been ransacked.

Second, for clarity, if either clause itself contains commas, you may need to use a semicolon before the conjunction.

EXAMPLE:

Because many diseases and insects cause serious damage to crops, special national legislation has been passed to provide for the quarantine of imported plants; and under provisions of various acts, inspectors are placed at ports of entry to prevent smugglers from bringing in plants that might be dangerous.

Use commas to separate the elements of a series.

EXAMPLES:

A full train crew consists of a motorman, a brakeman, a conductor, and two ticket takers.

The procedure requires that you open the outer cover plate, remove the thermostat, replace the broken switch, and then replace the thermostat.

Use a comma to separate a subordinate clause at the beginning of a sentence from the main clause.

EXAMPLES:

After Peter finished painting the bird feeder, he and Jack hung it from a limb of the oak tree.

When Pat explained to his mother that ten was the highest mark given on the entrance test, she breathed a sigh of relief.

If the subordinate clause follows the main clause, you do not need to set it off with a comma.

EXAMPLE:

Tim hopes to score well on the exam because he plans to go to an Ivy League school.

Use a comma after a long introductory phrase.

EXAMPLES:

In this impoverished region with its arid soil, a typical diet may contain only 800 calories per day.

At the height of the moral war against sensational journalism, Horace Greeley moved into the forefront of the journalistic picture.

Regardless of their length, use a comma after introductory gerunds, participles, and infinitives.

EXAMPLES:

Begun in 1981 and completed in 1985, the bridge provided the first link between the island and the mainland.

To slow the bleeding, Van tied a tourniquet around the lower portion of the leg.

Use commas to set off nonrestrictive clauses and phrases and other parenthetical elements.

EXAMPLES:

Niagara Falls, which forms part of the border between the United States and Canada, was the site of a sawmill built by the French in 1725.

The second Nicene Council, the seventh ecumenical council of the Church, was summoned by the Empress Irene and her son Constantine.

The last hope of the French expired when Metz, along with 180,000 soldiers, was surrendered by Bazaine.

Secretary of State Acheson, however, made a reasoned defense of the treaty.

(Nonrestrictive clauses and phrases are ones not essential to the meaning of the main clause. In general, if you can omit the material without changing the meaning of the main clause, then the material is nonrestrictive and should be set off by commas.)

These rules summarize the most important uses of commas. If you use them in just these situations, then you won't make a mistake in their use. In particular, do NOT use commas in the following situations.

Do not use a comma to separate a subject from its verb.

EXAMPLE:

Until the end of the 18th century, the only musicians in Norway, were simple unsophisticated peasants who traveled about.

(The underlined comma is incorrect.)

Do not use commas to set off restrictive or necessary clauses or phrases.

EXAMPLES:

Prizes will be awarded in each event, and the participant, who compiles the greatest overall total, will receive a special prize.

Since learning of the dangers of caffeine, neither my wife nor I have consumed any beverage, containing caffeine.

(The underlined commas are incorrect.)

Do not use a comma in place of a conjunction.

EXAMPLE:

After months of separation, Gauguin finally joined van Gogh in Arles in October of 1888, Gauguin left a few weeks later.

(The underlined comma is incorrect.)

The sentence is incorrect because clauses cannot be spliced together using only a comma. If you want to join two main clauses, you can use a conjunction (such as *and*) plus a comma or a semicolon. The sentence above could have been written: "After months of separation, Gauguin finally joined van Gogh in Arles in October of 1888, but Gauguin left a few weeks later."

2. Semicolons

One use of the semicolon has already been mentioned: Use a semicolon between main clauses linked by a coordinate conjunction (*and*, *but*, etc.) when the main clauses are complex, e.g., when they themselves contain commas. (See above.) Another use of semicolons is to separate two main clauses that are not linked by a coordinate conjunction.

EXAMPLES:

He grew up on a farm in Nebraska; he is now the captain of a Navy ship.

The Smithtown players cheered the referee's decision; the Stonybrook players booed it.

Notice that in these examples, each clause separated by the semicolon could stand alone as an independent sentence:

He grew up on a farm in Nebraska. He is now the captain of a Navy ship.

The Smithtown players cheered the referee's decision. The Stonybrook players booed it.

Unless each clause can function as an independent sentence, it probably is wrong to use a semicolon.

When John entered the room; everyone stood up.

Clem announced that the prize would be donated to Harbus House; a well-known charity.

The semicolons in the examples above are used incorrectly. Notice that the elements separated by the semicolons cannot stand as independent sentences.

When John entered the room. Everyone stood up.

Clem announced that the prize would be donated to Harbus House. A well-known charity.

The sentences can be corrected by using commas in place of the semicolons.

3. Colons

A colon may be used to introduce or to call attention to elaboration or explanation.

EXAMPLES:

The teacher announced that the course would require three papers: one on Shakespeare, one on Dickens, and one on a contemporary writer.

Will's suggestion was truly democratic: let everyone serve as chair for one meeting.

Be careful not to use a colon to introduce or call attention to material that is already signaled by some other element of the sentence.

EXAMPLES:

The seemingly tranquil lane has been the scene of many crimes including: two assaults, three robberies, and one murder.

In addition to test scores, college admissions officers take into consideration many other factors such as: grades, extracurricular activities, and letters of recommendation.

In the examples above, each colon is used incorrectly because the special material is already signaled by some other element in the sentence:

The seemingly tranquil lane has been the scene of many crimes including two assaults, three robberies, and one murder.

In addition to test scores, college admissions officers take into consideration many other factors such as grades, extracurricular activities, and letters of recommendation.

This shows that the colons in the original examples were superfluous and wrong.

4. Periods

Use a period to mark the end of a sentence that makes a statement, gives a command, or makes a polite request in the form of a question that does not require an answer.

EXAMPLE:

Peter notified Elaine, the guidance counselor, that he had been accepted.

Call if you are going to be late.

Would you please read that statement back to me.

5. *Parentheses*

Parentheses can be used to set off for emphasis or clarity an explanatory, illustrative, or parenthetical remark.

EXAMPLES:

Careful attention to the details of one's personal appearance (neatly pressed clothing, shined shoes, and a neat haircut) is an important part of preparing for a job interview.

Many colleges (including the nation's top schools) set aside a certain number of freshman seats for students who show academic promise in spite of low test scores.

Peanuts (blanched or lightly roasted) add an interesting texture and taste to garden salads.

This list is, of course, not exhaustive of all the rules of punctuation for the English language. It should, however, be sufficient for the exercise for which you are preparing. In other words, if you restrict your punctuation to commas, semicolons, colons, periods, and parentheses, and if you make sure that each instance of punctuation in your essays is consistent with the rules set forth above, then your essay will be correctly punctuated.

Essay-Writing Style

The final element on which your essays will be graded is style. Since writing style is a complex of many variables and evolves over time, there is not much that you can hope to accomplish by way of "test preparation" that will dramatically improve your writing style. In fact, one advantage of the templates presented for each of the two types of essays is that they minimize the role that style can play in your responses. Of course, some test candidates may choose to reject the use of the templates in favor of more flexibility, and those who have excellent writing skills may succeed. This flexibility, however, can be achieved only at considerable risk. While the templates may limit what you are able to do in terms of style, they also minimize the risk of error. Since they do leave so little room to maneuver, a candidate who follows them (even if not slavishly) can reasonably expect to write a fairly strong essay. Any other approach may result in an essay so deficient in terms of content and organization as to be considered "weak" by the graders.

Regardless of whether you intend to use the templates as presented, adapt them to your own style, or ignore them altogether, there are a few other points to keep in mind. First, you should not try to do too much. You will be working within a fairly restrictive time limit during which you must not only read and evaluate the topic but formulate and outline a position, and then write and edit the essay. A four- or five-paragraph essay is all most candidates will have time to write. Further, your essay will create a better impression if it has a beginning, a middle, and an end than if it is only a first paragraph full of grand promises that are never fulfilled.

Here is a good way of using the thirty minutes allotted for each essay:

Time in Minutes	Task
2	Read the topic and the directions. Make sure that your essay will be responsive to directions.
3	Make a list (either mental or on the scratch paper provided) of some ideas that you will use. Create an outline (either mental or on paper) of the essay.
20	Write the essay.
5	Proofread and edit the essay. Make corrections where necessary using the functionalities of the word processor.

Second, you should avoid trite and vague generalities. The topics that you will write on are not likely to involve "big" moral or political issues. Consider, for example, whether the following belongs in our essay on the "argument" topic above:

> Requiring airlines to install these devices would threaten the very basis of a free market economy and our American way of life.

The difficulty with this point is not that it is necessarily wrong but that it cannot be proved to be correct. Such broad statements have no place in your essay responses to the AWA prompts.

Analytical Writing Drills

1. Walk-Through Drill
2. Warm-Up Drill

This lesson includes two Analytical Writing drills. The first drill is a "walk-through," with a printed template so that you can "walk through" the writing of an essay. The other drill is a "warm-up" drill that you should do within the specified time limit. Use the lined pages that follow each sample topic to write your essay.

Walk-Through

> *Directions:* In this Walk-Through exercise, you are asked to write an essay on an "issue" topic. Unlike other Walk-Through exercises that you have done, this one should be done within the 30-minute time limit following the suggested breakdown given. You can then adjust the breakdown to meet your own individual needs.
>
> In addition to the topic, the Walk-Through exercise includes three lined pages on which to write the essay and a printed template. For this exercise, follow the printed template closely—copying verbatim those parts that are already written for you and inserting your own ideas into the designated spaces.

Analysis of an Issue

Sample Topic

Time: 30 minutes

People often complain that advertising is misleading and that products do not live up to the claims made by advertisers. Consequently, they say, advertising undermines consumer confidence in products and in business generally. What they fail to realize, however, is that aggressive advertising not only informs consumers of the existence of products of which they otherwise might not be aware, it also stimulates consumer demand for these products.

Which position do you find more persuasive, the complaint about misleading advertising or the response to it? Explain your position, using relevant reasons and/or examples taken from experience, observations, or readings.

Step 1   (2 minutes):
Read the topic and the instructions.

Step 2   (3 minutes):
A. Make a list of some ideas suggested by the topic.

_____

_____

_____

_____

_____

_____

_____

_____

B. What position will you take?

_____ I agree.   _____ I disagree.

C. What will be your three main reasons in support of that position?

_____

_____

_____

_____

_____

_____

_____

_____

D. Jot down two or three examples.

_____

_____

_____

_____

_____

_____

_____

_____

Step 3 **(20 minutes):**

Write your essay using the template provided either using a word processor or by hand using the lined paper provided.

Template

I (agree or disagree) with the complaint about misleading advertising for three reasons. First, (insert your first main reason). Second, (insert your second main reason). Third, (insert your third main reason).

In the first place, (restate your first main reason). (Add two sentences developing or giving examples of the first main idea.)

Second, (restate your second main reason). (Add two sentences developing or giving examples of the second main idea.)

Third, (restate your third main reason). (Add two sentences developing or giving examples of the third main idea.)

(Include a conclusionary paragraph if you wish.)

Step 4   (5 minutes):

Proofread your essay.

1. Does each sentence have a conjugated (main) verb?
2. Does each verb agree with its subject?
3. Does each pronoun have a referent (antecedent)?
4. Does each pronoun agree with its referent (antecedent)?
5. Do similar elements in each sentence have parallel form?
6. Do the modifiers make sense?
7. Does each sentence say what it means to say?
8. Is each sentence direct and concise?
9. Is the essay correctly punctuated?

Warm-Up Drill
Analysis of an Argument
Sample Topic
Time: 30 minutes

Directions: You have 30 minutes to write a critique of the argument presented below. Do not write on a topic other than the one assigned. Use the blank space on this page to make notes to yourself or to create an outline. Write your essay using either using a word processor or in hand using the lined paper provided on the following pages.

All buses used to transport children to and from public schools should be equipped with both lap and harness seat belts. The restraining system would virtually eliminate the danger that a child would be tossed from the seat and injured in the event of an accident.

Discuss the argument above. Analyze its logical structure and use of evidence. What, if anything, would make the argument more persuasive or would help you better to evaluate its conclusion?

Sample GMAT
CAT 1

Verbal Section

41 Questions—75 Minutes

> **General Directions:** To simulate the experience of taking the CAT, answer each question in order. Do not skip any questions, and do not go back to questions you have already answered.
>
> **Directions for sentence correction questions:** In questions of this type, either part or all of a sentence is underlined. The sentence is followed by five ways of wording the underlined part. The first answer choice always repeats the original; the other answer choices are different. If you think that the original phrasing is the best, choose the first answer. If you think one of the other answer choices is the best, select that choice. Indicate your answer by blackening the circle next to your choice.
>
> This section tests your ability to identify correct and effective expression. Evaluate the answer choices by the requirements of standard written English. Pay attention to elements of grammar, diction, (choice of words), and sentence construction. Select the answer choice that *best* expresses the meaning of the original sentence. The correct choice will be clear and precise and free of awkwardness, wordiness, or ambiguity.
>
> **Directions for critical reasoning questions:** Questions of this type ask you to analyze and evaluate the reasoning presented in short paragraphs or passages. For some questions, all of the answer choices may conceivably be answers to the question asked. You should select the *best* answer to the question; that is, an answer that does not require you to make assumptions that violate commonsense standards by being implausible, redundant, irrelevant or inconsistent. Indicate your answer by blackening the circle next to your choice.
>
> **Directions for reading comprehension questions:** Each passage is followed by questions or incomplete statements about it. Once you have read the passage, answer the question based upon what is stated or implied. Indicate your answer by blackening the circle next to your choice.

1. Because young girls were not expected to participate in sports, so they were never seriously trained to be athletes.

    (A) sports, so they
    (B) sports, and they
    (C) sports, and that
    (D) sports, they
    (E) sports, and so

2. Before the invention of television, radio was the chief form of at-home entertainment.

    (A) radio was the chief form of at-home entertainment
    (B) radio has been the chief form of at-home entertainment
    (C) radio, having been the chief form of at-home entertainment
    (D) the chief form of at-home entertainment is the radio
    (E) radio, a form of at-home entertainment, was the chief

3. Letters were received by the editor of the newspaper that complained of its editorial policy.

    (A) Letters were received by the editor of the newspaper that complained of its editorial policy.
    (B) Letters were received by the editor of the newspaper which complained of its editorial policy.
    (C) Letters were received by the editor of the newspaper complaining of their editorial policy.
    (D) The editor of the newspaper received letters that were complaining of the paper's editorial policy.
    (E) The editor of the newspaper received letters complaining of the paper's editorial policy.

GO ON TO NEXT PAGE

The editor of a newspaper received the following letter:

Dear Editor:

This holiday season I think we should make a serious effort to recapture the true spirit of giving. Each of us should resolve to give gifts and expect none. And if someone offers us a gift, we should refuse it and suggest that it be given to someone else. In this way, we would all experience a feeling of pure giving.

4. Which of the following statements points out the most serious logical flaw in the letter?

(A) If no one accepted any gifts, it would be impossible for anyone to give a gift.

(B) The holiday season is not the only time of year when people give and receive gifts.

(C) Often people receive gifts that are really not very useful, so it would not be a great sacrifice to part with them.

(D) Sometimes a person may make a gift to someone in the hope of later receiving something in exchange for it.

(E) Gift giving is a tradition that is thousands of years old and a characteristic of virtually every human community.

Recently credit card companies have come under attack by consumer groups who argue that the interest rates charged by these companies are unconscionably high. In fact, the rates are generally several percentage points above those charged by banks for ordinary personal loans. But consumer groups overlook the fact that credit cards afford the user great flexibility. A user can purchase an item while it is on sale. So the lower cost of the item offsets the extra cost of the credit.

5. The argument above makes which of the following assumptions?

(A) The cost savings of buying an item at a reduced price are at least equal to the excess interest that a consumer pays on purchases made with a credit card.

(B) A credit card application is not rejected unless the applicant has a long history of late payments and other credit problems.

(C) The prices of items on sale purchased by consumers are still sufficiently high to enable sellers to recoup their costs and make a modest profit.

(D) The consumers who make purchases of sale items with credit cards are persons who might not qualify for bank loans with a lower interest rate.

(E) The average outstanding balance of the ordinary credit card user is no greater than the total non-credit-card debt of the credit card user.

Bob and Cindy are each older than both Diane and Ellen.

6. If the statement above is true, then which of the following *additional* statements ensures the truth of the conclusion "Allen is older than Ellen"?

(A) Allen is younger than Bob.

(B) Cindy is older than Bob.

(C) Cindy is younger than Bob.

(D) Allen is older than Diane.

(E) Allen is older than Cindy.

Questions 7–9

Instead of casting aside traditional values, the Meiji Restoration of 1868 dismantled feudalism and modernized the country while preserving certain traditions as the foundations for a modern Japan. The oldest tradition and basis of the entire Japanese value system was respect for and even worship of the Emperor. During the early centuries of Japanese history, the Shinto cult, in which the imperial family traced its ancestry to the Sun Goddess, became the people's sustaining faith. Although later subordinated to imported Buddhism and Confucianism, Shintoism was perpetuated in Ise and Izumo until the Meiji modernizers established it as a quasi state religion.

Another enduring tradition was the hierarchical system of social relations based on feudalism and reinforced by Neo-Confucianism, which had been the official ideology of the pre-modern period. Confucianism prescribed a pattern of ethical conduct between groups of people within a fixed hierarchy. Four of the five Confucian relationships were vertical, requiring loyalty and obedience from the inferior toward the superior. Only the relationship between friend and friend was horizontal, and even there the emphasis was on reciprocal duties.

7. The passage mentions all of the following as being elements of Japanese society EXCEPT

(A) obedience to authority

(B) sense of duty

(C) respect for the Emperor

(D) concern for education

(E) loyalty to one's superiors

8. We may infer from the passage that those who led Japan into the modern age were concerned primarily with

(A) maintaining a stable society

(B) building a new industrial base

(C) expanding the nation's territory

(D) gaining new adherents of Confucianism

(E) creating a new middle class

9. The author makes which of the following statements about Shintoism?

   I. Prior to the Meiji Restoration it had been eclipsed by Buddhism and Confucianism.

   II. It was the source of reciprocal duties between friends.

   III. The Emperor was treated as an object of religious worship.

Ⓐ I only   Ⓑ II only   Ⓒ III only
Ⓓ I and III only   Ⓔ I, II, and III

10. Washington Irving's German-influenced stories were profoundly moving to Americans, <u>knowing more than most</u> Britons what it was to feel the trauma of rapid change, and Americans found in the lazy Rip a model for making a success of failure.

Ⓐ knowing more than most
Ⓑ who knew more then most
Ⓒ knowing more then most
Ⓓ most who knew more about what
Ⓔ who knew more than most

11. <u>In order to make skiing smoother, safer, and more enjoyable, a number of resorts have hired consultants</u> to design and sculpt the trails.

Ⓐ In order to make skiing smoother, safer, and more enjoyable, a number of resorts have hired consultants
Ⓑ In order to make skiing smoother, safer, and more enjoyable a number of consultants have been hired by resorts
Ⓒ In the interest of making skiing smoother, safer, and able to be enjoyed, a number of resorts have hired consultants
Ⓓ To make skiing smoother, safer, so that you can enjoy it, a number of resorts have hired consultants
Ⓔ To make skiing smoother, also safer and enjoyable, a number of resorts will have hired consultants

12. It is reported that some tribes in Africa used to eat the livers of their slain <u>enemies which they believed allowed them to ingest their courage.</u>

Ⓐ enemies which they believed allowed them to ingest their courage
Ⓑ enemies which they believed allowed them to ingest their enemies' courage
Ⓒ enemies which would, they believed, allow them to ingest their enemies' courage
Ⓓ enemies, an act they believed allowed them to ingest the courage of their enemies
Ⓔ enemies, an act they believed allowed them to ingest the enemy courage

Despite seductive advertisements, so-called low tar and nicotine cigarettes are really no safer than other cigarettes. The seemingly lower levels of tar and nicotine reported by the Federal Trade Commission are attributable to the FTC use of smoking machines, not human beings, to determine tar and nicotine levels. But people do not smoke like machines. A study of blood samples of smokers found no significant differences among smokers of the various brands and a direct relationship between nicotine intake and the number of cigarettes smoked, regardless of brand.

13. Someone wishing to defend a low tar and nicotine cigarette as a safer smoking alternative could point out that

Ⓐ most people who smoke give little consideration to the health risks involved in smoking
Ⓑ in confined spaces the health of even non-smokers is endangered by tobacco smoke
Ⓒ a smoker could choose to make his smoking habits similar to the methods of the testing machines
Ⓓ most cigarette companies offer smokers several different brands, including low tar and nicotine cigarettes
Ⓔ cigarette companies are required by law to include tar and nicotine content on the labels of cigarette packages

Many countries that rely on the United States for military assistance request the same sophisticated weapons systems used by United States forces. But experience shows the folly of this policy. Because their armed forces lack the training and parts needed to maintain them, the weapons systems are often totally ineffective when installed or become ineffective shortly thereafter.

14. The problem described above is most like which of the following situations?

Ⓐ An antique car collector who purchases two old sports cars of the same model and cannibalizes one for spare parts for the other
Ⓑ A business corporation that decides to lease a fleet of cars rather than purchase them with the understanding that the leasing company will service and repair them
Ⓒ A university physics professor who hires graduate students to do research work but finds that she must first train them in their new duties
Ⓓ A parent who purchases a personal computer for a child's education only to find that the available software is too complex for the child to use
Ⓔ A captain of a large ship who is forced to return to port for repairs after an accident caused by a failure of the ship's radar

GO ON TO NEXT PAGE

Dr. Esterhaus is an extremely competent administrator. In the twelve months following her appointment as Chief Executive Officer of the History Department, the number of applications for admission to the program was nearly 150 above that of the previous year.

15. The reasoning above makes which of the following assumptions?

    I. The increase in the number of applications for admission is attributable to Dr. Esterhaus's efforts.

    II. Dr. Esterhaus is well respected in the academic community as a history scholar.

    III. The number of applications for admission to a program is a good measure of the effectiveness of the Chief Executive Officer.

    (A) I only   (B) II only   (C) III only
    (D) I and III   (E) I, II, and III

Questions 16–18

The uniqueness of the Japanese character is the result of two seemingly contradictory forces: the strength of traditions and selective receptivity to foreign achievements and inventions. As early as the 1860s, there were counter movements to the traditional orientation. Yukichi Fukuzawa, the most eloquent spokesman of Japan's "Enlightenment," claimed, "The Confucian civilization of the East seems to me to lack two things possessed by Western civilization: science in the material sphere and a sense of independence in the spiritual sphere." Fukuzawa's great influence is found in the free and individualistic philosophy of the Education Code of 1872, but he was not able to prevent the government from turning back to the canons of Confucian thought in the Imperial Rescript of 1890. Another interlude of relative liberalism followed World War I, when the democratic idealism of President Woodrow Wilson had an important impact on Japanese intellectuals and, especially, students; but more important was the Leninist ideology of the 1917 Bolshevik Revolution. Again, in the early 1930s, nationalism and militarism became dominant, largely as a result of failing economic conditions.

Following the end of World War II, substantial changes were undertaken in Japan to liberate the individual from authoritarian restraints. The new democratic value system was accepted by many teachers, students, intellectuals, and old liberals, but it was not immediately embraced by the society as a whole. Japanese traditions were dominated by group values, and notions of personal freedom and individual rights were unfamiliar. Today, democratic processes are clearly evident in the widespread participation of the Japanese people in social and political life; yet, there is no universally accepted and stable value system. Values are constantly modified by strong infusions of Western ideas, both democratic and Marxist. School textbooks expound democratic principles, emphasizing equality over hierarchy and rationalism over tradition; but in practice these values are often misinterpreted and distorted, particularly by the youth who translate the individualistic and humanistic goals of democracy into egoistic and materialistic ones.

Most Japanese people have consciously rejected Confucianism, but vestiges of the old order remain. An important feature of relationships in many institutions such as political parties, large corporations, and university faculties is the *oyabun-kobun* or parent-child relation. A party leader, supervisor, or professor, in return for loyalty, protects those subordinate to him and takes general responsibility for their interests throughout their entire lives, an obligation that sometimes even extends to arranging marriages. The corresponding loyalty of the individual to his patron reinforces his allegiance to the group to which they both belong. A willingness to cooperate with other members of the group and to support without qualification the interests of the group in all its external relations is still a widely respected virtue. The *oyabun-kobun* creates ladders of mobility which an individual can ascend, rising as far as abilities permit, so long as he maintains successful personal ties with a superior in the vertical channel, the latter requirement usually taking precedence over a need for exceptional competence. As a consequence, there is little horizontal relationship between people even within the same profession.

16. Which of the following is most like the relationship of the *oyabun-kobun* described in the passage?

    (A) A political candidate and the voting public
    (B) A gifted scientist and his protégé
    (C) Two brothers who are partners in a business
    (D) A judge presiding at the trial of a criminal defendant
    (E) A leader of a musical ensemble who is also a musician in the group

17. The author implies that

    (A) decisions about promotions are often based on personal feelings
    (B) students and intellectuals do not understand the basic tenets of Western democracy
    (C) Western values have completely overwhelmed traditional Japanese attitudes
    (D) respect for authority was introduced into Japan following World War II
    (E) most Japanese workers are members of a single political party

18. It can be inferred that the Imperial Rescript of 1890

   (A) was a protest by liberals against the lack of individual liberty in Japan.
   (B) marked a return in government policies to conservative values
   (C) implemented the ideals set forth in the Education Code of 1872
   (D) was influenced by the Leninist ideology of the Bolshevik Revolution
   (E) prohibited the teaching of Western ideas in Japanese schools

19. By law, a qualified physician can only prescribe medicine, protecting the public.

   (A) By law, a qualified physician can only prescribe medicine, protecting the public.
   (B) By law, only a qualified physician can prescribe medicine, protecting the public.
   (C) By law, only a qualified physician can prescribe medicine which protects the public.
   (D) In order to protect the public, by law a qualified physician only can prescribe medicine.
   (E) In order to protect the public, by law only a qualified physician can prescribe medicine.

20. Improvements in economic theory and data gathering today makes possible more accurate to forecast than was possible even 20 years ago.

   (A) today makes possible more accurate to forecast than was
   (B) have made possible more accurate forecasts than were
   (C) today have made possible more accurate forecasts than was
   (D) today make possible more accurate forecasts than was
   (E) today make possible more accurate forecasting that were

21. After the Christmas tree was decorated, the guests were served the eggnog and then sang carols.

   (A) guests were served the eggnog and then sang carols
   (B) eggnog was served to the guests who sang carols
   (C) eggnog was served to the guests who then sang carols
   (D) guests were served the eggnog and singing carols
   (E) guests who then sang carols were served eggnog

The recent 40-percent reduction in airfares represents an attempt by the airlines to encourage impulse traveling. Because the lower-fare tickets need to be purchased only two days in advance of the flight, the companies hope to increase volume, thereby boosting overall revenues. The policy is ill-conceived, however, because business travelers, who would normally pay full fare, will now purchase discount fares, thus depressing revenues.

22. Which of the following, if true, would most weaken the argument above?

   (A) Some people would prefer to pay a higher fare if the additional cost ensured better schedules and service.
   (B) The number of business travelers who will purchase discount tickets is greater than the number of additional passengers who will be attracted by the lower fares.
   (C) An airplane must be operated at or near capacity for the airline to show a profit on a particular flight.
   (D) Impulse travelers are persons whose schedules are highly flexible and who are anxious to find lower fares.
   (E) Most business travelers must arrange their travel schedules more than two days in advance.

The United States Postal Service is drowning in junk mail. The average postal carrier delivers more junk mail, or third-class letters, than first-class mail. The result is a rapid decline in the quality of all postal services because first-class mail in effect subsidizes third-class mail.

23. Which of the following, if true, would most strengthen the argument above?

   (A) It costs six times as much to mail a three-ounce first-class letter as a three-ounce third-class letter, yet per piece handling cost for each is the same.
   (B) Members of the postal workers union have opposed deregulation of third-class delivery services because such a move threatens the jobs of postal workers.
   (C) Since private companies were allowed to compete with the Postal Service for overnight letter business, the Postal Service's share of that market fell off by 60 percent.
   (D) The cost of first-class postage has risen at a rate twice that of inflation while the delivery time for first-class mail has increased by 10 percent.
   (E) An audit conducted by the General Accounting Office revealed that 80 percent of all first-class letters are delivered within five days of postmark while only 20 percent of all third-class mail is delivered within five days of postmark.

GO ON TO NEXT PAGE

The bills produced by a truly great counterfeiter are never discovered. So a counterfeiter whose product has been learned to be fraudulent is not a very good counterfeiter. The truly great ones never get caught.

24. Which of the following arguments supports its conclusion in the same way as the argument above?

(A) This government agency has been infiltrated by spies from a foreign power. The three who were caught have given the names of several other spies.

(B) A reliable security guard always patrols his or her assigned territory. Ellen, who is a security guard, did not patrol her assigned territory. Therefore, Ellen is not a good security guard.

(C) Drug usage is on the increase. Over the past few years, drug enforcement agents have arrested more and more people attempting to smuggle drugs into the country.

(D) The CIA is accused of bungling its attempted covert operations in several foreign countries. But this is not fair to the CIA. The agency conducts many successful covert operations, but by definition, a successful covert operation never comes to light, so the agency cannot take credit for them.

(E) The state legislature should pass a law requiring all restaurants with a seating capacity of a certain minimum to set aside a section for non-smokers. There is ample scientific evidence that passive smoking is harmful to non-smokers.

Questions 25–27

In analyzing factors likely to induce depression it is useful to distinguish between "life events" and "life circumstances," both of which promote stress though in different ways. Stressful life events include divorce or loss of a spouse and loss of employment. Stress-inducing "life conditions" include single parenthood, low income, poor education, and responsibility for young children, circumstances that most often afflict the single-parent family head who is nearly always a woman. Any particular incident of depression is likely to include elements from both categories.

As expected, epidemiological studies show that more women than men exhibit signs of depression. The sex difference in rates of depression is also explained by a condition of learned helplessness. Society encourages women to be passive, not aggressive; not to seek power, but to trust others and to nurture others; to put the needs of others before their own; to appreciate mastery in others and not threaten them with their own. So any particular incident of depression may include a past history of learned helplessness as well as an immediate environmental agent of depression.

25. The main purpose of this passage is to

(A) describe the behavior of depressed people

(B) explain the biochemical causes of depression

(C) discuss the factors that contribute to depression

(D) analyze the different rates of depression in men and women

(E) identify the family situations that lead to depression

26. Which of the following best explains the distinction between a life circumstance and a life event?

(A) A life circumstance is a long-term condition, while a life event is a sudden change.

(B) Life circumstances occur less frequently but are more serious than life events.

(C) A life circumstance is learned behavior, and a life event is caused by an outside agent.

(D) A life circumstance can easily be controlled, but a life event cannot.

(E) A life circumstance is more likely to cause depression in women; a life event is more likely to cause depression in men.

27. Which of the following best explains the relationship between the first paragraph and the second paragraph of the passage?

(A) Statistics in the second paragraph support a contention made in the first paragraph.

(B) Information in the second paragraph helps to explain a phenomenon mentioned in the first paragraph.

(C) Studies cited in the second paragraph undermine the central point of the first paragraph.

(D) Arguments in the first paragraph contradict the arguments in the second paragraph.

(E) Examples given in the first paragraph illustrate points made in the second paragraph.

28. Horatio Greenough, considering by many to be the first American to become a professional sculptor, executed a bust of then President John Quincy Adams.

(A) considering by many to be the first American to become a professional sculptor

(B) considered by many to be the first American to become a professional sculptor

(C) considering by many to be the first American to have become a professional sculptor

(D) considered by many to be the first professional American sculptor

(E) considered by many to have become the first American professional sculptor

29. In no field of history has the search for logical explanation been so diligent <u>so much as</u> the study of the decline and fall of the Roman Empire.

 Ⓐ so much as
 Ⓑ as in
 Ⓒ for
 Ⓓ due to
 Ⓔ like

30. The viola, the alto member of the violin <u>family, having</u> four strings tuned C, G, D, A upward from the C below middle C (a fifth lower than the violin's strings).

 Ⓐ family, having
 Ⓑ family, had
 Ⓒ families, having
 Ⓓ family, having had
 Ⓔ family, has

Questions 31–32

Negative consumer reaction to a product is not generated solely by critical negative appraisal of a product's performance. Rather, negative reaction is generated by a perceived gap between consumer expectation and product performance. Businesses should use advertising to adjust consumer expectations to coincide with their products' performances.

31. Which of the following is (are) implied by the passage above?

 I. If consumer expectations are sufficiently reduced, then negative consumer reaction to products will disappear even though product performance remains unchanged.

 II. If product performances are sufficiently improved, negative consumer reaction to products will disappear no matter how high expectations remain.

 III. When consumer expectations about product performance increase, negative consumer reaction may persist despite improvements in product performance.

 Ⓐ I only Ⓑ III only Ⓒ I and III only
 Ⓓ II and III only Ⓔ I, II, and III

32. Which of the following, if true, would most weaken the argument above?

 Ⓐ Most consumers are able to make informed judgments about the actual performance of the products they purchase.
 Ⓑ The expectations of most consumers are influenced to a large extent by the claims made for those products by the manufacturers.
 Ⓒ Unless consumer expectations about a product are sufficiently high, consumers will not purchase that product.
 Ⓓ Government agencies prosecute businesses that make fraudulent advertising claims about product performances.
 Ⓔ Most consumers purchase products based upon their recognition of a particular brand name, not on a critical evaluation of the product's past performance.

Production of chlorofluorocarbons (CFCs) is believed to cause the breakdown of fragile ozone molecules in the Earth's atmosphere. During the 1970s, when production of CFCs was high, especially in the United States, scientists found that the quantity of ozone in the atmosphere dropped by an average of about 2 percent. In 1981, a ban on the use of CFCs in aerosol spray cans went into effect in the United States. In 1986, new measurements showed that ozone levels in the atmosphere had fallen by another 1 percent as compared to 1981.

33. Which of the following, if true, could help provide an explanation for this finding?

 I. Production of CFCs in Japan and Western Europe rose sharply between 1981 and 1986.

 II. Climatic changes occurring during the early 1980s have contributed to the breakdown of atmospheric ozone.

 III. During the early 1980s, several new and important uses were found for CFCs.

 Ⓐ I only Ⓑ III only Ⓒ I and III only
 Ⓓ II and III only Ⓔ I, II, and III

GO ON TO NEXT PAGE

34. Her dissertation was interesting and well-researched, but she lacked the organizational skills to make a convincing argument.

Ⓐ but she lacked the organizational skills to make a convincing argument

Ⓑ lacking the organizational skills making a convincing argument

Ⓒ but she also was lacking in organizational skills which would serve to make her argument more convincing

Ⓓ but having lacked the organizational skills of a convincing argument

Ⓔ but without a convincing argument as a result of organizational skills

35. Leprosy is not a highly contagious disease, yet it has always and will continue to be feared until a vaccine will have been developed.

Ⓐ has always and will continue to be feared until a vaccine will have been developed

Ⓑ is and always will continue to be feared until a vaccine is developed

Ⓒ continues being feared and will be feared by people until the development of a vaccine

Ⓓ has always been and will continue to be feared until a vaccine is developed

Ⓔ is always feared and until a vaccine is developed, will continue to be so

In a study of crime, it was estimated that over 60 percent of all major property crimes—auto thefts, burglaries, and robberies—in the city during 1996 were committed by a group of 350 persistent offenders. It was also found that over half of the major property crimes were committed by individuals who were addicted to drugs.

36. If the statements above are true, which of the following must also be true?

Ⓐ Some of the 350 persistent offenders in the city are also drug addicts.

Ⓑ All of the 350 persistent offenders in the city are also drug addicts.

Ⓒ Most drug addicts eventually become persistent offenders.

Ⓓ Most persistent offenders became criminals because they were drug addicts.

Ⓔ Persistent offenders and drug addicts do not commit crimes other than major property crimes.

During the past ten years, the number of semiconductors manufactured by the United States semiconductor industry has grown by 200 percent, but the number of semiconductors manufactured by the Japanese semiconductor industry has grown by 500 percent. Therefore, Japan now produces more semiconductors than the United States.

37. Which of the following, if true, most weakens the argument above?

Ⓐ In the past five years, the number of semiconductors manufactured by the United States semiconductor industry has grown by only 100 percent.

Ⓑ The dollar value of the semiconductors produced in the United States over the past ten years was greater than the dollar value of the semiconductors produced in Japan during the same time.

Ⓒ Exports of semiconductors today represent a higher proportion of total United States exports than they did ten years ago.

Ⓓ Ten years ago, the United States produced 90 percent of the world's semiconductors while Japan produced only two percent.

Ⓔ Ten years ago, Japan ranked fourth in the world in the production of semiconductors while the United States ranked first.

Government spending on education does not really benefit students. During the 1960s and 1970s, spending by the federal government on education programs rose by over 150 percent. During the same period, students' scores on standardized tests dropped nearly every year.

38. The argument above depends upon which of the following assumptions?

Ⓐ The scores students achieve on standardized examinations are a good measure of the effectiveness of educational programs.

Ⓑ During the 1960s and 1970s, progressively more students were able to take advantage of federally funded educational programs.

Ⓒ The proportion of the United States population classified as students did not increase appreciably during the 1960s and 1970s.

Ⓓ The money spent by the federal government on educational programs during the 1960s and 1970s could have been better spent on health and welfare programs.

Ⓔ The number of college graduates who chose teaching as a profession declined during the 1960s and 1970s.

Questions 39–41

The basic objective of the antitrust laws is to achieve desirable economic performance as measured by such criteria as efficient manufacturing and distributive processes, rapid technological progress, economic growth, and equity in the distribution of the fruits of progress. A society may achieve these objectives in a variety of ways. The government may specify performance by telling business what and how much to produce, or it may itself undertake the performance of certain functions. The basic philosophy of the antitrust laws, however, is to attempt to maintain sufficiently competitive market structure and market conduct to insure that private enterprise performs in a socially acceptable manner. The assumption is that we can avoid government intervention in the economically and politically hazardous thicket of specifying industrial performance by controlling certain aspects of industrial structure and competitive conduct. Hence, the antitrust approach is not regulation, per se.

Much of the job of antitrust enforcement involves formulating rules that govern the ways in which the competitive game is played. Economic theory suggests, and business experience verifies, that market structure plays a powerful role in determining or conditioning business conduct and that business conduct, in turn, determines the ultimate quality of industrial performance. This is not to say that an industry's structure and conduct are the only factors determining ultimate performance, but the available empirical evidence indicates that such structural characteristics as the height of entry barriers facing potential competitors, the degree of product differentiation, and the level of market concentration always are of some importance, and often are of decisive importance, in determining industry performance. There is also general agreement that certain forms of business conduct result in undesirable performance. For example, restrictive agreement among competitors may result in monopoly pricing even in industries that would otherwise generate competitive prices. Other forms of conduct may adversely affect market structure and thereby ultimate industry performance. Predatory pricing is an example. Although in the short run such conduct may give consumers low prices, it may also destroy competitors and result in higher prices in the long run.

Antitrust policy does not involve exhaustive investigation or analysis of all the factors that conceivably might have a bearing on industrial performance, nor does it involve direct specification of desired performance. This is both the great strength and the great weakness of the antitrust approach. Its strength derives from the fact that a maximum effect may flow from a minimum of government intervention. It is not necessary to assemble and maintain a vast bureaucracy that exercises continued intervention in and surveillance of the affairs of business. The Interstate Commerce Commission, whose major responsibilities involve setting of rates and other performance characteristics, has twice as many employees as the combined employees in antitrust enforcement at the Federal Trade Commission and the Department of Justice—and the ICC has responsibility for just a part of the field of transportation.

While the great virtue of the antitrust approach is that it requires a minimum of regulatory resources and intervention into business affairs, this is also its Achilles' heel. Because there are no precise causal links between market structure, conduct, and performance, rules of law controlling or modifying market structure and conduct are necessarily vulnerable to criticism.

39. The author of the passage is primarily concerned with
   - (A) arguing against direct government intervention in the marketplace
   - (B) explaining the underlying philosophy of the antitrust laws
   - (C) outlining different theories of government regulation of markets
   - (D) criticizing government agencies such as the Interstate Commerce Commission
   - (E) justifying the enforcement of antitrust legislation

40. It can be inferred from the passage that predatory pricing
   - (A) occurs only when a single firm has control of a large share of a market
   - (B) is a type of business conduct best eliminated by direct government regulation
   - (C) allows a large number of firms to distribute products over a broad region
   - (D) improves an industry's ability to deliver a variety of goods and services
   - (E) aims at eliminating competition so that the surviving firm can raise prices

41. The author would most likely agree with which of the following statements?
   - (A) An effective antitrust policy depends on having as much information about market structure and conduct as possible.
   - (B) An antitrust approach to controlling market structure and conduct is only marginally more effective than regulation.
   - (C) Direct government intervention in the marketplace is cumbersome and never warranted.
   - (D) Antitrust policies are inherently arbitrary because no one can be certain what factors influence market structure and conduct.
   - (E) Market structure and market conduct are two independent variables and must be regulated separately.

Stop: End of Verbal Section

Quantitative Section

37 Questions—75 Minutes

> ***General Directions:*** To simulate the experience of taking the CAT, answer each question in order. Do not skip any questions and do not go back to questions you have already answered.
>
> ***Directions for problem-solving questions:*** For this question type, select the best of the answer choices. Indicate your answer by blackening the circle next to your choice.
>
> *Numbers*: All numbers used are real numbers.
>
> *Figures*: The diagrams and figures that accompany these questions are for the purpose of providing information useful in solving the problems. The diagrams and figures are drawn as accurately as possible unless the figure is accompanied by a note stating that it is not drawn to scale. All figures are in a plane unless otherwise indicated.
>
> ***Directions for data sufficiency questions:*** Each question is followed by two numbered statements. You are to determine whether the data given in the statements are sufficient for answering the question. Use the data given, plus your knowledge of math and everyday facts, to choose among the five possible answers. Indicate your answer by blackening the circle next to your choice.
>
> *Numbers*: All values are real numbers.
>
> *Figures*: Any figures provided will not necessarily reflect the information given in the numbered statements, but they will reflect the information provided in the question. Unless otherwise indicated, all figures lie in a plane; all lines shown as straight are straight; and the positions of all points, angles, regions, etc., are correctly depicted.
>
> *Example:*
>
> In $\triangle ABC$, what is the value of x?
>
> (1) $y = 60$
>
> (2) $AB = BC$
>
> *Explanation*: Statement (1) is not sufficient to answer the question, for statement (1) provides no information about x or z. Statement (2) is not sufficient to answer the question. Statement (2) does establish that $y = z$, but that is not enough information to determine the value of x. Both statements together are sufficient to answer the question. Since $AB = BC$ and $y = z$, $z = 60$. Since $x + y + z = 180$, $x = 60$.

1. If $\dfrac{1}{x} + \dfrac{1}{x} = 8$, then $x =$

   Ⓐ $\dfrac{1}{4}$ Ⓑ $\dfrac{1}{2}$ Ⓒ 1   Ⓓ 2   Ⓔ 4

2. In a certain school, there are 600 boys and 400 girls. If 20 percent of the boys and 30 percent of the girls are on the honor roll, how many of the students are on the honor roll?

   Ⓐ 120   Ⓑ 175   Ⓒ 240   Ⓓ 250   Ⓔ 280

3. Three students are each scheduled to give a short speech at an assembly. In how many different orders can the speeches be scheduled?

   Ⓐ 12   Ⓑ 9   Ⓒ 6   Ⓓ 4   Ⓔ 3

4. Is $a > b$?

   (1) $a = b^2$

   (2) $a = b + 2$

   Ⓐ statement 1 alone is sufficient to answer the question, but statement 2 alone is not sufficient

   Ⓑ statement 2 alone is sufficient to answer the question, but statement 1 alone is not sufficient

   Ⓒ both statements together are needed to answer the question, but neither statement alone is sufficient

   Ⓓ either statement by itself is sufficient to answer the question

   Ⓔ not enough facts are given to answer the question

5. What is Steven's weight, in pounds?

(1) If Steven's weight, in pounds, is multiplied by 3, the result is 360.

(2) Half of Steven's weight in pounds plus 15 is equal to 75.

(A) statement 1 alone is sufficient to answer the question, but statement 2 alone is not sufficient

(B) statement 2 alone is sufficient to answer the question, but statement 1 alone is not sufficient

(C) both statements together are needed to answer the question, but neither statement alone is sufficient

(D) either statement by itself is sufficient to answer the question

(E) not enough facts are given to answer the question

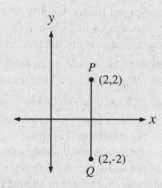

6. If points P and Q lie in the xy plane and have the coordinates shown above, what is the midpoint of PQ?

(A) $(-2, 0)$ (B) $(-2, 2)$ (C) $(0, 2)$
(D) $(2, 0)$ (E) $(2, 2)$

7. If xy is positive, which of the following CANNOT be true?

(A) $x > y > 0$ (B) $y > x > 0$ (C) $x > 0 > y$
(D) $0 > x > y$ (E) $0 > y > x$

8. If $30,000 \times 20 = 6 \times 10^n$, then $n =$

(A) 4   (B) 5   (C) 6   (D) 7   (E) 8

9. What is the value of $p - q$?

(1) $p + r = 12$.

(2) $r + q = 4$.

(A) statement 1 alone is sufficient to answer the question, but statement 2 alone is not sufficient

(B) statement 2 alone is sufficient to answer the question, but statement 1 alone is not sufficient

(C) both statements together are needed to answer the question, but neither statement alone is sufficient

(D) either statement by itself is sufficient to answer the question

(E) not enough facts are given to answer the question

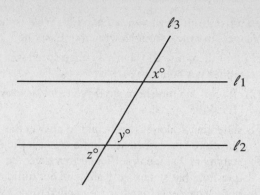

10. In the figure above, ℓ_1, ℓ_2, and ℓ_3 are straight lines. Does $x = z$?

(1) ℓ_1 and ℓ_2 are parallel.

(2) $x = y$

(A) statement 1 alone is sufficient to answer the question, but statement 2 alone is not sufficient

(B) statement 2 alone is sufficient to answer the question, but statement 1 alone is not sufficient

(C) both statements together are needed to answer the question, but neither statement alone is sufficient

(D) either statement by itself is sufficient to answer the question

(E) not enough facts are given to answer the question

11. The average (arithmetic mean) of Al's scores on three tests was 80. If the average of his scores on the first two tests was also 80, what was his score on the third test?

(A) 90   (B) 85   (C) 80   (D) 75

(E) Cannot be determined from the information given.

12. If 100 identical bricks weigh p pounds, then, in terms of p, 20 of these bricks weigh how many pounds?

(A) $\dfrac{p}{20}$ (B) $\dfrac{p}{5}$ (C) $20p$ (D) $\dfrac{5}{p}$ (E) $\dfrac{20}{p}$

13. If the distances between points P, Q, and R are equal, which of the following could be true?

I. P, Q, and R are points on a circle with center O.

II. P and Q are points on a circle with center R.

III. P, Q, and R are vertices of an equilateral triangle.

(A) I only   (B) I and II only   (C) I and III only
(D) II and III only   (E) I, II, and III

GO ON TO NEXT PAGE

14. Jan drove from Newtown to Eastville. What is the distance, in miles, from Newtown to Eastville?

    (1) For the entire trip, Jan's average speed was 50 miles per hour.

    (2) It took Jan nine hours to drive from Newtown to Eastville.

    Ⓐ statement 1 alone is sufficient to answer the question, but statement 2 alone is not sufficient

    Ⓑ statement 2 alone is sufficient to answer the question, but statement 1 alone is not sufficient

    Ⓒ both statements together are needed to answer the question, but neither statement alone is sufficient

    Ⓓ either statement by itself is sufficient to answer the question

    Ⓔ not enough facts are given to answer the question

15. N is a two-digit integer. Does $N = 81$?

    (1) The sum of the digits of N is 9.

    (2) N is divisible by 9.

    Ⓐ statement 1 alone is sufficient to answer the question, but statement 2 alone is not sufficient

    Ⓑ statement 2 alone is sufficient to answer the question, but statement 1 alone is not sufficient

    Ⓒ both statements together are needed to answer the question, but neither statement alone is sufficient

    Ⓓ either statement by itself is sufficient to answer the question

    Ⓔ not enough facts are given to answer the question

	Year					
	1960	1965	1970	1975	1980	1985
Price of a Certain Item	$2	$4	$7	$12	$20	$30

16. In the table above, the percent increase in the price of the item was greatest during which of the following periods?

    Ⓐ 1960–65　Ⓑ 1965–70　Ⓒ 1970–75
    Ⓓ 1975–80　Ⓔ 1980–85

17. Two cartons weigh $3x - 2$ and $2x - 3$. If the average weight of the cartons is 10, the heavier carton weighs how much more than the lighter carton?

    Ⓐ 2　Ⓑ 4　Ⓒ 5　Ⓓ 6　Ⓔ 10

18. A group of 15 students took a test that was scored from 0 to 100. If exactly 10 students scored 75 or more on the test, what is the *lowest* possible value for the average of the scores of all 15 students?

    Ⓐ 25　Ⓑ 50　Ⓒ 70　Ⓓ 75　Ⓔ 90

19. Do two lines, l_1 and l_2, drawn on a coordinate system intersect at the point (4, 7)?

    (1) l_1 is parallel to the y axis and l_2 is parallel to the x axis.

    (2) l_1 includes the point (4, 1) and l_2 includes the point (2, 7).

    Ⓐ statement 1 alone is sufficient to answer the question, but statement 2 alone is not sufficient

    Ⓑ statement 2 alone is sufficient to answer the question, but statement 1 alone is not sufficient

    Ⓒ both statements together are needed to answer the question, but neither statement alone is sufficient

    Ⓓ either statement by itself is sufficient to answer the question

    Ⓔ not enough facts are given to answer the question

20. Working together but independently, Scott and Eric can address X envelopes in 18 hours. How long would it take Scott working alone to address X envelopes?

    (1) In M minutes, Scott addresses three times as many envelopes as Eric addresses in M minutes.

    (2) Eric can address X envelopes in 72 hours.

    Ⓐ statement 1 alone is sufficient to answer the question, but statement 2 alone is not sufficient

    Ⓑ statement 2 alone is sufficient to answer the question, but statement 1 alone is not sufficient

    Ⓒ both statements together are needed to answer the question, but neither statement alone is sufficient

    Ⓓ either statement by itself is sufficient to answer the question

    Ⓔ not enough facts are given to answer the question

21. If a machine produces x units in t minutes and 30 seconds, what is its average operating speed in units per minute?

    Ⓐ $\dfrac{t+30}{x}$

    Ⓑ $\dfrac{x}{t+30}$

    Ⓒ $tx + \dfrac{1}{2}x$

    Ⓓ $\dfrac{t}{x} + \dfrac{1}{2}$

    Ⓔ $\dfrac{x}{t+\frac{1}{2}}$

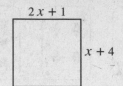

$2x + 1$

$x + 4$

22. If the figure above is a square, what is the perimeter of the figure?

    (A) 28   (B) 16   (C) 9   (D) 3
    (E) Cannot be determined from the information given.

23. A certain dairy packing plant has two machines, P and Q, that process milk at constant rates of 30 gallons per minute and 45 gallons per minute, respectively. A day's run of milk can be processed by machine P operating alone in 6 hours, by machine Q operating alone in 4 hours, or by both machines operating simultaneously in 2.4 hours. If a day's run of milk is processed using machine Q alone for half the time and both machines together for half the time, how many hours does it take to complete the run?

    (A) 1.5   (B) 3.0   (C) 3.75   (D) 4.2   (E) 5.0

24. If a commercial fertilizer called Green Grow is a mixture of compounds M and N, what percent of one bag of Green Grow, by weight, is nitrogen?

    (1) By weight, Green Grow consists of 7 parts M and 5 parts N.
    (2) By weight, 18 percent of compound N is nitrogen.

    (A) statement 1 alone is sufficient to answer the question, but statement 2 alone is not sufficient
    (B) statement 2 alone is sufficient to answer the question, but statement 1 alone is not sufficient
    (C) both statements together are needed to answer the question, but neither statement alone is sufficient
    (D) either statement by itself is sufficient to answer the question
    (E) not enough facts are given to answer the question

25. What is the average number of runs per game scored by the Bluebirds last season?

    (1) Last season, the Bluebirds played 120 games.
    (2) Last season, the Bluebirds scored four runs in exactly $\frac{1}{5}$ of their games, five runs in exactly $\frac{3}{4}$ of their games, and nine runs in exactly $\frac{1}{20}$ of their games.

    (A) statement 1 alone is sufficient to answer the question, but statement 2 alone is not sufficient
    (B) statement 2 alone is sufficient to answer the question, but statement 1 alone is not sufficient
    (C) both statements together are needed to answer the question, but neither statement alone is sufficient
    (D) either statement by itself is sufficient to answer the question
    (E) not enough facts are given to answer the question

26. In the figure above, O is the center of the larger circle. If the radius of the larger circle is r, what is the area of the shaded portion of the figure?

    (A) $\dfrac{\pi}{2}$ (B) $\dfrac{3\pi r}{4}$ (C) $\dfrac{\pi r}{2}$

    (D) $\dfrac{\pi r^2}{2}$ (E) $\dfrac{3\pi r^2}{4}$

27. If the cost of b books is d dollars, what is the cost, in dollars, of x books at the same rate?

    (A) xd (B) $\dfrac{xd}{b}$ (C) $\dfrac{bd}{x}$ (D) bx (E) $\dfrac{bx}{d}$

28. A contest winner is entitled to a prize of $21,000. She may take the entire prize at once, or she may elect to receive 10 percent of the prize at once and payments of $900 a month for 24 consecutive months. How much more will she receive if she elects to take the prize in installments than if she elects to take the entire prize at once?

    (A) $600   (B) $900   (C) $2,400
    (D) $2,700   (E) $3,000

29. In a certain election, how many votes did Smith receive for public office?

    (1) Smith received 5,676 votes, or 22 percent of the votes cast in District 1, and District 1 accounted for 15 percent of all votes cast in the election.
    (2) Smith received 45 percent of all votes cast in districts other than District 1.

    (A) statement 1 alone is sufficient to answer the question, but statement 2 alone is not sufficient
    (B) statement 2 alone is sufficient to answer the question, but statement 1 alone is not sufficient
    (C) both statements together are needed to answer the question, but neither statement alone is sufficient
    (D) either statement by itself is sufficient to answer the question
    (E) not enough facts are given to answer the question

GO ON TO NEXT PAGE

30. Is p a prime number?

(1) $p + 2$ is a prime number.

(2) $10 < p < 20$

Ⓐ statement 1 alone is sufficient to answer the question, but statement 2 alone is not sufficient

Ⓑ statement 2 alone is sufficient to answer the question, but statement 1 alone is not sufficient

Ⓒ both statements together are needed to answer the question, but neither statement alone is sufficient

Ⓓ either statement by itself is sufficient to answer the question

Ⓔ not enough facts are given to answer the question

31. In one classroom exactly one-half the seats are occupied. In another classroom with double the seating capacity of the first, exactly three-quarters of the seats are occupied. If the students from both rooms are transferred into a third, empty classroom that has a seating capacity exactly equal to the first two combined, what fraction of the seats in the third classroom is occupied?

Ⓐ $\frac{1}{4}$ Ⓑ $\frac{1}{3}$ Ⓒ $\frac{3}{8}$ Ⓓ $\frac{2}{3}$ Ⓔ $\frac{3}{4}$

32. If a bag of marbles contains only red, yellow, and blue marbles, and if there are twice as many yellow marbles as red marbles and three times as many blue marbles as yellow marbles in the bag, which of the following could be the number of marbles in the bag?

Ⓐ 24 Ⓑ 56 Ⓒ 80 Ⓓ 99 Ⓔ 115

33. The manager of a produce market purchased a quantity of tomatoes for $0.80 per pound. Due to improper handling, 10 percent of the tomatoes, by weight, were ruined and discarded. At what price per pound should the manager sell the remaining tomatoes if she wishes to make a profit on the sale of the tomatoes equal to 8 percent of the cost of the tomatoes?

Ⓐ $0.94 Ⓑ $0.96 Ⓒ $0.98
Ⓓ $1.00 Ⓔ $1.20

34. In a certain card game, an ace counts one point, face cards count ten points, and all other cards count their face values. A player must play at least one card on each turn, and his score on a turn is determined by the total point value of the cards played. If a player holds the cards shown above, how many different point totals are possible for him on his next turn?

Ⓐ 5 Ⓑ 6 Ⓒ 10 Ⓓ 20 Ⓔ 21

35. What percent of the students at College X are in-state students?

(1) At College X, the ratio of in-state students to out-of-state students is 3 to 7.

(2) Exactly 50 percent of the women and 25 percent of the men who are students at College X are in-state students.

Ⓐ statement 1 alone is sufficient to answer the question, but statement 2 alone is not sufficient

Ⓑ statement 2 alone is sufficient to answer the question, but statement 1 alone is not sufficient

Ⓒ both statements together are needed to answer the question, but neither statement alone is sufficient

Ⓓ either statement by itself is sufficient to answer the question

Ⓔ not enough facts are given to answer the question

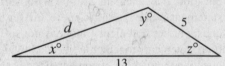

36. What is the area of the triangle above?

(1) $x + z = 90°$

(2) $169 - d^2 = 25$

Ⓐ statement 1 alone is sufficient to answer the question, but statement 2 alone is not sufficient

Ⓑ statement 2 alone is sufficient to answer the question, but statement 1 alone is not sufficient

Ⓒ both statements together are needed to answer the question, but neither statement alone is sufficient

Ⓓ either statement by itself is sufficient to answer the question

Ⓔ not enough facts are given to answer the question

37. For a certain calendar quarter, monthly sales by Vendor X were less in December than they were in October. Total monthly sales by Vendor X changed by what percent from October to November?

   (1) During October, Vendor X had total sales of $10,500, and during December, Vendor X had total sales of $9,000.

   (2) The decline in total sales from November to December was equal to the decline in total sales from October to December.

   Ⓐ statement 1 alone is sufficient to answer the question, but statement 2 alone is not sufficient

   Ⓑ statement 2 alone is sufficient to answer the question, but statement 1 alone is not sufficient

   Ⓒ both statements together are needed to answer the question, but neither statement alone is sufficient

   Ⓓ either statement by itself is sufficient to answer the question

   Ⓔ not enough facts are given to answer the question

Stop: End of Quantitative Section

Answer Key

VERBAL SECTION

1. D	15. D	29. B
2. A	16. B	30. E
3. E	17. A	31. B
4. A	18. B	32. C
5. A	19. E	33. E
6. E	20. B	34. A
7. D	21. C	35. D
8. A	22. E	36. A
9. D	23. A	37. D
10. E	24. D	38. A
11. A	25. C	39. B
12. D	26. A	40. E
13. C	27. B	41. A
14. D	28. B	

QUANTITATIVE SECTION

1. A	14. C	27. B
2. C	15. E	28. D
3. C	16. A	29. C
4. B	17. D	30. E
5. D	18. B	31. D
6. D	19. C	32. D
7. C	20. D	33. B
8. B	21. E	34. E
9. C	22. A	35. A
10. D	23. B	36. D
11. C	24. E	37. B
12. B	25. B	
13. E	26. E	

Explanatory Answers

VERBAL SECTION

1. Because young girls were not expected to participate in sports, so they were never seriously trained to be athletes.

   Ⓐ sports, so they
   Ⓑ sports, and they
   Ⓒ sports, and that
   Ⓓ sports, they
   Ⓔ sports, and so

   (D) The original sentence is incorrect because it contains a superfluous conjunction (*so*), which distorts the logical connection between the first clause and the second. (B) and (E) are incorrect for the same reason. As for (C), by replacing *so* with *that*, the main clause is reduced to the status of a noun clause, and the result is a sentence fragment rather than a complete sentence. (D) makes the needed correction.

2. Before the invention of television, radio was the chief form of at-home entertainment.

   Ⓐ radio was the chief form of at-home entertainment
   Ⓑ radio has been the chief form of at-home entertainment
   Ⓒ radio, having been the chief form of at-home entertainment
   Ⓓ the chief form of at-home entertainment is the radio
   Ⓔ radio, a form of at-home entertainment, was the chief

   (A) The original form of the sentence looks correct. It is best, however, to check the other sentences to be sure that your first assessment is correct. (B) is incorrect because there is no need to use the present perfect tense in this sentence where the simple past is needed. (C) is incorrect because it results in a sentence fragment instead of a sentence since (C) contains no conjugated verb. (D) is wrong because it is not logical to use the present tense to refer to what is obviously a past event. (E) is not idiomatic English and changes the intended meaning of the original.

3. Letters were received by the editor of the newspaper that complained of its editorial policy.

   Ⓐ Letters were received by the editor of the newspaper that complained of its editorial policy.
   Ⓑ Letters were received by the editor of the newspaper which complained of its editorial policy.
   Ⓒ Letters were received by the editor of the newspaper complaining of their editorial policy.
   Ⓓ The editor of the newspaper received letters that were complaining of the paper's editorial policy.
   Ⓔ The editor of the newspaper received letters complaining of the paper's editorial policy.

   (E) The original is incorrect because the modifier "that complained of its editorial policy" is too far removed from the word it modifies, *letters*. As written, the sentence seems to imply that the newspaper complained of its editorial policy. (B) and (C) fail to eliminate this ambiguity. (D) eliminates the ambiguity but is needlessly wordy. The best choice is (E). (E) corrects the error of the original and has two additional points in its favor. First, the thought is rendered directly instead of indirectly with the passive voice; and second, (E) uses the noun *paper's* instead of the pronoun *its*, which makes the sentence clearer.

The editor of a newspaper received the following letter:

Dear Editor:

   This holiday season I think we should make a serious effort to recapture the true spirit of giving. Each of us should resolve to give gifts and expect none. And if someone offers us a gift, we should refuse it and suggest that it be given to someone else. In this way, we would all experience a feeling of pure giving.

4. Which of the following statements points out the most serious logical flaw in the letter?

   Ⓐ If no one accepted any gifts, it would be impossible for anyone to give a gift.
   Ⓑ The holiday season is not the only time of year when people give and receive gifts.
   Ⓒ Often people receive gifts that are really not very useful, so it would not be a great sacrifice to part with them.
   Ⓓ Sometimes a person may make a gift to someone in the hope of later receiving something in exchange for it.
   Ⓔ Gift giving is a tradition that is thousands of years old and a characteristic of virtually every human community.

(A) There is a logical flaw in the argument. If everyone refused to accept gifts, there would be no one to whom to give gifts. Thus, the whole idea of gift giving breaks down. The reasoning put forth in the letter is internally inconsistent.

Recently credit card companies have come under attack by consumer groups who argue that the interest rates charged by these companies are unconscionably high. In fact, the rates are generally several percentage points above those charged by banks for ordinary personal loans. But consumer groups overlook the fact that credit cards afford the user great flexibility. A user can purchase an item while it is on sale. So the lower cost of the item offsets the extra cost of the credit.

5. The argument above makes which of the following assumptions?

   Ⓐ The cost savings of buying an item at a reduced price are at least equal to the excess interest that a consumer pays on purchases made with a credit card.
   Ⓑ A credit card application is not rejected unless the applicant has a long history of late payments and other credit problems.
   Ⓒ The prices of items on sale purchased by consumers are still sufficiently high to enable sellers to recoup their costs and make a modest profit.
   Ⓓ The consumers who make purchases of sale items with credit cards are persons who might not qualify for bank loans with a lower interest rate.
   Ⓔ The average outstanding balance of the ordinary credit card user is no greater than the total non-credit-card debt of the credit card user.

(A) The conclusion of the argument is that despite the comparatively high interest rates charged by credit card companies, on balance consumers are not harmed because they save money by buying items on sale. For this conclusion to be true, it must be the case that the amount of money saved by purchasing items on sale is sufficient to offset the additional cost of the credit. (A) makes this hidden assumption explicit. (B) and (C) are both fairly weak responses. As for (B), the speaker claims only that those who have and use credit cards are not disadvantaged by the high interest rates. He doesn't make any claim about the availability of cards. As for (C), the speaker claims only that items are offered on sale. He doesn't have to commit himself to any position on the wisdom of the seller's marketing strategy.

   (D) and (E) are somewhat attractive because they both mention the idea of ordinary loans and the idea of credit cards. The difficulty with (D) is that this is a position to which the speaker need not commit, and you can prove this by making the opposite assumption. Even if all credit card users could qualify for

ordinary bank loans, this doesn't affect the speaker's conclusion that the flexibility afforded by credit cards offsets the additional cost of using them. (E) is wrong for a similar reason; even if (E) is false, the conclusion of the argument is not affected one way or the other.

Bob and Cindy are each older than both Diane and Ellen.

6. If the statement above is true, then which of the following additional statements ensures the truth of the conclusion "Allen is older than Ellen"?

   Ⓐ Allen is younger than Bob.
   Ⓑ Cindy is older than Bob.
   Ⓒ Cindy is younger than Bob.
   Ⓓ Allen is older than Diane.
   Ⓔ Allen is older than Cindy.

(E) You may find that a simple diagram is useful:

$$(D + E) < (B + C)$$

Now test each answer choice:

(A) $A < (D + E) < (B + C)$

This shows that (A) does not guarantee that A is older than E.

   (B) and (C) must be incorrect since neither places A on the diagram. As for (D):

$$D < A < E < (B + C)$$

This shows that (D) does not guarantee that A is older than E. (E), however, does guarantee that A is older than E.

$$(D + E) < (B + C) < A$$

Even if A is not older than B, he must be older than E.

7. The passage mentions all of the following as being elements of Japanese society EXCEPT

   Ⓐ obedience to authority
   Ⓑ sense of duty
   Ⓒ respect for the Emperor
   Ⓓ concern for education
   Ⓔ loyalty to one's superiors

(D) This is a specific detail question—with a thought-reverser. So the correct answer will be the one idea not specifically mentioned in the passage, and this is "concern for education." Although this might very well be a part of Japanese society, the idea is not mentioned in this selection. The other four ideas are mentioned, (C) in the first paragraph and (A), (B), and (E) in the second paragraph.

8. We may infer from the passage that those who led Japan into the modern age were concerned primarily with

Ⓐ maintaining a stable society
Ⓑ building a new industrial base
Ⓒ expanding the nation's territory
Ⓓ gaining new adherents of Confucianism
Ⓔ creating a new middle class

(A) This is an idea question. The first paragraph tells us that the reformers were concerned to preserve traditions, and the two traditions described in the passage were designed to ensure stability. So we may infer that the reformers were primarily concerned to maintain stability.

(B) (D), and (E) are not mentioned by name in the passage, nor is there any information from which you can logically infer that these were concerns of the reformers. To be sure, it is logically possible that the reformers *might* have had these concerns, but the opposite is just as likely. Finally, though the author does mention Confucianism, it is cited as a source of traditional values. The quasi state religion established by the reformers was Shintoism.

9. The author makes which of the following statements about Shintoism?

I. Prior to the Meiji Restoration it had been eclipsed by Buddhism and Confucianism.

II. It was the source of reciprocal duties between friends.

III. The Emperor was treated as an object of religious worship.

Ⓐ I only   Ⓑ II only   Ⓒ III only
Ⓓ I and III only   Ⓔ I, II, and III

(D) This is a specific detail question, in the special format. Statement I is specifically mentioned in the first paragraph: Shintoism was subordinated to Buddhism and Confucianism. Thus we eliminate (B) and (C), since they do not include I.

Statement II is not mentioned as a feature of Shintoism. The requirement of reciprocal duties between friends is mentioned in the second paragraph as a feature of Confucianism. Watch out for this type of wrong answer.

As for III, this is clearly mentioned in the first paragraph as a feature of Shintoism.

10. Washington Irving's German-influenced stories were profoundly moving to Americans, <u>knowing more than most</u> Britons what it was to feel the trauma of rapid change, and Americans found in the lazy Rip a model for making a success of failure.

Ⓐ knowing more than most
Ⓑ who knew more then most
Ⓒ knowing more then most
Ⓓ most who knew more about what
Ⓔ who knew more than most

(E) (A) is wrong because there is no relative pronoun to refer to *Americans*. (B) corrects that error but introduces the unidiomatic phrase *more then* instead of *more than*. (C) combines the errors of the first two choices. (D) is hopelessly awkward and unidiomatic. (E) is correct and precise.

11. <u>In order to make skiing smoother, safer, and more enjoyable, a number of resorts have hired consultants</u> to design and sculpt the trails.

Ⓐ In order to make skiing smoother, safer, and more enjoyable, a number of resorts have hired consultants
Ⓑ In order to make skiing smoother, safer, and more enjoyable a number of consultants have been hired by resorts
Ⓒ In the interest of making skiing smoother, safer, and able to be enjoyed, a number of resorts have hired consultants
Ⓓ To make skiing smoother, safer, so that you can enjoy it, a number of resorts have hired consultants
Ⓔ To make skiing smoother, also safer and enjoyable, a number of resorts will have hired consultants

(A) The original sentence is correct. The sentence maintains parallel structure and the subject agrees with the verb. (B) is incorrect for two reasons. First, (B) switches to the indirect passive voice. As a result, (B) is not as concise as the original. Second, (B) changes the intended meaning of the original sentence. (C) and (D) are wrong because the resulting sentences would lack a parallel structure. (E) also introduces an error of parallelism and compounds the problem by using the future perfect tense.

12. It is reported that some tribes in Africa used to eat the livers of their slain <u>enemies which they believed allowed them to ingest their courage</u>.

Ⓐ enemies which they believed allowed them to ingest their courage
Ⓑ enemies which they believed allowed them to ingest their enemies' courage
Ⓒ enemies which would, they believed, allow them to ingest their enemies' courage
Ⓓ enemies, an act they believed allowed them to ingest the courage of their enemies
Ⓔ enemies, an act they believed allowed them to ingest the enemy courage

493

(D) The original sentence is incorrect because the relative pronoun *which* lacks a clear referent. *Which* ought to refer to something like *eating,* but there is no such noun in the sentence. (B) and (C) fail to correct this error. (D) and (E) both correct the error, but (E), by changing *enemies* to an adjective, creates an unidiomatic expression. Additionally, (D) is better than the original because by using the noun *enemies* instead of the pronoun *their,* it avoids a potential ambiguity. (Did the people hope to ingest their own courage or that of the enemy?)

Despite seductive advertisements, so-called low tar and nicotine cigarettes are really no safer than other cigarettes. The seemingly lower levels of tar and nicotine reported by the Federal Trade Commission are attributable to the FTC use of smoking machines, not human beings, to determine tar and nicotine levels. But people do not smoke like machines. A study of blood samples of smokers found no significant differences among smokers of the various brands and a direct relationship between nicotine intake and the number of cigarettes smoked, regardless of brand.

13. Someone wishing to defend a low tar and nicotine cigarette as a safer smoking alternative could point out that

   Ⓐ most people who smoke give little consideration to the health risks involved in smoking

   Ⓑ in confined spaces the health of even non-smokers is endangered by tobacco smoke

   Ⓒ a smoker could choose to make his smoking habits similar to the methods of the testing machines

   Ⓓ most cigarette companies offer smokers several different brands, including low tar and nicotine cigarettes

   Ⓔ cigarette companies are required by law to include tar and nicotine content on the labels of cigarette packages

(C) The logical structure of the original statement is an attempt to discredit an argument from analogy by pointing out that machines don't smoke like human beings. You could strengthen the argument under attack (that is, you can strengthen the claim that low tar and nicotine cigarettes are an improvement over regular cigarettes) by repairing the analogy. This is what (C) attempts to do. As for (A), asserting that smokers just don't care about their health is not going to do very much to repair the argument for the claim that low tar and nicotine cigarettes have health advantages. As for (D) and (E), these two fail to advance the issue, for neither is connected with the question of whether light cigarettes really have any significant advantage in terms of health. (B) is perhaps the second-best choice. You might attempt to defend light cigarettes by arguing that, even though they don't offer any real advantage over

regular cigarettes in terms of the health of the smoker, non-smokers might benefit from them if they are exposed to less tar and nicotine than they otherwise would be. There are two things wrong with this line of thinking. First, you would still have the burden of showing that so-called light cigarettes emit lower levels of tar and nicotine, but (B) doesn't make any such claim. Second, as a matter of test-taking strategy, you should prefer choice (C) because (C) comes to grips with the internal logical structure of the statement.

Many countries that rely on the United States for military assistance request the same sophisticated weapons systems used by United States forces. But experience shows the folly of this policy. Because their armed forces lack the training and parts needed to maintain them, the weapons systems are often totally ineffective when installed or become ineffective shortly thereafter.

14. The problem described above is most like which of the following situations?

   Ⓐ An antique car collector who purchases two old sports cars of the same model and cannibalizes one for spare parts for the other

   Ⓑ A business corporation that decides to lease a fleet of cars rather than purchase them with the understanding that the leasing company will service and repair them

   Ⓒ A university physics professor who hires graduate students to do research work but finds that she must first train them in their new duties

   Ⓓ A parent who purchases a personal computer for a child's education only to find that the available software is too complex for the child to use

   Ⓔ A captain of a large ship who is forced to return to port for repairs after an accident caused by a failure of the ship's radar

(D) This is a logical similarity question. The problem described by the initial statement is that the armed forces of the beneficiary nation lack the know-how needed to operate the sophisticated equipment. A similar situation is described by (D)—the child lacks the know-how to operate the computer.

Dr. Esterhaus is an extremely competent administrator. In the twelve months following her appointment as Chief Executive Officer of the History Department, the number of applications for admission to the program was nearly 150 above that of the previous year.

15. The reasoning above makes which of the following assumptions?

   I. The increase in the number of applications for admission is attributable to Dr. Esterhaus's efforts.

   II. Dr. Esterhaus is well respected in the academic community as a history scholar.

III. The number of applications for admission to a program is a good measure of the effectiveness of the Chief Executive Officer.

Ⓐ I only   Ⓑ II only   Ⓒ III only
Ⓓ I and III   Ⓔ I, II, and III

(D) This question asks that you identify hidden assumptions of the argument. The conclusion of the argument is that Dr. Esterhaus is an effective administrator, and the support for that conclusion is the explicit premise that, following her appointment, the number of applications increased. This assumes (as I points out) that Dr. Esterhaus was responsible for the increase. If the increase had some other cause, then the conclusion regarding Dr. Esterhaus's effectiveness would not follow. The argument also assumes (as III notes) that the number of applications received is a good measure of an administrator's effectiveness. If the number of applications received is not necessarily a good measure of effectiveness, then the conclusion does not follow from the premises. II, however, is not a hidden premise of the argument. Whether or not Dr. Esterhaus is a good scholar is irrelevant to her effectiveness as an administrator, at least as that term is used in the initial statement.

16. Which of the following is most like the relationship of the *oyabun-kobun* described in the passage?

Ⓐ A political candidate and the voting public
Ⓑ A gifted scientist and his protégé
Ⓒ Two brothers who are partners in a business
Ⓓ A judge presiding at the trial of a criminal defendant
Ⓔ A leader of a musical ensemble who is also a musician in the group

(B) This is a further application question. You must take what you have learned about the *oyabun-kobun* and apply it to a new situation. What are the defining characteristics of this relationship? First the *oyabun-kobun* is like a parent-child relationship; one person is superior to the other. On this ground, you can eliminate both (C) and (E). They describe situations in which people behave more or less as equals. Another aspect of the parent-child relationship is intimacy. So you can eliminate (A), which is a relationship between one and many. Although (D) describes a one-on-one situation in which one party is in charge, the situation lacks the element of intimacy. This leaves (B). And (B) describes a relationship that is personal, in which the interests of the parties are similar, and in which one party is superior to the other.

17. The author implies that

Ⓐ decisions about promotions are often based on personal feelings
Ⓑ students and intellectuals do not understand the basic tenets of Western democracy
Ⓒ Western values have completely overwhelmed traditional Japanese attitudes
Ⓓ respect for authority was introduced into Japan following World War II
Ⓔ most Japanese workers are members of a single political party

(A) This is an implied idea question. You will find the basis for the conclusion expressed in (A) in the final paragraph. There the author states that maintaining a successful personal relationship with a superior may be more important than having exceptional abilities. We can infer, therefore, that superiors may make decisions based on their personal preferences for subordinates.

(B) represents a misunderstanding of the second and third paragraphs. The author states that students and intellectuals did embrace the basic ideas of democracy, but young people have distorted certain Western ideas.

(C) is actually in contradiction to the passage. The second half of the selection is devoted to a discussion of the influence of traditional values. So Western influences cannot have completely obliterated those values.

(D) represents a misreading of the passage. Respect for authority is a traditional value which predates the introduction of democratic ideas following the war. As for (E), there is nothing in the passage to support such a conclusion. If you selected (E), probably you misread something in the discussion of the *oyabun-kobun*. Although someone in a political party may establish a parent-child relationship with a senior member of the party, this does not imply that everyone belongs to the same political party.

18. It can be inferred that the Imperial Rescript of 1890

Ⓐ was a protest by liberals against the lack of individual liberty in Japan.
Ⓑ marked a return in government policies to conservative values
Ⓒ implemented the ideals set forth in the Education Code of 1872
Ⓓ was influenced by the Leninist ideology of the Bolshevik Revolution
Ⓔ prohibited the teaching of Western ideas in Japanese schools

(B) This is an inference question based on the first paragraph. The key sentence is the one that reads, "[Fukuzawa] was not able to prevent the government from turning back to the canons of Confucian thought in the Imperial Rescript of 1890." Since Fukuzawa represented liberal thought and Confucianism was the source of traditional values, we can infer that the Imperial Rescript represented a return to traditional values. Thus, (A) and (C) both reach clearly wrong conclusions. (D) represents a confused reading of the selection. The Bolshevik Revolution did not occur until 1917. Finally, (E) represents the second most attractive answer. It at least has the merit of noting that the Imperial Rescript represented a reaction to liberal ideas. The difficulty with (E) is that it goes too far beyond the explicit text. While we can infer the general conclusion that the Imperial Rescript represented a reaction to liberal thinking, there is nothing in the selection to support the very specific conclusion given in (E).

19. By law, a qualified physician can only prescribe medicine, protecting the public.
    (A) By law, a qualified physician can only prescribe medicine, protecting the public.
    (B) By law, only a qualified physician can prescribe medicine, protecting the public.
    (C) By law, only a qualified physician can prescribe medicine which protects the public.
    (D) In order to protect the public, by law a qualified physician only can prescribe medicine.
    (E) In order to protect the public, by law only a qualified physician can prescribe medicine.

(E) The original sentence contains two ambiguities. First, the placement of the modifier *only* implies that the only legal action a physician can take is prescribing medicine, when the sentence really means to say that it is only physicians who can prescribe medicine. Second, the placement of the modifier *protecting the public* so close to *medicines* implies that medicine, not the law, is intended to protect the public. Only (E) corrects both of these errors.

20. Improvements in economic theory and data gathering today makes possible more accurate to forecast than was possible even 20 years ago.
    (A) today makes possible more accurate to forecast than was
    (B) have made possible more accurate forecasts than were
    (C) today have made possible more accurate forecasts than was
    (D) today make possible more accurate forecasts than was
    (E) today make possible more accurate forecasting that were

(B) The sentence suffers from three problems. One, the verb makes does not agree with its subject, which is *improvements*. Two, the *today* introduces a possible ambiguity, because its placement implies that the

sentence is talking about data gathered on a particular day; and, in any event, the *today* is superfluous. Three, the use of the infinitive *to forecast* is not idiomatic. Only (B) eliminates all three of the errors.

21. After the Christmas tree was decorated, the guests were served the eggnog and then sang carols.
    (A) guests were served the eggnog and then sang carols
    (B) eggnog was served to the guests who sang carols
    (C) eggnog was served to the guests who then sang carols
    (D) guests were served the eggnog and singing carols
    (E) guests who then sang carols were served eggnog

(C) The original suffers from a lack of parallelism. ("were served . . . and . . . sang . . ."). (B) corrects the problem of faulty parallelism but changes the meaning of the original by implying that only guests who were singing were given eggnog. (D) fails to correct the error of the original, and (E) is afflicted with the same ambiguity that afflicts (B). (C) corrects the problem of faulty parallelism without introducing any new error.

The recent 40-percent reduction in airfares represents an attempt by the airlines to encourage impulse traveling. Because the lower-fare tickets need to be purchased only two days in advance of the flight, the companies hope to increase volume, thereby boosting overall revenues. The policy is ill-conceived, however, because business travelers, who would normally pay full fare, will now purchase discount fares, thus depressing revenues.

22. Which of the following, if true, would most weaken the argument above?
    (A) Some people would prefer to pay a higher fare if the additional cost ensured better schedules and service.
    (B) The number of business travelers who will purchase discount tickets is greater than the number of additional passengers who will be attracted by the lower fares.
    (C) An airplane must be operated at or near capacity for the airline to show a profit on a particular flight.
    (D) Impulse travelers are persons whose schedules are highly flexible and who are anxious to find lower fares.
    (E) Most business travelers must arrange their travel schedules more than two days in advance.

(E) This item asks you to find a good attack on the initial argument, and, as you have been instructed, the correct answer to such an item is often the denial of a hidden assumption of the argument. This is why (E) is an effective attack. The conclusion of the argument is that the airlines will lose money. Why? Because business travelers will take advantage of the reduced fares.

This argument assumes, however, that business travelers are able to take advantage of the reduced fares. (E) attacks this hidden assumption by noting that business travelers must arrange their schedules in advance, which effectively precludes them from taking advantage of the lower fares. (A) may have some merit as a choice. You might argue that some people would avoid using discount fares, preferring better service. The difficulty with this line of thinking is that it attempts to provide a counterexample to a claim that is not universal in the first place. The speaker never claims that everyone will take advantage of the lower fares, only that enough people will to depress revenues. (B) seems to be the second-best choice because it at least has the merit of trying to come to grips with the logical structure of the initial statement. (It tries to analyze the probable effect of the new policy.) The difficulty with (B), and this is a fatal difficulty, is that (B) actually strengthens the initial argument. In essence, (B) is arguing that revenues will be depressed by the discount fares. (C) does not come to grips with the logic of the argument. The airlines' cost structure does not necessarily dictate consumer behavior. Finally, (D) just seems to provide a definition of *impulse traveler* that is consistent with the usage the speaker makes of that term, so (D) does not weaken the argument.

The United States Postal Service is drowning in junk mail. The average postal carrier delivers more junk mail, or third-class letters, than first-class mail. The result is a rapid decline in the quality of all postal services because first-class mail in effect subsidizes third-class mail.

23. Which of the following, if true, would most strengthen the argument above?

    Ⓐ It costs six times as much to mail a three-ounce first-class letter as a three-ounce third-class letter, yet per piece handling cost for each is the same.
    Ⓑ Members of the postal workers union have opposed deregulation of third-class delivery services because such a move threatens the jobs of postal workers.
    Ⓒ Since private companies were allowed to compete with the Postal Service for overnight letter business, the Postal Service's share of that market fell off by 60 percent.
    Ⓓ The cost of first-class postage has risen at a rate twice that of inflation while the delivery time for first-class mail has increased by 10 percent.
    Ⓔ An audit conducted by the General Accounting Office revealed that 80 percent of all first-class letters are delivered within five days of postmark while only 20 percent of all third-class mail is delivered within five days of postmark.

(A) This item asks for you to strengthen the argument, so the correct choice may articulate a hidden assumption of the argument. The conclusion of the argument is that the quality of postal service has declined. What has caused this? According to the argument, the decline in service stems from the fact that first-class mail subsidizes third-class mail. This assertion rests on the hidden assumption that funds that would otherwise be spent on first-class are being used to pay for the servicing of third-class mail. (A) correctly identifies this assumption; third-class mail doesn't pay for itself.

As for (B), the fact that the postal workers union opposes a change in policy doesn't reveal anything about the cost structure of the post office one way or the other. As for (C), the argument concerns the relationship between first- and third-class mail, so a point about overnight mail service is irrelevant. (D) at least has the merit of addressing the issue of the cost of first-class mail, but it is not clear how this bears on the question of whether first-class mail is subsidizing third-class mail. Finally, (F) is perhaps the second-best response. (E) at least makes an attempt to compare some aspect of first-class mail with third-class mail, but (E) (which refers to delivery time) doesn't analyze the relative cost of mailing and handling the two classes of mail.

The bills produced by a truly great counterfeiter are never discovered. So a counterfeiter whose product has been learned to be fraudulent is not a very good counterfeiter. The truly great ones never get caught.

24. Which of the following arguments supports its conclusion in the same way as the argument above?

    Ⓐ This government agency has been infiltrated by spies from a foreign power. The three who were caught have given the names of several other spies.
    Ⓑ A reliable security guard always patrols his or her assigned territory. Ellen, who is a security guard, did not patrol her assigned territory. Therefore, Ellen is not a good security guard.
    Ⓒ Drug usage is on the increase. Over the past few years, drug enforcement agents have arrested more and more people attempting to smuggle drugs into the country.
    Ⓓ The CIA is accused of bungling its attempted covert operations in several foreign countries. But this is not fair to the CIA. The agency conducts many successful covert operations, but by definition, a successful covert operation never comes to light, so the agency cannot take credit for them.
    Ⓔ The state legislature should pass a law requiring all restaurants with a seating capacity of a certain minimum to set aside a section for non-smokers. There is ample scientific evidence that passive smoking is harmful to non-smokers.

(D) The logical structure of the initial statement reminds me of what parents tell their children as the Christmas holiday approaches: Santa Claus is watching you, but no matter how quick you are, you'll never get a glimpse of him, because he's too fast. In other words, the claim that Santa Claus is watching is, in principle, unverifiable. So, too, is the claim in (D); there are CIA successes, but you can never learn about them because they are successful. None of the other choices exhibit this logical flaw.

25. The main purpose of this passage is to
    (A) describe the behavior of depressed people
    (B) explain the biochemical causes of depression
    (C) discuss the factors that contribute to depression
    (D) analyze the different rates of depression in men and women
    (E) identify the family situations that lead to depression

(C) This is a main idea question in sentence completion form. Unfortunately, we can't eliminate any choice on the basis of first words. *Describe, explain, discuss, analyze,* and *identify* all seem appropriate descriptions of the selection.

Next we take each choice as a whole. We eliminate (A) as going beyond the scope of the passage. Though the passage does discuss depression, it does not describe the *behavior* of people who suffer from depression. We eliminate (B) also as going beyond the scope of the passage. The author never even mentions biochemical causes.

(D) and (E) commit the opposite sin. (D) is too narrow. It mentions one point raised in the passage. The author discusses the causes of depression in general, not just the reason for the discrepancy in the incidence of depression between men and women. (E) is also too narrow. Family situations are only one of the factors discussed in the passage.

26. Which of the following best explains the distinction between a life circumstance and a life event?
    (A) A life circumstance is a long-term condition, while a life event is a sudden change.
    (B) Life circumstances occur less frequently but are more serious than life events.
    (C) A life circumstance is learned behavior, and a life event is caused by an outside agent.
    (D) A life circumstance can easily be controlled, but a life event cannot.
    (E) A life circumstance is more likely to cause depression in women; a life event is more likely to cause depression in men.

(A) This is a further application question, somewhat like a question that asks "with which of the following would the author agree." What does the passage say about life circumstances versus life events? Events are things like divorce or getting fired—things that happen suddenly. Circumstances are things like lack of education or income—long-term things. (A) best summarizes this distinction.

(B) is incorrect because the difference is the length of time the fact lasts. (C) is wrong and just confuses the second with the first paragraph. (E) makes the same kind of error.

Finally, (D) is wrong because there is no support for such a conclusion in the passage. Indeed, it seems that life circumstances such as lack of education or a low-paying job are not easily controlled.

27. Which of the following best explains the relationship between the first paragraph and the second paragraph of the passage?
    (A) Statistics in the second paragraph support a contention made in the first paragraph.
    (B) Information in the second paragraph helps to explain a phenomenon mentioned in the first paragraph.
    (C) Studies cited in the second paragraph undermine the central point of the first paragraph.
    (D) Arguments in the first paragraph contradict the arguments in the second paragraph.
    (E) Examples given in the first paragraph illustrate points made in the second paragraph.

(B) This is a logical structure question. It asks about the relation between the first paragraph and the second paragraph. What does the author intend to do in the second paragraph? The first sentence of the second paragraph refers again to the sex difference in depression, a point that was already mentioned in the first paragraph. Then the second paragraph continues to say that the difference is *also* explained by the phenomenon of learned helplessness. So the second paragraph provides further explanation of a phenomenon mentioned in the first paragraph.

(A) is incorrect since the second paragraph does not contain any statistics. Although the second paragraph does mention a study, and though the study itself might have used statistics, the passage in front of you doesn't use those numbers.

(C) is incorrect since the study that is mentioned in the second paragraph helps support and explain the first paragraph, not contradict it. (D) is incorrect for the same reason. The second paragraph is a continuation of a thought mentioned in the first paragraph. Finally, (E) is wrong since the examples mentioned in the first paragraph illustrate points made in the first paragraph—not the second paragraph.

28. Horatio Greenough, <u>considering by many to be the first American to become a professional sculptor,</u> executed a bust of then President John Quincy Adams.

    Ⓐ considering by many to be the first American to become a professional sculptor

    Ⓑ considered by many to be the first American to become a professional sculptor

    Ⓒ considering by many to be the first American to have become a professional sculptor

    Ⓓ considered by many to be the first professional American sculptor

    Ⓔ considered by many to have become the first American professional sculptor

(B) The use of *considering* in the original to mean "is considered" is not idiomatic. (B), (D), and (E) attempt to correct the error, but (D) and (E) make ambiguous the intended meaning of the original. Neither the phrase *first professional American sculptor* nor the phrase *first American professional sculptor* makes clear which of the two elements, *American* or *professional*, the speaker considers more important.

29. In no field of history has the search for logical explanation been so diligent <u>so much as</u> the study of the decline and fall of the Roman Empire.

    Ⓐ so much as

    Ⓑ as in

    Ⓒ for

    Ⓓ due to

    Ⓔ like

(B) The original sentence is not idiomatic. The correct expression is "so *x* as in *y*." Only (B) conforms to this: *so diligent as in the study.* . . . The original and the other choices all use faulty expressions that do not represent standard English usage.

30. The viola, the alto member of the violin <u>family, having</u> four strings tuned C, G, D, A upward from the C below middle C (a fifth lower than the violin's strings).

    Ⓐ family, having

    Ⓑ family, had

    Ⓒ families, having

    Ⓓ family, having had

    Ⓔ family, has

(E) The original is wrong because it is a sentence fragment—there is no main verb. (B) is incorrect because there is no need to use the past tense. (C) commits the same error as (B) and commits an additional error by making *family* plural. (The resulting phrase is not logical because there is but one violin family.) (D) is wrong because it too is a fragment. (E) is the correct choice because it has a conjugated verb in the correct tense.

Questions 31–32

Negative consumer reaction to a product is not generated solely by critical negative appraisal of a product's performance. Rather, negative reaction is generated by a perceived gap between consumer expectation and product performance. Businesses should use advertising to adjust consumer expectations to coincide with their products' performances.

31. Which of the following is (are) implied by the passage above?

    I. If consumer expectations are sufficiently reduced, then negative consumer reaction to products will disappear even though product performance remains unchanged.

    II. If product performances are sufficiently improved, negative consumer reaction to products will disappear no matter how high expectations remain.

    III. When consumer expectations about product performance increase, negative consumer reaction may persist despite improvements in product performance.

    Ⓐ I only   Ⓑ III only   Ⓒ I and III only

    Ⓓ II and III only   Ⓔ I, II, and III

(B) This item asks you to draw a further conclusion from the premises given. With an item like this, you must make sure that your further conclusions are adequately supported by the premises contained in the initial statement. In particular, you want to make sure your further conclusions do not go beyond the scope of the initial statement. It is for this reason that we can eliminate both I and II. The initial statement says that negative consumer reaction is a function of expectation as well as product performance. I makes the mistake of concluding that expectation is the sole factor in consumer reaction and that product performance is completely irrelevant—a conclusion not supported by the initial statement. II errs in the other direction. It concludes that performance is the only relevant factor and that expectations can be ignored—again, a conclusion that goes beyond the scope of the initial statement. III, however, is implied by the initial statement. Since two factors are operating to determine consumer reaction, adjusting the one but not the other may leave a residuum of dissatisfaction.

32. Which of the following, if true, would most weaken the argument above?

  (A) Most consumers are able to make informed judgments about the actual performance of the products they purchase.

  (B) The expectations of most consumers are influenced to a large extent by the claims made for those products by the manufacturers.

  (C) Unless consumer expectations about a product are sufficiently high, consumers will not purchase that product.

  (D) Government agencies prosecute businesses that make fraudulent advertising claims about product performances.

  (E) Most consumers purchase products based upon their recognition of a particular brand name, not on a critical evaluation of the product's past performance.

(C) A common way of attacking an argument that makes a proposal for some sort of policy is to determine whether the proposal would entail any unwanted side effects. This is the strategy employed by (C). The initial statement says, in effect, that by reducing consumer expectations, the consumer won't be disappointed in the product. An unwanted consequence of reducing expectations, however, may be that consumers simply will not buy the product in the first place.

Here, both (A) and (B) seem to support rather than weaken the argument. As for (A), it is a hidden assumption of the argument that consumers are able to make judgments about product quality. But this choice provides support for that assumption, so it strengthens rather than weakens the argument. (B) makes a similar error. The argument presupposes that it is possible to manipulate consumer expectations, but this choice strengthens that assumption. (D) is fairly clearly irrelevant to the issue raised in the initial statement. Finally, (E) is perhaps the second-best choice. It seems to say that consumers don't make judgments about quality; compare choice (A). The difficulty with (E) is that brand name comes to stand for performance expectation and that is presumably something that can be manipulated.

Production of chlorofluorocarbons (CFCs) is believed to cause the breakdown of fragile ozone molecules in the Earth's atmosphere. During the 1970s, when production of CFCs was high, especially in the United States, scientists found that the quantity of ozone in the atmosphere dropped by an average of about 2 percent. In 1981, a ban on the use of CFCs in aerosol spray cans went into effect in the United States. In 1986, new measurements showed that ozone levels in the atmosphere had fallen by another 1 percent as compared to 1981.

33. Which of the following, if true, could help provide an explanation for this finding?

  I. Production of CFCs in Japan and Western Europe rose sharply between 1981 and 1986.

  II. Climatic changes occurring during the early 1980s have contributed to the breakdown of atmospheric ozone.

  III. During the early 1980s, several new and important uses were found for CFCs.

  (A) I only (B) III only (C) I and III only
  (D) II and III only (E) I, II, and III

(E) This question asks that you find possible causal explanations for a phenomenon. Statement I is a possible explanation. For even though the United States may have reduced its production of CFCs, it is possible that production increased elsewhere and that this accounted for damage to the ozone layer. II is another possible explanation: natural phenomena were at work as well. Finally, III also is a possible explanation: although one use was prohibited, CFCs were manufactured in increasing amounts to satisfy other uses.

34. Her dissertation was interesting and well-researched, but she lacked the organizational skills to make a convincing argument.

  (A) but she lacked the organizational skills to make a convincing argument

  (B) lacking the organizational skills making a convincing argument

  (C) but she also was lacking in organizational skills which would serve to make her argument more convincing

  (D) but having lacked the organizational skills of a convincing argument

  (E) but without a convincing argument as a result of organizational skills

(A) The original sentence appears to be correct. (B) fails to make a logical statement by omitting the conjunction *but,* which shows the relationship between the clauses. (C) is wordy, the use of the word *also* is illogical, and the resulting sentence changes the intended meaning of the original by introducing the word *more* ("more convincing"). (D) creates an illogical sentence. It is not clear what lacks the organizational skills, and the resulting sentence implies that it is convincing arguments that have organizational skills, rather than the person who is making the argument. (E) is also illogical. It implies that it was because of organizational skills that there was no convincing argument. (A) makes it clear that the person doing the writing lacked organizational skills.

35. Leprosy is not a highly contagious disease, yet it <u>has always and will continue to be feared until a vaccine will have been developed.</u>

   Ⓐ has always and will continue to be feared until a vaccine will have been developed

   Ⓑ is and always will continue to be feared until a vaccine is developed

   Ⓒ continues being feared and will be feared by people until the development of a vaccine

   Ⓓ has always been and will continue to be feared until a vaccine is developed

   Ⓔ is always feared and until a vaccine is developed, will continue to be so

(D) The original sentence is incorrect because it includes an incomplete construction: "has always . . . to be feared." Also, the future perfect tense is inappropriate here. (B) is incorrect because it too has the incomplete construction. (C) is wrong because it is awkward and not idiomatic. (E) changes the meaning of the original sentence: Leprosy is not continually being feared. (E) is also awkwardly worded. (D) is the best choice because the construction is complete and the verb tense appropriate.

In a study of crime, it was estimated that over 60 percent of all major property crimes—auto thefts, burglaries, and robberies—in the city during 1996 were committed by a group of 350 persistent offenders. It was also found that over half of the major property crimes were committed by individuals who were addicted to drugs.

36. If the statements above are true, which of the following must also be true?

   Ⓐ Some of the 350 persistent offenders in the city are also drug addicts.

   Ⓑ All of the 350 persistent offenders in the city are also drug addicts.

   Ⓒ Most drug addicts eventually become persistent offenders.

   Ⓓ Most persistent offenders became criminals because they were drug addicts.

   Ⓔ Persistent offenders and drug addicts do not commit crimes other than major property crimes.

(A) We can eliminate (C), (D), and (E) because they go beyond the scope of the initial statement. There is just not enough evidence provided to support them. (A), however, is supported by the evidence cited. Since 60 percent of the crimes in question were committed by persistent offenders, and since over half were committed by drug addicts, there must be some overlap between the two populations. Thus, we can conclude that at least some of the persistent offenders are drug addicts. We cannot, however, conclude that all of the persistent offenders are drug addicts.

If this is not clear to you, try thinking of an analogous case. For example, in a certain group of ten people, six are wearing hats and five are wearing gloves. Thus, you know at least one person is wearing both.

   During the past ten years, the number of semiconductors manufactured by the United States semiconductor industry has grown by 200 percent, but the number of semiconductors manufactured by the Japanese semiconductor industry has grown by 500 percent. Therefore, Japan now produces more semiconductors than the United States.

37. Which of the following, if true, most weakens the argument above?

   Ⓐ In the past five years, the number of semiconductors manufactured by the United States semiconductor industry has grown by only 100 percent.

   Ⓑ The dollar value of the semiconductors produced in the United States over the past ten years was greater than the dollar value of the semiconductors produced in Japan during the same time.

   Ⓒ Exports of semiconductors today represent a higher proportion of total United States exports than they did ten years ago.

   Ⓓ Ten years ago, the United States produced 90 percent of the world's semiconductors while Japan produced only two percent.

   Ⓔ Ten years ago, Japan ranked fourth in the world in the production of semiconductors while the United States ranked first.

(D) The fallacy in the argument is the common one of confusing percents with absolute numbers. The conclusion of the argument is that Japan produces more semiconductors than the United States, but the support for that argument would be a comparison of the percentage increase. It is easy to illustrate the fallacy using numbers. Assume, for example, that ten years ago the United States produced 90 semiconductors and Japan produced only two semiconductors. Ten years later, given a 200-percent growth rate, the United States would produce 90 + 180 = 270 units. Given a 500-percent growth rate, Japan would produce 2 + 10 = 12 units. This explains why people on opposite sides of an issue reach seemingly different conclusions based on the same facts. For example:

X: During the past five years, we have held the line on costs. The cost of a subway token has increased by only 15 cents during this period.

Y: The cost of riding the subway has soared over the past five years by a whopping 25 percent.

   Both of the claims could very well be true, if the original cost of the token was 60 cents and the new cost is 75 cents. (D) correctly focuses on this fallacy. (A) does not contradict the statements contained in the argument. It is possible that the growth rate over the past five years was only half of what it was for the entire ten-year period. (B) doesn't come to grips with the argument, for the speaker has chosen to make a point about the number of semiconductors—not their dollar value. As for (C), this point may very well be true but it doesn't address the comparison made in the initial paragraph. Finally, as for (E), this, if anything, seems completely consistent with the information provided in the initial paragraph.

Government spending on education does not really benefit students. During the 1960s and 1970s, spending by the federal government on education programs rose by over 150 percent. During the same period, students' scores on standardized tests dropped nearly every year.

38. The argument above depends upon which of the following assumptions?

Ⓐ The scores students achieve on standardized examinations are a good measure of the effectiveness of educational programs.

Ⓑ During the 1960s and 1970s, progressively more students were able to take advantage of federally funded educational programs.

Ⓒ The proportion of the United States population classified as students did not increase appreciably during the 1960s and 1970s.

Ⓓ The money spent by the federal government on educational programs during the 1960s and 1970s could have been better spent on health and welfare programs.

Ⓔ The number of college graduates who chose teaching as a profession declined during the 1960s and 1970s.

(A) This item asks for you to identify a hidden premise of the argument. Examine the structure of the argument. The conclusion is "Government spending on education does not really benefit students." The explicit premises are (a) spending has increased and (b) standardized test scores have not. The conclusion rests upon the suppressed premise that standardized test scores are an appropriate measure of how well students are doing. (A) correctly points this out.

(B) is not completely irrelevant to the argument, but its significance is not clear. It could be used to support the argument: the money reached more and more students but still did no good. It could also be used to undermine the argument: The funds were not ineffective, but they were spread too thinly, so that overall results were disappointing. Since the point seems to cut both ways, we cannot say that it definitely weakens the argument.

(C) and (E) can be analyzed in the same way. Both are generally related to the problem discussed by the speaker, but it is not clear how each is directly

relevant to the point made. Finally, as for (D), the author is not necessarily committed to the view that the money could have been better spent elsewhere. The author might very well think that virtually all such spending is a waste.

39. The author of the passage is primarily concerned with

Ⓐ arguing against direct government intervention in the marketplace

Ⓑ explaining the underlying philosophy of the antitrust laws

Ⓒ outlining different theories of government regulation of markets

Ⓓ criticizing government agencies such as the Interstate Commerce Commission

Ⓔ justifying the enforcement of antitrust legislation

(B) This is a main idea question. In the first paragraph the author distinguishes antitrust actions from regulation per se. In the second paragraph he talks about the basic functioning of antitrust laws. In the third and fourth paragraphs, the author mentions some pros and cons of the antitrust philosophy. (B) provides the best description of this development. As for (A), you might argue that the author's favorable review of antitrust law implies that he would look with disfavor on direct intervention. And you might even cite his mention of the ICC. The difficulty with this reasoning is twofold. First, the author may not be opposed to all government intervention. He may, for example, regard the ICC as a necessary evil because antitrust laws would be ineffective in the transportation sector. Second, even if the first point is conceded, you still haven't found the main idea of the selection. The focus of the argument is antitrust, not regulation per se. (C) is wrong for this second reason as well. It is true that in the first paragraph the author does distinguish between antitrust and regulation, but the main focus of the passage then becomes antitrust. (D) is wrong for both of the reasons discussed in connection with choice (A): One, we can't be sure that the author is critical of the ICC; and two, this wouldn't be considered the main point of the selection anyway. Finally, (E) is wrong because the word *justification* is inappropriate. Further, while you might conclude from the passage that having a system of antitrust laws is justifiable, persuading you of that is not the author's burden.

40. It can be inferred from the passage that predatory pricing

Ⓐ occurs only when a single firm has control of a large share of a market

Ⓑ is a type of business conduct best eliminated by direct government regulation

Ⓒ allows a large number of firms to distribute products over a broad region

① improves an industry's ability to deliver a variety of goods and services

⑤ aims at eliminating competition so that the surviving firm can raise prices

(E) This is an implied idea question. The information we need is found at the end of the second paragraph. The author states that the effect of predatory pricing is to lower prices in the short run. This eliminate competition. Then the survivors raise prices. (E) describes this process. (A) is the second-best choice, but the word *only* makes it wrong. We can certainly infer that predatory pricing could occur when a single firm is very powerful, but we should not conclude that this is the only circumstance under which it occurs. It might also occur with two or three very powerful firms. (B) must be wrong because the author seems to think that this type of conduct is best controlled by the antitrust laws. (C) and (D) have nothing to do with the concept of predatory pricing. And from what we have just learned, nothing good comes from predatory pricing—at least not in the long run.

41. The author would most likely agree with which of the following statements?

Ⓐ An effective antitrust policy depends on having as much information about market structure and conduct as possible.

Ⓑ An antitrust approach to controlling market structure and conduct is only marginally more effective than regulation.

Ⓒ Direct government intervention in the marketplace is cumbersome and never warranted.

Ⓓ Antitrust policies are inherently arbitrary because no one can be certain what factors influence market structure and conduct.

Ⓔ Market structure and market conduct are two independent variables and must be regulated separately.

(A) This is a further application question. In the third and fourth paragraphs, the author makes the point that antitrust is not an exact science because there are no easily definable causal connections between market structure and conduct. Thus, the author would probably agree that your policy is only as good as the information you have. (B) overstates the case. Our analysis of the preceding question revealed that the author believes that antitrust policy is effective. (C) also overstates the author's case. The author would prefer to avoid direct intervention, but we should not conclude that the author believes intervention is NEVER justified. And (D) overstates the case. Although the author recognizes that antitrust policy cannot be perfect, he certainly doesn't regard it as arbitrary. As for (E),

the author would surely reject this statement, for he specifically states that structure can affect conduct and vice versa.

QUANTITATIVE SECTION

1. If $\dfrac{1}{x} + \dfrac{1}{x} = 8$, then $x =$

   Ⓐ $\dfrac{1}{4}$ Ⓑ $\dfrac{1}{2}$ Ⓒ 1   Ⓓ 2   Ⓔ 4

   (A) Here you have a single equation with one variable, so you might as well solve for x:

   $$\frac{1}{x} + \frac{1}{x} = 8$$

   $$\frac{2}{x} = 8$$

   $$x = \frac{1}{4}$$

   Or, you might have reasoned that $\dfrac{1}{x}$ and $\dfrac{1}{x}$ are equal, and since their sum is 8, $\dfrac{1}{x}$ must be 4. So the value of x must be $\dfrac{1}{4}$. And, of course, you could have substituted numbers, but this equation is so simple that one of the two techniques just described is more effective.

2. In a certain school, there are 600 boys and 400 girls. If 20 percent of the boys and 30 percent of the girls are on the honor roll, how many of the students are on the honor roll?

   Ⓐ 120   Ⓑ 175   Ⓒ 240   Ⓓ 250   Ⓔ 280

   (C) This question asks about percents. You must take a percent of a number:

   20% of 600 boys = 120 boys on the honor roll

   30% of 400 girls = 120 girls on the honor roll

   120 boys + 120 girls = 240 students on the honor roll

3. Three students are each scheduled to give a short speech at an assembly. In how many different orders can the speeches be scheduled?

   Ⓐ 12   Ⓑ 9   Ⓒ 6   Ⓓ 4   Ⓔ 3

   (C) At first you might think you need a fancy mathematical formula to solve this question. And, in fact, there is a branch of mathematics that studies such problems. (The procedures are called permutations and combinations.) But you don't need any special knowledge to answer this question. Assume that the three speakers are A, B, and C, and count on your fingers the number of possible orders: ABC, ACB, BAC, BCA, CAB, CBA.

4. Is $a > b$?

(1) $a = b^2$

(2) $a = b + 2$

Ⓐ statement 1 alone is sufficient to answer the question, but statement 2 alone is not sufficient

Ⓑ statement 2 alone is sufficient to answer the question, but statement 1 alone is not sufficient

Ⓒ both statements together are needed to answer the question, but neither statement alone is sufficient

Ⓓ either statement by itself is sufficient to answer the question

Ⓔ not enough facts are given to answer the question

(B) Test each of the numbered statements independently.

Statement (1) is not sufficient to answer the question. In the lesson on Data Sufficiency, you were advised to consider different possible values for a variable. Here it is possible that a and b are zero. It is also possible that a and b are positive fractions, for example, $\frac{1}{4} = (\frac{1}{2})^2$ (in which case b is actually larger than a).

Statement (2) is sufficient to answer the question, for statement (2) says, in effect, that a is 2 more than b.

Since (1) is not sufficient but (2) is, this item should be classified as (B).

5. What is Steven's weight, in pounds?

(1) If Steven's weight, in pounds, is multiplied by 3, the result is 360.

(2) Half of Steven's weight in pounds plus 15 is equal to 75.

Ⓐ statement 1 alone is sufficient to answer the question, but statement 2 alone is not sufficient

Ⓑ statement 2 alone is sufficient to answer the question, but statement 1 alone is not sufficient

Ⓒ both statements together are needed to answer the question, but neither statement alone is sufficient

Ⓓ either statement by itself is sufficient to answer the question

Ⓔ not enough facts are given to answer the question

(D) Test each statement by itself.

As for statement (1), let x be Steven's weight in pounds:

$3(x) = 360$

This is an equation in one variable, and this information is sufficient to answer the question. (Remember the "good enough" principle: You don't have to solve for x.)

As for statement (2), again let x be Steven's weight in pounds:

$\frac{1}{2}(x) + 15 = 75$

Again you have an equation in one variable, so you can solve for x.

Since (1) and (2) are each sufficient, the correct classification for this item is (D).

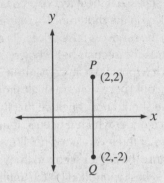

6. If points P and Q lie in the xy plane and have the coordinates shown above, what is the midpoint of PQ?

Ⓐ $(-2, 0)$ Ⓑ $(-2, 2)$ Ⓒ $(0, 2)$

Ⓓ $(2, 0)$ Ⓔ $(2, 2)$

(D) This question tests basic coordinate geometry. Since the x coordinate of both points is 2, the line runs parallel to the y axis. The x coordinate of the midpoint will also be 2. As for the y coordinate, the midpoint is halfway between 2 and –2, which is zero.

7. If xy is positive, which of the following CANNOT be true?

Ⓐ $x > y > 0$ Ⓑ $y > x > 0$ Ⓒ $x > 0 > y$

Ⓓ $0 > x > y$ Ⓔ $0 > y > x$

(C) This question tests the positive and negative properties of numbers. If xy is positive, then x and y both have the same sign. They might both be positive, or they might both be negative. And it doesn't make any difference which is larger. Thus, (A), (B), (D), and (E) can all be true. x and y cannot, however, have different signs, because a positive times a negative yields a negative result. And, of course, you could have tried substituting numbers. If $x > 0 > y$, then x could be 1 and y could be –1, and $1 \times -1 = -1$.

8. If $30,000 \times 20 = 6 \times 10^n$, then $n =$

Ⓐ 4   Ⓑ 5   Ⓒ 6   Ⓓ 7   Ⓔ 8

(B) This question tests powers. $30,000 \times 20 = 600,000 = 6 \times 10^5$ (one power of 10 for each zero).

9. What is the value of $p - q$?

   (1) $p + r = 12$.

   (2) $r + q = 4$.

  Ⓐ statement 1 alone is sufficient to answer the question, but statement 2 alone is not sufficient

  Ⓑ statement 2 alone is sufficient to answer the question, but statement 1 alone is not sufficient

  Ⓒ both statements together are needed to answer the question, but neither statement alone is sufficient

  Ⓓ either statement by itself is sufficient to answer the question

  Ⓔ not enough facts are given to answer the question

(C) Neither statement (1) nor statement (2) is, by itself, sufficient, but both statements taken together are sufficient. Treat the statements as simultaneous equations and subtract the second from the first:

$p + r = 12$

$-(q + r = 4)$

$p - q = 8$

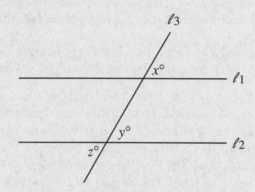

10. In the figure above, ℓ_1, ℓ_2, and ℓ_3 are straight lines. Does $x = z$?

   (1) ℓ_1 and ℓ_2 are parallel.

   (2) $x = y$

  Ⓐ statement 1 alone is sufficient to answer the question, but statement 2 alone is not sufficient

  Ⓑ statement 2 alone is sufficient to answer the question, but statement 1 alone is not sufficient

  Ⓒ both statements together are needed to answer the question, but neither statement alone is sufficient

  Ⓓ either statement by itself is sufficient to answer the question

  Ⓔ not enough facts are given to answer the question

(D) Test each statement.

  Statement (1) answers the question: yes, $x = z$. If ℓ_1 and ℓ_2 are parallel, then x and y must be equal. (This is the principle of "big angle/little angle" covered in the section on Holmes' attic in Lesson 17: When parallel lines are cut by a third line creating big and little angles, all big angles are equal, and all little angles are equal.)

And if $x = y$, then $x = z$. (Opposite or vertical angles are equal.)

  Statement (2) also answers the question. If x and y are equal, then, since y and z are equal, x and z must be equal.

11. The average (arithmetic mean) of Al's scores on three tests was 80. If the average of his scores on the first two tests was also 80, what was his score on the third test?

  Ⓐ 90 Ⓑ 85 Ⓒ 80 Ⓓ 75

  Ⓔ Cannot be determined from the information given.

(C) Use the procedure you learned for finding a missing element of an average. The total of all three numbers is $3 \times 80 = 240$. The total of the two numbers you know is $2 \times 80 = 160$. So the missing number is $240 - 160 = 80$. Or you might have used the "above and below" method. Since 80 is neither above nor below the average, the first two 80s are equal to the average, so the final number can be neither above nor below the average. It must be 80.

12. If 100 identical bricks weigh p pounds, then, in terms of p, 20 of these bricks weigh how many pounds?

  Ⓐ $\dfrac{p}{20}$ Ⓑ $\dfrac{p}{5}$ Ⓒ $20p$ Ⓓ $\dfrac{5}{p}$ Ⓔ $\dfrac{20}{p}$

(B) There are three ways of arriving at the solution. The simplest and most direct is to reason that if 100 bricks weigh p pounds, 20 bricks, which is $\frac{1}{5}$ of 100, must weigh $\frac{1}{5}$ of p.

  The same reasoning can be expressed using a direct proportion. The more bricks, the greater the weight, so

$$\frac{100}{20} = \frac{p}{x}$$

$100x = 20p$

$$x = \frac{20p}{100} = \frac{p}{5}$$

Finally, you could have substituted numbers. Assume that 100 bricks weigh 100 pounds, or 1 pound apiece. 20 bricks weigh 20 pounds. On the assumption that $p = 100$, the correct formula will generate the number 20.

13. If the distances between points P, Q, and R are equal, which of the following could be true?

  I. P, Q, and R are points on a circle with center O.

  II. P and Q are points on a circle with center R.

  III. P, Q, and R are vertices of an equilateral triangle.

  Ⓐ I only Ⓑ I and II only Ⓒ I and III only

  Ⓓ II and III only Ⓔ I, II, and III

(E) The following drawings show that I, II, and III are possible.

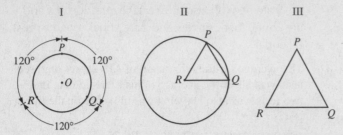

The thing to watch out for here is the Watson blunder. Both I and III are fairly obvious possibilities; II is more subtle. Since this is a problem of average difficulty, there must be something more to it than just I and III.

14. Jan drove from Newtown to Eastville. What is the distance, in miles, from Newtown to Eastville?

(1) For the entire trip, Jan's average speed was 50 miles per hour.

(2) It took Jan nine hours to drive from Newtown to Eastville.

Ⓐ statement 1 alone is sufficient to answer the question, but statement 2 alone is not sufficient

Ⓑ statement 2 alone is sufficient to answer the question, but statement 1 alone is not sufficient

Ⓒ both statements together are needed to answer the question, but neither statement alone is sufficient

Ⓓ either statement by itself is sufficient to answer the question

Ⓔ not enough facts are given to answer the question

(C) If you examine each statement independently of the other, you will see that neither (1) nor (2) is, by itself sufficient to answer the question: What is the distance? Taken together, however, the statements are sufficient:

distance = rate × time

distance = 50 miles per hour × 9 hours = 450 miles

(Of course, there is no need to do the multiplication.)

15. *N* is a two-digit integer. Does *N* = 81?

(1) The sum of the digits of *N* is 9.

(2) *N* is divisible by 9.

Ⓐ statement 1 alone is sufficient to answer the question, but statement 2 alone is not sufficient

Ⓑ statement 2 alone is sufficient to answer the question, but statement 1 alone is not sufficient

Ⓒ both statements together are needed to answer the question, but neither statement alone is sufficient

Ⓓ either statement by itself is sufficient to answer the question

Ⓔ not enough facts are given to answer the question

(E) Begin by testing each statement independently. Statement (1) is not sufficient to answer the question, for there are several two-digit numbers, the sums of which are 9, e.g., 18, 36, and 81. Nor is statement (2) sufficient, for there are several two-digit numbers that are divisible by 9, e.g., 18, 36, and 81. Even the two statements taken together are not sufficient to answer the question, as proved by the examples already given. The numbers 18, 27, 36, etc., all meet both of the conditions described by (1) and (2). Thus, the correct classification for this item is (E). (**Note:** Here is a little trick to help you if you ever see a problem like this again. If the sum of the digits of a number is divisible by 9, the number itself is also divisible by 9. Take, for example, the number 111,111,111. The sum of the digits is 9, and 111,111,111 ÷ 9 = 12, 345, 679.)

	Year					
	1960	1965	1970	1975	1980	1985
Price of a Certain Item	$2	$4	$7	$12	$20	$30

16. In the table above, the percent increase in the price of the item was greatest during which of the following periods?

Ⓐ 1960–65   Ⓑ 1965–70   Ⓒ 1970–75
Ⓓ 1975–80   Ⓔ 1980–85

(A) This problem can be solved with the "changeover" principle. But, you object, that means five different calculations. True, so look for an escape route: approximation. The percent increase in the period 1960–65 was $(\frac{4-2}{2}) = 100\%$. For the next period it was $\frac{3}{4}$, which is less than 100%. For the next it was $\frac{5}{7}$, which is less than 100%. For the next, $\frac{8}{12} = \frac{2}{3}$, which is less than 100%. And for the next period it was $\frac{10}{20}$, 50% less than 100%. The correct answer is (A).

17. Two cartons weigh $3x - 2$ and $2x - 3$. If the average weight of the cartons is 10, the heavier carton weighs how much more than the lighter carton?

Ⓐ 2   Ⓑ 4   Ⓒ 5   Ⓓ 6   Ⓔ 10

(D) The best approach to this question is simply to do the algebra. Since the average of $3x - 2$ and $2x - 3$ is 10, their sum is 20:

$3x - 2 + 2x - 3 = 20$

$5x - 5 = 20$

$5x = 25$

$x = 5$

So one of the packages weights $3(5) - 2 = 13$ pounds and the other weighs $2(5) - 3 = 7$ pounds. The difference between their weights is 6.

Testing choices would not be a good strategy for this question, because the question asks for the *difference* between the weights; so the choices are not possible weights of an individual package.

18. A group of 15 students took a test that was scored from 0 to 100. If exactly 10 students scored 75 or more on the test, what is the *lowest* possible value for the average of the scores of all 15 students?

Ⓐ 25   Ⓑ 50   Ⓒ 70   Ⓓ 75   Ⓔ 90

(B) This question is a variation on the theme of an average with missing elements. Since ten students have scores of 75 or more, the total of their scores is at least $10 \times 75 = 750$. Then, even assuming the other five students each scored 0, the average for the 15 would be at least $750 \div 15 = 50$.

19. Do two lines, ℓ_1 and ℓ_2, drawn on a coordinate system intersect at the point (4, 7)?

(1) ℓ_1 is parallel to the y axis and ℓ_2 is parallel to the x axis.

(2) ℓ_1 includes the point (4, 1) and ℓ_2 includes the point (2, 7).

Ⓐ statement 1 alone is sufficient to answer the question, but statement 2 alone is not sufficient
Ⓑ statement 2 alone is sufficient to answer the question, but statement 1 alone is not sufficient
Ⓒ both statements together are needed to answer the question, but neither statement alone is sufficient
Ⓓ either statement by itself is sufficient to answer the question
Ⓔ not enough facts are given to answer the question

(C) Statement (1) is not sufficient to answer the question. Given only that ℓ_1 is parallel to the y axis, ℓ_1 could be any line parallel to the y axis. Similarly, ℓ_2 could be any line parallel to the x axis. Statement (2) is also insufficient to answer the question, for there are an infinite number of lines that pass through the point (4, 1) and an infinite number of lines that pass through the point (2, 7). Both statements taken together, however, are sufficient to answer the question. If you know the slope of a line (the angle at which the line cuts the axes) and one pair of coordinates, you have enough information to plot all of the points of that line, for there is only one line that will pass through any particular point with that particular slope (at the particular angle). Since both statements taken together answer the question, the correct classification for this item is (C).

(Here, since ℓ_1 is parallel to the y axis and includes the point [4, 1] all of the points of ℓ_1 have coordinates of the form [4, y]. Similarly, since ℓ_2 is parallel to the x axis and includes the point [2, 7], all of the points of ℓ_2 have coordinates of the form [x, 7]. So the two lines

intersect at the point having coordinates [4, 7].)

20. Working together but independently, Scott and Eric can address X envelopes in 18 hours. How long would it take Scott working alone to address X envelopes?

(1) In M minutes, Scott addresses three times as many envelopes as Eric addresses in M minutes.

(2) Eric can address X envelopes in 72 hours.

Ⓐ statement 1 alone is sufficient to answer the question, but statement 2 alone is not sufficient
Ⓑ statement 2 alone is sufficient to answer the question, but statement 1 alone is not sufficient
Ⓒ both statements together are needed to answer the question, but neither statement alone is sufficient
Ⓓ either statement by itself is sufficient to answer the question
Ⓔ not enough facts are given to answer the question

(D) Here the question stem provides you with some very powerful information, and it is this information that makes each statement sufficient. We can summarize the information provided by the stem with the following equation:

$$S + E = \frac{X}{18}$$

where S and E stand for the rates at which envelopes are addressed by Scott and Eric, respectively. And we can summarize the information provided by statement (1) with an equation:

$$S = 3E$$

Therefore, $E = \frac{S}{3}$. Substituting $\frac{S}{3}$ for E in the first equation:

$$S + \frac{S}{3} = \frac{X}{18}$$

$$\frac{4S}{3} = \frac{X}{18}$$

$$(18)\frac{4S}{3} = X$$

$$24S = X$$

$$S = \frac{X}{24}$$

Since X is the number of envelopes that must be addressed and S is the rate at which Scott addresses them, it will take Scott 24 hours to address X envelopes.

Now examine statement (2). This statement establishes that E (the rate at which Eric works) is $\frac{X}{72}$:

$$E = \frac{X}{72}$$

Substituting this value for S in our initial equation:

$$S + \frac{X}{72} = \frac{X}{18}$$

$$S = \frac{X}{18} - \frac{X}{72}$$

$$S = \frac{X}{24}$$

So Scott addresses X envelopes in 24 hours.

Since each statement is, by itself, sufficient to answer the question, this item should be classified as (D).

21. If a machine produces x units in t minutes and 30 seconds, what is its average operating speed in units per minute?

Ⓐ $\dfrac{t + 30}{x}$

Ⓑ $\dfrac{x}{t + 30}$

Ⓒ $tx + \dfrac{1}{2}x$

Ⓓ $\dfrac{t}{x} + \dfrac{1}{2}$

Ⓔ $\dfrac{x}{t + \frac{1}{2}}$

(E) The operating speed is expressed in units per minute. The machine produces x units in t minutes plus $\frac{1}{2}$ minute, so the average operating speed is $\frac{x}{t + \frac{1}{2}}$.

Alternatively, you could try substituting some numbers.

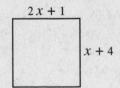

2x + 1

x + 4

22. If the figure above is a square, what is the perimeter of the figure?

Ⓐ 28   Ⓑ 16   Ⓒ 9   Ⓓ 3
Ⓔ Cannot be determined from the information given.

(A) First, a reminder not to pull a Watson. Since this is a difficult question, most people will not be able to answer it. It is therefore unlikely that the correct choice is (E).

The correct choice is (A). Since the figure is a square, the two sides are equal:

$$2x + 1 = x + 4$$

$$x = 3$$

Each side is $x + 4 = 3 + 4 = 7$, and the perimeter is $4(7) = 28$.

23. A certain dairy packing plant has two machines, P and Q, that process milk at constant rates of 30 gallons per minute and 45 gallons per minute, respectively. A day's run of milk can be processed by machine P operating alone in 6 hours, by machine Q operating alone in 4 hours, or by both machines operating simultaneously in 2.4 hours. If a day's run of milk is processed using machine Q alone for half the time and both machines together for half the time, how many hours does it take to complete the run?

Ⓐ 1.5   Ⓑ 3.0   Ⓒ 3.75   Ⓓ 4.2   Ⓔ 5.0

(B) This is a difficult problem. Here we can make use of Holmesian thinking. Machine Q alone can do the day's run in only 4 hours, and P and Q together can do the day's run in only 2.4 hours. If Q operates alone half the time and P and Q together half the time, then the running time will be less than that required for Q alone to do the job but longer than that required for P and Q working together to do the job. Thus, the time needed to do the run in the way described by the problem must be longer than 2.4 hours, but shorter than 4 hours. This reasoning disposes of choices (A), (D), and (E), and already we have a 50-50 chance of getting the right answer just by guessing.

Now we will work out the solution algebraically. Let T be the time it takes to do the run in the way described in the problem:

$0.5T(Q\text{'s rate}) + 0.5T(Q\text{'s Rate} + P\text{'s Rate}) = $ Day's Run

$0.5T(45\,\frac{\text{gal.}}{\text{min.}}) + 0.5T(75\,\frac{\text{gal.}}{\text{min.}}) = $ Day's Run

How much milk is processed in a day's run? According to the question stem, P working alone requires 6 hours to do a day's run. So a day's run must be

$6 \text{ hours} \times 60\,\frac{\text{min.}}{\text{hour.}} \times 30\,\frac{\text{gal.}}{\text{min.}} = 10{,}800 \text{ gallons}$

$0.5T(45) + 0.5T(75) = 10{,}800$

$22.50T + 37.50T = 10{,}800$

$60T = 10{,}800$

$T = 180$

The time required for the run is 180 minutes, or 3 hours.

24. If a commercial fertilizer called Green Grow is a mixture of compounds M and N, what percent of one bag of Green Grow, by weight, is nitrogen?

(1) By weight, Green Grow consists of 7 parts M and 5 parts N.

(2) By weight, 18 percent of compound N is nitrogen.

Ⓐ statement 1 alone is sufficient to answer the question, but statement 2 alone is not sufficient

Ⓑ statement 2 alone is sufficient to answer the question, but statement 1 alone is not sufficient

Ⓒ both statements together are needed to answer the question, but neither statement alone is sufficient

Ⓓ either statement by itself is sufficient to answer the question

Ⓔ not enough facts are given to answer the question

(E) Statement (1) alone is not sufficient to answer the question, because it provides no information about the nitrogen content of the compounds used in the fertilizer. Nor is statement (2) alone sufficient, even though it does provide information about the nitrogen content of one of the two compounds used in the fertilizer. Now we must ask whether the two statements together answer the question, and they do not. To find the nitrogen content of the fertilizer mixture, we would need not only the ratio of M and N but the nitrogen content of M as well as the nitrogen content of N.

25. What is the average number of runs per game scored by the Bluebirds last season?

(1) Last season, the Bluebirds played 120 games.

(2) Last season, the Bluebirds scored four runs in exactly $\frac{1}{5}$ of their games, five runs in exactly $\frac{3}{4}$ of their games, and nine runs in exactly $\frac{1}{20}$ of their games.

Ⓐ statement 1 alone is sufficient to answer the question, but statement 2 alone is not sufficient

Ⓑ statement 2 alone is sufficient to answer the question, but statement 1 alone is not sufficient

Ⓒ both statements together are needed to answer the question, but neither statement alone is sufficient

Ⓓ either statement by itself is sufficient to answer the question

Ⓔ not enough facts are given to answer the question

(B) Statement (1) is obviously not sufficient to answer the question, for it provides no information about runs scored. Next, look carefully at statement (2), ignoring entirely statement (1). Does statement (2) provide enough information to calculate the average number of runs per game? Yes, by setting up a weighted average:

$$\text{average} = \frac{4\left(\frac{1}{5}\right) + 5\left(\frac{3}{4}\right) + 9\left(\frac{1}{20}\right)}{1}$$

(Why a denominator of 1? Because $\frac{1}{5} + \frac{3}{4} + \frac{1}{20}$—the number of games—totals 1.) Now you should be able to see that it is possible to calculate the average using only statement (2). (It works out to five runs per game.)

Most people who miss this item probably classified it as a (C), believing mistakenly that it is necessary to know the total number of games to calculate the average. To avoid this mistake, make sure that you study each statement in isolation from the other. Here, when you study statement (2), don't be distracted by the fact that statement (1) provides the total number of games.

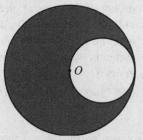

26. In the figure above, O is the center of the larger circle. If the radius of the larger circle is r, what is the area of the shaded portion of the figure?

Ⓐ $\frac{\pi}{2}$ Ⓑ $\frac{3\pi r}{4}$ Ⓒ $\frac{\pi r}{2}$ Ⓓ $\frac{\pi r^2}{2}$ Ⓔ $\frac{3\pi r^2}{4}$

(E) This is a typical shaded area problem. The area of the shaded portion of the figure is the area of the larger circle minus the area of the smaller circle:

Shaded Portion = Larger Circle – Smaller Circle

Since the radius of the larger circle is r, the larger circle has an area of πr^2. The radius of the larger circle is equal to the diameter of the smaller circle. Since the smaller circle has a diameter of r, it has a radius of $\frac{r}{2}$. And the area of the smaller circle is $\pi\left(\frac{r}{2}\right) = \frac{\pi r^2}{4}$. Now we can find the area of the shaded part of the figure:

$$\pi r - \frac{\pi r^2}{4} = \frac{3\pi r^2}{4}$$

27. If the cost of b books is d dollars, what is the cost, in dollars, of x books at the same rate?

Ⓐ xd Ⓑ $\frac{xd}{b}$ Ⓒ $\frac{bd}{x}$ Ⓓ bx Ⓔ $\frac{bx}{d}$

(B) You can set up an algebraic formula using a proportion:

$$\frac{b}{x} = \frac{d}{?}$$

where ? represents our unknown. Cross multiply:

$$b(?) = dx$$

Divide by b:

$$? = \frac{dx}{b}$$

Or you can assume numbers to test answer choices, a procedure you are familiar with by now.

28. A contest winner is entitled to a prize of $21,000. She may take the entire prize at once, or she may elect to receive 10 percent of the prize at once and payments of $900 a month for 24 consecutive months. How much more will she receive if she elects to take the prize in installments than if she elects to take the entire prize at once?

Ⓐ $600   Ⓑ $900   Ⓒ $2,400
Ⓓ $2,700   Ⓔ $3,000

(D) This problem is primarily a matter of bookkeeping. By taking the installment plan, the prize winner receives

$$0.10(\$21,000) + 24(\$900) = \$23,700$$

And

$$\$23,700 - \$21,000 = \$2,700$$

So she receives $2,700 more by choosing the installment plan.

29. In a certain election, how many votes did Smith receive for public office?

   (1) Smith received 5,676 votes, or 22 percent of the votes cast in District 1, and District 1 accounted for 15 percent of all votes cast in the election.

   (2) Smith received 45 percent of all votes cast in districts other than District 1.

Ⓐ statement 1 alone is sufficient to answer the question, but statement 2 alone is not sufficient
Ⓑ statement 2 alone is sufficient to answer the question, but statement 1 alone is not sufficient
Ⓒ both statements together are needed to answer the question, but neither statement alone is sufficient
Ⓓ either statement by itself is sufficient to answer the question
Ⓔ not enough facts are given to answer the question

(C) Statement (1) is not sufficient to answer the question. Statement (1) does provide information from which you can deduce the total number of votes cast (22 percent of 15 percent of Total Votes = 5,676), but (1) does not tell you what share of the non-District I votes Smith received. Statement (2) alone is not sufficient to answer the question, but statement (2)

supplies the information missing from (1). So both statements taken together are sufficient to answer the question. (Since 22 percent of 15 percent of Total Votes = 5,676, Total Votes = 172,000. Eighty-five percent of the total of 172,000 votes were cast outside of District I: 85% of 172,000 = 146,200. And Smith got 45 percent of those, or 65,790. So Smith's total vote count was 5,676 + 65,790 = 71,466.)

30. Is p a prime number?

   (1) $p + 2$ is a prime number.

   (2) $10 < p < 20$

Ⓐ statement 1 alone is sufficient to answer the question, but statement 2 alone is not sufficient
Ⓑ statement 2 alone is sufficient to answer the question, but statement 1 alone is not sufficient
Ⓒ both statements together are needed to answer the question, but neither statement alone is sufficient
Ⓓ either statement by itself is sufficient to answer the question
Ⓔ not enough facts are given to answer the question

(E) Statement (1) is not sufficient to answer the question, for there are many prime numbers p such that $p + 2$ is also a prime. For example, 1 and 3, 3 and 5, 5 and 7, 11 and 13, 101 and 103, and so on. Nor is Statement (2) sufficient to answer the question because there are four primes between 10 and 20: 11, 13, 17, and 19. Even both statements taken together are not sufficient to answer the question, for there are two primes between 10 and 20 such that the prime number plus 2 is also a prime: 11 (11 + 2 = 13); and 17 (17 + 2 = 19). Since the two statements do not fix a single, unique value for p, the correct classification of this item is (E).

31. In one classroom exactly one-half the seats are occupied. In another classroom with double the seating capacity of the first, exactly three-quarters of the seats are occupied. If the students from both rooms are transferred into a third, empty classroom that has a seating capacity exactly equal to the first two combined, what fraction of the seats in the third classroom is occupied?

Ⓐ $\frac{1}{4}$ Ⓑ $\frac{1}{3}$ Ⓒ $\frac{3}{8}$ Ⓓ $\frac{2}{3}$ Ⓔ $\frac{3}{4}$

(D) We are not told the actual capacities of the classrooms, so we can use an algebraic variable. Let c represent the capacity of the first classroom. On that assumption, the capacity of the second classroom is $2c$, and the capacity of the third classroom is the combined capacities of the first two: $c + 2c = 3c$. In the first classroom, one-half of the seats are occupied, or $\frac{1}{2}c$. In the second classroom, $\frac{3}{4}$ of $2c$ seats are occupied, or $\frac{3}{2}c$ seats. Together that makes:

$$\frac{1}{2}c + \frac{3}{2}c = 2c$$

Since the third and largest classroom has a capacity of $3c$, $2c$ out of $3c$ of its seats are filled:

$$\frac{2c}{3c} = \frac{2}{3}$$

As an alternative, you could use the Holmesian strategy of assuming some numbers. Assume that the first classroom seats 100 people. (Why 100? It's large enough to avoid the problem of fractions of students, and it's not so large as to be too cumbersome.) On the assumption that the first classroom seats 100, the second classroom seats 200, and the third classroom seats 300; and there are 50 students in the first classroom and 150 in the second. When those 200 students are transferred into the third classroom, 200 out of the 300 seats will be occupied; that is, $\frac{2}{3}$ of the seats will be occupied.

32. If a bag of marbles contains only red, yellow, and blue marbles, and if there are twice as many yellow marbles as red marbles and three times as many blue marbles as yellow marbles in the bag, which of the following could be the number of marbles in the bag?

Ⓐ 24　Ⓑ 56　Ⓒ 80　Ⓓ 99　Ⓔ 115

(D) The question tests your understanding of the concept of ratio parts. The ratio of yellow to red marbles is 2:1, and the ratio of blue to yellow marbles is 3:1. To find the ratio of blue to red marbles, you must do something that is similar to the procedure for finding a common denominator for adding fractions. Since the middle term is yellow marbles, multiply the second ratio by 2, so that the yellow marbles term is the same number in each ratio: blue: yellow = 3:1 = 6:2. So the ratio blue:yellow:red = 6:2:1. Since there are 6 + 2 + 1 = 0 parts in this ratio, the number of marbles must be divisible by 9. The only answer choice divisible by 9 is (D), 99. If there are 99 marbles in the bag, then there are 11 red marbles, 22 yellow marbles, and 66 blue marbles.

33. The manager of a produce market purchased a quantity of tomatoes for $0.80 per pound. Due to improper handling, 10 percent of the tomatoes, by weight, were ruined and discarded. At what price per pound should the manager sell the remaining tomatoes if she wishes to make a profit on the sale of the tomatoes equal to 8 percent of the cost of the tomatoes?

Ⓐ $0.94　Ⓑ $0.96　Ⓒ $0.98
Ⓓ $1.00　Ⓔ $1.20

(B) To solve the problem, we will use the letter T to represent the number of pounds of tomatoes and P to represent the price per pound that the manager should

charge. Now we will set up an equation. The general equation that governs all problems such as this is

Net = Gross – Cost

Cost here is T pounds of tomatoes at $0.80 per pound, which is $0.8T$:

Net = Gross – $0.8T$

The problem stipulates that Net should be 8 percent of the cost, so Net will be 8 percent of $0.8T = 0.064T$:

$$0.064T = \text{Gross} - 0.8T$$

As for Gross, the store will sell the tomatoes that remain at P dollars per pound, but only 90 percent of the tomatoes (by weight) are left. So the Gross will be

$0.9T(P)$
$$0.064T = 0.9T(P) - 0.8T$$

Now solve for P:

$$0.064T + 0.8T = 0.9T(P)$$

$$0.864 = 0.9T(P)$$

$$P = 0.96$$

Alternatively, you could assume a concrete number for the tomatoes. Assume that the store bought 1,000 pounds of tomatoes at $0.80 per pound, for a cost of $800. 100 pounds were ruined, so the manager has only 900 pounds to sell. She wishes to make a profit equal to 8 percent of $800, or $64, so she must sell the remaining tomatoes for $800 + $64 = $864. Thus, the price per pound should be $864 ÷ $900 = $0.96.

34. In a certain card game, an ace counts one point, face cards count ten points, and all other cards count their face values. A player must play at least one card on each turn, and his score on a turn is determined by the total point value of the cards played. If a player holds the cards shown above, how many different point totals are possible for him on his next turn?

Ⓐ 5　Ⓑ 6　Ⓒ 10　Ⓓ 20　Ⓔ 21

(E) One way of solving this problem is simply to work your way through all of the possible combinations of the points offered. For example, it is possible to score just 1 (with the ace), or 2 (with the deuce), or 5 (with the ace and the 4), or 7 (with the ace and the 6), and so on.

A more systematic approach is to ask yourself, is it possible to score 1? Yes. 2? Yes. 3? Yes. 4? Yes. 5? Yes. 6? Yes. And so on until you get to 21, the maximum that the player can score.

An even more elegant approach is to recognize that the even-numbered cards can combine to score all of the possible even numbers between 2 and 20, inclusive. Then the ace (which counts 1) makes it possible (using combinations of cards) to score all of the odd numbers between 1 and 21, inclusive. So there are 21 possible scores, 1–21, inclusive.

35. What percent of the students at College X are in-state students?

(1) At College X, the ratio of in-state students to out-of-state students is 3 to 7.

(2) Exactly 50 percent of the women and 25 percent of the men who are students at College X are in-state students.

Ⓐ statement 1 alone is sufficient to answer the question, but statement 2 alone is not sufficient

Ⓑ statement 2 alone is sufficient to answer the question, but statement 1 alone is not sufficient

Ⓒ both statements together are needed to answer the question, but neither statement alone is sufficient

Ⓓ either statement by itself is sufficient to answer the question

Ⓔ not enough facts are given to answer the question

(A) Statement (1) is sufficient to answer the question. As was pointed out in the lesson on Data Sufficiency, if you know the ratio between two quantities, you also know what percent one quantity is of the other, and also what percent each quantity is of the total. (In-state students account for $\frac{3}{10}$, or 30 percent of all students.) Statement (2), however, is not sufficient to answer the question. (2) establishes that the ratio of in-state students to total student population is

$$\frac{0.50W + 0.25M}{W + M}$$

where W and M represent the total number of women and total number of men students, respectively. But since you don't know the relationship between W and M, this information is not sufficient to answer the question asked. For example, if there are equal numbers of men and women at the college, then 37.5 percent of the students are in-state students. If $W = M$, then the ratio is

$$\frac{0.50W + 0.25W}{W + W} = \frac{0.75W}{2W} = 0.375 = 37.5\%$$

But if there are twice as many men as women, then in-state students account for $33\frac{1}{3}\%$ of all students. If $2W = M$, then

$$\frac{0.5W + 0.25W(2W)}{W + (2W)} = \frac{0.5W + 0.5W}{3W} = \frac{W}{3W} =$$

$$33\frac{1}{3}\%$$

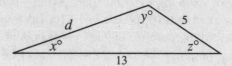

36. What is the area of the triangle above?

(1) $x + z = 90°$

(2) $169 - d^2 = 25$

Ⓐ statement 1 alone is sufficient to answer the question, but statement 2 alone is not sufficient

Ⓑ statement 2 alone is sufficient to answer the question, but statement 1 alone is not sufficient

Ⓒ both statements together are needed to answer the question, but neither statement alone is sufficient

Ⓓ either statement by itself is sufficient to answer the question

Ⓔ not enough facts are given to answer the question

(D) Statement (1) establishes that the triangle is a right triangle and that angle y is the right angle. Therefore it is possible to find the length of d using the Pythagorean Theorem. Once you know the length of d, you can use d and 5 as altitude and base to find the area of the triangle.

$$13^2 = d^2 + 5^2$$

$$169 = d^2 + 25$$

$$d^2 = 144$$

$$d = 12$$

The area of the triangle is $\frac{1}{2}(5)(12) = 30$.

Statement (2) is also sufficient to answer the question, for it also establishes that the sides of the triangle fit the Pythagorean Theorem, so the triangle must be a right triangle:

$$169 - d^2 = 25$$

$$13^2 - d^2 = 5^2$$

$$13^2 = 5^2 + d^2$$

Using the same reasoning as was applied to statement (1), it is possible to find the area of the triangle with this information.

37. For a certain calendar quarter, monthly sales by Vendor X were less in December than they were in October. Total monthly sales by Vendor X changed by what percent from October to November?

   (1)   During October, Vendor X had total sales of $10,500, and during December, Vendor X had total sales of $9,000.

   (2)   The decline in total sales from November to December was equal to the decline in total sales from October to December.

Ⓐ statement 1 alone is sufficient to answer the question, but statement 2 alone is not sufficient

Ⓑ statement 2 alone is sufficient to answer the question, but statement 1 alone is not sufficient

Ⓒ both statements together are needed to answer the question, but neither statement alone is sufficient

Ⓓ either statement by itself is sufficient to answer the question

Ⓔ not enough facts are given to answer the question

(B) Statement (1) is insufficient to answer the question because it provides no information about the specific period October to November. Statement (2), however, is sufficient, but you have to give the statement a careful reading to see this. Statement (2) says:

Nov. – Dec. = Oct. – Dec.

Nov. = Oct.

But for this to be true, (Oct. – Nov.) must be zero. So Statement (2) answers the question: there was no change.

Sample GMAT CAT 2

Verbal Section

41 Questions—75 Minutes

General Directions: To simulate the experience of taking the CAT, answer each question in order. Do not skip any questions, and do not go back to questions you have already answered.

Directions for sentence correction questions: In questions of this type, either part or all of a sentence is underlined. The sentence is followed by five ways of wording the underlined part. The first answer choice always repeats the original; the other answer choices are different. If you think that the original phrasing is the best, choose the first answer. If you think one of the other answer choices is the best, select that choice. Indicate your answer by blackening the circle next to your choice.

This section tests your ability to identify correct and effective expression. Evaluate the answer choices by the requirements of standard written English. Pay attention to elements of grammar, diction, (choice of words), and sentence construction. Select the answer choice that *best* expresses the meaning of the original sentence. The correct choice will be clear and precise and free of awkwardness, wordiness, or ambiguity.

Directions for critical reasoning questions: Questions of this type ask you to analyze and evaluate the reasoning presented in short paragraphs or passages. For some questions, all of the answer choices may conceivably be answers to the question asked. You should select the *best* answer to the question; that is, an answer that does not require you to make assumptions that violate commonsense standards by being implausible, redundant, irrelevant or inconsistent. Indicate your answer by blackening the circle next to your choice.

Directions for reading comprehension questions: Each passage is followed by questions or incomplete statements about it. Once you have read the passage, answer the question based upon what is stated or implied. Indicate your answer by blackening the circle next to your choice.

---

1. Henry David Thoreau was a philosopher as well as a naturalist; Gandhi read *Civil Disobedience* in 1906 and made it a major document in his struggle for Indian independence.

    Ⓐ read *Civil Disobedience* in 1906 and made it
    Ⓑ read *Civil Disobedience* in 1906 in order to make it into
    Ⓒ read *Civil Disobedience* and, in 1906, made it
    Ⓓ would have read *Civil Disobedience* in 1906 and would have made it
    Ⓔ reading *Civil Disobedience* in 1906 and making it

2. Some homeowners prefer gas heat to oil because there is no need for deliveries or no large storage tanks, with its being cheaper in most places.

    Ⓐ oil because there is no need for deliveries or no large storage tanks, with its being cheaper in most places
    Ⓑ oil because there is no need for deliveries or large storage tanks, and in most places gas is cheaper
    Ⓒ oil, being that there are no deliveries, no large storage tanks, and it is cheaper in most places
    Ⓓ oil, needing no deliveries or large storage tanks, and anyways gas is cheaper in most places
    Ⓔ oil, since gas is cheaper in most places and has no need of deliveries or large storage tanks

3. Although we now blame most catastrophes on "nature," thinkers in the Middle Ages thought every fire, earthquake, and disease to be the result of divine anger.

    Ⓐ Although we now blame most catastrophes on "nature,"
    Ⓑ Most catastrophes are now blamed on nature by us, and
    Ⓒ We now blame nature for catastrophes, moreover,
    Ⓓ Although nature is now blamed for most catastrophes by us,
    Ⓔ Now blaming most catastrophes on nature,

GO ON TO NEXT PAGE →

A Supreme Court justice once observed, "We are not the last word because we are infallible; we are infallible because we are the last word."

4. Which of the following most closely parallels the logic of the statement above?

(A) Congressperson: Although I may make some mistakes, I will always use my best judgment to protect the interests of my constituents.

(B) Teacher: My ideas may not always be correct, but students obey me because I am the teacher.

(C) Doctor: Doctors make life and death decisions every day, so we are the most powerful judges in this society.

(D) Lawyer: I cannot assure my client of victory, because I cannot predict with certainty what a judge will do.

(E) Pilot: In an emergency, the ground control crew is not in the plane with me, so I have to make the final decision and hope I have not made a mistake.

It is truly folly that when we are sick in fortune—often the surfeit of our own behavior—we make guilty of our disasters the sun, the moon, and the stars, as if we were villains of necessity, fools by heavenly compulsion, knaves and treacheries by spherical predominance, drunkards, liars, and adulterers by enforced obedience of planetary influence, and all that we are evil in by a divine thrusting on.

5. It can be inferred that the speaker above believes which of the following?

I. There is no substance to astrology. ✓

II. Many people are reluctant to accept the consequences of their actions.

III. Most people are evil.

(A) I only   (B) II only   (C) I and II only
(D) I and III only   (E) I, II, and III

Philosophical ideals, as they find embodiment in political action, cannot be confined to a single geographical region. This is particularly true where two countries undergo a period of parallel development. The seed will necessarily be blown to other regions where, if the conditions are favorable, it will take root. Nowhere is this seen better than in the Irish Revolution of the late 18th century. The seed of revolution blown from France found fertile ground and favorable climatic conditions in Ireland, so it flowered.

6. Which of the following, if true, most weakens the argument above?

(A) French political treatises were not widely read by most of Ireland's population.

(B) Conditions similar to those in Ireland and France existed at the same time in Poland and Austria, but those countries did not experience revolutions.

(C) Much of the revolutionary rhetoric in Ireland was drawn from the American Revolution.

(D) A substantial number of people in Ireland opposed the revolution.

(E) The revolt in Ireland ultimately failed because the English were too powerful.

Questions 7–9

The socialization process in America has historically been characterized by the interaction of clearly structured, well-organized groups that share a sense of mission about the future of the nation and codes of behavior with roots in common principals. Americans were a diverse people, but communities were bound by religious beliefs, ethnic backgrounds, and strong family relationships. The old configuration of socializing institutions no longer functions in the same way. Mobility is one factor in the changing picture. One fifth of all Americans change their residences every year, but they do not "pack" their culture. They simply move, breaking old community ties. There is no migration, just movement—motion without melody.

A second factor is depersonalization. Emerson once wrote that an institution is the lengthened shadow of one man. Today's institution is more likely to be the lengthened shadow of itself. The breakdown of the old configuration requires a reconceptualization of the whole socialization process, but the very fact of breakdown means that fewer and fewer people even understand what is required of a socialization process. By now the process of social decompression may be irreversible.

7. The main purpose of this passage is to

(A) describe the common roots of American citizens

(B) suggest patterns of behavior appropriate to the new social climate

(C) identify factors contributing to the breakdown of the socialization process

(D) describe the declining influence of religion in American life

(E) argue for a substantial change in public school curricula

8. The phrase "motion without melody" might be used to refer to which of the following events?

  Ⓐ Traveling abroad as part of a student exchange program

  Ⓑ Formation of ethnic communities in urban areas

  Ⓒ Relocation to a distant city to accept a job offer

  Ⓓ Moving to a bigger house in the same neighborhood

  Ⓔ Immigration of large groups of Europeans to America

9. The author cites Emerson in order to

  Ⓐ dramatize the power of bureaucracy in our society

  Ⓑ explain the importance of individual freedom

  Ⓒ demonstrate the need for the study of humanities in American schools

  Ⓓ highlight the progress that society has made since Emerson

  Ⓔ argue that all institutions should be run by an individual

10. To prove that acridines kill bacteria through asphyxiation rather than starvation (as is the case with sulfa drugs), Dr. Martin nearly spent ten years building an artificial chemical wall around the bacteria that deprives them of essential food.

  Ⓐ Dr. Martin nearly spent ten years building an artificial chemical wall around the bacteria

  Ⓑ building an artificial chemical wall around the bacteria was nearly Dr. Martin's task for ten years

  Ⓒ Dr. Martin spent nearly ten years building an artificial chemical wall around the bacteria

  Ⓓ nearly spending ten years, Dr. Martin built an artificial chemical wall around the bacteria

  Ⓔ ten years were nearly spent by Dr. Martin building an artificial chemical wall around the bacteria

11. The highly controversial proposal was voted against by the governor and whomever else favored conservation.

  Ⓐ The highly controversial proposal was voted against by the governor and whomever else favored conservation.

  Ⓑ The highly controversial proposal was voted against by the governor and whoever else favored conservation.

  Ⓒ The governor and everyone else who favored conservation voted against the highly controversial proposal.

  Ⓓ The governor and anyone else who favored conservation voted against the highly controversial proposal.

  Ⓔ Favoring conservation, the governor and everyone else voted against the highly controversial proposal.

12. Credit cards are now accepted in exchange for many goods and services around the world and in some countries, like the Americans, is used even more widely than cash.

  Ⓐ like the Americans, is used even more widely than

  Ⓑ like that of America, is used even more widely than

  Ⓒ as in America, are used even more widely than

  Ⓓ such as America, are used even more widely than

  Ⓔ such as America, are used even more widely as

If Peter graduated from college, he must have studied a foreign language.

13. Which of the following, if true, is sufficient to guarantee the truth of the statement above?

  Ⓐ Only college students study foreign languages.

  Ⓑ All foreign languages are studied by some college students.

  Ⓒ All college students are allowed to study a foreign language.

  Ⓓ All college students are required to study a foreign language before graduation.

  Ⓔ Some foreign languages are studied by no college students.

At a recent art auction, a large canvas painted in many colors sold for $100,000. At the same auction, a simple pen-and-ink drawing by the same artist sold for $105,000, because it was more beautiful. Whatever it is that is beauty, that is, whatever it is that we prize so highly, it is not necessarily the product of a lifetime of work but rather the gift of a moment.

14. The speaker above is making what point?

  Ⓐ Art collectors often do not know the true value of a work of art.

  Ⓑ Prices for rare objects of art are governed by market forces.

  Ⓒ What one person considers beautiful, another may consider not beautiful.

  Ⓓ Artistic achievement requires creative insight and not just technique.

  Ⓔ There is a direct correlation between the price of a work of art and the time the artist required to produce the object.

GO ON TO NEXT PAGE ⟹

All bushes that bear red roses have thorns. This bush has no thorns. Therefore, this bush cannot bear roses.

15. The logic of the argument above is most nearly paralleled by which of the following?

Ⓐ All Sandarac automobiles have three wheels. This car has three wheels. Therefore, this car is a Sandarac automobile.

Ⓑ All brides wear white. This woman is not wearing white. Therefore, this woman must be the maid of honor.

Ⓒ All professional tennis players use metal rackets. This player does not use a metal racket. Therefore, this player is not a professional tennis player.

Ⓓ All Scottish ivy is heliotropic. This plant is not heliotropic. Therefore, this plant is not ivy.

Ⓔ All pencils have rubber erasers. This eraser is not attached to a pencil. Therefore, this eraser is not made of rubber.

Questions 16–18

The health-care economy is replete with unusual and even unique economic relationships. One of the least understood involves the peculiar roles of producer or "provider" and purchaser or "consumer" in the typical doctor-patient relationship. In most sectors of the economy, it is the seller who attempts to attract a potential buyer with various inducements of price, quality, and utility, and it is the buyer who makes the decision. Where circumstances permit the buyer no choice because there is effectively only one seller and the product is relatively essential, government usually asserts monopoly and places the industry under price and other regulations. Neither of these conditions prevails in most of the health-care industry.

In the health-care industry, the doctor-patient relationship is the mirror image of the ordinary relationship between producer and consumer. Once an individual has chosen to see a physician—and even then there may be no real choice—it is the physician who usually makes all significant purchasing decisions: whether the patient should return "next Wednesday," whether X-rays are needed, whether drugs should be prescribed, etc. It is a rare and sophisticated patient who will challenge such professional decisions or raise in advance questions about price, especially when the ailment is regarded as serious.

This is particularly significant in relation to hospital care. The physician must certify the need for hospitalization, determine what procedures will be performed, and announce when the patient may be discharged. The patient may be consulted about some of these decisions, but in the main it is the doctor's judgments that are final. Little wonder then that in the eyes of the hospital it is the physician who is the real "consumer." As a consequence, the medical staff represents the "power center" in hospital policy and decision-making, not the administration.

Although usually there are in this situation four identifiable participants—the physician, the hospital, the patient, and the payer (generally an insurance carrier or government)—the physician makes the essential decisions for all of them. The hospital becomes an extension of the physician; the payer generally meets most of the bona fide bills generated by the physician/hospital; and for the most part the patient plays a passive role. In routine or minor illnesses, or just plain worries, the patient's options are, of course, much greater with respect to use and price. In illnesses that are of some significance, however, such choices tend to evaporate, and it is for these illnesses that the bulk of the health-care dollar is spent. We estimate that about 75–80 percent of health-care expenditures are determined by physicians, not patients. For this reason, economy measures directed at patients or the general public are relatively ineffective.

16. It can be inferred that doctors are able to determine hospital policies because

Ⓐ it is doctors who generate income for the hospital

Ⓑ most of a patient's bills are paid by his health insurance

Ⓒ hospital administrators lack the expertise to question medical decisions

Ⓓ a doctor is ultimately responsible for a patient's health

Ⓔ some patients might refuse to accept their physician's advice

17. The author is most probably leading up to

Ⓐ a proposal to control medical costs

Ⓑ a discussion of a new medical treatment

Ⓒ an analysis of the causes of inflation in the United States

Ⓓ a study of lawsuits against doctors for malpractice

Ⓔ a comparison of hospitals and factories

18. With which of the following statements would the author be likely to agree?

I. Most patients are reluctant to object to the course of treatment prescribed by a doctor or to question the cost of the services.

II. The more serious the illness of a patient, the less likely it is that the patient will object to the course of treatment prescribed or to question the cost of services.

III. The payer, whether insurance carrier or the government, is less likely to acquiesce to demands for payment when the illness of the patient is regarded as serious.

Ⓐ I only Ⓑ II only Ⓒ I and II only

Ⓓ II and III only Ⓔ I, II, and III

19. Persistence of vision, <u>the condition when your eyes bridge</u> the gaps of darkness between flashes of light, explains the seeming magic produced by the strobo-scope, an instrument that appears to freeze the swiftest motions while they are still going on.

Ⓐ the condition when your eyes bridge
Ⓑ when your eyes bridge
Ⓒ the condition of your eyes bridging
Ⓓ which occurs when your eyes bridge
Ⓔ occurring when your eyes bridge

20. <u>The delivery in large volume of certain welfare services are costly on account of the large number of public contact employees that are required by this.</u>

Ⓐ The delivery in large volume of certain welfare services are costly on account of the large number of public contact employees that are required by this.
Ⓑ The delivery of a large volume of certain welfare services are costly on account of the large number of public contact employees that this requires.
Ⓒ The delivery in large volume of certain welfare services is costly because of the large number of public contact employees that is required.
Ⓓ The delivery of certain welfare services in large volume is costly on account of the large numbers of public contact employees that is required.
Ⓔ To deliver certain welfare services in large volume is costly on account of that this requires a large number of public service employees.

21. Most department stores offer customers the option <u>that you may exchange your</u> purchases within ten days.

Ⓐ that you may exchange your
Ⓑ to exchange your
Ⓒ of exchanging your
Ⓓ that exchanges their
Ⓔ of exchanging

The single greatest weakness of American parties is their inability to achieve cohesion in the legislature. Although there is some measure of party unity, it is not uncommon for the majority party to be unable to implement important legislation. The unity is strongest during the election campaigns. After the primary elections, the losing candidates all promise their support to the party nominee. By the time the Congress convenes, however, the unity has dissipated. This phenomenon is attributable to the frag-mented nature of political parties. The national committees are no more than feudal lords who receive nominal fealty from their vassals. A congressperson builds his or her power upon a local base. Consequently, he or she is likely to be responsive to locally based special-interest groups. Evi-dence of this is seen in the differences in voting patterns between the upper and lower houses. In the Senate, where terms are longer, there is more party unity.

22. Which of the following, if true, would most strengthen the author's argument?

Ⓐ On 30 key issues, 18 of the 67 majority party members in the Senate voted against the party leaders.
Ⓑ On 30 key issues, 70 of the 305 majority party members in the House voted against the party leaders.
Ⓒ On 30 key issues, over half of the members of the minority party in both houses voted with the majority party against the leaders of the minority party.
Ⓓ On 30 key legislative proposals introduced by the president, only eight passed both houses.
Ⓔ On 30 key legislative proposals introduced by a president whose party controlled a majority of both houses, only four passed both houses.

Hamlet: Watchman, tell me of the night.
Horatio: I see nothing, my Prince.
Hamlet: Your eyes are much better than mine. In this darkness, I can scarcely see anything.

23. It can be inferred that the first speaker in the exchange above believes that

Ⓐ Horatio is not really the watchman
Ⓑ nothing is something that can be seen
Ⓒ something is more easily seen in darkness than in light
Ⓓ the night conceals a serious danger
Ⓔ the watchman is concealing something from him

GO ON TO NEXT PAGE

Senator: It is my understanding that you have memberships in several private clubs that do not allow anyone other than members of the white race to join. Can you reconcile this fact with your desire to be confirmed as Director of the Bureau of Racial Equality?

Nominee: Senator, that is no longer true. Last week I resigned my membership in those clubs.

24. Which of the following is the best explanation for why the senator might find the response to his question unsatisfactory?

   (A) The senator was concerned not so much with the nominee's present affiliations as with the nominee's attitudes on race relations.
   (B) The nominee is attempting to conceal his affiliations in clubs that refuse to accept non-whites for membership.
   (C) The nominee attempts to escape moral responsibility for his actions on the grounds that he was unaware that the clubs discriminated against non-whites.
   (D) The nominee believes incorrectly that the senator himself endorses the existence of clubs that select membership on the basis of race.
   (E) The nominee believes that the senator believes that there is no inconsistency between such memberships and being Director of the Bureau of Racial Equality.

Questions 25–27

In the course of billions of years, millions of stars may occasionally be concentrated into a region only a few light years across, causing them to collide with one another. Some of these collisions occur at high speeds, in which case the stars are partially or completely torn apart; while others are gentle bumps, and the stars coalesce. The bigger the star gets, the more likely it is to be hit again and the faster it grows until it reaches instability, collapses on itself, and forms a black hole. Once formed, a central "seed" black hole grows mainly through the accretion of gas accumulated in the nucleus, gas obtained from other disrupted stars, from supernova explosions, from stars torn apart by the gravitational field of the black hole, or from gas falling into the galaxy from outside. Perhaps an entire galaxy can collide with another galaxy, resulting in the transfer of large amounts of gas from one galaxy to another, providing a plentiful supply of gas for black holes.

   When most of the stars and gas in the core of a galaxy have been swallowed up by the black hole, the nucleus of the galaxy settles down to a relatively quiet existence. This is probably the state of the nucleus of our own galaxy, every hundred million years or so it may flare up to a brightness one hundred times its present level when a globular cluster or especially large gas cloud spirals into the nucleus.

25. This passage deals primarily with the
   (A) formation of galaxies
   (B) creation of black holes
   (C) life cycle of stars
   (D) physical properties of black holes
   (E) movement of interstellar gases

26. The author implies that
   (A) some galaxies have no black hole
   (B) the black hole at the center of our galaxy is extinct
   (C) our galaxy has never collided with any other galaxy
   (D) black holes eventually disappear
   (E) larger stars are less stable than smaller ones

27. The author's use of the word *seed* to describe newly formed black holes is most nearly like which of the following?
   (A) Plant seeds that are placed in the ground to grow into mature plants
   (B) The seed of an idea that is then developed by an individual thinker
   (C) A seed bed where large numbers of young plants are carefully cultivated
   (D) A seed pod that will burst, distributing great quantities of seeds
   (E) Government-supplied seed money for a project that will attract money from other sources

28. The Russian music of the nineteenth century <u>is richer and more varied than France</u>.
   (A) is richer and more varied than France
   (B) is richer and more varied than the music of France
   (C) is more rich and varied than France
   (D) is more rich and more varied than is the music of France
   (E) is more rich and varied in comparison to France

29. Many physicists think that at some time in the next century <u>we will not only discover life in other galaxies but will also communicate with them</u>.
   (A) we will not only discover life in other galaxies but will also communicate with them
   (B) we will discover not only life in other galaxies, but be able to communicate with it
   (C) we will not only discover life in other galaxies but we will be able to communicate with it
   (D) that not only will we be able to discover life in other galaxies but be able to communicate to them as well
   (E) not only to find life in other galaxies but to communicate with it as well

30. The most chance of being an insomniac is not the overworked executive or the student overwhelmed by studies but the bored housewife who feels unfilled.

   Ⓐ The most chance of being an insomniac is not the overworked executive or the student overwhelmed by studies but the bored housewife who feels unfilled.

   Ⓑ The highest degree of insomnia is not experienced by the overworked executive nor by the student overwhelmed by studies, but by the bored housewife who feels unfulfilled.

   Ⓒ Most insomniacs are not overworked executives or students overwhelmed by studies, yet they are bored housewives who feel unfulfilled.

   Ⓓ The greater degree of insomniacs are bored housewives who feels unfulfilled and not over-worked executives nor are they students over-whelmed by their studies.

   Ⓔ Insomniacs are, for the most part, bored house-wives who feel unfulfilled, not overworked executives or students overwhelmed by their studies.

Questions 31–32
Some snakes are amphibians.
Some amphibians are intelligent.
Some intelligent creatures are not snakes. ⋏

31. If the statements above are true, which of the follow-ing could also be true?

   Ⓐ No amphibians are intelligent.
   Ⓑ No snakes are amphibians.
   Ⓒ No intelligent creatures are amphibians
   Ⓓ No amphibians are snakes.
   Ⓔ All snakes are intelligent.

32. If the statements above are true, which of the follow-ing must be false?

   Ⓐ All snakes are not intelligent.
   Ⓑ All intelligent creatures are snakes. ⟶
   Ⓒ A rat is an amphibious snake.
   Ⓓ All amphibians are snakes.
   Ⓔ All intelligent creatures are amphibians.

I recall my first encounter with philosophy. Professor Elmendorff, who taught all of the introductory philosophy classes at the University, strode into the room and began, "The end of any philosophical inquiry is truth. Now, you may wonder why it is that a university, whose very reason for existence is the dissemination of learning, would offer a class in philosophy—not only allowing but even inviting the wolf into the fold. This has always been a great mystery to me."

33. It can be inferred that Professor Elmendorff believes that

   Ⓐ philosophy should not be a required course at the University
   Ⓑ philosophy has few if any practical applications
   Ⓒ truth and learning are not the same thing
   Ⓓ truth can be discovered only by the process of learning
   Ⓔ learning is more important than philosophy

34. According to a recent study by the Mayor's Task Force, the amount of homeless people in the city has tripled in the last ten years.

   Ⓐ the amount of homeless people in the city has
   Ⓑ the number of homeless people in the city has
   Ⓒ the amount of homeless people in the city have
   Ⓓ the number of homeless people in the city having
   Ⓔ the number of those people who are homeless in the city has

35. Many health-care professionals now advocate race walking as a form of exercise because it burns as many calories as jogging, works muscle groups that jogging does not, and the chances of stress-related injuries are reduced.

   Ⓐ and the chances of stress-related injuries are reduced
   Ⓑ and reduces the chances of stress-related injury
   Ⓒ reducing the chances of stress-related injury
   Ⓓ and the chances of a stress-related injury get reduced
   Ⓔ with a reduction of the chances of a stress-related injury

GO ON TO NEXT PAGE

Al: Why did you return my lawn mower with a broken blade?

David: First, I never borrowed your mower. Second, when I returned it, it wasn't broken. Third, when I borrowed it, it was already broken.

36. Which of the following best describes the weakness in David's response?

    Ⓐ It is internally inconsistent.
    Ⓑ It makes an unproved assumption.
    Ⓒ It contains circular reasoning.
    Ⓓ It leads to no definite conclusion.
    Ⓔ It seeks to evade the issue.

It is not always the case that the whole is equal to the sum of the parts. For example, we speak of Impressionist painting. The elements of such a painting are a certain choice of colors, the use of particular brush strokes and other techniques of paint application, and the selection of a certain subject matter. But the painting cannot be reduced to just these elements.

37. Which of the following would the speaker regard as most similar to the notion of Impressionist painting?

    Ⓐ The steps in a geometry proof
    Ⓑ The volumes in an encyclopedia
    Ⓒ The notion of a national character
    Ⓓ The instructions for assembling a toy
    Ⓔ The molecules that make up an atom

Although alcohol seems to make you sleepy, it is actually an antisoporific.

38. The logic of the statement above is most closely paralleled by the logic of which of the following statements?

    Ⓐ Although some people still believe in God, most people have accepted science as supreme.
    Ⓑ Although sea water will not quench thirst, it will extinguish fires.
    Ⓒ Although dry ice seems to burn the skin, it is actually quite cold.
    Ⓓ Although all states have a capital, no state has the same capital as any other.
    Ⓔ Although heroin induces a state of euphoria, the drug is highly addictive.

Questions 39–41

A National Industrial Conference Board study prepared by Bock and Forkas examined the relationship between average productivity measured in terms of labor inputs of the top companies in an industry and other companies in the same industry and the relationship between industry concentration and industry productivity. The study shows that, on the average, the top companies in an industry had higher rates of productivity than the remaining companies in the same industry and that the industries with the highest productivity tended, on the average, to have high concentration ratios. This prompted the nation's most sophisticated

weekly business magazine to title its story on the NICB study "Big-ness Means Efficiency."

The NICB study does find that there is a tendency for concentration to be higher in industries with high shipments per employee (or value added per employee) and lowest in industries with low shipments per employee. But this does not establish a causal link. The observed weak association between "productivity" and concentration is due mainly to two factors. First, the reason many industries are relatively unconcentrated is that the capital requirements for entry are very low. Frequently such industries are relatively labor-intensive and therefore have relatively low shipments or value added per employee—the measures of "productivity" used in the NICB study. It is not surprising, therefore, that the study found that of the 35 industries with the lowest productivity, 90 percent were located in areas such as textiles and apparel, lumber and wood products, and miscellaneous products such as lampshades and umbrellas. Once these industries are excluded from the analysis, the statistical association between concentration and shipments per employee disappears entirely, and that between concentration and value added per employee very nearly disappears. Additionally, the study's measure of "productivity" includes not only output per employee but also profits and advertising outlay per employee. (In some manufactured goods, advertising and profits may run as high as 50 percent of value added.) Hence, the higher productivity observed in the study is partly due to the presence of noncompetitive profits and greater advertising outlays in the more concentrated industries.

The NICB study also found that in 87 percent of the industries studied, the top four companies had greater "productivity" than other firms in their industries, but the observed association between size and productivity is misleading. Comparing the labor productivity of the top companies in a Census industry with "all others" generates questionable results. Often the smaller companies in a Census industry are actually in a different industry than the leading companies. For example, according to the Census of Manufacturers there are 158 companies competing with the four largest operators of blast furnaces and steel mills. Many of the smaller companies are actually in different, more labor-intensive industries than the top four. It is more relevant to compare large companies with medium-sized ones. When the top four are compared with the second four companies, their apparent superiority disappears. The one exception to this finding is consumer goods industries. This may seem surprising, since the requirements of large-scale production generally are less important in consumer goods than in producer goods industries. But the answer to this paradox lies in the fact that leading manufacturers of differentiated goods often have greater profits and advertising outlays than do smaller companies.

Finally, if the study's measure of productivity is a meaningful one, then the leading companies have such a decided advantage over their smaller rivals that they should be increasing their market share of the industry. Yet, since

1947 the leading companies have lost ground in most producer goods industries, the very industries where technology is most important. Only in consumer goods have they made net gains, but the reasons for this are not to be found in technology.

39. The primary purpose of the selection is to

    Ⓐ demonstrate that the NICB study does not prove that efficiency results from concentration

    Ⓑ argue that less concentrated industries are as efficient as highly concentrated ones

    Ⓒ prove that smaller companies are as efficient as the largest firms in any given industry

    Ⓓ explain why labor-intensive industries are likely to have low shipments per employee

    Ⓔ criticize the nation's leading business magazine for printing its story about the NICB study

40. According to the selection, the study tends to overstate shipments per employee in some industries because

    Ⓐ productivity included profits and advertising outlays

    Ⓑ capital requirements for entry are low

    Ⓒ the category "all other" industries is overly inclusive

    Ⓓ top companies, on the average, have higher rates of productivity

    Ⓔ low-productivity industries are relatively unconcentrated

41. In the final paragraph, the author

    Ⓐ indicts the motives of the people who prepared the NICB study

    Ⓑ criticizes the methodology of the NICB study

    Ⓒ offers affirmative evidence to disprove the conclusions of the NICB study

    Ⓓ cites other studies that contradict the conclusions of the NICB study

    Ⓔ describes the difference between consumer and producer goods industries

Stop: End of Verbal Section

Quantitative Section

37 Questions—75 Minutes

General Directions: To simulate the experience of taking the CAT, answer each question in order. Do not skip any questions and do not go back to questions you have already answered.

Directions for problem-solving questions: For this question type, select the best of the answer choices. Indicate your answer by blackening the circle next to your choice.

Numbers: All numbers used are real numbers.

Figures: The diagrams and figures that accompany these questions are for the purpose of providing information useful in solving the problems. The diagrams and figures are drawn as accurately as possible unless the figure is accompanied by a note stating that it is not drawn to scale. All figures are in a plane unless otherwise indicated.

Directions for data sufficiency questions: Each question is followed by two numbered statements. You are to determine whether the data given in the statements are sufficient for answering the question. Use the data given, plus your knowledge of math and everyday facts, to choose among the five possible answers. Indicate your answer by blackening the circle next to your choice.

Numbers: All values are real numbers.

Figures: Any figures provided will not necessarily reflect the information given in the numbered statements, but they will reflect the information provided in the question. Unless otherwise indicated, all figures lie in a plane; all lines shown as straight are straight; and the positions of all points, angles, regions, etc., are correctly depicted.

Example:

In $\triangle ABC$, what is the value of x?

(1) $y = 60$

(2) $AB = BC$

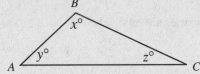

Explanation: Statement (1) is not sufficient to answer the question, for statement (1) provides no information about x or z. Statement (2) is not sufficient to answer the question. Statement (2) does establish that $y = z$, but that is not enough information to determine the value of x. Both statements together are sufficient to answer the question. Since $AB = BC$ and $y = z$, $z = 60$. Since $x + y + z = 180$, $x = 60$.

---

1. If five pounds of coffee cost $12, how much coffee can be purchased for $30?

    Ⓐ 7.2   Ⓑ 10   Ⓒ 12.5   Ⓓ 15   Ⓔ 18

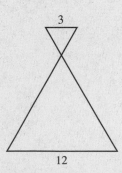

2. If the two triangles above are equilateral, what is the ratio of the perimeter of the smaller to that of the larger?

    Ⓐ $\frac{1}{36}$ Ⓑ $\frac{1}{15}$ Ⓒ $\frac{1}{9}$ Ⓓ $\frac{1}{4}$ Ⓔ $\frac{1}{3}$

3. If the perimeter of a rectangular playing field is 120 meters, which of the following could be the length of one of its sides?

    I. 20

    II. 40

    III. 60

    Ⓐ I only   Ⓑ I and II only   Ⓒ I and III only
    Ⓓ II and III only   Ⓔ I, II, and III

4. What number is Gary thinking of?

   (1) The number Gary is thinking of is less than 24.

   (2) The number Gary is thinking of is more than 22.

   Ⓐ statement 1 alone is sufficient to answer the question, but statement 2 alone is not sufficient

   Ⓑ statement 2 alone is sufficient to answer the question, but statement 1 alone is not sufficient

   Ⓒ both statements together are needed to answer the question, but neither statement alone is sufficient

   Ⓓ either statement by itself is sufficient to answer the question

   Ⓔ not enough facts are given to answer the question

5. Does Charlie weigh more than Nora?

   (1) Charlie and Nora together weigh 80 pounds.

   (2) Charlie's weight plus $1\frac{1}{2}$ pounds equals 50 percent of Nora's weight.

   Ⓐ statement 1 alone is sufficient to answer the question, but statement 2 alone is not sufficient

   Ⓑ statement 2 alone is sufficient to answer the question, but statement 1 alone is not sufficient

   Ⓒ both statements together are needed to answer the question, but neither statement alone is sufficient

   Ⓓ either statement by itself is sufficient to answer the question

   Ⓔ not enough facts are given to answer the question

6. If $\frac{1}{3}$ of a number is 2 more than $\frac{1}{5}$ of the number, what is the number?

   Ⓐ 3   Ⓑ 6   Ⓒ 12   Ⓓ 15   Ⓔ 24

7. In the figure above, if the triangle is equilateral and has a perimeter of 12, the perimeter of the square is

   Ⓐ 9   Ⓑ 12   Ⓒ 16   Ⓓ 20   Ⓔ 24

8. If $5x + 3y = 19$ and x and y are positive integers, then y could equal which of the following?

   Ⓐ 1   Ⓑ 2   Ⓒ 3   Ⓓ 4   Ⓔ 5

9. In 1994, Company x had gross revenues of $10,500,000. What were the gross sales of Company x in 1995?

   (1) Gross sales in 1994 were $2,100,000 more than gross sales in 1993.

   (2) The percent increase in gross sales from 1994 to 1995 was exactly one-half the percent increase in gross sales from 1993 to 1994.

   Ⓐ statement 1 alone is sufficient to answer the question, but statement 2 alone is not sufficient

   Ⓑ statement 2 alone is sufficient to answer the question, but statement 1 alone is not sufficient

   Ⓒ both statements together are needed to answer the question, but neither statement alone is sufficient

   Ⓓ either statement by itself is sufficient to answer the question

   Ⓔ not enough facts are given to answer the question

10. The total weight of three packages is 32 pounds. How much does the heaviest package weigh?

    (1) One of the packages weighs 7 pounds.

    (2) One of the packages weighs 18 pounds.

    Ⓐ statement 1 alone is sufficient to answer the question, but statement 2 alone is not sufficient

    Ⓑ statement 2 alone is sufficient to answer the question, but statement 1 alone is not sufficient

    Ⓒ both statements together are needed to answer the question, but neither statement alone is sufficient

    Ⓓ either statement by itself is sufficient to answer the question

    Ⓔ not enough facts are given to answer the question

11. At the first stop on her route, a driver unloaded two-fifths of the packages in her van. After she unloaded another three packages at her next stop, one-half of the original number of packages in the van remained. How many packages were in the van before the first delivery?

    Ⓐ 10   Ⓑ 18   Ⓒ 25   Ⓓ 30   Ⓔ 36

12. If m and n are negative numbers, which of the following must always be positive?

    I. $m - n$

    II. $m \times n$

    III. $m \div n$

    Ⓐ I only   Ⓑ II only   Ⓒ I and III only
    Ⓓ II and III only   Ⓔ I, II, and III

GO ON TO NEXT PAGE

13. $\dfrac{1}{1+\frac{1}{x}}$ is equal to which of the following?

    Ⓐ $x+1$ Ⓑ $\dfrac{1}{x+1}$ Ⓒ $\dfrac{x}{x+1}$

    Ⓓ $\dfrac{x+1}{x}$ Ⓔ x^2+x

14. What is the greatest integer that is less than n?

   (1) $n = \dfrac{13}{3}$

   (2) $n = \sqrt{169} \times \dfrac{1}{3}$

    Ⓐ statement 1 alone is sufficient to answer the question, but statement 2 alone is not sufficient
    Ⓑ statement 2 alone is sufficient to answer the question, but statement 1 alone is not sufficient
    Ⓒ both statements together are needed to answer the question, but neither statement alone is sufficient
    Ⓓ either statement by itself is sufficient to answer the question
    Ⓔ not enough facts are given to answer the question

15. Employees at a certain airline agreed to accept salary cuts. Was the amount of Mr. Thom's salary cut more than the amount of Mrs. Gershon's salary cut?

   (1) Mr. Thom's salary was cut by 12 percent.
   (2) Mrs. Gershon's salary was cut by 15 percent.

    Ⓐ statement 1 alone is sufficient to answer the question, but statement 2 alone is not sufficient
    Ⓑ statement 2 alone is sufficient to answer the question, but statement 1 alone is not sufficient
    Ⓒ both statements together are needed to answer the question, but neither statement alone is sufficient
    Ⓓ either statement by itself is sufficient to answer the question
    Ⓔ not enough facts are given to answer the question

16. If S is 150 percent of T, then T is what percent of $S+T$?

    Ⓐ $33\dfrac{1}{3}\%$ Ⓑ 40% Ⓒ 50%

    Ⓓ 75% Ⓔ 80%

17. If $\dfrac{5}{3} + \dfrac{x}{3} = 2$, then $x =$

    Ⓐ $\dfrac{5}{9}$ Ⓑ $\dfrac{3}{5}$ Ⓒ $\dfrac{5}{3}$ Ⓓ $\dfrac{5}{6}$ Ⓔ 1

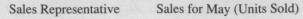

Sales Representative	Sales for May (Units Sold)
Victor	6
Mary	9
Randy	8
Sue	4
Carla	3

18. What was the average number of units sold by the sales representatives shown above?

    Ⓐ 4   Ⓑ 5   Ⓒ 6   Ⓓ 9   Ⓔ 30

19. What is the value of the integer x?

   (1) $8 < x^3 < 64$
   (2) $4 < x^2 < 16$

    Ⓐ statement 1 alone is sufficient to answer the question, but statement 2 alone is not sufficient
    Ⓑ statement 2 alone is sufficient to answer the question, but statement 1 alone is not sufficient
    Ⓒ both statements together are needed to answer the question, but neither statement alone is sufficient
    Ⓓ either statement by itself is sufficient to answer the question
    Ⓔ not enough facts are given to answer the question

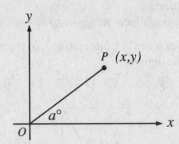

20. In the figure above, if O is the origin and point P has coordinates (x, y), is the length of segment OP greater than 5?

   (1) $a = 45°$
   (2) P is a point on a circle with center O and radius 7.5.

    Ⓐ statement 1 alone is sufficient to answer the question, but statement 2 alone is not sufficient
    Ⓑ statement 2 alone is sufficient to answer the question, but statement 1 alone is not sufficient
    Ⓒ both statements together are needed to answer the question, but neither statement alone is sufficient
    Ⓓ either statement by itself is sufficient to answer the question
    Ⓔ not enough facts are given to answer the question

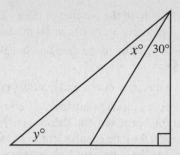

21. In the figure above, $x + y =$

Ⓐ 15° Ⓑ 30° Ⓒ 60° Ⓓ 90° Ⓔ 120°

22. Carl has only $5 bills and $10 bills in his wallet. If he has x $5 bills and ten more $10 bills than $5 bills, in terms of x, how much money, in dollars, does Carl have in his wallet?

Ⓐ 15x Ⓑ 15x + 10 Ⓒ 15x + 15
Ⓓ 15x + 100 Ⓔ 50x + 100

23. If x and y are positive integers and $\frac{x}{y} < 1$, which of the following is greater than 1?

Ⓐ $\frac{x}{2y}$ Ⓑ $\frac{\sqrt{x}}{y}$ Ⓒ $\left(\frac{x}{y}\right)^2$

Ⓓ $x - y$ Ⓔ $\frac{y}{x}$

24. Mr. Hayward bought a brooch and a necklace. If he paid 6-percent sales tax on each item, what was the cost of the necklace without the sales tax?

(1) The total cost of the two items plus the sales tax was $84.80.

(2) Mr. Hayward paid $21.20 for the brooch, including sales tax.

Ⓐ statement 1 alone is sufficient to answer the question, but statement 2 alone is not sufficient
Ⓑ statement 2 alone is sufficient to answer the question, but statement 1 alone is not sufficient
Ⓒ both statements together are needed to answer the question, but neither statement alone is sufficient
Ⓓ either statement by itself is sufficient to answer the question
Ⓔ not enough facts are given to answer the question

25. What is the circumference of a circle inscribed in a square?

(1) The diagonal of the square is 10.

(2) The perimeter of the square is $20\sqrt{2}$.

Ⓐ statement 1 alone is sufficient to answer the question, but statement 2 alone is not sufficient
Ⓑ statement 2 alone is sufficient to answer the question, but statement 1 alone is not sufficient
Ⓒ both statements together are needed to answer the question, but neither statement alone is sufficient
Ⓓ either statement by itself is sufficient to answer the question
Ⓔ not enough facts are given to answer the question

26. If $p = q + 2$ and $r = 2q^2$, then r =

Ⓐ $(p-2)^2$ Ⓑ $2(p-2)^2$ Ⓒ $\frac{p-2}{2}$

Ⓓ $\frac{p-2}{4}$ Ⓔ $\frac{(p-2)^2}{4}$

27. If a car travels at 40 kilometers per hour, how many *minutes* does it take the car to travel k kilometers?

Ⓐ $\frac{2k}{3}$ Ⓑ $\frac{3k}{2}$ Ⓒ $\frac{2}{3k}$ Ⓓ $\frac{3}{2k}$ Ⓔ 40k

28. If the spaces between the lettered points in the figure above are all equal, then $\frac{PT}{2} - \frac{QS}{2}$ is equal to which of the following?

Ⓐ $PS - QR$ Ⓑ $QR - QS$ Ⓒ PR
Ⓓ QT Ⓔ ST

29. How many square tiles were used to cover a certain windowless bathroom wall?

(1) The wall is 6 feet wide.

(2) The wall is 8 feet high.

Ⓐ statement 1 alone is sufficient to answer the question, but statement 2 alone is not sufficient
Ⓑ statement 2 alone is sufficient to answer the question, but statement 1 alone is not sufficient
Ⓒ both statements together are needed to answer the question, but neither statement alone is sufficient
Ⓓ either statement by itself is sufficient to answer the question
Ⓔ not enough facts are given to answer the question

30. At 1 p.m., train A leaves New York bound for Providence, and train B leaves Providence bound for New York along a track that runs beside that used by train A. If each train travels at a constant speed and the distance by rail from New York to Providence is 150 miles, how many miles from New York is train A when it meets train B?

(1) Train A and Train B travel at the same speed.

(2) Train A travels at a speed of 50 miles per hour.

Ⓐ statement 1 alone is sufficient to answer the question, but statement 2 alone is not sufficient
Ⓑ statement 2 alone is sufficient to answer the question, but statement 1 alone is not sufficient
Ⓒ both statements together are needed to answer the question, but neither statement alone is sufficient
Ⓓ either statement by itself is sufficient to answer the question
Ⓔ not enough facts are given to answer the question

GO ON TO NEXT PAGE ⟹

31. Exactly three years before the year in which Anna was born, the year was $1980 - x$. In terms of x, on Anna's twentieth birthday, the year will be

(A) $1977 + x$ (B) $1997 + x$ (C) $2003 - x$
(D) $2003 + x$ (E) $2006 + x$

32. If $x = k + \frac{1}{2} = \frac{k + 3}{2}$, then $x =$

(A) $\frac{1}{3}$ (B) $\frac{1}{2}$ (C) 1 (D) 2 (E) $\frac{5}{2}$

33. If $\frac{x}{z} = c$ and $\frac{y}{z} = c - 1$, then x and y are related in which of the following ways?

(A) $x = y - 1$ (B) $x = y + 1$ (C) $x = z + y$

(D) $x = z - y$ (E) $x = \frac{y}{1}$

34. A dean must select three students to serve on a committee. If she is considering five students, from how many possible threesomes must she choose?

(A) 2   (B) 3   (C) 10   (D) 15   (E) 18

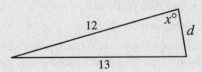

35. What is the area of the triangle above?

(1) $x = 90°$

(2) $d = 5$

Ⓐ statement 1 alone is sufficient to answer the question, but statement 2 alone is not sufficient
Ⓑ statement 2 alone is sufficient to answer the question, but statement 1 alone is not sufficient
Ⓒ both statements together are needed to answer the question, but neither statement alone is sufficient
Ⓓ either statement by itself is sufficient to answer the question
Ⓔ not enough facts are given to answer the question

36. What is the sum of the number of dimes and the number of quarters Steve has in his pocket?

(1) The total value of the coins in Steve's pocket is $3.55.

(2) Steve has only dimes and quarters in his pocket.

Ⓐ statement 1 alone is sufficient to answer the question, but statement 2 alone is not sufficient
Ⓑ statement 2 alone is sufficient to answer the question, but statement 1 alone is not sufficient
Ⓒ both statements together are needed to answer the question, but neither statement alone is sufficient
Ⓓ either statement by itself is sufficient to answer the question
Ⓔ not enough facts are given to answer the question

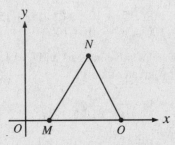

37. In the figure above, M and O are points on the x axis. What is the area of equilateral triangle MNO?

(1) The coordinates of point N are $(5, \sqrt{3})$.

(2) The coordinates of point M are $(\sqrt{3}, 0)$.

(A) statement 1 alone is sufficient to answer the question, but statement 2 alone is not sufficient
(B) statement 2 alone is sufficient to answer the question, but statement 1 alone is not sufficient
(C) both statements together are needed to answer the question, but neither statement alone is sufficient
(D) either statement by itself is sufficient to answer the question
(E) not enough facts are given to answer the question

Stop: End of Quantitative Section

Answer Key

VERBAL SECTION

1.	A	15.	D	29.	C
2.	B	16.	A	30.	E
3.	A	17.	A	31.	E
4.	B	18.	C	32.	B
5.	C	19.	D	33.	C
6.	B	20.	C	34.	B
7.	C	21.	E	35.	B
8.	C	22.	E	36.	A
9.	A	23.	B	37.	C
10.	C	24.	A	38.	C
11.	C	25.	B	39.	A
12.	D	26.	E	40.	A
13.	D	27.	E	41.	C
14.	D	28.	B		

QUANTITATIVE SECTION

1.	C	14.	D	27.	B
2.	D	15.	E	28.	E
3.	B	16.	B	29.	E
4.	E	17.	E	30.	A
5.	B	18.	C	31.	C
6.	D	19.	A	32.	E
7.	C	20.	B	33.	C
8.	C	21.	C	34.	C
9.	C	22.	D	35.	D
10.	B	23.	E	36.	E
11.	D	24.	C	37.	A
12.	D	25.	D		
13.	C	26.	B		

Explanatory Answers

VERBAL SECTION

1. Henry David Thoreau was a philosopher as well as a naturalist; Gandhi <u>read *Civil Disobedience* in 1906 and made it</u> a major document in his struggle for Indian independence.

   Ⓐ read *Civil Disobedience* in 1906 and made it
   Ⓑ read *Civil Disobedience* in 1906 in order to make it into
   Ⓒ read *Civil Disobedience* and, in 1906, made it
   Ⓓ would have read *Civil Disobedience* in 1906 and would have made it
   Ⓔ reading *Civil Disobedience* in 1906 and making it

   (A) The sentence is correct as originally written. (B) changes the meaning of the original by implying that Gandhi read *Civil Disobedience* with the objective of making it part of his struggle. (C), too, changes the meaning of the original by implying that it was in 1906 that Gandhi incorporated Thoreau's teachings into his struggle. The original states that it was in 1906 that Gandhi read the work. (D) also changes the meaning of the original. The use of the subjunctive (*would have*) implies that Gandhi did not read the work in 1906 because something prevented him from doing so. Finally, (E) eliminates the only conjugated verbs in the sentence. The result is a sentence fragment.

2. Some homeowners prefer gas heat to <u>oil because there is no need for deliveries or no large storage tanks, with its being cheaper in most places</u>.

   Ⓐ oil because there is no need for deliveries or no large storage tanks, with its being cheaper in most places
   Ⓑ oil because there is no need for deliveries or large storage tanks, and in most places gas is cheaper
   Ⓒ oil, being that there are no deliveries, no large storage tanks, and it is cheaper in most places
   Ⓓ oil, needing no deliveries or large storage tanks, and anyways gas is cheaper in most places
   Ⓔ oil, since gas is cheaper in most places and has no need of deliveries or large storage tanks

   (B) The original sentence contains two errors. First, there is the obvious error of a lack of logical structure. The *with its being cheaper* is tacked onto the sentence as an afterthought. Second, the original implies that with oil heat there is "no need for no large storage

tanks," a double negative. Only (B) corrects these errors without introducing a new error. (C) is wrong because this use of *being* is not acceptable in standard written English and because the resulting sentence suffers from a lack of parallelism. As for (D), the placement of the modifier ("needing no deliveries . . .") implies that it is oil that has these advantages rather than gas. Additionally, *anyways* is colloquial and not acceptable in standard written English. Finally, (E) makes an illogical statement by implying that gas, rather than the homeowner, wishes to avoid the problems associated with oil.

3. <u>Although we now blame most catastrophes on "nature,"</u> thinkers in the Middle Ages thought every fire, earthquake, and disease to be the result of divine anger.

   Ⓐ Although we now blame most catastrophes on "nature,"
   Ⓑ Most catastrophes are now blamed on nature by us, and
   Ⓒ We now blame nature for catastrophes, moreover,
   Ⓓ Although nature is now blamed for most catastrophes by us,
   Ⓔ Now blaming most catastrophes on nature,

   (A) The sentence appears correct as written. (B) is wrong because it needlessly switches to the passive voice and is awkwardly worded. Additionally, replacing *although* by *and* changes the logical relationship between those two clauses. (C) is incorrect for the reason just mentioned; *moreover* incorrectly expresses the relationship between the clauses. (D) is wrong because it switches needlessly to the passive voice and is awkward. Finally, (E) is incorrect because it changes the meaning of the original sentence and creates an illogical statement.

A Supreme Court justice once observed, "We are not the last word because we are infallible; we are infallible because we are the last word."

4. Which of the following most closely parallels the logic of the statement above?

   Ⓐ Congressperson: Although I may make some mistakes, I will always use my best judgment to protect the interests of my constituents.

   Ⓑ Teacher: My ideas may not always be correct, but students obey me because I am the teacher.

   Ⓒ Doctor: Doctors make life and death decisions every day, so we are the most powerful judges in this society.

   Ⓓ Lawyer: I cannot assure my client of victory, because I cannot predict with certainty what a judge will do.

   Ⓔ Pilot: In an emergency, the ground control crew is not in the plane with me, so I have to make the final decision and hope I have not made a mistake.

(B) The initial statement contains an interesting twist of reasoning. The Supreme Court justice is making the point that the Supreme Court is the highest authority. This doesn't mean that the court is infallible, but it does mean that it has the last word. In (B), the teacher makes a similar statement. The teacher will be obeyed because she is the highest authority for the students.

It is truly folly that when we are sick in fortune—often the surfeit of our own behavior—we make guilty of our disasters the sun, the moon, and the stars, as if we were villains of necessity, fools by heavenly compulsion, knaves and treacheries by spherical predominance, drunkards, liars, and adulterers by enforced obedience of planetary influence, and all that we are evil in by a divine thrusting on.

5. It can be inferred that the speaker above believes which of the following?

   I. There is no substance to astrology.

   II. Many people are reluctant to accept the consequences of their actions.

   III. Most people are evil.

   Ⓐ I only   Ⓑ II only   Ⓒ I and II only
   Ⓓ I and III only   Ⓔ I, II, and III

(C) This item is very much like something you would find in a Reading Comprehension section. You must read the paragraph and recognize that the speaker is criticizing the notion that the heavenly bodies influence human behavior. Therefore, the speaker probably would accept statement I. Also, the author implies that people attempt to escape the responsibility for their actions by blaming the influence of heavenly bodies. So II also would be endorsed by the speaker. III, however, overstates the case. The speaker does not imply that people are always evil, only that when they suffer misfortune or do something evil, they blame the stars.

Philosophical ideals, as they find embodiment in political action, cannot be confined to a single geographical region. This is particularly true where two countries undergo a period of parallel development. The seed will necessarily be blown to other regions where, if the conditions are favorable, it will take root. Nowhere is this seen better than in the Irish Revolution of the late 18th century. The seed of revolution blown from France found fertile ground and favorable climatic conditions in Ireland, so it flowered.

6. Which of the following, if true, most weakens the argument above?

   Ⓐ French political treatises were not widely read by most of Ireland's population.

   Ⓑ Conditions similar to those in Ireland and France existed at the same time in Poland and Austria, but those countries did not experience revolutions.

   Ⓒ Much of the revolutionary rhetoric in Ireland was drawn from the American Revolution.

   Ⓓ A substantial number of people in Ireland opposed the revolution.

   Ⓔ The revolt in Ireland ultimately failed because the English were too powerful.

(B) The author of the paragraph makes the general claim that revolution will spread from one country to another and documents that claim with a specific example. The best attack in this line of reasoning is provided by (B), which gives two counterexamples to the author's claim. (A) is, at best, a very weak attack. The author could turn aside this attack by simply saying, "But the leaders of the revolution were familiar with events in France." (C), too, is only a weak objection. The author could say, "It is true that the rhetoric was English, but the political ideas were derived from France." As for (D) and (E), the author doesn't contend that the revolution was successful, only that revolutionary activity occurred.

7. The main purpose of this passage is to

   Ⓐ describe the common roots of American citizens

   Ⓑ suggest patterns of behavior appropriate to the new social climate

   Ⓒ identify factors contributing to the breakdown of the socialization process

   Ⓓ describe the declining influence of religion in American life

   Ⓔ argue for a substantial change in public school curricula

(C) This is a main idea question in sentence completion format. You can eliminate (E) because "argue for a substantial change" is not an accurate description of the passage. The author specifies no such change. (B) fails for the same reason. The author does not suggest new patterns of behavior. Rather the passage is a discussion of the causes of the problem, and this is why (C) is the best choice.

You can eliminate (A) as too narrow. The first paragraph may touch on the idea of roots, but (A) is not the main theme of the selection. As for (D), the author does mention that the influence of religion as a socializing factor is declining, but this is one small point of the passage.

8. The phrase "motion without melody" might be used to refer to which of the following events?

Ⓐ Traveling abroad as part of a student exchange program
Ⓑ Formation of ethnic communities in urban areas
Ⓒ Relocation to a distant city to accept a job offer
Ⓓ Moving to a bigger house in the same neighborhood
Ⓔ Immigration of large groups of Europeans to America

(C) This is a further application question asking you to apply the idea of "motion without melody" to new situations. The author distinguishes between *movement* and *migration*. The difference is that movement occurs without regard to a person's traditions or values, whereas migration implies that a person takes with her or him a cultural heritage. So "motion without melody" refers to movement as opposed to migration.

Which of the choices best falls under the heading of "sheer motion"? (B) does not even contain the idea of movement, so you can eliminate it. Indeed, the formation of an ethnic group, in which traditions would continue, would not be movement.

The remaining choices all suggest change of location, but which lacks the "melody"? You can eliminate (A) for two reasons. First, the motion mentioned there is only temporary. A student would return home after a summer of traveling. Additionally, the idea of cultural exchange gives reason or "melody" to the movement. And you can eliminate (D) since the movement terminates in the same neighborhood; it is not an abandonment of ties. Finally, you can eliminate (E) since immigration of large groups allowed for the continuity of and preservation of traditions.

(C) is the example of motion without melody: relocating for economic reasons without regard to community ties.

9. The author cites Emerson in order to

Ⓐ dramatize the power of bureaucracy in our society
Ⓑ explain the importance of individual freedom
Ⓒ demonstrate the need for the study of humanities in American schools
Ⓓ highlight the progress that society has made since Emerson
Ⓔ argue that all institutions should be run by an individual

(A) This is a logical structure question asking *why* the author introduces his paraphrase of Emerson. In that paragraph, the author is talking about the power of institutions. When he says that an institution is likely to be a lengthening shadow of itself, he means that institutions become self-perpetuating. That is, they are no longer controlled and directed by an individual; individuals come and go, but the institution remains. This paraphrase of Emerson dramatizes the shift of social power from individuals to institutions, as correctly pointed out by (A).

(B), which makes a contrary claim, must be wrong. The author thinks that individuals are less free now because institutions now have the power once held by individuals. (D) must also be incorrect, since the author would not regard this shift as progress. (E) is wrong since the author does not state that things can be any different than they are. In other words, the author doesn't argue for *change* in institutions. Finally, (C) is wrong for a similar reason. The author does not call for such a proposal. further, the education that the author is talking about is not just formal education. He also has in mind the informal instruction once derived from institutions such as family and community.

10. To prove that acridines kill bacteria through asphyxiation rather than starvation (as is the case with sulfa drugs), <u>Dr. Martin nearly spent ten years building an artificial chemical wall around the bacteria</u> that deprives them of essential food.

Ⓐ Dr. Martin nearly spent ten years building an artificial chemical wall around the bacteria
Ⓑ building an artificial chemical wall around the bacteria was nearly Dr. Martin's task for ten years
Ⓒ Dr. Martin spent nearly ten years building an artificial chemical wall around the bacteria
Ⓓ nearly spending ten years, Dr. Martin built an artificial chemical wall around the bacteria
Ⓔ ten years were nearly spent by Dr. Martin building an artificial chemical wall around the bacteria

(C) The original sentence is incorrect because of a misplaced modifier. The sentence says that Dr. Martin *almost spent* ten years doing something, a construction which implies that he did not actually embark on the task. (Study the difference between the statements "I almost spent $10" and "I spent almost $10.") The sentence means to say that he spent almost ten years on the task. (B) is wrong because it changes the meaning of the sentence. Here, the *nearly* refers to his task and not the length of time it took to accomplish it. (D) is incorrect because it is susceptible to misreading. (D) implies that the process of asphyxiation took almost ten years. Additionally, the placement of the phrase *nearly spending ten years* is awkward. Finally, (E) is

534

wrong because it switches to the passive voice, and like the original implies that Dr. Martin did not actually undertake the task. (C) is correct because (C) makes it clear that the doctor spent almost ten years building the artificial wall.

11. The highly controversial proposal was voted against by the governor and whomever else favored conservation.

   Ⓐ The highly controversial proposal was voted against by the governor and whomever else favored conservation.

   Ⓑ The highly controversial proposal was voted against by the governor and whoever else favored conservation.

   Ⓒ The governor and everyone else who favored conservation voted against the highly controversial proposal.

   Ⓓ The governor and anyone else who favored conservation voted against the highly controversial proposal.

   Ⓔ Favoring conservation, the governor and everyone else voted against the highly controversial proposal.

(C) The original sentence is wrong on two counts. First, *whomever* is the wrong choice of pronouns for two reasons. One, *whomever* is intended to be the subject of the verb *favored*, so a subject case pronoun is needed. (The entire clause *whoever favored* is then the object of the preposition *by*.) Two, even *whoever* is an error in diction. The correct pronoun is *everyone*. Thus (B) and (D) are wrong. Second, the original sentence is awkward because it uses the indirect construction of the passive voice. Although (E) avoids the use of the passive voice, (E) changes the intended meaning of the original by asserting that everyone and the governor voted against the proposal. (C) is the best choice because it eliminates both of the problems of the original.

12. Credit cards are now accepted in exchange for many goods and services around the world and in some countries, like the Americans, is used even more widely than cash.

   Ⓐ like the Americans, is used even more widely than

   Ⓑ like that of America, is used even more widely than

   Ⓒ as in America, are used even more widely than

   Ⓓ such as America, are used even more widely than

   Ⓔ such as America, are used even more widely as

(D) The original sentence commits two errors. One, it sets up an illogical comparison between *countries* and *Americans*, a people. Two, the verb *is* fails to agree with its subject *cards*. (B) fails to correct the second error. Additionally, (B) is incorrect because *like* is unidiomatic here and the *that* doesn't refer to anything. (C) corrects the problem of agreement, but *as* is not

idiomatic. (The *as* seems to imply a similarity between two activities, but the sentence means to create a contrast between America, where credit cards have even more uses, and some other countries.) Finally, (E) implies that credit cards are used as cash more widely in America than in other countries, but the original means to say that in America credit cards are used more widely than cash.

If Peter graduated from college, he must have studied a foreign language.

13. Which of the following, if true, is sufficient to guarantee the truth of the statement above?

   Ⓐ Only college students study foreign languages.

   Ⓑ All foreign languages are studied by some college students.

   Ⓒ All college students are allowed to study a foreign language.

   Ⓓ All college students are required to study a foreign language before graduation.

   Ⓔ Some foreign languages are studied by no college students.

(D) The question stem really asks you to find a hidden assumption of the argument. The claim assumes that the status of being a college graduate is sufficient to guarantee that Peter studied a foreign language. So you need a premise that is tantamount to saying all college graduates have studied a foreign language. (D) provides the missing link.

At a recent art auction, a large canvas painted in many colors sold for $100,000. At the same auction, a simple pen-and-ink drawing by the same artist sold for $105,000, because it was more beautiful. Whatever it is that is beauty, that is, whatever it is that we prize so highly, it is not necessarily the product of a lifetime of work but rather the gift of a moment.

14. The speaker above is making what point?

   Ⓐ Art collectors often do not know the true value of a work of art.

   Ⓑ Prices for rare objects of art are governed by market forces.

   Ⓒ What one person considers beautiful, another may consider not beautiful.

   Ⓓ Artistic achievement requires creative insight and not just technique.

   Ⓔ There is a direct correlation between the price of a work of art and the time the artist required to produce the object.

(D) This question asks you to identify the conclusion of the argument. Although the conclusion is not signaled by any word such as *therefore*, it is contained in the final sentence of the paragraph: beauty is not necessarily the work of a lifetime but the gift of a moment. (D) best summarizes this idea. As for (A), the author does not imply any criticism of art collectors, and in fact seems to suggest that the prices paid were fair ones. As for (B), though the author might accept this statement, it is not the main point or conclusion of the argument as written. (C), too, might be a statement the author would accept, but (C) is not the conclusion of the argument as written. Finally, (E) seems to be directly contradicted by the passage.

All bushes that bear red roses have thorns. This bush has no thorns. Therefore, this bush cannot bear roses.

15. The logic of the argument above is most nearly paralleled by which of the following?

Ⓐ All Sandarac automobiles have three wheels. This car has three wheels. Therefore, this car is a Sandarac automobile.

Ⓑ All brides wear white. This woman is not wearing white. Therefore, this woman must be the maid of honor.

Ⓒ All professional tennis players use metal rackets. This player does not use a metal racket. Therefore, this player is not a professional tennis player.

Ⓓ All Scottish ivy is heliotropic. This plant is not heliotropic. Therefore, this plant is not ivy.

Ⓔ All pencils have rubber erasers. This eraser is not attached to a pencil. Therefore, this eraser is not made of rubber.

(D) This item asks you to find another argument that contains the same error found in the initial paragraph. You could describe the error of the initial paragraph as ambiguity, for the argument moves from a premise about "red rose bushes" to a conclusion about "rose bushes." (D) makes the same mistake. There the premise uses the term "Scottish ivy," but the conclusion uses the term "ivy."

16. It can be inferred that doctors are able to determine hospital policies because

Ⓐ it is doctors who generate income for the hospital

Ⓑ most of a patient's bills are paid by his health insurance

Ⓒ hospital administrators lack the expertise to question medical decisions

Ⓓ a doctor is ultimately responsible for a patient's health

Ⓔ some patients might refuse to accept their physician's advice

(A) This is an implied idea question. In the second paragraph, the author states that it is the physician who is the real "consumer." So it is not surprising that physicians would make key decisions. Although the author does not specifically say so, we may infer that physicians control power because they control the money. This is choice (A).

(B) mentions a related issue. But the author states that carriers are generally rubber stamps, paying whatever is approved by the physician. Thus, it is the physician, not the carrier, who has the real power. As for (C), this may very well be true in the real world, but this choice illustrates the limit of what is a correct answer to an implied idea question. The passage nowhere mentions anything about the expertise of hospital administrators nor anything related to that topic. (D) is arguably an explanation for the phenomenon mentioned. But it is not the one given by the author. The author cites economic factors, not professional ones; though this may be a true statement, it is not a response to the question asked.

Finally, as for (E), though it might be true that some patients do not follow their doctor's advice, this fact does not explain why doctors control hospital policies.

17. The author is most probably leading up to

Ⓐ a proposal to control medical costs

Ⓑ a discussion of a new medical treatment

Ⓒ an analysis of the causes of inflation in the United States

Ⓓ a study of lawsuits against doctors for malpractice

Ⓔ a comparison of hospitals and factories

(A) This is a further application question. The author concludes the passage with the statement that, because of the factors cited, cost control measures aimed at patients are ineffective. Patients do not decide what medical services to buy. Logically, the author could be leading up to a discussion of a plan to solve this problem. (B) would not be a logical extension of the argument. Though the passage discusses medicine, it analyzes the economics of health care, not medical knowledge. (C) goes beyond the scope of the passage. The selection focuses specifically on the problem of cost control in the health-care industry. As for (D), although in the real world medical malpractice suits may be tied to problems of cost control, there is nothing in the passage to suggest that this is the direction in which the author is moving. Finally, (E) is incorrect. The author analyzes the economics of the health-care industry. The initial comparison of this industry and the rest of the economy was made to introduce the reader to the special problems of the health-care industry.

18. With which of the following statements would the author be likely to agree?

  I. Most patients are reluctant to object to the course of treatment prescribed by a doctor or to question the cost of the services.

  II. The more serious the illness of a patient, the less likely it is that the patient will object to the course of treatment prescribed or to question the cost of services.

  III. The payer, whether insurance carrier or the government, is less likely to acquiesce to demands for payment when the illness of the patient is regarded as serious.

  Ⓐ I only   Ⓑ II only   Ⓒ I and II only
  Ⓓ II and III only   Ⓔ I, II, and III

  (C) This is a further application question. Statement I is something the author would agree with. In the second paragraph, the author states that it is a "rare and sophisticated" patient who challenges a doctor's decision regarding treatment. Thus, we can infer that the author believes that few people make such challenges; you can eliminate choices (B) and (D). Statement II is also something the author would accept, noting in that same sentence that this problem is particularly pronounced when the ailment is a serious one. Statement III, however, is not something the author would likely accept. In the fourth paragraph, the author states that the payer generally meets most of the bona fide bills of a patient. Here the author does not draw a distinction between serious and not-so-serious illnesses.

19. Persistence of vision, the condition when your eyes bridge the gaps of darkness between flashes of light, explains the seeming magic produced by the stroboscope, an instrument that appears to freeze the swiftest motions while they are still going on.

  Ⓐ the condition when your eyes bridge
  Ⓑ when your eyes bridge
  Ⓒ the condition of your eyes bridging
  Ⓓ which occurs when your eyes bridge
  Ⓔ occurring when your eyes bridge

  (D) The original sentence is incorrect because the conjunction *when* introduces an adverbial modifier, and an adverb cannot modify the noun *condition*. (B) commits a similar error, because the adverb seems to modify *persistence*, a noun. (C) is awkward and unidiomatic. And (E) changes the intended meaning of the sentence. The adjective clause set off by commas is intended as a definition of *persistence of vision*, not as an adjective describing it. (D) eliminates the error of the original and introduces no new error.

20. The delivery in large volume of certain welfare services are costly on account of the large number of public contact employees that are required by this.

  Ⓐ The delivery in large volume of certain welfare services are costly on account of the large number of public contact employees that are required by this.
  Ⓑ The delivery of a large volume of certain welfare services are costly on account of the large number of public contact employees that this requires.
  Ⓒ The delivery in large volume of certain welfare services is costly because of the large number of public contact employees that is required.
  Ⓓ The delivery of certain welfare services in large volume is costly on account of the large numbers of public contact employees that is required.
  Ⓔ To deliver certain welfare services in large volume is costly on account of that this requires a large number of public service employees.

  (C) The original sentence contains three errors. First *on account of* is not acceptable in standard written English as a substitute for *because*. Second, the verb *are* fails to agree with the subject of the sentence, *delivery*. Third, *this* does not have a clear referent. (If *this* is intended to refer to *delivery*, the additional pronoun is superfluous; but if *this* is not superfluous, it has nothing to refer to.) (B) corrects none of these errors. (D) corrects two of the errors but not the third and introduces a new error: *numbers*. Finally, (E) corrects only one of the errors and is awkwardly worded.

21. Most department stores offer customers the option that you may exchange your purchases within ten days.

  Ⓐ that you may exchange your
  Ⓑ to exchange your
  Ⓒ of exchanging your
  Ⓓ that exchanges their
  Ⓔ of exchanging

  (E) In the original, *that* seems to introduce a noun clause, but there is no logical function for a noun clause to fulfill in this sentence. The object of the verb *offer* is *option*, so a noun clause is out of place. (E) solves this problem by using a prepositional phrase (with the gerund *exchanging* as the object of the preposition *of*) that modifies *option* (stating what kind of option is available). Additionally, the pronouns *you* and *your* do not agree with their referent, *customers*. (B) and (C) solve the first problem but not the second, while (D) solves the second problem but not the first.

The single greatest weakness of American parties is their inability to achieve cohesion in the legislature. Although there is some measure of party unity, it is not uncommon for the majority party to be unable to implement important legislation. The unity is strongest during the election campaigns. After the primary elections, the losing candidates all promise their support to the party nominee. By the time the Congress convenes, however, the unity has dissipated. This phenomenon is attributable to the fragmented nature of political parties. The national committees are no more than feudal lords who receive nominal fealty from their vassals. A congressperson builds his or her power upon a local base. Consequently, he or she is likely to be responsive to locally based special-interest groups. Evidence of this is seen in the differences in voting patterns between the upper and lower houses. In the Senate, where terms are longer, there is more party unity.

22. Which of the following, if true, would most strengthen the author's argument?

Ⓐ On 30 key issues, 18 of the 67 majority party members in the Senate voted against the party leaders.

Ⓑ On 30 key issues, 70 of the 305 majority party members in the House voted against the party leaders.

Ⓒ On 30 key issues, over half of the members of the minority party in both houses voted with the majority party against the leaders of the minority party.

Ⓓ On 30 key legislative proposals introduced by the president, only eight passed both houses.

Ⓔ On 30 key legislative proposals introduced by a president whose party controlled a majority of both houses, only four passed both houses.

(E) The conclusion of the argument is contained in the first sentence of the initial paragraph: American political parties are not unified. The best support for this conclusion will be a statement that is evidence of this disunity. All of the choices provide some support for the author's claim because each shows that party members do not always toe the party line. (E), however, provides the greatest support. (E) clearly shows that the party leader was unable to control the members of his own party. As for (A) and (B), the defections mentioned here are insignificant when compared with those cited by (E). As for (D), this result could be explained by the fact that the president's party did not control the legislature. (C) is perhaps the second-best response. But to assess the real strength of (C) you would need to know how many key issues were decided. If there were 300 key issues during the period studied, and on only 30 of them party members did not vote with the party leaders, then that would not provide much strength for the author's position.

Hamlet: Watchman, tell me of the night.

Horatio: I see nothing, my Prince.

Hamlet: Your eyes are much better than mine. In this darkness, I can scarcely see anything.

23. It can be inferred that the first speaker in the exchange above believes that

Ⓐ Horatio is not really the watchman

Ⓑ nothing is something that can be seen

Ⓒ something is more easily seen in darkness than in light

Ⓓ the night conceals a serious danger

Ⓔ the watchman is concealing something from him

(B) The exchange contains ambiguity. The watchman says he sees nothing, meaning he doesn't see anything. The other speaker interprets the watchman's remark to mean that the watchman is able to see something he calls "nothing."

Senator: It is my understanding that you have memberships in several private clubs that do not allow anyone other than members of the white race to join. Can you reconcile this fact with your desire to be confirmed as Director of the Bureau of Racial Equality?

Nominee: Senator, that is no longer true. Last week I resigned my membership in those clubs.

24. Which of the following is the best explanation for why the senator might find the response to his question unsatisfactory?

Ⓐ The senator was concerned not so much with the nominee's present affiliations as with the nominee's attitudes on race relations.

Ⓑ The nominee is attempting to conceal his affiliations in clubs that refuse to accept non-whites for membership.

Ⓒ The nominee attempts to escape moral responsibility for his actions on the grounds that he was unaware that the clubs discriminated against non-whites.

Ⓓ The nominee believes incorrectly that the senator himself endorses the existence of clubs that select membership on the basis of race.

Ⓔ The nominee believes that the senator believes that there is no inconsistency between such memberships and being Director of the Bureau of Racial Equality.

(A) The nominee attempts a little fancy footwork to get around the issue. The senator has asked the nominee to explain how he could be a member of all-white clubs and still want to head an agency that is supposed to promote racial equality. The nominee attempts to evade the question by noting that he is no longer a member of the clubs. The issue, however, as (A) correctly points out, is the nominee's attitudes. As for (B) and (C), the nominee has implicitly admitted that he previously held such memberships and that he was aware of what those memberships signified. (D) and (E) are incorrect because the nominee evidently understands only too well that the senator does not endorse such clubs and, further, that the senator believes there is an inconsistency between membership in such clubs and the ability to head the Bureau.

25. This passage deals primarily with the
   (A) formation of galaxies
   (B) creation of black holes
   (C) life cycle of stars
   (D) physical properties of black holes
   (E) movement of interstellar gases

(B) This is a main idea question. The idea is to find a choice that summarizes the main theme of the selection by eliminating those that go beyond the scope of the passage or are too narrow in their description of the content of the passage.

(B) is the best choice. The author discusses how black holes are created. You can eliminate (A), since the author does not tell us how galaxies are first formed. Chronologically, the first events discussed by the passage are stellar collisions; therefore, the author treats a time when stars and galaxies already exist. The same is true of (C). The author does not tell us how stars are created, nor does he tell us what stages they pass through during their life cycles.

(D) goes beyond the scope of the passage. The author talks about the creation of black holes, but he does not describe their physical properties. Finally, (E) is just a small part of the passage. Though the author does mention that interstellar gas plays a role in the creation of black holes, this is but a minor point.

26. The author implies that
   (A) some galaxies have no black hole
   (B) the black hole at the center of our galaxy is extinct
   (C) our galaxy has never collided with any other galaxy
   (D) black holes eventually disappear
   (E) larger stars are less stable than smaller ones

(E) This is an implied idea question. We must test each choice to determine whether it is logically inferable from the passage. As for (A), the author says nothing to suggest that some galaxies do not have black holes. In fact, the first sentence of the second paragraph seems to suggest that every galaxy has one at its nucleus. As for (B), this is specifically contradicted by the passage. The black hole is there, ready to suck up anything that comes its way. It's not doing anything at the moment because it already swallowed up everything near it. As for (C), the author does state that galaxies may collide,

but there is nothing in the passage to support a conclusion one way or the other about our galaxy. As for (D), the author never implies that black holes eventually fade away. So far as we can tell, they may last forever. (E), however, is inferable. The third sentence states that the bigger the star grows, the less stable it becomes. We can infer from this that a larger star is less stable than a smaller one.

27. The author's use of the word *seed* to describe newly formed black holes is most nearly like which of the following?
   (A) Plant seeds that are placed in the ground to grow into mature plants
   (B) The seed of an idea that is then developed by an individual thinker
   (C) A seed bed where large numbers of young plants are carefully cultivated
   (D) A seed pod that will burst, distributing great quantities of seeds
   (E) Government-supplied seed money for a project that will attract money from other sources

(E) This is a further application question, and such questions are often the most difficult of all. Here you are asked to find an analogy to the idea of a "seed" black hole. What is the function of a "seed" black hole? It is the thing around which other gases coalesce. Through this process of accumulating debris from other sources, the hole grows. So there are two important elements: the thing grows, and it gets its material from outside sources.

First, we will eliminate (C) and (D) since they talk about many things growing in the same place or a single thing dividing into many parts. That is not what the black hole does.

Next, notice that (A) and (B) refer to growth, but the growth they describe comes from within. (E) describes a process whereby something grows because of contributions from another source. This is why (E) is the best analogy to a "seed" black hole. The black hole grows by attracting gases from other sources; seed money grows by attracting money from other sources.

28. The Russian music of the nineteenth century is richer and more varied than France.
   (A) is richer and more varied than France
   (B) is richer and more varied than the music of France
   (C) is more rich and varied than France
   (D) is more rich and more varied than is the music of France
   (E) is more rich and varied in comparison to France

(B) The original contains a faulty comparison: it attempts to compare Russian music to France (a country). (B) corrects this error by making it clear that two types of music are being compared. (C) fails to correct the faulty comparison. Additionally, (C) uses the awkward *more rich* in place of the preferable *richer*. (In English, the comparative of short adjectives is formed using the -er suffix.) (D), too, makes this error, and (D) is needlessly wordy compared to (B). Finally, (E) fails to correct the error of the original.

29. Many physicists think that at some time in the next century <u>we will not only discover life in other galaxies but will also communicate with them.</u>

   (A) we will not only discover life in other galaxies but will also communicate with them

   (B) we will discover not only life in other galaxies, but be able to communicate with it

   (C) we will not only discover life in other galaxies but we will be able to communicate with it

   (D) that not only will we be able to discover life in other galaxies but be able to communicate to them as well

   (E) not only to find life in other galaxies but to communicate with it as well

(C) The original contains an error of pronoun usage: *them* fails to agree in number with its referent, *life*. (C) solves this problem by substituting *it* for *them*. (B) corrects the error found in the original, but it changes the intended meaning of the original. (B) asserts that something in addition to life will be found in other galaxies. As for (D), the *that* seems to introduce a noun clause, but the noun clause has already been introduced by an earlier *that*. Thus, everything contained in (D) is left with no logical connection to the rest of the sentence. As for (E), since the *that* sets up a noun clause, you need a subject and a conjugated verb for the clause. The result of using (E) would be a phrase lacking a subject and a conjugated verb.

30. <u>The most chance of being an insomniac is not the overworked executive or the student overwhelmed by studies but the bored housewife who feels unfilled.</u>

   (A) The most chance of being an insomniac is not the overworked executive or the student overwhelmed by studies but the bored housewife who feels unfilled.

   (B) The highest degree of insomnia is not experienced by the overworked executive nor by the student overwhelmed by studies, but by the bored housewife who feels unfulfilled.

   (C) Most insomniacs are not overworked executives or students overwhelmed by studies, yet they are bored housewives who feel unfulfilled.

   (D) The greater degree of insomniacs are bored housewives who feels unfulfilled and not overworked executives nor are they students overwhelmed by their studies.

   (E) Insomniacs are, for the most part, bored housewives who feel unfulfilled, not overworked executives or students overwhelmed by their studies.

(E) The original sentence contains both an unidiomatic expression and an illogical assertion. First, the phrase *most chance* is simply not idiomatic. (The correct idiom would be *greatest chance*.) Additionally, the original sentence asserts that the chance (of being an insomniac) is a bored housewife. But there simply cannot be an identity between an abstract concept such as chance and a person. The second problem is solvable only by substantially reorganizing the sentence, as (E) does. (B) solves the problem of illogical expression but changes the intended meaning of the sentence. It seems to talk about the severity of the disorder rather than the frequency with which it afflicts members of certain groups. (C) solves the problems of the original but introduces a new error. *Yet* seems to signal a contrast, but the contrast has already been signaled by the *not* in the first clause. So *yet* has no logical role to play in the sentence. Finally, (D) makes the same error as (B) and is extremely awkward as well.

Questions 31–32

Some snakes are amphibians.
Some amphibians are intelligent.
Some intelligent creatures are not snakes.

31. If the statements above are true, which of the following could also be true?

   (A) No amphibians are intelligent.

   (B) No snakes are amphibians.

   (C) No intelligent creatures are amphibians

   (D) No amphibians are snakes.

   (E) All snakes are intelligent.

(E) Here you might want to make use of circle diagrams:

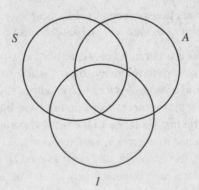

The three circles show the possible overlap of the categories "snakes," "amphibians," and "intelligent

540

creatures." Now enter on the diagram the information provided by the first statement:

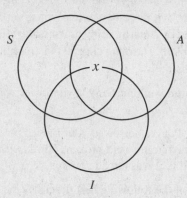

The *x* indicates that there is at least one individual in that region. I have placed the *x* on the circumference of the "intelligent creatures" circle, because we don't know whether the individual that is both a snake and an amphibian is also an intelligent creature. Now enter the information provided by the second statement:

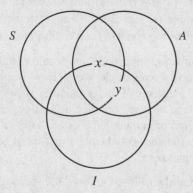

Again the *y* indicates that there is at least one individual who has the characteristics "amphibian" and "intelligent creature." And again, I have placed the *y* on one of the borderlines to indicate we don't know whether the individual shares the third characteristic as well. Finally, complete the diagram:

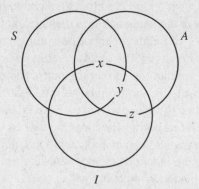

The diagram shows that (E) could be true. The *x* indicates that there is an individual that is both a snake and an amphibian. And it might belong in the circle for intelligent creatures as well—we don't know. The *y* might also be a snake, but if *y* is a snake, then *y* is also

intelligent. Therefore, the individual known to be a snake and the other individual that might be a snake could both be intelligent individuals. This leaves open the possibility that all snakes are intelligent. The other choices are not possible. As for the wrong choices, the diagram indicates that there is at least one individual that shares each of those pairs of characteristics.

32. If the statements above are true, which of the following must be false?

   Ⓐ All snakes are not intelligent.
   Ⓑ All intelligent creatures are snakes.
   Ⓒ A rat is an amphibious snake.
   Ⓓ All amphibians are snakes.
   Ⓔ All intelligent creatures are amphibians.

(B) The *z* indicates that there is at least one individual that is intelligent and not a snake. Therefore, it must be false that all intelligent creatures are snakes. (A) is equivalent to "no snakes are intelligent," and according to the diagram, that statement could be true (if the *x* falls outside of the circle for intelligent creatures). As for (C), we have no information about rats, so this statement could be true.

    As for (D), the *x* indicates there is at least one amphibian that is a snake, and the *y* indicates there is at least one individual that is both amphibian and intelligent, and it could also be a snake. And the *z* indicates there is a creature that is not a snake and might or might not be an amphibian. Thus it is possible for (D) to be true. Finally, as for (E), this could be true, depending on whether *x* belongs inside the amphibian circle.

    Using circle diagrams is one way to attack these two problems. You can also attack them by using verbal logic. You should use the technique you feel more comfortable with.

I recall my first encounter with philosophy. Professor Elmendorff, who taught all of the introductory philosophy classes at the University, strode into the room and began, "The end of any philosophical inquiry is truth. Now, you may wonder why it is that a university, whose very reason for existence is the dissemination of learning, would offer a class in philosophy—not only allowing but even inviting the wolf into the fold. This has always been a great mystery to me."

33. It can be inferred that Professor Elmendorff believes that

   Ⓐ philosophy should not be a required course at the University
   Ⓑ philosophy has few if any practical applications
   Ⓒ truth and learning are not the same thing
   Ⓓ truth can be discovered only by the process of learning
   Ⓔ learning is more important than philosophy

(C) The professor states that the goal of philosophy is truth and draws a distinction between truth and learning. Thus, (C) is the best response. As for (A), the professor seems to favor philosophy over learning. He probably thinks that the head of the University would not allow philosophy to be a required course, but this doesn't mean he believes philosophy should not be required. As for (B), this goes considerably beyond the scope of the initial paragraph. To be sure, you can probably make an argument the professor might accept this statement, but part of your justification will have to be that learning and truth are distinct. And that indicates that (B) is further removed from the explicit text, so (C) is a better choice. (D) and (E) must surely be false since the professor seems to accord priority to truth over learning.

34. According to a recent study by the Mayor's Task Force, the amount of homeless people in the city has tripled in the last ten years.

   Ⓐ the amount of homeless people in the city has
   Ⓑ the number of homeless people in the city has
   Ⓒ the amount of homeless people in the city have
   Ⓓ the number of homeless people in the city having
   Ⓔ the number of those people who are homeless in the city has

(B) The original sentence contains an error of usage. The word *amount* is used to describe mass or bulk quantities (quantities that do not come in discrete units), e.g., an amount of water or an amount of sand. Since people are countable, the correct word is *number*, e.g., a number of people, or a number of drops of water, or a number of grains of sand. (B), (D), and (E) make this correction. (D), however, uses the participle *having*, which leaves the sentence without a conjugated main verb, and (E) is needlessly wordy when compared with the correct choice.

35. Many health-care professionals now advocate race walking as a form of exercise because it burns as many calories as jogging, works muscle groups that jogging does not, and the chances of stress-related injuries are reduced.

   Ⓐ and the chances of stress-related injuries are reduced
   Ⓑ and reduces the chances of stress-related injury
   Ⓒ reducing the chances of stress-related injury
   Ⓓ and the chances of a stress-related injury get reduced
   Ⓔ with a reduction of the chances of a stress-related injury

(B) The original suffers from a lack of parallelism. In a series of verbs, such as *burns, works,* and *reduces,* the verbs must all have the same form. In the original, however, we have two active voice verbs in a series followed by a clause using the passive voice. (B) solves this problem. The other choices fail to supply the needed parallelism.

Al: Why did you return my lawn mower with a broken blade?

David: First, I never borrowed your mower. Second, when I returned it, it wasn't broken. Third, when I borrowed it, it was already broken.

36. Which of the following best describes the weakness in David's response?

   Ⓐ It is internally inconsistent.
   Ⓑ It makes an unproved assumption.
   Ⓒ It contains circular reasoning.
   Ⓓ It leads to no definite conclusion.
   Ⓔ It seeks to evade the issue.

(A) The speaker makes three different statements—all as assertions of fact. But the three statements cannot all be true, so the speaker has contradicted himself.

   It is not always the case that the whole is equal to the sum of the parts. For example, we speak of Impressionist painting. The elements of such a painting are a certain choice of colors, the use of particular brush strokes and other techniques of paint application, and the selection of a certain subject matter. But the painting cannot be reduced to just these elements.

37. Which of the following would the speaker regard as most similar to the notion of Impressionist painting?

   Ⓐ The steps in a geometry proof
   Ⓑ The volumes in an encyclopedia
   Ⓒ The notion of a national character
   Ⓓ The instructions for assembling a toy
   Ⓔ The molecules that make up an atom

(C) This is a kind of further application question. The point of the paragraph is that a concept that defines a school of painting cannot be completely reduced to other concepts. The speaker would say that the whole is more than the sum of the parts. The only situation given that is at all similar to the idea of a school of painting is the notion of a national character. So (C) is the best response. The ideas mentioned in each of the other choices can be reduced to individual parts, and once the individual components are isolated, there is nothing left to explain.

Although alcohol seems to make you sleepy, it is actually an antisoporific.

38. The logic of the statement above is most closely paralleled by the logic of which of the following statements?

Ⓐ Although some people still believe in God, most people have accepted science as supreme.

Ⓑ Although sea water will not quench thirst, it will extinguish fires.

Ⓒ Although dry ice seems to burn the skin, it is actually quite cold.

Ⓓ Although all states have a capital, no state has the same capital as any other.

Ⓔ Although heroin induces a state of euphoria, the drug is highly addictive.

(C) Although all of the answer choices have a grammatical structure similar to that of the initial statement, only one makes a claim that is substantively similar to the initial statement. The initial statement claims that X seems to have one characteristic but actually has the opposite—in other words, the sense is wrong. (C) makes a similar claim.

39. The primary purpose of the selection is to

Ⓐ demonstrate that the NICB study does not prove that efficiency results from concentration

Ⓑ argue that less concentrated industries are as efficient as highly concentrated ones

Ⓒ prove that smaller companies are as efficient as the largest firms in any given industry

Ⓓ explain why labor-intensive industries are likely to have low shipments per employee

Ⓔ criticize the nation's leading business magazine for printing its story about the NICB study

(A) This is a main idea question. The author begins by citing the NICB study. The study found correlations between concentration and productivity and between size and productivity. This prompted the NICB and the magazine to conclude that size equals efficiency. In the second paragraph the author attacks the study's claim that concentration is correlated with productivity; and in the third paragraph, he attacks the study's claim that size is correlated with productivity. In the final paragraph, the author directly contradicts the claim that size means efficiency. (A) best describes this development. (B) and (C) both overstate points made by the author. Even if they were toned down somewhat, neither could be considered the overall theme of the selection. (D) and (E) are only small points made in the passage.

40. According to the selection, the study tends to overstate shipments per employee in some industries because

Ⓐ productivity included profits and advertising outlays

Ⓑ capital requirements for entry are low

Ⓒ the category "all other" industries is overly inclusive

Ⓓ top companies, on the average, have higher rates of productivity

Ⓔ low-productivity industries are relatively unconcentrated

(A) This is a specific idea question. The last three sentences of the second paragraph specifically make the point suggested by (A). The other choices make statements that are to be found in the selection (made by the author or by the study), but those choices are not responsive to this question.

41. In the final paragraph, the author

Ⓐ indicts the motives of the people who prepared the NICB study

Ⓑ criticizes the methodology of the NICB study

Ⓒ offers affirmative evidence to disprove the conclusions of the NICB study

Ⓓ cites other studies that contradict the conclusions of the NICB study

Ⓔ describes the difference between consumer and producer goods industries

(C) This is a logical structure question. Having demolished the study in the second and third paragraphs, the author then goes one step further: not only does the study not prove that bigger is better, but it can be proven that bigger is not necessarily better. (C) describes this strategy. (A) is incorrect because the author carries out the attack in a very scholarly way—attacking the study itself, not the motives of those who wrote it. (B) correctly describes the second and third paragraphs, but not the final paragraph. (D) and (E) are incorrect because these ideas do not appear in the final paragraph.

QUANTITATIVE SECTION

1. If five pounds of coffee cost $12, how much coffee can be purchased for $30?

Ⓐ 7.2   Ⓑ 10   Ⓒ 12.5   Ⓓ 15   Ⓔ 18

(C) This question can be answered using "supermarket math." You find out how much coffee costs per pound: $\frac{\$12}{5}$ pounds = $2.40 per pound. Then you divide $30 by $2.40: $30 ÷ $2.40 = 12.5. The steps of the process can be represented in a single proportion:

$$\frac{\text{Cost } X}{\text{Cost } Y} = \frac{\text{Pounds } X}{\text{Pounds } Y}$$

$$\frac{\$12}{\$30} = \frac{5}{x}$$

$$12x = 5(30)$$

$$x = \frac{150}{12} = 12.5$$

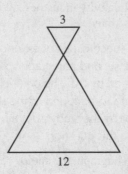

2. If the two triangles above are equilateral, what is the ratio of the perimeter of the smaller to that of the larger?

Ⓐ $\frac{1}{36}$ Ⓑ $\frac{1}{15}$ Ⓒ $\frac{1}{9}$ Ⓓ $\frac{1}{4}$ Ⓔ $\frac{1}{3}$

(D) Attack the question directly. Find the perimeter of each triangle. Since the triangles are equilateral, the smaller one has a perimeter of $3 + 3 + 3 = 9$, and the larger one has a perimeter of $12 + 12 + 12 = 36$. And $\frac{9}{36} = \frac{1}{4}$.

You might also have reasoned that since the triangles are equilateral, the ratio of their perimeters is the same as the ratio of their sides. So the ratio of their perimeters will also be $\frac{3}{12} = \frac{1}{4}$.

The second line of reasoning is more elegant (because it's simpler), but who needs elegance when the first line of attack is easily managed anyway?

3. If the perimeter of a rectangular playing field is 120 meters, which of the following could be the length of one of its sides?

I. 20

II. 40

III. 60

Ⓐ I only   Ⓑ I and II only   Ⓒ I and III only
Ⓓ II and III only   Ⓔ I, II, and III

(B) Just use numbers. As for I, a rectangle could have sides of 20 and 40: $20 + 20 + 40 + 40 = 120$. We see that it can also have a side of 40, so II is part of the correct answer. But what rectangle can have a side of 60 and a perimeter of only 120? It doesn't exist; $60 + 60 = 120$, so the other sides would be zero.

4. What number is Gary thinking of?

(1) The number Gary is thinking of is less than 24.

(2) The number Gary is thinking of is more than 22.

Ⓐ statement 1 alone is sufficient to answer the question, but statement 2 alone is not sufficient

Ⓑ statement 2 alone is sufficient to answer the question, but statement 1 alone is not sufficient

Ⓒ both statements together are needed to answer the question, but neither statement alone is sufficient

Ⓓ either statement by itself is sufficient to answer the question

Ⓔ not enough facts are given to answer the question

(E) Neither (1) nor (2) alone is sufficient to answer the question. Even taken together, the two statements are insufficient, for they establish only that $22 < x < 24$. (And the problem does not stipulate that Gary is thinking of an integer. He could be thinking of 22.25, 23, 23.95, etc.)

5. Does Charlie weigh more than Nora?

(1) Charlie and Nora together weigh 80 pounds.

(2) Charlie's weight plus $1\frac{1}{2}$ pounds equals 50 percent of Nora's weight.

Ⓐ statement 1 alone is sufficient to answer the question, but statement 2 alone is not sufficient

Ⓑ statement 2 alone is sufficient to answer the question, but statement 1 alone is not sufficient

Ⓒ both statements together are needed to answer the question, but neither statement alone is sufficient

Ⓓ either statement by itself is sufficient to answer the question

Ⓔ not enough facts are given to answer the question

(B) (1) is not sufficient to answer the question because it provides no information about the relative weights of Charlie and Nora. (2), however is sufficient, for (2) implies that Charlie weighs less than half of what Nora weighs. Algebraically, (2) states

$$C + 1\frac{1}{2} = 0.50N$$

where C and N represent the weights of Charlie and Nora, respectively.

Therefore,

$$2C + 3 = N$$

Since weights must be positive, this proves that C is less than N.

6. If $\frac{1}{3}$ of a number is 2 more than $\frac{1}{5}$ of the number, what is the number?

Ⓐ 3   Ⓑ 6   Ⓒ 12   Ⓓ 15   Ⓔ 24

(D) You can, if you insist, solve this problem with an equation:

$$\frac{1}{3}x - 2 = \frac{1}{5}x$$

$$\frac{1}{3}x - \frac{1}{5}x = 2$$

$$\frac{2}{15}x = 2$$

$$x = 15$$

But you can reach the same conclusion in your head by testing the answer choices. Start with (C). $\frac{1}{3}$ of 12 is 4 and $\frac{1}{6}$ of 12 is 2 and change. The difference is not 2; the difference is less than 2, so you need a larger number. Try 15. $\frac{1}{3}$ of 15 is 5; $\frac{1}{5}$ of 15 is 3; and 5 is 2 more than 3.

7. In the figure above, if the triangle is equilateral and has a perimeter of 12, the perimeter of the square is

Ⓐ 9   Ⓑ 12   Ⓒ 16   Ⓓ 20   Ⓔ 24

(C) This is a composite figure. One side of the equilateral triangle is also a side of the square. The triangle has a perimeter of 12, so each side is 4. If the square has a side of 4, then it has a perimeter of 4 + 4 + 4 + 4 = 16.

8. If $5x + 3y = 19$ and x and y are positive integers, then y could equal which of the following?

Ⓐ 1   Ⓑ 2   Ⓒ 3   Ⓓ 4   Ⓔ 5

(C) No need to devise a mathematical strategy for this question, just test the choices. You can start anywhere you want to. The correct choice is (C). If $y = 3$, then $5x + 3(3) = 19$, $5x = 10$, and $x = 2$, an integer.

9. In 1994, Company x had gross revenues of $10,500,000. What were the gross sales of Company x in 1995?

(1) Gross sales in 1994 were $2,100,000 more than gross sales in 1993.

(2) The percent increase in gross sales from 1994 to 1995 was exactly one-half the percent increase in gross sales from 1993 to 1994.

Ⓐ statement 1 alone is sufficient to answer the question, but statement 2 alone is not sufficient
Ⓑ statement 2 alone is sufficient to answer the question, but statement 1 alone is not sufficient
Ⓒ both statements together are needed to answer the question, but neither statement alone is sufficient
Ⓓ either statement by itself is sufficient to answer the question
Ⓔ not enough facts are given to answer the question

(C) (1) alone is not sufficient because it provides no information about sales in 1995. Nor is (2) alone sufficient. Although (2) implies that sales grew by the same percent from 1994 to 1995 as they did from 1993 to 1994, (2) doesn't quantify that increase, either in absolute or percent terms. Both statements taken together, however, are sufficient to answer the question. Using (1) with the information provided in the question stem, it is possible to calculate the percent increase in sales from 1993 to 1994; and that information coupled with the data provided by (2) can be used to calculate the increase in sales from 1994 to 1995. Because this is a data sufficiency item, there is no need to grind out the numbers, but for purposes of explanation, we will finish the calculation:

1993 Sales = $10,500,000 − $2,100,000 = $8,400,000

Percent Increase 1993 to 1994 = $\frac{\$2,100,000}{\$8,400,000}$ = 25%

1995 = (12.5% of $10,500,000) + $10,500,000 = $11,825,000

10. The total weight of three packages is 32 pounds. How much does the heaviest package weigh?

(1) One of the packages weighs 7 pounds.

(2) One of the packages weighs 18 pounds.

Ⓐ statement 1 alone is sufficient to answer the question, but statement 2 alone is not sufficient
Ⓑ statement 2 alone is sufficient to answer the question, but statement 1 alone is not sufficient
Ⓒ both statements together are needed to answer the question, but neither statement alone is sufficient
Ⓓ either statement by itself is sufficient to answer the question
Ⓔ not enough facts are given to answer the question

(B) (1) is not sufficient to answer the question. (2), however, is sufficient. Since 18 is more than half of 32, the 18-pound package must be the heaviest of the three.

11. At the first stop on her route, a driver unloaded two-fifths of the packages in her van. After she unloaded another three packages at her next stop, one-half of the original number of packages in the van remained. How many packages were in the van before the first delivery?

Ⓐ 10   Ⓑ 18   Ⓒ 25   Ⓓ 30   Ⓔ 36

(D) By now this problem should seem familiar to you. You can solve it with an equation:

$$x - \frac{2}{5}x - 3 = \frac{1}{2}x$$

$$\frac{3}{5}x - 3 = \frac{1}{2}x$$

$$\frac{3}{5}x - \frac{1}{2}x = 3$$

$$\frac{1}{10}x = 3$$

$$x = 30$$

Or, you can pick numbers and work backward.

12. If m and n are negative numbers, which of the following must always be positive?

 I. $m - n$

 II. $m \times n$

 III. $m \div n$

Ⓐ I only Ⓑ II only Ⓒ I and III only
Ⓓ II and III only Ⓔ I, II, and III

(D) This question tests properties of numbers. As for II, $m \times n$ is a negative times a negative, which always generates a positive number. As for III, $m \div n$ is a negative divided by a negative, which always generates a positive number. But $m - n$ may or may not generate a positive number. If m is larger than n, $m - n$ is positive; but if n is larger than m, $m - n$ is negative. Example: if $m = -2$ and $n = -1$, $-2 - (-1) = -2 + 1 = -1$.

13. $\dfrac{1}{1 + \frac{1}{x}}$ is equal to which of the following?

Ⓐ $x + 1$ Ⓑ $\dfrac{1}{x+1}$ Ⓒ $\dfrac{x}{x+1}$

Ⓓ $\dfrac{x+1}{x}$ Ⓔ $x^2 + x$

(C) This question asks you to rewrite the expression:

$$\frac{1}{1+\frac{1}{x}} = \frac{1}{\frac{x+1}{x}} = 1\left(\frac{x}{x+1}\right) = \frac{x}{x+1}$$

Or you could substitute numbers. If $x = 1$, then

$$\frac{1}{1+\frac{1}{x}} = \frac{1}{1+\frac{1}{1}} = \frac{1}{1+1} = \frac{1}{2}$$

On the assumption that $x = 1$, two answer choices generate the result $\frac{1}{2}$—(B) and (C). So try another number, say, $x = 2$. If $x = 2$, the correct answer should generate the value $\frac{2}{3}$. Now you can eliminate (B), and (C) must be correct.

14. What is the greatest integer that is less than n?

 (1) $n = \dfrac{13}{3}$

 (2) $n = \sqrt{169} \times \dfrac{1}{3}$

Ⓐ statement 1 alone is sufficient to answer the question, but statement 2 alone is not sufficient
Ⓑ statement 2 alone is sufficient to answer the question, but statement 1 alone is not sufficient
Ⓒ both statements together are needed to answer the question, but neither statement alone is sufficient
Ⓓ either statement by itself is sufficient to answer the question
Ⓔ not enough facts are given to answer the question

(D) Statement (1) is sufficient to answer the question. Since $\frac{13}{3} = 4\frac{1}{3}$, the greatest integer less than n is 4. (2) is also sufficient. $\sqrt{169} = 13$, and $13 \times \frac{1}{3} = \frac{13}{3}$. Therefore, (2) also establishes that the answer to the question is 4. (**Note:** The "$\sqrt{}$" indicates the positive root. The "$\pm$" symbol is used when solving an equation that has two roots.)

15. Employees at a certain airline agreed to accept salary cuts. Was the amount of Mr. Thom's salary cut more than the amount of Mrs. Gershon's salary cut?

 (1) Mr. Thom's salary was cut by 12 percent.

 (2) Mrs. Gershon's salary was cut by 15 percent.

Ⓐ statement 1 alone is sufficient to answer the question, but statement 2 alone is not sufficient
Ⓑ statement 2 alone is sufficient to answer the question, but statement 1 alone is not sufficient
Ⓒ both statements together are needed to answer the question, but neither statement alone is sufficient
Ⓓ either statement by itself is sufficient to answer the question
Ⓔ not enough facts are given to answer the question

(E) Neither statement alone can be sufficient, for each provides information about only one of the two persons. Even taken together, they are not sufficient, for they provide information about percent. The question asks for amount.

16. If S is 150 percent of T, then T is what percent of $S + T$?

Ⓐ $33\frac{1}{3}\%$ Ⓑ 40% Ⓒ 50%

Ⓓ 75% Ⓔ 80%

(B) You can solve this problem using S and T as unknowns. Since S is 150% of T, $S = 1.5T$. Then the question asks you to express $\frac{T}{S+T}$ as a percent. Just substitute $1.5T$ for S: $\frac{T}{1.5T+T} = \frac{T}{2.5T} = \frac{1}{2.5} = 40\%$. If you don't like working with letters, pick some numbers. Let T be 10 and S be 15. Then $\frac{T}{S+T} = \frac{10}{10+15} = \frac{10}{25} = 40\%$.

17. If $\frac{5}{3} + \frac{x}{3} = 2$, then $x =$

Ⓐ $\frac{5}{9}$ Ⓑ $\frac{3}{5}$ Ⓒ $\frac{5}{3}$ Ⓓ $\frac{5}{6}$ Ⓔ 1

(E) Solve for x:

$$\frac{5}{3} + \frac{x}{3} = 2$$

$$\frac{5+x}{3} = 2$$

$$5 + x = 2(3)$$

$$x = 6 - 5 = 1$$

If you look closely at the equation, you might be able to avoid doing all those steps. What number when added to $\frac{5}{3}$ makes 2, which is $\frac{6}{3}$? The answer is $\frac{1}{3}$. So x must be 1.

　　You might test the choices. If you do, start with the easiest value to work with, 1.

Sales Representative	Sales for May (Units Sold)
Victor	6
Mary	9
Randy	8
Sue	4
Carla	3

18. What was the average number of units sold by the sales representatives shown above?

Ⓐ 4 Ⓑ 5 Ⓒ 6 Ⓓ 9 Ⓔ 30

(C) Just calculate the average:

$$\frac{6+9+8+4+3}{5} = 6$$

19. What is the value of the integer x?

(1) $8 < x^3 < 64$

(2) $4 < x^2 < 16$

Ⓐ statement 1 alone is sufficient to answer the question, but statement 2 alone is not sufficient

Ⓑ statement 2 alone is sufficient to answer the question, but statement 1 alone is not sufficient

Ⓒ both statements together are needed to answer the question, but neither statement alone is sufficient

Ⓓ either statement by itself is sufficient to answer the question

Ⓔ not enough facts are given to answer the question

(A) (1) alone is sufficient to answer the question, for there is only one integer greater than 8 but less than 64 that is the cube of another number: 27. So (1) implies

that x is 3. Similarly, the only integral square greater than 4 and less than 16 is 9. (2), however, is not sufficient, for x could be either 3 or –3.

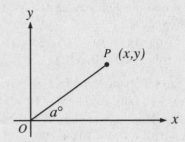

20. In the figure above, if O is the origin and point P has coordinates (x, y), is the length of segment OP greater than 5?

(1) $a = 45°$

(2) P is a point on a circle with center O and radius 7.5.

Ⓐ statement 1 alone is sufficient to answer the question, but statement 2 alone is not sufficient

Ⓑ statement 2 alone is sufficient to answer the question, but statement 1 alone is not sufficient

Ⓒ both statements together are needed to answer the question, but neither statement alone is sufficient

Ⓓ either statement by itself is sufficient to answer the question

Ⓔ not enough facts are given to answer the question

(B) (1) is not sufficient to answer the question, because it provides no information about the length of OP. (2), however, is sufficient. If P is a point on a circle with radius 7.5, then $OP = 7.5$

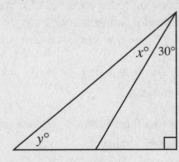

21. In the figure above, $x + y =$

Ⓐ 15° Ⓑ 30° Ⓒ 60° Ⓓ 90° Ⓔ 120°

(C)

$$x + y + 30 + 90 = 180$$

$$x + y = 180 - 120$$

$$x + y = 60$$

You can arrive at the same conclusion by estimating the size of x and the size of y. x appears to be equal to 30°, so assume x is approximately 30°. And y appears to be about 30°. Together they are about 60°. The only choice in the ballpark is (C), so (C) must be correct.

22. Carl has only $5 bills and $10 bills in his wallet. If he has x $5 bills and ten more $10 bills than $5 bills, in terms of x, how much money, in dollars, does Carl have in his wallet?

Ⓐ $15x$ Ⓑ $15x + 10$ Ⓒ $15x + 15$
Ⓓ $15x + 100$ Ⓔ $50x + 100$

(D) You can set up the formula. Carl has x $5 bills, or $5x$ dollars in $5 bills. And he has $10 + x$ $10 bills, or $10(x + 10) = 10x + 100$ dollars in $10 bills. Combine them: $5x + 10x + 100 = 15x + 100$.

You can also assume some numbers. To make it easy, assume Carl has one $5 bill; in other words, $x = 1$. Then he would have eleven $10 bills. The total amount would be $5 + 11(10) = 115$. So when $x = 1$, the correct formula will generate the value 115:

(A) $15(1) = 15$ (Wrong.)

(B) $15(1) + 10 = 25$ (Wrong.)

(C) $15(1) + 15 = 30$ (Wrong.)

(D) $15(1) + 100 = 115$ (Correct.)

(E) $50(1) + 100 = 150$ (Wrong.)

23. If x and y are positive integers and $\frac{x}{y} < 1$, which of the following is greater than 1?

Ⓐ $\frac{x}{2y}$ Ⓑ $\frac{\sqrt{x}}{y}$ Ⓒ $\left(\frac{x}{y}\right)^2$ Ⓓ $x - y$ Ⓔ $\frac{y}{x}$

(E) This question tests properties of numbers. Since x and y are positive integers such that $\frac{x}{y} < 1$, x must be less than y. Given that x is less than y,

(A) $\frac{x}{2y}$ is also less than 1, since $2y$ is a larger denominator than y;

(B) $\frac{\sqrt{x}}{y}$ is less than 1, since $\sqrt{x}$ is a smaller numerator than x;

(C) $\left(\frac{x}{y}\right)^2$ is less than 1, since the square of a fraction is smaller than the original fraction;

(D) $x - y$ is less than 1, since y is larger than x; but

(E) $\frac{y}{x}$ is greater than 1, since y is larger than x.

You can also use the technique of assuming some numbers. Assume that $x = 1$ and $y = 2$. Then,

(A) $\frac{1}{2}(2) = \frac{1}{4}$

(B) $\frac{\sqrt{1}}{2} = \frac{1}{2}$

(C) $\left(\frac{1}{2}\right)^2 = \frac{1}{4}$

(D) $1 - 2 = -1$

(E) $\frac{2}{1} = 2$, which is greater than 1.

24. Mr. Hayward bought a brooch and a necklace. If he paid 6-percent sales tax on each item, what was the cost of the necklace without the sales tax?

(1) The total cost of the two items plus the sales tax was $84.80.

(2) Mr. Hayward paid $21.20 for the brooch, including sales tax.

Ⓐ statement 1 alone is sufficient to answer the question, but statement 2 alone is not sufficient
Ⓑ statement 2 alone is sufficient to answer the question, but statement 1 alone is not sufficient
Ⓒ both statements together are needed to answer the question, but neither statement alone is sufficient
Ⓓ either statement by itself is sufficient to answer the question
Ⓔ not enough facts are given to answer the question

(C) Statement (1) is not sufficient because it provides no information about the relative cost of the two items. (2) alone is not sufficient because (2) provides no information about the cost of the necklace. Both statements together are sufficient for they imply that the cost of the necklace with the sales tax was $63.60. And

$63.60 = Cost + 0.06 Cost$

$63.60 = 1.06 Cost$

$Cost = 60

25. What is the circumference of a circle inscribed in a square?

(1) The diagonal of the square is 10.

(2) The perimeter of the square is $20\sqrt{2}$.

Ⓐ statement 1 alone is sufficient to answer the question, but statement 2 alone is not sufficient
Ⓑ statement 2 alone is sufficient to answer the question, but statement 1 alone is not sufficient
Ⓒ both statements together are needed to answer the question, but neither statement alone is sufficient
Ⓓ either statement by itself is sufficient to answer the question
Ⓔ not enough facts are given to answer the question

(D) To find the circumference of a circle, you need to know the radius. Statement (1) is sufficient, for (1) implies that the radius is $\frac{5\sqrt{2}}{2}$:

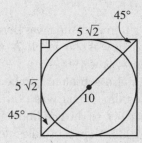

So the circumference of the circle must be $2\pi\left(\frac{5\sqrt{2}}{2}\right) =$ $5\sqrt{2}\pi$. Statement (2) also is sufficient. The side of the square is the diameter of the circle. (2) implies that the diameter of the circle is $20\sqrt{2} \div 4 = 5\sqrt{2}$, so the circumference is $5\sqrt{2}\pi$.

26. If $p = q + 2$ and $r = 2q^2$, then $r =$

Ⓐ $(p-2)^2$ Ⓑ $2(p-2)^2$ Ⓒ $\frac{p-2}{2}$

Ⓓ $\frac{p-2}{4}$ Ⓔ $\frac{(p-2)^2}{4}$

(B) Rewrite one equation so that its form corresponds to the other. If we are to have r expressed in terms of p, we need to express p in terms of $2q^2$.

$p = q + 2$

$p - 2 = q$

$(p-2)^2 = q^2$

$2(p-2)^2 = 2q^2$

$r = 2(p-2)^2$

You can also assume some values. Assume that $q = 1$. On that assumption, $p = (1) + 2 = 3$ and $r = 2(1)^2 = 2$. Using the value 3 for p in the correct answer choice will generate the number 2:

(A) $(3-2)^2 = 1^2 = 1$ (Wrong.)

(B) $2(3-2)^2 = 2(1)^2 = 2(1) = 2$ (Correct.)

(C) $\frac{2-2}{2} = \frac{0}{2} = 0$ (Wrong.)

(D) $\frac{2-2}{4} = \frac{0}{4} = 0$ (Wrong.)

(E) $\frac{(2-2)^2}{4} = \frac{0}{4} = 0$ (Wrong.)

27. If a car travels at 40 kilometers per hour, how many minutes does it take the car to travel k kilometers?

Ⓐ $\frac{2k}{3}$ Ⓑ $\frac{3k}{2}$ Ⓒ $\frac{2}{3k}$ Ⓓ $\frac{3}{2k}$ Ⓔ $40k$

(B) Create an algebraic formula by using a direct proportion.

$$\frac{\text{Kilometers}_1}{\text{Kilometers}_2} = \frac{\text{Time in Minutes}_1}{\text{Time in Minutes}_2}$$

$$\frac{40}{k} = \frac{60}{x}$$

where x is the number of minutes to travel k kilometers.

$40x = 60k$

$$x = \frac{60k}{40} = \frac{3k}{2}$$

You can also assume numbers. Assume that k is 40 kilometers. Since the car travels at 40 kilometers per hour, it will need one hour, or 60 minutes, to travel 40 kilometers. So on the assumption that $k = 40$, the correct choice will generate the number 60:

(A) $\frac{2(40)}{3} = \frac{80}{3}$ (Wrong.)

(B) $\frac{3(40)}{2} = \frac{120}{2} = 60$ (Correct.)

(C) $\frac{2}{3(40)} = \frac{2}{120}$ (Wrong.)

(D) $\frac{3}{2(40)} = \frac{3}{80}$ (Wrong.)

(E) $40(40) = 160$ (Wrong.)

$$\overset{P}{\bullet} \quad\quad \overset{Q}{\bullet} \quad\quad \overset{R}{\bullet} \quad\quad \overset{S}{\bullet} \quad\quad \overset{T}{\bullet}$$

28. If the spaces between the lettered points in the figure above are all equal, then $\frac{PT}{2} - \frac{QS}{2}$ is equal to which of the following?

Ⓐ $PS - QR$ Ⓑ $QR - QS$ Ⓒ PR
Ⓓ QT Ⓔ ST

(E) $\frac{PT}{2}$ is $\frac{1}{2}$ of the length of the entire segment. QS is $\frac{1}{2}$ the length of the segment, and $\frac{QS}{2}$ is $\frac{1}{4}$ of the segment. So $\frac{PT}{2} - \frac{QS}{2}$ is $\frac{1}{2}$ of the segment minus $\frac{1}{4}$ of the length of the segment, which is $\frac{1}{4}$ of the length of the segment. Only (E) is $\frac{1}{4}$ the length of the segment.

You can also assign numbers to the lengths. Assume that each segment is equal to 1. Then $PT = 4$, and $\frac{PT}{2} = 2$. And QS is 2, and $\frac{QS}{2} = 1$. Finally, $2 - 1 = 1$. So the correct answer choice should have a length of 1:

(A) $3 - 1 = 2$ (Wrong.)

(B) $1 - 2 = -1$ (Wrong.)

(C) 2 (Wrong.)

(D) 3 (Wrong.)

(E) 1 (Correct.)

29. How many square tiles were used to cover a certain windowless bathroom wall?

 (1) The wall is 6 feet wide.

 (2) The wall is 8 feet high.

Ⓐ statement 1 alone is sufficient to answer the question, but statement 2 alone is not sufficient

Ⓑ statement 2 alone is sufficient to answer the question, but statement 1 alone is not sufficient

Ⓒ both statements together are needed to answer the question, but neither statement alone is sufficient

Ⓓ either statement by itself is sufficient to answer the question

Ⓔ not enough facts are given to answer the question

(E) Statements (1) and (2) together provide the area of the wall that was covered with tile. But this information is not sufficient to determine how many tiles were used. A crucial piece of information is missing: the size of the tiles.

30. At 1 p.m., train A leaves New York bound for Providence, and train B leaves Providence bound for New York along a track that runs beside that used by train A. If each train travels at a constant speed and the distance by rail from New York to Providence is 150 miles, how many miles from New York is train A when it meets train B?

 (1) Train A and Train B travel at the same speed.

 (2) Train A travels at a speed of 50 miles per hour.

Ⓐ statement 1 alone is sufficient to answer the question, but statement 2 alone is not sufficient

Ⓑ statement 2 alone is sufficient to answer the question, but statement 1 alone is not sufficient

Ⓒ both statements together are needed to answer the question, but neither statement alone is sufficient

Ⓓ either statement by itself is sufficient to answer the question

Ⓔ not enough facts are given to answer the question

(A) Statement (1) is sufficient to answer the question. Since both trains leave their respective stations at the same time, traveling toward each other *at the same speed,* they will meet at the halfway point—75 miles from each city. Statement (2) is not sufficient to answer the question.

31. Exactly three years before the year in which Anna was born, the year was $1980 - x$. In terms of x, on Anna's twentieth birthday, the year will be

Ⓐ $1977 + x$ Ⓑ $1997 + x$ Ⓒ $2003 - x$
Ⓓ $2003 + x$ Ⓔ $2006 + x$

(C) Create a formula. Anna was born three years after $1980 - x$, so she was born in $1980 - x + 3$. Twenty years later the year will be $1980 - x + 3 + 20 = 2003 - x$.

You can also substitute numbers. Assume $x = 1$. And then assume Anna was born three years after $1980 - 1 = 1979$, so she was born in 1982. So she will turn 20 in 2002. Then substitute x for 1 in each of the answer choices.

(A) $1977 + 1 = 1978$ (Wrong.)

(B) $1997 + 1 = 1998$ (Wrong.)

(C) $2003 - 1 = 2002$ (Correct.)

(D) $2003 + 1 = 2004$ (Wrong.)

(E) $2006 + 1 = 2007$ (Wrong.)

32. If $x = k + \dfrac{1}{2} = \dfrac{k+3}{2}$, then $x =$

Ⓐ $\dfrac{1}{3}$ Ⓑ $\dfrac{1}{2}$ Ⓒ 1 Ⓓ 2 Ⓔ $\dfrac{5}{2}$

(E) You really have two equations:

$$x = k + \frac{1}{2} \text{ and } k + \frac{1}{2} = \frac{k+3}{2}$$

Solve for k:

$$k + \frac{1}{2} = \frac{k+3}{2}$$

$$2\left(k + \frac{1}{2}\right) = k + 3$$

$$2k + 1 = k + 3$$

$$k = 2$$

Now substitute 2 for k:

$$x = k + \frac{1}{2} = 2 + \frac{1}{2} = \frac{5}{2}$$

You can also try testing the choices, but the process is tedious. For example, assume that $x = 1$. On that assumption, the first equation gives the value of k as $\frac{1}{2}$, but when $\frac{1}{2}$ is substituted for k into the second equation, the second equation is false. So (C) is incorrect. (E), however, does work. If $x = \frac{5}{2}$, then the value of k in the first equation is 2. And substituting 2 for both k's in the second equation produces a true statement.

33. If $\frac{x}{z} = c$ and $\frac{y}{z} = c - 1$, then x and y are related in which of the following ways?

   Ⓐ $x = y - 1$ Ⓑ $x = y + 1$ Ⓒ $x = z + y$
   Ⓓ $x = z - y$ Ⓔ $x = \frac{y}{1}$

   (C) To relate x and y, you must use the term c. Since $\frac{y}{z} = c - 1$, $\frac{y}{z} + 1 = c$. Next,

   $$\frac{x}{z} = \frac{y}{z} + 1$$

   $$x = \left(\frac{y}{z} + 1\right)z$$

   $$x = y + z = z + y$$

   You can save some steps if you recognize that $\frac{x}{z}$ can be substituted directly for c in the second equation. You can avoid the algebra entirely by assuming some numbers. Suppose that $z = 2$ and $c = 3$. Then $x = 6$ and $y = 4$. Plug these numbers into the equations in the answer choices:

   (A) $6 = 4 - 1$ (False, so (A) is wrong.)

   (B) $6 = 4 + 1$ (False, so (B) is wrong.)

   (C) $6 = 4 + 2$ (True, so (C) is correct.)

   (D) $6 = 2 - 4$ (False, so (D) is wrong.)

   (E) $6 = \frac{4}{1}$ (False, so (E) is wrong.)

34. A dean must select three students to serve on a committee. If she is considering five students, from how many possible threesomes must she choose?

   Ⓐ 2   Ⓑ 3   Ⓒ 10   Ⓓ 15   Ⓔ 18

   (C) You can solve the problem by counting the possibilities. Let A, B, C, D, and E be the individuals. The possible committees are: ABC, ABD, ABE, ACD, ACE, ADE, BCD, BCE, BDE, and CDE.

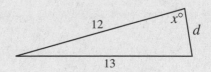

35. What is the area of the triangle above?

   (1) $x = 90°$

   (2) $d = 5$

   Ⓐ statement 1 alone is sufficient to answer the question, but statement 2 alone is not sufficient
   Ⓑ statement 2 alone is sufficient to answer the question, but statement 1 alone is not sufficient
   Ⓒ both statements together are needed to answer the question, but neither statement alone is sufficient
   Ⓓ either statement by itself is sufficient to answer the question
   Ⓔ not enough facts are given to answer the question

(D) Statement (1) alone is sufficient to answer the question, because (1) implies that the triangle is a right triangle and, further, that $d = 5$. d and 12 can then be used as an altitude and a base to find the area of the triangle: $\left(\frac{1}{2}\right)(5)(12) = 30$. Statement (2) alone is also sufficient. Assuming that $d = 5$, the measures of the sides of the triangle fit the Pythagorean Theorem ($5^2 + 12^2 = 13^2$), so the triangle is a right triangle. Given that $x = 90$, it is possible to find the area of the triangle.

36. What is the sum of the number of dimes and the number of quarters Steve has in his pocket?

   (1) The total value of the coins in Steve's pocket is $3.55.

   (2) Steve has only dimes and quarters in his pocket.

   Ⓐ statement 1 alone is sufficient to answer the question, but statement 2 alone is not sufficient
   Ⓑ statement 2 alone is sufficient to answer the question, but statement 1 alone is not sufficient
   Ⓒ both statements together are needed to answer the question, but neither statement alone is sufficient
   Ⓓ either statement by itself is sufficient to answer the question
   Ⓔ not enough facts are given to answer the question

(E) Neither statement (1) nor (2) alone is sufficient for obvious reasons, so the only question remaining is whether the two statements work together to answer the question. They do not. There are several combinations of dimes and quarters that total $3.55, for example, one quarter and 33 dimes, or 11 quarters and eight dimes.

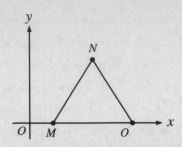

37. In the figure above, M and O are points on the x axis. What is the area of equilateral triangle MNO?

(1) The coordinates of point N are $(5, \sqrt{3})$.

(2) The coordinates of point M are $(\sqrt{3}, 0)$.

Ⓐ statement 1 alone is sufficient to answer the question, but statement 2 alone is not sufficient

Ⓑ statement 2 alone is sufficient to answer the question, but statement 1 alone is not sufficient

Ⓒ both statements together are needed to answer the question, but neither statement alone is sufficient

Ⓓ either statement by itself is sufficient to answer the question

Ⓔ not enough facts are given to answer the question

(A) It is a characteristic of an equilateral triangle that if you have information about one dimension or the area, it is possible to deduce the other relevant features of the triangle. Thus, statement (1) is sufficient to answer the question. Given that the y coordinate is $\sqrt{3}$:

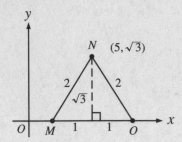

So the area of the triangle is $\sqrt{3}$. Statement (2), however, is not sufficient. Although (2) implies that point M is $\sqrt{3}$ removed from the origin, (2) supplies no information about the magnitude of any aspect of the triangle.

Sample GMAT
CAT 3

Verbal Section

41 Questions—75 Minutes

General Directions: To simulate the experience of taking the CAT, answer each question in order. Do not skip any questions, and do not go back to questions you have already answered.

Directions for sentence correction questions: In questions of this type, either part or all of a sentence is underlined. The sentence is followed by five ways of wording the underlined part. The first answer choice always repeats the original; the other answer choices are different. If you think that the original phrasing is the best, choose the first answer. If you think one of the other answer choices is the best, select that choice. Indicate your answer by blackening the circle next to your choice.

This section tests your ability to identify correct and effective expression. Evaluate the answer choices by the requirements of standard written English. Pay attention to elements of grammar, diction, (choice of words), and sentence construction. Select the answer choice that *best* expresses the meaning of the original sentence. The correct choice will be clear and precise and free of awkwardness, wordiness, or ambiguity.

Directions for critical reasoning questions: Questions of this type ask you to analyze and evaluate the reasoning presented in short paragraphs or passages. For some questions, all of the answer choices may conceivably be answers to the question asked. You should select the *best* answer to the question; that is, an answer that does not require you to make assumptions that violate commonsense standards by being implausible, redundant, irrelevant or inconsistent. Indicate your answer by blackening the circle next to your choice.

Directions for reading comprehension questions: Each passage is followed by questions or incomplete statements about it. Once you have read the passage, answer the question based upon what is stated or implied. Indicate your answer by blackening the circle next to your choice.

1. A baby boomer is defined to be one who is now in his or her mid-forties, who is concerned with raising a family, and who is upwardly mobile.

    (A) to be one who is now in his or her mid-forties, who is concerned with raising a family, and who
    (B) as those who are in their mid-forties, concerned with raising a family,
    (C) to be those that are in their mid-forties, concerned about the raising of a child, that
    (D) to be one who is in his or her mid-forties and concerned with the raising of a family and also who
    (E) as a person in his or her mid-forties, who is concerned with raising a family and who

2. The dropout rate in American schools is 10 times that of European nations.

    (A) that of European nations
    (B) what the rate is in Europe
    (C) that which it is in Europe
    (D) European nations'
    (E) that which they are in Europe

3. More and more fashion-conscious women are asking themselves if it is moral to wear clothing made from the skin of an animal.

    (A) if it is
    (B) about if it is
    (C) whether it is
    (D) as to whether or not it is
    (E) about whether it is

GO ON TO NEXT PAGE

Sid is traveling in the land of Sasnak. His destination is Nocam, but he has encountered a fork in the road and doesn't know which route leads to his destination. In the land of Sasnak there are two clans. Members of one clan always speak the truth; members of the other clan always speak the opposite of the truth. It is impossible to tell who is a member of which clan simply by looking at them. At the fork is a man, and Sid wants to ask him for directions.

4. The answer to which of the following questions, if asked by Sid, will ensure that Sid will find the right road?

   I. Is the left fork the road to Nocam?

   II. If I asked you whether the left fork is the road to Nocam, would you tell the truth?

   III. If I asked you whether the left fork is the road to Nocam, would you say yes?

   Ⓐ II only   Ⓑ III only   Ⓒ I and III only
   Ⓓ II and III only   Ⓔ I, II, and III

Questions 5 and 6

   (A) City Council member Ruth Jerome has intro-duced a proposal for commercial rent control that would limit the increases landlords can charge to small businesses. Of course, Ms. Jerome would favor such a plan because she and her husband own two small grocery stores.

   (B) On each of the three occasions I met John, he was wearing a hat. The first time it was a derby, the second time it was a beret, and the third time it was a baseball cap. I conclude, therefore, that John always wears a hat of some sort.

   (C) Mary has suggested that the Clippers finished in fifth place last season because they scored too few runs during the season. In fact, the Clip-pers' total run production for the season was the second highest in the league. So the Clippers failed to do better than fifth because their defense was inadequate.

   (D) Eighty-seven percent of the voters surveyed thought that Mr. Herman's views on foreign policy were better than those of Mr. Smith, and 91 percent thought Mr. Herman's views on domestic policy superior to those of Mr. Smith. On this basis, we can conclude that Mr. Herman is likely to make a better senator than Mr. Smith.

   (E) It is sometimes argued that the best way to stop drug-related crime is to legalize all drugs. But that's like giving away money to bank robbers and pickpockets.

5. Which of the arguments above relies upon a question-able analogy?

   Ⓐ   Ⓑ   Ⓒ   Ⓓ   Ⓔ

6. Which of the arguments above attacks the credibility of a person rather than the merits of a proposal?

   Ⓐ   Ⓑ   Ⓒ   Ⓓ   Ⓔ

Questions 7–9

The geological story of the Rocky Mountains is a long one, the details of which are lost in the passage of hundreds of millions of years. Some of the story has been put together by scientists from bits of scattered evidence that strongly indicate a certain chain of events, few of which can be proved to everyone's satisfaction. Most of the rocks in the Colorado region are crystalline and ancient. The gneiss and schist were, in part, once sediments formed in the seas—perhaps a billion years ago. These sediments were buried beneath thousands of feet of other sediments, cemented and hardened into layers of sedimentary rock and later squeezed, crushed, and elevated by slow, ceaselessly working earth forces that produced mountains. During this period, the sedimentary rocks were changed to harder metamorphic rocks, probably because of deep burial under tremendous pressure and considerable heat. Masses of molten rock welled up into these earlier deposits and hardened under the earth's surface. This later intrusive material is now exposed granite in many parts of the Rocky Mountains.

These ancient mountains were gradually worn away by wind, rain, and other agents of erosion, which must have attacked the surface of the earth as vigorously then as now. With the passage of millions of years, these mountains were gradually worn away until a new sea lapped over the land where mountains had been, and once again sediments were dropped in its bottom. This new invasion of the ocean affected the Colorado region during the many millions of years in which dinosaurs dominated the earth.

In response to little-understood rhythms of the earth's crust, which have lifted mountains ever so slowly at great intervals all over the world, the seas drained away as the crust rose again, and the rising land once more became subject to the ceaseless attack of erosion. This uplift—which began 60 million years ago—originated the system of mountain ranges and basins that today give Colorado its spectacular scenery and much of its climate.

7. The passage deals primarily with the

   Ⓐ scenic beauty of Colorado's mountains
   Ⓑ geological history of Colorado's mountains
   Ⓒ classification of rock types
   Ⓓ rhythms of the earth's crust
   Ⓔ era of the dinosaurs

8. According to the passage all of the following are true of metamorphic rock EXCEPT

   Ⓐ It is harder than sedimentary rock.
   Ⓑ It is formed from sedimentary rock.
   Ⓒ It is extremely old.
   Ⓓ It is a preliminary form of granite.
   Ⓔ It is created by extreme temperatures and high pressure.

9. The author regards the explanation he gives as

   (A) conclusively proven
   (B) complete fiction
   (C) highly tentative and unsupported by evidence
   (D) speculative but supported by evidence
   (E) certain but unprovable

10. This is the third straight Christmas season in which retail stores will experience a sharp drop in sales from the previous year.

    (A) in which retail stores will experience
    (B) in which retail stores experience
    (C) which retail stores will experience
    (D) of retail stores' experiencing
    (E) of experiencing by retail stores of

11. When used together, the cosmetic company claims that its products enhance the appearance of the skin by preventing blemishes and reducing signs of aging.

    (A) When used together, the cosmetic company claims that its products enhance the appearance of the skin by preventing blemishes and reducing signs of aging.
    (B) The cosmetic company claims that, when used together, the appearance of the skin will be enhanced by the products by their preventing blemishes and reducing signs of aging.
    (C) When used together, the products will enhance the appearance of the skin, also preventing blemishes and reducing signs of aging, or so the company claims.
    (D) According to the cosmetic company, when its products are used together, they will enhance the appearance of the skin, prevent blemishes, and reduce signs of aging.
    (E) According to the cosmetic company, when its products are used together, the appearance of the skin will be enhanced and blemishes will be prevented reducing the signs of aging.

12. Elizabeth I was a student of classical languages, and it was her who insisted that Greek and Latin were spoken at court.

    (A) it was her who insisted that Greek and Latin were spoken at court
    (B) it was she that insisted on the speaking of Greek and Latin at court
    (C) it was she who insisted that Greek and Latin be spoken at court
    (D) she insisted that, at court, Greek and Latin were spoken
    (E) she had insisted that Greek and Latin were to be spoken at court

Jorge: To be a good carpenter, one must have patience.

Gloria: That's not so; a good carpenter must also have the right tools.

13. Gloria has understood Jorge's statement to mean that

    (A) if a person is a good carpenter, she will have the right tools
    (B) if a person is a good carpenter, she will have patience
    (C) if a person has patience, she will be a good carpenter
    (D) if a person has the right tools, she will be a good carpenter
    (E) if a person does not have the right tools, she cannot be a good carpenter

   The country of West Umberland imports no copper. Private industry's use of copper in West Umberland equals 85 percent of the amount of copper produced by the country's mines each year, while government use of copper equals 23 percent of the amount of copper produced by the country's mines each year.

14. If the information above is true, which of the following conclusions can most reliably be drawn?

    (A) West Umberland imports copper ore from other countries.
    (B) Some copper in West Umberland is recycled.
    (C) West Umberland's industry wastes substantial amounts of copper.
    (D) Copper is in short supply in West Umberland.
    (E) Each year, West Umberland produces more copper than the previous year.

GO ON TO NEXT PAGE

At a time when New York City is going through a budgetary crisis, it is cutting its funding of the one agency that helps put more than half a billion dollars into its coffers: the Convention and Visitors Bureau. The proposed $1 million cut comes on the heels of last year's $250,000 funding cut. The debilitating effect of that cut is now obvious. Hotel occupancy rates shrank by 7 percent over last year, resulting in $10 million in taxes not realized by the city.

15. Which of the following, if true, would most weaken the argument above?

Ⓐ New York City spends less than other less populated cities such as Louisville and Dayton to attract visitors and conventions.

Ⓑ The proposed $1 million cut in the budget of the Convention and Visitors Bureau's budget would do little to help balance the city's budget.

Ⓒ The entire country is experiencing an economic downturn, and during an economic downturn people travel less than during times of prosperity.

Ⓓ Adverse publicity about the crime rate in New York discourages some people and organizations from visiting the city.

Ⓔ Many people and organizations would visit New York City even if it were not for the public relations efforts of the Convention and Visitors Bureau.

Questions 16–18

The National Security Act of 1947 created a national military establishment headed by a single Secretary of Defense. The legislation had been a year-and-a-half in the making—beginning when President Truman first recommended that the armed services be reorganized into a single department. During that period the President's concept of a unified armed service was torn apart and put back together several times, the final measure to emerge from Congress being a compromise. Most of the opposition to the bill came from the Navy and its numerous civilian spokesmen, including Secretary of the Navy James Forrestal. In support of unification (and a separate air force that was part of the unification package) were the Army air forces, the Army, and, most importantly, the President of the United States.

Passage of the bill did not bring an end to the bitter interservice disputes. Rather than unify, the act served only to federate the military services. It neither halted the rapid demobilization of the armed forces that followed World War II nor brought to the new national military establishment the loyalties of officers steeped in the traditions of the separate services. At a time when the balance of power in Europe and Asia was rapidly shifting, the services lacked any precise statement of United States foreign policy from the National Security Council on which to base future programs. The services bickered unceasingly over their respective roles and missions, already complicated by the Soviet nuclear capability that for the first time made the United States susceptible to devastating attack. Not even the appointment of Forrestal as First Secretary of Defense allayed the suspicions of naval officers and their supporters that the role of the U.S. Navy was threatened with permanent eclipse. Before the war of words died down, Forrestal himself was driven to resignation and then suicide.

By 1948, the United States military establishment was forced to make do with a budget approximately 10 percent of what it had been at its wartime peak. Meanwhile, the cost of weapons procurement was rising geometrically as the nation came to put more and more reliance on the atomic bomb and its delivery systems. These two factors inevitably made adversaries of the Navy and the Air Force as the battle between advocates of the B-36 and the supercarrier so amply demonstrates. Given severe fiscal restraints on the one hand, and on the other the nation's increasing reliance on strategic nuclear deterrence, the conflict between these two services over roles and missions was essentially a contest over slices of an ever-diminishing pie.

Yet if in the end neither service was the obvious victor, the principle of civilian dominance over the military clearly was. If there had ever been any danger that the United States military establishment might exploit, to the detriment of civilian control, the goodwill it enjoyed as a result of its victories in World War II, that danger disappeared in the interservice animosities engendered by the battle over unification.

16. Which of the following best describes the tone of the selection?

Ⓐ Analytical and confident
Ⓑ Resentful and defensive
Ⓒ Objective and speculative ♪
Ⓓ Tentative and skeptical
Ⓔ Persuasive and cynical

17. It can be inferred from the passage that Forrestal's appointment as Secretary of Defense was expected to

Ⓐ placate members of the Navy
Ⓑ result in decreased levels of defense spending
Ⓒ outrage advocates of the Army air forces
Ⓓ win Congressional approval of the unification plan
Ⓔ make Forrestal a Presidential candidate against Truman

18. With which of the following statements about defense unification would the author most likely agree?

Ⓐ Unification ultimately undermined United States military capability by inciting interservice rivalry.

Ⓑ The unification legislation was necessitated by the drastic decline in appropriations for the military services.

Ⓒ Although the unification was not entirely successful, it had the unexpected result of ensuring civilian control of the military.

Ⓓ In spite of the attempted unification, each service was still able to pursue its own objectives without interference from the other branches.

Ⓔ Unification was in the first place unwarranted and in the second place ineffective.

19. Although Beverly Sills never achieved superstar status in Europe or at the Metropolitan Opera, yet she was singing major roles at the City Opera during 20 years.

Ⓐ yet she was singing major roles at the City Opera during 20 years

Ⓑ she did sing major roles at the City Opera during 20 years

Ⓒ she sang major roles at the City Opera for 20 years

Ⓓ but she sang major roles at the City Opera for 20 years

Ⓔ yet for 20 years major roles had been sung by her at the City Opera

20. Although Mary Ann is not a great scholar, neither has she published any books, she has and always will be a great teacher and well-loved by her students.

Ⓐ scholar, neither has she published any books, she has and always will be

Ⓑ scholar, nor having published any books, she has been and always will be

Ⓒ scholar and she hasn't published any books, she has been and always will be

Ⓓ scholar nor published any books, still she has been and always will be

Ⓔ scholar nor has she published any books, but she has been and always will be

21. The great difference in interpretation between him and his immediate predecessor of the role of Anthony were the subject of last week's column by the well-known drama critic.

Ⓐ between him and his immediate predecessor of the role of Anthony were

Ⓑ between him and his immediate predecessor of the role of Anthony was

Ⓒ between he and his immediate predecessor of the role of Anthony were

Ⓓ among him and his immediate predecessor of the role of Anthony was

Ⓔ among him and his immediate predecessor of the role of Anthony were

Within a scheme of criminal penalties, some penalties are more severe than others. A logical consequence of this hierarchy is that one penalty must be the most severe or ultimate penalty. Since the death penalty is the ultimate penalty, we can see that the death penalty is justified as a matter of logic.

22. Which of the following observations most weakens the argument above?

Ⓐ Not everyone believes that the death penalty is effective in deterring crime.

Ⓑ Some people incorrectly convicted of a crime might receive the death penalty.

Ⓒ The most severe penalty in a system of punishments could be something other than the death penalty.

Ⓓ For a person serving a life sentence with no chance of parole, only the death penalty is greater punishment.

Ⓔ No two punishments can be ranked equally severe in their effects on a person.

Gloria's office is in Atlanta, but she must spend most of her time traveling. Every time I get a card from her, it has been mailed from some other city where she is staying on business.

23. It can be inferred from that passage above that Gloria

Ⓐ does not work in Atlanta

Ⓑ sends cards frequently

Ⓒ does not write letters

Ⓓ travels only on business

Ⓔ has offices in other cities

Advocates for the homeless attempt to portray homeless persons as victims of social and economic circumstances beyond their control. A recent survey of the homeless in major cities found that a high percentage are addicted to alcohol or other drugs. Rather than innocent victims, these are people who are solely responsible for their own plights.

24. Which of the following, if true, would most weaken the argument above?

Ⓐ A large number of homeless persons turn to drugs and alcohol out of despair after becoming homeless.

Ⓑ Several government programs are designed to help the homeless find jobs and new housing.

Ⓒ Most cities offer shelter to the homeless on a night-by-night basis.

Ⓓ Alcoholism and other drug addictions can cause erratic and even violent behavior.

Ⓔ As much as 60 percent of any community's homeless population are local people.

GO ON TO NEXT PAGE

Questions 25–27

Open government statues in California have proved both beneficial and harmful. In the energy commission, for example, as in other government commissions, nearly all decisions must be made in public session for which at least seven days' notice must be given. Which decisions can be made by the executive director and which are strictly reserved for the commission becomes quite important in this context. If something is a matter for the commission, there must be a public notice with attendant publicity and preparation of materials for distribution at the meeting. Furthermore, a commissioner may not meet informally with another commissioner nor with the executive director or any member of his staff to discuss commission activities. Such behavior would be a violation of open government statutes. Staff briefings must take place commissioner by commissioner or through a commissioner's advisors. More frequently, commissioners or their advisors contact the staff for information, but all such requests must be submitted in writing.

An example of the impact of open government on the operating procedures of a commission was illustrated by the energy commission's budgetary process. The budget for the commission, unlike that prepared in other state agencies, was prepared in public session by the five commissioners. The session was not simply a "review and comment" session since the commissioners had not previously discussed the budget. Every item proposed for the budget could be commented upon by anyone who attended the session.

Perhaps open government's effect has been greatest in the promulgation of rules and regulations. Complaints have arisen from several legislators and news media about the slowness of the energy commission in setting regulations. If, however, a commission attempts to handle fewer matters without input from state agencies and interested groups in open meetings, it will be criticized for circumventing the open government intentions. If present practices continue, the commission will continue to be criticized for moving too slowly.

25. The author is primarily concerned with discussing the
   (A) disadvantages of California's open government legislation
   (B) effect of an open government statute on California's energy commission
   (C) methods by which California energy commissioners obtain information
   (D) energy policies adopted by the California energy commission under the open government statute
   (E) political forces that shape California's energy policies

26. The passage implies the open government statute is intended to accomplish all of the following EXCEPT
   (A) to minimize the likelihood of secret political deals
   (B) to allow an opportunity for the public to influence government decisions
   (C) to ensure that government officials are held accountable for their policies
   (D) to guarantee that a government agency can respond quickly to a problem
   (E) to publicize governmental functions

27. The passage most strongly supports which of the following conclusions about a decision that is within the authority of the executive director of an agency?
   (A) It would be made more quickly than a decision reserved for a commission.
   (B) It would be made with the assistance of the agency's commissioners.
   (C) It would be a highly publicized event attended by members of the news media.
   (D) It would deal with a matter of greater importance than those handled by the commission.
   (E) It would be made only after the director had notified the commissioners and their aides in writing.

28. The English version of "Waiting for Godot," of which Beckett was the translator, was seen in a new production at the Performing Arts Center last year.
   (A) of which Beckett was the translator
   (B) which Beckett was the translator
   (C) having been translated by Beckett
   (D) that had been translated by Beckett
   (E) the translator Beckett

29. Accusing his opponent of falsifying his military record, it was clear that the Congressional race was heating up.
   (A) Accusing his opponent of falsifying his military record, it was clear that the Congressional race was heating up.
   (B) Accusing the other opponent of falsifying his military record, it was clear that the Congressional race heated up.
   (C) It was clear that the Congressional race was heating up when one candidate accused the other of falsifying his military record.
   (D) Having accused his opponent of falsifying his military record, it was clear that the Congressional race was heating up.
   (E) Once accused of falsifying his military record, it was clear that the Congressional race was heating up.

30. <u>Although she plays tennis as well, if not better than her sister,</u> her sister is the captain of the team.

 Ⓐ Although she plays tennis as well, if not better than her sister,

 Ⓑ Although she plays tennis as well as, if not better than, her sister,

 Ⓒ In spite of the fact of her playing tennis as well as, if not better than, her sister,

 Ⓓ She plays tennis as well, if not better, than her sister, but

 Ⓔ Playing tennis as well as, if not better than, her sister,

Several states have wisely refused to raise the highway speed limit above 55 miles per hour despite calls by motorists for an increase. Although the 55-mile-per-hour speed limit was initially enacted by the Federal government as a conservation measure, it soon became clear that a felicitous consequence of the measure was considerably fewer traffic fatalities.

31. The speaker above is arguing that states that have a 55-mile-per-hour highway speed limit should

 Ⓐ raise the highway speed limit

 Ⓑ further reduce the highway speed limit

 Ⓒ retain the 55-mile-per-hour highway speed limit

 Ⓓ enact other measures to improve fuel conservation

 Ⓔ find other ways of reducing highway fatalities

The quality of life provided by a government depends not so much upon its formal structure as upon the ability and temperament of those who serve as its officers.

32. The author of the paragraph above would most likely agree with which of the following statements?

 Ⓐ A written constitution is essential to ensure the liberty of citizens against a strong government.

 Ⓑ Universal suffrage is the best guarantee that the general will of the people will become legislation.

 Ⓒ A government with good leaders is likely to survive for a longer time than a government with incompetent leaders.

 Ⓓ Poor leadership in a hierarchical organization threatens the ability of the organization to achieve results.

 Ⓔ The quality of the leadership of a government is the main determinant of whether the citizens will be happy.

Your chart listing winners of the Most Valuable Player award states that one designated hitter won the award: Don Baylor in 1979. This is erroneous. No designated hitter has ever won the M. V. P., and it is extremely doubtful that a player who does not serve the team in the field will ever win it.

33. Which of the following, if true, would most strengthen the argument above?

 Ⓐ In 1979, Don Baylor played one game as first baseman.

 Ⓑ In 1979, Don Baylor played 97 games as an outfielder versus 65 as a designated hitter.

 Ⓒ Don Baylor won the Most Valuable Player award only once in his career.

 Ⓓ Of the two major baseball leagues, only the American League allows the use of a designated hitter.

 Ⓔ The Most Valuable Player award can be given to any player on the team.

34. <u>A discussion of our nation's foreign policy must begin with the fact of there being</u> an independent Western Europe which now thinks of itself in transnationalist terms.

 Ⓐ A discussion of our nation's foreign policy must begin with the fact of there being

 Ⓑ Beginning any discussion of our nation's foreign policy must be the fact of there being

 Ⓒ Any discussion of our nation's foreign policy must begin with the fact that there is

 Ⓓ Any discussion of our nation's foreign policy must begin by acknowledging the existence of

 Ⓔ To begin discussing our nation's foreign policy there must be an acknowledgment of the fact that

35. Interest rates on mortgages <u>have declined steadily during the first six months of this year but virtually remained unchanged</u> during the next three months.

 Ⓐ have declined steadily during the first six months of this year but virtually remained unchanged

 Ⓑ declined steadily during the first six months of this year but virtually remain unchanged

 Ⓒ steadily declined during the first six months of this year but remain virtually unchanged

 Ⓓ declined steadily during the first six months of this year but have remained virtually unchanging

 Ⓔ declined steadily during the first six months of this year but have remained virtually unchanged

GO ON TO NEXT PAGE

"Most people like pennies," says Hamilton Dix, spokesperson for the United States Mint. "We did a survey at the Epcot Center at Walt Disney World, and half of all the adults said they use pennies daily."

36. Which of the following observations most undermines the position of the speaker above?

    (A) Most of the people who visit Walt Disney World are on vacation.

    (B) The survey covered people only at a single location in one state.

    (C) The survey included adults visiting Epcot Center but not children.

    (D) The speaker is a representative of the agency that manufactures pennies.

    (E) Many purchases require the use of pennies either as payment or as change.

As a citizen who values individual rights, I am appalled at the growing use of random or mandatory drug testing. What is needed is a screening test for impaired function, not for drug use per se. For example, it would be easy to design a computerized test for reaction time. Such a test should be simple to administer and would be nonintrusive. Anyone failing the test could then be required to submit to the more invasive drug test.

37. Which of the following, if true, would most weaken the argument above?

    (A) Administrations of a reaction test could be arranged randomly, so that a drug user could not alter his or her habits.

    (B) A reaction test measures capacity only at that time, but a drug test may show that a person is likely to be a future risk.

    (C) The Supreme Court has refused to rule that mandatory drug tests for employees in sensitive positions are unconstitutional.

    (D) A person might fail a reaction test for a reason other than impairment due to the use of illegal drugs.

    (E) A person who has ingested an illegal substance might have sufficient self-control to pass a reaction test.

Computer colorization of black-and-white film is an important tool for making historical events seem real to students who live in an age of color movies and color television. A colorized version of the footage of Jack Ruby's assassination of Lee Harvey Oswald or of the first manned space shot will help students today understand what it was like for the millions of Americans who actually saw those events on television.

38. Which of the following, if true, most weakens the conclusion of the argument above?

    (A) The people who saw those events live saw them in black and white, not in color.

    (B) The events mentioned occurred before most of today's students were born.

    (C) Many important historical events were never recorded on film.

    (D) Modern techniques can improve the quality of the sound of old film footage.

    (E) Colorization can be accomplished by a computer process that is relatively inexpensive.

Questions 39–41

Is the Constitution of the United States a mechanism or an organism? Does it furnish for the American community a structure or a process? The Constitution is Newtonian in that it establishes a set of forces and counter-forces. These confer power and impose limitations on power, and one of the great virtues of the Newtonian model is that correctives can be self-generated. They do not have to be imposed from without. The homely illustration is the cutting of a pie into two pieces so that brother and sister will have equal shares. Rather than setting up a system of judicial review under an equal-protection clause—a device that might not work until the pie has become stale—you simply let one sibling cut the pie and the other choose a piece.

The Newtonian system assumes that each branch has a capacity to act that is commensurate with its authority to act and to improve its ability to discharge its constitutional responsibilities. For example, on the Congressional side, this means a rationalizing of the legislative process to improve its capability to formulate and carry through a legislative program that is coherent in policies and technically proficient. The goal involves better access to disinterested information through better research staffs and facilities, as well probably as the selection of committee chairs on a basis other than simple seniority. Other devices might alleviate the overburdened executive branch: a strengthened Cabinet, with a smaller, executive Cabinet of respected statesmen to serve as a link between the White House and the departments, and between the President and the Congress. No constitutional impediment stands in the way of any of the structural changes on either the legislative or the executive side.

In a Newtonian constitution, extraordinary force in one direction is likely to produce extraordinary, and sometimes excessive, force in another direction. In the early years of the New Deal, the Supreme Court, generally over the dissent of its most respected members, engaged in a series of judicial vetoes that reflected an unjudicial approach to the function of judging. The President, on his part, countered with the Court reorganization plan, which seriously threatened the independence of the judiciary. A Newtonian system demands constitutional morality. It would be possible, by excessive use of legal power, to bring the system to a standstill. Congress might refuse to appropriate for executive departments. The President might ignore Supreme Court decisions. The Court might declare unconstitutional all laws that a majority of its members would not have voted for. Without constitutional morality, the system breaks down.

The Constitution is also Darwinian and stresses process and adaptation. Justice Holmes remarked that "the provisions of the Constitution are not mathematical formulas having their essence in their form; they are organic living institutions." Growth and adaptation, to be sure, have sometimes been seen as mutations, threatening the constitutional order. Chief Justice Marshall, near the close of his life, viewing with despair the developments of the Jacksonian era, confided to Justice Story, "The Union has been preserved thus far by miracles. I fear they cannot continue."

It must be admitted that we have all too readily assigned responsibility for the Darwinian constitutional evolution to the Supreme Court. Congress has too often either neglected its opportunities and responsibilities or has acted tentatively. When Congress does legislate, it is apt to regard its own constitutional judgment as only provisional, to await as a matter of course a submission to the Supreme Court. A striking example is the recent campaign finance law. But in the final analysis, is the Constitution a mechanism or an organism? If light can be viewed as both wave and particles, depending on which analysis is the more serviceable for a given problem, why cannot the Constitution be seen as both a mechanism and an organism, a structure and a process?

39. The main purpose of the selection is to
   (A) discuss two models of constitutional law
   (B) criticize Congress and the executive branch for inaction
   (C) suggest a new role for the Supreme Court
   (D) challenge the validity of Supreme Court rulings
   (E) call for a revised Constitution

40. In the first paragraph, the author makes use of
   (A) circular reasoning
   (B) authority
   (C) analogy
   (D) generalization
   (E) ambiguity

41. The passage implies that
   (A) Congress is more important than either the executive or the judiciary
   (B) branches of government may have more constitutional authority than they use
   (C) the earliest Supreme Court justices were more sincere than today's justices
   (D) the Constitution sets up a very simple system for governmental decisions
   (E) constitutionally created hurdles block needed improvements in governmental efficiency

Stop: End of Verbal Section

Quantitative Section

37 Questions—75 Minutes

> *General Directions:* To simulate the experience of taking the CAT, answer each question in order. Do not skip any questions and do not go back to questions you have already answered.
>
> *Directions for problem-solving questions:* For this question type, select the best of the answer choices. Indicate your answer by blackening the circle next to your choice.
>
> *Numbers*: All numbers used are real numbers.
>
> *Figures*: The diagrams and figures that accompany these questions are for the purpose of providing information useful in solving the problems. The diagrams and figures are drawn as accurately as possible unless the figure is accompanied by a note stating that it is not drawn to scale. All figures are in a plane unless otherwise indicated.
>
> *Directions for data sufficiency questions:* Each question is followed by two numbered statements. You are to determine whether the data given in the statements are sufficient for answering the question. Use the data given, plus your knowledge of math and everyday facts, to choose among the five possible answers. Indicate your answer by blackening the circle next to your choice.
>
> *Numbers*: All values are real numbers.
>
> *Figures*: Any figures provided will not necessarily reflect the information given in the numbered statements, but they will reflect the information provided in the question. Unless otherwise indicated, all figures lie in a plane; all lines shown as straight are straight; and the positions of all points, angles, regions, etc., are correctly depicted.
>
> *Example:*
>
> In $\triangle ABC$, what is the value of x?
>
> (1) $y = 60$
> (2) $AB = BC$
>
>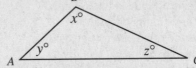
>
> *Explanation*: Statement (1) is not sufficient to answer the question, for statement (1) provides no information about x or z. Statement (2) is not sufficient to answer the question. Statement (2) does establish that $y = z$, but that is not enough information to determine the value of x. Both statements together are sufficient to answer the question. Since $AB = BC$ and $y = z$, $z = 60$. Since $x + y + z = 180$, $x = 60$.

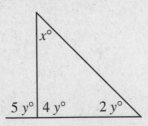

Note: Figure not drawn to scale

1. In the figure above, what is the value of $x°$?

    Ⓐ 15 Ⓑ 20 Ⓒ 30 Ⓓ 45 Ⓔ 60

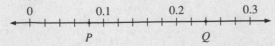

2. In the figure above, what is the length of PQ?

    Ⓐ 0.12 Ⓑ 0.16 Ⓒ 0.13 Ⓓ 0.11 Ⓔ 0.09

3. If the average (arithmetic mean) of $x, x, x, 56,$ and 58 is 51, then $x =$

    Ⓐ 43 Ⓑ 47 Ⓒ 49 Ⓓ 51 Ⓔ 53

4. What is the value of x?

    (1) $3x - 2 = 10$

    (2) $\dfrac{x}{10} = \dfrac{2}{5}$

    Ⓐ statement 1 alone is sufficient to answer the question, but statement 2 alone is not sufficient
    Ⓑ statement 2 alone is sufficient to answer the question, but statement 1 alone is not sufficient
    Ⓒ both statements together are needed to answer the question, but neither statement alone is sufficient
    Ⓓ either statement by itself is sufficient to answer the question
    Ⓔ not enough facts are given to answer the question

5. How many hardcover books does Greg have in his personal library?

   (1) Greg has three times as many paperbacks as hardcover books.

   (2) Greg has 24 more paperbacks than hardcover books.

   (A) statement 1 alone is sufficient to answer the question, but statement 2 alone is not sufficient

   (B) statement 2 alone is sufficient to answer the question, but statement 1 alone is not sufficient

   (C) both statements together are needed to answer the question, but neither statement alone is sufficient

   (D) either statement by itself is sufficient to answer the question

   (E) not enough facts are given to answer the question

6. For how many integers x is $-2 \le 2x \le 2$?

   (A) 1   (B) 2   (C) 3   (D) 4   (E) 5

7. If x is an odd integer, all of the following are odd EXCEPT

   (A) $x + 2$ (B) $3x + 2$ (C) $2x^2 + x$
   (D) $2x^3 + x$ (E) $3x^3 + x$

8. What is the sum of the areas of two squares with sides of 2 and 3, respectively?

   (A) 1   (B) 5   (C) 13   (D) 25   (E) 36

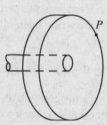

9. P is a point on the flywheel shown above. How far does P travel during five complete revolutions of the wheel?

   (1) The diameter of the wheel is 1 meter.

   (2) The wheel turns at the rate of 3,000 revolutions per minute.

   (A) statement 1 alone is sufficient to answer the question, but statement 2 alone is not sufficient

   (B) statement 2 alone is sufficient to answer the question, but statement 1 alone is not sufficient

   (C) both statements together are needed to answer the question, but neither statement alone is sufficient

   (D) either statement by itself is sufficient to answer the question

   (E) not enough facts are given to answer the question

10. $ABCD$ is a square. What is the area of $ABCD$?

    (1) $AB = 3$

    (2) $AC = 3\sqrt{2}$

    (A) statement 1 alone is sufficient to answer the question, but statement 2 alone is not sufficient

    (B) statement 2 alone is sufficient to answer the question, but statement 1 alone is not sufficient

    (C) both statements together are needed to answer the question, but neither statement alone is sufficient

    (D) either statement by itself is sufficient to answer the question

    (E) not enough facts are given to answer the question

11. If x is 80 percent of y, then y is what percent of x?

    (A) $133\dfrac{1}{3}\%$ (B) 125%   (C) 120%

    (D) 90%   (E) 80%

12. From which of the following statements can it be deduced that $m > n$?

    (A) $m + 1 = n$
    (B) $2m = n$
    (C) $m + n > 0$
    (D) $m - n > 0$
    (E) $mn > 0$

13. If for any number n, $\widehat{n}$ is defined as the least integer that is greater than or equal to n^2, then $\widehat{-1.1}$ =

    (A) -2 (B) -1 (C) 0   (D) 1   (E) 2

14. Is $xy > 0$?

    (1) $x^8 y^9 < 0$

    (2) $x^7 y^8 < 0$

    (A) statement 1 alone is sufficient to answer the question, but statement 2 alone is not sufficient

    (B) statement 2 alone is sufficient to answer the question, but statement 1 alone is not sufficient

    (C) both statements together are needed to answer the question, but neither statement alone is sufficient

    (D) either statement by itself is sufficient to answer the question

    (E) not enough facts are given to answer the question

GO ON TO NEXT PAGE

15. What is the value of N?

(1) $\dfrac{M}{M+N} = 5$

(2) $\dfrac{6M-24}{M+N} = 6$

Ⓐ statement 1 alone is sufficient to answer the question, but statement 2 alone is not sufficient

Ⓑ statement 2 alone is sufficient to answer the question, but statement 1 alone is not sufficient

Ⓒ both statements together are needed to answer the question, but neither statement alone is sufficient

Ⓓ either statement by itself is sufficient to answer the question

Ⓔ not enough facts are given to answer the question

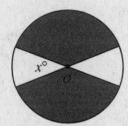

16. The above circle with center O has a radius of length 2. If the total area of the shaded regions is 3π, then $x =$

Ⓐ 270 Ⓑ 180 Ⓒ 120 Ⓓ 90 Ⓔ 45

17. If $\dfrac{1}{x}+\dfrac{1}{y}+\dfrac{1}{z}$, then $z =$

Ⓐ $\dfrac{1}{xy}$ Ⓑ xy Ⓒ $\dfrac{x+y}{xy}$

Ⓓ $\dfrac{xy}{x+y}$ Ⓔ $\dfrac{2xy}{x+y}$

18. In a certain clothing store, 60 percent of all the articles are imported and 20 percent of all the articles are priced at $100 or more. If 40 percent of the articles priced at $100 or more are imported, what percent of the articles priced *under* $100 are *not* imported?

Ⓐ 28% Ⓑ 12% Ⓒ 8% Ⓓ 4.8% Ⓔ 2%

19. If x is an integer such that $1 < x < 100$, what is the value of x?

(1) x is the square of an integer.

(2) x is the cube of an integer.

Ⓐ statement 1 alone is sufficient to answer the question, but statement 2 alone is not sufficient

Ⓑ statement 2 alone is sufficient to answer the question, but statement 1 alone is not sufficient

Ⓒ both statements together are needed to answer the question, but neither statement alone is sufficient

Ⓓ either statement by itself is sufficient to answer the question

Ⓔ not enough facts are given to answer the question

20. A group of 66 students is divided into three classes, each with a different number of students. How many students are in the largest class?

(1) One of the classes has two fewer students than the largest class.

(2) One of the classes has 21 students.

Ⓐ statement 1 alone is sufficient to answer the question, but statement 2 alone is not sufficient

Ⓑ statement 2 alone is sufficient to answer the question, but statement 1 alone is not sufficient

Ⓒ both statements together are needed to answer the question, but neither statement alone is sufficient

Ⓓ either statement by itself is sufficient to answer the question

Ⓔ not enough facts are given to answer the question

21. If $|r-6| = 5$ and $|2q-12| = 8$, what is the maximum value of $\dfrac{q}{r}$?

Ⓐ 2 Ⓑ $\dfrac{11}{2}$ Ⓒ 10 Ⓓ 11 Ⓔ 20

22. At the close of trading on Tuesday, the price per share of a certain stock was 20 percent less than the price per share at the close of trading on Monday. On Wednesday, the price per share at closing was 25 percent less than that on Tuesday. If on Thursday, the price per share at closing was equal to the closing price on Monday, what was the percent increase in the price per share of the stock from closing Wednesday to closing Thursday?

Ⓐ 45% Ⓑ $66\dfrac{2}{3}$% Ⓒ 75% Ⓓ 145% Ⓔ $166\dfrac{2}{3}$%

23. A hiker walked up a mountain path from a way station to an observation point and back to the way station by the same route. His average speed for the ascent was two miles per hour, and his average speed for the descent was four miles per hour. If the observation point is exactly three miles from the way station, what was the hiker's average speed, in miles per hour, for the entire trip?

Ⓐ $2\dfrac{2}{5}$ Ⓑ $2\dfrac{2}{3}$ Ⓒ 3 Ⓓ $3\dfrac{1}{3}$ Ⓔ $3\dfrac{3}{5}$

24. If the volume of a sphere is equal to its radius cubed multiplied by $\frac{4}{3}\pi$, what is the volume of sphere S?

   (1) The circumference of the largest circle that can be obtained by intersecting a plane with sphere S is 16π.

   (2) The length of a line segment connecting two points on the sphere and passing through the center of the sphere is 16.

   Ⓐ statement 1 alone is sufficient to answer the question, but statement 2 alone is not sufficient

   Ⓑ statement 2 alone is sufficient to answer the question, but statement 1 alone is not sufficient

   Ⓒ both statements together are needed to answer the question, but neither statement alone is sufficient

   Ⓓ either statement by itself is sufficient to answer the question

   Ⓔ not enough facts are given to answer the question

25. The six members of the student council of Westwood High School were asked to serve on three special committees. Each member of the student council volunteered to serve on at least one committee. How many students volunteered to serve on all three committees?

   (1) The following chart shows the number of students who volunteered to serve on each committee:

	Number of Volunteers
Activities Committee	3
Homecoming Committee	2
Welcoming Committee	4

   (2) Two students volunteered to serve on both the Activities Committee and the Welcoming Committee.

   Ⓐ statement 1 alone is sufficient to answer the question, but statement 2 alone is not sufficient

   Ⓑ statement 2 alone is sufficient to answer the question, but statement 1 alone is not sufficient

   Ⓒ both statements together are needed to answer the question, but neither statement alone is sufficient

   Ⓓ either statement by itself is sufficient to answer the question

   Ⓔ not enough facts are given to answer the question

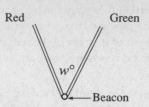

26. The figure above shows the beams from a beacon with two searchlights, one red and one green, which rotate at the same rate. If the red light rotates in a clockwise direction and the green light rotates in a counterclockwise direction, what is the number of degrees through which each light must rotate before the red beam and green beam are aligned a *second* time?

   Ⓐ $180° + w$ Ⓑ $180° - \dfrac{w}{2}$ Ⓒ $360° - \dfrac{w}{2}$

   Ⓓ $\dfrac{180° + w}{2}$ Ⓔ $\dfrac{360° + w}{2}$

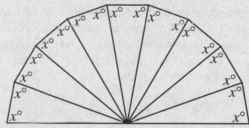

27. In the figure above, what is the average measure in degrees of the indicated angles?

   Ⓐ $105°$ Ⓑ $90°$ Ⓒ $80°$ Ⓓ $60°$ Ⓔ $45°$

28. If one star equals four circles and three circles equals four diamonds, what is the ratio star:diamond?

   Ⓐ 3:16   Ⓑ 1:3   Ⓒ 3:4   Ⓓ 3:1   Ⓔ 16:3

29. If $xy \neq 0$, what is the value of $\dfrac{(xy)^2 + x^2y^2}{x^2y^3}$?

   (1) $x = 2$

   (2) $y = 5$

   Ⓐ statement 1 alone is sufficient to answer the question, but statement 2 alone is not sufficient

   Ⓑ statement 2 alone is sufficient to answer the question, but statement 1 alone is not sufficient

   Ⓒ both statements together are needed to answer the question, but neither statement alone is sufficient

   Ⓓ either statement by itself is sufficient to answer the question

   Ⓔ not enough facts are given to answer the question

GO ON TO NEXT PAGE

30. When a certain fishing rod is purchased at the same time as a certain reel, the price of the rod is reduced by 25 percent of the cost of the reel. What is the total cost of the rod and reel if they are purchased at the same time?

    (1) When the rod and reel are purchased together, the price of the rod is reduced from $32 to $21.

    (2) If the rod and reel are purchased separately, the cost of the reel is $12 more than the cost of the rod.

    Ⓐ statement 1 alone is sufficient to answer the question, but statement 2 alone is not sufficient

    Ⓑ statement 2 alone is sufficient to answer the question, but statement 1 alone is not sufficient

    Ⓒ both statements together are needed to answer the question, but neither statement alone is sufficient

    Ⓓ either statement by itself is sufficient to answer the question

    Ⓔ not enough facts are given to answer the question

31. In 1996, 80 percent of the students at University Y were undergraduates. If 60 percent of the undergraduates at University Y were out-of-state students and 75 percent of all out-of-state students were undergraduates, what fraction of the students at University Y were out-of-state students?

    Ⓐ $\dfrac{16}{25}$ Ⓑ $\dfrac{3}{5}$ Ⓒ $\dfrac{1}{2}$ Ⓓ $\dfrac{12}{15}$ Ⓔ $\dfrac{1}{4}$

32. Georgette wished to use her videotape machine to record a 60-minute documentary scheduled to be aired at 10:30 P.M. At 8:00 that morning, she set the timer to begin taping at 10:30 P.M. the same day and to stop taping exactly 60 minutes later. If the timer on Georgette's videotape machine loses 30 seconds every hour and the documentary was aired on schedule, how much of the program following the documentary did the machine record?

    Ⓐ 6 minutes and 45 seconds
    Ⓑ 7 minutes
    Ⓒ 7 minutes and 15 seconds
    Ⓓ 7 minutes and 30 seconds
    Ⓔ 7 minutes and 45 seconds

33. A clock loses m minutes every h hours. If the clock shows the correct time at noon on Monday, what time will it show at noon on Wednesday of the same week?

    Ⓐ 48mh after noon

    Ⓑ $\dfrac{48m}{h}$ after noon

    Ⓒ $\dfrac{48h}{m}$ after noon

    Ⓓ $\dfrac{48m}{h}$ before noon

    Ⓔ $\dfrac{2,880h}{m}$ after noon

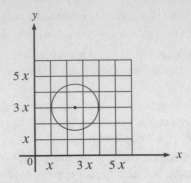

34. If the area of the circle above is 36π, what is the value of x?

    Ⓐ $\dfrac{3}{2}$ Ⓑ 2   Ⓒ 3   Ⓓ 4   Ⓔ $\dfrac{9}{2}$

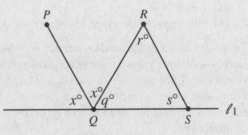

35. In the figure above, is PQ parallel to RS?

    (1) $QR = RS$

    (2) $q° = s°$

    Ⓐ statement 1 alone is sufficient to answer the question, but statement 2 alone is not sufficient

    Ⓑ statement 2 alone is sufficient to answer the question, but statement 1 alone is not sufficient

    Ⓒ both statements together are needed to answer the question, but neither statement alone is sufficient

    Ⓓ either statement by itself is sufficient to answer the question

    Ⓔ not enough facts are given to answer the question

36. The average of the salaries of the top four corporate officers of a company, the president, the vice-president, the secretary, and the comptroller, is $35,000. What is the president's salary?

    (1) The president's salary is the largest.

    (2) The average of the salaries of the vice-president, the secretary, and the comptroller is $32,000.

    Ⓐ statement 1 alone is sufficient to answer the question, but statement 2 alone is not sufficient

    Ⓑ statement 2 alone is sufficient to answer the question, but statement 1 alone is not sufficient

    Ⓒ both statements together are needed to answer the question, but neither statement alone is sufficient

    Ⓓ either statement by itself is sufficient to answer the question

    Ⓔ not enough facts are given to answer the question

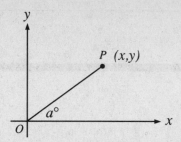

37. In the figure above, what is the length of *OP*?

   (1) $a = 60°$

   (2) $x = 3$

   Ⓐ statement 1 alone is sufficient to answer the
   question, but statement 2 alone is not sufficient
   Ⓑ statement 2 alone is sufficient to answer the
   question, but statement 1 alone is not sufficient
   Ⓒ both statements together are needed to answer the
   question, but neither statement alone is sufficient
   Ⓓ either statement by itself is sufficient to answer
   the question
   Ⓔ not enough facts are given to answer the question

Stop: End of Quantitative Section

Answer Key

VERBAL SECTION

1.	E	15.	C	29.	C
2.	A	16.	A	30.	B
3.	C	17.	A	31.	C
4.	B	18.	C	32.	E
5.	E	19.	C	33.	B
6.	A	20.	C	34.	D
7.	B	21.	B	35.	E
8.	D	22.	C	36.	E
9.	D	23.	B	37.	B
10.	A	24.	A	38.	A
11.	D	25.	B	39.	A
12.	C	26.	D	40.	C
13.	C	27.	A	41.	B
14.	B	28.	A		

QUANTITATIVE SECTION

1.	E	14.	C	27.	C
2.	B	15.	B	28.	E
3.	B	16.	E	29.	B
4.	D	17.	D	30.	A
5.	C	18.	A	31.	A
6.	C	19.	C	32.	E
7.	E	20.	C	33.	D
8.	C	21.	C	34.	D
9.	A	22.	B	35.	E
10.	D	23.	B	36.	B
11.	B	24.	D	37.	C
12.	D	25.	E		
13.	E	26.	E		

Explanatory Answers

VERBAL SECTION

1. A baby boomer is defined <u>to be one who is now in his or her mid-forties, who is concerned with raising a family, and who</u> is upwardly mobile.

   Ⓐ to be one who is now in his or her mid-forties, who is concerned with raising a family, and who

   Ⓑ as those who are in their mid-forties, concerned with raising a family,

   Ⓒ to be those that are in their mid-forties, concerned about the raising of a child, that

   Ⓓ to be one who is in his or her mid-forties and concerned with the raising of a family and also who

   Ⓔ as a person in his or her mid-forties, who is concerned with raising a family and who

   (E) The original contains two errors. First, the phrasing *is defined to be* is not idiomatic. The correct idiom is *defined as.* Second, the use of *one* is ambiguous: one what? (E) corrects both of these errors while preserving the parallelism of the original (which is correct on this count). (B) contains at least two weaknesses. First, the parallelism of the original is destroyed. Additionally, the use of *those* is no better than the use of *one:* those what? (C) fails to correct the first error of the original or to improve on the second. Additionally, (C) uses *that* to refer to people, another error. (D) fails to correct the error of the original and destroys the parallelism of the sentence.

2. The dropout rate in American schools is 10 times <u>that of European nations.</u>

   Ⓐ that of European nations

   Ⓑ what the rate is in Europe

   Ⓒ that which it is in Europe

   Ⓓ European nations'

   Ⓔ that which they are in Europe

   (A) The original is correct as written. (B) is needlessly indirect. Moreover, *what* cannot be substituted for *that.* (C) does not contain any dramatic error, but in this section conciseness counts. (C) is needlessly indirect compared to the original, and this makes it wrong. (As a matter of strategy, don't make a change unless you have reason for doing so.) (D) is wrong because the resulting sentence would set up an illogical comparison between *rate* and *nations.* (E) is wrong for the same reason that (C) is wrong and for the additional reason that *they* fails to agree with *rate.*

3. More and more fashion-conscious women are asking themselves <u>if it is</u> moral to wear clothing made from the skin of an animal.

   Ⓐ if it is

   Ⓑ about if it is

   Ⓒ whether it is

   Ⓓ as to whether or not it is

   Ⓔ about whether it is

   (C) The original contains a nonidiomatic expression. *If* does not have the meaning of *whether.* (C) provides the correct expression. The other choices are simply not idiomatic.

   Sid is traveling in the land of Sasnak. His destination is Nocam, but he has encountered a fork in the road and doesn't know which route leads to his destination. In the land of Sasnak there are two clans. Members of one clan always speak the truth; members of the other clan always speak the opposite of the truth. It is impossible to tell who is a member of which clan simply by looking at them. At the fork is a man, and Sid wants to ask him for directions.

4. The answer to which of the following questions, if asked by Sid, will ensure that Sid will find the right road?

   I. Is the left fork the road to Nocam?

   II. If I asked you whether the left fork is the road to Nocam, would you tell the truth?

   III. If I asked you whether the left fork is the road to Nocam, would you say yes?

   Ⓐ II only   Ⓑ III only   Ⓒ I and III only
   Ⓓ II and III only   Ⓔ I, II, and III

   (B) This question is a logical teaser. Try each question. Statement I won't do the trick. If the man is a member of the truth-telling clan, Sid will obviously get the right answer; but if the man is a member of the other clan, he will get the wrong answer. But he has no way of determining whether he is getting a right or wrong answer. Nor will statement II do the trick, because it doesn't even tell the man about the particular roads in question. Statement III, however, will solve Sid's problem. If the man is a member of the truth-telling clan, Sid will obviously get the right response. If the man is a member of the other clan, and if the left fork is the correct route, what will the man say? To answer the question "Is the left fork the correct route?" the liar would ordinarily respond "no," because it is the correct route. But if you ask at the same time "Would you say yes?" then the liar must respond "yes," because he would ordinarily say "no." Conversely, if the left fork is not the correct route, the liar will be tricked into saying "no." So regardless of the man's clan, Sid gets a "yes" response if the road is the right one and a "no" response if it is not.

Questions 5 and 6

(A) City Council member Ruth Jerome has introduced a proposal for commercial rent control that would limit the increases landlords can charge to small businesses. Of course, Ms. Jerome would favor such a plan because she and her husband own two small grocery stores.

(B) On each of the three occasions I met John, he was wearing a hat. The first time it was a derby, the second time it was a beret, and the third time it was a baseball cap. I conclude, therefore, that John always wears a hat of some sort.

(C) Mary has suggested that the Clippers finished in fifth place last season because they scored too few runs during the season. In fact, the Clippers' total run production for the season was the second highest in the league. So the Clippers failed to do better than fifth because their defense was inadequate.

(D) Eighty-seven percent of the voters surveyed thought that Mr. Herman's views on foreign policy were better than those of Mr. Smith, and 91 percent thought Mr. Herman's views on domestic policy superior to those of Mr. Smith. On this basis, we can conclude that Mr. Herman is likely to make a better senator than Mr. Smith.

(E) It is sometimes argued that the best way to stop drug-related crime is to legalize all drugs. But that's like giving away money to bank robbers and pickpockets.

5. Which of the arguments above relies upon a questionable analogy?

Ⓐ Ⓑ Ⓒ Ⓓ Ⓔ

(E) The argument presented in (E) likens the proposal to legalize drugs to a proposal to legalize bank robbery and pickpocketing. The best description of this kind of argument is analogy, and the analogy is very weak. The criminal aspect of the ordinary drug transaction is the transfer of a substance that is illegal. In a robbery, a legal item (money) is illegally transferred.

6. Which of the arguments above attacks the credibility of a person rather than the merits of a proposal?

Ⓐ Ⓑ Ⓒ Ⓓ Ⓔ

(A) In (A), the speaker never addresses the merits of the council member's proposal. The speaker just attacks her motivation for making it, hoping to discredit her.

7. The passage deals primarily with the

Ⓐ scenic beauty of Colorado's mountains
Ⓑ geological history of Colorado's mountains
Ⓒ classification of rock types
Ⓓ rhythms of the earth's crust
Ⓔ era of the dinosaurs

(B) This is a main idea question. You can eliminate (A) since the passage discusses geology, not scenery. (C) is too narrow. Though the author does mention different types of rocks, the distinctions are drawn in the service of a larger point, the history of the mountains. (D) and (E) can be eliminated for the same reason. The author mentions the rhythms of the earth's crust as part of the history, and the reference to dinosaurs is just to give the reader a point of reference.

8. According to the passage all of the following are true of metamorphic rock EXCEPT

Ⓐ It is harder than sedimentary rock.
Ⓑ It is formed from sedimentary rock.
Ⓒ It is extremely old.
Ⓓ It is a preliminary form of granite.
Ⓔ It is created by extreme temperatures and high pressure.

(D) This is a specific detail question. Everything you need to know about rocks is in the second paragraph. There the author states that metamorphic rock is ancient (C); that it is created from sedimentary rock (B); that it is harder than sedimentary rock (A); and that it is created by high temperatures and pressures (E). (D), however, is a misreading of that paragraph. Granite is "later intrusive material" and not a part of the evolution of metamorphic rock.

9. The author regards the explanation he gives as

Ⓐ conclusively proven
Ⓑ complete fiction
Ⓒ highly tentative and unsupported by evidence
Ⓓ speculative but supported by evidence
Ⓔ certain but unprovable

(D) This is an application question. In essence, the question is asking with which of the judgments would the author agree. In the first paragraph, the author states that the story is a long one, the details of which are not clear, but that there is scattered evidence that strongly suggests a theory. So both (A) and (B) overstate the point—in opposite directions. Scattered evidence and a good theory are not conclusive proof of anything, but neither are they total fiction. You can eliminate (C) and (E) for the same reasons.

10. This is the third straight Christmas season <u>in which retail stores will experience</u> a sharp drop in sales from the previous year.

   Ⓐ in which retail stores will experience
   Ⓑ in which retail stores experience
   Ⓒ which retail stores will experience
   Ⓓ of retail stores' experiencing
   Ⓔ of experiencing by retail stores of

(A) The original is correct as written. As for (B), the verb tense is inappropriate. (Your "ear" should convince you of this even though the technical explanation of the error is a little hard to come up with.) As for (C), here *which* seems to function as the subject of an adjective clause modifying *season,* but this leaves *stores* with no logical connection to the other words in the sentence. (D) and (E) are both awkward.

11. When used together, the cosmetic company claims that its products enhance the appearance of the skin by preventing blemishes and reducing signs of aging.

   Ⓐ When used together, the cosmetic company claims that its products enhance the appearance of the skin by preventing blemishes and reducing signs of aging.
   Ⓑ The cosmetic company claims that, when used together, the appearance of the skin will be enhanced by the products by their preventing blemishes and reducing signs of aging.
   Ⓒ When used together, the products will enhance the appearance of the skin, also preventing blemishes and reducing signs of aging, or so the company claims.
   Ⓓ According to the cosmetic company, when its products are used together, they will enhance the appearance of the skin, prevent blemishes, and reduce signs of aging.
   Ⓔ According to the cosmetic company, when its products are used together, the appearance of the skin will be enhanced and blemishes will be prevented reducing the signs of aging.

(D) The original sentence contains a misplaced modifier. The proximity of the phrase *when used together* to the phrase *cosmetic company* incorrectly suggests that the introductory phrase is intended to modify *company.* An error of this sort can usually be corrected only by restructuring the sentence, as (D) does. As for (B), the offending phrase is still incorrectly placed. In (B), the phrase seems to modify *appearance.* (C) solves the problem of the original but in doing so changes the intended meaning of the sentence. The original makes it clear that the products are intended to enhance the appearance of the skin by preventing blemishes and reducing the signs of aging. But (C) suggests that these are three separate advantages of the products. (E) makes a similar error.

12. Elizabeth I was a student of classical languages, and <u>it was her who insisted that Greek and Latin were spoken at court.</u>

   Ⓐ it was her who insisted that Greek and Latin were spoken at court
   Ⓑ it was she that insisted on the speaking of Greek and Latin at court
   Ⓒ it was she who insisted that Greek and Latin be spoken at court
   Ⓓ she insisted that, at court, Greek and Latin were spoken
   Ⓔ she had insisted that Greek and Latin were to be spoken at court

(C) The original contains two errors. First, since *her* functions as a predicate complement, you must use a nominative (or subject) case pronoun, in this instance *she.* Second, following a verb such as *insisted* you must use some form of the subjunctive. (The subjunctive is not a very important part of English usage, but it does come up occasionally. Remember the Beatles' "Let It Be"? (The song just would not sound the same with "Let it is" or "Let it was.") (B) corrects both errors but only at the price of using an awkward structure: *insisted on the speaking of.* Additionally, (B) is incorrect because it uses *that* to refer to a person. (D) fails to correct the second error; in addition, it creates a run-on sentence. (Technically, (D) results in a comma splice: two independent clauses joined by a comma without a conjunction.) (E) also results in a comma splice and uses an inappropriate verb tense. (The *had insisted* suggests that the second action occurred before the first.)

Jorge: To be a good carpenter, one must have patience.

Gloria: That's not so; a good carpenter must also have the right tools.

13. Gloria has understood Jorge's statement to mean that

   Ⓐ if a person is a good carpenter, she will have the right tools
   Ⓑ if a person is a good carpenter, she will have patience
   Ⓒ if a person has patience, she will be a good carpenter
   Ⓓ if a person has the right tools, she will be a good carpenter
   Ⓔ if a person does not have the right tools, she cannot be a good carpenter

(C) In this verbal exchange, Gloria has evidently misunderstood what Jorge has said. The best way to attack the problem is to put each choice into Jorge's mouth. When you find one that makes sense of Gloria's response, you've found the right response (*Jorge:* if a person has patience, she will be a good carpenter. *Gloria:* That's not so; a good carpenter must also have the right tools.) This exchange makes sense. Gloria believes that she is correcting Jorge: No, patience alone is not enough; you also need the right tools.

The country of West Umberland imports no copper. Private industry's use of copper in West Umberland equals 85 percent of the amount of copper produced by the country's mines each year, while government use of copper equals 23 percent of the amount of copper produced by the country's mines each year.

14. If the information above is true, which of the following conclusions can most reliably be drawn?

(A) West Umberland imports copper ore from other countries.
(B) Some copper in West Umberland is recycled.
(C) West Umberland's industry wastes substantial amounts of copper.
(D) Copper is in short supply in West Umberland.
(E) Each year, West Umberland produces more copper than the previous year.

(B) The paragraph asserts that West Umberland's use is equal to more than 100 percent of what its mines produce, so West Umberland must get some copper from a source other than its mines. The paragraph specifically denies that West Umberland imports any copper, so (A) must be wrong. Only (B) mentions a possible source for the extra copper. (C) uses the word *waste,* but there is nothing in the initial paragraph to support the conclusion that industry wastes copper. (D) is perhaps the second-best answer. When read carefully, however, it turns out to be wrong. (D) asserts that there is a shortage of copper. But the fact that a commodity is recycled does not necessarily mean it is in short supply. (Recycling may simply be cheaper than mining ore.) Finally, (E) is wrong because the paragraph implies no year-to-year comparison. It is conceivable, for all we are told, that both use and production of copper are falling steadily in West Umberland.

At a time when New York City is going through a budgetary crisis, it is cutting its funding of the one agency that helps put more than half a billion dollars into its coffers: the Convention and Visitors Bureau. The proposed $1 million cut comes on the heels of last year's $250,000 funding cut. The debilitating effect of that cut is now obvious. Hotel occupancy rates shrank by 7 percent over last year, resulting in $10 million in taxes not realized by the city.

15. Which of the following, if true, would most weaken the argument above?

(A) New York City spends less than other less populated cities such as Louisville and Dayton to attract visitors and conventions.
(B) The proposed $1 million cut in the budget of the Convention and Visitors Bureau's budget would do little to help balance the city's budget.

(C) The entire country is experiencing an economic downturn, and during an economic downturn people travel less than during times of prosperity.
(D) Adverse publicity about the crime rate in New York discourages some people and organizations from visiting the city.
(E) Many people and organizations would visit New York City even if it were not for the public relations efforts of the Convention and Visitors Bureau.

(C) The speaker asserts a causal connection between last year's cut of the Bureau's budget and the drop in tourism. The question stem then asks you to weaken this argument. Often, the correct answer to a question like this will be an alternative explanation for the phenomenon. (C) provides one: the drop is due to a general economic downturn, not to the cut in the Bureau's budget. (A) is irrelevant to the speaker's claim. The speaker has made a statement about what happened in New York—not in other cities. (B) and (E) both seem to strengthen the speaker's argument: (B) by stating that the city is being penny wise and pound foolish and (E) by stating that the Bureau is effective. (D) is perhaps the second-best response, for it might be read to suggest that adverse publicity is the reason for the drop. But notice that (D) talks about a chronic condition, so it does not explain the sudden one-year drop in tourism.

16. Which of the following best describes the tone of the selection?

(A) Analytical and confident
(B) Resentful and defensive
(C) Objective and speculative
(D) Tentative and skeptical
(E) Persuasive and cynical

(A) This is obviously a tone question. The treatment of the topic is scholarly and balanced, and the style of writing is aggressive (though not overly aggressive). Thus, (A) is the best description of the overall tone of the selection. (B) is incorrect on both counts. The author is analytical rather than resentful and confident rather than defensive. As for (C), though the tone of the selection could be described as objective, it cannot be described as speculative. As for (D), the tone is neither tentative (it is confident) nor skeptical (it is merely scholarly). Finally, as for (E), though the tone could be described as persuasive, it cannot be described as cynical.

17. It can be inferred from the passage that Forrestal's appointment as Secretary of Defense was expected to

(A) placate members of the Navy
(B) result in decreased levels of defense spending
(C) outrage advocates of the Army air forces
(D) win Congressional approval of the unification plan
(E) make Forrestal a Presidential candidate against Truman

(A) This is an implied idea. The reference you need is in the second paragraph. There the author states that not even the appointment of Forrestal allayed the suspicions of Navy officers and their allies. The words *not even* allow us to infer that the appointment of Forrestal was intended to have a placating effect on those people.

18. With which of the following statements about defense unification would the author most likely agree?

Ⓐ Unification ultimately undermined United States military capability by inciting interservice rivalry.

Ⓑ The unification legislation was necessitated by the drastic decline in appropriations for the military services.

Ⓒ Although the unification was not entirely successful, it had the unexpected result of ensuring civilian control of the military.

Ⓓ In spite of the attempted unification, each service was still able to pursue its own objectives without interference from the other branches.

Ⓔ Unification was in the first place unwarranted and in the second place ineffective.

(C) This is a further application question. In the closing paragraph the author states that an unexpected result of the unification battle was that the military would never be able to establish itself as a power independent of and outside civilian control.

19. Although Beverly Sills never achieved superstar status in Europe or at the Metropolitan Opera, <u>yet she was singing major roles at the City Opera during 20 years.</u>

Ⓐ yet she was singing major roles at the City Opera during 20 years

Ⓑ she did sing major roles at the City Opera during 20 years

Ⓒ she sang major roles at the City Opera for 20 years

Ⓓ but she sang major roles at the City Opera for 20 years

Ⓔ yet for 20 years major roles had been sung by her at the City Opera

(C) The original contains two errors. First, a contrast is signaled by the *although*, so the *yet* is superfluous and destroys the logical flow of the sentence. Second, *during* simply does not have a meaning appropriate to this sentence. And you might argue that the verb tense of *was singing* is out of place here. (You could make an argument that it is correct, but then the sentence would be saying something very strange. In any event, the verb tense of the correct choice is surely acceptable.) (B) fails to correct the second error. (D) corrects the second error, but substituting *but* for *yet* does not solve the problem of logical structure and even compounds that problem by creating an extremely awkward sentence.

20. Although Mary Ann is not a great <u>scholar, neither has she published any books, she has and always will be a</u> great teacher and well-loved by her students.

Ⓐ scholar, neither has she published any books, she has and always will be

Ⓑ scholar, nor having published any books, she has been and always will be

Ⓒ scholar and she hasn't published any books, she has been and always will be

Ⓓ scholar nor published any books, still she has been and always will be

Ⓔ scholar nor has she published any books, but she has been and always will be

(C) The sentence contains two errors. First, the clause introduced by *neither* has no clear, logical connection to the rest of the sentence. Second, the sentence contains an incomplete construction. It reads "she has . . . be a great teacher." (C) corrects the incomplete structure and gives the orphaned clause a clear connection to the rest of the sentence. (It is now one of two parallel dependent clauses governed by *although*.) (B) and (D) correct the second error but not the first. (E) suffers from two defects. First, the use of *nor* signals a contrast where one is not intended. (The first two ideas about Mary Ann are similar, not different.) Second, the *but* is superfluous and disrupts the logical flow of the sentence.

21. The great difference in interpretation <u>between him and his immediate predecessor of the role of Anthony were</u> the subject of last week's column by the well-known drama critic.

Ⓐ between him and his immediate predecessor of the role of Anthony were

Ⓑ between him and his immediate predecessor of the role of Anthony was

Ⓒ between he and his immediate predecessor of the role of Anthony were

Ⓓ among him and his immediate predecessor of the role of Anthony was

Ⓔ among him and his immediate predecessor of the role of Anthony were

(B) The original contains one error: the verb *were* does not agree with the subject *difference*. (B) makes the needed correction. (C) introduces a new error: *he* cannot be the object of the preposition *between*. And (D) and (E) introduce a new error. Here a comparison is made between two ideas (his interpretation and his predecessor's interpretation). *Between,* rather than *among,* is the appropriate word.

Within a scheme of criminal penalties, some penalties are more severe than others. A logical consequence of this hierarchy is that one penalty must be the most severe or ultimate penalty. Since the death penalty is the ultimate penalty, we can see that the death penalty is justified as a matter of logic.

22. Which of the following observations most weakens the argument above?

    (A) Not everyone believes that the death penalty is effective in deterring crime.
    (B) Some people incorrectly convicted of a crime might receive the death penalty.
    (C) The most severe penalty in a system of punishments could be something other than the death penalty.
    (D) For a person serving a life sentence with no chance of parole, only the death penalty is greater punishment.
    (E) No two punishments can be ranked equally severe in their effects on a person.

(C) The argument commits the fallacy of ambiguity. The speaker uses the term *ultimate* the first time to mean "most severe within the system." And it is true that in a system of punishments, there will be a most severe punishment. The second time, the speaker uses *ultimate* to mean "the most severe penalty possible." It is this equivocation that gives the argument its seemingly persuasive force. (A) is irrelevant to the speaker's claim. (If you picked [A], reread the choice carefully. [A] does not say that the death penalty is ineffective, only that some people don't believe that it is effective.) (B) is an argument that is often used by opponents of the death penalty, but it doesn't attack the logical structure of this particular argument. The observation made by (D) seems plausible, but it is irrelevant to the speaker's claim. Finally, (E) actually seems to strengthen that part of the speaker's claim that talks about a hierarchy of punishments.

Gloria's office is in Atlanta, but she must spend most of her time traveling. Every time I get a card from her, it has been mailed from some other city where she is staying on business.

23. It can be inferred from that passage above that Gloria

    (A) does not work in Atlanta
    (B) sends cards frequently
    (C) does not write letters
    (D) travels only on business
    (E) has offices in other cities

(B) This argument rests upon a suppressed or hidden premise. Gloria sends cards when she travels. (Gloria sends lots of cards.) Therefore, Gloria must travel a lot. (B) highlights this hidden assumption. (A) is specifically contradicted by the speaker's remarks. (C) is

outside the scope of the argument. The argument says that Gloria sends cards, not that she sends only cards. (D) makes the same kind of error. The speaker states that Gloria travels on business, not that she travels only on business. And (E) is wrong because the speaker says only that Gloria travels on business and nothing about where she does her work while traveling.

Advocates for the homeless attempt to portray homeless persons as victims of social and economic circumstances beyond their control. A recent survey of the homeless in major cities found that a high percentage are addicted to alcohol or other drugs. Rather than innocent victims, these are people who are solely responsible for their own plights.

24. Which of the following, if true, would most weaken the argument above?

    (A) A large number of homeless persons turn to drugs and alcohol out of despair after becoming homeless.
    (B) Several government programs are designed to help the homeless find jobs and new housing.
    (C) Most cities offer shelter to the homeless on a night-by-night basis.
    (D) Alcoholism and other drug addictions can cause erratic and even violent behavior.
    (E) As much as 60 percent of any community's homeless population are local people.

(A) This argument also rests upon a hidden assumption. The speaker must believe (though does not say so specifically) that the homeless people in question were addicted to drugs or alcohol before they became homeless. (A) attacks this premise by indicating that the addiction may have taken place after the homelessness occurred. (B), (C), and (E) are irrelevant to the speaker's claim. The speaker is talking about the causes of homelessness, not about what is done for the homeless after the fact nor about where the people lived when they had homes. (D) at least has the merit of focusing on addiction, but it, too, is irrelevant because it does not address the issue of addiction as a cause of homelessness.

25. The author is primarily concerned with discussing the

    (A) disadvantages of California's open government legislation
    (B) effect of an open government statute on California's energy commission
    (C) methods by which California energy commissioners obtain information
    (D) energy policies adopted by the California energy commission under the open government statute
    (E) political forces that shape California's energy policies

(B) The main point of the passage is introduced in the first two sentences: the open government statutes have good points and bad points, as shown by the example of the energy commission. (A) is wrong for two reasons. One, it fails to mention that the focus of the discussion is the example of the energy commission; and two, it fails to refer to the good points of the law. (C) is too narrow. The interaction between commission and staff is mentioned only by way of illustration. (D) is wrong because the focus is the process—not the final outcome. The author is concerned with *how* the decisions are made, not with their content. Finally, (E) is incorrect since the author analyzes the energy commission in terms of its structure, not political forces.

26. The passage implies the open government statute is intended to accomplish all of the following EXCEPT

    (A) to minimize the likelihood of secret political deals
    (B) to allow an opportunity for the public to influence government decisions
    (C) to ensure that government officials are held accountable for their policies
    (D) to guarantee that a government agency can respond quickly to a problem
    (E) to publicize governmental functions

    (D) This is an implied idea question that covers virtually the whole passage. The term "open government" provides a clue. The general idea of the law is to ensure that the workings of an agency are open to public scrutiny. So (C) and (E) must surely be purposes of the law.

    Beyond that, the second paragraph mentions that the law is so strict it prohibits private meetings between members of the commission. This fact, coupled with the general intent of an "open government" law, implies that it is intended to prevent private deals. So (A) is implied by the selection. (B) is supported by the last sentence of the third paragraph. A consequence of the law is that the public is given an opportunity to participate in the decision-making process.

    (D), however, is not implied by the passage. In fact, according to the last paragraph, the procedures required to implement the law have actually slowed the decision-making process.

27. The passage most strongly supports which of the following conclusions about a decision that is within the authority of the executive director of an agency?

    (A) It would be made more quickly than a decision reserved for a commission.
    (B) It would be made with the assistance of the agency's commissioners.
    (C) It would be a highly publicized event attended by members of the news media.
    (D) It would deal with a matter of greater importance than those handled by the commission.
    (E) It would be made only after the director had notified the commissioners and their aides in writing.

(A) This is a further application question. You must use what you have learned from the passage about the administrative process. In the first paragraph, the author says decisions can be classified according to whether they can be made by the executive director or must be reserved for the commission. If the matter can only be decided by the commission, then it must be done publicly. Later, the author points out that the requirements of publicity and public meetings slow the administrative process. We may conclude, therefore, that the executive director, because he or she is not bound by the open government requirements, can act more swiftly.

(B) and (C) are incorrect since a decision solely within the discretion of the executive director is made without the participation of the commission and the attendant publicity. As for (D), the "big decisions," like the entire budget, are the ones that must be done publicly. Finally, (E) is just a misreading of the passage. The passage mentions that requests for information from commissioners to staff must be in writing.

28. The English version of "Waiting for Godot," <u>of which Beckett was the translator</u>, was seen in a new production at the Performing Arts Center last year.

    (A) of which Beckett was the translator
    (B) which Beckett was the translator
    (C) having been translated by Beckett
    (D) that had been translated by Beckett
    (E) the translator Beckett

(A) The original is correct as written. As for (B), without the preposition, *which* seems to be the subject of the verb *was,* but this leaves the word *Beckett* with no connection to the rest of the sentence. (C) changes slightly the intended meaning of the sentence. In the original, the idea that Beckett produced the English translation is an aside, but the sentence implies that this notion is somehow necessary to the new production (rather than interesting but incidental). Remember, don't make a change from the original unless you have good reason for doing so. (D) is wrong because *that* would be used to introduce material essential to the sentence, not an aside. Finally, (E) is wrong because this phrase would have no logical connection to the rest of the sentence.

29. Accusing his opponent of falsifying his military record, it was clear that the Congressional race was heating up.

   (A) Accusing his opponent of falsifying his military record, it was clear that the Congressional race was heating up.

   (B) Accusing the other opponent of falsifying his military record, it was clear that the Congressional race heated up.

   (C) It was clear that the Congressional race was heating up when one candidate accused the other of falsifying his military record.

   (D) Having accused his opponent of falsifying his military record, it was clear that the Congressional race was heating up.

   (E) Once accused of falsifying his military record, it was clear that the Congressional race was heating up.

(C) The original sentence contains a dangling modifier. There is nothing for the phrase "accusing . . . record" to modify. (C) corrects this problem by substantially reordering the elements of the sentence. The remaining choices all include introductory phrases that have no clear relation to the rest of the sentence.

30. Although she plays tennis as well, if not better than her sister, her sister is the captain of the team.

   (A) Although she plays tennis as well, if not better than her sister,

   (B) Although she plays tennis as well as, if not better than, her sister,

   (C) In spite of the fact of her playing tennis as well as, if not better than, her sister,

   (D) She plays tennis as well, if not better, than her sister, but

   (E) Playing tennis as well as, if not better than, her sister,

(B) The original sentence contains an incomplete construction. It reads: "she plays as well . . . than her sister." (B) eliminates this problem. (C) completes the faulty construction, but the resulting sentence is wordy and awkward. (D) fails to correct the error of the original. As for (E), *playing* would seem to modify *she,* resulting in a sentence that is internally inconsistent.

Several states have wisely refused to raise the highway speed limit above 55 miles per hour despite calls by motorists for an increase. Although the 55-mile-per-hour speed limit was initially enacted by the Federal government as a conservation measure, it soon became clear that a felicitous consequence of the measure was considerably fewer traffic fatalities.

31. The speaker above is arguing that states that have a 55-mile-per-hour highway speed limit should

   (A) raise the highway speed limit

   (B) further reduce the highway speed limit

   (C) retain the 55-mile-per-hour highway speed limit

   (D) enact other measures to improve fuel conservation

   (E) find other ways of reducing highway fatalities

(C) The question asks that you state the speaker's conclusion. The speaker states that some states have "wisely" refused to raise the speed limit because a higher speed limit would result in more fatalities. (C) is most likely the conclusion of this thinking. (A) must surely be wrong because the speaker is clearly opposed to raising the speed limit. (B) overstates the speaker's case. The speaker may believe that 55 miles per hour is the optimum speed limit; it saves lives while not being overly inconvenient. (D) and (E) may be ideas that the speaker would endorse, but the evidence presented about the 55-mile-per-hour speed limit does not lead in either of these directions.

The quality of life provided by a government depends not so much upon its formal structure as upon the ability and temperament of those who serve as its officers.

32. The author of the paragraph above would most likely agree with which of the following statements?

   (A) A written constitution is essential to ensure the liberty of citizens against a strong government.

   (B) Universal suffrage is the best guarantee that the general will of the people will become legislation.

   (C) A government with good leaders is likely to survive for a longer time than a government with incompetent leaders.

   (D) Poor leadership in a hierarchical organization threatens the ability of the organization to achieve results.

   (E) The quality of the leadership of a government is the main determinant of whether the citizens will be happy.

(E) The initial statement asserts that the primary determinant of a government's ability to provide for its citizens is the skill of its administrators and not the formal structure of the government. Thus, (A) and (B) are incorrect. Those choices refer to formal elements of a government. (C) and (D) are more interesting but can be eliminated after careful reading. As for (C), the author states that the ability of the leaders determines the quality of life of the citizens—not whether the government will survive for a long period. It seems that (D) is the second-best choice. The author might very well apply his analysis of governmental structures to other hierarchical structures. But that requires that you go beyond the scope of the passage. By contrast, (E) is more clearly supported by the text because it is a statement about government. Another way of expressing this idea is to say that if (D) is arguably a correct choice, then (E) must be even better.

Your chart listing winners of the Most Valuable Player award states that one designated hitter won the award: Don Baylor in 1979. This is erroneous. No designated hitter has ever won the M. V. P., and it is extremely doubtful that a player who does not serve the team in the field will ever win it.

33. Which of the following, if true, would most strengthen the argument above?

   Ⓐ In 1979, Don Baylor played one game as first baseman.
   Ⓑ In 1979, Don Baylor played 97 games as an outfielder versus 65 as a designated hitter.
   Ⓒ Don Baylor won the Most Valuable Player award only once in his career.
   Ⓓ Of the two major baseball leagues, only the American League allows the use of a designated hitter.
   Ⓔ The Most Valuable Player award can be given to any player on the team.

(B) The argument as written is ambiguous. Is the speaker denying that Don Baylor was given the M.V.P. award in 1979, or is the speaker denying that Don Baylor was a designated hitter when he won it in 1979? If we adopt the first interpretation, there is no correct answer, so we must adopt the second interpretation. Now (B) appears to strengthen the argument: Don Baylor was an outfielder when he won the 1979 M.V.P., not a designated hitter. As for (A), this idea is consistent with the speaker's point but doesn't really strengthen the argument. The fact that Don Baylor played one game at first base doesn't prove that Don Baylor was not a designated hitter. (C) and (D) are irrelevant to the speaker's claim. Finally, as for (E), this point seems to suggest that it is theoretically possible for a designated hitter to be given the M.V.P. award, but that doesn't strengthen the argument that practically speaking, a designated hitter would never win the award.

34. A discussion of our nation's foreign policy must begin with the fact of there being an independent Western Europe which now thinks of itself in transnationalist terms.

   Ⓐ A discussion of our nation's foreign policy must begin with the fact of there being
   Ⓑ Beginning any discussion of our nation's foreign policy must be the fact of there being
   Ⓒ Any discussion of our nation's foreign policy must begin with the fact that there is
   Ⓓ Any discussion of our nation's foreign policy must begin by acknowledging the existence of
   Ⓔ To begin discussing our nation's foreign policy there must be an acknowledgment of the fact that

(D) The original contains two errors, one obvious, the other subtle. First, the phrase *of there being* is not idiomatic. Second, the phrasing *discussion must begin with the fact* doesn't really make a meaningful assertion. A discussion is an exchange of statements or ideas. Therefore, the beginning of a discussion can be a statement recognizing the existence of a fact, but the discussion cannot begin with a fact. (D) makes both the needed corrections. (B) fails to correct either error, and the resulting sentence is very awkward. (C) fails to correct the second error. (E) attempts to correct the second error, but not the first, and the resulting sentence is still very awkward.

35. Interest rates on mortgages have declined steadily during the first six months of this year but virtually remained unchanged during the next three months.

   Ⓐ have declined steadily during the first six months of this year but virtually remained unchanged
   Ⓑ declined steadily during the first six months of this year but virtually remain unchanged
   Ⓒ steadily declined during the first six months of this year but remain virtually unchanged
   Ⓓ declined steadily during the first six months of this year but have remained virtually unchanging
   Ⓔ declined steadily during the first six months of this year but have remained virtually unchanged

(E) The verb tenses in the original sentence reverse the temporal sequence. The use of the present perfect *have declined* suggests an action begun in the past but continuing into the future. But the intent of the sentence is to place the events of the first six months clearly in the past. (E) accomplishes this by using the simple past to describe the first six months and the present perfect to describe the latter events. (B) and (C) correct the one tense, but the use of the present *remain* is inappropriate to describe an event that belongs to the past. Additionally, the placement of *virtually* in (B) is incorrect. (*Virtually* is supposed to modify *unchanged,* not *remain.*) Finally, (D) is not idiomatic. (*Unchanging* has a meaning different from that of *unchanged.*)

"Most people like pennies," says Hamilton Dix, spokesperson for the United States Mint. "We did a survey at the Epcot Center at Walt Disney World, and half of all the adults said they use pennies daily."

36. Which of the following observations most undermines the position of the speaker above?

(A) Most of the people who visit Walt Disney World are on vacation.

(B) The survey covered people only at a single location in one state.

(C) The survey included adults visiting Epcot Center but not children.

(D) The speaker is a representative of the agency that manufactures pennies.

(E) Many purchases require the use of pennies either as payment or as change.

(E) The argument above is a non sequitur; that is, the conclusion does not follow from the premises. The speaker claims that people *like* pennies, but the proof for that claim is that people *use* pennies. A person might be compelled to do something that he or she doesn't like at all, as choice (E) suggests. It is difficult to imagine how (A) can be read to contradict the argument. To the extent that you read (A) as indicting the survey (vacationers are not representative of people in general?), (B) is surely a better choice. At least (B) suggests that there is something specifically wrong with the survey. The weakness with (B), however, is that it doesn't carry the issue far enough. To be an effective attack on the argument, (B) would have to explain why the people surveyed do not reflect the population as a whole. (C) is weak for the same reason: how does this prove that the survey is inaccurate? As for (D), this does constitute an attack on the argument by suggesting that the speaker may have some reason to misrepresent the results of the survey. The trouble with (D), however, is that it is nowhere nearly so powerful an attack as (E). Whereas (D) only hints that the speaker may be misrepresenting the results, (E) points out the logical fallacy in the argument.

As a citizen who values individual rights, I am appalled at the growing use of random or mandatory drug testing. What is needed is a screening test for impaired function, not for drug use per se. For example, it would be easy to design a computerized test for reaction time. Such a test should be simple to administer and would be nonintrusive. Anyone failing the test could then be required to submit to the more invasive drug test.

37. Which of the following, if true, would most weaken the argument above?

(A) Administrations of a reaction test could be arranged randomly, so that a drug user could not alter his or her habits.

(B) A reaction test measures capacity only at that time, but a drug test may show that a person is likely to be a future risk.

(C) The Supreme Court has refused to rule that mandatory drug tests for employees in sensitive positions are unconstitutional.

(D) A person might fail a reaction test for a reason other than impairment due to the use of illegal drugs.

(E) A person who has ingested an illegal substance might have sufficient self-control to pass a reaction test.

(B) The speaker's argument assumes that the purpose of drug testing is to detect impairment at a particular moment, but drug testing may also serve to identify persons who, though not impaired at the time of testing, might be impaired at some future time. This is in essence what (B) argues. (A) seems to strengthen the speaker's position by stating that the reaction test could be used effectively. (C) doesn't constitute an attack on the argument at all. The fact that the Supreme Court has not held mandatory testing unconstitutional does not mean that a reaction test is not a better alternative than mandatory drug testing. On the surface, (D) does seem to attack the speaker's position, but closer study shows that (D) is actually consistent with the spirit of the speaker's proposal. While it may be true that a person might incorrectly be required to take a drug test (because she or he failed the reaction test for a reason unrelated to drug use), even a flawed reaction test is less intrusive than mandatory drug testing: with a flawed reaction test, a few people are needlessly tested for drugs, but with mandatory drug testing everyone is subject to the drug test. Finally, (E) also seems to attack the speaker's argument by saying that the reaction test would not necessarily detect all drug use. But the speaker can easily absorb this attack: true, but if the person tested can pass the reaction test, then the person is not impaired and shouldn't be required to take the drug test.

Computer colorization of black-and-white film is an important tool for making historical events seem real to students who live in an age of color movies and color television. A colorized version of the footage of Jack Ruby's assassination of Lee Harvey Oswald or of the first manned space shot will help students today understand what it was like for the millions of Americans who actually saw those events on television.

38. Which of the following, if true, most weakens the conclusion of the argument above?

   Ⓐ The people who saw those events live saw them in black and white, not in color.

   Ⓑ The events mentioned occurred before most of today's students were born.

   Ⓒ Many important historical events were never recorded on film.

   Ⓓ Modern techniques can improve the quality of the sound of old film footage.

   Ⓔ Colorization can be accomplished by a computer process that is relatively inexpensive.

(A) The speaker argues that colorization of film footage of historical events will help students today understand what people who originally viewed those events on television felt. The fallacy in this argument is that the people who saw the original events saw them in black and white, not in color. So if you really want to understand what it was like to watch the first manned space shot on television, you should watch it in black and white. This is the point made by (A). (B) is simply irrelevant to the argument. That today's students were not yet born at the time of the events in question doesn't address the speaker's point that colorization would be a good way of educating those students. Similarly, (C) is irrelevant. The fact that some events were not recorded doesn't address the speaker's point that the film that does exist should be colorized. (D) seems to make the same kind of mistake as the initial paragraph. Improving the quality of the soundtrack of old film will not give the same impression as the original soundtrack. And finally, as for (E), the fact that colorization is technologically feasible is certainly not an argument against colorization.

39. The main purpose of the selection is to

   Ⓐ discuss two models of constitutional law

   Ⓑ criticize Congress and the executive branch for inaction

   Ⓒ suggest a new role for the Supreme Court

   Ⓓ challenge the validity of Supreme Court rulings

   Ⓔ call for a revised Constitution

(A) This is a main idea question. The author begins by asking which of two models better describes the Constitution. The selection then examines both models. And the author ends by creating an analogy between

constitutional theory and physics that suggests that both models have uses. The best description of this development is provided by (A). (B) is too narrow to be a correct description of the main idea of the selection. The author also criticizes the judiciary, and the main emphasis of the passage is theoretical. (C) is also too narrow. The author suggests obliquely that the Supreme Court has perhaps taken too much responsibility for evolving constitutional doctrine, but that is not the main point of the passage. Finally, (E) is surely wrong, for the author is concerned about how to interpret the existing Constitution.

40. In the first paragraph, the author makes use of

   Ⓐ circular reasoning

   Ⓑ authority

   Ⓒ analogy

   Ⓓ generalization

   Ⓔ ambiguity

(C) This is a logical structure question. In the first paragraph the author likens a certain view of the Constitution to dividing a pie between two siblings. The best description of this strategy is analogy.

41. The passage implies that

   Ⓐ Congress is more important than either the executive or the judiciary

   Ⓑ branches of government may have more constitutional authority than they use

   Ⓒ the earliest Supreme Court justices were more sincere than today's justices

   Ⓓ the Constitution sets up a very simple system for governmental decisions

   Ⓔ constitutionally created hurdles block needed improvements in governmental efficiency

(B) This is an inference question. In the second paragraph the author suggest some things that the executive and legislative branches might do to make government better, things that are constitutionally permissible. Thus, we can infer that the branches of government may have more authority than they are using. (A) is incorrect because the author seems to regard all three branches as equally important. (That is part of the Newtonian model.) (C) is wrong because the only part of the passage that even hints that judges might be "insincere" is the discussion about the New Deal decisions—and that compares members of the same Court. (D) must be incorrect because the author implies that the constitutional process is sufficiently complex that it cannot be explained by a single model. And our analysis of the correct choice shows that (E) is wrong. The author believes that governmental efficiency can be improved by taking constitutionally permissible action.

QUANTITATIVE SECTION

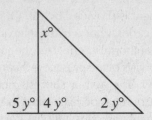

Note: Figure not drawn to scale

1. In the figure above, what is the value of $x°$?

Ⓐ 15 Ⓑ 20 Ⓒ 30 Ⓓ 45 Ⓔ 60

(E) First find the value of y:

$5y + 4y = 180$

$9y = 180$

$y = 20$

Next find the value of x:

$4y + 2y + x = 180$

$6y + x = 180$

$6(20°) + x = 180$

$120 + x = 180$

$x = 60$

2. In the figure above, what is the length of PQ?

Ⓐ 0.12 Ⓑ 0.16 Ⓒ 0.13 Ⓓ 0.11 Ⓔ 0.09

(B) The trick here is to recognize that each of the marks between the numbered marks is $\frac{1}{5}$ of the distance between the numbered marks. The distance between each numbered mark is 0.1, so each of the others is worth $0.1 \div 5 = 0.02$. So $PQ = 0.02 + 0.1 + 2(0.02) = 0.16$.

3. If the average (arithmetic mean) of x, x, x, 56, and 58 is 51, then $x =$

Ⓐ 43 Ⓑ 47 Ⓒ 49 Ⓓ 51 Ⓔ 53

(B) Use the technique for finding the missing elements of an average. The average of the five numbers is 51, so their sum is $5 \times 51 = 255$. The two known values total 114. So the remaining three numbers total $255 - 114 = 141$. And $141 \div 3 = 47$.

4. What is the value of x?

(1) $3x - 2 = 10$

(2) $\dfrac{x}{10} = \dfrac{2}{5}$

Ⓐ statement 1 alone is sufficient to answer the question, but statement 2 alone is not sufficient

Ⓑ statement 2 alone is sufficient to answer the question, but statement 1 alone is not sufficient

Ⓒ both statements together are needed to answer the question, but neither statement alone is sufficient

Ⓓ either statement by itself is sufficient to answer the question

Ⓔ not enough facts are given to answer the question

(D) Each statement is an equation with one variable, so each is, in and of itself, sufficient to provide the value of x:

$3x - 2 = 10$

$3x = 12$

$x = 4$

$\dfrac{x}{10} = \dfrac{2}{5}$

$x = \dfrac{2}{5}(10)$

$x = 4$

5. How many hardcover books does Greg have in his personal library?

(1) Greg has three times as many paperbacks as hardcover books.

(2) Greg has 24 more paperbacks than hardcover books.

Ⓐ statement 1 alone is sufficient to answer the question, but statement 2 alone is not sufficient

Ⓑ statement 2 alone is sufficient to answer the question, but statement 1 alone is not sufficient

Ⓒ both statements together are needed to answer the question, but neither statement alone is sufficient

Ⓓ either statement by itself is sufficient to answer the question

Ⓔ not enough facts are given to answer the question

(C) Neither statement alone is sufficient to answer the question, but both statements together are sufficient. The information can be expressed algebraically:

$P = 3H$

$P - H = 24$

(*P* represents the number of paperback books, and *H* the number of hardcover books.) We can treat these as simultaneous equations and solve for *H*:

$$P = 24 + H$$

$$24 + H = 3H$$

$$24 = 2H$$

$$H = 12$$

6. For how many integers *x* is $-2 \le 2x \le 2$?

Ⓐ 1   Ⓑ 2   Ⓒ 3   Ⓓ 4   Ⓔ 5

(C) *x* could be $-1, 0,$ or 1.

7. If *x* is an odd integer, all of the following are odd EXCEPT

Ⓐ $x + 2$ Ⓑ $3x + 2$ Ⓒ $2x^2 + x$
Ⓓ $2x^3 + x$ Ⓔ $3x^3 + x$

(E) You can reason to the conclusion using the properties of odd and even numbers. Or, you can just substitute a number for *x*. Say that $x = 1$, an odd number:

(A) $x + 2 = 1 + 2 = 3$ (Odd)

(B) $3x + 2 = 3(1) + 2 = 5$ (Odd)

(C) $2x^2 + x = 2(1)^2 + 1 = 2 + 1 = 3$ (Odd)

(D) $2x^3 + x = 2(1)^3 + 1 = 2 + 1 = 3$ (Odd)

(E) $3x^3 + x = 3(1)^3 + 1 = 3 + 1 = 4$ (Even)

8. What is the sum of the areas of two squares with sides of 2 and 3, respectively?

Ⓐ 1   Ⓑ 5   Ⓒ 13   Ⓓ 25   Ⓔ 36

(C) Just do the indicated operations. One square has an area of $2 \times 2 = 4$, the other an area of $3 \times 3 = 9$. The sum of their areas is $4 + 9 = 13$.

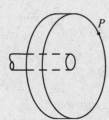

9. *P* is a point on the flywheel shown above. How far does *P* travel during five complete revolutions of the wheel?

(1) The diameter of the wheel is 1 meter.

(2) The wheel turns at the rate of 3,000 revolutions per minute.

Ⓐ statement 1 alone is sufficient to answer the question, but statement 2 alone is not sufficient

Ⓑ statement 2 alone is sufficient to answer the question, but statement 1 alone is not sufficient

Ⓒ both statements together are needed to answer the question, but neither statement alone is sufficient

Ⓓ either statement by itself is sufficient to answer the question

Ⓔ not enough facts are given to answer the question

(A) (1) is sufficient to answer the question. Since the diameter of the wheel is 1 meter, its circumference is $\pi(1) = \pi$. And since *P* is on the circumference of the wheel, during five complete revolutions of the wheel, *P* will travel $5 \times \pi$, or 5π meters. (2) is not sufficient to answer the question. To find the distance traveled by *P*, it is not necessary to know the speed at which *P* traveled.

10. *ABCD* is a square. What is the area of *ABCD*?

(1) $AB = 3$

(2) $AC = 3\sqrt{2}$

Ⓐ statement 1 alone is sufficient to answer the question, but statement 2 alone is not sufficient

Ⓑ statement 2 alone is sufficient to answer the question, but statement 1 alone is not sufficient

Ⓒ both statements together are needed to answer the question, but neither statement alone is sufficient

Ⓓ either statement by itself is sufficient to answer the question

Ⓔ not enough facts are given to answer the question

(D) Since *AB* is a side of a square, (1) implies Area = $3 \times 3 = 9$. So (1) is sufficient. (2) is also sufficient:

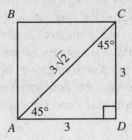

11. If *x* is 80 percent of *y*, then *y* is what percent of *x*?

Ⓐ $133\frac{1}{3}\%$ Ⓑ 125%   Ⓒ 120%
Ⓓ 90%   Ⓔ 80%

(B) Since *x* is 80 percent of *y*, $x = 0.8y$, and $y = \frac{x}{0.8} = 1.25x$. So *y* is 125% of *x*. Or, you can just use some numbers. Assume that *y* is 100. If $y = 100$, then $x = 80\%$ of $y = 80$. Finally, find what percent *y* is of *x*: $\frac{100}{80} = \frac{5}{4} = 1.25 = 125\%$.

12. From which of the following statements can it be deduced that $m > n$?

Ⓐ $m + 1 = n$
Ⓑ $2m = n$
Ⓒ $m + n > 0$
Ⓓ $m - n > 0$
Ⓔ $mn > 0$

(D) You can rewrite $m - n > 0$ by adding n to both sides: $m > n$. As for (A), this proves that $m < n$. As for (B), this proves nothing about m and n, since m and n might be either negative or positive. The same is true of (C), which is equivalent to $m > -n$. Finally, as for (E), you have neither relative values for m and n nor their signs.

13. If for any number n, ⓝ is defined as the least integer that is greater than or equal to n^2, then $=$ ⟨-1.1⟩
    Ⓐ -2 Ⓑ -1 Ⓒ 0 Ⓓ 1 Ⓔ 2

    (E) Here we have a defined function. Just do the indicated operation. $(-1.1)^2 = 1.21$, and the smallest integer greater than 1.21 is 2.

14. Is $xy > 0$?
    (1) $x^8 y^9 < 0$
    (2) $x^7 y^8 < 0$
    Ⓐ statement 1 alone is sufficient to answer the question, but statement 2 alone is not sufficient
    Ⓑ statement 2 alone is sufficient to answer the question, but statement 1 alone is not sufficient
    Ⓒ both statements together are needed to answer the question, but neither statement alone is sufficient
    Ⓓ either statement by itself is sufficient to answer the question
    Ⓔ not enough facts are given to answer the question

    (C) (1) is not sufficient to answer the question. Although (1) implies that y is negative (x^8 must be positive, but the entire expression is negative), this does not determine the sign of x. Similarly, (2) alone is not sufficient. (2) implies that x is negative (y^8 must be positive, but the entire expression is negative), but (2) implies nothing about the sign of y. Both statements taken together, however, imply that x and y are both negative. Therefore, $xy > 0$.

15. What is the value of N?
    (1) $\dfrac{M}{M+N} = 5$
    (2) $\dfrac{6M - 24}{M+N} = 6$
    Ⓐ statement 1 alone is sufficient to answer the question, but statement 2 alone is not sufficient
    Ⓑ statement 2 alone is sufficient to answer the question, but statement 1 alone is not sufficient
    Ⓒ both statements together are needed to answer the question, but neither statement alone is sufficient
    Ⓓ either statement by itself is sufficient to answer the question
    Ⓔ not enough facts are given to answer the question

    (B) Statement (1) is not sufficient, for you have only one equation but two variables. You can manipulate it:

$$M = 5(M + N)$$
$$M = 5M + 5N$$
$$-4M = +5N$$

But this does not establish the value of either M or N. Statement (2), however, can be manipulated to establish the value of N:

$$6M - 24 = 6(M + N)$$
$$6M - 24 = 6M + 6N$$
$$6N = -24$$
$$N = -4$$

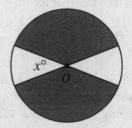

16. The above circle with center O has a radius of length 2. If the total area of the shaded regions is 3π, then $x =$
    Ⓐ 270 Ⓑ 180 Ⓒ 120 Ⓓ 90 Ⓔ 45

    (E) First, find the area of the circle: $\pi r^2 = \pi(2)^2 = 4\pi$. Since the shaded area is equal to 3π, it accounts for $\frac{3\pi}{4\pi} = \frac{3}{4}$ of the circle. So the unshaded area accounts for $\frac{1}{4}$ of the circle. This means that angle x plus the angle vertically opposite x are equal to $\frac{1}{4}$ of $360 = 90$. So $2x = 90$, and $x = 45$. Or, since the figure is drawn to scale, you could have relied on guestimation.

17. If $\dfrac{1}{x} + \dfrac{1}{y} = \dfrac{1}{z}$, then $z =$
    Ⓐ $\dfrac{1}{xy}$ Ⓑ xy Ⓒ $\dfrac{x+y}{xy}$
    Ⓓ $\dfrac{xy}{x+y}$ Ⓔ $\dfrac{2xy}{x+y}$

    (D) Rewrite the equation:

$$\frac{1}{x} + \frac{1}{y} = \frac{1}{z}$$

Add the fractions using the "flying x":

$$\frac{x+y}{xy} = \frac{1}{z}$$

Multiply both sides by z:

$$z\left(\frac{x+y}{xy}\right) = 1$$

Multiply both sides by $\dfrac{xy}{x+y}$

$$z = \dfrac{xy}{x+y}$$

Or, just assume some values. Assume that $x = 1$ and $y = 1$. On that assumption, $z = \frac{1}{2}$. Then substitute 1 for x and 1 for y into the choices. Only (D) generates the value $\frac{1}{2}$.

18. In a certain clothing store, 60 percent of all the articles are imported and 20 percent of all the articles are priced at $100 or more. If 40 percent of the articles priced at $100 or more are imported, what percent of the articles priced *under* $100 are *not* imported?

Ⓐ 28% Ⓑ 12% Ⓒ 8% Ⓓ 4.8% Ⓔ 2%

(A) Set up a table to show the possibilities:

	Imported	Not imported	Totals
$100 or more			
Less than $100			
Totals			

Now fill in the numbers that are given:

	Imported	Not imported	Totals
$100 or more			20%
Less than $100			
Totals	60%		

Since the total must equal 100%:

	Imported	Not imported	Totals
$100 or more			20%
Less than $100			80%
Totals	60%	40%	100%

Next, 40 percent of the articles priced at $100 or more are imported, and 40% of 20% = 8%:

	Imported	Not imported	Totals
$100 or more	8%		20%
Less than $100			80%
Totals	60%	40%	100%

By adding and subtracting, you can complete the table:

	Imported	Not imported	Totals
$100 or more	8%	12%	20%
Less than $100	52%	28%	80%
Totals	60%	40%	100%

You can reach the same conclusion by assuming some numbers.

19. If x is an integer such that $1 < x < 100$, what is the value of x?

(1) x is the square of an integer.

(2) x is the cube of an integer.

Ⓐ statement 1 alone is sufficient to answer the question, but statement 2 alone is not sufficient

Ⓑ statement 2 alone is sufficient to answer the question, but statement 1 alone is not sufficient

Ⓒ both statements together are needed to answer the question, but neither statement alone is sufficient

Ⓓ either statement by itself is sufficient to answer the question

Ⓔ not enough facts are given to answer the question

(C) Statement (1) is not sufficient, for x could be 4, 9, 16, 25, 36, 49, 64, or 81. Statement (2) is not sufficient, for x could be 8, 27, or 64. But the two statements taken together are sufficient because there is only one number, 64, that appears in both of the lists.

20. A group of 66 students is divided into three classes, each with a different number of students. How many students are in the largest class?

(1) One of the classes has two fewer students than the largest class.

(2) One of the classes has 21 students.

Ⓐ statement 1 alone is sufficient to answer the question, but statement 2 alone is not sufficient

Ⓑ statement 2 alone is sufficient to answer the question, but statement 1 alone is not sufficient

Ⓒ both statements together are needed to answer the question, but neither statement alone is sufficient

Ⓓ either statement by itself is sufficient to answer the question

Ⓔ not enough facts are given to answer the question

(C) Statement (1) is not sufficient to answer the question. Let a, b, and c represent the number of students in the three classes, and let c represent the number of students in the largest class. The question stem establishes that $a + b + c = 66$

Statement (1) says only:

$c = a + 2$

But these two equations are not sufficient to fix a value for c.

Nor is Statement (2) sufficient. But both statements together are sufficient to answer the question. The class with 21 students cannot be the largest class, for there are 66 students, so it must be either class a or class b. If it is class a, then the sizes of classes a, b, and c are 21, 22, and 23, respectively. Now assume that $b = 21$. If $b = 21$, then there are $66 - 21 = 45$ students in a and c combined. But the solutions for the equations

$a + c = 45$

$a + 2 = c$

are fractions, which proves that the three classes must have 21, 22, and 23 students. Therefore, the largest class has 23 students.

21. If $|r - 6| = 5$ and $|2q - 12| = 8$, what is the maximum value of $\frac{q}{r}$?

Ⓐ 2　　Ⓑ $\frac{11}{2}$　　Ⓒ 10　　Ⓓ 11　　Ⓔ 20

(C) The symbol "$|x|$" indicates absolute value, that is, the magnitude of a number without regard to the sign of the number. Thus, $|3| = 3$ and $|-3| = 3$, because both are a distance of 3 from zero on the number line (even though one is 3 removed from zero in a negative direction and the other 3 removed from zero in a positive direction). This symbol is not used very often on the exam.

If $|r - 6| = 5$, then either $r - 6 = 5$ or $r - 6 = -5$ (because $|5| = 5$ and $|-5| = 5$). Consequently, there are two possible values for r. Either

$r - 6 = 5$

$r = 11$

or

$r - 6 = -5$

$r = 1$

The same is true of $|2q - 12|$ and q. Either

$2q - 12 = 8$

$2q = 20$

$q = 10$

or

$2q - 12 = -8$

$2q = 4$

$q = 2$

So the possible values for r are 11 and 1, the possible values for q are 10 and 2, and the maximum possible value of $\frac{q}{r} = \frac{10}{1} = 10$.

22. At the close of trading on Tuesday, the price per share of a certain stock was 20 percent less than the price per share at the close of trading on Monday. On Wednesday, the price per share at closing was 25 percent less than that on Tuesday. If on Thursday, the price per share at closing was equal to the closing price on Monday, what was the percent increase in the price per share of the stock from closing Wednesday to closing Thursday?

Ⓐ 45%　Ⓑ $66\frac{2}{3}$%　Ⓒ 75%　Ⓓ 145%　Ⓔ $166\frac{2}{3}$%

(B) One way to attack this item is to assign a variable to represent the price of the stock on Monday, say, M. By the close of trading on Tuesday, the price of the stock had dropped by 20% to $0.80M$. Then, during Wednesday's trading, $0.80M$ dropped by 25 percent: $0.80M - (0.25 \times 0.80M) = 0.60M$. And on Thursday, the price rose from $0.60M$ to M. You can use the "change over" strategy to find the percent increase:

$$\frac{\text{Change}}{\text{Original Total}} = \frac{M - 0.60M}{0.60M} = \frac{0.40M}{0.60M} = \frac{2}{3}$$

$$= 66\frac{2}{3}\%$$

Of course, you don't really need to use a letter variable. You can reach the same conclusion just by assuming a value for the original price of the stock, say,

$100. By the close of trading on Tuesday, the price dropped by 20 percent, to $80. Then, on Wednesday, it dropped another 25 percent, to $60. And on Thursday it rose to $100. The percent increase from $60 to $100 is $\frac{$40}{$60}$, or $66\frac{2}{3}\%$.

23. A hiker walked up a mountain path from a way station to an observation point and back to the way station by the same route. His average speed for the ascent was two miles per hour, and his average speed for the descent was four miles per hour. If the observation point is exactly three miles from the way station, what was the hiker's average speed, in miles per hour, for the entire trip?

Ⓐ $2\frac{2}{5}$　Ⓑ $2\frac{2}{3}$　Ⓒ 3　Ⓓ $3\frac{1}{3}$　Ⓔ $3\frac{3}{5}$

(B) The correct attack on this item is to use the general formula: rate = $\frac{\text{distance}}{\text{time}}$. The distance covered is easy enough to calculate: $2 \times 3 = 6$ miles. To find the time required for the trip, you use the formula time = $\frac{\text{distance}}{\text{rate}}$, which is a variation on the first formula. For the trip up, the time is: $\frac{3\text{ miles}}{2\text{ miles/hour}} = \frac{3}{2}$ hours, and for the trip down, the time is $\frac{3\text{ miles}}{4\text{ miles/hour}} = \frac{3}{4}$ hours. So the total time for the trip is $\frac{3}{2} + \frac{3}{4} = \frac{9}{4}$ hours. And the average speed for the entire trip was $\frac{6\text{ miles}}{\frac{9}{4}\text{ hours}} = \frac{24}{9} = 2\frac{2}{3}$ miles per hour.

24. If the volume of a sphere is equal to its radius cubed multiplied by $\frac{4}{3}\pi$, what is the volume of sphere S?

(1) The circumference of the largest circle that can be obtained by intersecting a plane with sphere S is 16π.

(2) The length of a line segment connecting two points on the sphere and passing through the center of the sphere is 16.

Ⓐ statement 1 alone is sufficient to answer the question, but statement 2 alone is not sufficient

Ⓑ statement 2 alone is sufficient to answer the question, but statement 1 alone is not sufficient

Ⓒ both statements together are needed to answer the question, but neither statement alone is sufficient

Ⓓ either statement by itself is sufficient to answer the question

Ⓔ not enough facts are given to answer the question

(D) Statement (1) is sufficient to answer the question, for it establishes that the circumference of the sphere is 16π:

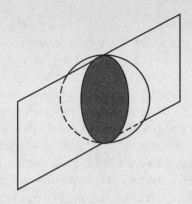

As the question stem makes clear, to find the volume of a sphere, you need only to know the radius. And if you know that the circumference of the sphere is 16π, you can find the radius:

$C = 2\pi r$

$16\pi = 2\pi r$

$r = 8$

Statement (2) is also sufficient because it establishes that the diameter of the sphere is 16, so the radius must be 8.

25. The six members of the student council of Westwood High School were asked to serve on three special committees. Each member of the student council volunteered to serve on at least one committee. How many students volunteered to serve on all three committees?

(1) The following chart shows the number of students who volunteered to serve on each committee:

	Number of Volunteers
Activities Committee	3
Homecoming Committee	2
Welcoming Committee	4

(2) Two students volunteered to serve on both the Activities Committee and the Welcoming Committee.

Ⓐ statement 1 alone is sufficient to answer the question, but statement 2 alone is not sufficient

Ⓑ statement 2 alone is sufficient to answer the question, but statement 1 alone is not sufficient

Ⓒ both statements together are needed to answer the question, but neither statement alone is sufficient

Ⓓ either statement by itself is sufficient to answer the question

Ⓔ not enough facts are given to answer the question

(E) Statement (1) is not sufficient to answer the question. It establishes that the six students volunteered for a total of nine positions, and this means that some students volunteered for more than one committee. But it is possible that three students volunteered for two committees, or that one student volunteered for three committees and one student for two committees.

Nor is Statement (2) by itself sufficient. Do the statements together answer the question? No. It is possible that one of the two students who volunteered for the Activities Committee and the Welcoming Committee also volunteered for the Homecoming Committee, but it is also possible that a third student volunteered for a second committee.

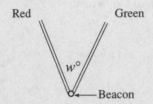

Red   Green

$w°$

Beacon

26. The figure above shows the beams from a beacon with two searchlights, one red and one green, which rotate at the same rate. If the red light rotates in a clockwise direction and the green light rotates in a counterclockwise direction, what is the number of degrees through which each light must rotate before the red beam and green beam are aligned a *second* time?

  Ⓐ $180° + w$ Ⓑ $180° - \dfrac{w}{2}$ Ⓒ $360° - \dfrac{w}{2}$

  Ⓓ $\dfrac{180° + w}{2}$ Ⓔ $\dfrac{360° + w}{2}$

(E) First, determine the position of the beams the second time that they are aligned:

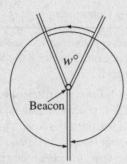

$w°$

Beacon

Each beam must rotate through 180° plus $\frac{1}{2}$ of w, and that is choice (E).

As an alternative, you might assume a value for w. Assume, for example, that $w = 60°$. Each beam would have to rotate through $\frac{1}{2}$ of w, or 30°, plus 180°, or

210°. Using this assumption, substitute 30° into each choice until you find the one that generates the value 210°.

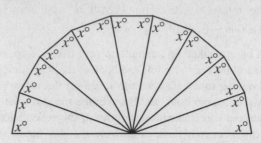

27. In the figure above, what is the average measure in degrees of the indicated angles?

  Ⓐ 105° Ⓑ 90°   Ⓒ 80°   Ⓓ 60°   Ⓔ 45°

(C) The sum of all the angles marked x plus the unmarked angles is the sum of the angles contained in nine triangles: 9(180) = 1620. The unmarked angles form a straight line, so their sum is 180. The sum of the remaining angles is 1620 – 180 = 1440. Since there are 18 angles marked x, x is 1440 ÷ 18 = 80.

Or you might have reasoned that the unmarked angles are equal. Since nine of them form a straight line, each is 180 ÷ 9 = 20. In each triangle, you have $x + x + 20 = 180$, so $2x = 160$ and $x = 160 ÷ 2 = 80$.

A much simpler solution to this difficult problem is estimation. Those angles look to be slightly less than 90°, so (A), (B), and (D) are wrong. As for (E), this is a difficult problem, so (E) is unlikely. And the figure is drawn to scale. (There is no warning note.)

28. If one star equals four circles and three circles equals four diamonds, what is the ratio star:diamond?

  Ⓐ 3:16 Ⓑ 1:3   Ⓒ 3:4   Ⓓ 3:1   Ⓔ 16:3

(E) Using the letters s for star, c for circle, and d for diamond, we do the following:

$1s = 4c$ and $3c = 4d$

$3s = 12c$ and $12c = 16d$

So $3s = 12c = 16d$, and $3s = 16d$.

$3s = 16d$

$\dfrac{3s}{d} = \dfrac{16}{1}$

$\dfrac{s}{d} = \dfrac{16}{3}$

So the ratio of star:diamond is 16:3.

29. If $xy \neq 0$, what is the value of $\dfrac{(xy)^2 + x^2 y^2}{x^2 y^3}$?

   (1) $x = 2$

   (2) $y = 5$

Ⓐ statement 1 alone is sufficient to answer the question, but statement 2 alone is not sufficient

Ⓑ statement 2 alone is sufficient to answer the question, but statement 1 alone is not sufficient

Ⓒ both statements together are needed to answer the question, but neither statement alone is sufficient

Ⓓ either statement by itself is sufficient to answer the question

Ⓔ not enough facts are given to answer the question

(B) Before you can determine the sufficiency of the statements, you must first ask whether the expression to be evaluated can be simplified. It can:

$$\frac{(xy)^2 + x^2 y^2}{x^2 y^3} = \frac{x^2 y^2 + x^2 y^2}{x^2 y^3} = \frac{y^2 + y^2}{y^3} = \frac{2}{y}$$

Given this simplification, it is obvious that (1) alone is not sufficient to answer the question asked, but (2) is.

30. When a certain fishing rod is purchased at the same time as a certain reel, the price of the rod is reduced by 25 percent of the cost of the reel. What is the total cost of the rod and reel if they are purchased at the same time?

   (1) When the rod and reel are purchased together, the price of the rod is reduced from $32 to $21.

   (2) If the rod and reel are purchased separately, the cost of the reel is $12 more than the cost of the rod.

Ⓐ statement 1 alone is sufficient to answer the question, but statement 2 alone is not sufficient

Ⓑ statement 2 alone is sufficient to answer the question, but statement 1 alone is not sufficient

Ⓒ both statements together are needed to answer the question, but neither statement alone is sufficient

Ⓓ either statement by itself is sufficient to answer the question

Ⓔ not enough facts are given to answer the question

(A) Statement (1) is sufficient to answer the question. Since the cost of the rod is reduced by 25 percent of the cost of the reel, (1) implies that the cost of the reel is $44 ($32 − $21 = $11 = 25% of $44). So the cost of the two items when purchased together is $21 + $44 = $65. Statement (2), however, is not sufficient, for it provides no information about the price when the two items are purchased together. (**Note:** If you selected choice (C) for this item, make sure you judge the sufficiency of each statement in isolation before you ask whether the two together are sufficient to answer the question.)

31. In 1996, 80 percent of the students at University Y were undergraduates. If 60 percent of the undergraduates at University Y were out-of-state students and 75 percent of all out-of-state students were undergraduates, what fraction of the students at University Y were out-of-state students?

Ⓐ $\dfrac{16}{25}$ Ⓑ $\dfrac{3}{5}$ Ⓒ $\dfrac{1}{2}$ Ⓓ $\dfrac{12}{15}$ Ⓔ $\dfrac{1}{4}$

(A) Let the letter T represent the total number of students at University Y. The question stem states that $0.8T$ were undergraduates and that 0.6 of that total, or $0.48T$, were undergraduates from out of state. Then, we know that this $0.48T$ represents 75 percent of all out-of-state students.

$0.48T = 0.75$ of out-of-state students

So

out-of-state students $= 0.64T = \dfrac{16}{25} T$

Therefore, out-of-state students accounted for $\dfrac{16}{25}$ of all students at the university.

32. Georgette wished to use her videotape machine to record a 60-minute documentary scheduled to be aired at 10:30 P.M. At 8:00 that morning, she set the timer to begin taping at 10:30 P.M. the same day and to stop taping exactly 60 minutes later. If the timer on Georgette's videotape machine loses 30 seconds every hour and the documentary was aired on schedule, how much of the program following the documentary did the machine record?

Ⓐ 6 minutes and 45 seconds

Ⓑ 7 minutes

Ⓒ 7 minutes and 15 seconds

Ⓓ 7 minutes and 30 seconds

Ⓔ 7 minutes and 45 seconds

(E) First, the timer on the machine is set at 8 A.M., to begin at 10:30 P.M., or 14.5 hours later. Since the timer loses 0.5 minutes each hour, it begins $0.5 \times 14.5 = 7.25$ minutes late. Many people who miss this question stop here and select choice (C), reasoning that the tape began 7.25 minutes late, so it taped 7.25 minutes of the following show. But there is something more to it.

    The machine was programmed to run for 60 minutes; but since the timer loses 30 seconds per hour, it doesn't stop the recording until one hour and 30 seconds have elapsed. So the tape records an extra 30 seconds in addition to the 7.25 minutes, or 7 minutes and 45 seconds.

33. A clock loses *m* minutes every *h* hours. If the clock shows the correct time at noon on Monday, what time will it show at noon on Wednesday of the same week?

Ⓐ 48*mh* after noon

Ⓑ $\dfrac{48m}{h}$ after noon

Ⓒ $\dfrac{48h}{m}$ after noon

Ⓓ $\dfrac{48m}{h}$ before noon

Ⓔ $\dfrac{2,880h}{m}$ after noon

(D) Since the clock loses *m* minutes per *h* hours, during the 48-hour period specified, it will lose $48\left(\dfrac{m}{h}\right) = \dfrac{48m}{h}$ minutes. Therefore, at noon on Wednesday the clock will actually read $\dfrac{48m}{h}$ minutes before noon.

You can arrive at the same conclusion by assuming some numbers. Assume that the clock loses 5 minutes every 48 hours. (Why 48 hours? Because that's the number of hours during the time period specified in the problem, so it's a convenient assumption.) At noon on Wednesday, the clock should read 5 minutes before noon. Substitute the values 5 for *m* and 48 for *h* into the choices, and the correct choice will generate the value 5 before noon:

(A) 48*mh* after noon = 48(5)(48) after noon

(Incorrect)

(B) $\dfrac{48m}{h}$ after noon = $\dfrac{48(5)}{5}$ = 5 after noon

(Incorrect)

(C) $\dfrac{48h}{m}$ after noon = $\dfrac{48(48)}{5}$ after noon

(Incorrect)

(D) $\dfrac{48m}{h}$ before noon = $\dfrac{48(5)}{48}$ = 5 before noon

(Correct)

(E) $\dfrac{2,880h}{m}$ after noon = $\dfrac{2,880(48)}{5}$ after noon

(Incorrect)

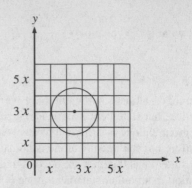

34. If the area of the circle above is 36π, what is the value of *x*?

Ⓐ $\dfrac{3}{2}$ Ⓑ 2   Ⓒ 3   Ⓓ 4   Ⓔ $\dfrac{9}{2}$

(D) The diameter of the circle is $4x - x = 3x$, so the radius is $\dfrac{3x}{2}$. Since the area of the circle is 36π,

$$\text{Area} = \pi r^2$$

$$\text{Area} = \pi\left(\dfrac{3x}{2}\right)^2$$

$$36\pi = \pi\left(\dfrac{3x}{2}\right)^2$$

$$36 = \left(\dfrac{3x}{2}\right)^2$$

$$36 = \dfrac{9x^2}{4}$$

$$x^2 = \dfrac{36(4)}{9}$$

$$x = \sqrt{\dfrac{36(4)}{9}}$$

$$x = \dfrac{6(2)}{3} = 4$$

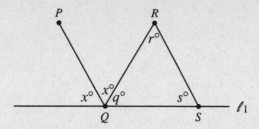

35. In the figure above, is PQ parallel to RS?

   (1) $QR = RS$

   (2) $q° = s°$

Ⓐ statement 1 alone is sufficient to answer the question, but statement 2 alone is not sufficient

Ⓑ statement 2 alone is sufficient to answer the question, but statement 1 alone is not sufficient

Ⓒ both statements together are needed to answer the question, but neither statement alone is sufficient

Ⓓ either statement by itself is sufficient to answer the question

Ⓔ not enough facts are given to answer the question

(E) Statement (1) alone is not sufficient to answer the question. Although (1) implies that $q = s$, those are not angles that would dictate whether PQ is parallel to RS. Statement (2) is insufficient for essentially the same reason. Finally, since the two statements are each insufficient for essentially the same reason, neither can supply information for the other, so the correct classification of this item must be (E).

36. The average of the salaries of the top four corporate officers of a company, the president, the vice-president, the secretary, and the comptroller, is $35,000. What is the president's salary?

   (1) The president's salary is the largest.

   (2) The average of the salaries of the vice-president, the secretary, and the comptroller is $32,000.

Ⓐ statement 1 alone is sufficient to answer the question, but statement 2 alone is not sufficient

Ⓑ statement 2 alone is sufficient to answer the question, but statement 1 alone is not sufficient

Ⓒ both statements together are needed to answer the question, but neither statement alone is sufficient

Ⓓ either statement by itself is sufficient to answer the question

Ⓔ not enough facts are given to answer the question

(B) Statement (1) is not sufficient. But statement (2) is. Expressed algebraically, (2) implies

$$\frac{VP + S + C}{3} = 32,000$$

$$VP + S + C = 96,000$$

where VP, S, and C represent the salaries of the vice-president, the secretary, and the comptroller, respectively. The question stem stipulates that the average salary of the four officers is $35,000. Therefore, the total of their salaries is $4 \times \$35,000 = \$140,000$. Then, as (2) implies, the total of the salaries of the vice-president, the secretary, and the comptroller is $3 \times \$32,000 = \$96,000$. Therefore, the salary of the president is $\$140,000 - \$96,000 = \$44,000$.

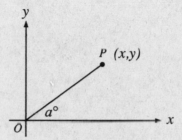

37. In the figure above, what is the length of OP?

   (1) $a = 60°$

   (2) $x = 3$

Ⓐ statement 1 alone is sufficient to answer the question, but statement 2 alone is not sufficient

Ⓑ statement 2 alone is sufficient to answer the question, but statement 1 alone is not sufficient

Ⓒ both statements together are needed to answer the question, but neither statement alone is sufficient

Ⓓ either statement by itself is sufficient to answer the question

Ⓔ not enough facts are given to answer the question

(C) Neither (1) nor (2) alone is sufficient to determine the length of OP. But both together are sufficient:

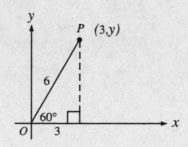

Sample GMAT
CAT 4

Verbal Section

41 Questions—75 Minutes

General Directions: To simulate the experience of taking the CAT, answer each question in order. Do not skip any questions, and do not go back to questions you have already answered.

Directions for sentence correction questions: In questions of this type, either part or all of a sentence is underlined. The sentence is followed by five ways of wording the underlined part. The first answer choice always repeats the original; the other answer choices are different. If you think that the original phrasing is the best, choose the first answer. If you think one of the other answer choices is the best, select that choice. Indicate your answer by blackening the circle next to your choice.

This section tests your ability to identify correct and effective expression. Evaluate the answer choices by the requirements of standard written English. Pay attention to elements of grammar, diction, (choice of words), and sentence construction. Select the answer choice that *best* expresses the meaning of the original sentence. The correct choice will be clear and precise and free of awkwardness, wordiness, or ambiguity.

Directions for critical reasoning questions: Questions of this type ask you to analyze and evaluate the reasoning presented in short paragraphs or passages. For some questions, all of the answer choices may conceivably be answers to the question asked. You should select the *best* answer to the question; that is, an answer that does not require you to make assumptions that violate commonsense standards by being implausible, redundant, irrelevant or inconsistent. Indicate your answer by blackening the circle next to your choice.

Directions for reading comprehension questions: Each passage is followed by questions or incomplete statements about it. Once you have read the passage, answer the question based upon what is stated or implied. Indicate your answer by blackening the circle next to your choice.

---

1. Many thoroughbred handicappers believe that a horse's chance of winning a race depends not so much on the final times of his previous races <u>but instead</u> on his class, an unquantifiable factor that is the horse's determination to win.

    (A) but instead
    (B) rather than
    (C) so much as
    (D) than
    (E) as

2. Three hundred years ago, famine was a periodic experience which came so <u>regular that people accepted periods of extreme hunger as normal.</u>

    (A) regular that people accepted periods of extreme hunger as normal
    (B) regularly that people accepted periods of extreme hunger as normal
    (C) regularly that people normally accepted periods of extreme hunger
    (D) regularly as people accepted periods of extreme hunger as normal
    (E) regularly since people accepted periods of extreme hunger as normal

3. In accentual-syllabic versification, the basic unit of measurement is the <u>foot, which consists of</u> one accented syllable accompanied by one or two unaccented syllables.

    (A) foot, which consists of
    (B) foot, which consists in
    (C) foot, which consisting of
    (D) foot that consists of
    (E) foot, which includes

    If Karen was selected for the committee, she must be a sophomore.

4. The statement above makes which of the following assumptions?

    (A) Only Karen can be selected for the committee.
    (B) Only sophomores can be selected for the committee.
    (C) Some sophomores must be selected for the committee.
    (D) Some sophomores might not be selected for the committee.
    (E) Karen did not refuse to serve on the committee.

GO ON TO NEXT PAGE

The use of statistical data gathered from historical sources such as census reports and commercial registers and analyzed with the help of sophisticated computer programs has permeated the study of history in recent years. Now it would appear that the new statistical methods have begun to generate major breakthroughs in historical research, which brings us to Dr. Kramer's fascinating new book on the nineteenth-century settlement of the American frontier.

5. Which of the following conclusions is best supported by the passage above?

Ⓐ Statistical data from historical sources are the single most important form of information underpinning current historical research.

Ⓑ Dr. Kramer is the first major historian to apply the new statistical techniques to the study of the settlement of the American frontier.

Ⓒ Historians have begun to make major contributions to the science of statistical analysis.

Ⓓ Today, writers of histories must be skilled as computer programmers as well as knowledgeable about a particular era of history.

Ⓔ Dr. Kramer's book offers important new insights into its subject, based on analysis of historical statistics.

Some people oppose college admissions programs for minority students on the ground that merit alone—as measured by high school grades, scores on entrance exams, and other objective standards—should be used in admissions decisions. This argument ignores the facts that non-merit factors have always been considered by colleges, for instance, the applicant's place of origin, whether a parent is a graduate of the college, and so on. These subjective factors are usually such as to exclude minority group students.

6. Which of the following would best complete the paragraph above?

Ⓐ Therefore, merit plays no substantive role in the majority of college admissions decisions.

Ⓑ Therefore, subjective factors should be completely removed from the college admissions process.

Ⓒ Therefore, the concept of merit is merely a subterfuge by which minority students may be excluded.

Ⓓ Therefore, it is not appropriate to use special admissions programs for minority students to help redress an imbalance.

Ⓔ Therefore, high school grades alone are an inadequate measure of a student's past academic performance.

Questions 7–9

Synchrotron radiation is the name given to pulses of intense X-rays created by electrons circulating within a large evacuated storage ring at nearly the speed of light. Compared with conventional sources, these electron rings produce a much more intense, highly collimated beam of X-rays. Additionally, synchrotron radiation is tunable. By using a monochromonator, a researcher can select X-rays of specific wavelengths or energies.

Synchrotron radiation can decipher structural changes during a reaction such as cellular respiration. Data gathered with an array of time-resolved spectroscopic methods, for example, can provide glimpses of local molecular events— the breaking of chemical bonds and the formation of intermediate compounds—that may transpire within a few millionths of a second.

The biggest payoff from the gain in beam intensity, however, will be the enhanced sensitivity of measurements that will maintain the high precision in the high-resolution data of atomic distances on the order of 0.02 to 0.05 angstroms. When working with less powerful machines, researchers compensate for deficiencies in beam intensity by preparing samples that contain high concentrations of protein. The high concentration increases the strength of the signals emanating from the sample when it is exposed to a beam. But many macromolecules cannot be highly concentrated; and when extracted proteins can be concentrated, the sample is not likely to represent conditions in the living membranes, where proteins are scattered over a large area.

7. The author is primarily concerned with describing

Ⓐ a new scientific theory
Ⓑ the properties of X-rays
Ⓒ the structure of proteins
Ⓓ the functioning of cells
Ⓔ an instrument for scientific research

8. According to the passage, researchers using conventional X-ray sources to study proteins use highly concentrated examples in order to

Ⓐ simulate the conditions in living cells
Ⓑ obtain a larger picture of the sample
Ⓒ condense several experiments into a short span of time
Ⓓ allow for respiration by sample components
Ⓔ compensate for the inadequacy of the X-ray beam

9. The passage makes all of the following statements about synchrotron radiation EXCEPT

Ⓐ The length of the waves that make up the beam can be controlled.
Ⓑ The beam is more intense than that of conventional X-ray sources.
Ⓒ It yields more precise data than conventional X-ray sources.
Ⓓ It is less dangerous to researchers than conventional X-ray sources.
Ⓔ It is composed of pulsating X-rays.

10. The Puritan was composed of two different men: the one all self-abasement and penitence; the other, proud and inflexible.

 Ⓐ the one all self-abasement and penitence
 Ⓑ one of them all self-abasement and penitence
 Ⓒ the one self-abasing and penitent
 Ⓓ the one self-abasement and penitence
 Ⓔ self-abasing and penitent

11. In 1896, when she began studying the effects of radium, Marie Curie was building on the work of Roentgen and Becquerel.

 Ⓐ In 1896, when she began studying the effects of radium
 Ⓑ In 1896, beginning to study the effects of radium
 Ⓒ Beginning to study the effects of radium in 1896
 Ⓓ Since she began to study the effects of radium in 1896
 Ⓔ In order to begin to study the effects of radium in 1896

12. Having been forbidden by Church law to marry, it was not unusual for a priest during the Middle Ages to sire a family.

 Ⓐ Having been forbidden by Church law to marry, it was not unusual for a priest during the Middle Ages to sire a family.
 Ⓑ Forbidden by Church law to marry, it was not unusual for a priest during the Middle Ages to sire a family.
 Ⓒ Although they were forbidden by Church law to marry, it was not unusual for a priest during the Middle Ages to sire a family.
 Ⓓ Although a priest was forbidden by Church law to marry, it was not unusual for him during the Middle Ages to sire a family.
 Ⓔ Although they were forbidden by Church law to marry, it was not unusual for priests during the Middle Ages to sire families.

Government involvement in industry is more detrimental than helpful to that industry. As proof of this, consider two comparable industries: urban mass transit and the airline business. The former has generally been subsidized and operated by local governments, and in most cities service is poor and deteriorating. By contrast, the privately owned and operated airlines earn profits and provide, for the most part, fast and efficient service.

13. Which of the following, if true, would LEAST weaken the argument above?

 Ⓐ Passenger complaints about airline scheduling and service have increased rapidly and are now greater than ever before.
 Ⓑ Privately owned mass transit systems do not have problems similar to those of government-operated systems.
 Ⓒ The government subsidizes airport construction and operation and offers tax breaks to airlines.
 Ⓓ Technological advances in air travel have allowed airlines to operate more efficiently, but no similar advances have occurred in rail travel.
 Ⓔ On average, airline ticket prices have increased faster than mass transit fares over the past ten years.

Neither artifacts, personal messages, nor historical documents from any human civilization would be likely to have any meaning for intelligent extraterrestrial beings. Therefore, the probe to be sent into interstellar space in the hope that alien beings may find it will contain a plaque inscribed with certain scientific and mathematical formulas, for example, a statement of the value of π or the molecular weight of water.

14. The argument above depends upon which of the following assumptions?

 Ⓐ Somewhere in the universe there is at least one intelligent race other than the human race living of Earth.
 Ⓑ Extraterrestrial beings probably have civilizations that are not as technically advanced as those on Earth.
 Ⓒ Life on other worlds is likely to be dependent upon the presence of water just as it is on Earth.
 Ⓓ Intelligent beings on other worlds have probably developed means of interstellar space travel.
 Ⓔ Some symbols used by human beings will be meaningful to intelligent extraterrestrial beings.

GO ON TO NEXT PAGE

Studies of twins separated at or shortly after birth have played a major role in attempts to measure the relative influence of genetic and environmental factors on personal development. Those who consider environment all-important would predict that separately reared twins would exhibit no more similarity than another two unrelated individuals brought up under the same conditions. The data do not support this extreme position, but neither do they support the opposite fallacy, the belief that "genetics is destiny."

15. Which of the following statements would be the most reasonable conclusion to draw from the argument above?

  (A) More study of the relationship between genetics and environment is needed before it can be determined whether one or the other of the two extreme positions is correct.

  (B) Studies of twins separated at birth show that environmental factors are the most important factor in later personal development.

  (C) Twin studies suggest that both genetic and environmental factors play an important part in the development of personality.

  (D) Attempts to modify personal development by making changes in the environment of an individual are misguided and doomed to failure.

  (E) Twin studies are inherently unsatisfactory as a research tool because of the ambiguity that infects the results obtained.

Questions 16–18

The geological story of the Rocky Mountains is a long one, the details of which are lost in the passage of hundreds of millions of years. Some of the story has been put together by scientists from bits of scattered evidence that strongly indicates a certain chain of events, few of which can be proved to everyone's satisfaction. Most of the rocks in the Colorado region are crystalline and ancient. The gneiss and schist were, in part, once sediments formed in the seas—perhaps a billion years ago. These sediments were buried beneath thousands of feet of other sediments, cemented and hardened into layers of sedimentary rock, and later squeezed, crushed, and elevated by slow, ceaselessly working earth forces, which produced mountains. During this period, the sedimentary rocks were changed to harder metamorphic rocks, probably because of deep burial under tremendous pressure and considerable heat. Masses of molten rock welled up into these earlier deposits and hardened under the earth's surface. This later intrusive material is now exposed granite in many parts of the Rocky Mountains.

These ancient mountains were gradually worn away by wind, rain, and other agents of erosion, which must have attacked the surface of the earth as vigorously then as now. With the passage of millions of years, these mountains were gradually worn away until a new sea lapped over the land where mountains had been, and once again sediments were dropped in its bottom. This new invasion of the ocean affected the Colorado region during the many millions of years in which dinosaurs dominated the earth.

In response to little-understood rhythms of the earth's crust, which have lifted mountains ever so slowly at great intervals all over the world, the seas drained away as the crust rose again, and the rising land once more became subject to the ceaseless attack of erosion. This uplift—which began 60 million years ago—originated the system of mountain ranges and basins that today give Colorado its spectacular scenery and much of its climate. This great period of mountain-making is called the Laramide Revolution, from its early recognition in the Laramie Basin region of Wyoming. This uplift continued intermittently for many millions of years, but eventually these rocks too will be stripped away by erosion, though this will require millions of years.

An unusual feature of the present landscape is the peneplain, or rolling, sometimes flattened character of many mountain summits. These peneplains appear to be all that is left of an old land surface that may once have been continuous far eastward over the area occupied today by the Great Plains. Their presence suggests that the range had been worn down by erosion to a fairly flat upland a few million years ago; then renewed uplifting occurred, and streams draining the highland gradually cut canyons two or three thousand feet into the elevated surface. These canyons were filled by glaciers at intervals during the ice age. The glaciers, moving under their own great weight, gradually broadened, deepened, and straightened the twists and turns of the original river-cut valleys, and bit by bit scooped out cirques (or bowls) at the glacier sources, and at the lower altitudes the landscape is dotted with moraines.

16. As described by the selection, the sequence of events leading to the present landscape was

  (A) erosion, uplift, submersion, uplift, erosion, submersion

  (B) uplift, submersion, erosion, uplift, submersion, erosion

  (C) submersion, erosion, uplift, submersion, erosion, uplift,

  (D) submersion, uplift, erosion, submersion, erosion, uplift,

  (E) submersion, uplift, erosion, submersion, uplift, erosion

17. The author mentions which of the following as forces that shaped the appearance of the landscape?

  I. Volcanic eruption
  II. Erosion
  III. Glacial activity

  (A) II only   (B) I and II only   (C) I and III only
  (D) II and III only   (E) I, II, and III

18. The author would likely agree with which of the following statements?

   I. The present appearance of the landscape is only temporary.

  II. The present appearance of the landscape is the product of natural forces.

 III. Any changes that will occur in the appearance of the landscape cannot be predicted.

  Ⓐ I only   Ⓑ II only   Ⓒ I and II only
  Ⓓ I and III only   Ⓔ I, II, and III

19. The singing teachers of the old Italian school taught <u>little more but</u> breath control because they believed that with proper breath control, all other technical problems could be easily solved.

  Ⓐ little more but
  Ⓑ little more than
  Ⓒ little more as
  Ⓓ more than a little
  Ⓔ rather than

20. In the early stages of the development of the common law, <u>equitable remedies were available only in the courts of the Chancery and not in the courts of law, such as injunctions.</u>

  Ⓐ equitable remedies were available only in the courts of the Chancery and not in the courts of law, such as injunctions
  Ⓑ equitable remedies, such as injunctions, were available only in the courts of the Chancery and not in the courts of law
  Ⓒ only equitable remedies, such as injunctions, were available in the courts of the Chancery and not in the courts of law
  Ⓓ the availability of equitable remedies, such as injunctions, was restricted to the courts of Chancery and not to the courts of law
  Ⓔ equitable remedies, such as injunctions, were not available in the courts of law but only in the courts of Chancery

21. These extensive forest reserves must be defended from the acquisitive hands of those whose ruthless axes <u>would destroy the trees and</u> expose the land to the ravages of sun and rain.

  Ⓐ would destroy the trees and
  Ⓑ will destroy the trees and
  Ⓒ would destroy the trees to
  Ⓓ would destroy the trees which would
  Ⓔ would destroy the trees that could

We hear it said that, for all the social progress America has made over the past thirty years—for all the toppling of racial and ethnic barriers that we have witnessed—this remains an inherently racist society in which the white majority has never fully accepted the equal humanity of the minority. Those who repeat this slander against America ignore the fact that, as I write, the most popular television program in the country focuses on the lives of a proud middle-class black family, whose members have become some of the best-recognized—and most widely admired—people in America.

22. The argument above assumes that

  Ⓐ television acting is a challenging and financially rewarding profession
  Ⓑ thirty years ago a television show with black characters would not have been popular
  Ⓒ those who label America a racist society seek to foment unrest and disrupt the fabric of American society
  Ⓓ a person's attitude toward a character on a television show is like his attitude toward real people with similar characteristics
  Ⓔ the television program is more popular among white viewers than among black viewers

Foods that are high in fat, salt, or sugar content have been shown to be deleterious to health. If the government can forbid the sale to minors of other harmful products, such as cigarettes and alcoholic beverages, why not treat dangerous foods the same way? Children under 18 should be allowed to purchase only foods that are nutritious and healthful.

23. The author of the statement above makes his point primarily by

  Ⓐ analyzing a cause and effect relationship
  Ⓑ drawing an analogy
  Ⓒ appealing to the emotions of the audience
  Ⓓ offering a counterexample
  Ⓔ making a generalization

GO ON TO NEXT PAGE ⇒

By studying census data, demographers are able to develop lists of counties and communities throughout the country whose populations have specific economic characteristics—for example, high or low median age, large numbers of families with children, a high percentage of two-career couples, or particularly affluent households. Lists such as these can be especially useful to political organizations that are promoting candidates who have particular appeal to voters with specific characteristics.

24. Which of the following, if true, best supports the claim that the demographic information mentioned in the passage may be valuable to political organizations?

    (A) Affluent citizens are known to be more likely to vote in local elections than are those who are less affluent.
    (B) Because census data are compiled by the federal government, they must legally be made available to all who request them.
    (C) Voters tend to be heavily influenced in their thinking by the opinions and preferences of their friends and neighbors.
    (D) Research shows that the economic and social characteristics of differing groups can be closely correlated with specific political views.
    (E) Several of today's most significant political issues have particular impact on the interests of families with children.

Questions 25–27

Ultrasonography works much like sonar. High-frequency sound waves are bounced off surfaces to compose a two-dimensional picture of anatomical structure. Since it became generally available about ten years ago, diagnostic ultrasound has gained increasing acceptance in the American medical community. Its low cost and apparent safety have made it one of the most frequently used methods of imaging in the United States, rivaling conventional radiography in popularity. Because ultrasonography does not utilize ionizing radiation, diagnostic ultrasound is particularly attractive to obstetricians and gynecologists who are concerned with protecting the fetus or the patient's fertility. This aspect of ultrasound, however, can also be a disadvantage.

Because X-rays pass through every type of tissue, images show the varying absorption of the radiation—more for bones, less for soft tissue. But virtually all of the ultrasonic waves that encounter bone or an air pocket are reflected. Therefore, the adult brain cannot be imaged because ultrasound cannot penetrate the completely formed skull. Similarly, the lungs cannot be imaged because ultrasonic waves are almost totally reflected by the air passages called bronchi, bronchioles, and alveoli.

Nevertheless, ultrasound can provide information that is as good or better than that supplied by X-radiography when imaging certain tissues, including those of the heart, abdomen, and fetus. It can be used to guide amniocentesis to assess gestational age, and to evaluate bleeding during

pregnancy, as well as to determine the location of the fetus, and monitor fetal presentation, growth, and anatomy.

25. The author's primary concern is to

    (A) define medical terminology
    (B) defend the use of radiography
    (C) encourage the use of ultrasonography
    (D) discuss a new medical technology
    (E) warn about a health hazard

26. The passage states that which of the following is (are) differences between conventional radiography and ultrasonography?

    I. Ultrasonography is more expensive than conventional radiography.
    II. Conventional radiography depends upon ionizing radiation; ultrasonography does not.
    III. The image of conventional radiography is created by the part of the beam that passes through the patient's body; the image of ultrasonography by the part of the beam that bounces back.

    (A) I only   (B) II only   (C) III only
    (D) I and III only   (E) II and III only

27. It can be inferred from the passage that some physicians prefer to use ultrasound when a patient is pregnant because

    (A) X-rays are absorbed by the skull
    (B) ultrasound is inexpensive
    (C) X-rays cannot penetrate the womb
    (D) ultrasound is more widely available
    (E) X-rays pose a hazard to the fetus

28. Smart investors realized early on that the compact disk, on which music is recorded in a digital code to be read by a laser, would soon become the most common form of recorded music, eventually replacing records and tapes altogether.

    (A) music, eventually replacing
    (B) music, and eventually replacing
    (C) music that eventually replaces
    (D) music by eventually replacing
    (E) music to eventually replace

29. Good American English is simply good English; that of London and Sydney differ no more from Boston and Chicago than the types of houses in which people live.

    (A) differ no more from
    (B) differs no more from
    (C) differ no more than
    (D) differs no more from that of
    (E) differ no more from those of

30. <u>Arturo Toscanini, well known for his sharp tongue as well as his musical genius, once cowed a famous singer</u> with the remark that there were for him no stars except those in the heavens.

   Ⓐ Arturo Toscanini, well known for his sharp tongue as well as his musical genius, once cowed a famous singer

   Ⓑ Arturo Toscanini, well known for his sharp tongue as well than his musical genius, cowed once a famous singer

   Ⓒ Arturo Toscanini's well known sharp tongue as well as his musical genius once cowed a famous singer

   Ⓓ Arturo Toscanini, who had a well-known sharp tongue as well as musical genius, once cowed a famous singer

   Ⓔ Well known for his sharp tongue as well as his musical genius, a famous singer was once cowed by Arturo Toscanini

Some people oppose testing of employees for use of illegal drugs on the ground that the tests sometimes produce false results. These fears are without basis. The newest tests can detect over ninety-nine percent of the cases in which a person has used one of the most common illegal drugs at any time during the previous 48 hours.

31. Which of the following, if true, would most weaken the argument above?

   Ⓐ The best drug tests available today return a significant number of positive results even when the person has not used drugs.

   Ⓑ The best drug tests available today cannot reliably identify every form of illegal drug that a person might have used.

   Ⓒ The best drug tests available today cannot identify an illegal drug if the subject took that drug more than 48 hours prior to the test.

   Ⓓ An employee who occasionally uses an illegal drug may still be a valuable worker.

   Ⓔ Some employers still continue to use older and less reliable drug tests.

One of the most influential studies of the ancient construction known as Stonehenge was conducted by Professor Gerald Hawkins. Hawkins used computer calculations to compare the locations of stones in Stonehenge with the positions of stars, planets, and the sun at the time the structure was built. He concluded that the stones could have been used to mark viewing angles along which the rising and setting of heavenly bodies could be observed, making Stonehenge a kind of primitive "computer" for predicting astronomical events.

32. Which of the following, if true, most seriously weakens Hawkins' argument?

   Ⓐ There is no reliable scientific evidence that the ancient people who built Stonehenge worshipped heavenly bodies.

   Ⓑ Hawkins' computer calculations, though on their face accurate, have not been independently verified.

   Ⓒ The positions of heavenly bodies have shifted slightly in the thousands of years since Stonehenge was built.

   Ⓓ The fragility of the already damaged stones of Stonehenge has caused authorities to limit the access of scholars to the site.

   Ⓔ Any structure as complex as that of Stonehenge must inevitably contain some astronomical viewing angles even if they were not intended by the builders.

The tendency toward political tyranny increases in periods of economic collapse. When most people have homes and jobs and when families anticipate a better life for their children, citizens support moderate policies that promise peaceful growth and gradual development. When work is scarce, prices are rising, and prospects for the future seem bleak, desperate measures begin to seem attractive, and the would-be totalitarian's promise of drastic upheaval holds appeal.

33. The claim made in the argument above would be most seriously weakened by evidence of which of the following?

   Ⓐ Countries undergoing economic collapse in which democratic institutions were strengthened.

   Ⓑ Countries in which periods of drastic economic change had little apparent political effect.

   Ⓒ Countries in which totalitarian governments were established with little basis in popular support.

   Ⓓ Examples of tyrannical governments that arose during periods of prosperity.

   Ⓔ Examples of totalitarian leaders who actually kept the promises they made before attaining power.

GO ON TO NEXT PAGE

34. Concrete is an artificial engineering material made from a mixture of portland cement, water, fine and coarse aggregates, <u>having a small</u> amount of air.

    Ⓐ having a small
    Ⓑ having added a small
    Ⓒ adding a small
    Ⓓ and a little
    Ⓔ and a small

35. During the Middle Ages, literacy was defined as <u>one who could read and write</u> Latin.

    Ⓐ one who could read and write
    Ⓑ one who would read and write
    Ⓒ reading and writing
    Ⓓ those who could read and write
    Ⓔ the ability to read and write

A basic social function of the university is to provide a setting within which all points of view may be freely debated, including those whose radical nature may offend some or even most members of the community. Unfortunately, this mandate includes totalitarian views that might themselves threaten the freedom and diversity of expression to which the university is dedicated.

36. The speaker in the paragraph above is most concerned with discussing a(n)

    Ⓐ dilemma
    Ⓑ contradiction
    Ⓒ paradox
    Ⓓ analogy
    Ⓔ generalization

Questions 37 and 38

Colleges are doing a poor job of imparting basic skills. According to a recent survey of personnel directors of major corporations, large numbers of entry-level workers lack ability in writing, mathematics, and reasoning skills.

37. Which of the following must be true if the argument above is valid?

    Ⓐ College students today are no longer required to take courses in basic skills.
    Ⓑ Few entry-level workers today have college degrees.
    Ⓒ Basic skills in writing, mathematics, and reasoning are important for success in most jobs.
    Ⓓ Entry-level workers at major corporations are generally representative of today's college graduates.
    Ⓔ College students in the past received better training in basic skills than students of today.

38. Which of the following questions would be most relevant in determining the validity of the argument above?

    Ⓐ What kinds of training programs are provided by major corporations for their entry-level workers?
    Ⓑ Do colleges have the responsibility for teaching students basic skills in writing, mathematics, and reasoning?
    Ⓒ How closely correlated are workers' levels of skill in writing, mathematics, and reasoning?
    Ⓓ Do major corporations today demand a higher level of basic skills from entry-level workers than in the past?
    Ⓔ How do the skill levels of workers at major corporations compare with those at smaller companies?

Questions 39–41

What we expect of translation is a reasonable facsimile of something that might have been said in our language, but there is involved in this notion of reasonable facsimile a debate between critics as to what constitutes a reasonable facsimile. Most of us at heart belong to the "soft-line" party: a given translation may not be exactly "living language," but the facsimile is generally reasonable. The "hard-line" party aims only for the good translation. The majority of readers never notice the difference, as they read passively, often missing stylistic integrity so long as the story holds them. Additionally, a literature like Japanese may even be treated to an "exoticism handicap."

Whether or not one agrees with Roy A. Miller's postulation of an attitude of mysticism by the Japanese toward their own language, it is true that the Japanese have special feelings toward the possibilities of their language and its relation to life and art, and these feelings have an effect on what Japanese writers write about and how they write. Many of the special language relationships are not immediately available to the non-Japanese (which is only to say that the Japanese language, like every other, has some unique features). For example, in my own work on Dazai Osamu, I have found how close to the sense of the rhythms of spoken Japanese his writing is, and how hard that is to duplicate in English. Juda's cackling hysterically, "Heh, heh, heh" (in *Kakekomi uttae*), or the coy poutings of a schoolgirl (in *Joseito*) have what Masao Miyoshi has called, in *Accomplices of Silence*, an "embarrassing" quality. It is, however, the embarrassment of recognition that the reader of Japanese feels. The moments simply do not work in English.

Even the orthography of written Japanese is a resource not open to us. Tanizaki Jun'ichiro, who elsewhere laments the poverty of "indigenous" Japanese vocabulary, writes in *Bunsho tokuhon* of the contribution to literary effect—to "meaning," if you will—made simply by the way a Japanese author chooses to "spell" a word. In Shiga Naoya's *Kinosaki nite*, for example, the onomatopoeic "bu—n" with which a honey bee takes flight has a different feeling for having been written in *hiragana* instead of *katakana*. I read, and I am convinced. Arishima Takeo uses onomatopoeic words in his children's story *Hitofusa no budo*, and the effect is not one of baby talk, but of gentleness and intimacy that automatically pulls the reader into the world of childhood fears, tragedies, and consolations, memories of which lie close under the surface of every adult psyche.

This, of course, is hard to reproduce in translation, although translators labor hard to do so. George Steiner speaks of an "intentional strangeness," a "creative dislocation," that sometimes is invoked in the attempt. He cites Chateaubriand's 1836 translation of Milton's *Paradise Lost*, for which Chateaubriand "created" a Latinate French to approximate Milton's special English as an example of just such a successful act of creation. He also laments what he calls the "'moon in pond like blossom weary' school of instant exotica," with which we are perhaps all too familiar.

39. The author is primarily concerned with
Ⓐ criticizing translators who do not faithfully reproduce the style of works written in another language
Ⓑ suggesting that Japanese literature is more complex than English literature
Ⓒ arguing that no translation can do justice to a work written in another language
Ⓓ demonstrating that Japanese literature is particularly difficult to translate into English
Ⓔ discussing some of the problems of translating Japanese literature into English

40. The author cites Shiga Naoya's *Kinosaki nite* in order to
Ⓐ illustrate the effect that Japanese orthography has on meaning
Ⓑ demonstrate the poverty of indigenous Japanese vocabulary
Ⓒ prove that it is difficult to translate Japanese into English
Ⓓ acquaint the reader with an important work of Japanese literature
Ⓔ impress upon the reader the importance of faithfully translating a work from one language into another

41. It can be inferred that the "exoticism handicap" mentioned by the author is
Ⓐ the tendency of some translators of Japanese to render Japanese literature in a needlessly awkward style
Ⓑ the attempt of Japanese writers to create for their readers a world characterized by mysticism
Ⓒ the lack of literal, word-for-word translational equivalents for Japanese and English vocabulary
Ⓓ the expectation of many English readers that Japanese literature can only be understood by someone who speaks Japanese
Ⓔ the difficulty a Japanese reader encounters in trying to penetrate the meaning of difficult Japanese poets

Stop: End of Verbal Section

Quantitative Section

37 Questions—75 Minutes

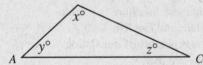
1. $121,212 + (2 \times 10^4) =$

    Ⓐ 321,212   Ⓑ 141,212   Ⓒ 123,212
    Ⓓ 121,412   Ⓔ 121,232

2. If $6x + 3 = 21$, then $2x + 1 =$

    Ⓐ 2   Ⓑ 3   Ⓒ 4   Ⓓ 6   Ⓔ 7

3. Jack, Ken, Larry, and Mike are $j, k, l,$ and m years old, respectively. If $j < k < l < m,$ which of the following *could* be true?

    Ⓐ $k = j + l$
    Ⓑ $j = k + l$
    Ⓒ $j + k = l + m$
    Ⓓ $j + k + m = l$
    Ⓔ $j + m = k + l$

4. Bob and Carol took out installment loans to purchase cars. Which loan has the greater outstanding balance?

    (1) Bob borrowed $5,000 for two years at 2.5% interest.

    (2) Carol borrowed $6,000 for three years at 3% interest.

    Ⓐ statement 1 alone is sufficient to answer the question, but statement 2 alone is not sufficient
    Ⓑ statement 2 alone is sufficient to answer the question, but statement 1 alone is not sufficient
    Ⓒ both statements together are needed to answer the question, but neither statement alone is sufficient
    Ⓓ either statement by itself is sufficient to answer the question
    Ⓔ not enough facts are given to answer the question

5. Is $x = 0$?

   (1) $x \cdot y = x$

   (2) $x + y = y$

   Ⓐ statement 1 alone is sufficient to answer the question, but statement 2 alone is not sufficient

   Ⓑ statement 2 alone is sufficient to answer the question, but statement 1 alone is not sufficient

   Ⓒ both statements together are needed to answer the question, but neither statement alone is sufficient

   Ⓓ either statement by itself is sufficient to answer the question

   Ⓔ not enough facts are given to answer the question

6. Of the following, which is greater than $\frac{1}{2}$?

   Ⓐ $\frac{9}{19}$ Ⓑ $\frac{7}{15}$ Ⓒ $\frac{4}{9}$ Ⓓ $\frac{6}{11}$ Ⓔ $\frac{3}{7}$

7. Out of a group of 360 students, exactly 18 are on the track team. What percent of the students are on the track team?

   Ⓐ 5% Ⓑ 10% Ⓒ 12% Ⓓ 20% Ⓔ 25%

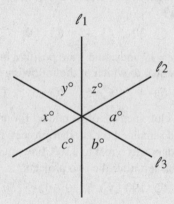

8. In the figure above, three lines intersect as shown. Which of the following must be true?

   I. $a = x$

   II. $y + z = b + c$

   III. $x + a = y + b$

   Ⓐ I only Ⓑ II only Ⓒ I and II only

   Ⓓ I and III only Ⓔ I, II, and III

9. A certain mix of nuts contains only pecans, walnuts, and cashews. How many pounds of pecans are contained in 12 pounds of the mix?

   (1) The weight of the pecans in the mix is equal to the weight of the cashews.

   (2) By weight, the mix is $\frac{1}{6}$ walnuts and $\frac{5}{12}$ cashews.

   Ⓐ statement 1 alone is sufficient to answer the question, but statement 2 alone is not sufficient

   Ⓑ statement 2 alone is sufficient to answer the question, but statement 1 alone is not sufficient

   Ⓒ both statements together are needed to answer the question, but neither statement alone is sufficient

   Ⓓ either statement by itself is sufficient to answer the question

   Ⓔ not enough facts are given to answer the question

10. Is Z an odd integer?

   (1) $\frac{Z}{3}$ is an odd integer.

   (2) $3Z$ is an odd integer.

   Ⓐ statement 1 alone is sufficient to answer the question, but statement 2 alone is not sufficient

   Ⓑ statement 2 alone is sufficient to answer the question, but statement 1 alone is not sufficient

   Ⓒ both statements together are needed to answer the question, but neither statement alone is sufficient

   Ⓓ either statement by itself is sufficient to answer the question

   Ⓔ not enough facts are given to answer the question

11. The average (arithmetic mean) height of four buildings is 20 meters. If three of the buildings have a height of 16 meters, what is the height, in meters, of the fourth building?

   Ⓐ 32 Ⓑ 28 Ⓒ 24 Ⓓ 22 Ⓔ 18

12. The perimeter of the square above is

   Ⓐ 1 Ⓑ $\sqrt{2}$ Ⓒ 4 Ⓓ $4\sqrt{2}$ Ⓔ 8

GO ON TO NEXT PAGE

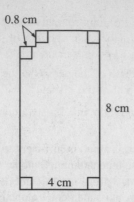

0.8 cm

8 cm

4 cm

13. The figure above is a scale drawing of the floor of a dining hall. If 1 centimeter on the drawing represents 5 meters, what is the area, in square meters, of the floor?

Ⓐ 144   Ⓑ 156   Ⓒ 784   Ⓓ 796   Ⓔ 800

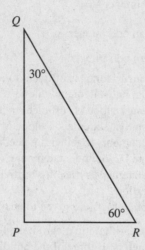

Q

30°

60°

P   R

14. In triangle PQR shown above, what is the length of QP?

(1) $PR = 6$

(2) $QR = 12$

Ⓐ statement 1 alone is sufficient to answer the question, but statement 2 alone is not sufficient
Ⓑ statement 2 alone is sufficient to answer the question, but statement 1 alone is not sufficient
Ⓒ both statements together are needed to answer the question, but neither statement alone is sufficient
Ⓓ either statement by itself is sufficient to answer the question
Ⓔ not enough facts are given to answer the question

15. If N is an integer greater than 1,000, what is the value of the units digit of N?

(1) N is divisible by 12.

(2) N is a power of 6.

Ⓐ statement 1 alone is sufficient to answer the question, but statement 2 alone is not sufficient
Ⓑ statement 2 alone is sufficient to answer the question, but statement 1 alone is not sufficient
Ⓒ both statements together are needed to answer the question, but neither statement alone is sufficient
Ⓓ either statement by itself is sufficient to answer the question
Ⓔ not enough facts are given to answer the question

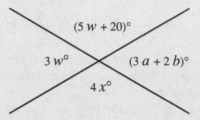

$(5w + 20)°$

$3w°$ $(3a + 2b)°$

$4x°$

16. If two straight lines intersect as shown, what is the value of x?

Ⓐ 15   Ⓑ 30   Ⓒ 45   Ⓓ 60   Ⓔ 75

17. If $2x + 3y = 19$ and x and y are positive integers, x could be equal to which of the following?

Ⓐ 3   Ⓑ 4   Ⓒ 5   Ⓓ 6   Ⓔ 7

18. A school club spent $\frac{2}{5}$ of its budget for one project and $\frac{1}{3}$ of what remained for another project. If the club's entire budget was equal to $300, how much of the budget was left after the two projects?

Ⓐ $60   Ⓑ $90   Ⓒ $120   Ⓓ $180   Ⓔ $240

19. Is $\frac{a}{b}$ an integer?

(1) $\frac{4a}{b}$ is an integer.

(2) $\frac{4b}{a}$ is an integer.

Ⓐ statement 1 alone is sufficient to answer the question, but statement 2 alone is not sufficient
Ⓑ statement 2 alone is sufficient to answer the question, but statement 1 alone is not sufficient
Ⓒ both statements together are needed to answer the question, but neither statement alone is sufficient
Ⓓ either statement by itself is sufficient to answer the question
Ⓔ not enough facts are given to answer the question

20. The figure above shows a square inscribed in a circle. What is the area of the shaded part of the figure?

   (1) The area of the square is 8.

   (2) The area of the circle is 4π.

   Ⓐ statement 1 alone is sufficient to answer the question, but statement 2 alone is not sufficient

   Ⓑ statement 2 alone is sufficient to answer the question, but statement 1 alone is not sufficient

   Ⓒ both statements together are needed to answer the question, but neither statement alone is sufficient

   Ⓓ either statement by itself is sufficient to answer the question

   Ⓔ not enough facts are given to answer the question

21. If the cost of N nails is C cents, what is the cost *in dollars* of X nails?

   Ⓐ $100CX$ Ⓑ $\dfrac{100CX}{N}$ Ⓒ $\dfrac{100NX}{C}$

   Ⓓ $\dfrac{NX}{100C}$ Ⓔ $\dfrac{CX}{100N}$

22. If $a^2 b^3 c < 0$, which of the following must be true?

   Ⓐ $b^3 < 0$ Ⓑ $b^2 c < 0$ Ⓒ $b < 0$
   Ⓓ $c < 0$ Ⓔ $bc < 0$

23. During a certain shift, a quality control inspector inspected 6 out of every 30 items produced. What was the ratio of inspected to uninspected items during that shift?

   Ⓐ 1:4 Ⓑ 1:5 Ⓒ 1:6 Ⓓ 5:1 Ⓔ 6:1

24. In a group of 18 professional drivers, some have a chauffeur's license, some have a taxi license, and some have both. How many members of the group have both a chauffeur's license and a taxi license?

   (1) Twice as many members of the group have a taxi license as have a chauffeur's license.

   (2) Eight members of the group have a chauffeur's license.

   Ⓐ statement 1 alone is sufficient to answer the question, but statement 2 alone is not sufficient

   Ⓑ statement 2 alone is sufficient to answer the question, but statement 1 alone is not sufficient

   Ⓒ both statements together are needed to answer the question, but neither statement alone is sufficient

   Ⓓ either statement by itself is sufficient to answer the question

   Ⓔ not enough facts are given to answer the question

25. n is a positive integer. What is the remainder when n is divided by 6?

   (1) n is a multiple of 3.

   (2) When n is divided by 2, the remainder is 1.

   Ⓐ statement 1 alone is sufficient to answer the question, but statement 2 alone is not sufficient

   Ⓑ statement 2 alone is sufficient to answer the question, but statement 1 alone is not sufficient

   Ⓒ both statements together are needed to answer the question, but neither statement alone is sufficient

   Ⓓ either statement by itself is sufficient to answer the question

   Ⓔ not enough facts are given to answer the question

26. For which of the following pairs of numbers is it true that their sum is 9 times their product?

   Ⓐ $1, \dfrac{1}{9}$ Ⓑ $1, \dfrac{1}{8}$ Ⓒ $1, \dfrac{1}{19}$ Ⓓ $1, 8$ Ⓔ $1, 9$

27. The price of a book, after it was reduced by one-third, is B dollars. What was the price of the book, in dollars, before the reduction?

   Ⓐ $\dfrac{2B}{3}$ Ⓑ $\dfrac{3B}{4}$ Ⓒ $\dfrac{6B}{5}$

   Ⓓ $\dfrac{4B}{3}$ Ⓔ $\dfrac{3B}{2}$

28. Y years ago, Tom was three times as old as Julie was. If Julie is now 20 years old, how old is Tom in terms of Y?

   Ⓐ $60 + 2Y$ Ⓑ $30 + 2Y$ Ⓒ $30 - 2Y$
   Ⓓ $60 - 2Y$ Ⓔ $60 - 3Y$

29. Is $n > 1$?

   (1) $1 > \dfrac{1}{n}$

   (2) $n > 0$

   Ⓐ statement 1 alone is sufficient to answer the question, but statement 2 alone is not sufficient

   Ⓑ statement 2 alone is sufficient to answer the question, but statement 1 alone is not sufficient

   Ⓒ both statements together are needed to answer the question, but neither statement alone is sufficient

   Ⓓ either statement by itself is sufficient to answer the question

   Ⓔ not enough facts are given to answer the question

GO ON TO NEXT PAGE

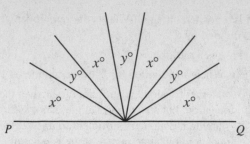

30. In the figure above, PQ is a line segment. What is the value of x?

   (1) $x - y = 10$
   (2) $y = 20$

   Ⓐ statement 1 alone is sufficient to answer the question, but statement 2 alone is not sufficient
   Ⓑ statement 2 alone is sufficient to answer the question, but statement 1 alone is not sufficient
   Ⓒ both statements together are needed to answer the question, but neither statement alone is sufficient
   Ⓓ either statement by itself is sufficient to answer the question
   Ⓔ not enough facts are given to answer the question

31. If S is the sum of x consecutive integers, S must be even if x is a multiple of

   Ⓐ 6   Ⓑ 5   Ⓒ 4   Ⓓ 3   Ⓔ 2

32. One pound of peanuts is added to a bin containing only cashews, and the resulting nut mix is 20 percent peanuts by weight. How many more pounds of peanuts must be added to the bin to create a mix that is 60 percent peanuts, by weight?

   Ⓐ 2   Ⓑ 3   Ⓒ 4.75   Ⓓ 5   Ⓔ 5.25

33. If $x^5 = 4$ and $x^4 = \dfrac{5}{y}$, then what is x in terms of y?

   Ⓐ $20y$ Ⓑ $\dfrac{25y}{16}$ Ⓒ $\dfrac{5y}{4}$ Ⓓ y Ⓔ $\dfrac{4y}{5}$

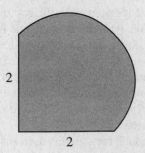

2

2

34. If the figure above is composed of a semicircle and a right triangle, what is the area of the shaded region?

   Ⓐ $\pi + \sqrt{2}$ Ⓑ $\pi + 2$ Ⓒ $2\pi + 1$
   Ⓓ $\sqrt{2\pi} + 1$ Ⓔ $\sqrt{2\pi} + \sqrt{2}$

35. Profits of corporation X over a three-year period averaged $1.2 million. If the corporation had profits in all three years, in which of the years were profits the greatest?

   (1) In the third year, the profits of corporation X were twice the average of its profits for the first two years.
   (2) Profits of corporation X were three times as great in the second year and four times as great in the third year as in the first.

   Ⓐ statement 1 alone is sufficient to answer the question, but statement 2 alone is not sufficient
   Ⓑ statement 2 alone is sufficient to answer the question, but statement 1 alone is not sufficient
   Ⓒ both statements together are needed to answer the question, but neither statement alone is sufficient
   Ⓓ either statement by itself is sufficient to answer the question
   Ⓔ not enough facts are given to answer the question

36. In the correct addition shown above, the symbols represent different nonzero digits. What is the number represented by ● ◆?

   (1) ■ $= 2 \times$ ▲
   (2) 10 ● $+$ ◆ $= 95$

   Ⓐ statement 1 alone is sufficient to answer the question, but statement 2 alone is not sufficient
   Ⓑ statement 2 alone is sufficient to answer the question, but statement 1 alone is not sufficient
   Ⓒ both statements together are needed to answer the question, but neither statement alone is sufficient
   Ⓓ either statement by itself is sufficient to answer the question
   Ⓔ not enough facts are given to answer the question

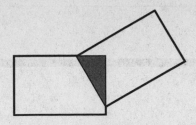

37. In the figure above, two rectangles, each with the same dimensions, overlap. If the perimeter of each rectangle is 28, what is the total length of the heavy-line segments?

  (1) The shaded region has an area of 4.

  (2) The shaded region has a perimeter of 12.

Ⓐ statement 1 alone is sufficient to answer the question, but statement 2 alone is not sufficient

Ⓑ statement 2 alone is sufficient to answer the question, but statement 1 alone is not sufficient

Ⓒ both statements together are needed to answer the question, but neither statement alone is sufficient

Ⓓ either statement by itself is sufficient to answer the question

Ⓔ not enough facts are given to answer the question

Stop: End of Quantitative Section

Answer Key

VERBAL SECTION

1.	E	15.	C	29.	D
2.	B	16.	E	30.	A
3.	A	17.	D	31.	A
4.	B	18.	C	32.	E
5.	E	19.	B	33.	A
6.	D	20.	B	34.	E
7.	E	21.	A	35.	E
8.	E	22.	D	36.	A
9.	D	23.	B	37.	D
10.	C	24.	D	38.	B
11.	A	25.	D	39.	E
12.	E	26.	E	40.	A
13.	B	27.	E	41.	A
14.	E	28.	A		

QUANTITATIVE SECTION

1.	B	14.	D	26.	B
2.	E	15.	B	27.	E
3.	E	16.	B	28.	D
4.	E	17.	C	29.	C
5.	B	18.	C	30.	D
6.	D	19.	E	31.	C
7.	A	20.	D	32.	D
8.	C	21.	E	33.	E
9.	B	22.	E	34.	B
10.	A	23.	A	35.	D
11.	A	24.	C	36.	B
12.	C	25.	C	37.	B
13.	C				

Explanatory Answers

VERBAL SECTION

1. Many thoroughbred handicappers believe that a horse's chance of winning a race depends not so much on the final times of his previous races <u>but instead</u> on his class, an unquantifiable factor that is the horse's determination to win.

   Ⓐ but instead
   Ⓑ rather than
   Ⓒ so much as
   Ⓓ than
   Ⓔ as

   (E) The construction "not so much . . . but instead" is not idiomatic. The correct expression is "not so much . . . as."

2. Three hundred years ago, famine was a periodic experience which came so <u>regular that people accepted periods of extreme hunger as normal.</u>

   Ⓐ regular that people accepted periods of extreme hunger as normal
   Ⓑ regularly that people accepted periods of extreme hunger as normal
   Ⓒ regularly that people normally accepted periods of extreme hunger
   Ⓓ regularly as people accepted periods of extreme hunger as normal
   Ⓔ regularly since people accepted periods of extreme hunger as normal

   (B) The original sentence contains one error. The adjective *regular* is intended to modify the verb *came*, but an adjective cannot modify a verb. The correct word is the adverb *regularly*. (B) makes the needed change and introduces no new error. (C), (D), and (E) also make the needed change, but each of them also changes the intended meaning of the original.

3. In accentual-syllabic versification, the basic unit of measurement is the <u>foot, which consists of</u> one accented syllable accompanied by one or two unaccented syllables.

   Ⓐ foot, which consists of
   Ⓑ foot, which consists in
   Ⓒ foot, which consisting of
   Ⓓ foot that consists of
   Ⓔ foot, which includes

   (A) The original sentence is correct. (B) is incorrect because the correct idiom to describe the parts of which something is made is *consists of,* not *consists in.* (C) is ungrammatical. The relative pronoun *which* requires a conjugated verb. (D) changes the meaning of the original sentence by suggesting that accentual-syllabic versification employs a particular kind of foot to the exclusion of other kinds. (E), too, changes the meaning of the original. The use of *includes* implies that the foot may consist of other elements not mentioned in the sentence.

   If Karen was selected for the committee, she must be a sophomore.

4. The statement above makes which of the following assumptions?

   Ⓐ Only Karen can be selected for the committee.
   Ⓑ Only sophomores can be selected for the committee.
   Ⓒ Some sophomores must be selected for the committee.
   Ⓓ Some sophomores might not be selected for the committee.
   Ⓔ Karen did not refuse to serve on the committee.

   (B) This item asks you to find a hidden assumption of the initial argument. The argument is very brief, only one sentence long, but it still has a premise and a conclusion. The conclusion is "Karen must be a sophomore," and the premise is "Karen was selected for the committee." Thus, the argument has the structure:

   Premise: Karen was selected for the committee.

   Conclusion: Karen must be a sophomore.

   The hidden assumption of this argument is articulated by (B).

The use of statistical data gathered from historical sources such as census reports and commercial registers and analyzed with the help of sophisticated computer programs has permeated the study of history in recent years. Now it would appear that the new statistical methods have begun to generate major breakthroughs in historical research, which brings us to Dr. Kramer's fascinating new book on the nineteenth-century settlement of the American frontier.

5. Which of the following conclusions is best supported by the passage above?

   (A) Statistical data from historical sources are the single most important form of information underpinning current historical research.
   (B) Dr. Kramer is the first major historian to apply the new statistical techniques to the study of the settlement of the American frontier.
   (C) Historians have begun to make major contributions to the science of statistical analysis.
   (D) Today, writers of histories must be skilled as computer programmers as well as knowledgeable about a particular era of history.
   (E) Dr. Kramer's book offers important new insights into its subject, based on analysis of historical statistics.

(E) This question asks you to draw a further conclusion from the paragraph. When you analyze a question like this, look for an answer choice that is well supported by the text and does not go very far beyond its explicit wording. (E) is a good choice. The paragraph claims that statistical analyses of old records are now generating important research. Then the author says, "which brings us to Dr. Kramer's new book." From this, we can infer that Dr. Kramer's new book is an example of the general trend cited by the author.

(A) overstates the author's point. The author does not claim that this new research technique is now the single most important source of historical research. (B) avoids the error of (A), but makes a different mistake. To be sure, Dr. Kramer's book is evidently an example of the general trend described by the author, but there is nothing in the paragraph to suggest that Dr. Kramer is the very first to use it. Choice (C) gets the causal sequence reversed. Existing statistical methods are now being applied to historical research, but the paragraph does not say that historians discovered new statistical techniques. Finally, (D) overstates the case. Though the new research technique requires researchers who understand statistics, this does not necessarily mean that they have to be able to program a computer.

Some people oppose college admissions programs for minority students on the ground that merit alone—as measured by high school grades, scores on entrance exams, and other objective standards—should be used in admissions decisions. This argument ignores the facts that non-merit factors have always been considered by colleges, for instance, the applicant's place of origin, whether a parent is a graduate of the college, and so on. These subjective factors are usually such as to exclude minority group students.

6. Which of the following would best complete the paragraph above?

   (A) Therefore, merit plays no substantive role in the majority of college admissions decisions.
   (B) Therefore, subjective factors should be completely removed from the college admissions process.
   (C) Therefore, the concept of merit is merely a subterfuge by which minority students may be excluded.
   (D) Therefore, it is not appropriate to use special admissions programs for minority students to help redress an imbalance.
   (E) Therefore, high school grades alone are an inadequate measure of a student's past academic performance.

(D) This question asks that you draw a conclusion. Eliminate (A) because it goes too far beyond the text. The paragraph suggests that factors other than merit play a role in admissions decisions, but not that merit plays absolutely no role at all. (B) makes a recommendation, but one that is not strongly supported by the text (especially given the recommendation made by [D]). The author says that colleges use subjective factors, but there is nothing to suggest the author favors eliminating them from the admission decision entirely—as opposed to using them in a new way. (C) really overstates the author's case. Nothing in the paragraph suggests a conclusion that uses emotional terms such as *subterfuge.* Though the author would surely endorse (E), it is not the point toward which this paragraph is leading. The point toward which the paragraph is leading is nicely stated by (D). The author cites a position: some people oppose the use of special admissions criteria. The author then notes that colleges have always used subjective considerations. Given the opening sentence of the paragraph, (D) is a conclusion toward which the author is probably working.

7. The author is primarily concerned with describing

   (A) a new scientific theory
   (B) the properties of X-rays
   (C) the structure of proteins
   (D) the functioning of cells
   (E) an instrument for scientific research

(E) This is a main idea question. The focus of the passage is on the use of synchrotron radiation for research. (E) correctly describes this focus. (A) is incorrect because the discussion is not about a theory but a research instrument. (B) is incorrect because the discussion about the properties of X-rays is incidental to the main point of the passage. The author mentions X-rays because synchrotron radiation is made up of X-rays, but the main point of the passage is not a discussion of the properties of X-rays per se. As for (C) and (D), these are mentioned in the passage as possible research topics that might be investigated by using synchrotron radiation, but neither is the main point of the selection.

8. According to the passage, researchers using conventional X-ray sources to study proteins use highly concentrated examples in order to
   - Ⓐ simulate the conditions in living cells
   - Ⓑ obtain a larger picture of the sample
   - Ⓒ condense several experiments into a short span of time
   - Ⓓ allow for respiration by sample components
   - Ⓔ compensate for the inadequacy of the X-ray beam

(E) This is a specific detail question. In the third paragraph the author specifically states that concentrated samples are used to compensate for the weakness in the beam generated by conventional X-ray sources. (A) is specifically contradicted by the passage, since the greater concentration makes conditions in the lab unlike actual conditions. As for (B) and (C), the author does not state that the technique gives a picture of larger size, nor that concentrating a sample makes an experiment run faster. Finally, (D) is inconsistent with what the author says about high concentrations making conditions in the lab unlike those actually found in the cell. Concentration interferes with normal functions.

9. The passage makes all of the following statements about synchrotron radiation EXCEPT
   - Ⓐ The length of the waves that make up the beam can be controlled.
   - Ⓑ The beam is more intense than that of conventional X-ray sources.
   - Ⓒ It yields more precise data than conventional X-ray sources.
   - Ⓓ It is less dangerous to researchers than conventional X-ray sources.
   - Ⓔ It is composed of pulsating X-rays.

(D) This is a specific idea question with a thought-reverser. The correct choice is the one not mentioned in the passage. (A), (B), (C), and (E) are all specifically stated in the passage. Nowhere in the passage, however, does the author say anything about any hazards posed by X-rays.

10. The Puritan was composed of two different men: the one all self-abasement and penitence; the other, proud and inflexible.
   - Ⓐ the one all self-abasement and penitence
   - Ⓑ one of them all self-abasement and penitence
   - Ⓒ the one self-abasing and penitent
   - Ⓓ the one self-abasement and penitence
   - Ⓔ self-abasing and penitent

(C) The sentence suffers from a lack of parallelism. The elements used to complete the structure "the one . . . the other . . ." should have similar parts of speech. Since *proud* and *inflexible* are adjectives, the correct choice of words is *self-abasing* and *penitent*. Only (C) and (E) make the needed correction, but (E) leaves the phrase *self-abasing and penitent* with no clear logical connection to the other elements of the sentence.

11. In 1896, when she began studying the effects of radium, Marie Curie was building on the work of Roentgen and Becquerel.
   - Ⓐ In 1896, when she began studying the effects of radium
   - Ⓑ In 1896, beginning to study the effects of radium
   - Ⓒ Beginning to study the effects of radium in 1896
   - Ⓓ Since she began to study the effects of radium in 1896
   - Ⓔ In order to begin to study the effects of radium in 1896

(A) The original sentence is correct. (B) and (C) are incorrect for the same reason: *beginning* is a participle used as an adjective and must modify *Marie Curie,* but the (B) and (C) phrases incorrectly use *beginning* to modify the verb in the main clause *to study.* (D) and (E) both change the meaning of the original sentence.

12. Having been forbidden by Church law to marry, it was not unusual for a priest during the Middle Ages to sire a family.
   - Ⓐ Having been forbidden by Church law to marry, it was not unusual for a priest during the Middle Ages to sire a family.
   - Ⓑ Forbidden by Church law to marry, it was not unusual for a priest during the Middle Ages to sire a family.
   - Ⓒ Although they were forbidden by Church law to marry, it was not unusual for a priest during the Middle Ages to sire a family.
   - Ⓓ Although a priest was forbidden by Church law to marry, it was not unusual for him during the Middle Ages to sire a family.
   - Ⓔ Although they were forbidden by Church law to marry, it was not unusual for priests during the Middle Ages to sire families.

(E) The original sentence commits an error of logical expression. The sentence means to contrast two ideas, but rendering the first idea (priests were forbidden to marry) as a phrase modifying *priest* suggests the two ideas are similar, not dissimilar. (B) is incorrect for the same reason: it fails to provide the needed contrast between the two ideas. (C), (D), and (E) all provide the needed contrast, but (C) and (D) make other errors. In (C), *they* is intended to refer to *priest,* so there is a failure of agreement. And (D) changes the intended meaning of the original by implying that there was a single priest who sired several families.

Government involvement in industry is more detrimental than helpful to that industry. As proof of this, consider two comparable industries: urban mass transit and the airline business. The former has generally been subsidized and operated by local governments, and in most cities service is poor and deteriorating. By contrast, the privately owned and operated airlines earn profits and provide, for the most part, fast and efficient service.

13. Which of the following, if true, would LEAST weaken the argument above?

    Ⓐ Passenger complaints about airline scheduling and service have increased rapidly and are now greater than ever before.
    Ⓑ Privately owned mass transit systems do not have problems similar to those of government-operated systems.
    Ⓒ The government subsidizes airport construction and operation and offers tax breaks to airlines.
    Ⓓ Technological advances in air travel have allowed airlines to operate more efficiently, but no similar advances have occurred in rail travel.
    Ⓔ On average, airline ticket prices have increased faster than mass transit fares over the past ten years.

(B) This question asks you to attack the argument. The conclusion of the argument is contained in the first sentence: government involvement is harmful. The proof of this conclusion is a comparison of urban mass transit and airlines. The author claims that the quality of service provided by urban mass transit, which receives government aid, is deteriorating while costs have increased. On the other hand, according to the argument, the airlines, which receive no government aid, provide good service and make a profit.

(A) provides a good attack on this final point: airline service is not that good. (C) attacks the argument by claiming that the successful operations of the airlines are actually dependent upon government support and involvement. (D) attacks the argument by

pointing to an alternative causal explanation: it is not management but technological breakthroughs that account for the difference. Finally, (E) argues that the economic performance of airlines is, in at least one respect, no better than that of urban mass transit.

(B) actually strengthens the argument by suggesting that government interference is the cause of the differences in performances between government-owned rapid transit and privately owned airlines; publicly owned mass transit has these problems, but privately owned mass transit does not.

Neither artifacts, personal messages, nor historical documents from any human civilization would be likely to have any meaning for intelligent extraterrestrial beings. Therefore, the probe to be sent into interstellar space in the hope that alien beings may find it will contain a plaque inscribed with certain scientific and mathematical formulas, for example, a statement of the value of π or the molecular weight of water.

14. The argument above depends upon which of the following assumptions?

    Ⓐ Somewhere in the universe there is at least one intelligent race other than the human race living of Earth.
    Ⓑ Extraterrestrial beings probably have civilizations that are not as technically advanced as those on Earth.
    Ⓒ Life on other worlds is likely to be dependent upon the presence of water just as it is on Earth.
    Ⓓ Intelligent beings on other worlds have probably developed means of interstellar space travel.
    Ⓔ Some symbols used by human beings will be meaningful to intelligent extraterrestrial beings.

(E) This question asks you to find a hidden assumption of the argument. The conclusion of the argument (although not stated very precisely) is that alien beings will be able to read mathematical and scientific formulas. But these formulas are written in human symbols. Thus, the argument implicitly presupposes that the aliens will be able to read (at least some) symbols used by humans.

(A) is incorrect, for the probe is launched with the hope that such races exist. But that they exist is just that—a hope, not a presupposition. As for (B) and (D), the argument depends upon the assumption that an alien race is different—not that it is less or more technically advanced than we are. Finally, as for (C), though one of the formulas is the molecular weight of water, the argument assumes only that alien races would recognize it as the molecular weight of water—not that they depend on water in the same way that we do.

Studies of twins separated at or shortly after birth have played a major role in attempts to measure the relative influence of genetic and environmental factors on personal development. Those who consider environment all-important would predict that separately reared twins would exhibit no more similarity than another two unrelated individuals brought up under the same conditions. The data do not support this extreme position, but neither do they support the opposite fallacy, the belief that "genetics is destiny."

15. Which of the following statements would be the most reasonable conclusion to draw from the argument above?

    Ⓐ More study of the relationship between genetics and environment is needed before it can be determined whether one or the other of the two extreme positions is correct.

    Ⓑ Studies of twins separated at birth show that environmental factors are the most important factor in later personal development.

    Ⓒ Twin studies suggest that both genetic and environmental factors play an important part in the development of personality.

    Ⓓ Attempts to modify personal development by making changes in the environment of an individual are misguided and doomed to failure.

    Ⓔ Twin studies are inherently unsatisfactory as a research tool because of the ambiguity that infects the results obtained.

    (C) This item asks you to draw a further conclusion from the initial paragraph. The speaker mentions two competing theories; heredity is all-important and environment is all-important. The evidence provided by studies of twins, according to the author, does not support either view. The most reasonable conclusion to draw is that the truth is somewhere in between—as (C) suggests. You can eliminate (A) because the author does not believe either of the extreme positions is correct. For the same reason, you can eliminate both (B) and (D). Finally, as for (E), nothing in the paragraph suggests that the studies are unreliable.

16. As described by the selection, the sequence of events leading to the present landscape was

    Ⓐ erosion, uplift, submersion, uplift, erosion, submersion

    Ⓑ uplift, submersion, erosion, uplift, submersion, erosion

    Ⓒ submersion, erosion, uplift, submersion, erosion, uplift,

    Ⓓ submersion, uplift, erosion, submersion, erosion, uplift,

    Ⓔ submersion, uplift, erosion, submersion, uplift, erosion

(E) This is a specific idea question. According to the second paragraph, the process begins under water, so you eliminate (A) and (B). The next stage is elevation or uplift, so eliminate (C). Then, according to the third paragraph, there is the process of erosion and another submersion, and then another elevation and erosion. (E) correctly describes the process.

17. The author mentions which of the following as forces that shaped the appearance of the landscape?

    I. Volcanic eruption

    II. Erosion

    III. Glacial activity

    Ⓐ II only   Ⓑ I and II only   Ⓒ I and III only
    Ⓓ II and III only   Ⓔ I, II, and III

(D) In the second paragraph the author mentions erosion, so II must be part of the correct choice. In the last paragraph the author mentions the fact that canyons were filled by glaciers and that the glaciers broadened and deepened and scooped out cirques or bowls. So III must be part of the correct choice. As for I, although the author mentions masses of molten rock welling up and hardening under the earth's surface, he does not mention volcanic eruption as one of the forces that shaped the landscape.

18. The author would likely agree with which of the following statements?

    I. The present appearance of the landscape is only temporary.

    II. The present appearance of the landscape is the product of natural forces.

    III. Any changes that will occur in the appearance of the landscape cannot be predicted.

    Ⓐ I only   Ⓑ II only   Ⓒ I and II only
    Ⓓ I and III only   Ⓔ I, II, and III

(C) The author would probably agree with the first statement because one of the main ideas of the passage is that the landscape changed several times over the last millions of years. And he would also agree with II, since the forces he describes are natural forces, (he never states that the landscape has been altered by the activities of man). He would not, however, agree with III, since at the end of the fourth paragraph he makes a prediction about the change of the appearance of the landscape. He says that the rocks of Colorado will eventually be stripped away by erosion, although that process will require millions of years.

19. The singing teachers of the old Italian school taught <u>little more but</u> breath control because they believed that with proper breath control, all other technical problems could be easily solved.

    Ⓐ little more but
    Ⓑ little more than
    Ⓒ little more as
    Ⓓ more than a little
    Ⓔ rather than

(B) The original sentence is not idiomatic. The correct idiom is not *little more but,* it is *little more than.* Choice (D) is idiomatic but changes the intended meaning of the original; while the remaining choices, like the original, are not idiomatic.

20. In the early stages of the development of the common law, <u>equitable remedies were available only in the courts of the Chancery and not in the courts of law, such as injunctions.</u>

    Ⓐ equitable remedies were available only in the courts of the Chancery and not in the courts of law, such as injunctions
    Ⓑ equitable remedies, such as injunctions, were available only in the courts of the Chancery and not in the courts of law
    Ⓒ only equitable remedies, such as injunctions, were available in the courts of the Chancery and not in the courts of law
    Ⓓ the availability of equitable remedies, such as injunctions, was restricted to the courts of Chancery and not to the courts of law
    Ⓔ equitable remedies, such as injunctions, were not available in the courts of law but only in the courts of Chancery

(B) The original sentence makes an illogical assertion. The placement of the phrase *such as injunctions* suggests that injunctions are a type of court. (B) corrects this false impression by relocating the phrase closer to what it is intended to modify. The other three choices correct this problem but introduce new mistakes. (C) changes the intended meaning of the original by implying that the equitable remedies were the only remedies available in courts of Chancery. Additionally, the new placement of *only* isolates the phrase *and not in the courts of law,* leaving it disconnected from the rest of the sentence. As for (D), the construction "availability of . . ." is wordy and awkward. Additionally, the resulting sentence would read "the availability . . . was restricted . . . not to. . . ." This phrasing implies that the availability of equitable remedies was not restricted in courts of law, an extremely awkward sentence that seems to contradict the intended meaning of the original. Finally, (E) makes a similar error. The resulting sentence would read "equitable remedies . . . were not available . . . only in courts of Chancery."

21. These extensive forest reserves must be defended from the acquisitive hands of those whose ruthless axes <u>would destroy the trees and</u> expose the land to the ravages of sun and rain.

    Ⓐ would destroy the trees and
    Ⓑ will destroy the trees and
    Ⓒ would destroy the trees to
    Ⓓ would destroy the trees which would
    Ⓔ would destroy the trees that could

(A) The original sentence is correct. As for (B), the change from the subjunctive *(would)* to the indicative *(will)* is incorrect, because the original clearly implies that the destruction is contingent, not certain. (C) implies that cutting the trees is a means of exposing the land, a shift from the meaning of the original. (D) is needlessly wordy, and (E) changes the intended meaning of the original by implying that the cutting of the trees might or might not expose the land (whereas the original states categorically that the result would follow).

We hear it said that, for all the social progress America has made over the past thirty years—for all the toppling of racial and ethnic barriers that we have witnessed—this remains an inherently racist society in which the white majority has never fully accepted the equal humanity of the minority. Those who repeat this slander against America ignore the fact that, as I write, the most popular television program in the country focuses on the lives of a proud middle-class black family, whose members have become some of the best-recognized—and most widely admired—people in America.

22. The argument above assumes that

    Ⓐ television acting is a challenging and financially rewarding profession
    Ⓑ thirty years ago a television show with black characters would not have been popular
    Ⓒ those who label America a racist society seek to foment unrest and disrupt the fabric of American society
    Ⓓ a person's attitude toward a character on a television show is like his attitude toward real people with similar characteristics
    Ⓔ the television program is more popular among white viewers than among black viewers

(D) This question asks that you find a hidden assumption of the argument. The conclusion of the argument is that America is not a racist society (or at least not so racist as some would contend). The proof for this conclusion is that a popular television show depicts successful black people. Thus, the argument implicitly assumes that what people find attractive in a television character, they also find attractive in a real person—a point made by (D).

As for (A), the important fact, according to the speaker, is that the fictional characters are successful—not that the actors are successful. On first reading, (B) might seem to be an implicit assumption of the argument, but a closer reading shows that it is not. You might think that the author is logically committed to the proposition that black characters would not have been popular thirty years ago. (Otherwise, why would the fact that this particular series is popular indicate that racism is on the decline?) The difficulty with (B) is that it fails to distinguish between possible portrayals of black characters, and one of the most important features of the argument is that the characters mentioned are successful. Thus, the author might allow that thirty years ago there were popular black characters but these were racist stereotypes. (C) overstates the case. Although there is some indication in the paragraph that the author regards this as an emotional issue (he uses the term *slander*), (C) goes too far beyond the text. Finally, as for (E), this is not an idea to which the author is logically committed. The author could allow that white and black viewers alike enjoy the program and still argue that the fact that, since whites like it at all, it shows that racism is on the wane.

Foods that are high in fat, salt, or sugar content have been shown to be deleterious to health. If the government can forbid the sale to minors of other harmful products, such as cigarettes and alcoholic beverages, why not treat dangerous foods the same way? Children under 18 should be allowed to purchase only foods that are nutritious and healthful.

23. The author of the statement above makes his point primarily by
    Ⓐ analyzing a cause and effect relationship
    Ⓑ drawing an analogy
    Ⓒ appealing to the emotions of the audience
    Ⓓ offering a counterexample
    Ⓔ making a generalization

(B) The speaker draws an analogy between harmful substances such as tobacco and alcohol and foods that might be harmful. Admittedly, the argument from analogy is not very persuasive, but (B) does correctly describe the form of the argument.

By studying census data, demographers are able to develop lists of counties and communities throughout the country whose populations have specific economic characteristics—for example, high or low median age, large numbers of families with children, a high percentage of two-career couples, or particularly affluent households. Lists such as these can be especially useful to political organizations that are promoting candidates who have particular appeal to voters with specific characteristics.

24. Which of the following, if true, best supports the claim that the demographic information mentioned in the passage may be valuable to political organizations?
    Ⓐ Affluent citizens are known to be more likely to vote in local elections than are those who are less affluent.
    Ⓑ Because census data are compiled by the federal government, they must legally be made available to all who request them.
    Ⓒ Voters tend to be heavily influenced in their thinking by the opinions and preferences of their friends and neighbors.
    Ⓓ Research shows that the economic and social characteristics of differing groups can be closely correlated with specific political views.
    Ⓔ Several of today's most significant political issues have particular impact on the interests of families with children.

(D) This item asks us to strengthen the argument, so we are anticipating an answer choice that proves a hidden assumption of the argument. The conclusion of the argument is that the lists mentioned can be helpful to political organizations in targeting certain voters. Since the lists contain demographic information, the speaker must believe that demographic characteristics can be used to predict voting patterns. (D) provides support for this critical assumption. (A) uses language that is generally relevant to the argument, but (A) doesn't weaken or strengthen the argument. One way of proving this to yourself is to try to explain how (A) is relevant to the argument. Then try to explain how the negation of (A) is also relevant to the argument. Both (A) and its negation are equally uninteresting. As for (B), this may be true of census data, but it does not explain why lists of demographic characteristics would be valuable to political organizations. As for (C), this at least has the merit of suggesting that demographic information (who the neighbors are and what they think) may have something to do with voting patterns. And, in the absence of (D), you might make a good argument for the correctness of (C). The difficulty with (C) is that it merely suggests that demographic data is important, whereas (D) states this specifically. So on balance (D) is a better choice than (C).

Finally, as for (E), to the extent that you can argue that it would be useful to know which families have children because they might be predisposed to vote a certain way on some issues, you are really making an argument for (D).

25. The author's primary concern is to
   (A) define medical terminology
   (B) defend the use of radiography
   (C) encourage the use of ultrasonography
   (D) discuss a new medical technology
   (E) warn about a health hazard

(D) This is a main idea question presented in the form of a sentence completion. You can eliminate (E) because the first word is not descriptive of the selection. The selection is not intended to warn.

Then (A) can be eliminated because the main point of the passage is not to define terms. Although the author does define ultrasonography in the opening paragraph, that is a small part of the passage. You can eliminate (B) because the focus of the passage is ultrasonography, not radiography. (C) should be eliminated because the author's main purpose is not to encourage the use of ultrasonography. When the author describes the advantages of ultrasonography, he is not trying to sell the reader on the technique; he is informing the reader. This is why (D) best describes the overall theme of the passage. The author discusses this new medical technology.

26. The passage states that which of the following is (are) differences between conventional radiography and ultrasonography?
   I. Ultrasonography is more expensive than conventional radiography.
   II. Conventional radiography depends upon ionizing radiation; ultrasonography does not.
   III. The image of conventional radiography is created by the part of the beam that passes through the patient's body; the image of ultrasonography by the part of the beam that bounces back.

   (A) I only   (B) II only   (C) III only
   (D) I and III only   (E) II and III only

(E) This is a specific idea question. The elements of the correct answer must be mentioned somewhere in the selection. As for statement I, the author specifically states that ultrasonography is not expensive (first paragraph), so I is not part of the correct choice. (And you eliminate [A] and [D].) As for II, the author states in the first paragraph that ultrasonography "does not utilize ionizing radiation." (Now that you know II is part of the correct answer, you eliminate [C] as well.) Finally,

III is also mentioned in the passage in the final paragraph. There the author states that X-ray images show how much radiation was absorbed, while ultrasound pictures are compiled from the reflected waves.

27. It can be inferred from the passage that some physicians prefer to use ultrasound when a patient is pregnant because
   (A) X-rays are absorbed by the skull
   (B) ultrasound is inexpensive
   (C) X-rays cannot penetrate the womb
   (D) ultrasound is more widely available
   (E) X-rays pose a hazard to the fetus

(E) This is an implied idea question. In the final sentence of the first paragraph the author states that doctors who are concerned about the health of a fetus use ultrasound rather than radiography. Although the passage does not specifically state that X-rays are hazardous, we may infer from this statement that they are.

As for (A), while it is true that X-rays are absorbed by bone and therefore by the skull, that does not explain why a doctor uses one technique over the other on a pregnant patient. As for (B), though the author does say that ultrasonography is not expensive, cost is not the reason the technique is particularly attractive to doctors attending pregnant women. (C) is incorrect for the very reason that X-rays can and do penetrate the womb, thereby posing a threat to the fetus. Finally, (D) like (B) is contradicted by the first paragraph of the selection.

28. Smart investors realized early on that the compact disk, on which music is recorded in a digital code to be read by a laser, would soon become the most common form of recorded <u>music, eventually replacing</u> records and tapes altogether.
   (A) music, eventually replacing
   (B) music, and eventually replacing
   (C) music that eventually replaces
   (D) music by eventually replacing
   (E) music to eventually replace

(A) The original sentence is correct. (B) is incorrect, for the two parts of a compound verb must have similar verb forms. (C) and (D) both change the meaning of the original by implying that the compact disk was but one form of recorded music that would replace records and disks, namely, the most common form. (E) also changes the meaning of the original because (E) implies that the compact disk would become the most common form of recorded music only by replacing the others. But the original clearly implies that the compact disk would become the most common form and then replace records and tapes altogether. (*Most common* does not necessarily mean "sole.")

29. Good American English is simply good English; that of London and Sydney differ no more from Boston and Chicago than the types of houses in which people live.

    Ⓐ differ no more from
    Ⓑ differs no more from
    Ⓒ differ no more than
    Ⓓ differs no more from that of
    Ⓔ differ no more from those of

(D) The original sentence asserts an illogical comparison between the English spoken in London and Sydney and two other cities, Boston and Chicago. Additionally, the verb *differ* fails to agree in number with its subject, *that*. (B) corrects the second error but not the first. (C) corrects neither error and creates an unidiomatic expression. (E) corrects both errors but in doing so makes a new mistake. *Those* refers to *English*.

30. Arturo Toscanini, well known for his sharp tongue as well as his musical genius, once cowed a famous singer with the remark that there were for him no stars except those in the heavens.

    Ⓐ Arturo Toscanini, well known for his sharp tongue as well as his musical genius, once cowed a famous singer
    Ⓑ Arturo Toscanini, well known for his sharp tongue as well than his musical genius, cowed once a famous singer
    Ⓒ Arturo Toscanini's well known sharp tongue as well as his musical genius once cowed a famous singer
    Ⓓ Arturo Toscanini, who had a well-known sharp tongue as well as musical genius, once cowed a famous singer
    Ⓔ Well known for his sharp tongue as well as his musical genius, a famous singer was once cowed by Arturo Toscanini

(A) The original sentence is correct. (B) introduces two new errors. First, the phrase *as well than* is not idiomatic; and second, the placement of *once* here is not as idiomatic as the placement of *once* in the original. (C) changes the meaning of the original by making *tongue* and *musical genius* the agents who act (instead of the person who acts.) (D) is awkward compared to the original, and (E) contains a misplaced modifier that changes the meaning of the original by implying that it was the singer who possessed the sharp tongue and musical genius.

Some people oppose testing of employees for use of illegal drugs on the ground that the tests sometimes produce false results. These fears are without basis. The newest tests can detect over ninety-nine percent of the cases in which a person has used one of the most common illegal drugs at any time during the previous 48 hours.

31. Which of the following, if true, would most weaken the argument above?

    Ⓐ The best drug tests available today return a significant number of positive results even when the person has not used drugs.
    Ⓑ The best drug tests available today cannot reliably identify every form of illegal drug that a person might have used.
    Ⓒ The best drug tests available today cannot identify an illegal drug if the subject took that drug more than 48 hours prior to the test.
    Ⓓ An employee who occasionally uses an illegal drug may still be a valuable worker.
    Ⓔ Some employers still continue to use older and less reliable drug tests.

(A) The argument claims that drug testing is fairly reliable, and the proof given for this is that the tests are able to detect accurately when someone has used drugs within a certain time period before the test. The difficulty with this analysis is that it addresses only half of the issue of reliability. The real concern over drug testing is not whether the tests return a positive most or all of the time that the person tested has used drugs, but whether the tests return a positive on only those occasions. This is the issue of false positives, and (A) points out that this is a weakness in the argument about reliability.

(B) and (C) are incorrect for the same reason. Each does cite a weakness in drug testing, but the wording of the speaker's claim really pre-empts these objections. The speaker says that drug testing is fairly reliable for the most common illegal drugs taken within a certain time before the test. (D) makes a claim that is irrelevant to the issue of reliability. As for (E), the fact that some employers use unreliable tests does not weaken the author's claim that reliable tests are available.

One of the most influential studies of the ancient construction known as Stonehenge was conducted by Professor Gerald Hawkins. Hawkins used computer calculations to compare the locations of stones in Stonehenge with the positions of stars, planets, and the sun at the time the structure was built. He concluded that the stones could have been used to mark viewing angles along which the rising and setting of heavenly bodies could be observed, making Stonehenge a kind of primitive "computer" for predicting astronomical events.

32. Which of the following, if true, most seriously weakens Hawkins' argument?

Ⓐ There is no reliable scientific evidence that the ancient people who built Stonehenge worshipped heavenly bodies.

Ⓑ Hawkins' computer calculations, though on their face accurate, have not been independently verified.

Ⓒ The positions of heavenly bodies have shifted slightly in the thousands of years since Stonehenge was built.

Ⓓ The fragility of the already damaged stones of Stonehenge has caused authorities to limit the access of scholars to the site.

Ⓔ Any structure as complex as that of Stonehenge must inevitably contain some astronomical viewing angles even if they were not intended by the builders.

(E) One of the techniques discussed in the chapter on logical reasoning is to attack an argument by looking for an alternative causal explanation. This is what choice (E) does. Hawkins explains the structure at Stonehenge by reference to the intentions of the builders. (E) suggests that a different explanation is possible; the viewing lines are merely coincidence.

(A) is a fairly weak attack on the argument. A people might construct something with astronomical significance even if they did not worship heavenly bodies. (B), too, is not much of an attack on the argument, for even if true, it does not mean that Hawkins is wrong. (C) would be more interesting if Hawkins had contended that Stonehenge has no astronomical significance. A good attack on that argument would then explain that the lines of viewing had significance thousands of years ago, even if they do not have significance now. But (C) does nothing to the argument actually made by Hawkins. (D) is very much like (B).

The tendency toward political tyranny increases in periods of economic collapse. When most people have homes and jobs and when families anticipate a better life for their children, citizens support moderate policies that promise peaceful growth and gradual development. When work is scarce, prices are rising, and prospects for the future seem bleak, desperate measures begin to seem attractive, and the would-be totalitarian's promise of drastic upheaval holds appeal.

33. The claim made in the argument above would be most seriously weakened by evidence of which of the following?

Ⓐ Countries undergoing economic collapse in which democratic institutions were strengthened.

Ⓑ Countries in which periods of drastic economic change had little apparent political effect.

Ⓒ Countries in which totalitarian governments were established with little basis in popular support.

Ⓓ Examples of tyrannical governments that arose during periods of prosperity.

Ⓔ Examples of totalitarian leaders who actually kept the promises they made before attaining power.

(A) To answer this item correctly, you have to read the initial paragraph with some care. The conclusion of the argument is contained in the first sentence: poor economic conditions are conducive to the rise of tyranny. Counterexamples in which poor economic conditions actually lead to a strengthening of democratic institutions would be the best refutation of this theory. (A) provides them.

(D) is surely the second-best answer but would have been more nearly correct if the conclusion of the initial paragraph had been "During times of economic prosperity, tyranny rarely flourishes." That is not the conclusion of the initial paragraph, although it is an idea related to the topic discussed in the paragraph and an idea the author would probably accept. (A) is a stronger attack than (D) because (A) aims at the precise conclusion of the argument and not at a collateral issue.

(B), (C), and (E) are weaker responses. (B) is generally related to the topic of the paragraph, but (B) doesn't specify as ([A] and [D] do) the kinds of economic changes that occurred. As for (C), the author would probably respond to this statement by agreeing that it is possible for tyrannies to exist without popular support, but he claims only that when economic conditions are poor, they receive popular support. Finally, as for (E), the author never analyzes the features of tyrannical government.

34. Concrete is an artificial engineering material made from a mixture of portland cement, water, fine and coarse aggregates, <u>having a small</u> amount of air.

    Ⓐ having a small
    Ⓑ having added a small
    Ⓒ adding a small
    Ⓓ and a little
    Ⓔ and a small

(E) The original sentence suffers from faulty parallelism. The sequence of ingredients consists of four nouns and a verb. Both (D) and (E) solve the problem of parallelism, but the phrase *little amount* is not idiomatic.

35. During the Middle Ages, literacy was defined as <u>one who could read and write</u> Latin.

    Ⓐ one who could read and write
    Ⓑ one who would read and write
    Ⓒ reading and writing
    Ⓓ those who could read and write
    Ⓔ the ability to read and write

(E) The sentence is guilty of illogical expression, for it asserts an equivalence between *literacy* and *one*, a person. (B) and (D) fail to correct this problem. (C) creates a new illogical expression by asserting equivalence between literacy and two activities, *reading and writing*. (E) makes a logical assertion by equating *literacy* with *ability*.

A basic social function of the university is to provide a setting within which all points of view may be freely debated, including those whose radical nature may offend some or even most members of the community. Unfortunately, this mandate includes totalitarian views that might themselves threaten the freedom and diversity of expression to which the university is dedicated.

36. The speaker in the paragraph above is most concerned with discussing a(n)

    Ⓐ dilemma
    Ⓑ contradiction
    Ⓒ paradox
    Ⓓ analogy
    Ⓔ generalization

(A) Let's begin by eliminating (D) and (E), since they are fairly obviously not descriptions of the paragraph. The remaining choices, (A), (B), and (C), are fairly close.

What makes this item difficult is the fact that dilemma, contradiction, and paradox share a common logical feature. Each involves a pair of ideas. Dilemma is the best description of the problem discussed in the initial paragraph, because the paragraph describes two possible courses of action, neither of which is a happy choice. On the one hand, the university cannot suppress ideas without failing in its function. On the other hand, the university cannot allow the expression of

totalitarian ideas without also jeopardizing its function. This "damned if you do, and damned if you don't" is the defining characteristic of a dilemma.

A contradiction, on the other hand, is simply the conjunction of two statements, the one of which is the negative to the other: "I will go, but I won't go." A paradox is a special logical form, the most famous example of which is the Liar's Paradox:
The sentence you are now reading is false.

Questions 37 and 38
Colleges are doing a poor job of imparting basic skills. According to a recent survey of personnel directors of major corporations, large numbers of entry-level workers lack ability in writing, mathematics, and reasoning skills.

37. Which of the following must be true if the argument above is valid?

    Ⓐ College students today are no longer required to take courses in basic skills.
    Ⓑ Few entry-level workers today have college degrees.
    Ⓒ Basic skills in writing, mathematics, and reasoning are important for success in most jobs.
    Ⓓ Entry-level workers at major corporations are generally representative of today's college graduates.
    Ⓔ College students in the past received better training in basic skills than students of today.

(D) This question asks you to identify a hidden assumption of the argument. Test each of the choices to see whether or not the author is committed to that idea. As for (A), the author says only that colleges today are not teaching important basic skills, and that's as far as he needs to go. For his purposes, he doesn't need to explain the cause of that failure, so (A) is not an idea the author is necessarily committed to. As for (B), the author is committed to the idea that some entry-level workers have college degrees. Otherwise, it would be irrational to blame the colleges for the workers' lack of training. As for (C), although the author might agree that these skills are important, he is not logically committed to this idea by the structure of the argument. The author says only that entry-level workers in large corporations lack these important skills—not that the skills are important for most jobs. Finally, (E) has some merit, for, given the general tone of the paragraph, this is something we might anticipate the author would endorse. But again, he is not committed to this idea by the structure of the argument. (The author could conceivably believe that colleges have always done a poor job of teaching basic skills.) (D) is an idea the author is committed to. The conclusion of the argument is "Colleges are doing a poor job." The evidence for this conclusion is "This group of people is poorly trained." For this conclusion to follow, the group cited must be representative of college graduates in general.

38. Which of the following questions would be most relevant in determining the validity of the argument above?

Ⓐ What kinds of training programs are provided by major corporations for their entry-level workers?

Ⓑ Do colleges have the responsibility for teaching students basic skills in writing, mathematics, and reasoning?

Ⓒ How closely correlated are workers' levels of skill in writing, mathematics, and reasoning?

Ⓓ Do major corporations today demand a higher level of basic skills from entry-level workers than in the past?

Ⓔ How do the skill levels of workers at major corporations compare with those at smaller companies?

(B) This question focuses upon a hidden assumption of the argument. The conclusion of the argument is that colleges are doing a poor job of teaching basic skills, and the evidence for this is that certain college graduates today lack these skills. Obviously, the argument rests upon the implicit premise that it is the job of the colleges to provide these skills. (Otherwise, the author would not blame the colleges.)

The question posed by (A) is not immediately relevant to the argument. Whether or not corporations are forced to provide training programs is not relevant to the issue of whether or not new workers come to them with basic skills. As for (C), the author says that college graduates are weak in all three areas, but he does not need to insist that there is a correlation of skills in these three areas. He might very well think that the three areas are completely independent of each other and that colleges are failing on three different counts—not just on one. As for (D), we noted in the discussion of the preceding item that the author does not imply a comparison of the quality of college education today with that of an earlier time. Be careful that you don't read something into the paragraph that is not there. To be sure, many people might use the information provided to support an argument having the form "Things today are much worse than they used to be . . . ," but this is not the argument advanced in this particular case. Finally, as for (E), the author focuses on entry-level workers, not on workers in general.

39. The author is primarily concerned with

Ⓐ criticizing translators who do not faithfully reproduce the style of works written in another language

Ⓑ suggesting that Japanese literature is more complex than English literature

Ⓒ arguing that no translation can do justice to a work written in another language

Ⓓ demonstrating that Japanese literature is particularly difficult to translate into English

Ⓔ discussing some of the problems of translating Japanese literature into English

(E) This is a main idea question. (A) is not correct because although the author discusses the difficulty of making a translation, he does not criticize translators. In fact, he seems sympathetic to their problems since he is a translator himself. (B) is not correct since he mentions the fact that all languages have their particular difficulties and uses the poetry of Milton—an English poet—as an example of a difficult text to translate. (C) is wrong because although the author says it is difficult to do justice to a work in another language, he refers to some translations that are successful—those that please the "hard-liners," for instance. He also mentions Chateaubriand's translation of *Paradise Lost* as a successful translation. (D) is incorrect because although the author mentions some of the difficulties of translating Japanese into English, the point of the passage is not that Japanese is particularly difficult—just that it is difficult in particular ways. (E) is the correct answer.

40. The author cites Shiga Naoya's *Kinosaki nite* in order to

Ⓐ illustrate the effect that Japanese orthography has on meaning

Ⓑ demonstrate the poverty of indigenous Japanese vocabulary

Ⓒ prove that it is difficult to translate Japanese into English

Ⓓ acquaint the reader with an important work of Japanese literature

Ⓔ impress upon the reader the importance of faithfully translating a work from one language into another

(A) This is a logical detail question. The author uses an example taken from *Kinosaki nite* to illustrate the onomatopoeic effect of writing a word in one system of orthography rather than another. (B) is incorrect because although the author mentions the fact that a Japanese writer laments the poverty of indigenous Japanese vocabulary, this is not the point of his example. In fact, the example actually demonstrates a certain richness of the Japanese language. (C) is incorrect because the example has nothing to do with translation. It is an example of an effect rendered in Japanese. (D) is not correct since the reader actually learns nothing at all about this work of literature except that this literary device appears in it. Finally, (E) is wrong because, again, the example has nothing to do with the translation.

41. It can be inferred that the "exoticism handicap" mentioned by the author is

   Ⓐ the tendency of some translators of Japanese to render Japanese literature in a needlessly awkward style
   Ⓑ the attempt of Japanese writers to create for their readers a world characterized by mysticism
   Ⓒ the lack of literal, word-for-word translational equivalents for Japanese and English vocabulary
   Ⓓ the expectation of many English readers that Japanese literature can only be understood by someone who speaks Japanese
   Ⓔ the difficulty a Japanese reader encounters in trying to penetrate the meaning of difficult Japanese poets

   (A) This is an implied idea question. (B) cannot be correct since the handicap referred to is the result of translating the poetry, not the result of the Japanese writer's intention. (C) is incorrect because although there may be no word-for-word equivalents, that is a general problem of translation, not just a problem of translating Japanese into English. (D) is incorrect because the handicap is not related to the expectations of the reader. (E) is obviously incorrect since the problem is related to translation and has nothing to do with the problems of a Japanese reader reading in Japanese. The example quote by the author is obviously a translator's attempt to make the English sound "oriental," or what a Western audience thinks "oriental" sounds like. So (A) is the correct response.

QUANTITATIVE SECTION

1. $121,212 + (2 \times 10^4) =$

   Ⓐ 321,212 Ⓑ 141,212 Ⓒ 123,212
   Ⓓ 121,412 Ⓔ 121,232

   (B) $2 \times 10^4 = 20,000$, and $121,212 + 20,000 = 141,212$

2. If $6x + 3 = 21$, then $2x + 1 =$

   Ⓐ 2 Ⓑ 3 Ⓒ 4 Ⓓ 6 Ⓔ 7

   (E) Solve for x:

   $6x + 3 = 21$

   $6x = 18$

   $x = 3$

   So $2x + 1 = 2(3) + 1 = 7$.

3. Jack, Ken, Larry, and Mike are j, k, l, and m years old, respectively. If $j < k < l < m$, which of the following *could* be true?

   Ⓐ $k = j + l$
   Ⓑ $j = k + l$
   Ⓒ $j + k = l + m$
   Ⓓ $j + k + m = l$
   Ⓔ $j + m = k + l$

   (E) You can reason in general terms to the correct answer. As for (A), since k is less than l, k cannot be equal to l plus something. The same reasoning applies to (B), (C), and (D). (E), however, could be true. For example, if Jack is 5 and Ken is 10 and Larry is 15 and Mike is 20, then $5 + 20 = 10 + 15$.

4. Bob and Carol took out installment loans to purchase cars. Which loan has the greater outstanding balance?

   (1) Bob borrowed $5,000 for two years at 2.5% interest.

   (2) Carol borrowed $6,000 for three years at 3% interest.

   Ⓐ statement 1 alone is sufficient to answer the question, but statement 2 alone is not sufficient
   Ⓑ statement 2 alone is sufficient to answer the question, but statement 1 alone is not sufficient
   Ⓒ both statements together are needed to answer the question, but neither statement alone is sufficient
   Ⓓ either statement by itself is sufficient to answer the question
   Ⓔ not enough facts are given to answer the question

   (E) Although the two statements provide information about the amount borrowed and the terms of the loans, neither statement provides any information about the amount of the loan that remains unpaid.

5. Is $x = 0$?

   (1) $x \cdot y = x$

   (2) $x + y = y$

   Ⓐ statement 1 alone is sufficient to answer the question, but statement 2 alone is not sufficient
   Ⓑ statement 2 alone is sufficient to answer the question, but statement 1 alone is not sufficient
   Ⓒ both statements together are needed to answer the question, but neither statement alone is sufficient
   Ⓓ either statement by itself is sufficient to answer the question
   Ⓔ not enough facts are given to answer the question

   (B) (1) is not sufficient to answer the question. While it is true that x could be 0 ($0 \cdot y = 0$), x could also be any number, provided that y is 1 ($x \cdot 1 = x$). (2) is sufficient to answer the question:

   $x + y = y$

   $x = 0$

6. Of the following, which is greater than $\frac{1}{2}$?

(A) $\frac{9}{19}$ (B) $\frac{7}{15}$ (C) $\frac{4}{9}$ (D) $\frac{6}{11}$ (E) $\frac{3}{7}$

(D) Use $\frac{1}{2}$ as a benchmark, and reason in this way: Eliminate (A), since $\frac{9}{18} = \frac{1}{2}$, $\frac{9}{19}$ is less than $\frac{1}{2}$. Continue eliminating choices until you are left with (D).

7. Out of a group of 360 students, exactly 18 are on the track team. What percent of the students are on the track team?

(A) 5%   (B) 10%   (C) 12%   (D) 20%   (E) 25%

(A) Use the "this-of-that" strategy:

$$\frac{\text{this}}{\text{that}} = \frac{\text{students on track team}}{\text{total students}} = \frac{18}{360} =$$
$$\frac{1}{20} = 5\%$$

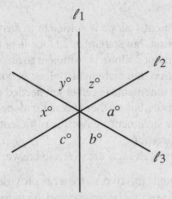

8. In the figure above, three lines intersect as shown. Which of the following must be true?

 I. $a = x$

 II. $y + z = b + c$

 III. $x + a = y + b$

(A) I only   (B) II only   (C) I and II only
(D) I and III only   (E) I, II, and III

(C) Equation I must be true because a and x are vertically opposite each other. Similarly, II must be true because y and b are equal and z and c are equal. III, however, is not necessarily true. x and a are equal and y and b are equal, but you don't have information on which to base a conclusion about the relationship between x and y or that between a and b.

9. A certain mix of nuts contains only pecans, walnuts, and cashews. How many pounds of pecans are contained in 12 pounds of the mix?

 (1) The weight of the pecans in the mix is equal to the weight of the cashews.

 (2) By weight, the mix is $\frac{1}{6}$ walnuts and $\frac{5}{12}$ cashews.

(A) statement 1 alone is sufficient to answer the question, but statement 2 alone is not sufficient

(B) statement 2 alone is sufficient to answer the question, but statement 1 alone is not sufficient

(C) both statements together are needed to answer the question, but neither statement alone is sufficient

(D) either statement by itself is sufficient to answer the question

(E) not enough facts are given to answer the question

(B) (1) is not sufficient to answer the question, for it provides no information about the portion of the mix that is walnuts. For example, the mix could consist of 11 pounds of walnuts and $\frac{1}{2}$ pound each of pecans and cashews, or the mix could consist of 4 pounds of each type of nut. (2), however, is by itself sufficient to answer the question. Since there are only three types of nuts in the mix, (2) implies that $1 - \left(\frac{1}{6} + \frac{5}{12}\right) = \frac{5}{12}$, by weight, is pecans. The batch of the mix contains $\frac{5}{12} \times 12 = 5$ pounds of pecans.

10. Is Z an odd integer?

 (1) $\frac{Z}{3}$ is an odd integer.

 (2) $3Z$ is an odd integer.

(A) statement 1 alone is sufficient to answer the question, but statement 2 alone is not sufficient

(B) statement 2 alone is sufficient to answer the question, but statement 1 alone is not sufficient

(C) both statements together are needed to answer the question, but neither statement alone is sufficient

(D) either statement by itself is sufficient to answer the question

(E) not enough facts are given to answer the question

(A) (1) is sufficient to answer the question. Since $\frac{Z}{3}$ is an odd integer, Z is equal to 3 times an odd integer; and the product of an odd integer and another odd integer is also odd. So Z is odd. (2), by itself, is not sufficient to answer the question. Although Z might be an odd integer, Z might also be a fraction ($3(\frac{5}{3}) = 5$).

11. The average (arithmetic mean) height of four buildings is 20 meters. If three of the buildings have a height of 16 meters, what is the height, in meters, of the fourth building?

(A) 32   (B) 28   (C) 24   (D) 22   (E) 18

(A) Use the method for finding the missing element of an average. Since the average height of all four buildings is 20, the sum of the heights of all four is $4 \times 20 = 80$. The three known heights total $3 \times 16 = 48$. So the missing value is $80 - 48 = 32$.

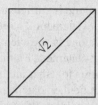

12. The perimeter of the square above is

Ⓐ 1   Ⓑ $\sqrt{2}$ Ⓒ 4   Ⓓ $4\sqrt{2}$ Ⓔ 8

(C) The diagonal of a square creates an isosceles right triangle, so the side of the square is equal to $\frac{1}{2} \times \sqrt{2} \times \sqrt{2} = 1$. Since the side has a length of 1, the perimeter of the square is $4(1) = 4$

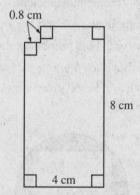

13. The figure above is a scale drawing of the floor of a dining hall. If 1 centimeter on the drawing represents 5 meters, what is the area, in square meters, of the floor?

Ⓐ 144   Ⓑ 156   Ⓒ 784   Ⓓ 796   Ⓔ 800

(C) If the floor were a perfect rectangle, it would have a width of $4 \times 5 = 20$ meters, a length of $8 \times 5 = 40$ meters, and a total area of $20 \times 40 = 800$ square meters. But the floor is not a perfect rectangle. Its actual area is smaller.

Subtract the area of the missing "corner." It has actual dimensions of $0.8 \times 5 = 4$, so its actual area is $16.800 - 16 = 784$.

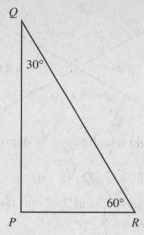

14. In triangle *PQR* shown above, what is the length of *QP*?

(1) $PR = 6$

(2) $QR = 12$

Ⓐ statement 1 alone is sufficient to answer the question, but statement 2 alone is not sufficient

Ⓑ statement 2 alone is sufficient to answer the question, but statement 1 alone is not sufficient

Ⓒ both statements together are needed to answer the question, but neither statement alone is sufficient

Ⓓ either statement by itself is sufficient to answer the question

Ⓔ not enough facts are given to answer the question

(D) This is a 30°-60°-90° triangle, so the sides must be in the ratio of $1 : \sqrt{3} : 2$. Therefore, if you know the length of any side, you can determine the length of the other two sides. Thus, (1) implies that $QP = 6\sqrt{3}$, and (2) implies that $QP = 6\sqrt{3}$. So each statement is, by itself, sufficient to answer the question asked.

15. If *N* is an integer greater than 1,000, what is the value of the units digit of *N*?

(1) *N* is divisible by 12.

(2) *N* is a power of 6.

Ⓐ statement 1 alone is sufficient to answer the question, but statement 2 alone is not sufficient

Ⓑ statement 2 alone is sufficient to answer the question, but statement 1 alone is not sufficient

Ⓒ both statements together are needed to answer the question, but neither statement alone is sufficient

Ⓓ either statement by itself is sufficient to answer the question

Ⓔ not enough facts are given to answer the question

(B) (1) is not sufficient, for a number divisible by 12 could have any even number (including zero) as its units digit. (2), however, is sufficient to answer the question. Every power of 6 has 6 as its units digit, e.g., $6^2 = 36$, $6^3 = 216$, etc.

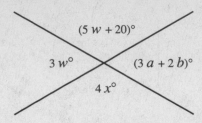

16. If two straight lines intersect as shown, what is the value of x?

    Ⓐ 15   Ⓑ 30   Ⓒ 45   Ⓓ 60   Ⓔ 75

    (B) The angles labeled $3w°$ *and* $(5w + 20)°$ form a straight line:

    $3w + (5w + 20) = 180$

    $8w + 20 = 180$

    $8w = 160$

    $w = 20$

    And the angles labeled $3w°$ and $4x°$ also form a straight line:

    $3w + 4x = 180$

    $3(20) + 4x = 180$

    $60 + 4x = 180$

    $4x = 120$

    $x = 30$

    You can also guestimate the value of x. The angle labeled $4x$ appears to be 120°, so x must be about 30°.

17. If $2x + 3y = 19$ and x and y are positive integers, x could be equal to which of the following?

    Ⓐ 3   Ⓑ 4   Ⓒ 5   Ⓓ 6   Ⓔ 7

    (C) You might reason that the only permissible values for x are those which, when multiplied by 2 and subtracted from 19, yield a number that is divisible by 3. That's a lot of reasoning. Just "test the test." Try (A). If x is 3, then $2x$ is 6, and $3y = 13$. But then y cannot be an integer, so (A) is wrong. The correct answer is (C). If x is 5, then $3y = 9$, and $y = 3$, an integer.

18. A school club spent $\frac{2}{5}$ of its budget for one project and $\frac{1}{3}$ of what remained for another project. If the club's entire budget was equal to $300, how much of the budget was left after the two projects?

    Ⓐ $60   Ⓑ $90   Ⓒ $120   Ⓓ $180   Ⓔ $240

    (C) If the club spent $\frac{2}{5}$ of the budget on the first project, it was left with $\frac{3}{5}$ of $300 = $180. If it spent $\frac{1}{3}$ of $180, it was left with $180 - $60 = $120.

19. Is $\frac{a}{b}$ an integer?

    (1) $\frac{4a}{b}$ is an integer.

    (2) $\frac{4b}{a}$ is an integer.

    Ⓐ statement 1 alone is sufficient to answer the question, but statement 2 alone is not sufficient
    Ⓑ statement 2 alone is sufficient to answer the question, but statement 1 alone is not sufficient
    Ⓒ both statements together are needed to answer the question, but neither statement alone is sufficient
    Ⓓ either statement by itself is sufficient to answer the question
    Ⓔ not enough facts are given to answer the question

    (E) Neither statement alone is sufficient to answer the question. A number of the form $\frac{4a}{b}$ may be an integer $\left(\frac{4(2)}{4}\right)$, even though $\frac{a}{b}$ is not an integer $\left(\frac{2}{4}\right)$. Nor are both statements together sufficient. $\frac{a}{b}$ might be an integer; for example, if $a = 2$ and $b = 1$ (and these values are consistent with both numbered statements), then $\frac{a}{b}$ is an integer. But if $a = 1$ and $b = 2$ (values also consistent with both numbered statements), then $\frac{a}{b}$ is not an integer.

20. The figure above shows a square inscribed in a circle. What is the area of the shaded part of the figure?

    (1) The area of the square is 8.

    (2) The area of the circle is 4π.

    Ⓐ statement 1 alone is sufficient to answer the question, but statement 2 alone is not sufficient
    Ⓑ statement 2 alone is sufficient to answer the question, but statement 1 alone is not sufficient
    Ⓒ both statements together are needed to answer the question, but neither statement alone is sufficient
    Ⓓ either statement by itself is sufficient to answer the question
    Ⓔ not enough facts are given to answer the question

    (D) This problem underscores the importance of examining each statement independently of the other. The shaded portion of the figure has an area equal to that of the circle minus that of the square, but you don't need both statements to find the value of the shaded area. (1) is, by itself, sufficient to answer the question, for (1) implies that the side of the square is $2\sqrt{2}$, so the diagonal of the square must be 4. Since the diagonal of the square is also the diameter of the circle, the circle has an area of 4π. The shaded area is $4\pi - 8$. (2) by itself, is also sufficient. (2) implies that the radius of the circle is 2. Since the diameter of the circle is also the diagonal of the square, the diagonal of the square is 4. If the diagonal of the square is 4, then the side of the square is $2\sqrt{2}$, and the area of the square is 8. Again, we reach the conclusion that the shaded area is $4\pi - 8$.

Since each statement alone is sufficient to answer the question, this item should be classified as a (D). If you missed this item by selecting (C), remember to study each statement in isolation before you start asking whether the statements work together to provide an answer.

21. If the cost of N nails is C cents, what is the cost *in dollars* of X nails?

Ⓐ $100CX$ Ⓑ $\dfrac{100CX}{N}$ Ⓒ $\dfrac{100NX}{C}$

Ⓓ $\dfrac{NX}{100C}$ Ⓔ $\dfrac{CX}{100N}$

(E) You can create a formula by setting up a direct proportion:

$$\frac{N}{C} = \frac{X}{100z}$$

Where z is the cost of N nails in dollars:

$100zN = CX$

$z = \dfrac{CX}{100N}$

Or, you can use the technique of assuming some values for the variables.

22. If $a^2b^3c < 0$, which of the following must be true?

Ⓐ $b^3 < 0$ Ⓑ $b^2c < 0$ Ⓒ $b < 0$
Ⓓ $c < 0$ Ⓔ $bc < 0$

(E) Since the expression is less than zero, either one or the other of the factors must be negative. a^2 cannot be negative. So either b^3 is negative or c is negative, but not both. And this means either b or c is negative, but not both. So bc must be negative. You can eliminate (A), (B), (C), and (D) since they might be, but are not necessarily, true.

23. During a certain shift, a quality control inspector inspected 6 out of every 30 items produced. What was the ratio of inspected to uninspected items during that shift?

Ⓐ 1:4   Ⓑ 1:5   Ⓒ 1:6   Ⓓ 5:1   Ⓔ 6:1

(A) Since 6 items out of 30 are inspected, $30 - 6 = 24$ are not inspected, and the ratio 6:24 is equal to 1:4.

24. In a group of 18 professional drivers, some have a chauffeur's license, some have a taxi license, and some have both. How many members of the group have both a chauffeur's license and a taxi license?

(1) Twice as many members of the group have a taxi license as have a chauffeur's license.

(2) Eight members of the group have a chauffeur's license.

Ⓐ statement 1 alone is sufficient to answer the question, but statement 2 alone is not sufficient

Ⓑ statement 2 alone is sufficient to answer the question, but statement 1 alone is not sufficient

Ⓒ both statements together are needed to answer the question, but neither statement alone is sufficient

Ⓓ either statement by itself is sufficient to answer the question

Ⓔ not enough facts are given to answer the question

(C) (1) alone is not sufficient to answer the question, for it provides no information about the number of people who have which licenses. It is possible that seven people have a chauffeur's license and 14 people a taxi license, or that eight people have a chauffeur's license and 16 people a taxi license, or that nine people have a chauffeur's license and 18 people a taxi license. Nor is (2) alone sufficient since (2) provides no information about the number of taxi licenses. The two statements together do provide enough information to answer the question. If eight people have a chauffeur's license, then 16 people have a taxi license. That is a total of 24 licenses held by a group of only 18 people. Therefore, $24 - 18 = 6$ people who hold two licenses.

25. n is a positive integer. What is the remainder when n is divided by 6?

(1) n is a multiple of 3.

(2) When n is divided by 2, the remainder is 1.

Ⓐ statement 1 alone is sufficient to answer the question, but statement 2 alone is not sufficient

Ⓑ statement 2 alone is sufficient to answer the question, but statement 1 alone is not sufficient

Ⓒ both statements together are needed to answer the question, but neither statement alone is sufficient

Ⓓ either statement by itself is sufficient to answer the question

Ⓔ not enough facts are given to answer the question

(C) (1) alone is not sufficient to answer the question. Since $6 = 2 \times 3$, some multiples of 3 are divisible by 6, in which case the remainder is zero; and other multiples of 3 are not divisible by 6, in which case the result of dividing by 3 includes a remainder of 3. Nor is (2) alone sufficient, for (2) implies only that n is odd. Although no odd number is divisible by 6 (because $6 = 2 \times 3$ and any number divisible by 2 is even), the remainder that results from division by 6 depends on the odd number divided. The remainder when 9 is divided by 6 is 3, but the remainder when 11 is divided by 6 is 5. Both statements together, however, do answer the question. If n is an odd multiple of 3, then the remainder when n is divided by 6 must be 3.

26. For which of the following pairs of numbers is it true that their sum is 9 times their product?

    Ⓐ $1, \dfrac{1}{9}$ Ⓑ $1, \dfrac{1}{8}$ Ⓒ $1, \dfrac{1}{19}$ Ⓓ $1, 8$ Ⓔ $1, 9$

    (B) Just test the choices. The sum of 1 and $\frac{1}{8}$ is $\frac{9}{8}$ which is 9 times the product of 1 and $\frac{1}{8}$, which is $\frac{1}{8}$.

27. The price of a book, after it was reduced by one-third, is B dollars. What was the price of the book, in dollars, before the reduction?

    Ⓐ $\dfrac{2B}{3}$ Ⓑ $\dfrac{3B}{4}$ Ⓒ $\dfrac{6B}{5}$ Ⓓ $\dfrac{4B}{3}$ Ⓔ $\dfrac{3B}{2}$

    (E) You can set up an equation here:

    $$\text{Original price} - \frac{1}{3}\,\text{Original price} = B$$

    $$O - \frac{1}{3}O = B$$

    $$\frac{2}{3}O = B$$

    $$O = \frac{3B}{2}$$

    Or you can assume some numbers, a technique we have used often.

28. Y years ago, Tom was three times as old as Julie was. If Julie is now 20 years old, how old is Tom in terms of Y?

    Ⓐ $60 + 2Y$ Ⓑ $30 + 2Y$ Ⓒ $30 - 2Y$
    Ⓓ $60 - 2Y$ Ⓔ $60 - 3Y$

    (D) You can set up the formula by reasoning as follows. Tom's age minus Y years is equal to three times Julie's age, minus Y years:

    $$T - Y = 3(20 - Y)$$

    $$T - Y = 60 - 3Y$$

    $$T = 60 - 2Y$$

    You can reach the same conclusion by assuming some values and substituting them into the formulas.

29. Is $n > 1$?

    (1) $1 > \dfrac{1}{n}$

    (2) $n > 0$

    Ⓐ statement 1 alone is sufficient to answer the question, but statement 2 alone is not sufficient
    Ⓑ statement 2 alone is sufficient to answer the question, but statement 1 alone is not sufficient
    Ⓒ both statements together are needed to answer the question, but neither statement alone is sufficient
    Ⓓ either statement by itself is sufficient to answer the question
    Ⓔ not enough facts are given to answer the question

    (C) (1) is not sufficient to answer the question. n might be a negative number. (Don't make the mistake of multiplying that inequality by n, because you don't know whether or not n is positive.) Nor is (2) by itself sufficient. Both statements taken together do answer the question. Given that n is positive, you can manipulate the inequality in (1):

    $$1 > \frac{1}{n}$$

    $$n > 1$$

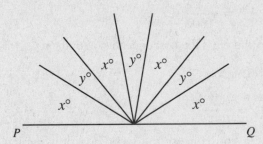

30. In the figure above, PQ is a line segment. What is the value of x?

    (1) $x - y = 10$

    (2) $y = 20$

    Ⓐ statement 1 alone is sufficient to answer the question, but statement 2 alone is not sufficient
    Ⓑ statement 2 alone is sufficient to answer the question, but statement 1 alone is not sufficient
    Ⓒ both statements together are needed to answer the question, but neither statement alone is sufficient
    Ⓓ either statement by itself is sufficient to answer the question
    Ⓔ not enough facts are given to answer the question

    (D) Since PQ is a line segment, the figure implies

    $$x + y + x + y + x + y + x = 180$$

    $$4x + 3y = 180$$

(1), when coupled with the information provided by the figure, is sufficient to answer the question, for we have two equations and only two variables:

$x - y = 10$

$x - 10 = y$

$4x + 3(x - 10) = 180$

$7x - 30 = 180$

$7x = 210$

$x = 30$

(2) is also sufficient by the same reasoning:

$4x + 3(20) = 180$

$4x = 120$

$x = 30$

31. If S is the sum of x consecutive integers, S must be even if x is a multiple of

Ⓐ 6   Ⓑ 5   Ⓒ 4   Ⓓ 3   Ⓔ 2

(C) The sum of four consecutive integers must always be even. You have two even numbers and an odd number added to an odd number, which yields another even number.

32. One pound of peanuts is added to a bin containing only cashews, and the resulting nut mix is 20 percent peanuts by weight. How many more pounds of peanuts must be added to the bin to create a mix that is 60 percent peanuts, by weight?

Ⓐ 2   Ⓑ 3   Ⓒ 4.75   Ⓓ 5   Ⓔ 5.25

(D) First, find the weight of the cashews in the existing mix. To do this, create an equation to express the idea "one pound of peanuts is equal to 20% of the combined weight of the peanuts and the cashews":

$1 = 0.2 (1 + C)$

$1 = 0.2 + 0.2C$

$0.2C = 0.8$

$C = 4$

The existing mix contains 4 pounds of cashews and 1 pound of peanuts. Next, set up an equation to express the idea "How many pounds of peanuts when combined with the peanuts already in the mix will equal 60% of the combined weight of the cashews, the peanuts already in the mix, plus the peanuts added to the mix?":

$P + 1 = 0.60(P + 1 + 4)$

$P + 1 = 0.6P + 3$

$0.4P = 2$

$P = 5$

33. If $x^5 = 4$ and $x^4 = \dfrac{5}{y}$, then what is x in terms of y?

Ⓐ $20y$ Ⓑ $\dfrac{25y}{16}$ Ⓒ $\dfrac{5y}{4}$ Ⓓ y Ⓔ $\dfrac{4y}{5}$

(E) Here you are asked to express x in terms of y. If you start trying to work with fifth and fourth roots, you will soon find that you're getting nowhere. Look for a way to make a direct substitution. If you only had x^4 in the first equation rather than x^5, things would be easy, so rewrite the first equation. Factor x^5 into x times x^4. The first equation can be rewritten:

$x(x^4) = 4$

$x^4 = \dfrac{4}{x}$

Now make a direct substitution of $\dfrac{4}{x}$ for x^4 in the second equation:

$\dfrac{4}{x} = \dfrac{5}{y}$

$4y = 5x$

$x = \dfrac{4y}{5}$

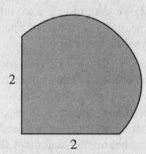

34. If the figure above is composed of a semicircle and a right triangle, what is the area of the shaded region?

Ⓐ $\pi + \sqrt{2}$ Ⓑ $\pi + 2$ Ⓒ $2\pi + 1$
Ⓓ $\sqrt{2\pi} + 1$ Ⓔ $\sqrt{2\pi} + \sqrt{2}$

(B) This is a composite figure of a 45°-45°-90° triangle plus a semicircle. The shaded area is the sum of the area of the triangle and the area of the semicircle.

First, calculate the area of the triangle. Since this is a right triangle, you can use the two sides forming the right angle as altitude and base: area of triangle =

$\dfrac{1}{2} \times 2 \times 2 = \dfrac{1}{2} \times 4 = 2.$

The diameter of the circle is the hypotenuse of that triangle, and the hypotenuse of a 45°-45°-90° triangle is equal to the length of the side times $\sqrt{2}$. The hypotenuse is therefore equal to $2 \times \sqrt{2} = 2\sqrt{2}$. The diameter of the semicircle is $2\sqrt{2}$, so the radius is $\sqrt{2}$. The area of an entire circle with that radius is $\pi\left(\sqrt{2}\right)^2 = 2\pi$. But the figure is a semicircle with an area only half that of a full circle: $2\pi \div 2 = \pi$.

Thus, the area of the composite figure is $\pi + 2$.

There are two ways of "meastimating" the correct answer. You can use the value of 2 to "meastimate" the length of the radius of the semicircle. And here's an even neater trick. The semicircle must have an area slightly larger than that of the triangle:

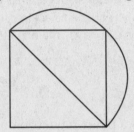

This means that the composite figure has an area somewhat more than 5. That has to be choice (B).

35. Profits of corporation X over a three-year period averaged \$1.2 million. If the corporation had profits in all three years, in which of the years were profits the greatest?

(1) In the third year, the profits of corporation X were twice the average of its profits for the first two years.

(2) Profits of corporation X were three times as great in the second year and four times as great in the third year as in the first.

Ⓐ statement 1 alone is sufficient to answer the question, but statement 2 alone is not sufficient

Ⓑ statement 2 alone is sufficient to answer the question, but statement 1 alone is not sufficient

Ⓒ both statements together are needed to answer the question, but neither statement alone is sufficient

Ⓓ either statement by itself is sufficient to answer the question

Ⓔ not enough facts are given to answer the question

(D) (1) is sufficient to answer the question. (1) implies

$$\text{Third Year} = 2\left(\frac{\text{First Year} + \text{Second Year}}{2}\right)$$

Third Year = First Year + Second Year

Therefore, profits in the third year were greater than those in the other two years. Similarly, (2) is also sufficient. (2) establishes

Second Year = 3 × First Year

Third Year = 4 × First Year

So the profits in the third year were the greatest.

36. In the correct addition shown above, the symbols represent different nonzero digits. What is the number represented by ● ◆?

(1) ■ = 2 × ▲

(2) 10 ● + ◆ = 95

Ⓐ statement 1 alone is sufficient to answer the question, but statement 2 alone is not sufficient

Ⓑ statement 2 alone is sufficient to answer the question, but statement 1 alone is not sufficient

Ⓒ both statements together are needed to answer the question, but neither statement alone is sufficient

Ⓓ either statement by itself is sufficient to answer the question

Ⓔ not enough facts are given to answer the question

(B) This question may seem a little less strange if we do away with the funny symbols and instead use a for ■, b for ▲, c for ●, and d for ◆. The question stem implies

$(10a + 2) + (30 + b) = 10c + d$

(1) is not sufficient to answer the question, for even substituting $2b$ for a, we still have an equation with three variables. (2), however, is sufficient, for (2) implies that ● = 9 and ◆ = 5, so ●◆ = 95.

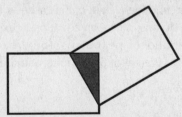

37. In the figure above, two rectangles, each with the same dimensions, overlap. If the perimeter of each rectangle is 28, what is the total length of the heavy-line segments?

(1) The shaded region has an area of 4.

(2) The shaded region has a perimeter of 12.

Ⓐ statement 1 alone is sufficient to answer the question, but statement 2 alone is not sufficient

Ⓑ statement 2 alone is sufficient to answer the question, but statement 1 alone is not sufficient

Ⓒ both statements together are needed to answer the question, but neither statement alone is sufficient

Ⓓ either statement by itself is sufficient to answer the question

Ⓔ not enough facts are given to answer the question

(B) (1) alone is not sufficient, since (1) provides no information about the perimeter of the shaded part of the figure. (2), however, is sufficient. The length of the heavy-line segments is equal to the combined perimeters of the two rectangles minus the perimeter of the shaded area:

$2 \times 28 - 12 = 44$

Sample GMAT
CAT 5

Verbal Section

41 Questions—75 Minutes

1. Ballet dancers warm up before each performance by doing a series of pliés and stretching exercises, and it reduces the chance of injury.

    (A) exercises, and it reduces
    (B) exercises, which reduces
    (C) exercises, reducing
    (D) exercises; the routine reduces
    (E) exercises, so the routine reduces

2. Unlike the French, the German art songs are dramatic and sometimes almost operatic.

    (A) Unlike the French, the German art songs are dramatic and sometimes almost operatic.
    (B) Unlike the French art songs, the German art songs are dramatic and sometimes almost operatic.
    (C) The German art songs, unlike the French, are dramatic and sometimes almost operatic.
    (D) The German art songs are dramatic and sometimes almost operatic, unlike the French.
    (E) The German art songs, which are dramatic and sometimes almost operatic, are unlike the French.

3. An airline may overbook a flight to ensure a full passenger load, but it is required to pay compensation to any passenger who cannot be accommodated on that flight.

    (A) to ensure a full passenger load, but it is required to pay compensation to
    (B) ensuring a full passenger load, but it is required to pay compensation to
    (C) to ensure a full passenger load, since compensation is required to
    (D) to ensure a full passenger load, which is required to pay compensation to
    (E) to ensure a full passenger load and pay compensation to

GO ON TO NEXT PAGE

In an attempt to predict the future course of consumer spending, *Investment Monthly* magazine surveyed its readers. Of those surveyed, over 60 percent reported that they planned to buy a new automobile or at least one major appliance within the next three months. From these results, the magazine concluded that consumer spending for the next quarter was likely to be high.

4. Which of the following, if true, would most weaken the conclusion above?

    Ⓐ The cost of a new automobile is much greater than that of a major appliance.

    Ⓑ A person who plans to make a major purchase at some time in the future may not yet have settled on a brand.

    Ⓒ The readers of *Investment Monthly* are more affluent than the average consumer.

    Ⓓ Some of the items to be purchased will be imports and will not stimulate markets in the United States.

    Ⓔ Not all readers of *Investment Monthly* magazine responded to the survey.

Questions 5–6

Every member of the New York Burros, a team in the Big Apple Softball League, who wears wristbands when batting wears either red wristbands or white wristbands.

5. If the statement above is true, which of the following must be true?

    I. A member of the New York Burros who does not wear red wristbands while batting wears white wristbands while batting.

    II. No member of the New York Burros wears blue wristbands while batting.

    III. Some members of the New York Burros do not wear wristbands when batting.

    Ⓐ I only   Ⓑ II only   Ⓒ III only
    Ⓓ I and III only   Ⓔ I, II, and III

6. If any player in the Big Apple Softball League who wears red wristbands while batting also wears blue batting gloves, and if no member of the New York Burros wears blue batting gloves, which of the following must be true?

    Ⓐ Every member of the New York Burros wears white wristbands when batting.

    Ⓑ No member of the New York Burros wears blue batting gloves.

    Ⓒ Some members of the New York Burros wear red wristbands when batting.

    Ⓓ Some members of the New York Burros do not wear batting gloves.

    Ⓔ Every member of the New York Burros who wears wristbands wears white wristbands when batting.

Questions 7–9

One continuing problem in labor-management relations is the "us/them" mentality. In addition to fiscal constraints, continuing problems with the Fair Labor Standards Act, bad faith negotiations, bad management practices, poor union leadership, and a continued loss of management prerogatives will all combine to produce forces which will cause a significant increase in disruptive job actions in the near future. Neither side is blameless. The tragedy of the situation is that the impact of poor labor management relations is relatively predictable and is thus avoidable.

Since the economic situation will not improve significantly in the next few years, the pressure on the part of union leaders to obtain more benefits for their members will be frustrated. As a result of the PATCO strike, management has learned that times are conducive to regaining prerogatives lost during the previous decade. The stage for confrontation between labor and management in the public sector is set, and in many areas, only requires an incident to force disruptive job actions. The only solution to this seemingly intractable problem lies in the area of skilled negotiations and good faith bargaining. This requires commitment on the part of management and labor to live up to the terms of existing contracts.

7. It can be inferred that the PATCO strike

    Ⓐ was an example of bad faith negotiations

    Ⓑ lasted only a brief period

    Ⓒ was the fault of incompetent management

    Ⓓ violated the provisions of the Fair Labor Standards Act

    Ⓔ resulted in a victory for management

8. The author's discussion of labor management relations can best be described as

    Ⓐ extremely pro-labor

    Ⓑ mildly pro-labor

    Ⓒ neutral

    Ⓓ mildly pro-management

    Ⓔ extremely pro-management

9. The author implies that if the economic conditions improve,

    Ⓐ management will lose much of its power

    Ⓑ labor leaders will not seek more benefits

    Ⓒ labor-management tensions will decline

    Ⓓ the Fair Labor Standards Act will be repealed

    Ⓔ labor will win a voice in management

10. It is typical of the high soprano voice, <u>like</u> the highest voices within each vocal range, to be lighter in weight and more flexible.

    Ⓐ like

    Ⓑ as

    Ⓒ like it is of

    Ⓓ as it is of

    Ⓔ similar to

11. The earliest texts in cuneiform script are about 5,000 years old, having antedated the use of the first alphabets by some 1,500 years.

    Ⓐ old, having antedated the use
    Ⓑ old, having antedated the invention
    Ⓒ old, antedating the use
    Ⓓ old and antedate the use
    Ⓔ old and antedate the invention

12. After her admission to the bar, Margaret, herself a childless attorney's only daughter, specialized in adoption and family law.

    Ⓐ Margaret, herself a childless attorney's only daughter
    Ⓑ Margaret herself, a childless attorney's only daughter
    Ⓒ Margaret, herself the childless and only daughter of an attorney
    Ⓓ Margaret, only a childless attorney's daughter herself
    Ⓔ Margaret, herself, only a daughter of a childless attorney

A bill now pending before the Congress would give physicians the option of prescribing heroin as a painkiller for terminally ill patients. The Congress should refuse to pass the bill because there is a serious danger that the heroin would be stolen and wind up being sold on the streets.

13. Which of the following, if true, would most weaken the argument above?

    Ⓐ Other prescription painkillers are available for terminally ill patients that in most cases provide relief of pain as effective as that provided by heroin.
    Ⓑ The addictive effects of heroin are inconsequential considering that the patients who would be scheduled for treatment are terminally ill.
    Ⓒ The amount of heroin that would be required for terminally ill patients is insignificant when compared with the amount of heroin sold illegally.
    Ⓓ Heroin sold illegally varies widely in quality and purity and can easily cause death by overdose because it is taken without proper measurement.
    Ⓔ Over the past five years, the number of deaths attributable to heroin overdose has declined slightly, but the total number of deaths by drug overdose has increased significantly because of increased use of cocaine.

It used to be said that artistic creativity is the province solely of human beings and that it is, in fact, one of the marks that distinguishes humans from all other creatures. Today, cleverly programmed computers can create images that are indistinguishable from paintings by contemporary abstract artists. Thus, the traditional argument that artistic creativity is the province of humans is proved incorrect.

14. Which of the following, if true, most weakens the argument above?

    Ⓐ Most human beings have never produced a creative work that others would regard as a work of art.
    Ⓑ The image produced by a computer is an image that it was directed to create by the human programmer.
    Ⓒ Many people are unfamiliar with abstract art and so are unable to distinguish good modern art from bad modern art.
    Ⓓ Human beings engage in many activities other than the creation of art, activities such as production, warfare, and building.
    Ⓔ A program designed to produce a computerized image will produce the same image on any computer that can accept the program.

The right to work under humane conditions is a fundamental right of all people. Therefore, all men and women have the right to a job and to decent conditions of employment.

15. Which of the following arguments most closely parallels the reasoning of the argument above?

    Ⓐ The expression of anger is a natural instinct of human beings who feel threatened. Therefore, Smith is not to be blamed for expressing anger when she felt threatened.
    Ⓑ Johnson is one of the most honest legislative leaders ever to serve this state. Therefore, Johnson could not have committed the dishonest acts of which he has been accused.
    Ⓒ The Bill of Rights protects the free practice of religion in this country. Therefore, all people have the right to worship God in a manner of their own choosing.
    Ⓓ Children are human beings who have the potential for adult behavior. Therefore, any right or privilege that is granted to adults ought, in fairness, to be granted to children as well.
    Ⓔ The President has the duty of defending the country from any external enemy. Therefore, the President acted properly in ordering our army to repel the invading forces.

GO ON TO NEXT PAGE ⇨

Questions 16–18

Behavior is one of two general responses available to endothermic (warm-blooded) species for the regulation of body temperature, the other being innate (reflexive) mechanisms of heat production and heat loss. Human beings rely primarily on the first to provide a hospitable thermal microclimate for themselves, in which the transfer of heat between the body and the environment is accomplished with minimal involvement of innate mechanisms of heat production and loss. Thermoregulatory behavior *anticipates* hypothermia, and the organism adjusts its behavior to avoid becoming hypothermic: it removes layers of clothing, it goes for a cool swim, etc. The organism can also respond to changes in the temperature of the body core, as is the case during exercise; but such responses result from the direct stimulation of thermoreceptors distributed widely within the central nervous system, and the ability of these mechanisms to help the organism adjust to gross changes in its environment is limited.

Until recently it was assumed that organisms respond to microwave radiation in the same way that they respond to temperature changes caused by other forms of radiation. After all, the argument runs, microwaves are radiation and heat body tissues. This theory ignores the fact that the stimulus to a behavioral response is normally a temperature change that occurs at the surface of the organism. The thermoreceptors that prompt behavioral changes are located within the first millimeter of the skin's surface, but the energy of a microwave field may be selectively deposited in deep tissues, effectively bypassing these thermoreceptors, particularly if the field is at near-resonant frequencies. The resulting temperature profile may well be a kind of reverse thermal gradient in which the deep tissues are warmed more than those of the surface. Since the heat is not conducted outward to the surface to stimulate the appropriate receptors, the organism does not "appreciate" this stimulation in the same way that it "appreciates" heating and cooling of the skin. In theory, the internal organs of a human being or an animal could be quite literally cooked well-done before the animal even realizes that the balance of its thermomicroclimate has been disturbed.

Until a few years ago, microwave irradiations at equivalent plane-wave power densities of about 100 mW/cm^2 were considered unequivocally to produce "thermal" effects; irradiations within the range of 10 to 100 mW/cm^2 might or might not produce "thermal" effects; while effects observed at power densities below 10 mW/cm^2 were assumed to be "nonthermal" in nature. Experiments have shown this to be an oversimplification, and a recent report suggests that fields as weak as 1 mW/cm^2 can be thermogenic. When the heat generated in the tissues by an imposed radio frequency (plus the heat generated by metabolism) exceeds the heat-loss capabilities of the organism, the thermoregulatory system has been compromised. Yet surprisingly, not long ago, an increase in the internal body temperature was regarded merely as "evidence" of a thermal effect.

16. The author is primarily concerned with

(A) showing that behavior is a more effective way of controlling bodily temperature than innate mechanisms

(B) criticizing researchers who will not discard their theories about the effects of microwave radiation on organisms

(C) demonstrating that effects of microwave radiation are different from those of other forms of radiation

(D) analyzing the mechanism by which an organism maintains its bodily temperature in a changing thermal environment

(E) discussing the importance of thermoreceptors in the control of the internal temperature of an organism

17. The author makes which of the following points about innate mechanisms for heat production?

I. They are governed by thermoreceptors inside the body of the organism rather than at the surface.

II. They are a less effective means of compensating for gross changes in temperature than behavioral strategies.

III. They are not affected by microwave radiation.

(A) I only   (B) I and II only   (C) I and III only
(D) II and III only   (E) I, II, and III

18. Which of the following would be the most logical topic for the author to take up in the paragraph following the final paragraph of the selection?

(A) A suggestion for new research to be done on the effects of microwaves on animals and human beings

(B) An analysis of the differences between microwave radiation and other forms of radiation

(C) A proposal that the use of microwave radiation be prohibited because it is dangerous

(D) A survey of the literature on the effects of microwave radiation on human beings

(E) A discussion of the strategies used by various species to control hypothermia

19. A survey of over 1,000 people conducted by a marketing firm determined that people over the age of 40 do not like cherry cola as <u>well as people under the age of 20.</u>

(A) well as people under the age of 20
(B) much as people under the age of 20
(C) many people under the age of 20 do
(D) well than people under the age of 20 do
(E) much as people under the age of 20 do

20. Baker was perhaps not the most gifted soloist in the orchestra, but the conductor felt <u>what was lacking in his technical skill was more than made up by</u> the passion with which he played the music.

 Ⓐ what was lacking in his technical skill was more than made up by

 Ⓑ what he lacked in technical skill was more than made up by

 Ⓒ whatever was lacking in his technical skill was more than made up by

 Ⓓ whatever he lacked in technical skill was more than made up for by

 Ⓔ whatever he lacked in technical skill he more than made up by

21. <u>Although few outside of academe have heard of him today, William Dean Howells</u> was among America's most successful literary critics and novelists.

 Ⓐ Although few outside of academe have heard of him today, William Dean Howells

 Ⓑ However difficult it may be to find someone outside of academe who has heard of him today, William Dean Howells

 Ⓒ As difficult as it is to find someone outside of academe who has heard of him today, William Dean Howells

 Ⓓ William Dean Howells is not heard of by very many outside of academe today, but he

 Ⓔ Although today William Dean Howells is not heard of by very many people outside of academe, he

  Amid great fanfare, the Taxi and Limousine Commission announced last June that a new dress code for taxi drivers would be incorporated into the Commission's rules. After six months, no driver has lost his license or even been fined under the new dress code. Evidently, drivers have chosen to comply with the new dress code.

22. Which of the following, if true, would most weaken the argument above?

 Ⓐ Prior to the announcement of the new dress code, an average of 16 cab drivers each month lost their licenses for various violations of the Commission's rules.

 Ⓑ Inspectors routinely stop cab drivers to inspect licenses, safety, and cleanliness of the vehicle and the driver's record of fares.

 Ⓒ City prosecutors have refused to prosecute drivers cited under the new dress code because they believe that the law is unconstitutional.

 Ⓓ A survey of passengers who say they regularly use taxi cabs shows that 45 percent of the riders don't believe that drivers are better dressed.

 Ⓔ During July and August, the number of cab drivers available for work is less than that during the other months of the year.

Questions 23–24

  The existence of our state's inefficient and wasteful automobile accident liability system can be easily explained. As long as most of our legislators are lawyers, the system will never be reformed, because litigation creates more work for lawyers.

23. Which of the following, if true, would most weaken the argument above?

 Ⓐ Most judges in the state are members of the legal profession as well.

 Ⓑ Few of the state's legislators are among the relatively small percentage of lawyers who handle automobile accident cases.

 Ⓒ Under the customary fee arrangement, a lawyer receives one-third of any monetary award made to a client.

 Ⓓ The state legislature allocates funds to pay for defense attorneys who represent indigent clients.

 Ⓔ Any reform legislation could be vetoed by the governor of the state, who is also an attorney.

24. The argument above rests on the assumption that

 Ⓐ given the opportunity, most lawyers would want to be members of the state legislature.

 Ⓑ legislation to reform the state's automobile accident liability system could be introduced by a legislator who is not a lawyer.

 Ⓒ state laws set minimum fees that attorneys are permitted to charge in cases arising from automobile accidents.

 Ⓓ the state's automobile accident liability system encourages litigation.

 Ⓔ state laws governing the ownership and operation of motor vehicles encourage unsafe driving practices.

Questions 25–27

In 1792, George Washington received the unanimous vote of the electors, Federalist and Republican alike. But the struggle over the vice-presidency hinted at the rekindling of old divisions and antagonism sparked by Alexander Hamilton's system. Southern planters who in 1789 had been eager to cooperate with the moneyed men of the North, parted with them when they realized that the policies designed to benefit Northern merchants and bankers brought no profit to them as landed aristocrats. Although in 1792 they were willing to continue with Washington, they were not as willing to go along with Vice-President John Adams. If the Federalists were to have the first office, then the followers of Jefferson—who had already come to call themselves Republicans in contradistinction to the unpopular term anti-Federalist, insisted that they were to command the second office.

  The Republicans waged a losing campaign for the second office, but the campaign proved that when the

GO ON TO NEXT PAGE ⟩

Republicans became better organized nationally, they would be a power political force. This did not take long. In 1793, England declared war on republican France over the guillotining of Louis XVI, and in 1794 John Jay's treaty seemed to suggest a sympathetic policy toward monarchical and conservative England, instead of republican, liberty-loving France. The treaty gave the Republicans a sense of mission. The contest was now between the Republicans, "lovers of liberty," and the Monocrats.

25. Which of the following titles best describes the content of the passage?

    Ⓐ The Origins of Jefferson's Republican Party
    Ⓑ Jefferson's Defeat in the 1792 Election
    Ⓒ The Legacy of Hamilton's Political System
    Ⓓ Political Differences between the Rich and the Poor
    Ⓔ Political Issues Separating the Federalists and the Republicans

26. According to the passage, all of the following are true of the Republicans EXCEPT

    Ⓐ They opposed the moneyed interests of the North.
    Ⓑ They were led by Thomas Jefferson.
    Ⓒ They disapproved of the French Revolution.
    Ⓓ They and the Federalists supported the same candidate for President in 1792.
    Ⓔ They were initially called Anti-Federalists.

27. The passage implies that Thomas Jefferson was unsuccessful in his 1792 bid for the vice-presidency because the Republican Party

    Ⓐ did not have its own presidential candidate
    Ⓑ was not as well organized as the Federalists
    Ⓒ refused to support John Adams
    Ⓓ appealed to workers in the North
    Ⓔ agreed to support George Washington's bid for the presidency

28. Although the stock market seems to offer the possibility of great personal gain, you must understand that to invest in stocks is accepting the risk of financial ruin as well.

    Ⓐ is accepting the risk of financial ruin as well
    Ⓑ is to accept the risk of financial ruin as well
    Ⓒ is to accept the risk as well as financial ruin
    Ⓓ are accepting the risk of financial ruin as well
    Ⓔ are to accept the risk of financial ruin as well

29. Since the past twenty years, thousands of magnificent United States elms have been killed by infestations of the tiny European bark beetle.

    Ⓐ Since the past twenty years
    Ⓑ Since twenty years have passed
    Ⓒ During the past twenty years
    Ⓓ Twenty years ago
    Ⓔ After twenty years

30. The new biography of Thomas Jefferson contains some startling insights about the man who was the primary author of the Declaration of Independence.

    Ⓐ about the man who was the primary author
    Ⓑ into the man who was the primary author
    Ⓒ into the character of the man who was the primary author
    Ⓓ into the character of a man who was the primary author
    Ⓔ about the man who was primarily the author

Questions 31–32
Premises: All weavers are members of the union.

          Some carders are women.

          Some weavers are women.

          All union members are covered by health insurance.

          No carders are covered by health insurance.

31. All of the following conclusions can be drawn from the statements above EXCEPT

    Ⓐ All weavers are covered by health insurance.
    Ⓑ Some women are covered by health insurance.
    Ⓒ Some women are not covered by health insurance.
    Ⓓ Some members of the union are not covered by health insurance.
    Ⓔ No carders are members of the union.

32. Which of the following workers would provide a counterexample to the statements above?

    Ⓐ A man who is a carder
    Ⓑ A weaver who is not covered by health insurance
    Ⓒ A carder who is not covered by health insurance
    Ⓓ A worker covered by health insurance who is not a weaver
    Ⓔ A worker covered by health insurance who is not a carder

    The Olympic Games represent a first step in the historic movement away from war and toward the substitution for war of peaceful competition among nations. Just as professional sports in the United States provide a field in which local, regional, and even racial and ethnic hostilities may be sublimated and expressed in a controlled, harmless form, so international athletic competition may help to abolish war between nations by providing a sphere in which chauvinistic hostilities may be harmlessly discharged.

33. Which of the following, if true, would weaken the argument in the passage?

    Ⓐ The existence of professional sports in the United States has not completely eliminated regional and ethnic conflicts.
    Ⓑ The Olympic Games themselves generate intense international rivalries and emotional responses by spectators.

Ⓒ On several occasions, the Olympic Games have been canceled or reduced in scope because of international conflicts or wars.

Ⓓ Unlike professional sports, the Olympic Games are conducted on a purely amateur, not-for-profit basis.

Ⓔ War is caused primarily by objective conflicts between nations over political and economic advantages.

34. <u>Although completely withered</u>, the botanists were able to conclude from what remained of the flower that the species was very rare.

Ⓐ Although completely withered
Ⓑ Although totally withered
Ⓒ Although withering completely
Ⓓ Although it was completely withered
Ⓔ While it withered completely

35. Four days a week, parking is permitted only on alternate sides of the street <u>on account of enabling</u> the mechanical street sweepers to pass close to the curbs.

Ⓐ on account of enabling
Ⓑ for the reason of enabling
Ⓒ to permit
Ⓓ so as to allow
Ⓔ therefore allowing

Psychology originated in the attempts of researchers to describe, record, classify, and explain their own mental impressions, thoughts, and feelings and those of others as they described them verbally. It matured into a science only when the reliance on subjective impressions was gradually abandoned and researchers concentrated on human behavior. Then, psychology truly became a science of mental activity.

36. The passage above assumes that

I. it is not possible to observe episodes of mental activity directly
II. early research was unreliable because researchers gave less-than-candid accounts of their mental experiences
III. human behavior is an expression of mental activity

Ⓐ I only   Ⓑ III only   Ⓒ I and II only
Ⓓ I and III only   Ⓔ II and III only

Many people who describe themselves as authors do not belong in that category at all, since writing is not their main source of income.

37. The paragraph above makes the assumption that

Ⓐ many of those who consider themselves authors lack the skills and training needed to write professionally
Ⓑ the average income of professional writers is higher than that for most other professions
Ⓒ professional authors are motivated to become writers primarily by the prospect of financial gain
Ⓓ to be considered an author a person must publish writings on a regular basis
Ⓔ a person cannot be considered an author unless he or she derives most of his or her income from writing

A poll taken ten days before the election showed that 36 percent of the people surveyed planned to vote for Green and 42 percent planned to vote for his opponent. When the votes were finally tallied, Green received 52 percent of the vote, while his opponent received only 46 percent. Thus, the survey method used for the preelection poll was flawed.

38. Which of the following, if true, would most weaken the conclusion of the argument above?

Ⓐ A poll taken 21 days before the election showed that 32 percent of the people surveyed planned to vote for Green.
Ⓑ At the time the preelection poll was taken, many voters had not yet made up their minds about which candidate to vote for.
Ⓒ During the week just before the election, Green's opponent received an important endorsement from a major newspaper.
Ⓓ The voter turnout for the election in question was extremely light due to inclement weather.
Ⓔ The preelection survey also questioned voters about their attitudes toward a referendum authorizing the legislature to legalize pari-mutuel gambling.

Questions 39–41

Antitrust suits are easy to bring and costly to defend. The defendant's exposure includes treble damages, injunction, and plaintiff's attorney's fees. The defendant bears the principal burden of discovery and must pay his or her own attorneys. The plaintiff can litigate on a comparative shoestring and may pass even these costs on to the defendant. Thus, one firm may find suing its business rival a worthwhile strategic move. If the plaintiff wins, the rival is burdened; if the litigation drags on, the rival is burdened; and if the rival backs off from the challenged conduct to relieve these burdens, the plaintiff may benefit from a reduction in competition. Even the sharing of information in discovery may help rivals to collude. It seems possible,

GO ON TO NEXT PAGE

then, that the filing of an antitrust suit might tend to lessen competition in violation of the antitrust laws themselves. Is such conduct actionable?

We protect untruth, if at all, only because of concern that attempts to separate truth from untruth will lead to condemnation of truth by mistake and will prompt people to be too cautious and thus desist from making even true-because-debatable statements. A rule that requires someone to spend hours in research or contemplation before speaking, the better to avoid untruthful statements, raises the costs of all speech and ensures that we will have less of it. The compromise struck in the constitutional libel cases is a rule that discriminates honest statements—those that are not made recklessly or with knowledge of falsehood—from deliberately untruthful ones. All but the deliberately untruthful are protected.

Similarly, we protect petitioning the government by interest groups for private favors, if at all, only to give shelter to other speech. There is no abstract First Amendment right to seek transfer payments or economic rents. The framers of the Constitution saw political and economic factions as a danger to be overcome, not as a desirable end. They divided the powers of government in the belief that this would reduce the power of self-interested factions. They wrote constitutional prohibitions such as the contract clause in the hope that the limits on the power of government to transfer wealth and undercut property would aid the welfare of all. Yet a court cannot confidently separate appeals for transfers and other rents from the kind of appeals to the joint welfare that the First Amendment was designed to protect. There may be no line between the two, let alone a line that could be maintained in litigation. Thus, the Constitution protects both kinds of petitions. This protection requires "victims" to bear some or all of the costs of the political process, whether wisely or selfishly used. Similarly, they must bear part of the cost of the judicial process under the American rule. The next question is whether there is a good parallel in antitrust to the "honest statement" rule used in libel to allocate these costs.

We may quickly discard a rule that turns on whether the plaintiff (or administrative protestant) wins on the merits. That would be the equivalent of a "truth" rule for other First Amendment purposes; it would impose excessive risks or resort to the political and judicial process. We may also discard a rule that turns on whether the plaintiff or protestant had a colorable claim, something that could survive dismissal on the pleading. Noncolorable claims impose no loss on business rivals, because they may be disposed of by court or agency quickly. The only claims we need to worry about are the ones with just enough merit to linger and impose loss on one's rivals.

The tort of abuse of process offers a useful way to strike the balance. It is tortuous—and the injured party can recover damages for any loss—to employ litigation in pursuit of an objective other than the one ostensibly sought. This tort offers the victim of an illegitimate suit the protection of the law yet does not endanger First Amendment rights.

39. Which of the following best describes the primary purpose of the passage?

Ⓐ Antitrust claims may be used as a weapon by one business entity against its competitors.

Ⓑ The tort of abuse of process is the best way to discourage spurious antitrust suits.

Ⓒ The First Amendment does not necessarily protect statements that are untrue.

Ⓓ Antitrust suits can impose considerable economic burdens on those sued.

Ⓔ Some businesses may file antitrust claims against competitors to reduce competition.

40. According to the passage, the American rule requires

Ⓐ plaintiffs to prove the truth of their claims

Ⓑ defendants to pay their own costs in litigation

Ⓒ each party to a lawsuit to pay the other's costs

Ⓓ a judge to determine which party is at fault

Ⓔ the government to grant favors to petitioners

41. It can be inferred from the passage that a "truth" rule would

Ⓐ impose liability for litigation costs on a plaintiff if the plaintiff lost

Ⓑ create a buffer zone between statements that are true and those that are honest but untrue

Ⓒ increase the economic and financial risks incurred by defendants in antitrust suits

Ⓓ encourage businesses to file frivolous antitrust claims against rival businesses

Ⓔ reduce the power of the government to control markets through antitrust policy

Stop: End of Verbal Section

Quantitative Section

37 Questions—75 Minutes

General Directions: To simulate the experience of taking the CAT, answer each question in order. Do not skip any questions and do not go back to questions you have already answered.

Directions for problem-solving questions: For this question type, select the best of the answer choices. Indicate your answer by blackening the circle next to your choice.

Numbers: All numbers used are real numbers.

Figures: The diagrams and figures that accompany these questions are for the purpose of providing information useful in solving the problems. The diagrams and figures are drawn as accurately as possible unless the figure is accompanied by a note stating that it is not drawn to scale. All figures are in a plane unless otherwise indicated.

Directions for data sufficiency questions: Each question is followed by two numbered statements. You are to determine whether the data given in the statements are sufficient for answering the question. Use the data given, plus your knowledge of math and everyday facts, to choose among the five possible answers. Indicate your answer by blackening the circle next to your choice.

Numbers: All values are real numbers.

Figures: Any figures provided will not necessarily reflect the information given in the numbered statements, but they will reflect the information provided in the question. Unless otherwise indicated, all figures lie in a plane; all lines shown as straight are straight; and the positions of all points, angles, regions, etc., are correctly depicted.

Example:

In $\triangle ABC$, what is the value of x?

(1) $y = 60$

(2) $AB = BC$

Explanation: Statement (1) is not sufficient to answer the question, for statement (1) provides no information about x or z. Statement (2) is not sufficient to answer the question. Statement (2) does establish that $y = z$, but that is not enough information to determine the value of x. Both statements together are sufficient to answer the question. Since $AB = BC$ and $y = z$, $z = 60$. Since $x + y + z = 180$, $x = 60$.

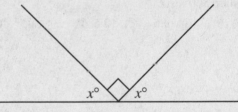

1. In the figure above, $x =$

　Ⓐ 30　Ⓑ 45　Ⓒ 60　Ⓓ 75　Ⓔ 90

2. In a certain game, a person's age is multiplied by 2 and then the product is divided by 3. If the result of performing the operations on John's age is 12, what is John's age?

　Ⓐ 2　Ⓑ 8　Ⓒ 12　Ⓓ 18　Ⓔ 36

3. n is a positive integer. If n is a multiple of 6 and a multiple of 9, what is the least possible value of n?

　Ⓐ 12　Ⓑ 18　Ⓒ 27　Ⓓ 36　Ⓔ 54

4. Is x divisible by 70?

　(1) x is divisible by 2 and 5.

　(2) x is divisible by 2 and 7.

　Ⓐ statement 1 alone is sufficient to answer the question, but statement 2 alone is not sufficient

　Ⓑ statement 2 alone is sufficient to answer the question, but statement 1 alone is not sufficient

　Ⓒ both statements together are needed to answer the question, but neither statement alone is sufficient

　Ⓓ either statement by itself is sufficient to answer the question

　Ⓔ not enough facts are given to answer the question

GO ON TO NEXT PAGE

5. Does Bob have more records in his record collection than Linda has in hers?

   (1) Christina has more records in her collection than Linda.

   (2) Bob has fewer records in his collection than Christina.

   Ⓐ statement 1 alone is sufficient to answer the question, but statement 2 alone is not sufficient

   Ⓑ statement 2 alone is sufficient to answer the question, but statement 1 alone is not sufficient

   Ⓒ both statements together are needed to answer the question, but neither statement alone is sufficient

   Ⓓ either statement by itself is sufficient to answer the question

   Ⓔ not enough facts are given to answer the question

6. For any positive integer k, $\langle k \rangle = k^2 - k$. What is the value of $\langle 2 \rangle$?

   Ⓐ 0 Ⓑ 1 Ⓒ 2 Ⓓ 4 Ⓔ 8

List X	List Y
1	1
2	2
3	3
4	4

7. For how many different ordered pairs (x, y) where x is a number selected from List X and y is a number selected from list Y, is $x - y > 0$?

   Ⓐ 24 Ⓑ 18 Ⓒ 15 Ⓓ 12 Ⓔ 6

8. A student receives an average of 75 on three exams that are scored on a scale of 0 to 100. If one of her test scores was 75, what is the lowest possible score she could have received on any of the three tests?

   Ⓐ 0 Ⓑ 1 Ⓒ 25 Ⓓ 40 Ⓔ 50

9. A class of 30 children took a test. What was the average test score of the students in the class?

   (1) The highest score was 40.

   (2) The lowest score was 10.

   Ⓐ statement 1 alone is sufficient to answer the question, but statement 2 alone is not sufficient

   Ⓑ statement 2 alone is sufficient to answer the question, but statement 1 alone is not sufficient

   Ⓒ both statements together are needed to answer the question, but neither statement alone is sufficient

   Ⓓ either statement by itself is sufficient to answer the question

   Ⓔ not enough facts are given to answer the question

10. Allen and Chris founded a company in 1990. In which year did the company's profits first exceed $100,000?

    (1) In 1990, the company had profits of $15,000, and in every year after that profits were double those of the previous year.

    (2) In 1992, the company had profits of $60,000.

    Ⓐ statement 1 alone is sufficient to answer the question, but statement 2 alone is not sufficient

    Ⓑ statement 2 alone is sufficient to answer the question, but statement 1 alone is not sufficient

    Ⓒ both statements together are needed to answer the question, but neither statement alone is sufficient

    Ⓓ either statement by itself is sufficient to answer the question

    Ⓔ not enough facts are given to answer the question

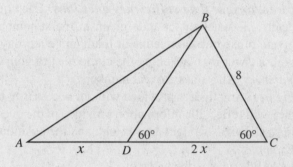

11. In ABC above, what is the length of side AC?

    Ⓐ 4 Ⓑ 8 Ⓒ 12 Ⓓ 18 Ⓔ 20

12. If $x + 1 + 2x + 2 + 3x + 3 = 6$, $x =$

    Ⓐ −2 Ⓑ 0 Ⓒ 1 Ⓓ 6 Ⓔ 12

13. If a horse gallops at an average speed of 40 feet per second, how many seconds will it take the horse to gallop 500 feet?

    Ⓐ 8 Ⓑ 9.5 Ⓒ 12.5 Ⓓ 20 Ⓔ 40

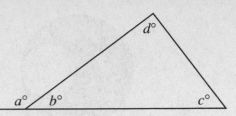

14. In the figure above, what is the value of d?

(1) $b + c = 90$

(2) $c + a = 180$

Ⓐ statement 1 alone is sufficient to answer the question, but statement 2 alone is not sufficient

Ⓑ statement 2 alone is sufficient to answer the question, but statement 1 alone is not sufficient

Ⓒ both statements together are needed to answer the question, but neither statement alone is sufficient

Ⓓ either statement by itself is sufficient to answer the question

Ⓔ not enough facts are given to answer the question

15. Is x an integer?

(1) $x > 0$

(2) $3^2 + 4^2 = x^2$

Ⓐ statement 1 alone is sufficient to answer the question, but statement 2 alone is not sufficient

Ⓑ statement 2 alone is sufficient to answer the question, but statement 1 alone is not sufficient

Ⓒ both statements together are needed to answer the question, but neither statement alone is sufficient

Ⓓ either statement by itself is sufficient to answer the question

Ⓔ not enough facts are given to answer the question

16. If 1 mill = 0.1 cents, how many mills are there in $3.13?

Ⓐ 0.313   Ⓑ 3.13   Ⓒ 31.3
Ⓓ 313   Ⓔ 3,130

17. Which of the following is a pair of numbers that are not equal?

Ⓐ $\frac{63}{6}, \frac{21}{2}$ Ⓑ 0.3%, 0.003   Ⓒ $\frac{44}{77}, \frac{4}{7}$

Ⓓ $\frac{3}{8}, 0.375$ Ⓔ $\sqrt{3^2}, 9$

18. If $\frac{64}{x} - 6 = 2$, then $x =$

Ⓐ 8   Ⓑ 12   Ⓒ 16   Ⓓ 24   Ⓔ 32

19. What is the volume of cube C?

(1) The total surface area of C is 54 square inches.

(2) The area of each face of C is 9 square inches.

Ⓐ statement 1 alone is sufficient to answer the question, but statement 2 alone is not sufficient

Ⓑ statement 2 alone is sufficient to answer the question, but statement 1 alone is not sufficient

Ⓒ both statements together are needed to answer the question, but neither statement alone is sufficient

Ⓓ either statement by itself is sufficient to answer the question

Ⓔ not enough facts are given to answer the question

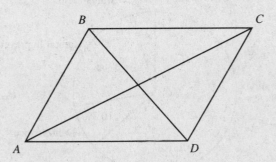

20. In the figure above, what is the ratio

$$\frac{\text{Area of Triangle } ABD}{\text{Area of Triangle } ACD}?$$

(1) $AB \parallel CD$

(2) $BC \parallel AD$

Ⓐ statement 1 alone is sufficient to answer the question, but statement 2 alone is not sufficient

Ⓑ statement 2 alone is sufficient to answer the question, but statement 1 alone is not sufficient

Ⓒ both statements together are needed to answer the question, but neither statement alone is sufficient

Ⓓ either statement by itself is sufficient to answer the question

Ⓔ not enough facts are given to answer the question

21. If x, y, and z are consecutive integers and $x > y > z$, then $(x - y)(x - z)(y - z) =$

Ⓐ –2   Ⓑ –1   Ⓒ 0   Ⓓ 1   Ⓔ 2

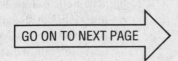

Questions 22–23

For all positive integers n,

$n = 2n$ if n is even
$n = 3n$ if n is odd

22. If n is a prime number greater than 4, $(n-1) =$

(A) $3n$ (B) $2n$ (C) $3n-3$ (D) $2n-2$ (E) n

23. $③ \cdot ④ =$

(A) ⑥ (B) ⑦ (C) ⑫ (D) ⑱ (E) ㊱

BUDGET FOR DAY SCHOOL D

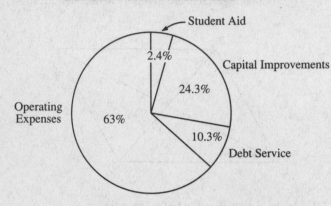

24. How much money did Day School D spend on operating expenses?

(1) The total budget for the school was $9 million.

(2) The school spent $216,000 on student aid.

(A) statement 1 alone is sufficient to answer the question, but statement 2 alone is not sufficient
(B) statement 2 alone is sufficient to answer the question, but statement 1 alone is not sufficient
(C) both statements together are needed to answer the question, but neither statement alone is sufficient
(D) either statement by itself is sufficient to answer the question
(E) not enough facts are given to answer the question

25. What is the value of the integer N?

(1) N is an integer multiple of 2 and 3.

(2) $30 < N < 70$

(A) statement 1 alone is sufficient to answer the question, but statement 2 alone is not sufficient
(B) statement 2 alone is sufficient to answer the question, but statement 1 alone is not sufficient
(C) both statements together are needed to answer the question, but neither statement alone is sufficient
(D) either statement by itself is sufficient to answer the question
(E) not enough facts are given to answer the question

26. If $\dfrac{x}{z} = k$ and $\dfrac{y}{z} = k - 1$, $x =$

(A) $y - 1$ (B) $y + 1$ (C) $y + z$

(D) $z - y$ (E) $\dfrac{y}{z}$

27. In the figure above, O is the center of the circle. What is the ratio of the area of the shaded portion of the figure to the area of the unshaded portion of the figure?

(A) 4:1 (B) π:1 (C) 3:1 (D) 5:2 (E) 2:1

28. If x is 25% of y, y is what percent of x?

(A) 400% (B) 300% (C) 250%
(D) 125% (E) 75%

29. How much money is saved by buying a box of a dozen donuts instead of buying 12 donuts singly?

(1) When purchased in a box of 12, the cost of each donut is $0.05 less than if purchased singly.

(2) The price of a box of a dozen donuts is $2.40.

(A) statement 1 alone is sufficient to answer the question, but statement 2 alone is not sufficient
(B) statement 2 alone is sufficient to answer the question, but statement 1 alone is not sufficient
(C) both statements together are needed to answer the question, but neither statement alone is sufficient
(D) either statement by itself is sufficient to answer the question
(E) not enough facts are given to answer the question

30. What is the value of $a^4 - b^4$?

(1) $a^2 + b^2 = 24$

(2) $a^2 - b^2 = 0$

(A) statement 1 alone is sufficient to answer the question, but statement 2 alone is not sufficient
(B) statement 2 alone is sufficient to answer the question, but statement 1 alone is not sufficient
(C) both statements together are needed to answer the question, but neither statement alone is sufficient
(D) either statement by itself is sufficient to answer the question
(E) not enough facts are given to answer the question

31. If x is an integer which is a multiple of both 9 and 5, which of the following must be true?

I. x is equal to 45.

II. x is a multiple of 15.

III. x is odd.

(A) I only (B) II only (C) III only
(D) II and III only (E) I, II, and III

32. If the radius of circle O is 20 percent less than the radius of circle P, the area of circle O is what percent of the area of circle P?

Ⓐ 60%   Ⓑ 64%   Ⓒ 72%
Ⓓ 80%   Ⓔ 120%

33. If the average (arithmetic mean) of 20, 23, 24, x and y = 26 and $\frac{x}{y} = \frac{3}{4}$, $x =$

Ⓐ 25   Ⓑ 27   Ⓒ 36   Ⓓ 41   Ⓔ 63

34. If a cube has a side of length 2, what is the distance from any vertex to the center of the cube?

Ⓐ $\frac{\sqrt{2}}{2}$ Ⓑ $\sqrt{3}$ Ⓒ $2\sqrt{2}$ Ⓓ $2\sqrt{3}$ Ⓔ $\frac{3}{2}$

35. Daniel invested a total of $10,000 for a period of one year. Part of the money he put into an investment that earned 6 percent simple interest, and the rest of the money into an investment that earned 8 percent simple interest. How much money did he put into the investment that earned 6 percent?

(1) The total interest earned on the $10,000 for the year was $640.

(2) The dollar value of the investment that earned 8 percent was one-fourth the dollar value of the investment that earned 6 percent.

Ⓐ statement 1 alone is sufficient to answer the question, but statement 2 alone is not sufficient
Ⓑ statement 2 alone is sufficient to answer the question, but statement 1 alone is not sufficient
Ⓒ both statements together are needed to answer the question, but neither statement alone is sufficient
Ⓓ either statement by itself is sufficient to answer the question
Ⓔ not enough facts are given to answer the question

36. Is x greater than y?

(1) $3x = 4y$

(2) $x = \frac{k}{3}$, $y = \frac{k}{4}$, and $k > 0$

Ⓐ statement 1 alone is sufficient to answer the question, but statement 2 alone is not sufficient
Ⓑ statement 2 alone is sufficient to answer the question, but statement 1 alone is not sufficient
Ⓒ both statements together are needed to answer the question, but neither statement alone is sufficient
Ⓓ either statement by itself is sufficient to answer the question
Ⓔ not enough facts are given to answer the question

37. Is the perimeter of a rectangular yard greater than 60 meters?

(1) The two shorter sides of the yard are each 15 meters long.

(2) The length of the yard is 3 meters longer than the width of the yard.

Ⓐ statement 1 alone is sufficient to answer the question, but statement 2 alone is not sufficient
Ⓑ statement 2 alone is sufficient to answer the question, but statement 1 alone is not sufficient
Ⓒ both statements together are needed to answer the question, but neither statement alone is sufficient
Ⓓ either statement by itself is sufficient to answer the question
Ⓔ not enough facts are given to answer the question

Stop: End of Quantitative Section

Answer Key

VERBAL SECTION

1.	D	15.	C	29.	C
2.	B	16.	C	30.	C
3.	A	17.	B	31.	D
4.	C	18.	A	32.	B
5.	B	19.	E	33.	E
6.	E	20.	D	34.	D
7.	E	21.	A	35.	C
8.	C	22.	C	36.	D
9.	C	23.	B	37.	E
10.	D	24.	D	38.	B
11.	E	25.	A	39.	B
12.	C	26.	C	40.	B
13.	C	27.	B	41.	A
14.	B	28.	B		

QUANTITATIVE SECTION

1.	B	14.	A	27.	C
2.	D	15.	B	28.	A
3.	B	16.	E	29.	A
4.	C	17.	E	30.	B
5.	E	18.	A	31.	B
6.	C	19.	D	32.	B
7.	E	20.	B	33.	B
8.	E	21.	E	34.	B
9.	E	22.	D	35.	D
10.	A	23.	E	36.	B
11.	C	24.	D	37.	A
12.	B	25.	E		
13.	C	26.	C		

Explanatory Answers

VERBAL SECTION

1. Ballet dancers warm up before each performance by doing a series of pliés and stretching <u>exercises, and it reduces</u> the chance of injury.

    Ⓐ exercises, and it reduces
    Ⓑ exercises, which reduces
    Ⓒ exercises, reducing
    Ⓓ exercises; the routine reduces
    Ⓔ exercises, so the routine reduces

    (D) In the original sentence, *it* lacks a referent. *It* seems to refer to something in the first part of the sentence, but there is no noun there that it can replace. (B) suffers from the same problem. As for (C), it is not clear what *reducing* (an adjective) is intended to modify. Both (D) and (E) solve the problem of faulty reference, but (E) changes the intended meaning of the original.

2. <u>Unlike the French, the German art songs are dramatic and sometimes almost operatic.</u>

    Ⓐ Unlike the French, the German art songs are dramatic and sometimes almost operatic.
    Ⓑ Unlike the French art songs, the German art songs are dramatic and sometimes almost operatic.
    Ⓒ The German art songs, unlike the French, are dramatic and sometimes almost operatic.
    Ⓓ The German art songs are dramatic and sometimes almost operatic, unlike the French.
    Ⓔ The German art songs, which are dramatic and sometimes almost operatic, are unlike the French.

    (B) The sentence sets up an illogical comparison between German art songs and the French (people). Only (B) eliminates this problem.

3. An airline may overbook a flight <u>to ensure a full passenger load, but it is required to pay compensation to</u> any passenger who cannot be accommodated on that flight.

    Ⓐ to ensure a full passenger load, but it is required to pay compensation to
    Ⓑ ensuring a full passenger load, but it is required to pay compensation to
    Ⓒ to ensure a full passenger load, since compensation is required to
    Ⓓ to ensure a full passenger load, which is required to pay compensation to
    Ⓔ to ensure a full passenger load and pay compensation to

    (A) The original sentence is correct. (B) is ambiguous, for it fails to state clearly that overbooking is the means of ensuring a full passenger load. (C) changes the meaning of the original by subordinating the second idea to the first idea. As for (D), the *which* lacks any clear referent. And finally, (E) changes the meaning of the original by implying that an airline overbooks in order to pay compensation to passengers who are bumped.

In an attempt to predict the future course of consumer spending, *Investment Monthly* magazine surveyed its readers. Of those surveyed, over 60 percent reported that they planned to buy a new automobile or at least one major appliance within the next three months. From these results, the magazine concluded that consumer spending for the next quarter was likely to be high.

4. Which of the following, if true, would most weaken the conclusion above?

    Ⓐ The cost of a new automobile is much greater than that of a major appliance.
    Ⓑ A person who plans to make a major purchase at some time in the future may not yet have settled on a brand.
    Ⓒ The readers of *Investment Monthly* are more affluent than the average consumer.
    Ⓓ Some of the items to be purchased will be imports and will not stimulate markets in the United States.
    Ⓔ Not all readers of *Investment Monthly* magazine responded to the survey.

    (C) The strength of a generalization depends on the representativeness of the examples on which it is based. Here the conclusion is that consumer spending in general will be high for the upcoming quarter, and the basis for that general conclusion is a sampling of readers of a magazine called *Investment Monthly.*

    (C) attacks the generalization by suggesting that the sample is not representative of consumers in general. (A), (B), and (D) are all irrelevant to the argument, since the speaker does not distinguish types of consumer purchases, e. g., automobile versus refrigerator, Brand X versus Brand Y, or imported versus domestically produced goods. (E) is perhaps the second-best answer, for at least it has the merit of addressing the sampling procedure. (E), however, represents a questioning of the argument rather than an outright attack. Even if the survey covered only a part of the readership, if that survey was unbiased, the fact that not everyone responded is not important. (E) would have been a much stronger answer had it been phrased "Only the wealthiest readers responded." But then, that would be very much like (C), and the test writers would never include two answers so similar to each other.

Questions 5–6

Every member of the New York Burros, a team in the Big Apple Softball League, who wears wristbands when batting wears either red wristbands or white wristbands.

5. If the statement above is true, which of the following must be true?

    I. A member of the New York Burros who does not wear red wristbands while batting wears white wristbands while batting.

    II. No member of the New York Burros wears blue wristbands while batting.

    III. Some members of the New York Burros do not wear wristbands when batting.

    (A) I only   (B) II only   (C) III only
    (D) I and III only   (E) I, II, and III

    (B) The result of your attack on a question like this usually depends on a careful reading of the initial statements. I and III are not inferable for essentially the same reason. The initial statement has the general form "All individuals with characteristic X also have characteristic Y or Z." (All individuals who wear wristbands while batting wear either red or white ones.) But you cannot infer from such a statement that everyone in the population has characteristic X, so you cannot infer that everyone in the population has characteristic Y or Z. On the other hand, you cannot conclude that some individuals do not have characteristic X. Therefore, neither I nor III is inferable. II, however, is inferable. Any Burro who wears wristbands while batting wears either red ones or white ones. So no Burro wears blue wristbands while batting.

6. If any player in the Big Apple Softball League who wears red wristbands while batting also wears blue batting gloves, and if no member of the New York Burros wears blue batting gloves, which of the following must be true?

    (A) Every member of the New York Burros wears white wristbands when batting.
    (B) No member of the New York Burros wears blue batting gloves.
    (C) Some members of the New York Burros wear red wristbands when batting.
    (D) Some members of the New York Burros do not wear batting gloves.
    (E) Every member of the New York Burros who wears wristbands wears white wristbands when batting.

(E) What can be inferred using the additional information? Since no Burro wears blue batting gloves, no Burro wears red wristbands when batting. Coupling this conclusion with the initial statements, we can infer that those Burros who wear wristbands while batting wear white wristbands. This is the conclusion set forth in (E). (A) is incorrect for the same reason that statement I of the preceding item is not inferable. As for (B), the reasoning just adduced shows that it is possible for a Burro to wear blue batting gloves, provided he is also wearing white wristbands. (C) is necessarily false (given the additional information of this question stem). Finally, (D) is not inferable. Although (D) is possibly true, it is not necessarily true.

7. It can be inferred that the PATCO strike

    (A) was an example of bad faith negotiations
    (B) lasted only a brief period
    (C) was the fault of incompetent management
    (D) violated the provisions of the Fair Labor Standards Act
    (E) resulted in a victory for management

(E) This is an inference question. The author states that a result of the PATCO strike is that management can now expect to regain some of the power it gave up to labor in earlier decades. So you may infer that the outcome of that strike was favorable to management. This is the description given by (E). As for (A), though the author mentions bad faith negotiations in the first paragraph, there is nothing to connect that concept with the example mentioned in the second paragraph. As for (B), nothing in the passage supports a conclusion one way or the other about the length of the strike, as opposed to its outcome. (C) and (D) make the same mistake as (A). Though they are ideas mentioned in the passage, there is nothing to connect them with the example of the PATCO strike.

8. The author's discussion of labor management relations can best be described as

    (A) extremely pro-labor
    (B) mildly pro-labor
    (C) neutral
    (D) mildly pro-management
    (E) extremely pro-management

(C) This is an attitude question, and the choices have already been arranged for you on a spectrum. You can eliminate all but (C) because the author says nothing to indicate he favors one side over the other. In fact, statements such as "neither side is blameless" specifically attest to his neutrality.

9. The author implies that if the economic conditions improve,

    Ⓐ management will lose much of its power
    Ⓑ labor leaders will not seek more benefits
    Ⓒ labor-management tensions will decline
    Ⓓ the Fair Labor Standards Act will be repealed
    Ⓔ labor will win a voice in management

(C) This is an implied idea question. The first sentence of the second paragraph states that *since* the economic situation will not improve, union leaders will be frustrated. So the stage is set for confrontation. We may infer, therefore, that if economic conditions were better, labor would be happier, and tensions would be lessened. This is choice (C). (A) carries this line of reasoning too far. We can infer that better economic conditions would prevent management from recouping its losses, but we cannot infer that better economic conditions will cause further erosion of management's position. As for (B), the opposite conclusion seems inferable. When economic circumstances are good, labor demands more. As for (E), there is nothing to connect this idea mentioned in the first paragraph with the line of reasoning in the second. Finally, (D) makes the same mistake as (A).

10. It is typical of the high soprano voice, <u>like</u> the highest voices within each vocal range, to be lighter in weight and more flexible.

    Ⓐ like
    Ⓑ as
    Ⓒ like it is of
    Ⓓ as it is of
    Ⓔ similar to

(D) The original sentence is not idiomatic. *Like* implies a comparison between the high soprano voice and the highest voices in the other ranges, but the sentence means to create a comparison between the typical features of the high soprano voice (lightness and flexibility) and the typical features of the high voices in the other ranges. (D) is the correct idiom for making the comparison.

11. The earliest texts in cuneiform script are about 5,000 years <u>old, having antedated the use</u> of the first alphabets by some 1,500 years.

    Ⓐ old, having antedated the use
    Ⓑ old, having antedated the invention
    Ⓒ old, antedating the use
    Ⓓ old and antedate the use
    Ⓔ old and antedate the invention

(E) The original sentence contains two problems of diction or word meaning. First, *antedate* means "to come before"; therefore, the *having* is not only superfluous, but the phrase *having antedated* is almost like saying "having had come before," a verb tense inconsistent with the rest of the sentence.

    Additionally, *use* implies an ongoing condition, but the sentence means to say that the cuneiform texts were written before a certain time in history, the date alphabets were invented or first used.

12. After her admission to the bar, <u>Margaret, herself a childless attorney's only daughter</u>, specialized in adoption and family law.

    Ⓐ Margaret, herself a childless attorney's only daughter
    Ⓑ Margaret herself, a childless attorney's only daughter
    Ⓒ Margaret, herself the childless and only daughter of an attorney
    Ⓓ Margaret, only a childless attorney's daughter herself
    Ⓔ Margaret, herself, only a daughter of a childless attorney

(C) The original sentence is ambiguous. As written, it seems to imply that Margaret was the daughter of a childless woman—a logical contradiction. Only (C) clears up this ambiguity.

A bill now pending before the Congress would give physicians the option of prescribing heroin as a painkiller for terminally ill patients. The Congress should refuse to pass the bill because there is a serious danger that the heroin would be stolen and wind up being sold on the streets.

13. Which of the following, if true, would most weaken the argument above?

    Ⓐ Other prescription painkillers are available for terminally ill patients that in most cases provide relief of pain as effective as that provided by heroin.
    Ⓑ The addictive effects of heroin are inconsequential considering that the patients who would be scheduled for treatment are terminally ill.
    Ⓒ The amount of heroin that would be required for terminally ill patients is insignificant when compared with the amount of heroin sold illegally.
    Ⓓ Heroin sold illegally varies widely in quality and purity and can easily cause death by overdose because it is taken without proper measurement.
    Ⓔ Over the past five years, the number of deaths attributable to heroin overdose has declined slightly, but the total number of deaths by drug overdose has increased significantly because of increased use of cocaine.

(C) The speaker opposes the proposal of a limited legalization of heroin because he or she fears that any quantities earmarked for legal use might be diverted to illegal street sales. And this is a legitimate objection to the plan. (C), however, points out that although the objection is not illogical, it is not a serious objection because of the limited quantities that would be required. (A) does not weaken the speaker's objection. If anything, the point made by (A) strengthens the speaker's objection by claiming that there is no particular need for legalized heroin. (B) is generally related to the topic of the initial paragraph, but (B) seems to be a response to a possible objection to the plan to legalize heroin. As such, it is a point that a defender of the plan might make, but it is not a response to the particular point made in this initial paragraph. (D) and (E) may both be true, but they aren't arguments directed against the use of legalized heroin.

It used to be said that artistic creativity is the province solely of human beings and that it is, in fact, one of the marks that distinguishes humans from all other creatures. Today, cleverly programmed computers can create images that are indistinguishable from paintings by contemporary abstract artists. Thus, the traditional argument that artistic creativity is the province of humans is proved incorrect.

14.   Which of the following, if true, most weakens the argument above?

Ⓐ   Most human beings have never produced a creative work that others would regard as a work of art.

Ⓑ   The image produced by a computer is an image that it was directed to create by the human programmer.

Ⓒ   Many people are unfamiliar with abstract art and so are unable to distinguish good modern art from bad modern art.

Ⓓ   Human beings engage in many activities other than the creation of art, activities such as production, warfare, and building.

Ⓔ   A program designed to produce a computerized image will produce the same image on any computer that can accept the program.

(B) The point of the initial argument is that computers can generate what seems to be art and that artistic creativity is therefore not just the province of humans. (B) weakens the argument by attacking the evidence for the claim, namely, that computers can generate art. It does this not by denying that art emerges from a computer, but by arguing that it is not the machine but a human being who is ultimately responsible for the image. (A) sounds like an attack on the argument only if you misread the argument. The speaker attacks the claim "Only humans can produce art," not the claim "All humans produce art." (C) and (D) are incorrect for substantially the same reason. The claim under attack is not "Everyone has good artistic judgment" nor "Humans create only art." Finally, as for (E), this idea, if anything, seems to strengthen rather than weaken the

speaker's point by suggesting that computer-generated images are produced by a purely mechanical process completely devoid of any creative urge.

The right to work under humane conditions is a fundamental right of all people. Therefore, all men and women have the right to a job and to decent conditions of employment.

15.   Which of the following arguments most closely parallels the reasoning of the argument above?

Ⓐ   The expression of anger is a natural instinct of human beings who feel threatened. Therefore, Smith is not to be blamed for expressing anger when she felt threatened.

Ⓑ   Johnson is one of the most honest legislative leaders ever to serve this state. Therefore, Johnson could not have committed the dishonest acts of which he has been accused.

Ⓒ   The Bill of Rights protects the free practice of religion in this country. Therefore, all people have the right to worship God in a manner of their own choosing.

Ⓓ   Children are human beings who have the potential for adult behavior. Therefore, any right or privilege that is granted to adults ought, in fairness, to be granted to children as well.

Ⓔ   The President has the duty of defending the country from any external enemy. Therefore, the President acted properly in ordering our army to repel the invading forces.

(C) The initial argument is not very complex. The conclusion really amounts to little more than a restatement of the premise. (C) parallels this structure, because the conclusion of (C) is little more than a restatement of the premise. The other four choices do not parallel the initial argument as closely because in each of the other four choices the conclusion is something more than a restatement of the premise.

16.   The author is primarily concerned with

Ⓐ   showing that behavior is a more effective way of controlling bodily temperature than innate mechanisms

Ⓑ   criticizing researchers who will not discard their theories about the effects of microwave radiation on organisms

Ⓒ   demonstrating that effects of microwave radiation are different from those of other forms of radiation

Ⓓ   analyzing the mechanism by which an organism maintains its bodily temperature in a changing thermal environment

Ⓔ   discussing the importance of thermoreceptors in the control of the internal temperature of an organism

(C) This is a main idea question. Choice (A) describes a point made in the selection (in the last sentence in the first paragraph), but that idea is not the overall or main point of the selection. The idea suggested by choice (B) is certainly one that is consistent with the overall tone of the passage, but again, the idea is not the main point of the selection. The author is not just concerned with criticizing those who won't abandon their theories; he is more concerned with demonstrating that those theories are in fact wrong. And this is the idea mentioned by (C): the main point of the passage is that the popular theories are incorrect. Choices (D) and (E) are like choice (A). They mention ideas covered in the passage, but neither describes the main point of the passage.

17. The author makes which of the following points about innate mechanisms for heat production?

    I. They are governed by thermoreceptors inside the body of the organism rather than at the surface.

    II. They are a less effective means of compensating for gross changes in temperature than behavioral strategies.

    III. They are not affected by microwave radiation.

    Ⓐ I only   Ⓑ I and II only   Ⓒ I and III only
    Ⓓ II and III only   Ⓔ I, II, and III

(B) This is a specific detail question. In the opening sentence, the author establishes that there are two general responses available to warm-blooded animals for regulating body temperature: behavior and innate mechanisms. The author goes on to state that humans rely primarily on the first type of response but adds that the organism also responds to changes in temperature in the core of the body (the second type of response) and that these changes are triggered by thermoreceptors distributed throughout the central nervous system. Thus, statement I must be part of the correct answer choice. In the final sentence of the first paragraph, the author states that the second type of mechanism for regulating temperature is less effective for adjusting to gross changes in temperature than the first type. Thus, II must be part of the correct response. Finally, the author does not state that the internal thermoreceptors are not affected by microwave radiation. The problem cited by the author is not that internal thermoreceptors do not respond to changes in the temperature of the core of the body but that they do not trigger the type of response needed to counteract gross changes in environmental temperatures.

18. Which of the following would be the most logical topic for the author to take up in the paragraph following the final paragraph of the selection?

    Ⓐ A suggestion for new research to be done on the effects of microwaves on animals and human beings

    Ⓑ An analysis of the differences between microwave radiation and other forms of radiation

    Ⓒ A proposal that the use of microwave radiation be prohibited because it is dangerous

    Ⓓ A survey of the literature on the effects of microwave radiation on human beings

    Ⓔ A discussion of the strategies used by various species to control hypothermia

(A) This is a further application question. Since the last paragraph deals with a recent report suggesting that previous assumptions about microwaves were incorrect, the author would probably go on to talk about the need for more research. (B) is incorrect because the author is dealing with microwave radiation and there would be no reason at this point to compare it to other forms of radiation. Besides, the author made the comparison earlier in the passage. (C) is incorrect because it overstates the case. There is no evidence to suggest that microwave radiation is so dangerous that it should be prohibited—just understood and regulated. (D) is incorrect because clearly the author is concerned with new information about microwave radiation. He has already suggested that what we now believe is erroneous. Finally, (E) is incorrect because a discussion of the strategies used by various species to control hypothermia would not follow logically from his remarks that microwave radiation has not been correctly understood. In any event, the discussion of such strategies early in the passage is intended to set the stage for the main point of the selection.

19. A survey of over 1,000 people conducted by a marketing firm determined that people over the age of 40 do not like cherry cola as <u>well as people under the age of 20</u>.

    Ⓐ well as people under the age of 20
    Ⓑ much as people under the age of 20
    Ⓒ many people under the age of 20 do
    Ⓓ well than people under the age of 20 do
    Ⓔ much as people under the age of 20 do

(E) The original sentence is ambiguous. It seems to set up a comparison between cherry cola and people under the age of 20. (B) fails to eliminate this ambiguity. (C) eliminates the ambiguity but changes the intended meaning of the original. In (D), the phrase *as well than* is not idiomatic. (E) eliminates this ambiguity in the original.

20. Baker was perhaps not the most gifted soloist in the orchestra, but the conductor felt <u>what was lacking in his technical skill was more than made up by</u> the passion with which he played the music.

   Ⓐ what was lacking in his technical skill was more than made up by

   Ⓑ what he lacked in technical skill was more than made up by

   Ⓒ whatever was lacking in his technical skill was more than made up by

   Ⓓ whatever he lacked in technical skill was more than made up for by

   Ⓔ whatever he lacked in technical skill he more than made up by

(D) The original sentence is defective in two respects. First, the sentence states that Baker's weaknesses were made up by the passion with which he played. The sentence means to say that his weaknesses were made up for (compensated for) by his passion. Additionally, the use of *what* implies that there are clearly identifiable weaknesses in Baker's playing, but the sentence doesn't name those. *Whatever* is more idiomatic because it carries the sense of indefiniteness that is required here. (B) fails to correct either error. (C), (D), and (E) all correct the second error, but (C) and (E) fail to correct the first error.

21. <u>Although few outside of academe have heard of him today, William Dean Howells</u> was among America's most successful literary critics and novelists.

   Ⓐ Although few outside of academe have heard of him today, William Dean Howells

   Ⓑ However difficult it may be to find someone outside of academe who has heard of him today, William Dean Howells

   Ⓒ As difficult as it is to find someone outside of academe who has heard of him today, William Dean Howells

   Ⓓ William Dean Howells is not heard of by very many outside of academe today, but he

   Ⓔ Although today William Dean Howells is not heard of by very many people outside of academe, he

(A) The original sentence is correct. By comparison, the other choices are excessively wordy, awkward, and nonidiomatic. It would be a tedious task to detail every shortcoming of the wrong answers, and I will not undertake to do so. If you selected a choice other than (A), compare your choice with the original and try to determine for yourself the respects in which the original is superior.

Amid great fanfare, the Taxi and Limousine Commission announced last June that a new dress code for taxi drivers would be incorporated into the Commission's rules. After six months, no driver has lost his license or even been fined under the new dress code. Evidently, drivers have chosen to comply with the new dress code.

22. Which of the following, if true, would most weaken the argument above?

   Ⓐ Prior to the announcement of the new dress code, an average of 16 cab drivers each month lost their licenses for various violations of the Commission's rules.

   Ⓑ Inspectors routinely stop cab drivers to inspect licenses, safety, and cleanliness of the vehicle and the driver's record of fares.

   Ⓒ City prosecutors have refused to prosecute drivers cited under the new dress code because they believe that the law is unconstitutional.

   Ⓓ A survey of passengers who say they regularly use taxi cabs shows that 45 percent of the riders don't believe that drivers are better dressed.

   Ⓔ During July and August, the number of cab drivers available for work is less than that during the other months of the year.

(C) This item asks you to find an alternative causal explanation for the phenomenon described. (C) provides an alternative explanation: There have been no convictions not because drivers have complied with the law but because the law has not been enforced. As for (A), the fact that drivers were in the past disciplined for other reasons has no bearing on the patterns of enforcement of the dress code. As for (B), this idea seems to strengthen rather than weaken the argument by suggesting that inspectors are in a position to detect violations of the dress code. (D) is perhaps the second-best answer, for (D) at least has the merit of suggesting that drivers are not better dressed. But (D) relies on a survey of attitudes, and the attitudes might or might not be well founded. A driver might be in compliance with a dress code and still not meet a passenger's expectation of "better dressed." Finally, it is difficult to imagine how (E) could be construed to be an attack on the argument.

Questions 23–24

The existence of our state's inefficient and wasteful automobile accident liability system can be easily explained. As long as most of our legislators are lawyers, the system will never be reformed, because litigation creates more work for lawyers.

23. Which of the following, if true, would most weaken the argument above?

    Ⓐ Most judges in the state are members of the legal profession as well.

    Ⓑ Few of the state's legislators are among the relatively small percentage of lawyers who handle automobile accident cases.

    Ⓒ Under the customary fee arrangement, a lawyer receives one-third of any monetary award made to a client.

    Ⓓ The state legislature allocates funds to pay for defense attorneys who represent indigent clients.

    Ⓔ Any reform legislation could be vetoed by the governor of the state, who is also an attorney.

    (B) The initial argument tries to provide an explanation for a certain situation: The lawyers in the legislature refuse to reform the law because reform would reduce the income of lawyers. In other words, the initial argument suggests that the lawyers in the legislature act out of self-interest. The argument implicitly assumes that the lawyers in the legislature derive financial benefit from the existing laws. (B) attacks this hidden assumption of the argument. The remaining answer choices are generally relevant to the topic of the initial paragraph but do not constitute an attack on the speaker's reasoning.

24. The argument above rests on the assumption that

    Ⓐ given the opportunity, most lawyers would want to be members of the state legislature.

    Ⓑ legislation to reform the state's automobile accident liability system could be introduced by a legislator who is not a lawyer.

    Ⓒ state laws set minimum fees that attorneys are permitted to charge in cases arising from automobile accidents.

    Ⓓ the state's automobile accident liability system encourages litigation.

    Ⓔ state laws governing the ownership and operation of motor vehicles encourage unsafe driving practices.

    (D) The argument above has the structure: Litigation creates work for lawyers; therefore, these laws will not be reformed. The speaker apparently believes, though he does not say so explicitly, that the existing system of laws encourages litigation. Thus, (D) highlights a suppressed premise of the argument. The speaker is not, however, logically committed to the idea mentioned in (A). Instead, the speaker is committed only to the proposition that those lawyers who are legislators refuse to reform the laws. As for (B), this might be a way of attacking the speaker's position (though probably not a very effective way of attacking it), so (B) is not a hidden assumption made by the speaker. As for (C), if this were true, the speaker's position would probably be strengthened somewhat; but the speaker is not logically committed to each and every point that might help his position. Finally, (E) seems to represent a misreading of the initial paragraph. The author is not claiming that existing laws cause accidents, only that those accidents that do occur often become the basis for litigation.

25. Which of the following titles best describes the content of the passage?

    Ⓐ The Origins of Jefferson's Republican Party

    Ⓑ Jefferson's Defeat in the 1792 Election

    Ⓒ The Legacy of Hamilton's Political System

    Ⓓ Political Differences between the Rich and the Poor

    Ⓔ Political Issues Separating the Federalists and the Republicans

    (A) This is a main idea question that asks for the best title. The passage discusses the founding and initial stages of the political party of Thomas Jefferson, later called the Republicans. So (A) correctly describes the content of the passage.

26. According to the passage, all of the following are true of the Republicans EXCEPT

    Ⓐ They opposed the moneyed interests of the North.

    Ⓑ They were led by Thomas Jefferson.

    Ⓒ They disapproved of the French Revolution.

    Ⓓ They and the Federalists supported the same candidate for President in 1792.

    Ⓔ They were initially called Anti-Federalists.

    (C) This is a specific detail question with a thought-reverser. All of the statements are mentioned in the passage except for (C). In the final paragraph the author states that the Republicans were sympathetic to the French Revolution.

27. The passage implies that Thomas Jefferson was unsuccessful in his 1792 bid for the vice-presidency because the Republican Party

    Ⓐ did not have its own presidential candidate

    Ⓑ was not as well organized as the Federalists

    Ⓒ refused to support John Adams

    Ⓓ appealed to workers in the North

    Ⓔ agreed to support George Washington's bid for the presidency

(B) This is an implied idea question. The author never specifically provides the reason for Jefferson's defeat, but he does say, in the second paragraph, that when the Republicans became better organized nationally, the Federalists would have a serious challenge. We may infer from this that it was the lack of organization that led to Jefferson's defeat.

28. Although the stock market seems to offer the possibility of great personal gain, you must understand that to invest in stocks is accepting the risk of financial ruin as well.

   Ⓐ is accepting the risk of financial ruin as well
   Ⓑ is to accept the risk of financial ruin as well
   Ⓒ is to accept the risk as well as financial ruin
   Ⓓ are accepting the risk of financial ruin as well
   Ⓔ are to accept the risk of financial ruin as well

(B) The original sentence suffers from faulty parallelism, "to invest . . . is accepting. . . ." (B), (C), and (E) make the needed correction; (D) does not. (C), however, changes the meaning of the original sentence, so (C) is wrong. And (E) introduces an error of subject-verb agreement by changing *is* to *are.* The subject of *is* is *to invest,* which requires a singular verb.

29. Since the past twenty years, thousands of magnificent United States elms have been killed by infestations of the tiny European bark beetle.

   Ⓐ Since the past twenty years
   Ⓑ Since twenty years have passed
   Ⓒ During the past twenty years
   Ⓓ Twenty years ago
   Ⓔ After twenty years

(C) The underlined portion of the original sentence is not idiomatic English. The correct preposition is *during.* The original sentence uses *since* as a preposition, but (B) uses *since* as a conjunction. As a conjunction, *since* implies a causal or explanatory connection. Therefore, (B) implies that it is because twenty years have passed that the trees have died, a change from the intended meaning of the original. (D), too, changes the intended meaning of the original by implying that the loss of the trees occurred during some completed time period twenty years in the past. (E), too, changes the intended meaning of the original. (E) implies that some event occurred twenty years ago and that only now are the trees dying.

30. The new biography of Thomas Jefferson contains some startling insights about the man who was the primary author of the Declaration of Independence.

   Ⓐ about the man who was the primary author
   Ⓑ into the man who was the primary author
   Ⓒ into the character of the man who was the primary author
   Ⓓ into the character of a man who was the primary author
   Ⓔ about the man who was primarily the author

(C) The underlined portion of the original sentence contains one error. The correct English idiom is not "insights about" but "insights into." (B) makes this correction, but (B) implies that the insights were provided into the man himself (the body). (C), (D), and (E) each makes the needed correction while avoiding this ambiguity. (D), however, changes slightly the intended meaning of the original sentence. The use of *a* rather than *the* makes the fact that Jefferson wrote the Declaration of Independence incidental rather than vital to Jefferson's identity. (Compare "He is a man in a blue suit" with "He is the man in the blue suit.") Finally, (E) changes radically the intended meaning of the original by suggesting that Jefferson's main task in life was to write the Declaration of Independence.

Questions 31–32
Premises: All weavers are members of the union.

            Some carders are women.

            Some weavers are women.

            All union members are covered by health insurance.

            No carders are covered by health insurance.

31. All of the following conclusions can be drawn from the statements above EXCEPT

   Ⓐ All weavers are covered by health insurance.
   Ⓑ Some women are covered by health insurance.
   Ⓒ Some women are not covered by health insurance.
   Ⓓ Some members of the union are not covered by health insurance.
   Ⓔ No carders are members of the union.

(D) (D) cannot be inferred from the statements. In fact, the fourth statement implies that (D) is false. As for (A), since all weavers are union members and all union members are covered by health insurance, it follows that all weavers are covered by health insurance. As for (B), since some women are weavers and all weavers are covered by health insurance, it follows that some women are covered by health insurance. As for (C), since some women are carders and no carder is covered by health insurance, it follows that some women are not covered by health insurance. Finally, as for (E), since no carder is covered by health insurance but all union members are covered by health insurance, it follows that no carder is a member of the union.

32. Which of the following workers would provide a counterexample to the statements above?

    (A) A man who is a carder
    (B) A weaver who is not covered by health insurance
    (C) A carder who is not covered by health insurance
    (D) A worker covered by health insurance who is not a weaver
    (E) A worker covered by health insurance who is not a carder

    (B) (B) provides a counterexample to the first and fourth statements. Those two statements together imply that all weavers are covered by health insurance.

The Olympic Games represent a first step in the historic movement away from war and toward the substitution for war of peaceful competition among nations. Just as professional sports in the United States provide a field in which local, regional, and even racial and ethnic hostilities may be sublimated and expressed in a controlled, harmless form, so international athletic competition may help to abolish war between nations by providing a sphere in which chauvinistic hostilities may be harmlessly discharged.

33. Which of the following, if true, would weaken the argument in the passage?

    (A) The existence of professional sports in the United States has not completely eliminated regional and ethnic conflicts.
    (B) The Olympic Games themselves generate intense international rivalries and emotional responses by spectators.
    (C) On several occasions, the Olympic Games have been canceled or reduced in scope because of international conflicts or wars.
    (D) Unlike professional sports, the Olympic Games are conducted on a purely amateur, not-for-profit basis.
    (E) War is caused primarily by objective conflicts between nations over political and economic advantages.

    (E) The argument implicitly assumes that nations are moved to go to war by the same emotions that generate regional and ethnic rivalries, and (E) attacks this hidden premise. (A) may be read as weakening the argument, but the attack is not very serious. The speaker could easily reply, "That's true. I didn't claim that sports can eliminate all conflict. I claimed only that they may help accomplish that." As for (B), the speaker could also claim that this idea is consistent with his argument: "True, but these emotional responses are controlled and channeled into an acceptable outlet." As for (C), the speaker argues that the games could have a

certain effect, but the speaker does not claim that the games will necessarily take place. Finally, while (D) is generally relevant to the topic of the initial paragraph, it is difficult to see the immediate relevance of this idea to the initial argument.

34. <u>Although completely withered</u>, the botanists were able to conclude from what remained of the flower that the species was very rare.

    (A) Although completely withered
    (B) Although totally withered
    (C) Although withering completely
    (D) Although it was completely withered
    (E) While it withered completely

    (D) The original sentence contains a dangling modifier and seems to imply that it is the botanists who are withered. (B), (C), and (E) fail to eliminate this ambiguity. (D) corrects the error of the original by inserting the pronoun *it,* which must refer to *flower.*

35. Four days a week, parking is permitted only on alternate sides of the street <u>on account of enabling</u> the mechanical street sweepers to pass close to the curbs.

    (A) on account of enabling
    (B) for the reason of enabling
    (C) to permit
    (D) so as to allow
    (E) therefore allowing

    (C) This item is primarily a test of idiom. Neither (A) nor (B) is idiomatic. (D) is needlessly wordy when compared to (C). As for (E), the placement of *allowing* seems to suggest that the word is the participle of *to allow* and is used as an adjective. But there is nothing for the adjective to modify.

Psychology originated in the attempts of researchers to describe, record, classify, and explain their own mental impressions, thoughts, and feelings and those of others as they described them verbally. It matured into a science only when the reliance on subjective impressions was gradually abandoned and researchers concentrated on human behavior. Then, psychology truly became a science of mental activity.

36. The passage above assumes that

    I. it is not possible to observe episodes of mental activity directly
    II. early research was unreliable because researchers gave less-than-candid accounts of their mental experiences
    III. human behavior is an expression of mental activity

    (A) I only   (B) III only   (C) I and II only
    (D) I and III only   (E) II and III only

    (D) This question asks that you identify suppressed premises of the argument. Statement I is a suppressed premise. The speaker claims that psychology could become a science only when researchers abandoned the attempt to study mental impressions. Thus, the speaker evidently believes that mental impressions are not observable as scientific phenomena. Similarly, III, too, is a suppressed premise. The speaker claims that psychology became a true science of mental activity only when it concentrated on observable events such as human behavior. Thus, the speaker must believe that behavior is tied to mental activity. Finally, II is not a suppressed premise of the argument. The weakness of early psychology, according to the speaker, was that it tried to study subjective impressions rather than observable phenomena. A subjective impression is just that, regardless of whether the person describing the feeling is being candid or not.

Many people who describe themselves as authors do not belong in that category at all, since writing is not their main source of income.

37. The paragraph above makes the assumption that

  Ⓐ many of those who consider themselves authors lack the skills and training needed to write professionally
  Ⓑ the average income of professional writers is higher than that for most other professions
  Ⓒ professional authors are motivated to become writers primarily by the prospect of financial gain
  Ⓓ to be considered an author a person must publish writings on a regular basis
  Ⓔ a person cannot be considered an author unless he or she derives most of his or her income from writing

(E) The initial argument has the structure: Writing is not the main source of income for a certain group of people; therefore, these people are not really authors. The argument implicitly assumes that a person is not an author unless he derives most of his income from writing. (A) is not an assumption of the argument. The speaker assumes only that such people do not derive most of their income from writing, not that they cannot do so. As for the remaining choices, the speaker's definition of *author* requires that a person derive most of his income from writing, not that he have a large income, nor that the prospect of financial gain be his motivation for writing, nor that the income derive from a series of regularly published writings.

A poll taken ten days before the election showed that 36 percent of the people surveyed planned to vote for Green and 42 percent planned to vote for his opponent. When the votes were finally tallied, Green received 52 percent of the vote, while his opponent received only 46 percent. Thus, the survey method used for the preelection poll was flawed.

38. Which of the following, if true, would most weaken the conclusion of the argument above?

  Ⓐ A poll taken 21 days before the election showed that 32 percent of the people surveyed planned to vote for Green.
  Ⓑ At the time the preelection poll was taken, many voters had not yet made up their minds about which candidate to vote for.
  Ⓒ During the week just before the election, Green's opponent received an important endorsement from a major newspaper.
  Ⓓ The voter turnout for the election in question was extremely light due to inclement weather.
  Ⓔ The preelection survey also questioned voters about their attitudes toward a referendum authorizing the legislature to legalize pari-mutuel gambling.

(B) This question asks you to find an alternative explanation (an explanation for the result other than a flawed study). (B) provides this alternative. The findings were correct as reported: at the time of the survey, 36 percent of the people were committed to Green and 42 percent were committed to Green's opponent (36% + 42% = 78%), but over the next ten days, many of those who were previously undecided determined to vote for Green. As for (A), while this is consistent with the results and suggests that Green was picking up votes as the election date grew nearer, this does not explain what happened in the ten days between the date of the survey and the election. As for (C), this seems to strengthen the conclusion that the survey was inaccurate, for this suggests that Green's opponent should have had even more votes than predicted by the survey. As for (D), weather certainly could affect the outcome of the election, but it's impossible to say given the available facts which of the candidates (if either) would have been aided by a light turnout. Therefore, this idea neither weakens nor strengthens the argument. Finally, (E) is generally related to the topic of the passage but has no bearing on the specific issue being discussed.

39. Which of the following best describes the primary purpose of the passage?

  Ⓐ Antitrust claims may be used as a weapon by one business entity against its competitors.

  Ⓑ The tort of abuse of process is the best way to discourage spurious antitrust suits.

  Ⓒ The First Amendment does not necessarily protect statements that are untrue.

  Ⓓ Antitrust suits can impose considerable economic burdens on those sued.

  Ⓔ Some businesses may file antitrust claims against competitors to reduce competition.

(B) This is a main idea question. The author begins by noting that antitrust laws may be unfairly used by one business against another. In the final sentence of that paragraph, the author asks what we can do about this problem. The second, third, and fourth paragraphs discuss some philosophical problems associated with discouraging parties from seeking government relief (either legislative or judicial). Finally, the author concludes that the best solution is the tort of abuse of process: it won't deter people from filing claims, but it will protect innocent defendants. The other choices do refer to ideas mentioned in the selection, but none of them describes the overall development of the selection. In short, the other choices are too narrow.

40. According to the passage, the American rule requires

  Ⓐ plaintiffs to prove the truth of their claims

  Ⓑ defendants to pay their own costs in litigation

  Ⓒ each party to a lawsuit to pay the other's costs

  Ⓓ a judge to determine which party is at fault

  Ⓔ the government to grant favors to petitioners

(B) This is a specific detail question. Use the wording of the question to find the material you need. You will find it at the end of the third paragraph. The author states that under the American rule, the "victim" may have to bear some of the cost of the dispute. The "victim" is the defendant. So the American rule requires defendants to bear their own costs.

41. It can be inferred from the passage that a "truth" rule would

  Ⓐ impose liability for litigation costs on a plaintiff if the plaintiff lost

  Ⓑ create a buffer zone between statements that are true and those that are honest but untrue

  Ⓒ increase the economic and financial risks incurred by defendants in antitrust suits

  Ⓓ encourage businesses to file frivolous antitrust claims against rival businesses

  Ⓔ reduce the power of the government to control markets through antitrust policy

(A) This is an implied idea question. At the end of the third paragraph, the author is wrestling with the problem of how to allocate costs in an antitrust suit. At the beginning of the fourth paragraph, he says we must reject a rule that would impose costs on a plaintiff simply because the plaintiff does not win. The next sentence refers to this as the "truth" rule. Thus, we can infer that the "truth" rule would require the plaintiff to pay all costs if it doesn't win. (B) is surely wrong because a "truth" rule would impose risks on speech. (C) is incorrect because the rule would increase the risk for plaintiffs and reduce the risk for defendants and potential defendants. (D) is incorrect because the rule, by placing the risk on the plaintiff, would discourage suits. Finally, (E) is wrong because the rule as applied to antitrust law would affect the parties, not the government.

QUANTITATIVE SECTION

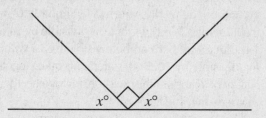

1. In the figure above, $x =$

  Ⓐ 30 Ⓑ 45 Ⓒ 60 Ⓓ 75 Ⓔ 90

(B) $x + 90 + x = 180$

$2x = 90$

$x = 45$

2. In a certain game, a person's age is multiplied by 2 and then the product is divided by 3. If the result of performing the operations on John's age is 12, what is John's age?

  Ⓐ 2 Ⓑ 8 Ⓒ 12 Ⓓ 18 Ⓔ 36

(D) You can set up an equation:

$$\frac{2J}{3} = 12$$

$2J = 36$

$J = 18$

Or you could just test answer choices until you found one that worked. 18 times 2 is 36, and 36 divided by 3 is 12.

3. n is a positive integer. If n is a multiple of 6 and a multiple of 9, what is the least possible value of n?

  Ⓐ 12 Ⓑ 18 Ⓒ 27 Ⓓ 36 Ⓔ 54

(B) Just test choices until you find the smallest available value that is divisible by both 6 and 9. The answer is 18.

4. Is x divisible by 70?
    (1) x is divisible by 2 and 5.
    (2) x is divisible by 2 and 7.
    Ⓐ statement 1 alone is sufficient to answer the question, but statement 2 alone is not sufficient
    Ⓑ statement 2 alone is sufficient to answer the question, but statement 1 alone is not sufficient
    Ⓒ both statements together are needed to answer the question, but neither statement alone is sufficient
    Ⓓ either statement by itself is sufficient to answer the question
    Ⓔ not enough facts are given to answer the question

(C) Statement (1) alone is not sufficient to answer the question. Statement (1) does imply that x is divisible by 10 ($2 \times 5 = 10$), but a number can be divisible by 10 without being divisible by 70. Similarly, (2) alone is insufficient. (2) implies that x is divisible by 14 ($2 \times 7 = 14$), but a number can be divisible by 14 without being divisible by 70. Both statements taken together are sufficient to answer the question, for together they imply that x is divisible by 70 ($2 \times 5 \times 7 = 70$).

5. Does Bob have more records in his record collection than Linda has in hers?
    (1) Christina has more records in her collection than Linda.
    (2) Bob has fewer records in his collection than Christina.
    Ⓐ statement 1 alone is sufficient to answer the question, but statement 2 alone is not sufficient
    Ⓑ statement 2 alone is sufficient to answer the question, but statement 1 alone is not sufficient
    Ⓒ both statements together are needed to answer the question, but neither statement alone is sufficient
    Ⓓ either statement by itself is sufficient to answer the question
    Ⓔ not enough facts are given to answer the question

(E) Neither (1) nor (2) alone can be sufficient, because neither provides a basis for comparing the number of records in Bob's collection with the number in Linda's collection. Nor are the two together sufficient. Although the two statements together establish that both Bob and Linda have fewer records than Christina, that is not sufficient to answer the question asked.

6. For any positive integer k, $\langle k \rangle = k^2 - k$. What is the value of $\langle 2 \rangle$?
    Ⓐ 0   Ⓑ 1   Ⓒ 2   Ⓓ 4   Ⓔ 8

(C) Here we have a defined function problem. Do the indicated operation:

$2 = 2^2 - 2 = 2$

And when that operation is repeated (as required by the problem), the result is still 2.

List X	List Y
1	1
2	2
3	3
4	4

7. For how many different ordered pairs (x, y) where x is a number selected from List X and y is a number selected from list Y, is $x - y > 0$?
    Ⓐ 24   Ⓑ 18   Ⓒ 15   Ⓓ 12   Ⓔ 6

(E) Just count the pairs that fit the requirement:

$(2,1), (3,1), (3,2), (4,1), (4,2), (4,3)$

8. A student receives an average of 75 on three exams that are scored on a scale of 0 to 100. If one of her test scores was 75, what is the lowest possible score she could have received on any of the three tests?
    Ⓐ 0   Ⓑ 1   Ⓒ 25   Ⓓ 40   Ⓔ 50

(E) Use the technique for finding a missing element in an average. Since the three scores average 75, the student earned a total score of $3 \times 75 = 225$. We know that one score is 75, and $225 - 75 = 150$. The maximum she could receive on any test is 100, and $150 - 100 = 50$. So the lowest score she could have received (and still maintain a 75 average) is 50.

9. A class of 30 children took a test. What was the average test score of the students in the class?
    (1) The highest score was 40.
    (2) The lowest score was 10.
    Ⓐ statement 1 alone is sufficient to answer the question, but statement 2 alone is not sufficient
    Ⓑ statement 2 alone is sufficient to answer the question, but statement 1 alone is not sufficient
    Ⓒ both statements together are needed to answer the question, but neither statement alone is sufficient
    Ⓓ either statement by itself is sufficient to answer the question
    Ⓔ not enough facts are given to answer the question

(E) Neither (1) nor (2) is sufficient to answer the question. And even taken together the statements are insufficient, because they do not provide any information about the scores of the other 28 children.

10. Allen and Chris founded a company in 1990. In which year did the company's profits first exceed $100,000?

   (1) In 1990, the company had profits of $15,000, and in every year after that profits were double those of the previous year.

   (2) In 1992, the company had profits of $60,000.

  Ⓐ statement 1 alone is sufficient to answer the question, but statement 2 alone is not sufficient

  Ⓑ statement 2 alone is sufficient to answer the question, but statement 1 alone is not sufficient

  Ⓒ both statements together are needed to answer the question, but neither statement alone is sufficient

  Ⓓ either statement by itself is sufficient to answer the question

  Ⓔ not enough facts are given to answer the question

(A) Statement (1) is sufficient to answer the question. In 1991, profits were $30,000; in 1992, $60,000; and in 1993, $120,000. So it was in 1993 that profits first exceeded $100,000. Statement (2), however, is not sufficient to answer the question. Since (1) alone is sufficient to answer but (2) is not, this item should be classified as (A).

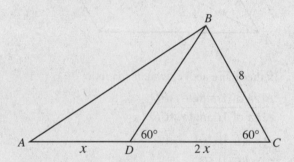

11. In ABC above, what is the length of side AC?

  Ⓐ 4   Ⓑ 8   Ⓒ 12   Ⓓ 18   Ⓔ 20

(C) The triangle on the right is an equilateral triangle, so $2x = 8$, which means that $x = 4$. So the length of AC is $8 + 4 = 12$.

12. If $x + 1 + 2x + 2 + 3x + 3 = 6$, $x =$

  Ⓐ –2   Ⓑ 0   Ⓒ 1   Ⓓ 6   Ⓔ 12

(B) Just do the indicated operations:

$$x + 1 + 2x + 2 + 3x + 3 = 6$$

$$6x + 6 = 6$$

$$6x = 0$$

$$x = 0$$

13. If a horse gallops at an average speed of 40 feet per second, how many seconds will it take the horse to gallop 500 feet?

  Ⓐ 8   Ⓑ 9.5   Ⓒ 12.5   Ⓓ 20   Ⓔ 40

(C) The easiest solution is to use a direct proportion:

$$\frac{40 \text{ feet}}{500 \text{ feet}} = \frac{1 \text{ seconds}}{x \text{ seconds}}$$

$$\frac{40}{500} = \frac{1}{x}$$

$$40x = 500$$

$$x = 12.5 \text{ seconds}$$

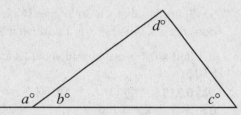

14. In the figure above, what is the value of d?

  (1) $b + c = 90$

  (2) $c + a = 180$

  Ⓐ statement 1 alone is sufficient to answer the question, but statement 2 alone is not sufficient

  Ⓓ statement 2 alone is sufficient to answer the question, but statement 1 alone is not sufficient

  Ⓒ both statements together are needed to answer the question, but neither statement alone is sufficient

  Ⓓ either statement by itself is sufficient to answer the question

  Ⓔ not enough facts are given to answer the question

(A) Statement (1) is sufficient. Since the sum of the degree measures of the interior angles of a triangle is 180:

$$b + c + d = 180$$

Then, given that $b + c = 90$:

$$(b + c) + d = 180$$

$$90 + d = 180$$

$$d = 90$$

(2), however, is not sufficient to answer the question.

15. Is x an integer?

  (1) $x > 0$

  (2) $3^2 + 4^2 = x^2$

  Ⓐ statement 1 alone is sufficient to answer the question, but statement 2 alone is not sufficient

  Ⓑ statement 2 alone is sufficient to answer the question, but statement 1 alone is not sufficient

  Ⓒ both statements together are needed to answer the question, but neither statement alone is sufficient

  Ⓓ either statement by itself is sufficient to answer the question

  Ⓔ not enough facts are given to answer the question

(B) (1) alone is not sufficient to answer the question, for (1) implies only that x is a positive number, not that x is an integer. (2) alone, however, is sufficient to answer the question:

$$3^2 + 4^2 = x^2$$

$$x^2 = 25$$

$$x = +5 \text{ or } x = -5$$

So (2) implies that x is an integer. (Note: The question does not ask whether x is a positive integer.)

16. If 1 mill = 0.1 cents, how many mills are there in $3.13?

    (A) 0.313   (B) 3.13   (C) 31.3
    (D) 313   (E) 3,130

    (E) This question just asks you to manipulate the decimal point: $3.13 = 313$ cents, and $313 \div 0.1 = 3,130$.

17. Which of the following is a pair of numbers that are not equal?

    (A) $\dfrac{63}{6}, \dfrac{21}{2}$ (B) $0.3\%, 0.003$ (C) $\dfrac{44}{77}, \dfrac{4}{7}$

    (D) $\dfrac{3}{8}, 0.375$ (E) $\sqrt{3^2}, 9$

    (E) Don't bother with any fancy mathematic theorizing. Just test the test. $\sqrt{3^2} = 3$, which is *not* equal to 9.

18. If $\dfrac{64}{x} - 6 = 2$, then $x =$

    (A) 8   (B) 12   (C) 16   (D) 24   (E) 32

    (A) Here is a simple equation with one variable, so solve for x:

    $$\frac{64}{x} - 6 = 2$$

    $$\frac{64}{x} = 8$$

    $$8x = 64$$

    $$x = 8$$

19. What is the volume of cube C?

    (1) The total surface area of C is 54 square inches.

    (2) The area of each face of C is 9 square inches.

    (A) statement 1 alone is sufficient to answer the question, but statement 2 alone is not sufficient
    (B) statement 2 alone is sufficient to answer the question, but statement 1 alone is not sufficient
    (C) both statements together are needed to answer the question, but neither statement alone is sufficient
    (D) either statement by itself is sufficient to answer the question
    (E) not enough facts are given to answer the question

(D) Statement (1) alone is sufficient to answer the question. The surface area of a cube is composed of six equal faces, and each of those faces is a square. So (1) implies that the edge of the cube has a length of 3:

$$54 = 6 \times \text{edge} \times \text{edge}$$

$$9 = \text{edge}^2$$

$$\text{edge} = 3$$

(2) also is sufficient, for it too implies that the length of the edge is 3:

$$\text{Area} = \text{edge} \times \text{edge}$$

$$9 = \text{edge}^2$$

$$\text{edge} = 3$$

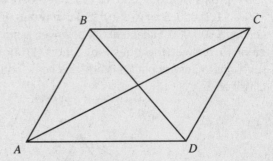

20. In the figure above, what is the ratio

    $$\frac{\text{Area of Triangle } ABD}{\text{Area of Triangle } ACD}?$$

    (1) $AB \parallel CD$

    (2) $BC \parallel AD$

    (A) statement 1 alone is sufficient to answer the question, but statement 2 alone is not sufficient
    (B) statement 2 alone is sufficient to answer the question, but statement 1 alone is not sufficient
    (C) both statements together are needed to answer the question, but neither statement alone is sufficient
    (D) either statement by itself is sufficient to answer the question
    (E) not enough facts are given to answer the question

    (B) Since the triangles share a common base, they will have the same area provided that they have altitudes of equal length. That (1) alone is not sufficient to answer the question can be demonstrated by the technique of distorting the figure:

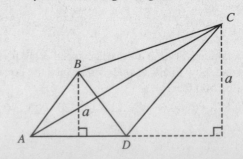

Even though $AB \parallel CD$ in each of the figures, the length of the altitudes of the two triangles may or may not be equal. (2), however, is sufficient to answer the question, for (2) implies that the two altitudes have the same length:

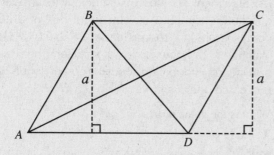

21. If x, y, and z are consecutive integers and $x > y > z$, then $(x - y)(x - z)(y - z) =$

Ⓐ –2 Ⓑ –1 Ⓒ 0 Ⓓ 1 Ⓔ 2

(E) You can solve this problem by setting up equations. Since x, y, and z are consecutive integers and since $x > y > z$, $y = x - 1$ and $z = x - 2$.

$(x - (x - 1))(x - (x - 2))((x - 1) - (x - 2)) =$

$(x - x + 1)(x - x + 2)(x - 1 - x + 2) =$

$(1)(2)(1) = 2$

You can reach the same conclusion with a bit less effort just by assuming some numbers for x, y, and z. Say $x = 3$, $y = 2$, and $z = 1$. The result of plugging those numbers into the expression in the problem is 2.

Questions 22–23

For all positive integers ⓝ,

ⓝ $= 2n$ if n is even
ⓝ $= 3n$ if n is odd

22. If n is a prime number greater than 4, ⓝⓝ $=$

Ⓐ $3n$ Ⓑ $2n$ Ⓒ $3n - 3$ Ⓓ $2n - 2$ Ⓔ n

(D) If n is a prime number greater than 4 the next smaller number must be an even number. And ⓝ $= 2n$ when n is even, so $n - 1 = 2n - 2$.

23. ③·④ $=$

Ⓐ⑥ Ⓑ⑦ Ⓒ⑫ Ⓓ⑱ Ⓔ㊱

(E) First, perform the function on the values given:

③ $= 3 \times 3 = 9$

④ $= 2 \times 4 = 8$

So ③ · ④ $= 72$

Now you can reason that since 72 is an even number, it is the result of performing the function on a number $\frac{1}{2}$ of 72, and $\frac{1}{2}$ of 72 = 36. Or you can test answer choices until you find one that generates the value 72.

BUDGET FOR DAY SCHOOL D

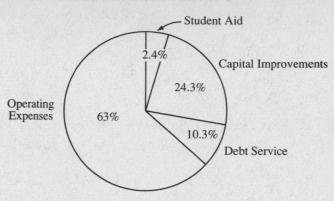

24. How much money did Day School D spend on operating expenses?

(1) The total budget for the school was $9 million.

(2) The school spent $216,000 on student aid.

Ⓐ statement 1 alone is sufficient to answer the question, but statement 2 alone is not sufficient

Ⓑ statement 2 alone is sufficient to answer the question, but statement 1 alone is not sufficient

Ⓒ both statements together are needed to answer the question, but neither statement alone is sufficient

Ⓓ either statement by itself is sufficient to answer the question

Ⓔ not enough facts are given to answer the question

(D) Statement (1) alone is sufficient to answer the question. Operating expenses were 63% of $9,000,000 = $5,670,000. Statement (2) is also sufficient, for (2) implies that the total budget was $9,000,000:

2.4% of Total = $216,000

$0.024T = $216,000$

$T = $9,000,000$

And as shown above, that additional information, when coupled with the data provided by the chart, is sufficient to answer the question.

25. What is the value of the integer N?

(1) N is an integer multiple of 2 and 3.

(2) $30 < N < 70$

Ⓐ statement 1 alone is sufficient to answer the question, but statement 2 alone is not sufficient

Ⓑ statement 2 alone is sufficient to answer the question, but statement 1 alone is not sufficient

Ⓒ both statements together are needed to answer the question, but neither statement alone is sufficient

Ⓓ either statement by itself is sufficient to answer the question

Ⓔ not enough facts are given to answer the question

(E) Neither (1) nor (2) alone is sufficient to answer the question, and even taken together they do not provide enough information to answer the question. Although

(1) implies that N must be a multiple of 6, there are 6 numbers between 30 and 70 that are divisible by 6.

26. If $\frac{x}{z} = k$ and $\frac{y}{z} = k - 1$, $x =$

(A) $y - 1$ (B) $y + 1$ (C) $y + z$

(D) $z - y$ (E) $\frac{y}{z}$

(C) Use the method for solving simultaneous equations. Since $\frac{y}{z} = k - 1$, $k = \frac{y}{z} + 1$. And since $\frac{x}{z} = k$:

$$\frac{x}{z} = \frac{y}{z} + 1$$

$$x = z\left(\frac{y}{z} + 1\right)$$

$$x = y + z$$

27. In the figure above, O is the center of the circle. What is the ratio of the area of the shaded portion of the figure to the area of the unshaded portion of the figure?

(A) 4:1   (B) π:1   (C) 3:1   (D) 5:2   (E) 2:1

(C) Let r be the radius of the smaller circle. Its area is πr^2. Then the radius of the larger circle is $2r$, and its area is $\pi(2r)^2 = 4\pi r^2$. The shaded part of the diagram is the larger circle minus the smaller one, so the area of the shaded part of the diagram is $4\pi r^2 - \pi r^2 = 3\pi r^2$, and the ratio of the shaded area to the unshaded area is 3:1.

28. If x is 25% of y, y is what percent of x?

(A) 400%   (B) 300%   (C) 250%
(D) 125%   (E) 75%

(A) If $x = 0.25y$, $y = \frac{x}{0.25} = 4x$, so y is 400 percent of x.

29. How much money is saved by buying a box of a dozen donuts instead of buying 12 donuts singly?

(1) When purchased in a box of 12, the cost of each donut is $0.05 less than if purchased singly.

(2) The price of a box of a dozen donuts is $2.40.

(A) statement 1 alone is sufficient to answer the question, but statement 2 alone is not sufficient

(B) statement 2 alone is sufficient to answer the question, but statement 1 alone is not sufficient

(C) both statements together are needed to answer the question, but neither statement alone is sufficient

(D) either statement by itself is sufficient to answer the question

(E) not enough facts are given to answer the question

(A) Statement (1) alone is sufficient to answer the question. (1) implies that buying a box of a dozen donuts results in a cost savings of $12 \times \$0.05 = \$0.60$. Statement (2), however, is not sufficient, because (2) provides no information about the cost of donuts when purchased one at a time.

30. What is the value of $a^4 - b^4$?

(1) $a^2 + b^2 = 24$

(2) $a^2 - b^2 = 0$

(A) statement 1 alone is sufficient to answer the question, but statement 2 alone is not sufficient

(B) statement 2 alone is sufficient to answer the question, but statement 1 alone is not sufficient

(C) both statements together are needed to answer the question, but neither statement alone is sufficient

(D) either statement by itself is sufficient to answer the question

(E) not enough facts are given to answer the question

(B) The expression $a^4 - b^4$ is the difference between two squares and can be factored:

$$a^4 - b^4 = (a^2 + b^2)(a^2 - b^2)$$

Statement (1) alone is not sufficient to fix the value of the expression, but (2) is.

If $a^2 - b^2 = 0$:

$$a^4 - b^4 = (a^2 + b^2)(0) = 0$$

31. If x is an integer which is a multiple of both 9 and 5, which of the following must be true?

I. x is equal to 45.

II. x is a multiple of 15.

III. x is odd.

(A) I only   (B) II only   (C) III only
(D) II and III only   (E) I, II, and III

(B) Since 3 is a factor of 9 and 5 is a factor of 5, any multiple of both 9 and 5 will be a multiple of 15, so II is a correct choice. I, however is not correct. x could be any multiple of 45, e.g., 90, which also proves that III is not a correct choice.

32. If the radius of circle O is 20 percent less than the radius of circle P, the area of circle O is what percent of the area of circle P?

(A) 60%   (B) 64%   (C) 72%
(D) 80%   (E) 120%

(B) Let r be the radius of P, the larger circle. It has an area of πr^2. Then the radius of O, the smaller circle, will be $0.8r$, and it will have an area of $\pi(0.8r)^2 = 0.64\pi r^2$. Thus, the area of the smaller circle is only 64% of that of the larger circle.

33. If the average (arithmetic mean) of 20, 23, 24, x and y = 26 and $\frac{x}{y} = \frac{3}{4}$, $x =$

    Ⓐ 25   Ⓑ 27   Ⓒ 36   Ⓓ 41   Ⓔ 63

    (B) Solve using the technique for finding the missing element of an average. Since the average of the five numbers is 26, their sum is $26 \times 5 = 130$. The sum of 20, 23, and 24 is 67, and $130 - 67 = 63$, so $x + y = 63$. Now you can use the method for solving simultaneous equations. x is equal to 27 and y is equal to 36.

34. If a cube has a side of length 2, what is the distance from any vertex to the center of the cube?

    Ⓐ $\frac{\sqrt{2}}{2}$ Ⓑ $\sqrt{3}$ Ⓒ $2\sqrt{2}$ Ⓓ $2\sqrt{3}$ Ⓔ $\frac{3}{2}$

    (B) This problem really needs a diagram:

    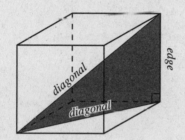

    Notice that the diagonal of the face, the edge of the cube, and the diagonal of the cube form a right triangle, the hypotenuse of which is the diagonal of the cube. Since the edge has a length of 2, the diagonal of the face has a length of $2\sqrt{2}$. Now use the Pythagorean Theorem:

    $2^2 + (2\sqrt{2})^2 = d^2$

    $4 + 8 = d^2$

    $d^2 = 12$

    $d = \sqrt{12} = 2\sqrt{3}$

    This is the length of the diagonal. The distance from any vertex to the center of the cube is one-half of that, or $\sqrt{3}$.

35. Daniel invested a total of $10,000 for a period of one year. Part of the money he put into an investment that earned 6 percent simple interest, and the rest of the money into an investment that earned 8 percent simple interest. How much money did he put into the investment that earned 6 percent?

    (1) The total interest earned on the $10,000 for the year was $640.

    (2) The dollar value of the investment that earned 8 percent was one-fourth the dollar value of the investment that earned 6 percent.

    Ⓐ statement 1 alone is sufficient to answer the question, but statement 2 alone is not sufficient

    Ⓑ statement 2 alone is sufficient to answer the question, but statement 1 alone is not sufficient

    Ⓒ both statements together are needed to answer the question, but neither statement alone is sufficient

    Ⓓ either statement by itself is sufficient to answer the question

    Ⓔ not enough facts are given to answer the question

    (D) Statement (1) alone is sufficient to answer the question, for you can set up simultaneous equations. Let x stand for the amount invested at 6 percent and y for the amount invested at 8 percent. Since a total of $10,000 was invested at both rates:

    $x + y = \$10,000$

    Then, $(x)(0.06)$ plus $(y)(0.08)$ is the total amount of interest earned:

    $0.06x + 0.08y = \$640$

    Using the first equation, redefine y in terms of x:

    $y = \$10,000 - x$

    And substitute this value for y in the second equation:

    $0.06x + 0.08(\$10,000 - x) = \$640$

    $0.06x + \$800 - 0.08x = \$640$

    $0.02x = \$160$

    $x = \$8,000$

    Statement (2) is also sufficient. Again, let x stand for the amount that earned 6 percent and y for the amount that earned 8 percent. (2) implies:

    $y = \frac{1}{4}x$

Given that $x + y = \$10,000$:

$$\frac{1}{4}x + x = \$10,000$$

$$\frac{5}{4}x = \$10,000$$

$$x = \$8,000$$

36. Is x greater than y?

(1) $3x = 4y$

(2) $x = \dfrac{k}{3}$, $y = \dfrac{k}{4}$, and $k > 0$

Ⓐ statement 1 alone is sufficient to answer the question, but statement 2 alone is not sufficient

Ⓑ statement 2 alone is sufficient to answer the question, but statement 1 alone is not sufficient

Ⓒ both statements together are needed to answer the question, but neither statement alone is sufficient

Ⓓ either statement by itself is sufficient to answer the question

Ⓔ not enough facts are given to answer the question

(B) Statement (1) alone is not sufficient. If x and y are positive, then given that $3x = 4y$, x is larger than y. But if x and y are negative, then given that $3x = 4y$, y is larger than x. (For example, x might be -4 and y -3.) Statement (2), however, is sufficient to answer the question. Since $x = \frac{k}{3}$, $3x = k$, and since $y = \frac{k}{4}$, $4y = k$. This implies that $3x = 4y$. And here it is stipulated that k is positive, which means that both x and y must also be positive. Therefore, (2) implies that x is greater than y.

37. Is the perimeter of a rectangular yard greater than 60 meters?

(1) The two shorter sides of the yard are each 15 meters long.

(2) The length of the yard is 3 meters longer than the width of the yard.

Ⓐ statement 1 alone is sufficient to answer the question, but statement 2 alone is not sufficient

Ⓑ statement 2 alone is sufficient to answer the question, but statement 1 alone is not sufficient

Ⓒ both statements together are needed to answer the question, but neither statement alone is sufficient

Ⓓ either statement by itself is sufficient to answer the question

Ⓔ not enough facts are given to answer the question

(A) Statement (1) is sufficient to answer the question. The sum of the lengths of the two shorter sides must be less than half of the perimeter of the rectangle. Since $15 + 15 = 30$, the total perimeter of the yard must be more than twice 30. (2), however, is not sufficient to answer the question, for (2) provides no information about the actual length of either side.

Sample GMAT
CAT 6

Verbal Section:

41 Questions—75 Minutes

1. What I would call personal style depends not so much on the actual clothing you wear but one's choice of items such as jewelry and makeup.

    (A) but one's choice of
    (B) but one's choosing
    (C) but your choice of
    (D) as your choice of
    (E) as your choosing

2. The actual votes cast by incumbents can provide voters with a more accurate picture of their attitudes than the speeches they make while campaigning for reelection.

    (A) their attitudes than the speeches they make
    (B) the attitudes of incumbents than the speeches they make
    (C) the attitudes of incumbents than do the speeches they make
    (D) the attitudes of incumbents than do the speeches
    (E) the attitudes of incumbents than the speeches

3. With the writing of *Huckleberry Finn,* it marked the first time that the American vernacular was used in a novel.

    (A) With the writing of *Huckleberry Finn,* it marked the first time that the American vernacular was used in a novel.
    (B) Marking the first time that the American vernacular was used in a novel was *Huckleberry Finn.*
    (C) The writing of *Huckleberry Finn,* a novel, was the first time that the American vernacular was used.
    (D) The writing of *Huckleberry Finn* marked the first time that the American vernacular was used in a novel.
    (E) The first time that the American vernacular was used in a novel was *Huckleberry Finn.*

GO ON TO NEXT PAGE

Bernie was stopped on the street by a man in dark glasses. The man offered to sell Bernie an Epsilon watch, which normally retails for $750, for $50. Bernie gave the man $50 for the watch. Later that day, Bernie learned the watch was actually an Upsilon watch, which normally retails for $19.95.

4. Which of the following adages is an appropriate criticism of Bernie's action?

   I. You must look before you leap.

   II. A fool and his money are soon parted.

   III. There is a sucker born every minute.

   IV. Nothing ventured; nothing gained.

    (A) I and II only
    (B) I and IV only
    (C) I, II, and III only
    (D) II, III, and IV only
    (E) I, II, III, and IV

The governor claims that the state faces a drought and has implemented new water-use restrictions; but that's just a move to get some free publicity for his re-election campaign. So far this year we have had 3.5 inches of rain, slightly more than the average amount of rain for the same period over the last three years.

5. Which of the following, if true, would most weaken the conclusion of the argument above?

    (A) The governor did not declare drought emergencies in the previous three years.
    (B) City officials who have the authority to mandate water-use restrictions have not done so.
    (C) The snowmelt that usually contributes significantly to the state's reservoirs is several inches below normal.
    (D) The amount of water the state can draw from rivers that cross state boundaries is limited by federal law.
    (E) Water-use restrictions are short-term measures and do little to reduce long-term water consumption.

Clean-Well is a company that offers cleaning services. The agency's fee is $25 per hour per employee used to do a job plus $5 car fare for each employee. Customers must provide cleaning supplies. I use the service to clean the windows of my store. Over the years, I have found that one worker can do the job in eight hours, while two workers can do the job in only three hours, making it cheaper to hire two workers than one. I conclude that two workers function as a team, making them more efficient than a single worker.

6. Which of the following, if true, would most weaken the conclusion of the argument above?

    (A) The cost of cleaning supplies to do the job is the same for one worker as for a team of two workers.
    (B) At the end of an eight-hour day a worker is $\frac{1}{3}$ less efficient than at the beginning of the day.
    (C) The workers provided by the service are paid only $7 of the $25-per-hour charge assessed by the company.
    (D) A team of four workers requires two hours and thirty minutes to complete the job.
    (E) A team of two workers from a competitor of Clean-Well will take four hours to do the job.

Questions 7–9

The radio waves emitted by supernova remnants are produced by the synchrotron process, named after a phenomenon first observed in synchrotron particle accelerators, namely the emission of strongly polarized radiation by very energetic electrons spiraling along a magnetic field. Every supernova remnant somehow produces large quantities of extremely high-energy particles. But how do they do it?

The initial explosion cannot explain the high-energy particles observed in supernova remnants. Particles produced that way will quickly lose their energy as they cool in the expanding cloud. In the Vela supernova remnant, a pulsar, or rapidly rotating neutron star, is generating large quantities of high-energy particles, but this object appears to be the exception rather than the rule. In most cases, the acceleration of particles to high energies must have something to do with the shock wave produced by the supernova explosion.

It has been suggested that these fragments represent turbulent magnetic eddies and that charged particles are accelerated to very high energies through collisions with the fragments. The acceleration process is analogous to that of a Ping-Pong ball moving through a collection of randomly moving bowling balls. Over the course of many collisions, the Ping-Pong ball will be accelerated to a very high speed. It is too early to say definitely that the size and number of fragments are adequate to generate the high-energy electrons and magnetic field necessary to explain the radio emission, but a preliminary analysis looks promising.

7. The author develops the passage by

   Ⓐ raising an issue and discussing both sides of it
   Ⓑ logically deducing conclusions from a premise
   Ⓒ explaining a known sequence of events
   Ⓓ providing a list of examples to illustrate an idea
   Ⓔ posing a question and giving a tentative answer

8. Which of the following best describes the logical development of the second paragraph?

   Ⓐ The author presents a theory and refutes it.
   Ⓑ The author presents a theory and gives evidence to support it.
   Ⓒ The author relies on authority to prove his point.
   Ⓓ The author invites the reader to form his or her own conclusion.
   Ⓔ The author uncovers the hidden ambiguity in a statement.

9. The author regards the conclusions advanced in the third paragraph of the passage as

   Ⓐ unproved but likely
   Ⓑ unsubstantiated but doubtful
   Ⓒ conclusively demonstrated
   Ⓓ true by definition
   Ⓔ idle speculation

10. Parents and teachers are becoming increasingly concerned about protecting children and the drugs which are available to them, and several parent-teacher organizations dedicated to educating children to the dangers of drugs have recently been formed.

   Ⓐ protecting children and the drugs which are available to them
   Ⓑ protection of children and the drugs which are available to them
   Ⓒ protecting children from their availability to drugs
   Ⓓ protecting children and the drugs' availability to them
   Ⓔ protecting children from the drugs available to them

11. Although today it is cost-effective to make perfumes with synthetic ingredients, they used to make the classic fragrances from flowers only and other natural essences.

   Ⓐ they used to make the classic fragrances from flowers only
   Ⓑ the classic fragrances used to be made only from flowers
   Ⓒ the classic fragrances used to be made by them only from flowers
   Ⓓ the classic fragrances used to be made from flowers only
   Ⓔ only flowers used to make the classic fragrances

12. Appearing to be the only candidate whose views would be acceptable to its membership, the Youth Caucus finally endorsed George Avery for City Council.

   Ⓐ Appearing to be
   Ⓑ Seeming to be
   Ⓒ Because he appeared to be
   Ⓓ Because he seemed
   Ⓔ Being

In general, the per-hour cost of operating a device by solar energy is more expensive than using the power supplied by the public utility. But for some purposes, such as adding a new outdoor light to a house, a solar-powered unit is actually cheaper.

13. Which of the following, if true, probably underlies the conclusion above?

   Ⓐ Solar energy is more efficient in the southern latitudes than in the northern latitudes.
   Ⓑ A solar-powered light is a self-contained unit and does not require the installation of a power line.
   Ⓒ New technology will eventually reduce the cost of solar power below that of other energy sources.
   Ⓓ The most costly components of any solar-powered system are the solar cells that convert sunlight to electricity.
   Ⓔ A solar-powered system can be installed only in areas that receive considerable direct sunlight.

The Commission on Public Service recently recommended that federal judges be given a substantial pay increase. For many years, however, there have been many applicants for each new vacancy on the federal bench, proving that a pay increase is not needed.

14. Which of the following, if true, most weakens the argument above?

   Ⓐ Salaries for federal judges are higher than those for state and municipal judges.
   Ⓑ Salaries for the federal judiciary are established by the legislative branch.
   Ⓒ A federal judgeship is a very prestigious position in the legal community.
   Ⓓ Salaries for federal judges are too low to attract qualified lawyers.
   Ⓔ Most federal judges are former practitioners, teachers, or state judges.

GO ON TO NEXT PAGE

When it rains, my car gets wet. Since it hasn't rained recently, my car can't be wet.

15. Which of the following is logically most similar to the argument above?

(A) Whenever critics give a play a favorable review, people go to see it; Pinter's new play did not receive favorable reviews, so I doubt that anyone will go to see it.

(B) Whenever people go to see a play, critics give it a favorable review; people did go to see Pinter's new play, so it did get a favorable review.

(C) Whenever critics give a play a favorable review, people go to see it; Pinter's new play got favorable reviews, so people will probably go see it.

(D) Whenever a play is given favorable reviews by the critics, people go to see it; since people are going to see Pinter's new play, it will probably get favorable reviews.

(E) Whenever critics give a play a favorable review, people go to see it; people are not going to see Pinter's new play, so it did not get favorable reviews.

Questions 16–18

At Nuremberg, 210 individuals were tried before thirteen military tribunals. The International Military Tribunal (IMT) tried the major German war criminals, including Hermann Goering, Rudolph Hess, and Joachim von Ribbentrop, from November 1945 to October 1946. Subsequently, another 185 defendants, grouped by organization or by type of crime, were tried before twelve United States military tribunals. Robert H. Jackson, the United States chief of counsel and an associate justice of the United States Supreme Court, decided for the IMT that in order to obtain convictions of the officials who gave the orders but did not themselves execute them, the prosecution would rely heavily upon documentary evidence. Such evidence was presumably more persuasive than affidavits and direct testimony of witnesses who might easily be brought by defense lawyers to waver in their statements.

In the course of the various trials, the prosecution chose from the millions of records available to them about 18,000 to be presented as evidence. Only 2,500 of these were affidavits or interrogation transcripts. Of the total number of defense exhibits, about one-half were affidavits. The rest of the documentary evidence came from a variety of sources, often from the defendant's personal files, the materials in the tribunal library file, and prosecution records and resources. Heavy reliance on the latter often placed the defense in a position of dependence on the good will of the prosecution.

The prosecution staff of the IMT established an elaborate system requiring the cooperation of many government agencies for processing documents, and the prosecution at the 12 United States trials at Nuremberg inherited this system. The resources of the defense were, of course, considerably more limited. Though defendants were given the right to present evidence to the tribunal, they were often compelled to engage in a long and often futile struggle to obtain records. Rulings were often affected by factors not directly related to courtroom and document-handling procedures. Some former members of the IMT defense counsel had acquired more expertise than others by defending several of the accused before the various United States tribunals at different times. As the crimes of the Nazis became more remote in time and the differences among the Allies in the cold-war period increased, a strong, rearmed Germany that could serve as an integral part of Western European defense became desirable. Correspondingly, it became difficult to try German military leaders before United States military tribunals while reestablishing a German military force. Sentences were progressively lightened and procedures softened. Sometimes, however, the nature of the crimes committed precluded the chance of the defendants to receive lighter sentences. Many harsh sentences resulted from the trial of 24 SS Einsatzgruppen for exterminating approximately one million Soviet citizens. In general, SS defendants received severe sentences, often the death penalty, and had greater difficulty in obtaining documents than other defendants.

The judges themselves were also of considerable importance. Judge Toms, from Michigan's third judicial district, Judge Phillips, from North Carolina's thirteenth district, Judge Musamanno, from the court of common pleas in Pennsylvania, and John J. Speight, admitted to the bar of Alabama, adjudicated the Milch and Pohl cases. In addition, judges Musamanno and Speight were on the bench in the Ohlendorf case. Their rulings on document-handling procedures were often more rigid and disadvantageous to defendants than were those of other judges. Among the latter were judges Wennerstrum, Shake, and Christianson of the Supreme Court of Minnesota, who presided over the Weizaecker case.

Although one might say that greater lenience in document procedures might have resulted in better defense, considering the crimes charged, there is no assurance that even the most liberal procedure would have produced exonerating records. The prosecution's greater control of documents in the earlier cases, acting under rules similar to adversary proceedings, tainted the trials. Yet, despite these flaws, the procedures devised at Nuremberg pioneered the massive use of records as court evidence with large groups of defendants. In the face of the terrible hatred engendered by the inhumanities of the Second World War, the tribunals succeeded in dispensing, essentially, justice.

16. The author is primarily concerned with

(A) describing a historical event
(B) developing a theory of jurisdprudence
(C) analyzing courtroom procedures
(D) criticizing a government policy
(E) interpreting a legal principle

17. According to the passage, defendants at the Nuremberg trials

    Ⓐ were not given the opportunity to present evidence
    Ⓑ frequently had difficulty obtaining documents
    Ⓒ were not represented by counsel
    Ⓓ were tried in absentia
    Ⓔ were prosecuted by officers of the United States military

18. The author would be most likely to agree with which of the following statements?

    Ⓐ Members of the SS were unfairly punished more severely than other war criminals.
    Ⓑ The IMT was more effective than the 12 United States military tribunals.
    Ⓒ Many war criminals would have received harsher sentences had they been tried earlier.
    Ⓓ Counsel who represented the defendants at Nuremberg were often incompetent.
    Ⓔ Trial by documentary evidence is inherently prejudicial to the rights of a defendant.

19. Modern theories of criminal justice view rehabilitation as the goal of the penal system and aim at <u>restoration of the offender to society rather as</u> merely punishing him.

    Ⓐ restoration of the offender to society rather as
    Ⓑ restoring of the offender to society rather than
    Ⓒ restoring the offender to society rather as
    Ⓓ restoring the offender to society rather than
    Ⓔ restoration of the offender to society rather as

20. Approximately 20,000 meteors enter the earth's atmosphere every day, <u>but very few of them reach the earth's surface on the grounds that they</u> are consumed by frictional heat long before they reach the earth.

    Ⓐ but very few of them reach the earth's surface on the grounds that they
    Ⓑ but very few of them reach the earth's surface because most
    Ⓒ but very few of them reach the earth's surface because they
    Ⓓ with very few of them reaching the earth's surface on account of they
    Ⓔ since very few of them reach the earth's surface because most

21. The major national leaders consulted consider solar power economically infeasible at present but <u>that it will be so</u> in the future.

    Ⓐ that it will be so
    Ⓑ that it would be so
    Ⓒ believe that it will be so
    Ⓓ believe that it will be economically feasible
    Ⓔ believe that economic feasibility will be achieved

"Channel One" is a 12-minute school news show that includes two minutes of commercials. The show's producers offer high schools $50,000 worth of television equipment to air the program. Many parents and teachers oppose the use of commercial television in schools, arguing that advertisements are tantamount to indoctrination. But students are already familiar with television commercials and know how to distinguish programming from advertising.

22. The argument assumes that

    Ⓐ the effects of an advertisement viewed in a classroom would be similar to those of the same advertisement viewed at home
    Ⓑ many educators would be willing to allow the indoctrination of students in exchange for new equipment for their schools
    Ⓒ television advertising is a more effective way of promoting a product to high school students than print advertising
    Ⓓ high school students are sufficiently interested in world affairs to learn from a television news program
    Ⓔ a television news program produced especially for high school students is an effective teaching tool

Questions 23–24

The spate of terrorist acts against airlines and their passengers raises a new question: should government officials be forced to disclose the fact that they have received warning of an impending terrorist attack? The answer is "yes." The government currently releases information about the health hazards of smoking, the ecological dangers of pesticides, and the health consequences of food.

23. The argument above relies primarily on

    Ⓐ circular reasoning
    Ⓑ generalization
    Ⓒ authority
    Ⓓ analogy
    Ⓔ causal analysis

24. All of the following, if true, would weaken the argument above EXCEPT

    Ⓐ Public disclosure of threats would encourage more threats by giving terrorists greater publicity.
    Ⓑ Information about terrorist acts is gained from intelligence gathering, not research studies.
    Ⓒ Information about possible terrorist acts is routinely distributed to the staff of U.S. embassies.
    Ⓓ Making public terrorist threats would allow terrorists to identify sources who had leaked the information.
    Ⓔ Public disclosure of threats would encourage false threats designed to disrupt air travel.

GO ON TO NEXT PAGE ⇨

Questions 25–27

The two principal ways in which immigrant groups adjust to the dominant culture of the host country are assimilation and acculturation. Some ethnic groups appear to have been almost completely assimilated, but Puerto Ricans remain a clearly identifiable minority community.

Puerto Ricans have followed the examples of previous immigrant groups by clustering in their own ethnic communities. They have created islands within a city where Spanish is spoken, native foods are available, Latin music is heard and other elements of the island life style are evident. The cultural familiarity of the *barrio* keeps many Puerto Ricans from leaving even when they can find better housing elsewhere, and this slows the process of assimilation.

Additionally, Puerto Ricans are a short plane trip from their homeland. There is a constant two-way flow between this country and the island that disrupts the assimilation process. And with the trend toward ethnic pride and cultural pluralism, pride in Puerto Rican cultural roots has been strengthened. Had the extreme anti-foreigner sentiment of the 1940s persisted, Puerto Ricans may well have had to assimilate sooner, as did many other ethnic groups.

The term *acculturation* rather than assimilation would be used to describe the Puerto Rican experience on the mainland of the United States. Genuine assimilation has not taken place until an immigrant is able to function in the host community without encountering prejudice or discrimination. The problem of hostility in an alien world does not disappear with acculturation: there remains the painful reality of deprivation of status and social rejection.

25. According to the passage, the process of assimilation is complete only when an immigrant

    Ⓐ applies for citizenship
    Ⓑ learns to speak English
    Ⓒ no longer actively preserves the native culture
    Ⓓ can freely participate in the greater society
    Ⓔ finds employment in the host country

26. According to the passage, Puerto Ricans have not been assimilate for which of the following reasons?

    I. The physical proximity of Puerto Rico helps to maintain strong ties to their homeland.
    II. The prevailing social and political climate is conducive to the survival of a distinct ethnic identity.
    III. Puerto Ricans prefer to live in cultural enclaves where elements of the Puerto Rican life style abound.

    Ⓐ I only   Ⓑ III only   Ⓒ I and II only
    Ⓓ II and III only   Ⓔ I, II, and III

27. The author is primarily concerned with

    Ⓐ explaining why Puerto Ricans have not been assimilated
    Ⓑ analyzing the process of acculturation of immigrant groups
    Ⓒ discussing social problems created by discrimination against Puerto Ricans
    Ⓓ comparing the experience of Puerto Ricans with that of other immigrant groups
    Ⓔ describing some of the important features of Puerto Rican culture

28. Puritan fanatics brought to civil and military affairs a coolness of judgment and mutability of purpose that some writers have thought inconsistent with their religious zeal, <u>but which was in fact a natural outgrowth of it.</u>

    Ⓐ but which was in fact a natural outgrowth of it
    Ⓑ but which were in fact a natural outgrowth of it
    Ⓒ but which were in fact natural outgrowths of it
    Ⓓ but it was in fact a natural outgrowth of them
    Ⓔ which was in fact a natural outgrowth of it

29. In the past few years, significant changes have taken place in the organization of our <u>economy that will profoundly affect the character of our labor unions as well as influencing</u> consumer and industrial life.

    Ⓐ economy that will profoundly affect the character of our labor unions as well as influencing
    Ⓑ economy that will profoundly affect the character of our labor unions as well as influence
    Ⓒ economy; these changes will profoundly affect the character of our labor unions and influence
    Ⓓ economy, and that will profoundly affect the character of our labor unions as well as influence
    Ⓔ economy, changes that will profoundly affect the character of our labor unions as well as to influence

30. Americans give pride of place to the value of individual liberty, and we find <u>especially unintelligible the infliction of suffering</u> on the innocent.

    Ⓐ especially unintelligible the infliction of suffering
    Ⓑ especial unintelligible the infliction of suffering
    Ⓒ especially unintelligible suffrage that is inflicted
    Ⓓ especially unintelligible the suffering that is inflicted
    Ⓔ especially unintelligible the inflicting to suffer

Some residents of San Juan Capistrano, California, have suggested that government take some action to prevent the swallows from returning there each year because the birds constitute a nuisance. This suggestion ignores the important role the birds play in the environment. Swallows feed almost exclusively on flying insects, including many species that are annoying or harmful to human beings. The abundance of the birds in that region indicates an abundance of insects that are controlled through predation.

31. The speaker above implies that

    (A) without swallows, the region would be infested with insects
    (B) the majority of residents favor limiting the swallow population
    (C) the economic damage caused by the swallows is negligible
    (D) swallows are less destructive than other species of birds
    (E) pesticides would be ineffective against the species of insects eaten by the swallows

Susan: International Cosmetics is marketing a new treatment for cellulite called Fango Italiano. It's a cream that is spread on the affected area, allowed to dry, and then washed off. The treatment is very expensive— $250 per month—but it comes with a money-back guarantee. If Fango Italiano doesn't reduce your cellulite, the company will give you all of your money back. Since the company gives such a guarantee, the treatment must work.

Tom: I doubt that the treatment works. "Fango" is just the Italian word for *mud*. But it does seem to me that the company has found a brilliant marketing scheme. People who are so worried about their physical appearance that they are willing to spend $250 a month to get rid of cellulite are people who, while using the treatment, will also start eating less and exercising more. Thus, the treatment will appear to be successful and International Cosmetics will be that much richer.

32. Which of the following best characterizes the position Tom takes with regard to Susan's statement?

    (A) He denies that Fango Italiano will be effective and questions whether or not International Cosmetics really intends to refund the money of dissatisfied customers.
    (B) He denies that International Cosmetics really intends to market Fango Italiano, but suspects that the treatment is not effective.
    (C) He questions whether or not the treatment is effective and denies that it is possible to do anything about cellulite.
    (D) He agrees that people who purchase Fango Italiano may very well lose cellulite, but is skeptical that the treatment will be the reason.
    (E) He argues that $250 per month is too expensive for a treatment for cellulite and encourages people with cellulite to eat less and exercise more.

The National Research Council has recommended against requiring seat belts in school buses because only one life would be saved per year at a cost of $40 million annually. This analysis is shortsighted. Children who are required to use seat belts in school buses will remember to use them when they are old enough to drive.

33. The speaker above assumes that

    (A) installing seat belts in school buses will not cost $40 million per year
    (B) requiring seat belts in school buses would save many lives each year
    (C) most schoolchildren are transported to and from school in buses
    (D) states should require the use of seat belts in private vehicles
    (E) behavior learned as a child may affect adulthood behavior

34. Curfews, <u>which were initially enacted as a precaution against fire</u>, were common in towns and cities throughout Europe in the Middle Ages.

    (A) which were initially enacted as a precaution against fire
    (B) which were enacted as an initial precaution against fire
    (C) which were a precaution initially enacted against fire
    (D) enacted as a precaution initially against fire
    (E) enacted initially against fire

35. The nuclear accident at Chernobyl released clouds of radioactive particles into the <u>atmosphere, contaminating agricultural products grown within much of the Ukraine, as well as products grown in countries as far away</u> as Italy.

    (A) atmosphere, contaminating agricultural products grown within much of the Ukraine, as well as products grown in countries as far away as
    (B) atmosphere, to contaminate agricultural products growing within much of the Ukraine, as well as products growing in countries as far away as
    (C) atmosphere, while contaminating agricultural products growing within much of the Ukraine, as well as products growing in countries as far away than
    (D) atmosphere, contaminating agricultural products grown within much of the Ukraine, as well as far away than
    (E) atmosphere, contaminating agricultural products grown within much of the Ukraine, as well as

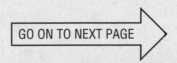
GO ON TO NEXT PAGE

A decade ago, "earn your age" was the immediate goal of every recent business school graduate. For example, a 26-year-old M.B.A. expected to earn $26,000 per year. This standard no longer holds true in America—a newly graduated M.B.A. in America would want to earn much more—but it is still the norm in England. It seems, therefore, that a starting M.B.A. in America is economically better off than one in England.

36. Which of the following, if true, most weakens the argument above?

(A) Many students from England earn their M.B.A.s in the United States.

(B) Most students in American business schools have had prior work experience.

(C) The British pound is worth almost twice as much as the American dollar.

(D) Graduates from American law schools earn more than graduates from American business schools.

(E) England produces fewer M.B.A.s each year than the United States.

The United States is currently faced with a shortage of qualified math and science teachers. A Rand Corporation study indicates that graduates of traditional undergraduate schools of education are expected to fill only half the 20,000 vacancies for math and science teachers. One way of addressing this problem is to provide scholarships for math and science majors to finish their educations and graduate without accumulating massive debts. If they are freed of the burdens of college loans, they will be more likely to consider careers in teaching.

37. Which of the following, if true, would most weaken the argument above?

(A) Public school teachers earn starting salaries that are well above the average wage in the United States.

(B) Large numbers of graduates in math and science in prior years created a surplus pool from which teaching jobs are filled.

(C) The cost of an undergraduate education in math or science is comparable to that for other majors.

(D) Faculty at colleges and universities generally earn higher salaries than teachers in public schools.

(E) There is no shortage of teachers in areas such as history, literature, and vocational training.

Helium-filled balloons rise because helium is a light gas, much lighter than air. Glass tubes filled with neon gas can be charged with electricity to make light, so neon is also a light gas. Therefore, there is one respect in which both helium gas and neon gas are alike: they are both light gases.

38. Which of the following arguments most closely parallels the argument above?

(A) The Empire State Building is a tall building, and Peter is a tall man. Therefore, there is one respect in which both the Empire State Building and Peter are alike: they are both tall.

(B) Mary is a law school professor, and her daughter is a medical school professor. So there is one respect in which Mary and her daughter are alike: they are both professors.

(C) A good steak must be rare, and total lunar eclipses are rare. So there is one respect in which a good steak and total lunar eclipses are alike: they are both rare.

(D) All whales are mammals, and all bats are mammals. Since all mammals are warm-blooded, there is one respect in which whales and bats are alike: they are both warm-blooded.

(E) Susan ate half of the melon, and Nancy ate the other half of the melon. So there is one respect in which Susan and Nancy are alike: each ate half a melon.

Questions 39–41

A fundamental principle of pharmacology is that all drugs have multiple actions. Actions that are desirable in the treatment of disease are considered therapeutic, while those that are undesirable or pose risks to the patient are called "effects." Adverse drug effects range from the trivial, for example, nausea or dry mouth, to the serious, such as massive gastrointestinal bleeding or thromboembolism; and some drugs can be lethal. Therefore, an effective system for the detection of adverse drug effects is an important component of the health-care system of any advanced nation. Much of the research conducted on new drugs aims at identifying the conditions of use that maximize beneficial effects and minimize the risk of adverse effects. The intent of drug labeling is to reflect this body of knowledge accurately so that physicians can properly prescribe the drug or, if it is to be sold without prescription, so that consumers can properly use the drug.

The current system of drug investigation in the United States has proved very useful and accurate in identifying the common side effects associated with new prescription drugs. By the time a new drug is approved by the Food and Drug Administration, its side effects are usually well described in the package insert for physicians. The investigational process, however, cannot be counted on to detect all adverse effects because of the relatively small number of patients involved in premarketing studies and the relatively short duration of the studies. Animal toxicology studies are, of course, done prior to marketing in an attempt to identify any potential for toxicity, but negative results do not guarantee the safety of a drug in humans, as evidenced by such well-known examples as the birth deformities due to thalidomide.

This recognition prompted the establishment in many countries of programs to which physicians report adverse drug effects. The United States and other countries also send reports to an international program operated by the World Health Organization. These programs, however, are voluntary reporting programs and are intended to serve a limited goal: alerting a government or private agency to adverse drug effects detected by physicians in the course of practice. Other approaches must be used to confirm suspected drug reactions and to estimate incidence rates. These other approaches include conducting retrospective control studies, for example, the studies associating endometrial cancer with estrogen use, and systematically monitoring hospitalized patients to determine the incidence of acute common side effects, as typified by the Boston Collaborative Drug Surveillance Program.

Thus, the overall drug surveillance system of the United States is composed of a set of information bases, special studies, and monitoring programs, each contributing in its own way to our knowledge about marketed drugs. The system is decentralized among a number of governmental units and is not administered as a coordinated function. Still, it would be inappropriate at this time to attempt to unite all of the disparate elements into a comprehensive surveillance program. Instead, the challenge is to improve each segment of the system and to take advantage of new computer strategies to improve coordination and communication.

39. The author's primary concern is to discuss

(A) methods for testing the effects of new drugs on humans
(B) the importance of having accurate information about the effects of drugs
(C) procedures for determining the long-term effects of new drugs
(D) attempts to curb the abuse of prescription drugs
(E) the difference between the therapeutic and nontherapeutic actions of drugs

40. The author introduces the example of thalidomide to show that some

(A) drugs do not have the same actions in humans that they do in animals
(B) drug testing procedures are ignored by careless laboratory workers
(C) drugs have no therapeutic value for humans
(D) drugs have adverse side effects as well as beneficial actions
(E) physicians prescribe drugs without first reading the manufacturer's recommendations

41. The author is most probably leading up to a discussion of some suggestions about how to

(A) centralize authority for drug surveillance in the United States
(B) centralize authority for drug surveillance among international agencies
(C) coordinate better the sharing of information among the drug surveillance agencies
(D) eliminate the availability and sale of certain drugs now on the market
(E) improve drug-testing procedures to detect dangerous effects before drugs are approved

Stop: End of Verbal Section

Quantitative Section

37 Questions—75 Minutes

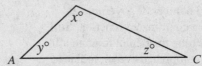
1. If $x + 2 = 3x + 10$, then $x =$

    ⓐ –8 ⓑ –4 ⓒ 2 ⓓ 6 ⓔ 12

2. 10^3 is what percent of 10^5?

    ⓐ 0.01% ⓑ 0.1% ⓒ 1%
    ⓓ 10% ⓔ 100%

3. From 1996 to 1997, the size of the student body at Midvale High School increased by 30 percent. If the size of the student body in 1997 was 4,550, what was the size of the student body in 1996?

    ⓐ 3,185 ⓑ 3,350 ⓒ 3,500
    ⓓ 3,600 ⓔ 3,650

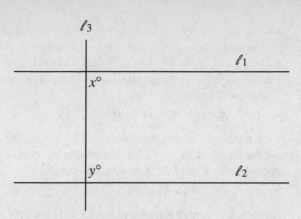

4. In the figure above, l_1 and l_2 intersect l_3. Do l_1 and l_2 intersect to the right of l_3?

   (1) $x > y$

   (2) $x + y < 180$

   Ⓐ statement 1 alone is sufficient to answer the question, but statement 2 alone is not sufficient
   Ⓑ statement 2 alone is sufficient to answer the question, but statement 1 alone is not sufficient
   Ⓒ both statements together are needed to answer the question, but neither statement alone is sufficient
   Ⓓ either statement by itself is sufficient to answer the question
   Ⓔ not enough facts are given to answer the question

5. What is the value of $(p + q)(r + s)$?

   (1) $p(r + s) = 5$ and $q(r + s) = 3$.

   (2) $(p + q) = 8$

   Ⓐ statement 1 alone is sufficient to answer the question, but statement 2 alone is not sufficient
   Ⓑ statement 2 alone is sufficient to answer the question, but statement 1 alone is not sufficient
   Ⓒ both statements together are needed to answer the question, but neither statement alone is sufficient
   Ⓓ either statement by itself is sufficient to answer the question
   Ⓔ not enough facts are given to answer the question

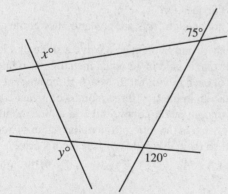

Note: Figure not drawn to scale.

6. In the figure above, $x - y =$
   Ⓐ 45   Ⓑ 90   Ⓒ 135   Ⓓ 180   Ⓔ 195

7. What percent of 16 is $\sqrt{16}$?

   Ⓐ $12\frac{1}{2}\%$ Ⓑ 25%   Ⓒ $33\frac{1}{3}\%$ Ⓓ 50%   Ⓔ $66\frac{2}{3}\%$

8. $x = yz$ and $x \neq 0$. If the y term of the equation is multiplied by 5 and the z term of the equation is also multiplied by 5, then, to preserve the statement of equality, it is necessary to

   Ⓐ multiply the x term by 5
   Ⓑ multiply the x term by 10
   Ⓒ multiply the x term by 25
   Ⓓ divide the x term by 1
   Ⓔ divide the x term by 25

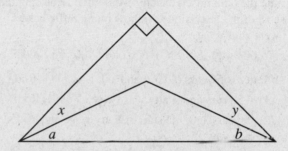

9. In the figure above, what is the value of $x + y$?

   (1) $a = 2b$

   (2) $a + b = 45$

   Ⓐ statement 1 alone is sufficient to answer the question, but statement 2 alone is not sufficient
   Ⓑ statement 2 alone is sufficient to answer the question, but statement 1 alone is not sufficient
   Ⓒ both statements together are needed to answer the question, but neither statement alone is sufficient
   Ⓓ either statement by itself is sufficient to answer the question
   Ⓔ not enough facts are given to answer the question

10. What is the sum of 3 consecutive integers?

   (1) The ratio of the least of the three integers to the greatest is 2.

   (2) The sum of the 3 integers is less than the average of the three integers.

   Ⓐ statement 1 alone is sufficient to answer the question, but statement 2 alone is not sufficient
   Ⓑ statement 2 alone is sufficient to answer the question, but statement 1 alone is not sufficient
   Ⓒ both statements together are needed to answer the question, but neither statement alone is sufficient
   Ⓓ either statement by itself is sufficient to answer the question
   Ⓔ not enough facts are given to answer the question

GO ON TO NEXT PAGE

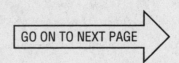

11. If $0 < x < 1$, which of the following is the greatest?

   (A) x^2 (B) x (C) $\dfrac{1}{x}$ (D) $\dfrac{1}{x^2}$ (E) $\dfrac{1}{x^3}$

12. If m is an integer, which of the following must be an *odd* integer?

   (A) $\dfrac{m}{2}$ (B) $2m+1$ (C) $3m$

   (D) $3m+1$ (E) m^2

13. A civic club sold raffle tickets to raise $450 for a charity. The winning prize was a television set that cost the club $150. If the raffle tickets cost $0.75 each and the club raised exactly $450 (after deducting the cost of the television set), how many raffle tickets were sold?

   (A) 60 (B) 80 (C) 600 (D) 700 (E) 800

14. If Patty is 5 years older than Rod, how old is Rod?

   (1) 15 years ago, Patty was twice as old as Rod.
   (2) 5 years ago, the sum of Patty's age and Rod's age was 35.

   (A) statement 1 alone is sufficient to answer the question, but statement 2 alone is not sufficient
   (B) statement 2 alone is sufficient to answer the question, but statement 1 alone is not sufficient
   (C) both statements together are needed to answer the question, but neither statement alone is sufficient
   (D) either statement by itself is sufficient to answer the question
   (E) not enough facts are given to answer the question

15. 149 people were aboard Flight 222 when it arrived at Los Angeles from New York City with Chicago as the only intermediate stop. How many people first boarded the flight in Chicago?

   (1) 170 people were aboard the flight when it left New York City.
   (2) 23 people from the flight deplaned in Chicago and did not reboard.

   (A) statement 1 alone is sufficient to answer the question, but statement 2 alone is not sufficient
   (B) statement 2 alone is sufficient to answer the question, but statement 1 alone is not sufficient
   (C) both statements together are needed to answer the question, but neither statement alone is sufficient
   (D) either statement by itself is sufficient to answer the question
   (E) not enough facts are given to answer the question

16. If $\dfrac{6a(b+3)}{3b(2a+4)} = \dfrac{3}{4}$, then $\dfrac{a}{b} =$

   (A) 4 (B) 3 (C) $\dfrac{4}{3}$ (D) $\dfrac{3}{4}$
   (E) cannot be determined from the information given.

17. A bicyclist rode from point A to point B in 90 minutes. The return trip along the same route took only 45 minutes. If the distance from A to B is 36 miles, what was the bicyclist's average speed, in miles per hour, for the entire trip?

   (A) 16 (B) 24 (C) 30 (D) 32 (E) 36

18. If the width of a rectangle is increased by 10 percent and the length is increased by 40 percent, by what percent is the area of the rectangle increased?

   (A) 4% (B) 16% (C) 36% (D) 54% (E) 66%

19. Was Mark's average running speed for the first hour of his 26-mile marathon 11 miles per hour?

   (1) He ran the entire 26 miles in 2.5 hours.
   (2) He ran the last 15 miles in 1.5 hours.

   (A) statement 1 alone is sufficient to answer the question, but statement 2 alone is not sufficient
   (B) statement 2 alone is sufficient to answer the question, but statement 1 alone is not sufficient
   (C) both statements together are needed to answer the question, but neither statement alone is sufficient
   (D) either statement by itself is sufficient to answer the question
   (E) not enough facts are given to answer the question

20. A certain packing crate contains between 50 and 60 books. How many books are there in the packing crate?

   (1) If the books are counted out by threes, there will be one book left over.
   (2) If the books are counted out by sixes, there will be one book left over.

   (A) statement 1 alone is sufficient to answer the question, but statement 2 alone is not sufficient
   (B) statement 2 alone is sufficient to answer the question, but statement 1 alone is not sufficient
   (C) both statements together are needed to answer the question, but neither statement alone is sufficient
   (D) either statement by itself is sufficient to answer the question
   (E) not enough facts are given to answer the question

21. Elizabeth and Scott each receive a share of a lottery prize that is paid in 12 equal installments on the last day of each month for 20 years. If the amount paid to Elizabeth in the first three months of a year is equal to the amount paid to Scott in the first nine months of a year, what is the ratio of the dollar value of Scott's prize to the dollar value of Elizabeth's prize?

   (A) 1:3 (B) 7:11 (C) 2:3 (D) 9:13 (E) 3:4

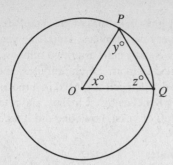

Note: Figure not drawn to scale.

22. In the figure above, O is the center of the circle. If $PQ > OP$, which of the following must be true?

   I. $y = z$
   II. $y < 60$
   III. $x < y + z$

   Ⓐ I only   Ⓑ II only   Ⓒ I and II only
   Ⓓ I and III only   Ⓔ I, II, and III

23. Forty percent of the employees of a certain company are men, and 75 percent of the men earn more than $25,000 per year. If 45 percent of all the company's employees earn more than $25,000 per year, what fraction of the women employed by the company earn $25,000 per year or less?

   Ⓐ $\dfrac{2}{11}$ Ⓑ $\dfrac{1}{4}$ Ⓒ $\dfrac{1}{3}$ Ⓓ $\dfrac{2}{3}$ Ⓔ $\dfrac{3}{4}$

24. If N and P denote the nonzero digits of a four-digit number $NNPP$, is $NNPP$ divisible by 4?

   (1) NPP is divisible by 8.
   (2) NPP is divisible by 4.

   Ⓐ statement 1 alone is sufficient to answer the question, but statement 2 alone is not sufficient
   Ⓑ statement 2 alone is sufficient to answer the question, but statement 1 alone is not sufficient
   Ⓒ both statements together are needed to answer the question, but neither statement alone is sufficient
   Ⓓ either statement by itself is sufficient to answer the question
   Ⓔ not enough facts are given to answer the question

25. A supermarket sells both a leading brand of laundry powder and its own brand of laundry powder. On all sizes of the leading brand it makes a profit of 15 percent of cost per box. On all sizes of its own brand it makes a profit of 10 percent of cost per box. For a certain month, from the sales of which of the two brands does the supermarket realize the greater profit?

   (1) Ounce for ounce, the supermarket pays a higher wholesale price for the leading brand than it does for its own brand.
   (2) Ounce for ounce, the supermarket sells 25 percent more of its own brand than of the leading brand.

   Ⓐ statement 1 alone is sufficient to answer the question, but statement 2 alone is not sufficient
   Ⓑ statement 2 alone is sufficient to answer the question, but statement 1 alone is not sufficient
   Ⓒ both statements together are needed to answer the question, but neither statement alone is sufficient
   Ⓓ either statement by itself is sufficient to answer the question
   Ⓕ not enough facts are given to answer the question

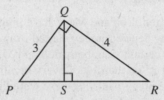

26. In the figure above, what is the length of QS?

   Ⓐ $\dfrac{25}{3}$ Ⓑ $\dfrac{20}{3}$ Ⓒ $\dfrac{15}{4}$ Ⓓ $\dfrac{12}{5}$ Ⓔ $\dfrac{7}{5}$

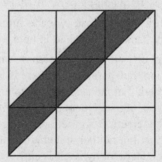

27. The figure above shows a square piece of land that is divided into nine smaller square lots. The shaded portion is a railroad right-of-way. If the area of the shaded portion of the figure is 5 square miles, what is the area, in square miles, of the entire piece of land?

   Ⓐ 9   Ⓑ 10   Ⓒ 13   Ⓓ 18   Ⓔ 36

GO ON TO NEXT PAGE

28. Cars are entering the parking lot of a suburban shopping mall at the rate of one car every three seconds and leaving at the rate of one car every seven seconds. The parking lot is filling at a rate of approximately one car every

    (A) 6 seconds   (B) $5\frac{1}{3}$ seconds   (C) $5\frac{1}{4}$ seconds

    (D) $3\frac{3}{7}$ seconds   (E) $2\frac{1}{10}$ seconds

29. If S is a sequence of numbers the first term of which is 1 and each succeeding term of which is x more than the preceding term, what is the value of x?

    (1) The sum of the third and fourth terms of S is 22.

    (2) The sum of the second and ninth terms of S is 39.

    (A) statement 1 alone is sufficient to answer the question, but statement 2 alone is not sufficient
    (B) statement 2 alone is sufficient to answer the question, but statement 1 alone is not sufficient
    (C) both statements together are needed to answer the question, but neither statement alone is sufficient
    (D) either statement by itself is sufficient to answer the question
    (E) not enough facts are given to answer the question

30. Two children, Bob and Mary, have piggy banks into which they deposit money earned from doing odd jobs. In a certain year, both Bob and Mary each deposited $5 on the first of every month into their respective piggy banks. If these were the only deposits made into the piggy banks during the year, on December 31 does Bob have more money in his piggy bank than Mary has in her piggy bank? (Assume no withdrawals.)

    (1) On March 15 Bob had three times as much money in his piggy bank as Mary had in hers.

    (2) On June 15 Bob had twice as much money in his piggy bank as Mary had in hers.

    (A) statement 1 alone is sufficient to answer the question, but statement 2 alone is not sufficient
    (B) statement 2 alone is sufficient to answer the question, but statement 1 alone is not sufficient
    (C) both statements together are needed to answer the question, but neither statement alone is sufficient
    (D) either statement by itself is sufficient to answer the question
    (E) not enough facts are given to answer the question

31. $(3508)^2 - (3510 \times 3508) =$

    (A) 7020
    (B) 0
    (C) −2
    (D) −3508
    (E) −7016

32. A new fast-growing strain of yeast cells reproduces by dividing every two minutes. Thus, one yeast cell becomes two yeast cells after two minutes, four after four minutes, eight after eight minutes, and so on. If one newly divided cell is placed in a rectangular vat 6 inches by 8 inches by 12 inches, and after one hour the vat is full of yeast, how long did it take to fill half the vat?

    (A) 15 minutes
    (B) 24 minutes
    (C) 30 minutes
    (D) 48 minutes
    (E) 58 minutes

33. For a certain concert, 560 tickets were sold for a total of $2,150. If an orchestra seat sold for twice the balcony seat price of $2.50, how many of the tickets sold were balcony seat tickets?

    (A) 235
    (B) 260
    (C) 300
    (D) 325
    (E) 358

34. At the beginning of a class, a classroom has 3 empty chairs and all students are seated. No student leaves the classroom, and additional students equal to 20 percent of the number of students already seated enter the class late and fill the empty chairs. What is the total number of chairs in the classroom?

    (A) 18
    (B) 15
    (C) 10
    (D) 6
    (E) 3

35. Is $a > 0$?

    (1) $-2a < 0$

    (2) $5a > 0$

    (A) statement 1 alone is sufficient to answer the question, but statement 2 alone is not sufficient
    (B) statement 2 alone is sufficient to answer the question, but statement 1 alone is not sufficient
    (C) both statements together are needed to answer the question, but neither statement alone is sufficient
    (D) either statement by itself is sufficient to answer the question
    (E) not enough facts are given to answer the question

36. An elevator in a large office building contains riders who range in weight from 95 to 205 pounds. How many riders are in the elevator?

   (1) The total weight of all the elevator riders is 1500 pounds.

   (2) The maximum capacity of the elevator is 1600 pounds.

  Ⓐ statement 1 alone is sufficient to answer the question, but statement 2 alone is not sufficient

  Ⓑ statement 2 alone is sufficient to answer the question, but statement 1 alone is not sufficient

  Ⓒ both statements together are needed to answer the question, but neither statement alone is sufficient

  Ⓓ either statement by itself is sufficient to answer the question

  Ⓔ not enough facts are given to answer the question

37. A company's profit was $600,000 in 1990. What was its profit in 1991?

   (1) There was a 20 percent increase in income in 1991.

   (2) There was a 25 percent increase in costs in 1991.

  Ⓐ statement 1 alone is sufficient to answer the question, but statement 2 alone is not sufficient

  Ⓑ statement 2 alone is sufficient to answer the question, but statement 1 alone is not sufficient

  Ⓒ both statements together are needed to answer the question, but neither statement alone is sufficient

  Ⓓ either statement by itself is sufficient to answer the question

  Ⓔ not enough facts are given to answer the question

Stop: End of Quantitative Section

Answer Key

VERBAL SECTION

1.	D	15.	A	29.	C
2.	C	16.	A	30.	A
3.	D	17.	B	31.	A
4.	C	18.	C	32.	D
5.	C	19.	D	33.	E
6.	B	20.	B	34.	A
7.	E	21.	D	35.	A
8.	A	22.	A	36.	C
9.	A	23.	D	37.	B
10.	E	24.	C	38.	C
11.	B	25.	D	39.	B
12.	C	26.	E	40.	A
13.	B	27.	A	41.	C
14.	D	28.	C		

QUANTITATIVE SECTION

1.	B	14.	D	27.	D
2.	C	15.	C	28.	C
3.	C	16.	E	29.	D
4.	B	17.	D	30.	D
5.	A	18.	D	31.	E
6.	A	19.	C	32.	E
7.	B	20.	B	33.	B
8.	C	21.	A	34.	A
9.	B	22.	C	35.	D
10.	A	23.	E	36.	E
11.	E	24.	D	37.	E
12.	B	25.	E		
13.	E	26.	D		

Explanatory Answers

VERBAL SECTION

1. What I would call personal style depends not so much on the actual clothing you wear <u>but one's choice of</u> items such as jewelry and makeup.

   Ⓐ but one's choice of
   Ⓑ but one's choosing
   Ⓒ but your choice of
   Ⓓ as your choice of
   Ⓔ as your choosing

   (D) The underlined portion of the original sentence contains two errors. First, the construction "not so much this *but* that" is not idiomatic. The correct idiom is "not so much this *as* that." Second, the underlined part uses the pronoun *one*, but *one* is intended to refer to *you*. (D) and (E) correct both these errors. (E), however, changes the intended meaning of the original. It is not the mere fact someone makes a decision that is important (as [E] implies); rather, the important thing is the outcome of the decision. And the word *choice* refers to the result of the decision, e.g., "her choice was the blue pendant."

2. The actual votes cast by incumbents can provide voters with a more accurate picture of <u>their attitudes than the speeches they make</u> while campaigning for reelection.

   Ⓐ their attitudes than the speeches they make
   Ⓑ the attitudes of incumbents than the speeches they make
   Ⓒ the attitudes of incumbents than do the speeches they make
   Ⓓ the attitudes of incumbents than do the speeches
   Ⓔ the attitudes of incumbents than the speeches

   (C) The original sentence contains two errors. First, it attempts an illogical comparison: the actual votes provide a better picture of attitudes than speeches. To correct this problem, a *do* must be placed after *than*. Second, the pronoun *their* doesn't have a clear referent. (It is not immediately clear whether *their* refers to incumbents or voters.) This problem can be corrected by using a noun in place of *their*. (B) and (E) make only one of the needed corrections. (D) makes both corrections, but (D) introduces a new error. (D) implies that the speeches are campaigning.

3. <u>With the writing of *Huckleberry Finn*, it marked the first time that the American vernacular was used in a novel.</u>

   Ⓐ With the writing of *Huckleberry Finn*, it marked the first time that the American vernacular was used in a novel.
   Ⓑ Marking the first time that the American vernacular was used in a novel was *Huckleberry Finn*.
   Ⓒ The writing of *Huckleberry Finn*, a novel, was the first time that the American vernacular was used.
   Ⓓ The writing of *Huckleberry Finn* marked the first time that the American vernacular was used in a novel.
   Ⓔ The first time that the American vernacular was used in a novel was *Huckleberry Finn*.

   (D) The main problem with the original sentence is that *it* has no referent. (B) eliminates the problematic pronoun usage, but the resulting sentence is extremely awkward. Stripped to its essentials, (B) has the structure "Marking the first time . . . was *Huckleberry Finn*." (C) changes the intended meaning of the original, for (C) implies that the American vernacular had never been used before in any way—not just that it had never before been used in a novel. Finally, (E) asserts an illogical equivalence between an event and a book: "The first time . . . was *Huckleberry Finn*."

Bernie was stopped on the street by a man in dark glasses. The man offered to sell Bernie an Epsilon watch, which normally retails for $750, for $50. Bernie gave the man $50 for the watch. Later that day, Bernie learned the watch was actually an Upsilon watch, which normally retails for $19.95.

4. Which of the following adages is an appropriate criticism of Bernie's action?

   I. You must look before you leap.
   II. A fool and his money are soon parted.
   III. There is a sucker born every minute.
   IV. Nothing ventured; nothing gained.

   Ⓐ I and II only
   Ⓑ I and IV only
   Ⓒ I, II, and III only
   Ⓓ II, III, and IV only
   Ⓔ I, II, III, and IV

   (C) Bernie was obviously conned. You could use I, II, and III to criticize Bernie's behavior because each of those adages cautions against being overly trusting.

IV, however, could only be used to *defend* Bernie's behavior—not to criticize it.

The governor claims that the state faces a drought and has implemented new water-use restrictions; but that's just a move to get some free publicity for his re-election campaign. So far this year we have had 3.5 inches of rain, slightly more than the average amount of rain for the same period over the last three years.

5. Which of the following, if true, would most weaken the conclusion of the argument above?

Ⓐ The governor did not declare drought emergencies in the previous three years.

Ⓑ City officials who have the authority to mandate water-use restrictions have not done so.

Ⓒ The snowmelt that usually contributes significantly to the state's reservoirs is several inches below normal.

Ⓓ The amount of water the state can draw from rivers that cross state boundaries is limited by federal law.

Ⓔ Water-use restrictions are short-term measures and do little to reduce long-term water consumption.

(C) The argument above depends upon a hidden and unsupported assumption: rainfall is the only source of water for the reservoirs. (C) effectively attacks the argument by attacking this hidden assumption. (A) is an interesting observation, but it is difficult to see in which direction it cuts. Does (A) tend to show that the governor is declaring a drought emergency in this year as a political maneuver, or does it tend to show that this year there really is a drought? As for (B), if this has any relevance at all, it actually strengthens the argument: if city officials have not declared a drought emergency, then maybe there really is no emergency. (D) and (E) mention ideas that are generally related to the problem discussed by the speaker, but they have no specific relevance to the points made by him.

Clean-Well is a company that offers cleaning services. The agency's fee is $25 per hour per employee used to do a job plus $5 car fare for each employee. Customers must provide cleaning supplies. I use the service to clean the windows of my store. Over the years, I have found that one worker can do the job in eight hours, while two workers can do the job in only three hours, making it cheaper to hire two workers than one. I conclude that two workers function as a team, making them more efficient than a single worker.

6. Which of the following, if true, would most weaken the conclusion of the argument above?

Ⓐ The cost of cleaning supplies to do the job is the same for one worker as for a team of two workers.

Ⓑ At the end of an eight-hour day a worker is $\frac{1}{3}$ less efficient than at the beginning of the day.

Ⓒ The workers provided by the service are paid only $7 of the $25-per-hour charge assessed by the company.

Ⓓ A team of four workers requires two hours and thirty minutes to complete the job.

Ⓔ A team of two workers from a competitor of Clean-Well will take four hours to do the job.

(B) Begin your attack on this item by finding the conclusion of the argument. It's not difficult to find, for the speaker signals it with the phrase "I conclude that." The conclusion is that a team of workers requires fewer working hours to complete the project than a single worker because they work as a team. One way of attacking this argument is to look for an alternative causal linkage. (B) does this. The real reason that two workers take less time is that they are fresher. Each works only three hours, while a single worker works eight hours, becoming less efficient later in the day. (A), (C), and (E) have nothing to do with why two workers from Clean-Well appear to be more efficient than a single worker. (D) is probably the second-best answer choice here. The group of four workers requires a total of ten hours to do the job, and this suggests that four workers may not be an efficient team. But the speaker has made a point about a group of two people working as a team. He might readily acknowledge that four is too large a group to work as a team, but that point does not score against his explanation about the efficiency of a two-person work group.

7. The author develops the passage by

Ⓐ raising an issue and discussing both sides of it

Ⓑ logically deducing conclusions from a premise

Ⓒ explaining a known sequence of events

Ⓓ providing a list of examples to illustrate an idea

Ⓔ posing a question and giving a tentative answer

(E) This is a logical structure question that asks about the overall development of the selection. In the first paragraph, the author explicitly poses a question. In the second paragraph, he dismisses one possible answer as incorrect. But in the final paragraph, he provides a possible answer. (E) is a particularly appropriate description of the structure of the passage because it recognizes that the answer the author provides is tentative.

8. Which of the following best describes the logical development of the second paragraph?

Ⓐ The author presents a theory and refutes it.

Ⓑ The author presents a theory and gives evidence to support it.

Ⓒ The author relies on authority to prove his point.

Ⓓ The author invites the reader to form his or her own conclusion.

Ⓔ The author uncovers the hidden ambiguity in a statement.

(A) This is a logical structure question. We have already noted that the author presents the hypothesis in paragraph two in order to disprove it. (A) correctly describes this structure.

9. The author regards the conclusions advanced in the third paragraph of the passage as

   Ⓐ unproved but likely
   Ⓑ unsubstantiated but doubtful
   Ⓒ conclusively demonstrated
   Ⓓ true by definition
   Ⓔ idle speculation

(A) This is an attitude question. In the final paragraph, the author specifically says, "it is too early to say definitely," but concludes with the remark that the theory seems "promising." So the author recognizes that the theory is as yet unproved but expresses his confidence in its correctness.

10. Parents and teachers are becoming increasingly concerned about <u>protecting children and the drugs which are available to them</u>, and several parent-teacher organizations dedicated to educating children to the dangers of drugs have recently been formed.

   Ⓐ protecting children and the drugs which are available to them
   Ⓑ protection of children and the drugs which are available to them
   Ⓒ protecting children from their availability to drugs
   Ⓓ protecting children and the drugs' availability to them
   Ⓔ protecting children from the drugs available to them

(E) In the original sentence, *protecting* seems to include as one of its objects *drugs*. Thus, the sentence seems to assert that parents are concerned about protecting drugs. (B) fails to eliminate this ambiguity. (C), (D), and (E) all eliminate the ambiguity, but (C) and (D) introduce new errors. (C) makes an error of logical expression, for the drugs are available to the children, not, as (C) suggests, vice versa. As for (D), the phrase "drugs' availability to them" is awkward.

11. Although today it is cost-effective to make perfumes with synthetic ingredients, <u>they used to make the classic fragrances from flowers only</u> and other natural essences.

   Ⓐ they used to make the classic fragrances from flowers only
   Ⓑ the classic fragrances used to be made only from flowers
   Ⓒ the classic fragrances used to be made by them only from flowers
   Ⓓ the classic fragrances used to be made from flowers only
   Ⓔ only flowers used to make the classic fragrances

(B) The original contains two errors. First, *they* has no referent. Second, the placement of *only* implies that the fragrances were manufactured solely from flowers, but the sentence clearly states that other natural essences were also used. Only (B) eliminates both of these errors. (C) eliminates the second error but it fails to eliminate the first because *them* has no referent. (D) eliminates the first error but not the second. Finally, (E) changes the intended meaning of the original by implying that the flowers are responsible for the manufacture of the fragrances and the other natural essences.

12. <u>Appearing to be</u> the only candidate whose views would be acceptable to its membership, the Youth Caucus finally endorsed George Avery for City Council.

   Ⓐ Appearing to be
   Ⓑ Seeming to be
   Ⓒ Because he appeared to be
   Ⓓ Because he seemed
   Ⓔ Being

(C) The sentence is afflicted with a dangling modifier and implies that the Youth Caucus was itself a candidate. (B) and (E) fail to correct the error, and *being* would probably not be acceptable in any event. (C) and (D) both make the needed correction, but *to be* is needed to complete the predicate initiated by *seemed*.

In general, the per-hour cost of operating a device by solar energy is more expensive than using the power supplied by the public utility. But for some purposes, such as adding a new outdoor light to a house, a solar-powered unit is actually cheaper.

13. Which of the following, if true, probably underlies the conclusion above?

   Ⓐ Solar energy is more efficient in the southern latitudes than in the northern latitudes.
   Ⓑ A solar-powered light is a self-contained unit and does not require the installation of a power line.
   Ⓒ New technology will eventually reduce the cost of solar power below that of other energy sources.
   Ⓓ The most costly components of any solar-powered system are the solar cells that convert sunlight to electricity.
   Ⓔ A solar-powered system can be installed only in areas that receive considerable direct sunlight.

(B) The speaker notes that the cost of electricity supplied by a public utility is generally lower than that for solar power but concludes that there are some exceptions to this rule, such as an outdoor light. Why would an outdoor light be such an exception? (B) gives us a possible explanation: it doesn't incur the cost of running a wire. (A) is irrelevant, since the speaker does not contrast solar power in northern and southern latitudes. (C) is also irrelevant, since the speaker is talking about technology that is presently in use. (D) helps explain why solar power is generally more expensive but doesn't explain why the exception mentioned is an exception to the general rule. Finally, (E) certainly discusses a limitation of solar power, but it does nothing to explain the exception mentioned by the speaker.

The Commission on Public Service recently recommended that federal judges be given a substantial pay increase. For many years, however, there have been many applicants for each new vacancy on the federal bench, proving that a pay increase is not needed.

14. Which of the following, if true, most weakens the argument above?

 Ⓐ Salaries for federal judges are higher than those for state and municipal judges.

 Ⓑ Salaries for the federal judiciary are established by the legislative branch.

 Ⓒ A federal judgeship is a very prestigious position in the legal community.

 Ⓓ Salaries for federal judges are too low to attract qualified lawyers.

 Ⓔ Most federal judges are former practitioners, teachers, or state judges.

(D) The speaker argues that there is no need to raise salaries for federal judges because there are many applicants who want these positions at existing salaries. The problem with this reasoning is that it equates quantity with quality.

(D) focuses on this weakness. As for (A), this idea seems to strengthen the speaker's claim; you don't need to raise salaries for federal judges because their salaries are already higher than those for other judges. (B) has nothing to do with the question of whether or not judges should be given raises. (C) seems to strengthen the speaker's claim: you don't need to raise salaries because the prestige of the position is sufficient to ensure that qualified applicants will seek federal judgeships. Finally, (E) is irrelevant to the speaker's claim.

When it rains, my car gets wet. Since it hasn't rained recently, my car can't be wet.

15. Which of the following is logically most similar to the argument above?

 Ⓐ Whenever critics give a play a favorable review, people go to see it; Pinter's new play did not receive favorable reviews, so I doubt that anyone will go to see it.

 Ⓑ Whenever people go to see a play, critics give it a favorable review; people did go to see Pinter's new play, so it did get a favorable review.

 Ⓒ Whenever critics give a play a favorable review, people go to see it; Pinter's new play got favorable reviews, so people will probably go see it.

 Ⓓ Whenever a play is given favorable reviews by the critics, people go to see it; since people are going to see Pinter's new play, it will probably get favorable reviews.

 Ⓔ Whenever critics give a play a favorable review, people go to see it; people are not going to see Pinter's new play, so it did not get favorable reviews.

(A) The fallacy of the initial argument is confusing a sufficient with a necessary cause. A sufficient cause is an event that is sufficient to guarantee some effect; for example, rain is a sufficient cause for getting a car wet. A necessary cause is one that is required for some event; for example, oxygen is a necessary condition for combustion. The initial argument mentions a sufficient cause (rain will wet a car) but erroneously concludes that that cause is a necessary cause (a car might be hosed down). (A) parallels this error.

According to (A), favorable reviews are sufficient to prompt people to see a play. (A) goes on to say that since the play did not receive favorable reviews, people will not go to see it. But favorable reviews are a sufficient cause for people's going to see the play, not a necessary cause.

16. The author is primarily concerned with

 Ⓐ describing a historical event
 Ⓑ developing a theory of jurisdprudence
 Ⓒ analyzing courtroom procedures
 Ⓓ criticizing a government policy
 Ⓔ interpreting a legal principle

(A) This is a main idea question. Using the first words of the choices, you should be able to eliminate (D). Although the author does make one or two remarks that are critical of the tribunals, it is not the main purpose of the passage to criticize anything. The first words of the remaining choices are consistent with the development of the passage, so we must look at those choices in their entirety. The best choice is (A). The author treats the Nuremberg trials as a historical occurrence. We can eliminate (B) as too broad. Though the topic of the selection is law, the author is not concerned with the broad topic of jurisprudence. (C), too, is overly broad. The selection does talk about problems of proof at the Nuremberg trials, but those problems were unique to those tribunals. So the phrase "courtroom procedures" is not particularly apt. And we eliminate (E) because the author doesn't mention any legal principle as such.

17. According to the passage, defendants at the Nuremberg trials

(A) were not given the opportunity to present evidence
(B) frequently had difficulty obtaining documents
(C) were not represented by counsel
(D) were tried in absentia
(E) were prosecuted by officers of the United States military

(B) This is a specific detail question. In the third paragraph, the author specifically states that procedures established to handle documents made it difficult for the defense to get access to the documents. (A) is specifically contradicted by the selection. The defendants did present evidence. As for (C), the passage specifically refers to defense counsel in the third paragraph. As for (D), though the passage doesn't specifically state that the defendants were present at the trials, it doesn't state that they were absent either. Finally, (E) is perhaps the most attractive of the wrong answers because the passage talks about "military tribunals." But the passage doesn't specifically state that the lawyers who prosecuted the cases were themselves members of the military. In fact, it indicates that the head of the prosecution for the IMT was a justice of the Supreme Court of the United States.

18. The author would be most likely to agree with which of the following statements?

(A) Members of the SS were unfairly punished more severely than other war criminals.
(B) The IMT was more effective than the 12 United States military tribunals.
(C) Many war criminals would have received harsher sentences had they been tried earlier.
(D) Counsel who represented the defendants at Nuremberg were often incompetent.
(E) Trial by documentary evidence is inherently prejudicial to the rights of a defendant.

(C) This is a further application question. In the third paragraph, the author notes that the passing of time and changing political conditions resulted in lighter sentences. We can conclude that had defendants been tried before these factors began to mitigate the severity of the sentencing process, they would have received stiffer sentences. Thus, the author would endorse the statement suggested by (C). You can eliminate (A) because it uses the word *unfairly*. While the author acknowledges that members of the SS were generally treated more harshly, the author does not suggest that the difference was in any way unfair. As for (B), the author does mention that the IMT tried the major war criminals, but that does not mean it was any more effective than the other tribunals. As for (D), the author acknowledges that defense counsel often had difficulty obtaining documents, but the difficulty is attributed to the procedures, not to any lack of ability on the part of the lawyers. And it is true that the author later states that some defense counsel were more experienced with the procedures than others (and more effective), but that does not mean that those who were new to the procedures were not competent. Finally, (E) seems to be contradicted by the selection.

19. Modern theories of criminal justice view rehabilitation as the goal of the penal system and aim at <u>restoration of the offender to society rather as</u> merely punishing him.

(A) restoration of the offender to society rather as
(B) restoring of the offender to society rather than
(C) restoring the offender to society rather as
(D) restoring the offender to society rather than
(E) restoration of the offender to society rather as

(D) The original sentence contains two errors. One, there is a failure of parallelism between *restoration* and *punishing*. Two, the expression *rather* is not idiomatic. The correct idiom is *rather than*. Only (B) and (D) make both the needed changes, but the inclusion of *of* following *restoring* in (B) results in a construction that is not idiomatic.

20. Approximately 20,000 meteors enter the earth's atmosphere every day, <u>but very few of them reach the earth's surface on the grounds that they</u> are consumed by frictional heat long before they reach the earth.

(A) but very few of them reach the earth's surface on the grounds that they
(B) but very few of them reach the earth's surface because most
(C) but very few of them reach the earth's surface because they
(D) with very few of them reaching the earth's surface on account of they
(E) since very few of them reach the earth's surface because most

(B) The original sentence contains two errors. First, the placement of the phrase "on the grounds that" implies that this is the mechanism by which a meteor might be expected to reach the earth's surface even though most fail to do so. Second, *they* lacks a clear referent (because of the proximity of *them* to *few*). (B) corrects both of these problems without introducing any new difficulties. (C) corrects the first problem but not the second. It is still not clear which type of meteor is referred to by *they*; those that reach the earth's surface or those that do not? (D) fails to correct the second error, and its attempt to correct the first error fails because *on account of* is not an acceptable substitute for *because*. Additionally, by eliminating *but* in favor of *with*, (D) creates a prepositional phrase that doesn't have a clear connection to any other element in the sentence. Finally, though (E) makes the needed correction, it is guilty of illogical subordination. The *since* implies that 20,000 meteors per day enter the atmosphere because most are burned up.

21. The major national leaders consulted consider solar power economically infeasible at present but <u>that it will be so in the future.</u>

 (A) that it will be so
 (B) that it would be so
 (C) believe that it will be so
 (D) believe that it will be economically feasible
 (E) believe that economic feasibility will be achieved

(D) The original suffers from two problems. First the part of the sentence following *but* needs a verb. As written, the sentence has the structure: "leaders consider . . . but that it will be so." To complete the parallel construction, you need a verb rather than a noun clause. Second, the sentence contains a problem of logical expression. As written, *so* evidently refers to *economically infeasible,* but then the sentence asserts: "leaders consider it is economically infeasible today but will be economically infeasible in the future." (B) fails to correct either error. (C) corrects the first but not the second error. (E) attempts to correct both errors, but the resulting sentence is extremely awkward. (D) corrects both errors and avoids the awkwardness of (E).

"Channel One" is a 12-minute school news show that includes two minutes of commercials. The show's producers offer high schools $50,000 worth of television equipment to air the program. Many parents and teachers oppose the use of commercial television in schools, arguing that advertisements are tantamount to indoctrination. But students are already familiar with television commercials and know how to distinguish programming from advertising.

22. The argument assumes that

 (A) the effects of an advertisement viewed in a classroom would be similar to those of the same advertisement viewed at home
 (B) many educators would be willing to allow the indoctrination of students in exchange for new equipment for their schools
 (C) television advertising is a more effective way of promoting a product to high school students than print advertising
 (D) high school students are sufficiently interested in world affairs to learn from a television news program
 (E) a television news program produced especially for high school students is an effective teaching tool

(A) The speaker addresses a concern voiced by some parents and teachers about commercial television in school. She argues that students already understand the difference between commercials and programming. But this argument depends upon the unsupported assumption that the student will be able to apply that distinction in the classroom situation. You might argue on the other side that students have been taught to accept information provided in a classroom setting and that they will not be able to draw the distinction as easily. So the speaker is logically committed to the idea expressed by (A), not to the ideas expressed by the other choices. As for (B), the speaker assumes that indoctrination will not be a necessary consequence of the new program (not that educators are willing to accept the indoctrination). As for (C), the speaker is not committed to any comparison between print and television advertising. As for (D) and (E), the speaker does not commit herself one way or the other on the effectiveness of the program.

Questions 23–24

 The spate of terrorist acts against airlines and their passengers raises a new question: should government officials be forced to disclose the fact that they have received warning of an impending terrorist attack? The answer is "yes." The government currently releases information about the health hazards of smoking, the ecological dangers of pesticides, and the health consequences of food.

23. The argument above relies primarily on

 (A) circular reasoning
 (B) generalization
 (C) authority
 (D) analogy
 (E) causal analysis

(D) The author draws an analogy between releasing information about terrorist threats and the publication of warnings of other types. For an explanation of the meanings of the other terms, consult the lessons on logical reasoning in the instructional portion of this book.

24. All of the following, if true, would weaken the argument above EXCEPT

 (A) Public disclosure of threats would encourage more threats by giving terrorists greater publicity.
 (B) Information about terrorist acts is gained from intelligence gathering, not research studies.
 (C) Information about possible terrorist acts is routinely distributed to the staff of U.S. embassies.
 (D) Making public terrorist threats would allow terrorists to identify sources who had leaked the information.
 (E) Public disclosure of threats would encourage false threats designed to disrupt air travel.

(C) Choices (A) and (E) clearly undermine the speaker's proposal, for they point out disadvantages associated with releasing the information. (D) also undermines the argument, for (D) suggests that sources of information would dry up. And since this argument is based on an analogy, (B) also weakens the argument by pointing out a dissimilarity between the two situations compared. (C), however, actually seems to strengthen the argument; the information is already available to some and should be available to others.

25. According to the passage, the process of assimilation is complete only when an immigrant

(A) applies for citizenship
(B) learns to speak English
(C) no longer actively preserves the native culture
(D) can freely participate in the greater society
(E) finds employment in the host country

(D) This is a specific detail question. In the final paragraph, the author states that the process of assimilation is not complete until an immigrant can function in the host country without fear of prejudice or discrimination.

26. According to the passage, Puerto Ricans have not been assimilate for which of the following reasons?

I. The physical proximity of Puerto Rico helps to maintain strong ties to their homeland.
II. The prevailing social and political climate is conducive to the survival of a distinct ethnic identity.
III. Puerto Ricans prefer to live in cultural enclaves where elements of the Puerto Rican life style abound.

(A) I only   (B) III only   (C) I and II only
(D) II and III only   (E) I, II, and III

(E) This is a specific idea question. In the third paragraph the author mentions both statements I and II. In the second paragraph he specifically mentions III.

27. The author is primarily concerned with

(A) explaining why Puerto Ricans have not been assimilated
(B) analyzing the process of acculturation of immigrant groups
(C) discussing social problems created by discrimination against Puerto Ricans
(D) comparing the experience of Puerto Ricans with that of other immigrant groups
(E) describing some of the important features of Puerto Rican culture

(A) This is a main idea question. The passage discusses the difference between assimilation and acculturation as it applies to the Puerto Rican community. The author's conclusion is that Puerto Ricans have been

acculturated but not assimilated, so (A) correctly describes the main point of the passage. (B) is too broad. The author focuses on Puerto Rican immigrants. (C) goes beyond the scope of the passage. Though the author implies that groups not yet assimilated may be victims of prejudice, this is not the main point of the passage. As for (D), the passing reference to the similarities of immigrant experience (each group establishes its own communities) is not the main point of the passage. Similarly, (E), the passing mention of some elements of Puerto Rican culture, is not the main point.

28. Puritan fanatics brought to civil and military affairs a coolness of judgment and mutability of purpose that some writers have thought inconsistent with their religious zeal, but which was in fact a natural outgrowth of it.

(A) but which was in fact a natural outgrowth of it
(B) but which were in fact a natural outgrowth of it
(C) but which were in fact natural outgrowths of it
(D) but it was in fact a natural outgrowth of them
(E) which was in fact a natural outgrowth of it

(C) The original contains an error of subject-verb agreement. *Which* refers to *coolness* and to *mutability,* and *so* requires a plural verb. Additionally, the original sets up an equivalence between those two elements and a natural outgrowth. Only (B) and (C) correct the first error, and only (C) corrects the second. (D) and (E) are incorrect for the further reason that they distort the intended meaning of the original sentence.

29. In the past few years, significant changes have taken place in the organization of our economy that will profoundly affect the character of our labor unions as well as influencing consumer and industrial life.

(A) economy that will profoundly affect the character of our labor unions as well as influencing
(B) economy that will profoundly affect the character of our labor unions as well as influence
(C) economy; these changes will profoundly affect the character of our labor unions and influence
(D) economy, and that will profoundly affect the character of our labor unions as well as influence
(E) economy, changes that will profoundly affect the character of our labor unions as well as to influence

(C) The sentence contains two errors. First, the relative pronoun *that* has no clear referent. Its proximity to *economy* suggests that it is intended to refer to that word, but the rest of the sentence shows it is intended to refer to *changes.*

Second, the sentence suffers from faulty parallelism: "affect . . . influencing." (B) corrects only the second error. (D) makes an attempt to correct both but fails on the first count; there is still nothing for *that* to refer to. (E) attempts to correct both errors, but the *to influence* fails to supply the needed parallelism. (C) corrects both of the errors without introducing any new error.

30. Americans give pride of place to the value of individual liberty, and we find <u>especially unintelligible the infliction of suffering</u> on the innocent.

    Ⓐ especially unintelligible the infliction of suffering
    Ⓑ especial unintelligible the infliction of suffering
    Ⓒ especially unintelligible suffrage that is inflicted
    Ⓓ especially unintelligible the suffering that is inflicted
    Ⓔ especially unintelligible the inflicting to suffer

    (A) The original sentence contains no error. (B), however, introduces a new error by changing the adverb *especially* to an adjective. Only an adverb can be used to modify an adjective. (C) contains an error of diction. Suffrage is the right to vote. (D) changes the intended meaning of the original. It is not that Americans find unintelligible the suffering of people; rather, Americans find unintelligible the infliction of that suffering. Finally, (E) is simply not idiomatic.

    Some residents of San Juan Capistrano, California, have suggested that government take some action to prevent the swallows from returning there each year because the birds constitute a nuisance. This suggestion ignores the important role the birds play in the environment. Swallows feed almost exclusively on flying insects, including many species that are annoying or harmful to human beings. The abundance of the birds in that region indicates an abundance of insects that are controlled through predation.

31. The speaker above implies that

    Ⓐ without swallows, the region would be infested with insects
    Ⓑ the majority of residents favor limiting the swallow population
    Ⓒ the economic damage caused by the swallows is negligible
    Ⓓ swallows are less destructive than other species of birds
    Ⓔ pesticides would be ineffective against the species of insects eaten by the swallows

    (A) The speaker argues that swallows help to control a large insect population. Thus, we can infer that without the swallows the insect population would be considerably larger than it is. So (A) is a conclusion that can be drawn from the material given. (B) cannot be logically inferred. The speaker refers to "some residents" only. As for (C), the speaker implies that the harm of attacking the swallows would not be negligible. As for (D), no such comparison is implied by the initial paragraph. (E) is perhaps the second-best answer, but

carefully compare (A) and (E). Had (E) read "the city would have to use pesticides to combat the insects," then (E) would be more nearly correct. Notice, however, that this is not what (E) says.

Susan: International Cosmetics is marketing a new treatment for cellulite called Fango Italiano. It's a cream that is spread on the affected area, allowed to dry, and then washed off. The treatment is very expensive—$250 per month—but it comes with a money-back guarantee. If Fango Italiano doesn't reduce your cellulite, the company will give you all of your money back. Since the company gives such a guarantee, the treatment must work.

Tom: I doubt that the treatment works. "Fango" is just the Italian word for *mud*. But it does seem to me that the company has found a brilliant marketing scheme. People who are so worried about their physical appearance that they are willing to spend $250 a month to get rid of cellulite are people who, while using the treatment, will also start eating less and exercising more. Thus, the treatment will appear to be successful and International Cosmetics will be that much richer.

32. Which of the following best characterizes the position Tom takes with regard to Susan's statement?

    Ⓐ He denies that Fango Italiano will be effective and questions whether or not International Cosmetics really intends to refund the money of dissatisfied customers.
    Ⓑ He denies that International Cosmetics really intends to market Fango Italiano, but suspects that the treatment is not effective.
    Ⓒ He questions whether or not the treatment is effective and denies that it is possible to do anything about cellulite.
    Ⓓ He agrees that people who purchase Fango Italiano may very well lose cellulite, but is skeptical that the treatment will be the reason.
    Ⓔ He argues that $250 per month is too expensive for a treatment for cellulite and encourages people with cellulite to eat less and exercise more.

    (D) In the very first sentence of Tom's statement, he says that he doubts the treatment will be effective. He goes on to explain that he imagines that the people who use the treatment will lose cellulite because they are the people who have probably also made a decision to begin losing weight and toning muscle. (D) best describes this position (Tom finds a different causal linkage). (B) captures Tom's skepticism regarding the effectiveness of the treatment, but Tom does not suggest that the company will not actually market the product. In fact, his statement that the company will be richer because of its sales indicates that he thinks the company *will* market the product. As for (A), although Tom seems to think that the company will market the product, it is not the case that he believes the company will not honor the guarantee. Rather, Tom evidently thinks the company will not often *have* to honor the guarantee because the treatment will seem to be effective. As for (C), while Tom evidently thinks the treatment will not be effective, it is not the case that he thinks there is no effective treatment for cellulite. He thinks that dieting and exercise will be effective. Finally, as for (E), while it is true that Tom thinks that dieting and exercise are effective treatments for cellulite, he does not encourage anyone to undertake such a regimen.

The National Research Council has recommended against requiring seat belts in school buses because only one life would be saved per year at a cost of $40 million annually. This analysis is shortsighted. Children who are required to use seat belts in school buses will remember to use them when they are old enough to drive.

33. The speaker above assumes that

   Ⓐ installing seat belts in school buses will not cost $40 million per year

   Ⓑ requiring seat belts in school buses would save many lives each year

   Ⓒ most schoolchildren are transported to and from school in buses

   Ⓓ states should require the use of seat belts in private vehicles

   Ⓔ behavior learned as a child may affect adulthood behavior

(E) The question asks you to find a hidden assumption of the argument. The speaker assumes, without saying so specifically, that what a person learns as a child will carry over to adulthood. (A) and (B) are incorrect because the speaker does not choose to quarrel with the specifics of the report. As for (C), the speaker does claim that the policy would benefit a certain group of the population, but she is not logically committed to any position on the number of persons in that group. As for (D), the speaker might very well accept this notion, but it has nothing to do with putting seat belts in school buses.

34. Curfews, which were initially enacted as a precaution against fire, were common in towns and cities throughout Europe in the Middle Ages.

   Ⓐ which were initially enacted as a precaution against fire

   Ⓑ which were enacted as an initial precaution against fire

   Ⓒ which were a precaution initially enacted against fire

   Ⓓ enacted as a precaution initially against fire

   Ⓔ enacted initially against fire

(A) The original sentence is correct. Choice (B) changes the intended meaning of the original sentence by implying that curfews were a first-line defense against fires. The phrase "enacted against fire," used in (C), (D), and (E), is not idiomatic.

35. The nuclear accident at Chernobyl released clouds of radioactive particles into the atmosphere, contaminating agricultural products grown within much of the Ukraine, as well as products grown in countries as far away as Italy.

   Ⓐ atmosphere, contaminating agricultural products grown within much of the Ukraine, as well as products grown in countries as far away as

   Ⓑ atmosphere, to contaminate agricultural products growing within much of the Ukraine, as well as products growing in countries as far away as

   Ⓒ atmosphere, while contaminating agricultural products growing within much of the Ukraine, as well as products growing in countries as far away than

   Ⓓ atmosphere, contaminating agricultural products grown within much of the Ukraine, as well as far away than

   Ⓔ atmosphere, contaminating agricultural products grown within much of the Ukraine, as well as

(A) The original sentence is correct as originally written, and each of the other choices introduces an error. (B) changes the meaning of the original by implying that the radioactivity was released for the specific purpose of contaminating the agricultural products mentioned. (C), too, changes the meaning of the original by implying that the contamination was a simultaneous effect of the release of the radioactivity rather than a result that followed later. (D) illogically implies that the agricultural products of the Ukraine are grown in other countries. Finally, (E) implies that the radioactivity contaminated Italy, the country, not just the agricultural products grown there.

A decade ago, "earn your age" was the immediate goal of every recent business school graduate. For example, a 26-year-old M.B.A. expected to earn $26,000 per year. This standard no longer holds true in America—a newly graduated M.B.A. in America would want to earn much more—but it is still the norm in England. It seems, therefore, that a starting M.B.A. in America is economically better off than one in England.

36. Which of the following, if true, most weakens the argument above?

Ⓐ Many students from England earn their M.B.A.s in the United States.

Ⓑ Most students in American business schools have had prior work experience.

Ⓒ The British pound is worth almost twice as much as the American dollar.

Ⓓ Graduates from American law schools earn more than graduates from American business schools.

Ⓔ England produces fewer M.B.A.s each year than the United States.

(C) This problem involves a cute little twist of reasoning; and once you see that, the problem becomes easy. The speaker is saying that "earn your age" is the standard in England and concludes on that basis that M.B.A.s are paid less in England. The fallacy is that there is a big difference between earning 26,000 dollars and 26,000 pounds—as (C) points out.

The United States is currently faced with a shortage of qualified math and science teachers. A Rand Corporation study indicates that graduates of traditional undergraduate schools of education are expected to fill only half the 20,000 vacancies for math and science teachers. One way of addressing this problem is to provide scholarships for math and science majors to finish their educations and graduate without accumulating massive debts. If they are freed of the burdens of college loans, they will be more likely to consider careers in teaching.

37. Which of the following, if true, would most weaken the argument above?

Ⓐ Public school teachers earn starting salaries that are well above the average wage in the United States.

Ⓑ Large numbers of graduates in math and science in prior years created a surplus pool from which teaching jobs are filled.

Ⓒ The cost of an undergraduate education in math or science is comparable to that for other majors.

Ⓓ Faculty at colleges and universities generally earn higher salaries than teachers in public schools.

Ⓔ There is no shortage of teachers in areas such as history, literature, and vocational training.

(B) The correct answer to a "weakening" question often attacks a hidden premise of the argument. Here the speaker claims that there is a shortage of math and

science teachers because there are not enough math and science majors now. This assumes that the only source of math and science teachers is the math and science majors now graduating. (B) attacks this assumption: there is another source of math and science teachers. The other choices make statements that are generally related to the ideas of teaching and recruitment but do not address the specific claims of this speaker.

Helium-filled balloons rise because helium is a light gas, much lighter than air. Glass tubes filled with neon gas can be charged with electricity to make light, so neon is also a light gas. Therefore, there is one respect in which both helium gas and neon gas are alike: they are both light gases.

38. Which of the following arguments most closely parallels the argument above?

Ⓐ The Empire State Building is a tall building, and Peter is a tall man. Therefore, there is one respect in which both the Empire State Building and Peter are alike: they are both tall.

Ⓑ Mary is a law school professor, and her daughter is a medical school professor. So there is one respect in which Mary and her daughter are alike: they are both professors.

Ⓒ A good steak must be rare, and total lunar eclipses are rare. So there is one respect in which a good steak and total lunar eclipses are alike: they are both rare.

Ⓓ All whales are mammals, and all bats are mammals. Since all mammals are warm-blooded, there is one respect in which whales and bats are alike: they are both warm-blooded.

Ⓔ Susan ate half of the melon, and Nancy ate the other half of the melon. So there is one respect in which Susan and Nancy are alike: each ate half a melon.

(C) This is a logical similarity question. The most striking thing about the stimulus argument is that it uses a term in an ambiguous fashion. It uses *light* the first time to mean "lacking weight," but it uses the word the second time to mean "illumination." Only (C) contains a similar error. The first use of *rare* means "undercooked," while its second use means "not common."

39. The author's primary concern is to discuss

Ⓐ methods for testing the effects of new drugs on humans

Ⓑ the importance of having accurate information about the effects of drugs

Ⓒ procedures for determining the long-term effects of new drugs

Ⓓ attempts to curb the abuse of prescription drugs

Ⓔ the difference between the therapeutic and nontherapeutic actions of drugs

(B) This is a main idea question. (B) correctly describes the overall point of the passage. The author starts by stating that all drugs have both good and bad effects and that correct use of a drug requires balancing the effects. For such a balancing to take place, it is essential to have good information about how the drugs work. Some of this can be obtained prior to approval of the drug, but some information will not become available until after years of use.

(A) is incorrect, for the different methods for testing drugs are mentioned only as a part of the development just described. The author is not concerned with talking about how drugs are tested but about why it is important that they be tested. (C) is incorrect for the same reason.

As for (E), this is the starting point for the discussion—not its main point. Finally, as for (D), drug abuse is not discussed in the passage at all.

40. The author introduces the example of thalidomide to show that some
    Ⓐ drugs do not have the same actions in humans that they do in animals
    Ⓑ drug testing procedures are ignored by careless laboratory workers
    Ⓒ drugs have no therapeutic value for humans
    Ⓓ drugs have adverse side effects as well as beneficial actions
    Ⓔ physicians prescribe drugs without first reading the manufacturer's recommendations

(A) This is a logical detail question. The author introduces thalidomide when he is discussing animal studies. He says the fact that a drug shows no dangerous effects in animals does not necessarily mean that it will not adversely affect humans. Then he gives the example. Thus, the example proves that a drug does not necessarily work in humans the same way it does in animals.

41. The author is most probably leading up to a discussion of some suggestions about how to
    Ⓐ centralize authority for drug surveillance in the United States
    Ⓑ centralize authority for drug surveillance among international agencies
    Ⓒ coordinate better the sharing of information among the drug surveillance agencies
    Ⓓ eliminate the availability and sale of certain drugs now on the market
    Ⓔ improve drug-testing procedures to detect dangerous effects before drugs are approved

(C) This is a further application question. In the last paragraph the author suggests that uniting disparate elements into a comprehensive surveillance program is inappropriate at this time. This eliminates choices (A)

and (B). He suggests, however, that improvements are possible in each segment of the system and urges reliance on computers to improve coordination and communication, so (C) is the correct answer. (D) is wrong because although the author might advocate the elimination of the availability of certain drugs, that is not what the passage is leading up to. As for (E), although the author acknowledges that preapproval studies are not infallible, this notion is too narrow in scope to be the next logical topic for discussion.

QUANTITATIVE SECTION

1. If $x + 2 = 3x + 10$, then $x =$
   Ⓐ -8　Ⓑ -4　Ⓒ 2　Ⓓ 6　Ⓔ 12

   (B) This problem asks you to solve a simple equation with only one variable, so the direct attack is surely the best. Just solve for x:

   $$x + 2 = 3x + 10$$
   $$2 - 10 = 3x - x$$
   $$-8 = 2x$$
   $$2x = -8$$
   $$x = -4$$

2. 10^3 is what percent of 10^5?
   Ⓐ 0.01%　Ⓑ 0.1%　Ⓒ 1%
   Ⓓ 10%　Ⓔ 100%

   (C) This question has the form "this is what percent of that?" Create a fraction in which the object of the preposition *of* is the denominator and the other number in the question is the numerator:

   $$\frac{10^3}{10^5} = \frac{1,000}{100,000} = \frac{1}{100} = 1\%$$

3. From 1996 to 1997, the size of the student body at Midvale High School increased by 30 percent. If the size of the student body in 1997 was 4,550, what was the size of the student body in 1996?
   Ⓐ $3,185$　Ⓑ $3,350$　Ⓒ $3,500$
   Ⓓ $3,600$　Ⓔ $3,650$

   (C) One way of attacking this question is to set up an equation:

   $$1996 + 30\% \text{ of } 1996 = 1997$$
   $$x + 30\% \text{ of } x = 4,550$$
   $$x + 0.30x = 4,550$$
   $$1.3x = 4,550$$
   $$x = 3,500$$

Alternatively, you could just work backward from the answer choices, starting with (C). Assume that the student population in 1996 was 3,500. Thirty percent of 3,500 is 1,050 and 3,500 + 1,050 = 4,550—which proves that (C) is the correct response.

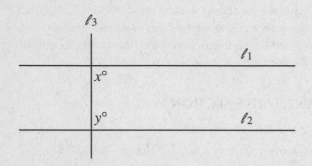

4. In the figure above, l_1 and l_2 intersect l_3. Do l_1 and l_2 intersect to the right of l_3?

(1) $x > y$

(2) $x + y < 180$

Ⓐ statement 1 alone is sufficient to answer the question, but statement 2 alone is not sufficient

Ⓑ statement 2 alone is sufficient to answer the question, but statement 1 alone is not sufficient

Ⓒ both statements together are needed to answer the question, but neither statement alone is sufficient

Ⓓ either statement by itself is sufficient to answer the question

Ⓔ not enough facts are given to answer the question

(B) Statement (1) is not sufficient as the following figures make clear:

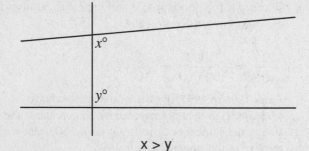

x > y

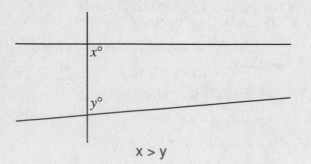

x > y

Statement (2), however, is sufficient. If $x + y$ were equal to 180, then l_1 and l_2 would be parallel and would not meet. Since $x + y$ is less than 180, l_1 and l_2 must eventually intersect to the right of l_3.

5. What is the value of $(p + q)(r + s)$?

(1) $p(r + s) = 5$ and $q(r + s) = 3$.

(2) $(p + q) = 8$

Ⓐ statement 1 alone is sufficient to answer the question, but statement 2 alone is not sufficient

Ⓑ statement 2 alone is sufficient to answer the question, but statement 1 alone is not sufficient

Ⓒ both statements together are needed to answer the question, but neither statement alone is sufficient

Ⓓ either statement by itself is sufficient to answer the question

Ⓔ not enough facts are given to answer the question

(A) First, perform the indicated operation:

$$(p + q)(r + s) = pr + ps + qr + qs$$

Statement (1) alone is sufficient to answer the question:

$$p(r + s) = pr + ps$$

$$q(r + s) = qr + qs$$

So the value of the expression in the question stem is 5 + 3 = 8. Statement (2), however, is not sufficient to answer the question.

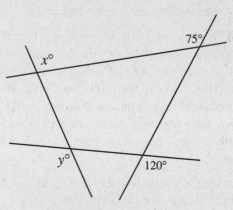

Note: Figure not drawn to scale.

6. In the figure above, $x - y =$

Ⓐ 45   Ⓑ 90   Ⓒ 135   Ⓓ 180   Ⓔ 195

(A) One of the most important things to remember about a problem like this is that the problem has been constructed so that you can find the solution. Even if you don't see the final solution when you begin your analysis, be confident that a solution can be found. Play around with formulas that you know until you find a starting point.

Here you have a quadrilateral. One of the interior angles of the quadrilateral is equal to y (vertical angles are equal), and another interior angle is equal to $120°$ (for the same reason). That's a good start. Next, x plus an angle we'll call p makes a straight line, so $x + p = 180°$ and $p = 180° - x$; and $75°$ plus an angle we'll call q makes a straight line, so $75° + q = 180°$ and $q = 180° - 75° = 105°$.

Now let's put all of this information together. The sum of the four interior angles is $360°$.

$$(180° - x) + 105° + y + 120° = 360°$$

$$180° - x + 105° + y + 120° = 360°$$

$$-x + y = 360° - 180° - 105° - 120°$$

$$-x + y = -45°$$

$$x - y = 45°$$

7. What percent of 16 is $\sqrt{16}$?

Ⓐ $12\frac{1}{2}\%$ Ⓑ 25% Ⓒ $33\frac{1}{3}\%$ Ⓓ 50% Ⓔ $66\frac{2}{3}\%$

(B) This question has the general form "this is what percent of that?" Set up a fraction and convert that fraction to a percent:

$$\frac{\sqrt{16}}{16} = \frac{4}{16} = \frac{1}{4} = 25\%$$

8. $x = yz$ and $x \neq 0$. If the y term of the equation is multiplied by 5 and the z term of the equation is also multiplied by 5, then, to preserve the statement of equality, it is necessary to

Ⓐ multiply the x term by 5
Ⓑ multiply the x term by 10
Ⓒ multiply the x term by 25
Ⓓ divide the x term by 1
Ⓔ divide the x term by 25

(C) This question tests your knowledge of the basic procedures for manipulating an equation. Remember that you can do the same thing to both sides of an equation (except divide by zero). If you multiply one side of an equation by 5, then you must do the same thing to the other side of the equation. Similarly, if you multiply one side of the equation by 5 and then again by 5, you must multiply the other side by $5 \times 5 = 25$.

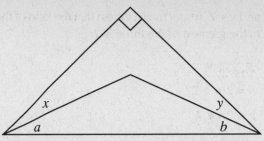

9. In the figure above, what is the value of $x + y$?

(1) $a = 2b$

(2) $a + b = 45$

Ⓐ statement 1 alone is sufficient to answer the question, but statement 2 alone is not sufficient
Ⓑ statement 2 alone is sufficient to answer the question, but statement 1 alone is not sufficient
Ⓒ both statements together are needed to answer the question, but neither statement alone is sufficient
Ⓓ either statement by itself is sufficient to answer the question
Ⓔ not enough facts are given to answer the question

(B) Statement (1) is not sufficient to answer the question, for (1) provides no information about the size of x and y. Statement (2), however, is sufficient. Since the figure is a triangle:

$$90 + (a + x) + (b + y) = 180$$

$$(a + x) + (b + y) = 90$$

$$a + b + x + y = 90$$

Since $a + b = 45$:

$$45 + x + y = 90$$

$$x + y = 45$$

10. What is the sum of 3 consecutive integers?

(1) The ratio of the least of the three integers to the greatest is 2.

(2) The sum of the 3 integers is less than the average of the three integers.

Ⓐ statement 1 alone is sufficient to answer the question, but statement 2 alone is not sufficient
Ⓑ statement 2 alone is sufficient to answer the question, but statement 1 alone is not sufficient
Ⓒ both statements together are needed to answer the question, but neither statement alone is sufficient
Ⓓ either statement by itself is sufficient to answer the question
Ⓔ not enough facts are given to answer the question

(A) Statement (1) alone is sufficient to answer the question. Let n represent the smallest of the three integers. Since these are consecutive integers, the second and third integers in the sequence can be defined as $n + 1$

and $n + 2$, respectively. Given that the ratio of the least to the greatest of the three is 2:

$$\frac{n}{(n+2)} = 2$$

$$n = 2(n + 2)$$

$$n = 2n + 4$$

$$-n = 4$$

$$n = -4$$

So the smallest of the integers is –4, and the other two integers are –3, and –2. Therefore, the sum of the three is –9.

Statement (2), however, is not sufficient to answer the question. The sum of any three consecutive, negative integers is less than the average of the three integers. For example, the sum of –3, –2, and –1 is –6, the average is –2, and –6 < –2.

11. If $0 < x < 1$, which of the following is the greatest?

Ⓐ x^2　　Ⓑ x　　Ⓒ $\dfrac{1}{x}$　　Ⓓ $\dfrac{1}{x^2}$　　Ⓔ $\dfrac{1}{x^3}$

(E) One way of solving this problem is to use a benchmark. The question stem stipulates that x is a fraction. Start by asking yourself how choice (B) differs from choice (A). Choice (A), x^2, is a fraction squared, and choice (B), x, is simply that fraction. The result of squaring a fraction is smaller than the original fraction, so eliminate (A) in favor of (B). Now compare (C) with (B). (C), $\dfrac{1}{x}$, is the reciprocal of a fraction (like dividing 1 by a fraction), so (C) must be larger than (B). Next compare (D) with (C). As you raise a fraction to a power, the product gets smaller, so x^2 is smaller than x. So (C) and (D) are both fractions with numerator 1, but the denominator of (D) is smaller than the denominator of (C). Therefore, (D) is larger than (C). Finally, since x^3 is smaller than x^2, (E) must be larger than (D).

That's a lot of explanation. You might be more comfortable using the Holmesian strategy of assuming numbers. Just pick a value for x, say $\frac{1}{2}$:

(A) $x^2 = \left(\dfrac{1}{2}\right)^2 = \dfrac{1}{4}$

(B) $x = \dfrac{1}{2}$

(C) $\dfrac{1}{x} = \dfrac{1}{\left(\dfrac{1}{2}\right)} = 2$

(D) $\dfrac{1}{x^2} = \dfrac{1}{\left(\dfrac{1}{2}\right)^2} = \dfrac{1}{\left(\dfrac{1}{4}\right)} = 4$

(E) $\dfrac{1}{x^3} = \dfrac{1}{\left(\dfrac{1}{2}\right)^3} = \dfrac{1}{\left(\dfrac{1}{8}\right)} = 8$

Thus, (E) is the largest.

12. If m is an integer, which of the following must be an *odd* integer?

Ⓐ $\dfrac{m}{2}$　　Ⓑ $2m + 1$　　Ⓒ $3m$

Ⓓ $3m + 1$　　Ⓔ m^2

(B) One way to attack this item is to reason abstractly about the properties of odd and even integers. As for (A), since m is simply an integer, $\frac{m}{2}$ might be an integer (either even or odd) or a fraction. As for (B), $2m$ must be an even integer, and that means that $2m + 1$ is odd. As for (C), if m is odd, then $3m$ is also odd, but if m is even, then $3m$ is also even. You can extend this reasoning to (D). If $3m$ is odd, then $3m + 1$ is even; but if $3m$ is even, then $3m + 1$ is odd. Finally, as for (E), if m is even, then m^2 is also even; but if m is odd, m^2 is also odd.

You could reach the same conclusion by using the Holmesian strategy of assuming some concrete values for the variables. For example, assume that $m = 1$:

(A) $\dfrac{m}{2} = \dfrac{1}{2}$ (a fraction, not odd)

(B) $2m + 1 = 2(1) + 1 = 3$ (odd)

(C) $3m = 3(1) = 3$ (odd)

(D) $3m + 1 = 3(1) + 1 = 3 + 1 = 4$ (even)

(E) $m^2 = 1^2 = 1$ (odd)

Thus far, we have eliminated two choices, (A) and (D), so we will try another number: $m = 2$.

(B) $2m + 1 = 2(2) + 1 = 5$ (odd)

(C) $3m = 3(2) = 6$ (even)

(E) $m^2 = 2^2 = 4$ (even)

(B) is the only expression left that generates an odd number, so (B) must be correct.

13. A civic club sold raffle tickets to raise $450 for a charity. The winning prize was a television set that cost the club $150. If the raffle tickets cost $0.75 each and the club raised exactly $450 (after deducting the cost of the television set), how many raffle tickets were sold?

Ⓐ 60 Ⓑ 80 Ⓒ 600 Ⓓ 700 Ⓔ 800

(E) This is really just a bookkeeping problem. If the club cleared $450 after paying for the television set, the club must have raised $450 + $150 = $600. Since raffle tickets cost $0.75 each, the club sold $600 ÷ $0.75 = 800 tickets.

Alternatively, you could have worked backward from the answer choices (one of those important Holmesian strategies). Start with (C). Assume that the club sold 600 tickets. That would mean it had gross receipts of 600 × $0.75 = $450. Although $450 equals the net fund-raising effort, it doesn't cover the cost of the prize, so (C) is too small. Test (D). Assume that 700 tickets were sold: 700 × $0.75 = $525. Deduct the cost of the television: $525 − $150 = $375. But $375 is less than $450, so this proves that the one remaining choice must be correct. (Still not persuaded? Work out the figures yourself for (E).)

14. If Patty is 5 years older than Rod, how old is Rod?

(1) 15 years ago, Patty was twice as old as Rod.

(2) 5 years ago, the sum of Patty's age and Rod's age was 35.

Ⓐ statement 1 alone is sufficient to answer the question, but statement 2 alone is not sufficient
Ⓑ statement 2 alone is sufficient to answer the question, but statement 1 alone is not sufficient
Ⓒ both statements together are needed to answer the question, but neither statement alone is sufficient
Ⓓ either statement by itself is sufficient to answer the question
Ⓔ not enough facts are given to answer the question

(D) Statement (1) is sufficient to answer the question. Let P and R represent the present ages of Patty and Rod, respectively. The question stem establishes:

$P = R + 5$

And statement (1) establishes:

$P - 15 = 2(R - 15)$

We now have two equations and only two variables:

$P = R + 5$

$P - 15 = 2(R - 15)$

Solve for R:

$(R + 5) - 15 = 2(R - 15)$

$R - 10 = 2R - 30$

$R = 20$

A similar line of reasoning shows that statement (2) is also sufficient. Using P and R again, we represent the information provided by (2) as follows:

$(P - 5) + (R - 5) = 35$

$P + R = 45$

Couple this new equation with the one used above to describe the information contained in the question stem and solve for R:

$P + R = 45$

$(R + 5) + R = 35$

$2R = 40$

$R = 20$

15. 149 people were aboard Flight 222 when it arrived at Los Angeles from New York City with Chicago as the only intermediate stop. How many people first boarded the flight in Chicago?

(1) 170 people were aboard the flight when it left New York City.

(2) 23 people from the flight deplaned in Chicago and did not reboard.

Ⓐ statement 1 alone is sufficient to answer the question, but statement 2 alone is not sufficient
Ⓑ statement 2 alone is sufficient to answer the question, but statement 1 alone is not sufficient
Ⓒ both statements together are needed to answer the question, but neither statement alone is sufficient
Ⓓ either statement by itself is sufficient to answer the question
Ⓔ not enough facts are given to answer the question

(C) We are asked to determine how many people first boarded the flight in Chicago. (1) is not sufficient by itself. Though we know that 149 people were aboard the plane when it arrived in Los Angeles and (1) specifies the number on board when it left New York City, we cannot assume that those people on the plane when it arrived in Los Angeles were originally on board when the flight left New York City because the flight stopped in Chicago. Nor is (2) sufficient by itself, for we need to know how many passengers were on board when the flight left New York City. Both statements together, however, are sufficient. If we know how many people were on board when the flight left New York City, how many got off in Chicago, and how many arrived in Los

Angeles, simple arithmetic will tell us how many first boarded in Chicago (though, of course, there is no reason to do the arithmetic).

16. If $\dfrac{6a(b+3)}{3b(2a+4)} = \dfrac{3}{4}$, then $\dfrac{a}{b} =$

Ⓐ 4   Ⓑ 3   Ⓒ $\dfrac{4}{3}$ Ⓓ $\dfrac{3}{4}$

Ⓔ Cannot be determined from the information given.

(**E**) This item is a little tricky. The correct attack is to manipulate the equation to see if you can simplify expressions and get a value for $\frac{a}{b}$:

$$\frac{6a(b+3)}{3b(2a+4)} = \frac{3}{4}$$

$$\frac{2a(b+3)}{b(2a+4)} = \frac{3}{4}$$

Cross-multiply:

$$(4)(2a)(b+3) = 3(b)(2a+4)$$

$$8a(b+3) = 3b(2a+4)$$

$$8ab + 24a = 6ab + 12b$$

$$2ab + 24a = 12b$$

Because of the ab term, you cannot get the ratio $a{:}b$.

17. A bicyclist rode from point A to point B in 90 minutes. The return trip along the same route took only 45 minutes. If the distance from A to B is 36 miles, what was the bicyclist's average speed, in miles per hour, for the entire trip?

Ⓐ 16   Ⓑ 24   Ⓒ 30   Ⓓ 32   Ⓔ 36

(**D**) Once you get your calculation set up, this problem is fairly easy. The total distance traveled was 72 miles and the total time elapsed was 135 minutes, or 2.25 hours:

$$\text{rate} = \frac{\text{distance}}{\text{time}}$$

$$\text{rate} = \frac{72}{2.25} = 32 \text{ miles per hour}$$

18. If the width of a rectangle is increased by 10 percent and the length is increased by 40 percent, by what percent is the area of the rectangle increased?

Ⓐ 4%   Ⓑ 16%   Ⓒ 36%   Ⓓ 54%   Ⓔ 66%

(**D**) One way to handle this problem is to solve it algebraically. Let W be the original width of the rectangle and L its original length. The original area was just $W \times L$, or WL. Now, we assume that the width increased by 10%, to $1.1W$, and that the length increased by 40%, to $1.4L$. The new area is

$$1.1W \times 1.4L = 1.54WL$$

Since the question asks about percent increase, you can use the "change over" strategy developed in the math lessons:

$$\frac{\text{change}}{\text{over}} = \frac{1.54WL - WL}{WL} = \frac{0.54W}{WL} =$$

$0.54 = 54\%$

Alternatively, you could always assign some real number to W and L. For example, assume that the width and the length of the original rectangle are both 1. (Yes, the width and the length could both be the same. A square is, after all, a rectangle, and the question does not stipulate that the width and length are different.) On that assumption, the area of the original rectangle is $1 \times 1 = 1$. Then W becomes 1.1 and L becomes 1.4. The new area is $1.1 \times 1.4 = 1.54$. Thus, the area increases by $\frac{1.54-1}{1} = 0.54 = 54\%$

19. Was Mark's average running speed for the first hour of his 26-mile marathon 11 miles per hour?

  (1) He ran the entire 26 miles in 2.5 hours.

  (2) He ran the last 15 miles in 1.5 hours.

Ⓐ statement 1 alone is sufficient to answer the question, but statement 2 alone is not sufficient

Ⓑ statement 2 alone is sufficient to answer the question, but statement 1 alone is not sufficient

Ⓒ both statements together are needed to answer the question, but neither statement alone is sufficient

Ⓓ either statement by itself is sufficient to answer the question

Ⓔ not enough facts are given to answer the question

(**C**) We are asked a yes or no question: Was the speed 11 MPH for the first hour? (1) is not sufficient, for we cannot assume that Mark maintained a constant pace for the entire 2.5 hours. (2) is not sufficient, for it gives us Mark's running speed for the last 15 miles and for the last 1.5 hours. Both statements taken together, however, answer the question. From (1) we learn that the total running time was 2.5 hours. From (2) we learn that the last 15 miles were covered in 1.5 hours. This means that the first 11 miles were covered in the first hour. This is sufficient to answer the question posed. Incidentally, the answer to the question is yes, but that is a step we do not have to take within the Data Sufficiency format.

20. A certain packing crate contains between 50 and 60 books. How many books are there in the packing crate?

    (1) If the books are counted out by threes, there will be one book left over.

    (2) If the books are counted out by sixes, there will be one book left over.

Ⓐ statement 1 alone is sufficient to answer the question, but statement 2 alone is not sufficient

Ⓑ statement 2 alone is sufficient to answer the question, but statement 1 alone is not sufficient

Ⓒ both statements together are needed to answer the question, but neither statement alone is sufficient

Ⓓ either statement by itself is sufficient to answer the question

Ⓔ not enough facts are given to answer the question

(**B**) Here the question is really asking whether we can pinpoint one integer between 50 and 60. (1) is not sufficient since it establishes that the number of books is 52, 55, or 58. (2), however, is sufficient. There is only one number between 50 and 60 which is one greater than a number divisible by 6. That number is 55 ($54 ÷ 6 = 9$, then adding 1 makes the number 55). So (2) alone is sufficient to establish the exact number of books in the crate, but (1) alone is not sufficient.

21. Elizabeth and Scott each receive a share of a lottery prize that is paid in 12 equal installments on the last day of each month for 20 years. If the amount paid to Elizabeth in the first three months of a year is equal to the amount paid to Scott in the first nine months of a year, what is the ratio of the dollar value of Scott's prize to the dollar value of Elizabeth's prize?

Ⓐ 1:3   Ⓑ 7:11   Ⓒ 2:3   Ⓓ 9:13   Ⓔ 3:4

(**A**) One way to attack this item is to set up an equation. Let E represent the size of Elizabeth's prize and S the size of Scott's prize. Since there are 12 months in a year,

$$\frac{3}{12}E = \frac{9}{12}S$$

$$\frac{1}{4}E = \frac{3}{4}S$$

Multiply both sides of the equation by $\frac{4}{3}$:

$$\left(\frac{4}{3}\right)\left(\frac{1}{4}\right)E = S$$

$$\frac{1}{3}E = S$$

$$\frac{1}{3} = \frac{S}{E}$$

The ratio of Scott's prize to Elizabeth's prize is 1:3.

You can reach the same conclusion by assuming some numbers. Since you are dealing here with months in a year, it will be convenient to assume numbers that are divisible by 12. Assume that Scott's prize is only $12 per year. On that assumption, he gets $1 per month and $9 in the first nine months of the year. And on that assumption, Elizabeth gets $9 in the first three months, or $3 per month. Thus, Elizabeth would get $3 × 12, or $36 per year. Since Scott gets $12 per year (for 20 years) and Elizabeth gets $36 per year (for 20 years), the ratio of Scott's prize to Elizabeth's prize is 12:36 or 1:3.

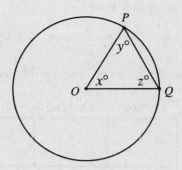

Note: Figure not drawn to scale.

22. In the figure above, O is the center of the circle. If $PQ > OP$, which of the following must be true?

   I. $y = z$

   II. $y < 60$

   III. $x < y + z$

Ⓐ I only   Ⓑ II only   Ⓒ I and II only
Ⓓ I and III only   Ⓔ I, II, and III

(**C**) The note accompanying the figure states that it is not drawn to scale. In such cases, it is often helpful to ask what the figure would look like if it were drawn to scale. OP and OQ are radii of the circle and must be equal in length. If PQ is longer than the radii, the figure should look like this:

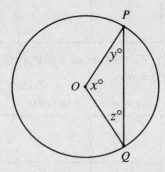

This may suggest to you the correct answer. As for I, since OP and OQ are equal, y and z must be equal (they are angles opposite equal sides in the same triangle). As for II, y must be less than 60°, as the redrawn figure suggests. (The technical reason for this is that PQ is stipulated to be the longest side of the triangle, so angle *POQ* must be more than 60°.) As for III, although you know that $x > 60°$, you don't know whether x is less than, greater than, or equal to the sum of the other two angles. For example, x could be 90° and y and z each 45°, in which case $x = y + z$. Or x might be 120° and y and z each 30°, in which case $x > y + z$.

23. Forty percent of the employees of a certain company are men, and 75 percent of the men earn more than $25,000 per year. If 45 percent of all the company's employees earn more than $25,000 per year, what fraction of the women employed by the company earn $25,000 per year or less?

Ⓐ $\dfrac{2}{11}$ Ⓑ $\dfrac{1}{4}$ Ⓒ $\dfrac{1}{3}$ Ⓓ $\dfrac{2}{3}$ Ⓔ $\dfrac{3}{4}$

(**E**) A table will help you organize the information:

	>$25,000	≦$25,000	Total
Men			
Women			
Total			

Enter the information supplied by the question stem. Since 40 percent of the employees are men,

	>$25,000	≦$25,000	Total
Men			.40
Women			
Total			

And since 75 percent of those men earn more than $25,000 per year,

	>$25,000	≦$25,000	Total
Men	.30		.40
Women			
Total			

We are already in a position to draw some further conclusions. First, since 40 percent of the employees are men, 60 percent are women:

	>$25,000	≦$25,000	Total
Men	.30		.40
Women			.60
Total			1.00

And

	>$25,000	≦$25,000	Total
Men	.30	.10	.40
Women			.60
Total			1.00

Next, the question stem stipulates that 45 percent of all employees earn more than $25,000.

	>$25,000	≦$25,000	Total
Men	.30	.10	.40
Women			.60
Total	.45		1.00

Using the table, we can deduce

	>$25,000	≦$25,000	Total
Men	.30	.10	.40
Women	.15	.45	.60
Total	.45	.55	1.00

Thus, 60 percent of the people employed at the company are women, and 45 percent of the people employed at the company are women who earn $25,000 or less. The answer to the question is $\frac{45\%}{60\%} = \frac{3}{4}$.

24. If N and P denote the nonzero digits of a four-digit number $NNPP$, is $NNPP$ divisible by 4?

   (1) NPP is divisible by 8.

   (2) NPP is divisible by 4.

  Ⓐ statement 1 alone is sufficient to answer the question, but statement 2 alone is not sufficient

  Ⓑ statement 2 alone is sufficient to answer the question, but statement 1 alone is not sufficient

  Ⓒ both statements together are needed to answer the question, but neither statement alone is sufficient

  Ⓓ either statement by itself is sufficient to answer the question

  Ⓔ not enough facts are given to answer the question

(D) The question asks whether $NNPP$ is divisible by 4. We can analyze the problem as follows. (1) is sufficient for the following reason: What is the difference between NPP and $NNPP$? Obviously, the extra N on the left of the number. But what does that mean? Since it is located in the fourth place to the left of the decimal point, it means "$N \times 1000$." Therefore, $NPP + (N \times 1000) = NNPP$. We are told in (1) that NPP is divisible by 8, so $NNPP$ will be divisible by 8 provided that $N \times 1000$ is also divisible by 8. Since 1000 is divisible by 8, $N \times 1000$ will be divisible by 8, so $NNPP$ must also be divisible by 8. And if a number is divisible by 8, it must be divisible by 4 as well. So (1) is sufficient. The same reasoning can be used to show that (2) is sufficient. Since $N \times 1000$ is divisible by 4 and since NPP is divisible by 4, $NPP + (N \times 1000)$ or $NNPP$, must also be divisible by 4.

25. A supermarket sells both a leading brand of laundry powder and its own brand of laundry powder. On all sizes of the leading brand it makes a profit of 15 percent of cost per box. On all sizes of its own brand it makes a profit of 10 percent of cost per box. For a certain month, from the sales of which of the two brands does the supermarket realize the greater profit?

   (1) Ounce for ounce, the supermarket pays a higher wholesale price for the leading brand than it does for its own brand.

   (2) Ounce for ounce, the supermarket sells 25 percent more of its own brand than of the leading brand.

  Ⓐ statement 1 alone is sufficient to answer the question, but statement 2 alone is not sufficient

  Ⓑ statement 2 alone is sufficient to answer the question, but statement 1 alone is not sufficient

  Ⓒ both statements together are needed to answer the question, but neither statement alone is sufficient

  Ⓓ either statement by itself is sufficient to answer the question

  Ⓔ not enough facts are given to answer the question

(E) The question requires that we determine which brand accounted for the greater dollar profit. It should be fairly clear that (1) will not do the trick because it does not tell us how much of each was sold. (2) also is insufficient since it does not establish the wholesale price, and without that we cannot compute the dollar profit per item. The question is now whether both statements together answer the question. A moment's reflection will show the answer is no. (1), coupled with information provided in the stem, establishes that the monetary profit is higher on the name-brand items. But how much greater? If we sell enough of the generic brand, we will make more money on the generic brand. But how much is enough? That will depend on the difference in the per item profit. And that critical piece of information is missing.

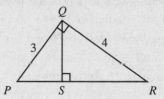

26. In the figure above, what is the length of QS?

  Ⓐ $\dfrac{25}{3}$ Ⓑ $\dfrac{20}{3}$ Ⓒ $\dfrac{15}{4}$ Ⓓ $\dfrac{12}{5}$ Ⓔ $\dfrac{7}{5}$

(D) There are at least three ways to solve this problem. One is to set up a complicated set of equations using the Pythagorean Theorem. Let's not even attempt that.

A second and more manageable attack is to recognize that the two legs of a right triangle can be treated as altitude and base for the purpose of computing the area of the triangle. Therefore, the area of the triangle is 6. And since PR can also be regarded as a base of the triangle,

$$\frac{1}{2}(QS)(PR) = 6$$

You should recognize that PR is 5 (either by using the Pythagorean Theorem to find that $PR = 5$ or by remembering that 3, 4, and 5 are "magic" numbers). Thus,

$$\frac{1}{2}(QS)(5) = 6$$

$$QS = \frac{12}{5}$$

Even that may be difficult to find, given the time constraints of the test, so Holmes would use an alternative strategy: guestimation. There is no note stating that the figure is not drawn to scale, so just measure the length of QS. Then compare that distance to a known distance. QS appears to be slightly more than 2, so the correct choice must be (D).

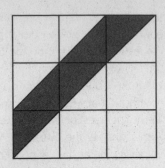

27. The figure above shows a square piece of land that is divided into nine smaller square lots. The shaded portion is a railroad right-of-way. If the area of the shaded portion of the figure is 5 square miles, what is the area, in square miles, of the entire piece of land?

Ⓐ 9　　Ⓑ 10　　Ⓒ 13　　Ⓓ 18　　Ⓔ 36

(D) The easiest way to handle this problem is to recognize that the shaded area takes up half of five of the squares, so the shaded area is $\frac{5}{2} \div 9 = \frac{5}{18}$ of the entire piece of land. Since $\frac{5}{18}$ of the total is equal to 5, the total is equal to 18 square miles.

28. Cars are entering the parking lot of a suburban shopping mall at the rate of one car every three seconds and leaving at the rate of one car every seven seconds. The parking lot is filling at a rate of approximately one car every

Ⓐ 6 seconds　　Ⓑ $5\frac{1}{3}$ seconds　　Ⓒ $5\frac{1}{4}$ seconds

Ⓓ $3\frac{3}{7}$ seconds　　Ⓔ $2\frac{1}{10}$ seconds

(C) Set up an equation:

$$\frac{1 \text{ car}}{3 \text{ seconds}} - \left(\frac{1 \text{ car}}{7 \text{ seconds}}\right) = \frac{1 \text{ car}}{x \text{ seconds}}$$

$$\frac{1}{3} - \frac{1}{7} = \frac{1}{x}$$

$$\frac{4}{21} = \frac{1}{x}$$

$$x = \frac{21}{4}$$

$$x = 5\frac{1}{4}$$

29. If S is a sequence of numbers the first term of which is 1 and each succeeding term of which is x more than the preceding term, what is the value of x?

(1) The sum of the third and fourth terms of S is 22.

(2) The sum of the second and ninth terms of S is 39.

Ⓐ statement 1 alone is sufficient to answer the question, but statement 2 alone is not sufficient

Ⓑ statement 2 alone is sufficient to answer the question, but statement 1 alone is not sufficient

Ⓒ both statements together are needed to answer the question, but neither statement alone is sufficient

Ⓓ either statement by itself is sufficient to answer the question

Ⓔ not enough facts are given to answer the question

(D) This question is actually easier than it might, at first glance, seem to be. We have a sequence in which each succeeding term is related to the preceding term in this way:

$$1; 1 + x; 1 + x + (x); 1 + 2x + (x) \ldots$$

Thus, if we are told the sum of any two terms in the sequence, we can construct an equation with x as the only variable, and then solve for x. For example, the third term is $1 + 2x$ (as shown), so the fourth term must be $1 + 3x$. If $(1 + 2x) + (1 + 3x) = 22$, then $x = 4$. So (1) is sufficient. (2) must also be sufficient. Though the equation for (2) would be a bit more complex, we could still solve for x. Remember that once you recognize this you are finished.

30. Two children, Bob and Mary, have piggy banks into which they deposit money earned from doing odd jobs. In a certain year, both Bob and Mary each deposited $5 on the first of every month into their respective piggy banks. If these were the only deposits made into the piggy banks during the year, on December 31 does Bob have more money in his piggy bank than Mary has in her piggy bank? (Assume no withdrawals.)

(1) On March 15 Bob had three times as much money in his piggy bank as Mary had in hers.

(2) On June 15 Bob had twice as much money in his piggy bank as Mary had in hers.

Ⓐ statement 1 alone is sufficient to answer the question, but statement 2 alone is not sufficient

Ⓑ statement 2 alone is sufficient to answer the question, but statement 1 alone is not sufficient

Ⓒ both statements together are needed to answer the question, but neither statement alone is sufficient

Ⓓ either statement by itself is sufficient to answer the question

Ⓔ not enough facts are given to answer the question

(D) This question also is much easier than it at first appears to be. The question asks us to compare the amount of money Bob has at the end of the year with the amount Mary has at the end of the year. Now, the only deposits made during the year are those in the amount of $5 made on the first of each month. In other words, both Bob and Mary deposit the same amount during the year. How then could there be any difference in the totals at the end of the year? The only difference between the two would have to be the result of some residual funds already in the bank at the start of the year. (1) establishes that after three deposits Bob had more money than Mary. (2) establishes a similar conclusion. But for Bob to have had more money than Mary at any time, it must be that Bob had more than Mary to begin with. Consequently, both statements establish that Bob will finish the year with more money than Mary (since each deposits 12 × $5). Now, it would be a more difficult task to calculate exactly how much each began and ended with. It could be done using simultaneous equations, but that is not relevant to the problem given the phrasing of the question.

31. $(3508)^2 - (3510 \times 3508) =$

   (A) 7020
   (B) 0
   (C) −2
   (D) −3508
   (E) −7016

   (E) In a problem such as this, which appears to involve considerable arithmetic, always look for a shortcut. If you recognize that 3510 × 3508 is the same as (3508 + 2)(3508), which equals (3508 × 3508) + (3508 × 2), the problem becomes much easier. We then have $(3508)^2 - (3510 \times 3508) = (3508 \times 3508) - [(3508 \times 3508) + (2 \times 3508)] = -(2 \times 3508) = -7016$.

32. A new fast-growing strain of yeast cells reproduces by dividing every two minutes. Thus, one yeast cell becomes two yeast cells after two minutes, four after four minutes, eight after eight minutes, and so on. If one newly divided cell is placed in a rectangular vat 6 inches by 8 inches by 12 inches, and after one hour the vat is full of yeast, how long did it take to fill half the vat?

   (A) 15 minutes
   (B) 24 minutes
   (C) 30 minutes
   (D) 48 minutes
   (E) 58 minutes

   (E) This problem is actually quite easy if you think to apply some backward reasoning to its solution. If the vat is full after one hour, then 2 minutes earlier it must have been half-full, since the cells double every 2 minutes. Two minutes earlier than an hour later is 58 minutes later. Note that the dimensions of the vat are

irrelevant to the answer to this question. If the vat is full after 1 hour, it will be half-full after 58 minutes regardless of the capacity of the vat.

33. For a certain concert, 560 tickets were sold for a total of $2,150. If an orchestra seat sold for twice the balcony seat price of $2.50, how many of the tickets sold were balcony seat tickets?

   (A) 235
   (B) 260
   (C) 300
   (D) 325
   (E) 358

   (B) One way of attacking this question is to use simultaneous equations. Let x be the number of balcony tickets sold and y the number of orchestra tickets sold. How many tickets were sold in total? The answer is 560, the sum of the number of balcony and the number of orchestra tickets: $x + y = 560$. How much was taken in? $2,150. Where did it come from? It came from x tickets at $2.50 and y tickets at $5.00: $2.50x + 5.00y = 2150$. Now, both of the statements are true:

   $x + y = 560$

   $2.5x + 5y = 2150$

   And that is why we call these statements simultaneous equations—both are true at the same time. Now, we use algebraic techniques to solve for x:

   Isolating y: $y = 560 - x$

   Substituting for y: $2.5x + 5(560 - x) = 2150$

   Solving for x:

   $2.5x + 2800 - 5x = 2150$

   $-2.5x = -650$

   $x = 260$

   For the "mathophobes," this question can be attacked by testing answer choices. Begin with (C). Assume that 300 tickets were sold at $2.50 each. How many tickets were then sold at $5.00? 260. So what would be total revenues? (300 @ $2.50) + (260 @ $5.00) = $2,050. But that is not equal to $2,150; it is $100 short. So, did we assume too few or too many cheap tickets? Obviously, we assumed too many cheap tickets, so you would test the next smaller answer, (B). A quick calculation will show that (B) is the correct answer.

34. At the beginning of a class, a classroom has 3 empty chairs and all students are seated. No student leaves the classroom, and additional students equal to 20 percent of the number of students already seated enter the class late and fill the empty chairs. What is the total number of chairs in the classroom?

Ⓐ 18
Ⓑ 15
Ⓒ 10
Ⓓ 6
Ⓔ 3

(A) As with many problems on the test, there is more than one line of attack that can be used. One way of approaching this question is to set up an algebraic statement. Let x designate the number of students already seated at the beginning of class; then the three additional late-comers are equal to 20 percent of that.

So: $.20x = 3$

And $x = 15$

The number of students originally seated was 15. But the question asks not about the number originally seated, but about the total number of chairs in the classroom. So we must add in the three late-comers, and $15 + 3 = 18$.

35. Is $a > 0$?

(1) $-2a < 0$

(2) $5a > 0$

Ⓐ statement 1 alone is sufficient to answer the question, but statement 2 alone is not sufficient
Ⓑ statement 2 alone is sufficient to answer the question, but statement 1 alone is not sufficient
Ⓒ both statements together are needed to answer the question, but neither statement alone is sufficient
Ⓓ either statement by itself is sufficient to answer the question
Ⓔ not enough facts are given to answer the question

(D) If -2 times a is negative, then a must be positive because only a negative times a positive will yield a negative, so (1) is sufficient. If 5 times a is positive, then a must be positive, so (2) is sufficient.

36. An elevator in a large office building contains riders who range in weight from 95 to 205 pounds. How many riders are in the elevator?

(1) The total weight of all the elevator riders is 1500 pounds.

(2) The maximum capacity of the elevator is 1600 pounds.

Ⓐ statement 1 alone is sufficient to answer the question, but statement 2 alone is not sufficient
Ⓑ statement 2 alone is sufficient to answer the question, but statement 1 alone is not sufficient

Ⓒ both statements together are needed to answer the question, but neither statement alone is sufficient
Ⓓ either statement by itself is sufficient to answer the question
Ⓔ not enough facts are given to answer the question

(E) Knowing the range of weights does not give us the average weight, which is what we would need to obtain the number of riders from (1), by division. (2) is simply irrelevant.

37. A company's profit was $600,000 in 1990. What was its profit in 1991?

(1) There was a 20 percent increase in income in 1991.

(2) There was a 25 percent increase in costs in 1991.

Ⓐ statement 1 alone is sufficient to answer the question, but statement 2 alone is not sufficient
Ⓑ statement 2 alone is sufficient to answer the question, but statement 1 alone is not sufficient
Ⓒ both statements together are needed to answer the question, but neither statement alone is sufficient
Ⓓ either statement by itself is sufficient to answer the question
Ⓔ not enough facts are given to answer the question

(E) Profit = Income – Costs, so we need to know income and costs. Neither proposition by itself will allow us to compute the 1991 costs and income. The information in (1) and (2) together gives us only percentage increases. Without the actual 1990 income and cost numbers, we cannot calculate 1991 income and costs. If the percentage increases for costs and income had been the same, then you could have computed the new profit. For example, if both costs and income had increased by 50 percent, then the profit would also have increased by 50 percent. With the given information, it is not enough. For example, if in 1990 income were $1,000,000 and the costs were $400,000 (for a 1990 profit of $600,000), the 1991 income would be $1,200,000 and the 1991 costs would be $500,000, for a 1991 profit of $700,000. If the 1990 figures were $10,000,000 – $9,400,000 = $600,000, then 1991 would be $12,000,000 – $11,750,000 = $250,000. This shows that you don't even know whether the profit is larger or smaller in 1991.